BUDDHIST SPIRITUALITY

Indian, Southeast Asian, Tibetan, and Early Chinese

World Spirituality

An Encyclopedic History of the Religious Quest

1. Asian Archaic Spirituality
2. European Archaic Spirituality
3. African and Oceanic Spirituality
4. South and Meso-American Native Spirituality
5. North American Indian Spirituality
6. Hindu Spirituality: Vedas through Vedanta
7. Hindu Spirituality: Postclassical and Modern
8. Buddhist Spirituality: Indian, Southeast Asian, Tibetan, and Early Chinese
9. Buddhist Spirituality: Ch'an, East Asian, and Contemporary
10. Taoist Spirituality
11. Confucian Spirituality
12. Ancient Near Eastern Spirituality: Zoroastrian, Sumerian, Assyro-Babylonian, Hittite
13. Jewish Spirituality: From the Bible to the Middle Ages
14. Jewish Spirituality: From the Sixteenth-Century Revival to the Present
15. Classical Mediterranean Spirituality: Egyptian, Greek, Roman
16. Christian Spirituality: Origins to the Twelfth Century
17. Christian Spirituality: High Middle Ages and Reformation
18. Christian Spirituality: Post-Reformation and Modern
19. Islamic Spirituality: Foundations
20. Islamic Spirituality: Manifestations
21. Modern Esoteric Spirituality
22. Spirituality and the Secular Quest
23. Encounter of Spiritualities: Past to Present
24. Encounter of Spiritualities: Present to Future
25. Dictionary of World Spirituality

Volume 8 of

World Spirituality:
An Encyclopedic History
of the Religious Quest

BUDDHIST SPIRITUALITY

Indian, Southeast Asian, Tibetan, and Early Chinese

Edited by
Takeuchi Yoshinori

in association with
Jan Van Bragt, James W. Heisig,
Joseph S. O'Leary, and Paul L. Swanson

CROSSROAD • NEW YORK

The Crossroad Publishing Company
370 Lexington Avenue, New York, NY 10017

World Spirituality, Volume 8
Diane Apostolos-Cappadona, Art Editor

Printed in the United States of America

Library of Congress Cataloging-in-Publication Data

Buddhist spirituality : Indian, Southeast Asian, Tibetan, and early Chinese / edited by Takeuchi Yoshinori, in association with Jan Van Bragt . . . [et al.].
p. cm.–(World spirituality ; v. 8-)
Includes bibliographical references and index.
Contents: 1. India, Southeast Asia, Tibet, China–
ISBN 0-8245-1277-4; 0-8245-1452-1 (pbk.)
1. Buddhism–History I. Takeuchi, Yoshinori, 1913-
II. Bragt, Jan van. III. Series: World Spirituality ; v. 8, etc.
BQ266.B834 1993
294.3'095–dc20 93-9360

Contents

Preface to the Series

THE PRESENT VOLUME is part of a series entitled World Spirituality: An Encyclopedic History of the Religious Quest, which seeks to present the spiritual wisdom of the human race in its historical unfolding. Although each of the volumes can be read on its own terms, taken together they provide a comprehensive picture of the spiritual strivings of the human community as a whole—from prehistoric times, through the great religions, to the meeting of traditions at the present.

Drawing upon the highest level of scholarship around the world, the series gathers together and presents in a single collection the richness of the spiritual heritage of the human race. It is designed to reflect the autonomy of each tradition in its historical development, but at the same time to present the entire story of the human spiritual quest. The first five volumes deal with the spiritualities of archaic peoples in Asia, Europe, Africa, Oceania, and North and South America. Most of these have ceased to exist as living traditions, although some perdure among tribal peoples throughout the world. However, the archaic level of spirituality survives within the later traditions as a foundational stratum, preserved in ritual and myth. Individual volumes or combinations of volumes are devoted to the major traditions: Hindu, Buddhist, Taoist, Confucian, Jewish, Christian, and Islamic. Included within the series are the Jain, Sikh, and Zoroastrian traditions. In order to complete the story, the series includes traditions that have not survived but have exercised important influence on living traditions—such as Egyptian, Sumerian, classical Greek and Roman. A volume is devoted to modern esoteric movements and another to modern secular movements.

Having presented the history of the various traditions, the series devotes two volumes to the meeting of spiritualities. The first surveys the meeting of spiritualities from the past to the present, exploring common themes that

A longer version of this preface may be found in Christian Spirituality: Origins to the Twelfth Century, *the first published volume in the series.*

can provide the basis for a positive encounter, for example, symbols, rituals, techniques. Finally, the series closes with a dictionary of world spirituality.

Each volume is edited by a specialist or a team of specialists who have gathered a number of contributors to write articles in their fields of specialization. As in this volume, the articles are not brief entries but substantial studies of an area of spirituality within a given tradition. An effort has been made to choose editors and contributors who have a cultural and religious grounding within the tradition studied and at the same time possess the scholarly objectivity to present the material to a larger forum of readers. For several years some five hundred scholars around the world have been working on the project.

In the planning of the project, no attempt was made to arrive at a common definition of spirituality that would be accepted by all in precisely the same way. The term "spirituality," or an equivalent, is not found in a number of the traditions. Yet from the outset, there was a consensus among the editors about what was in general intended by the term. It was left to each tradition to clarify its own understanding of this meaning and to the editors to express this in the introduction to their volumes. As a working hypothesis, the following description was used to launch the project:

> The series focuses on that inner dimension of the person called by certain traditions "the spirit." This spiritual core is the deepest center of the person. It is here that the person is open to the transcendent dimension; it is here that the person experiences ultimate reality. The series explores the discovery of this core, the dynamics of its development, and its journey to the ultimate goal. It deals with prayer, spiritual direction, the various maps of the spiritual journey, and the methods of advancement in the spiritual ascent.

By presenting the ancient spiritual wisdom in an academic perspective, the series can fulfill a number of needs. It can provide readers with a spiritual inventory of the richness of their own traditions, informing them at the same time of the richness of other traditions. It can give structure and order, meaning and direction to the vast amount of information with which we are often overwhelmed in the computer age. By drawing the material into the focus of world spirituality, it can provide a perspective for understanding one's place in the larger process. For it may well be that the meeting of spiritual paths—the assimilation not only of one's own spiritual heritage but of that of the human community as a whole—is the distinctive spiritual journey of our time.

EWERT COUSINS

Introduction

OF ALL THE GREAT RELIGIONS, it is Buddhism that has focused most intensively on that aspect of religion which we call spirituality. No religion has set a higher value on states of spiritual insight and liberation, and none has set forth so methodically and with such a wealth of critical reflection the various paths and disciplines by which such states are reached, as well as the ontological and psychological underpinnings that make those states so valuable and those paths so effective. In Buddhism, "spirituality"—perhaps the Sanskrit term *bhāvanā,* or "cultivation," is the closest equivalent—is not a merely interior reality or a mere escape from ordinary existence. It does not presuppose any dualism between the spiritual realm and that of the senses, or between a sacred dimension and the profane world. Rather:

> It aims at cleansing the mind of impurities and disturbances, such as lustful desires, hatred, ill-will, indolence, worries and restlessness, sceptical doubts, and cultivating such qualities as concentration, awareness, intelligence, will, energy, the analytical faculty, confidence, joy, tranquility, leading finally to the attainment of highest wisdom which sees the nature of things as they are, and realizes the Ultimate Truth, Nirvāṇa.[1]

In a word, the freedom attained in Buddhist practice is knowledge of reality, or rather it is reality itself, existence freed from the illusions and passions that bind us to a world of ignorance and suffering.

However dimly most people in non-Buddhist countries apprehend the doctrinal content of Buddhism, the conviction of its depth and wisdom is shared almost instinctively by men and women everywhere. Buddhist scholars and spiritual writers, of course, welcome this worldwide goodwill, but not without a certain reserve that is often difficult for the non-Buddhist

*The present volume covers the earlier career of Buddhism as it unfolded in India, Southeast Asia, Tibet, and China. Volume Two will take up further developments in China, Korea, and Japan, including Ch'an (Zen). It will also contain material on the spirituality of new Buddhist religious movements and a comprehensive treatment of Buddhist iconography.

to appreciate—and indeed may even look like cultural or religious elitism. Simply put, the fear is that popular interreligious culture, in the rush to get to the "core" of Buddhist truth, is content to plunder a few valuable ideas or practices that can be absorbed easily into other traditions, bypassing the specific character of the transformation Buddhism aims at and the disciplines required to achieve it.

In none of its historical forms is Buddhism easy to grasp, and the great diversity of its teachings can be mastered only if we are ready to survey the entire tradition from end to end, chronologically and geographically. The present collection has attempted to do this, though it does not aim at the fuller understanding that could be achieved by setting Buddhism in its wider interreligious context. The reader of the volumes on Hinduism in this collection may recognize the Vedic elements that shaped the teachings of the Buddha himself and early Buddhism, or the Hindu devotionalism that helped shape the later Mahāyāna ("Greater Vehicle") Buddhism. The assortment of folk beliefs and practices that became a part of the Buddhist tradition as it spread south across India and into Southeast Asia, and north into Central Asia, Tibet, Mongolia, China, Korea, and Japan, creates a variegated picture which our contributors have had to deal with briskly in order to keep the focus on the spiritual quest that has traditionally been seen as the core of the religion. The encounter of Buddhism with the indigenous literary and religious traditions of China, where its sacred texts were translated to become a major force in a quite different intellectual history, is perhaps the most dramatic chapter in this development, and a full understanding of this metamorphosis requires a thorough understanding of the Confucian and Taoist traditions as well.

In focusing on the upper reaches of Buddhist spirituality, our contributors have brought two themes in particular into special prominence: *meditation* and *emptiness*. If the reader keeps these topics firmly in view, the other matters discussed in these pages will be seen to converge on them and to draw significance from them. The resultant portrait may reflect the bias of current Western interest, for these two themes provide only one possible solution to the problem of identifying the distinctive core of Buddhist spirituality. Yet in the present Western perspective, characterized by the popularity of Vipassanā and Zen techniques of meditation and by intense academic interest in "emptiness" as a philosophical topic, if not as a spiritual practice, these two themes have acquired a special valency and offer a promising point of entry into the immense and often unfamiliar world of Buddhist thought.

What Is Buddhism?

Before discussing the topics of meditation and emptiness, it is necessary to set forth some very basic notions, drawing both on the Pāli Canon (the major source for early Buddhist teachings) and sources in Sanskrit.

What is Buddhism? The classical answer: To be Buddhist is to take refuge in three supreme, salutary realities: the Buddha, the Dharma, and the Saṅgha. These are prized as the "three jewels" beyond all price.

The *Buddha* (literally, the "awakened one") refers primarily to the historical figure of Gautama Siddhārtha, or Śākyamuni (sage of the Śākya clan), who attained Buddhahood in the last of his many births, but also to other figures who are believed to have preceded him in the past or to follow him in the future. Some branches of Mahāyāna Buddhism posit a whole host of Buddhas living in all places and at all times. The term "Buddha" has also been understood in Mahāyāna thought as the ultimate goal toward which all beings must strive, a perfect reality preexisting all historical Buddhas. This supreme goal, transcending the meager life of the individual yet belonging intimately to each individual, is imaged as a force that drives us beyond death, through repeated cycles of birth and rebirth, or as an innate capacity, a "Buddha-nature," that inclines all beings toward the same end. The perfection of being that the historical Buddha realized in his enlightenment is seen in Mahāyāna as a universal human vocation.

The *Dharma* (Sanskrit) or *Dhamma* (Pāli) is the Teaching, the vision of reality taught by the Buddha, who, just before his decease, spoke to his sorrowful disciples in these words:

> Dwell making yourselves your island (support), making yourselves, not anyone else, your refuge; making the Dhamma your island (support), the Dhamma your refuge, nothing else your refuge.[2]

Dharma thus refers to all the teachings of the Buddha, recorded in the sūtras or sacred scriptures of Buddhism (an amorphous collection of thousands of works transmitted in over a dozen languages over more than two thousand years). But it is also interpreted, especially in Mahāyāna Buddhism, as meaning "things just as they are," ultimate reality, discovered and illuminated by Śākyamuni but not in any sense dependent on his historical experience.

The best-known formulation of the Dharma is known as the *Four Truths*, expounded by the Buddha at Benares immediately after his enlightenment:

> Life is full of suffering;
> suffering is caused by craving for the things of life;

> suffering can be stopped by the renunciation of this craving; and there is a path that leads to the cessation of suffering, namely, the *Eightfold Path* of right views, right intention, right speech, right conduct, right livelihood, right effort, right mindfulness, right concentration.

The first of the Four Truths, the universality of suffering, is a stumbling block for many on their first encounter with Buddhism; yet it is presented not as a piece of willful pessimism but as the finding of advanced spiritual insight:

> It is difficult to shoot from a distance arrow after arrow through a narrow key hole, and miss not once. It is more difficult to shoot and penetrate with the tip of a hair split a hundred times a piece of hair similarly split. It is still more difficult to penetrate to the fact that "all this is ill."[3]

It was insight into suffering that led Gautama to abandon his worldly life and embark on the ascetic quest:

> When I consider the impermanence of everything in this world, then I can find no delight in it. . . . If people, doomed to undergo old age, illness, and death, are carefree in their enjoyment with others who are in the same position, they behave like birds and beasts. . . . By contrast I become frightened and greatly alarmed when I reflect on the dangers of old age, death, and disease. I find neither peace nor contentment, and enjoyment is quite out of the question, for the world looks to me as if ablaze with an all-consuming fire.[4]

His solution to the problem of existence, attained in the night of his enlightenment, his entry into the bliss of nirvāṇa, exposes both the causes and the cure of this suffering:

> A pleasant sensation originates in dependence on contact with pleasant objects; but when that contact with pleasant objects ceases, the feeling sprung from that contact, the pleasant sensation that originated in dependence on contact with pleasant objects, ceases and comes to an end. . . .
>
> Perceiving this, the learned and noble disciple conceives an aversion for contact, conceives an aversion for sensation, conceives an aversion for perception, conceives an aversion for the predispositions, conceives an aversion for consciousness. And in conceiving this aversion he becomes divested of passion, and by the absence of passion he becomes free, and when he is free he becomes aware that he is free; and he knows that rebirth is exhausted, that he has lived the holy life, that he has done what it behooved him to do, and that he is no more for this world.[5]

This is one of the innumerable passages in the Pāli Canon that exposes the basic ontological vision of early Buddhism, namely, the doctrine of *dependent co-origination.* The doctrine teaches that all things come into being and pass out of being by way of a chain of interlocked, mutually conditioning events, culminating in ignorance. In its standard form it has twelve links: ignorance, volitional actions, consciousness, psychophysical phenomena, the sense faculties, contact, sensation, thirst, clinging, the process of becoming, birth, and pain-and-death. Each of these conditions exists only in interdependence on all the others; together they constitute the world of saṃsara, the realm of illusion and suffering in which the unenlightened live.

The dispassionate tone of such analyses may be disconcerting, but it is permeated by the joy of those who have found spiritual freedom, who have lit up the sure path through the thickets of craving, aversion, and illusion into the clear light of spiritual day. The immense influence of these teachings owes nothing to a superficial attractiveness of presentation but can be explained only by their effects. The value of the dry catechetical lists which fill so many pages in the Pāli Canon, like that of medical treatises, lies in their efficacity for healing, for cutting off passions and defilements. The diagnosis is gloomy enough, yet persuasive; the cure prescribed is lucid, comprehensive, and can be worked out in a variety of practical styles.

Another formula said to capture the core of the second jewel of Buddhism is the *Threefold Seal of Dharma* (three marks of existence): the impermanence of all conditioned things; the universality of suffering; and the absence of a permanent self. Some sources add a fourth seal—the tranquillity of nirvāṇa—the goal of all Buddhist practice. The denial of a substantial self, another stumbling block, is perhaps more plausible to the Western mind today than it has previously seemed.

> According to the teaching of the Buddha, the idea of self is an imaginary, false belief which has no corresponding reality, and it produces harmful thoughts of "me" and "mine," selfish desire, craving, attachment, hatred, ill-will, conceit, pride, egoism, and other defilements, impurities and problems. It is the source of all the troubles in the world from personal conflicts to wars between nations. In short, to this false view can be traced all the evil in the world.[6]

The final jewel, the Saṅgha, refers to the community of those who follow the Buddha and the Dharma. In the narrow sense it refers to the monks and nuns who have "left home to live in homelessness," and who find their home in the Buddhist precepts. These rules, known as the Vinaya, incorporate the strictest practice of the "path" to enlightenment and deliverance that was followed by Śākyamuni himself. The precepts are only one part of the life of the Saṅgha. They find their fulfillment in meditation, which includes both the practice of trying to center the mind and the mindfulness of one for whom the art has become a habit; and in wisdom, the insight that comes through keeping the precepts and cultivating meditation. The wisdom of the detached, awakened mind-body is, we might say, the heart of Buddhist spirituality.

Meditation: Early Buddhism and the Theravāda Tradition

Meditation is a central theme in the essays in Part 1 of this collection. It is in meditation that one makes one's own the insights of the Buddha and that one discovers the meaning of the dry texts of the scriptures. The doctrinal context in which the practice of meditation acquires its crucial status is surveyed in G. C. Pande's essay on the teaching of the Buddha and its development in the debates between the various Indian schools or sects of the first Buddhist centuries. Focusing closely on the meditative realization of Buddhist truth, Paul Griffiths brings into relief some basic structures of the teaching on meditation which culminated in the summas of Buddhaghosa (fifth century C.E.). Griffiths identifies and describes the varieties, methods, and stages of meditation, which he characterizes as "a self-conscious attempt to alter, in a systematic and thoroughgoing way, the practitioner's perceptual, cognitive, and affective experience."

The prowess of the Abhidharma thinkers in psychological and ontological analysis, evoked by Sakurabe Hajime, owes much to this schooling in meditative attention. To some, these highly technical speculations may seem to lack the warmth or passion of true religious spirituality, but to many in Buddhist history they have symbolized the very pinnacle of spiritual development. In a wide-ranging panorama Robert Thurman explains the role of monastic life in the unfolding of Buddhist spiritual endeavor—this essay looks forward to the entire later course of the tradition, and its lessons should be kept in mind in most later chapters.

Winston King reveals the vitality of this tradition of meditation in the lands of Southeast Asia, where the Theravāda tradition, based exclusively on the Pāli Canon, continues to flourish. The centrality of meditation, usually in monastic settings, is not unrelated to the cultural and social vitality Buddhism has manifested in these countries, as shown also in the accounts of Thai Buddhism by Sunthorn Na-Rangsi and Sulak Sivaraksa and in Maeda Egaku's outline of developments in Sri Lanka.

The supreme illusion that meditation seeks to overcome is the belief in a substantial self, which is the source of all the distracting thoughts and desires that cloud the practitioners' vision and, more generally, of that preoccupation with "self" which makes our lives superficial and uncreative. The struggle with this illusion prepares the ground for the rhetoric of emptiness in which, later, the Mahāyāna tradition is steeped. As distracting self-consciousness recedes, the mind is freed for compassion with all living things, practiced in the "four Sublime States" (*brahma-vihāra*): extending unlimited, universal love and goodwill (*mettā*) to all living beings without any kind of discrimination, "just as a mother loves her only child"; compassion (*karuṇā*) for all living beings who are suffering, in trouble and affliction; sympathetic joy (*muditā*) in others' success, welfare, and happiness; and equanimity (*upekkhā*) in all vicissitudes of life.[7]

Meditation releases a nondiscursive awareness of present reality, bringing the mind back from its compulsive straying to unreal imagined realms of past or future. Yet this purification and concentration of mind are not hostile to the proper use of discursive thought. Philosophical analysis can be a powerful auxiliary weapon in the struggle to overcome illusion and craving. For though Buddhism has known revolts against excessively scholastic developments—Nāgārjuna's critique of the Abhidharmists, for example, or the Zen revolt against the complexity of Chinese Buddhist learning and speculation—it has never known that opposition between *religion* and *philosophy*, or between faith and reason, which is a recurring theme in the West. From the time that the ancient Greeks sought to replace poetry, divine revelations, myth, and symbol with nature, history, science, and fact, religion has had to walk a narrow line between crippling refusal of intellectual progress and no less crippling surrender to its absolute control. Buddhism knew no such problem: the Buddhist philosopher was always religious, and the search for insight was an essential element in this religion; even to state this fact is to introduce a dichotomy where none exists.

The general editor of the two Buddhist volumes of this Encyclopedia of World Spirituality, Takeuchi Yoshinori, writes:

> In Buddhism religion and philosophy are like a tree that forks into two from its base. Both stem from the same roots and both are nourished by the same sap. To be sure, religion forms the main trunk and philosophy its branch, but the two remain intimately connected to each other. There have been times in the long history of Buddhism in which a pruning of the philosophical branch has helped the trunk to flourish, and other times at which the philosophical branch stood in full bloom while the trunk had become hollowed out. But by and large the two have shared together the common fate of the same tree, through its flower and its decay—two partners locked together in dialogue. Religion reflects on its own essence through philosophy and thereby deepens and renews its vitality. It is like the steady flow of water gushing forth from an underground spring; at the same time as the steady stream of water continues to purify and freshen the water that flowed before it, it also goes on boring its own well deeper into the earth. . . .

> Strictly speaking, Buddhism has nothing like what Saint Paul refers to as the "folly of the cross." This is both its weakness and its strength and has led Buddhist philosophy in a direction different from Western philosophy and theology. That is to say, the religious experience of the "folly of the cross" set philosophy and religion in opposition to each other in the West, establishing the autonomy of reason to criticize religion from the outside; but at the same time this basic opposition led to a new, albeit secondary, relationship between philosophy and theology, a mutuality grounded in a common concern with metaphysics. . . .
>
> Originally philosophy served as an inner principle of religion for Buddhism, not as an outside critic, even though it has often functioned as a means of criticizing the obscurantism of religion. That is to say, philosophy in Buddhism is not speculation or metaphysical contemplation but rather a metanoia of thinking, a conversion within reflective thought that signals a return to the authentic self. . . . For Buddhism this "metanoesis" represents the true meaning of enlightenment to the truth of religion.[8]

It is clear that philosophy, thus understood, conduces to meditation and that the clear-eyed attainment of the spiritually liberated person is the summit of philosophy rather than its abolition.

Another dichotomy that has plagued Western spirituality and that seems to be ignored or overcome in Buddhist meditation is the mind/body dualism, which also goes back to the Greeks. The notion of the modern individual who is the subject of spirituality carries in it vestiges of centuries of debate on the reality and structures of a "soul" or life-giving principle that makes mere corporeality distinctively human. Whether the animating principle was *located in* the body or simply *participated in* by the body, the opposition has been crucial to religion in the West; and the denial of the principle all but entailed the rejection of religion as well. In modern times the related opposition between unconscious and conscious mind has become a useful model for progress in the spiritual life, but always as something "higher" than the body. In contrast, in the most exemplary forms of Buddhist meditation, the body has been seen as the locus of insight and experience, inseparably one with mind. Whether the senses are harnessed so as to enhance the experience of the mind, as in Tibetan tantric tradition, or starved for the sake of depriving the mind of its preoccupations, as in Zen, in each case the practice involves mind and body in an undifferentiated unity.

Buddhist meditation is not only a path to enlightenment of mind; it also effects a transformation of the affective life at its very roots. It replaces an attitude of *clinging* with one of *letting go.* Renunciation of the world and the appetites that incline us toward losing ourselves in the enjoyment of it is not seen as a mere technique for purifying the mind and spirit. From early on, the philosophical tradition in Buddhism has taken liberation from attachment as the foundation for a range of psychological, epistemological, and even ontological theories. Again, as this tradition of detachment expands and articulates itself across the whole range of thought it gives rise to the dominant intuition of *emptiness.* The emptiness of all things is the objective correlative of the freedom of the one who has let go of all attachments.

Emptiness

Emptiness (Skt. *śūnyatā*) is a recurrent theme in the second and third parts of this volume, which deal with the Mahāyāna movement in India and its acculturation in Tibet and China. Proclaiming itself the "Greater Vehicle" capable of ferrying all sentient beings to the other shore of Buddhahood, laity no less than monks, Mahāyāna owed its unprecedented missionary outreach to the range of its imaginative vision and the flexibility of its interpretative procedures. The resultant diversity of its forms—the multiplicity of Buddhas and bodhisattvas (one who embodies the ideals of one on the path to Buddhahood), objects and forms of worship, types of meditation—staggers the imagination. Yet a certain spiritual homogeneity may be detected, not only in the renewed stress on the cardinal Buddhist virtues of Wisdom and Compassion, and on their inseparability, but also in the haunting and fascinating theme of emptiness.

Kajiyama Yūichi explains the social and cultural background of the rise of Mahāyāna in the first centuries C.E., an event about which much remains obscure. The family of sūtras known as "Perfection of Wisdom" (*prajñāpāramitā*) centers on the insight that all things are "empty," that nothing exists independently, autonomously, or eternally.

Devotion to quasi-divinized Buddhas and bodhisattvas, a prominent trait of Mahāyāna religiosity, is much in evidence in the *Lotus Sūtra,* one of the best-known and most revered scriptures among Buddhists in China and Japan, presented here by Michael Pye. One can see how the leavening of devotionalism with the consciousness of emptiness allowed the fruitful coexistence of sophisticated and popular religion, legitimated by the idea of "skillful means" (*upāya*) which finds its classic presentation here. The sūtra also teaches universal Buddhahood, a higher goal than the arhatship, or sainthood, aimed at in early Buddhism.

Nagao Gadjin examines the *Vimalakīrti Sūtra,* a text that he claims is "more empty" than the Prajñāpāramitā sūtras. This sūtra was never the prime focus of a Buddhist school in the sense that it never gave rise to a "Vimalakīrti Sect," but the story of its lay protagonist and its teaching of nonduality made it a popular and influential text in East Asia. Awareness of nonduality is equivalent to awareness of emptiness. The image of Vimalakīrti, asked for a final word by the participants in a lengthy philosophical debate and responding with a resounding silence, is dear to Mahāyāna Buddhists.

From a literary point of view, the Vimalakīrti Sūtra is one of the Mahāyāna texts that is most attractive to Western tastes. It conveys in a series of memorable, and often rather humorous, scenes the poetry, joy, and freedom associated with emptiness and shows how the practice of compassion is grounded in the wisdom of emptiness:

> "Mañjuśrī, a bodhisattva should regard all living beings as a wise man regards the reflection of the moon in water or as magicians regard men created by magic. He should regard them as being like a face in a mirror; like the water of a mirage; like the sound of an echo; like a mass of clouds in the sky; like the previous moment of a ball of foam; like the appearance and disappearance of a bubble of water; like the core of a plantain tree; like a flash of lightning; like the fifth great element. . . ."
>
> "Noble sir, if a bodhisattva considers all living beings in such a way, how does he generate the great love toward them?"
>
> "Mañjuśrī, when a Bodhisattva considers all living beings in this way, he thinks: 'Just as I have realized the Dharma, so should I teach it to living beings.' Thereby, he generates the love that is truly a refuge for all living beings; the love that is peaceful because free of grasping; the love that is not feverish, because free of passions; the love that accords with reality because it is equanimous in all three times; the love that is without conflict because free of the violence of the passions; the love that is nondual because it is involved neither with the external nor with the internal; . . . the Buddha's love that causes living things to awaken from their sleep; . . . the love that is never exhausted because it acknowledges voidness and selflessness."[9]

The teaching of emptiness was given a firm logical underpinning in the *Mūlamadhyamaka-kārikā* of Nāgārjuna (second-third centuries C.E.), who subjected basic Buddhist concepts to a radical logical analysis with the purpose of demonstrating the emptiness of all things. Since all things arise in dependent co-origination, all things are empty of self-nature or own-being; emptiness is the true nature of the real, which cannot be grasped in our words or concepts but only in a meditation that leaves thought behind. Tachikawa Musashi describes the Mādhyamika or "Middle Way" tradition issuing from Nāgārjuna, showing how its logic overcomes all forms of dualistic thinking; Nāgārjuna and his commentators, far from dissolving logic in mystical intuition, clarified that intuition by the very relentless rigor of their logical argumentation.

The other great school of Mahāyāna philosophy, the Yogācāra or mind-only school, founded by Asaṅga and Vasubandhu (fifth century C.E.), is often seen as reacting against the "nihilistic" perils of Nāgārjuna and his followers and as propounding instead an idealist account of the self-contained nature of consciousness. However, as John Keenan shows in his fresh approach to this school, they accepted the essential teaching of the Mādhyamika philosophers but rooted it in a doctrine of mind. The most intensive developments in Buddhist logic are associated with this school, and Ernst Steinkellner's essay provides a glimpse into the workings of these subtle epistemologists.

The expansive vision and rich imagery of the *Avataṁsaka Sūtra*, an "encyclopedic compendium of Mahāyāna Buddhism," was also favored in East Asia, where it came to full flower. Luis Gómez discusses the dazzling play of perspectives in the *Avataṁsaka* (known in Chinese as Hua-yen and in Japanese as Kegon), describing the various vows of bodhisattvas, the quest for truth by a layman named Sudhana, and the stages of spiritual progress. This enormous sūtra was the foundation of the most brilliant form of speculative Buddhism in China, here examined by Taitetsu Unno, along with two other great movements of Chinese Buddhist thought. His discussion of these schools shows how philosophic scholasticism serves as a vehicle for spirituality and remains anchored in meditation, in such a way that the dichotomy between teaching and practice is never drawn. On the contrary, the two are like the two wings of a bird. If either is lacking, the religious quest never gets off the ground. This image is also emphasized by Chih-i, the sixth-century founder of the T'ien-t'ai school, whom Paul Swanson introduces in the context of a more general treatment of emptiness in early Chinese Buddhism.

Absent from all these systems is any notion corresponding to the God of the monotheistic religions. Aside from certain devotional ways of thought that appear to begin in the Chinese tradition of Pure Land Buddhism, the least philosophical of the Mahāyāna schools, described here by Roger Corless, the idea of a personal relationship with an absolute being in another, transcendent world is foreign to Buddhism. This does not mean, however, that one can speak of Buddhism as a simple "atheism," radically contradicting theistic spirituality. In the end it is not a question so much of denying the existence of a supreme being as charting a quite different map of spiritual reality.

The Mādhyamika philosophy continued as a major intellectual force in Tibet, where it was associated with what at first might seem something entirely alien to it, the exuberant Tantric tradition, whose emphasis on ritual and practice had widespread appeal, not least because of its affinities with popular indigenous practices. Tantric practices consist basically of manual gestures (*mudrā*), chanting ritual formulas (*dhāraṇī*), and mental concentration on graphic representations of the Dharma (*maṇḍala*). The Indian origins and the Chinese career of this third major path of Mahāyāna Buddhism—the Vajrayāna, or "Diamond Vehicle"—are traced by Paul Watt, and its Tibetan flowering is chronicled with zest by Alex Wayman.

In China, too, the philosophy of emptiness developed in rich and unexpected ways. Of great interest is its hybridization with the Taoist concept of nothingness, which is traced in intricate detail by Whalen Lai, who discusses China's "extravagant flight of the spirit during its medieval Buddhist period, which lasted from the third to the twelfth centuries." He sees Buddhism in China neither as an Indianization of China nor merely as a tailoring of the Dharma to local tastes, but as a "dynamic unfolding of the Dharma."

It is important for understanding Buddhist spirituality to be aware that emptiness is not merely a theoretical tour de force. Even in its most lofty flights of speculation, Buddhism has always—at least in principle—made orthodoxy subservient to orthopraxis. By this is not meant a social morality that insists on putting doctrinal convictions to work in practice, but rather learning that what one experiences in religious practice is itself the truth of doctrine. Many of what may appear to be secondary, "practical" questions to the Western intellectual tradition are so central in Buddhism as to make the concerns of the latter appear secondary and "speculative."

It is alien to Buddhism to think in terms of logic alone, separating the study of what is true from the exploration of the path to spiritual freedom. Liberation and transformation are the goal and the element of all Buddhist philosophy. If the tradition has never lacked those who deliberately cultivate a speculative or scholastic approach for religious ends, it has also been constant in its vigilance against the danger of being drowned in academic pursuits and forgetting the essential concern with liberation. The philosophy of emptiness is in fact developed entirely as a series of defenses against this danger, a motivation that may excuse what many critics of the Mādhyamika thinkers saw as their excesses.

Thus, while Western metaphysics has developed a sophisticated array of alternative accounts of *being* and *essences,* the philosophical schools of Mahāyāna Buddhism have developed a no less impressive and pluralistic array of theories about *nothingness* and *emptiness.* Much that appears repetitious is so because the significance of the minor difference is lost on the non-Buddhist, while much that appears simplistic and uncritical is so because the Buddhist tradition has focused its sights elsewhere.

Aware of the provisional status of language, Buddhism was able to take in its stride many notions and practices of a kind often proscribed as heretical or superstitious in the West. The Asian cultures that accepted Buddhism and blended it synergistically with their indigenous traditions never produced the kind of "underground" movements that have been so significant in Western religious history. The streams of gnosticism, mysticism, alchemy, magic, spiritism, and even folklore that have provided a kind of countercurrent to official Christianity from early in its history are not present in the same way in the Buddhist world. These elements are not absent from Buddhism, of course, and in fact have become integral parts of the Buddhist tradition in many cultures and function as useful ways of making contact with the minds and hearts of ordinary people. The conviction that all things are empty allows religious language and gestures to be regarded as lacking any intrinsic substance, as belonging, like all language, to the register of conventional rather than absolute truth, and therefore as being useful as a "skillful means" for leading to enlightenment even when they take what may seem coarse and materialistic forms.

The Staff of the Nanzan Institute for Religion and Culture
Nagoya, Japan

Notes

1. Walpola Rahula, *What the Buddha Taught* (New York: Grove Press, 1974) 68.
2. *Mahāparinibbāna-sutta,* as quoted in Rahula, *What the Buddha Taught,* 61.
3. Quoted in Edward Conze, *Buddhism: Its Essence and Development* (London: Faber, 1951) 45.
4. Quoted in Edward Conze, *Buddhist Scriptures* (Harmondsworth: Penguin, 1959) 40–41.
5. *Samyutta-Nikāya,* in Henry Clarke Warren, *Buddhism in Translations* (reprint, New York: Atheneum, 1977) 152.
6. Rahula, *What the Buddha Taught,* 51.
7. Ibid., 75.
8. Takeuchi Yoshinori, *The Heart of Buddhism* (New York: Crossroad, 1983) 3–4.
9. *The Holy Teaching of Vimalakīrti,* trans. Robert A. F. Thurman (University Park, PA: Pennsylvania State University Press, 1976) 56–57.

Bibliography

Corless, Roger J. *The Vision of Buddhism.* New York: Paragon House, 1989.
The Dhammapada: The Path of Perfection. Translated by Juan Mascaró. Harmondsworth: Penguin, 1973.
Gombrich, Richard. *Theravada Buddhism.* London: Routledge & Kegan Paul, 1988.

Harvey, B. Peter. *An Introduction to Buddhism: Teachings, History and Practices.* Cambridge: Cambridge University Press, 1990.
Nyanaponika Thera. *Heart of Buddhist Meditation.* 3rd ed. London: Rider, 1962.
Williams, Paul. *Mahāyāna Buddhism: The Doctrinal Foundations.* London: Routledge, 1989.

Part One

EARLY BUDDHISM AND THERAVĀDA

1

The Message of Gotama Buddha and Its Earliest Interpretations

G. C. Pande

THE IMMEDIATE CONTEXT of the emergence of Buddhism in India in the fifth century B.C.E. is the śramaṇa movement, in which independent ascetics freed themselves from Vedic authority, brahmanic ritualism, and conservative social tradition and established communities for the purpose of exploring new paths to spiritual liberation. The fatalist Ājīvakas, the naturalist Lokāyatas, the Agnostic school, the Jains, and the Buddhists are the foremost of these groups. The teaching, dhamma (Skt. *dharma*),[1] of the latter group is closely associated with the life of its founder Gotama, acclaimed as a Buddha, or awakened one. Already in the earliest sources, his biography, or the fragments of it which they present, has become an exemplification of the Dhamma and the way to liberation, nibbāna. Chief among these sources are the scriptures (*sutta*) of the *Sutta-piṭaka,* the first of the Three Baskets (Tripiṭaka) into which the canons of the early schools of Buddhism are divided. For the present account, we may rely exclusively on the Pāli Canon of the Theravāda school.

Gotama's Conversion

Very few strictly historical details of Siddhattha Gotama the Buddha's life can be gleaned. He was born about 566 B.C.E. in Lumbinī near Kapilavatthu, the principal city of the Sākyas, in present-day Nepal. The Sākyas were a republican clan, and the Buddha belonged to one of their ruling families. At the age of twenty-nine he "went forth" to live a homeless existence. His conversion to spiritual life is said to have resulted from his perception of the suffering of old age, disease, and death on the one hand and of the peace of world-renouncing ascetics on the other.

> Narrow is the household life, a path of dust . . . , nor is it easy while dwelling in a house to lead the Brahma-faring completely fulfilled, utterly purified,

> polished like a conch-shell. Suppose now that I, having cut off hair and beard, having clothed myself in saffron garments, should go forth from home into homelessness? Thus he considered and went forth.[2]

> There came to me the thought: "Why do I, being of a nature to be reborn, being subject to death, to sorrow, to the impurities, thus search after things of like nature? What if I, being myself of such nature, and seeing the disadvantage of what is subject to rebirth, were to search after the unsurpassed, perfect security, which is nibbāna!"–Then, brethren, some time after this, when I was a young lad, a black-haired stripling, endowed with happy youth, in the first flush of manhood, against my mother's and my father's wish, who lamented with tearful eyes, I had the hair of head and face shaved off, I donned the saffron robes, I went forth from my home to the homeless life.[3]

What led the Buddha to this renunciation was a spiritual sensitivity outraged by the vanity of egoistic and sensual pursuits and by the universality of mutability and disquiet, strife, and suffering. This transforming experience of *dukkha* was his discovery of the first of the four noble (ariyan) truths, namely: (1) the nature of *dukkha;* (2) its origination; (3) its cessation; (4) the path to this cessation. Rather than translate *dukkha* as "pain" or "suffering," one ought rather to use the term "ill" or "disvalue," indicating that the truth of *dukkha* is registered not by feelings but by spiritual insight. Identifying it with mere physical or emotional suffering, C. A. F. Rhys Davids thought that since *dukkha* was not a "distinctively spiritual ill," the first noble truth could not be an original principle of Buddhism but must be a later monastic addition.[4] Attempts to define *dukkha* simply in terms of socially structured suffering are similarly misleading. Nor can it be conceived simply as unrest or agitation, though these are essential aspects of it. Disagreeable sensations, emotional suffering, or social deprivations may occasion spiritual dissatisfaction with the habitual life of the body and the mind, individual and social. To speak of *dukkha* in this sense is not to speak of discontent of body and mind, but rather of discontent with body and mind, an existential suffering grounded in the temporality of human existence.

The universality of *dukkha–sabbaṃ dukkhaṃ*–was not a tenet peculiar to Buddhism but was quite widespread among Indian sects. The Theravādins rejected the interpretation propounded by some Buddhist schools that this doctrine implied there could be no pleasure in the world. If there were no pleasure, how could there be any attachment? To avoid confusion a distinction was made between types of suffering. *Dukkha-dukkhatā* is the pain of disagreeable sensations and is known to everyone. *Pariṇāma-dukkhatā* is the pain caused by the passing away of pleasure and happiness. *Saṃkhāra-dukkhatā* is the subtlest form of "pain," fully appreciated only by the spiritually discerning. It is the pain caused by the inherent restlessness and transitoriness of all phenomena. Experience and all its elements are composites, ceaselessly arising and passing away. As attention is focused on this restlessness of conscious being, an excruciating experience of pain is produced. This is a pain from which there can be no relief except through a total inner detachment. The renunciation of worldly life, of family ties, property, and social position, of pleasure-seeking and egoistic ambitions is the first step in this direction.

The Noble Quest

The Buddha spent the next six years in the study of spiritual practices. His two principal teachers taught him the attainments that Buddhism classifies as the third and fourth of the formless meditations. In these the mind withdraws from external objects until it rests in virtual objectlessness. In the third formless meditation, taught by Āḷāra Kālāma, the mind rests in simple emptiness or nothingness. The Buddha mastered this but felt dissatisfied, because, while it led the mind away from the bustle and distraction of external life for a time, it did not lead to dispassion or higher knowledge, or remove the roots of passion: "This *dhamma* does not conduce to disregard nor to dispassion nor to stopping nor to tranquillity nor to super-knowledge nor to awakening nor to nibbāna, but only as far as reaching the plane of neither-perception-nor-non-perception."[5] Such concentration of abstracted consciousness did not eradicate the passions and hence could not yield lasting peace. In the fourth formless meditation, taught by Uddaka Rāmaputta, the indrawn consciousness becomes so subtle that despite its continued existence its presence cannot be noticed distinctly, and one attains "the sphere of neither ideation nor non-ideation." The Buddha found that it suffered the same defect as the attainment mastered earlier.

The Buddha now devoted himself to the practice of austerities, common among the śramaṇa groups:

> I was unclothed, flouting life's decencies, licking my hands (after meals), not one to come when asked to do so. . . . I was one who subsisted on forest roots and fruits, eating the fruits that had fallen. . . . I became one who stood upright, refusing a seat; I became one who squats on his haunches, intent on the practice of squatting. I became one for covered thorns, I made my bed on covered thorns . . . on my body there accumulated the dust and dirt of years, so that it fell off in shreds.[6]

He practiced extreme solitude, fleeing from all human contact. He exposed himself to extreme heat and cold:

> Now scorched, now cold, alone in terrifying forest,
> Naked and sitting fireless, the sage is intent on his quest.[7]

He lay down in a charnel field upon bones of corpses and bore with equanimity the insults and torments people heaped upon him.

He strove to still his mind by sheer effort and resolution and through practices described as follows in a dialogue between the Buddha and a Jain controversialist:

> So I, Aggivessana, with my teeth clenched, with my tongue pressed against the palate, by mind subdued, restrained and dominated my mind. . . . When I had stopped breathing in and breathing out through the mouth and through the nose, there came to be an exceedingly loud noise of winds escaping by the auditory passages. . . . When I had stopped breathing in and breathing out through the mouth and through the nose and through the ears, exceedingly loud winds rent my head. . . . Unsluggish energy came to be stirred up in me, unmuddled mindfulness set up, yet my body was turbulent, not calmed, because I was harassed in striving by striving against that very pain. . . . Because I ate so little, all my limbs became like the joints of withered creepers . . . my gaunt ribs became like the crazy rafters of a tumble-down shed . . . the pupils of my eyes appeared lying low and deep. . . . Some recluses . . . in the past have experienced feelings that were acute, painful, sharp, severe; but this is paramount, nor is there worse than this. . . . But I, by this severe austerity, do not reach states of further-men, the excellent knowledge and vision befitting the ariyans. Could there be another way to awakening?[8]

So he abandoned the path of austerities and was given up by his companions as an apostate.

Enlightenment

That severe physical austerities do not constitute a spiritually fruitful path became a cardinal principle of the Buddha's teachings. The "middle path" advocated in the First Sermon counsels avoidance of the two extremes of ease and enjoyment on the one hand and of severe austerities and self-torture on the other. A lute is melodious only when its strings are neither slack nor overstrung.[9] Spiritual practice requires a well-tuned body and mind, neither torpid nor overwrought. The Buddha finally reached his goal through the practice of jhāna, translated as "concentration" or "meditation." In choosing the path of jhāna, the Buddha shed the ascetic fear of all kinds of happiness. "Now, am I afraid of that happiness which is happiness apart from sense-pleasures, apart from unskilled states of mind?"[10] Such non-sensual happiness is characteristic of the early stages of jhāna. Through the practice of jhāna he overcame Māra (a tempter figure who represents desire and death) and attained *saṃbodhi* (awakening, enlightenment). It is interesting to note that the Buddha's contemporary Nigaṇṭha Nātaputta claimed to have attained spiritual perfection through the practice of severe austerities and that this remains a cardinal principle of Jainism.

1. The Birth of the Future Buddha at Lumbinī.

The four jhānas are described as follows:

> But when I, Aggivessana, had taken some material nourishment, having picked up strength, aloof from pleasures of the senses, aloof from unskilled states of mind, I entered on and abided in the first meditation which is accompanied by initial thought and discursive thought, is born of aloofness, and is rapturous and joyful. . . .
>
> By allaying initial thought and discursive thought, with the mind subjectively tranquillised and fixed on one point, I entered on and abided in the second meditation which is devoid of initial and discursive thought, is born of concentration, and is rapturous and joyful. . . .
>
> By the fading out of rapture I dwelt with equanimity, attentive and clearly conscious, and I experienced in my person that joy of which the ariyans say: "Joyful lives he who has equanimity and is mindful," and I entered on and abided in the third meditation. . . .
>
> By getting rid of joy and by getting rid of anguish, by the going down of former pleasures and sorrows, I entered into and abided in the fourth meditation which has neither anguish nor joy and which is entirely purified by equanimity and mindfulness.[11]

Having reached the fourth jhāna, the Buddha's mind became "quite purified, quite clarified, without blemish, without defilement, grown soft and workable, fixed, immovable."[12] He acquired the knowledge of his previous existences, of the rise and fall of beings, and of the destruction of the cankers of sense pleasure, becoming, and ignorance.

> Destroyed is birth, brought to a close is the Brahma-faring, done is what was to be done, there is no more of being such and such. This, Aggivessana, was the third knowledge attained by me in the third watch of the night; ignorance was dispelled, knowledge arose, darkness was dispelled, light arose, even as I abided diligent, ardent, self-resolute.[13]

Saṃbodhi constitutes the foundational experience for the Buddhist tradition of spirituality. On its basis the Buddha preached, and it has always been the goal of Buddhist spiritual aspirants. In enlightenment the mind is in a state of illumining concentration. It reflects transcendent quiescence and is omniscient, capable of illumining any object to which it turns. The totality of objects as thus apprehended is radically different from the finite world accessible to common sense. All finitizing and objectivizing movement of the mind is arrested, and the mind rests in its original state, "luminous, ethereal." Enlightenment is an intuitive experience, beyond words and thought, a synoptic vision of reality in its twofold aspect, timeless and temporal:

> I have attained to the Dhamma, profound, difficult to see, difficult to understand, quiet, excellent, beyond thought, subtle, knowable only by the knowledgeable. . . . Difficult to see is this stance: contingent or dependent origination;

this stance too is difficult to see: the quiescence of all composite conditions, the abandonment of all accidents, the cessation of desire, passionlessness, cessation, nibbāna.[14]

Here the content of enlightenment, or the Dhamma, is reflectively formulated in terms of the principles of dependent origination and nibbāna, the former emphasizing the contingency and orderedness of temporal phenomena, the latter the transcendence of the timeless. After his awakening the Buddha is said to have exclaimed, "When the elements are revealed to the strenuous meditating seer, his doubts are all removed since he knows the phenomena along with their causes."[15] Elsewhere his first words are said to have been the following:

Seeking the builder of the house
I have run through the cycle of many births.
Ill is birth over and over again,
House-builder, you are seen,
You will build a house no more.
All your rafters are broken,
The peak of the roof is ruined,
The mind is freed from its accumulations,
It has reached the cessation of desires.
(*Dhammapada* 11.8–9)

The Buddha's Teaching

How was the Buddha to communicate his transcendental vision? It was beyond word and thought, and the people were sunk in the mad pursuit of the world. His reluctance to return to the world and preach was natural. It is said that Brahma entreated him to preach and that he agreed to do so out of compassion. This scene symbolizes the superhuman compassion that bridges the vast gulf between the eternal silence of transcendental wisdom and the preaching of the truth in the world. Wisdom alone would have led to total silence. It is compassion that made the historic ministry of the Buddha possible.

The Buddha was able to communicate spiritual truth by a reinterpretation of the role of words. The current Vedic theory was that truth is beheld by seers clothed *ab initio* in words. Others have to grasp the truth in and through these perennial words. The Buddha, however, wanted people to remember his teaching in their own dialects. Truth has to be realized directly and personally. The Buddha can only point the way. He sought to confine himself to practical directions avoiding verbal and conceptual pictures of the truth. Words and concepts, since they are derived from ordinary experience, cannot be applied to transcendental truth. Hence the Buddha refused to answer questions about what transcends ordinary experience and preserved a noble silence about such speculative issues as whether the world is permanent or impermanent, finite or infinite, whether the soul is the same as the body or different, whether the Tathāgata survives death or not; since these questions did not contribute to dispassion or enlightenment, he classified them as *abyākata* (unanalyzed, unexplained). What he had promised to explain were the four truths. If someone is hit by a poisoned arrow, should the physician conduct a detailed inquiry into the circumstances of the person or of the manufacture of the arrow, leaving the patient to die without treatment? The Buddha's practical directions are addressed to the spiritual cure of humankind, not to idle speculation.[16]

The spirituality that the Buddha inculcated may be characterized as follows: Spiritual life consists in the effort to move away from ignorance to wisdom. This effort has two principal dimensions: the cultivation of serenity and the cultivation of insight. Ignorance is the mistaken belief in the selfhood of body and mind, which leads to involvement in egoism, passions, actions, and repeated birth and death. Wisdom is insight into the three characteristics of all existence–no-self (*anattā*), impermanence (*anicca*), and *dukkha*–and the direct experience of timeless reality, leading to liberation and lasting peace. The diverse classifications, explanations, and elaborations of these principles in the accounts of the Buddha's teaching provide the basis for later sectarian differences. Mahāyāna resolved these inconsistencies by the theory that the Buddha taught differently to different persons according to their inclination and abilities.

The distinctiveness of the Buddha's teachings may be judged from their contrast with beliefs and practices then current. In the Vedic tradition one sought the immortality of the soul through the appeasement of gods by prayer and ritual, which have no place in the Buddha's teaching. In marked contrast to the Jains, who focused on perfecting the individual soul, the Buddha did not accept a permanent individual spiritual substance. By inner serenity and watchfulness one can discern the non-selfhood of body and mind. As an aid to this insight an objective analysis of the human being as an aggregate of physical and mental factors was encouraged:

> "What do you think about this, monks? Is body permanent or impermanent?"
> "Impermanent, Lord."
> "But is that which is impermanent painful or pleasurable?"
> "Painful, Lord."
> "But is it fit to consider that which is impermanent, painful, of a nature to change, as 'This is mine, this am I, this is my self'?"
> "It is not, Lord."[17]

The question is repeated for the other four skandhas—feeling, perception, habitual tendencies, consciousness. Although the Buddha shunned speculation, a distinctive philosophical method and vision underlie this practice of meditative analysis. The universal orderedness of phenomena is assumed. The mind is treated simply as conditioned happening.

These foundations of Buddhist spirituality were not secured by faith in tradition or any literal revelation. Whereas Vedic rituals were performed in view of invisible results, the Buddha's spiritual path involves a constant transformation of one's self-consciousness with evident results. Nevertheless, it would be incorrect to think of the Buddha as lying totally outside ancient spiritual tradition. He was seen as freshly proclaiming the ancient highway to nibbāna. What the Buddha preached was held to be part of an ancient spiritual tradition forgotten or allowed to lapse into disuse. Confirmation by tradition strengthens the credibility of personal testimony. But the tradition in question here is essentially invisible and nonhistorical. It is also incorrect to say that Buddhism excludes the notion of grace. As the supreme teacher, the Buddha himself functioned as a channel of grace. Moreover, the very fact that people sunk in ignorance and passions are enabled to reach transcendent knowledge attests to the spontaneously illumining power of reality; this is of the order of grace.[18] In reciting the words "I take refuge in the Buddha, the Dhamma, the Saṅgha," the spiritual aspirant is linked to the Three Jewels as channels of grace. This aspect of Buddhism is greatly elaborated in the Mahāyāna schools.

The Middle Way and Nibbāna

In the First Sermon, given to five monks after his enlightenment, the Buddha presents his Dhamma as a middle way between the extremes of sensual indulgence and ascetic self-affliction:

> And what, monks, is this middle course fully awakened to by the Truthfinder, making for vision, making for knowledge, which conduces to calming, to super-knowledge, to awakening, to nirvana? It is this ariyan eightfold Way itself, that is to say: right view, right thought, right speech, right action, right mode of living, right endeavour, right mindfulness, right concentration.[19]

The term "middle way" can also mean the avoidance of the extremes of eternalism (*sassatavāda*) and materialistic annihilationism (*ucchedavāda*); in this sense it is identified with dependent co-arising, *paṭiccasamuppāda*. Some take this to mean that the concept of the stream of psychic becoming should replace the notion of a permanent soul substance and its materialistic denial. The Mahāyāna interpretation represented by Nāgārjuna is superior: it holds that neither being nor non-being can truly be predicated of the flux of contingent and relative phenomena. While dependent co-arising is a central teaching of the Buddha, its importance waned in the scholastic analysis of the Abhidharma schools in favor of a more general theory of causes and conditions. In Mahāyāna it was revived as a principle of dialectical relativity, revealing the emptiness of phenomena. In the Buddha's teaching, dependent co-arising is the essential character of the phenomenal world. It explains the genesis of *dukkha* and the necessary order which links different mental states. The full chain of twelves causes (*nidāna*) is a standard item of Buddhist dogmatics:

> Conditioned by ignorance activities come to pass; conditioned by activities consciousness, conditioned by consciousness name-and-shape, conditioned by name-and-shape sense, conditioned by sense contact, conditioned by contact feeling, conditioned by feeling craving, conditioned by craving grasping, conditioned by grasping becoming, conditioned by becoming birth, conditioned by birth old age-and-death, grief, lamenting, suffering, sorrow, despair come to pass. Such is the uprising of this entire mass of ill. This, brethren, is called [causal] happening.
>
> But from the utter fading away and ceasing of ignorance [comes] ceasing of activities; from ceasing of activities ceasing of consciousness. . . .[20]

Knowledge of this law of enchainment gives one the possibility of self-liberation. Desisting from worldly actions, curbing desires, and ultimately destroying ignorance through the cultivation of wisdom, one can break the links of one's bondage.

Nibbāna is the goal of spiritual striving. A correct appreciation of its nature is necessary to understand the orientation and value of Buddhist spirituality. Nibbāna is not mere annihilation: that would be *ucchedavāda,* which the Buddha repeatedly condemned. No Buddhist school except the Sautrāntikas hold nibbāna to be merely negative. Negative epithets prevail in accounts of it, both because it means cessation of the life of suffering, desires, and ignorance, and because, not being a phenomenal, finite object, it can only be described through negations and contrasts. Nibbāna is the eternal beacon for spiritual practice:

> Monks, there is a not-born, a not-become, a not-made, a not-compounded. Monks, if that unborn, not-become, not-made, not-compounded were not, there would be apparent no escape from this here that is born, become, made, compounded.[21]

The reason why nibbāna is so often grasped as a void is because it is thought that the doctrine of no-self implies that there can be nothing left after the bodily and mental aggregates cease. However, this doctrine is not a denial of the continuity of spiritual life (saṃsāra) and moral responsibility after death (kamma). Nor does it deny the reality of a transcendent and eternal principle attainable through spiritual effort. It rejects the substantial conception of the soul and the selfhood of mutable aggregates so that detachment from them can be cultivated. Its context is spiritual practice, not a naturalist or positivist critique of metaphysics.

The Way of Liberation

Buddhist spirituality thus begins with a radical analysis of the chain of human bondage. Depending on a beginningless ignorance arises name-and-form, a world of individual persons and thence pleasure and pain, love and hate. Craving and striving, we lay down the burden of one life only to pick up that of another. The eightfold path methodically reverses this chain of causes, beginning from the liberating vantage-point of right view, as opposed to the ignorance from which bondage originated. Founded on this lucid analysis, spiritual practice is a gradual and systematic training in which personal effort is as indispensable as competent guidance.[22] First, actions are controlled by moral rules. Then the mind is stilled so that the turbulence of desires and passions subsides. Finally, the cultivation of insight leads to wisdom and the eradication of ignorance. These three stages of spiritual life are named *sīla*, samādhi, and *paññā*.[23]

But the Buddha did not map out the spiritual path in any fixed formula. His Dhamma is an inspiration, not a detailed manual. In one scheme thirty-seven elements conducive to enlightenment are inculcated: four applications of mindfulness, four right exertions, four bases of psychic powers, five faculties, five powers, seven factors of wisdom, and the eightfold path. The four applications of mindfulness apply it to the body, the sensations, mental states, and phenomena respectively. The four right exertions, to prevent the rise of evil states, to suppress evil states that have arisen, to promote the rise of good states, and to maintain them, are an elaboration of the right exertion that is part of the eightfold path. The four bases of psychic powers—concentration on right willing, effort, thought, and investigation—are connected with right resolution and right exertion. The five faculties and the five powers are identical: faith, will, mindfulness, concentration, and wisdom. The seven factors of wisdom are mindfulness, investigation of the law, energy, rapture, repose, concentration, and equanimity. The various lists overlap and represent diverse schematizations of the elements of the path taken as a whole or in parts.

In Buddha's own realization faith played little part. He preached in opposition to established faiths. He claimed to teach a doctrine that anybody could directly realize for himself, and he criticized the brahmins and the Jains for their reliance on faith and tradition.[24] Yet faith (*saddhā*), in the sense of heartfelt inner commitment to the spiritual life, rather than belief based on authority, is counted as an essential ingredient of the spiritual orientation. Buddhist faith is conative, not cognitive. The enthusiastic adoption of spiritual life has to be followed by a determined effort of the will. *Vāyāma* (exertion), *viriya* (energy), *padhāna* (effort), *parakkama* (application of will), *utthāna* (initiative) are some of the terms used. This attitude differed sharply from the predeterminism of the Ājīvakas and the reliance on grace proclaimed in some Upanishads. In ordinary life we are creatures of habit shaped by ignorance and passion. To overcome this inertia, we need continuing effort and application of the will. Spiritual life requires the effort to practice ideals that are at variance with habitual inclinations. Ordinarily the mind is beset by distraction. Desire as thirst (*taṇhā*) rules the mind, flitting here and there like a butterfly. To overcome it, constant vigilance and mindfulness (*sati*) are required. But before much progress can be made in mindfulness and concentration (samādhi), it is necessary that a suitable moral culture be firmly adopted. The regulation and purification of conduct precede concentration and insight.

Moral Culture

The lack of theological and metaphysical dogmas in the path inculcated by the Buddha does not mean that it consists merely in ethical practice. Such practice is the necessary beginning of Buddhist spiritual culture, but not its culmination. Right conduct is not merely the adoption of clearly formulated rules but also of the attitude of moderation, in opposition to a lazy slavery to sense impressions and impulses. Mere formalism, ethical or ritual, is condemned.[25] Some brahmins recommended the total deprivation of the senses as a method of controlling them.[26] The Buddha rejected this in favor of an analytical attitude toward sense impressions so as to "divert the complex impacts of the external world from kindling delusions and passions, and convert them into the cool judgments of the intellect."[27] These prescriptions rest on a distinctive psychoethical approach to action. Moral values are not sundered from the factual psychology of action, and good and evil are focused by the intuitive, introspective perception of motives that move the will to action. The will may be moved by the evil motives—desire, hatred, or delusion—or by their opposites—compassion, nonviolence, equanimity—which are intrinsically good. The distinction between good and evil thus rests on one between higher and lower motives.

Moral law is not simply a formal obligation which leaves facts untouched,

2. *An Unidentified Scene from the Life of the Buddha,* 2nd–3rd century C.E. Kushāṇa period (ca. 50 C.E. —mid 5th century). Sculpture—Pakastani (Gandhāra). Silvery dark grey phyllite. 22 1/2 x 36 inches.

but a cosmically operative natural law, perceived by wisdom and expressed in appropriate sequences of action and experience. Good actions lead to happiness, and bad actions lead to unhappiness. Motiveless actions do not produce any affective consequences. The correlation of actions with consequences, however, is not directly perceptible because of the complexity of motives and the fact that the results of actions are worked out in long chains of life and death. Only the Buddha can perceive the working out of the law of kamma. It remains his firm teaching that men are constituted by their kamma. Their proper inheritance consists of their own past kamma.

Moral culture thus involves the adoption of rules, the purification of motives, and ultimately the transcendence of kamma. The adoption of the precepts is the beginning of *sīla*. Five of these are fundamental and are common to lay followers as well as monks: refraining (1) from injury to living things, (2) from taking what is not given, (3) from sexual misconduct, (4) from falsehood, (5) from liquors that induce forgetfulness. The first four were universally accepted in ancient Indian spirituality and may even be described as universal presuppositions of spiritual culture. The recognition of the natural rights of life, property, and fair dealings is implicit here. Additional rules for the monks included refraining (6) from untimely food, (7) from seeing the performance of dancers, musicians, and jesters, (8) from adorning the body, (9) from the use of high and comfortable beds, (10) from accepting gold and silver. Other lists of *sīlas* replace the fifth lay precept with (5) refraining from slander, and add refraining (6) from harsh speech, (7) from frivolous talk, (8) from covetousness, (9) from malice, and (10) from false views. The monk is in addition subject to the basic rules called *pātimokkha,* collectively recited at the fortnightly ceremony called *uposatha,* at which monks who had transgressed were required to confess and accept the punishment prescribed by the local Saṅgha. Other rules, dealing with such details as the personal goods allowed to be used by monks or their medical treatment in case of illness, were collected in the Vinaya; these gradually became more extensive, and more liberal than those followed by sects such as the Jains and the Ājīvakas. The Buddha is said to have charged these sects with tormenting themselves in this life without freeing themselves from suffering in the next.

Buddhist morality consists in "avoiding evil, promoting the good, and purifying the heart." Avoiding ascetic self-torment and ritualism, Buddhist morality is distinguished by its moderation, rationality, and introspection. Though rejecting self-mortification, it is an ascetic path inasmuch as it prescribes self-discipline and rejects the worldly end of gratification. As a householder, one lives in the world without pursuing it and cultivates truth, nonviolence, respect for the property of others, and marital fidelity, accepting only the right methods of livelihood and practicing liberality and compassion. The Sermon to Sigāla sketches the practices appropriate to a householder, centering on restraint and purification of the heart.[28]

Spiritual Concentration

The purification of the heart can be helped by certain exercises of contemplation, notably the four *brahmavihāras,* the divine (brahmic) states, also practiced in Hinduism: meditation on love (*mettā*), compassion (*karuṇā*), sympathetic enjoyment (*muditā*), and equanimity (*upekkhā*).[29] Love is defined as pure goodwill, the desire of bringing welfare and good to fellow human beings. The meditation on love begins by reflecting on the evils of hate and the advantages of forbearance. One may recollect sayings like "Friend, a man who is overcome by hate and whose mind is assailed by hate kills beings." "Him I call a brahmin who is strong in forbearance, who makes an army of it." Next one concentrates on an appropriate object of love so that the feeling of love suffuses the mind. The object of love is then universalized and the feeling of love deepened till a trance is reached. One begins by thinking of oneself and then one recalls the similarity between oneself and others, thus extending goodwill to others and overcoming the diverse barriers to this extension. "And how, monks, does a monk live suffusing a quarter of the globe with a heart full of love? Just as on seeing a dear charming person one would fall in love, so he suffuses all beings with love." During this process one must avoid the resurgence of ill will and anger. The admonitions in the parable of the saw may be dwelt upon: "Monks, were spies and thieves with a double-handled saw to cut the various limbs of a man, and he were to be angry in mind thereat, he on that account would not be a follower of my religion." As one reaches contemplative trance, one "abides suffusing wholeheartedly the whole wide world, above, below, around, and everywhere with heart full of love, far-reaching, grown great, and beyond measure, without enmity, without ill will." Such a person is happy awake and asleep, dear to all beings, and goes to Brahma's heaven after death.

The meditation on pity begins with reflection on the ills of not pitying and on the blessings of pity. The first object of pity is a person placed in evil circumstances. "And how does the monk live suffusing one quarter of the globe with heart full of pity? As on seeing a person in poor circumstances, of evil ways, he should show pity, so he suffuses all beings with pity." After developing pity with respect to a person suffering in misery, one should develop the same sentiment with respect to those who are dear, or neutral, and lastly, with respect to an enemy. (It is worth noting that Mahāyāna, distinguishing between *karuṇā* and *mahākaruṇā*, regarded this conception of compassion as a limited one, in that it describes a psychic sentiment to be developed on the way to nibbāna and takes for granted the reality of individual persons.) To develop sympathetic gladness, one may begin with the thought of a very dear friend. "As, on seeing a person, loved, lovable, he would be joyful, so he suffuses all beings with sympathy." Having reached the third jhāna in any of the preceding, one may proceed to develop equanimity. "As, on seeing a person neither lovable nor unlovable, he would be even-minded, so he suffuses all beings with even-mindedness." It arises from realizing that all beings are fashioned by their actions, that the moral law determines their condition. It is an attitude of centered objectivity.

The *brahmavihāras* are a link between *śīla* and samādhi. Love, compassion, sympathy, and equanimity are inherently spiritualizing forms of awareness transforming the subject, not merely sentiments approved socially. Another equally important practice which promotes concentration is the cultivation of mindfulness, of which the most famous form is the mindfulness of breathing (*ānāpānasati*).

> Respiration mindfulness, monks, developed and repeatedly practiced, is of great fruit, of great benefit; respiration-mindfulness, developed and repeatedly practiced, perfects the four foundations of mindfulness; the four foundations of mindfulness perfect the seven factors of enlightenment factors; the seven factors of enlightenment perfect clear vision and deliverance.[30]

The monk wishing to practice mindfulness sits cross-legged with body erect. He breathes in and breathes out mindfully, noticing whether the breath is long or short. He notices the whole process of breathing, calming the bodily formations. He then combines the mindfulness of breathing with the noticing of subjective feelings. Later he notices the passage of thoughts, and finally he notices the impermanence, fading, and cessation of phenomena. This practice has a close affinity to Yogic *prāṇāyāma.* In modern times U Sobhana Mahathera of Burma has revived, refined, and popularized it.[31] The practice is specially recommended to those who are bewildered or suffering from delusion (*moha*). A modern mind will be convinced of its amazing efficacy only through actual experience, which, however, is not difficult to acquire.

Jhāna, which has a central place in the Buddhist cultivation of mental serenity and insight, is not unique to Buddhism, but the Buddha advocated jhāna in a distinctive manner, as the intuition by the purified and still mind of the evanescence, determinate orderedness, non-selfhood of all phenomena, especially mental phenomena. It is such an intuition alone that can lead the mind to its noumenal effulgence and total detachment. Jhāna was used by different sects for a variety of purposes—for reaching this or that divine world, for the acquisition of supernormal powers, for the sake of enjoyable experience, for communication with the true self or inner reality. The Buddha, however, advocated it for the realization of spiritual learning (*vijjā*) culminating in bodhi. The nearest parallel to this is found in Sāṃkhya Yoga, which also had the four jhānas. In the first jhāna, as we have seen, the practitioner is freed from passions and evil states but is in possession of thought and a pleasure born of discrimination. In the second jhāna, the movement of thought ceases, but the rapturous pleasure born of concentration continues. In the third the experience of rapture is left behind but the physical sensation of pleasure continues. In the fourth all pleasure is dropped and only an even-minded concentration remains. In the early canonical texts, it is in this state that Buddha attained Enlightenment. The usual accounts of jhāna, however, add to these four jhānas of the world of form the four formless meditations, whereby one dwells in the spheres of ethereal infinity, the infinity of consciousness, nothingness, and neither ideation nor non-ideation, respectively. Sometimes a ninth attainment is added, called the cessation of thought and feeling. Some have tried to see it as the attainment of nibbāna, but this is unlikely.

A distinction is sometimes made between the cultivation of serenity (*samatha*) and insight (*vipassanā*). Sayadaw writes:

> There are two kinds of Meditation-development, viz., tranquillity and insight. A person who, of these two, has first developed tranquillity, and after having established himself in either Access Concentration or Full Concentration, subsequently contemplates the five groups of Grasping, is called a *samatha-yānika,* i.e., one who has tranquillity as his vehicle. A person who, without developing either of these concentrations, contemplates the five groups of Grasping, is called a *suddhavipassanā-yanika,* i.e., one who has pure insight as his vehicle.

Actually the difference between the two paths is only at the stage of commencement, for at some point in jhāna one has to meditate on truth, while those who start with such meditation are bound to tranquillize their minds if their meditation is sufficiently serious. Both paths culminate in the intuition of truth. This is possible because in Buddhist spiritual practice the objects of meditation are not transcendent or verbal entities but basically psychic phenomena to be discerned with clarity and without prejudice. The hallmark (*lakkhaṇa*) of that which is evil and from which detachment is sought is impermanence. Whatever is impermanent is causally determined and devoid of selfhood. It is only through the direct inward perception of these truths with respect to the elements of experience that one can finally still and free the mind. This is possible because of the nature of the mind, luminous in itself but covered by desires arising from the misapprehension of the nature of things.

Four stages of spiritual development are distinguished. The realization of the noble truth of suffering enables one to enter the stream of spirituality leading to nibbāna. When the first three fetters—delusion of the self, doubt about Buddha and his teachings, belief in the efficacy of rites and ceremonies—are removed, one becomes a stream-runner, whose salvation is assured within seven births. The next stage is that of "one who will have but one more birth" and the third that of "one who will not be reborn again." During these stages one eradicates the fetters of lust and hatred. The fourth path is that of the worthy one or arahant, who is freed from the fetters of love of life in the form world, pride, self-righteousness, ignorance. Thus, arahantship is freedom from the ten fetters. The image of the arahant as one who has given up all desires, passions, and egoism and dwells and moves in imperturbable peace is a perpetual spiritual inspiration. The path of arahantship culminates in nibbāna, whose facets are indicated by the endless names the early Buddhists found for it: emancipation, island of refuge, end of craving, state of purity, the supreme, the transcendent, the uncreate, the tranquil, the unchanging, the going-out, the unshaken, the imperishable, the ambrosia. These are relational descriptions of nibbāna as the goal of spiritual practice. What nibbāna is in itself lies beyond speech and thought.

The Buddha's Followers and the First Differences in Interpretation

The Buddha died, or rather attained final and complete nibbāna, nibbāna freed from the residual substrate of the physical and mental constituents, at Kusinārā about the age of eighty. His last days are recorded in the *Mahāparinibbāna-suttanta*, which gives his final utterance as "Decay is inherent in all composite things; work with diligence."[32] The Buddha's followers had come from all sections of society and included kings, queens, generals, rich bankers, smiths, courtesans, slave women, fishermen, barbers, robbers. Once they joined the order all were considered equal, and for many the Buddhist Saṅgha brought liberation from the constraints of a caste society. While some scholars have attempted to connect particular followers of the Buddha with specific Buddhist doctrines, such attempts remain highly speculative. Nor does the tradition preserve much about the individual spiritual practices and experiences of these followers. The commentaries give biographical details about the Buddha's followers but do not claim any doctrinal or spiritual originality for them, for the tradition supposes the entire corpus of canonical writings to be directly or indirectly the word of the Buddha, and does not distinguish between his teachings and their later development by his followers. Historically, such a distinction is more than likely. Only a detailed

3. The Stūpa at Bodhgayā, the site of the Buddha's Enlightenment.

4. Stupā and gate at Sāñchī from the Aśoka period.

stratification of the canon can clarify it. Preliminary investigations in this direction show that the Buddha's message was developed through elaboration and systematization, through the introduction of metaphysical elements, and through a growing emphasis on a negative and analytical outlook. The attempt at systematization was equally extended to spiritual practice and monastic discipline. While the seminal notions of *dukkha,* dependent co-arising, ultimate peace, the middle path, and meditation were doubtless formulated by the Buddha, he refrained from metaphysical speculation of the kind already found in the canon.

Some instances may be given of what was undoubtedly taught by the Buddha and what came to be formulated by his followers through elaboration and analysis. In the *Aṭṭhakavagga,* one of the oldest and most authentic parts of the *Suttanipāta,* the Buddha speaks of man as bound and tormented in the world by pleasures and desire. Egoism, worldly consciousness, speculation, and encumbrances must be given up. The state which one reaches is neither the self nor not self. It is a state where there is not the slightest mental construction. The *Pārāyanavagga* develops this theme in a more metaphysical way. In these texts the spiritual subject is man or consciousness (*vinnāna*); his accidents are name-and-form. The doctrine of the five aggregates as constituting man is thus a later development of name-and-form. In Abhidhamma the aggregates are further subdivided into many elements (dhamma). This analytical tendency makes the concept of *anattā* more pronounced and negative. The spiritual practice of meditating on mental and physical phenomena as non-self lay behind this tendency toward an analytical outlook and a negativism that virtually became an end in itself.

Instead of nominating a successor, the Buddha declared that the Dhamma was to be the one leader of the order.

> The venerable Ānanda addressed the Exalted One, and said: . . . "Though at the sight of the sickness of the Exalted One my body became weak as a creeper, . . . I took some little comfort from the thought that the Exalted One would not pass away until at least he had left instructions as touching the Order." "What then, Ānanda? Does the Order expect that of me? I have preached the truth without making any distinction between exoteric and esoteric doctrine; for in respect of the truths, Ānanda, the Tathāgata has no such thing as the closed fist of a teacher, who keeps some things back. . . . Now the Tathāgata, Ānanda, thinks not that it is he who should lead the brotherhood, or that the Order is dependent upon him. Why then should he leave any instructions in any matter concerning the Order? . . . Therefore, O Ānanda, be ye lamps unto yourselves. Be ye a refuge to yourselves. Betake yourselves to no external refuge. Hold fast to the Truth as a lamp. Hold fast as a refuge to the Truth. Look not for any refuge to anyone besides yourselves.[33]

Moreover, instead of leaving behind any clear-cut compilation of Dhamma, the Buddha authorized minor modifications of the law: "When I am gone, Ānanda, let the Order, if it should so wish, abolish all the lesser and minor precepts."[34] This created a fluid situation. The First Council was held at Rājagṛha shortly after the death of the Buddha, on the initiative of Mahākassapa, in order to secure an agreed canon consisting of the words of the Buddha, which would be binding on all. The Venerable Upāli was questioned by Mahākassapa on the rules of discipline or Vinaya. Ānanda was similarly questioned on the principles of the faith or Dhamma. As a result the basic texts of Vinaya and Dhamma or *Suttapiṭaka* were compiled. There is no reference in these accounts, the earliest being in the Vinaya itself, to any compilation of the *Abhidhamma-piṭaka.* The issue of the abrogation of minor rules came up before the Council, but it was decided not to abrogate anything because it was feared that once begun such a process might continue indefinitely and threaten the major rules also. The appeal to all leading monks to agree to the conclusions of the Council was largely successful, but there were some dissenters.

The Second Council, held at Veśāli a hundred years later, was momentous enough to occasion the addition of a postscript describing its proceedings to the Vinaya as collected by the First Council.[35] The Council dealt with the controversy occasioned by ten new practices that the Saṅgha at Veśāli had adopted. These included the storing of a personal supply of salt; eating after midday provided that the shadow did not exceed two fingers; eating a second time if one went to a different village; taking the permission after doing an act; imitating worldly conduct during one's life as a householder; drinking a mixture of milk and curd after meals; drinking liquor by sipping it like a leech; the use of a seat or mat without a border; the acceptance of gold, silver, and other valuable goods and money. It is possible to discover important issues behind some of these apparent trivialities if they are seen as debating points to prepare the ground for others. Several of the disputed points concern exigencies of illness, especially the permission to use tonics and digestives of different kinds, some of which had been permitted by the Buddha himself. There might be a similar rational motive for eating after midday or on a journey. Some looked on such disciplinary latitude as a dangerous deviation, yet rigidity in minor matters did not really fit the original spirit of Buddhism. In the Vedic faith the rationally unintelligible parts of prescriptions were justified by reference to the unseen merit they acquired. The Buddha, however, had appealed to reason and personal experience, encouraging flexibility in regard to minor rules.

Some scholars have suggested that the real issue at the Council was an opposition between local and central authority.[36] In reality, however, the Saṅgha did not have any organized central authority, except when a General

Council was held or when some great ruler decided to intervene in its affairs. Normally the Saṅgha existed as an autonomously run local unit. These units were regarded as units of one universal ecclesia subject to the one Dhamma. Nevertheless, regional and local differences, especially with respect to monastic practice, were bound to arise. Since the Second Council was the last really ecumenical one and conciliar authority did not develop as a regular governing force, the problem of conflict between regional and central authority does not arise. The ultrademocratic spirit of the Saṅgha excluded the idea of centralized or personalized control. Some scholars have suspected that the option of accepting gold and silver in alms showed a significant growth of luxury reflecting spiritual decline. Yet, although the growth of economic and urban life coupled with lay patronage must have brought some change in monastic life, there is no real evidence of a correlative spiritual decline.

The Early Schools

The emergence of new forms of spirituality, prototypes of Mahāyāna or "greater vehicle" Buddhism, can be seen as the major silent force shaping the rise of the diverse sects and schools. The great King Aśoka had Moggaliputta Tissa convene the Third Council at Pātaliputta in 236 or 250 B.C.E. in order to put an end to sectarian controversies and to purify the Saṅgha by expelling schismatics.[37] This council no longer embodied a united Buddhism but principally represented one sect, the Sthaviras, who upheld traditional orthodoxy against the Mahāsāṅghika, Sarvāstivāda (Pāli: Sabbatthivāda, from *sabbam atthi*, "everything exists") and Puggalavāda (personalist) groups which had seceded in the century or so since the Second Council. The council is remembered only in the Singhalese Theravāda tradition; its debates are recorded in the *Katthavatthu* (Points of Controversy), one of the books of the *Abhidhamma-piṭaka.*

Traditionally eighteen schools of early Buddhism are counted; the fragmentary surviving accounts of their teachings form a confusing patchwork. The Singhalese tradition traces the secession of the Mahāsāṅghika sect from the Sthaviras to the Second Council. More plausible is the tradition preserved by Tibetan historians to the effect that the Mahāsāṅghikas emerged at an assembly at Pātaliputta in 349 B.C.E. They accepted the Five Points of Mahādeva, which liberalized the qualifications for arahantship in a way unacceptable to the Sthavira group representing the traditional teaching. Another major split was occasioned by Vātsīputra, who believed that underlying the five skandhas was an ineffable person (*puggala*)—not, however, to be identified with the substantial soul (*attā*) rejected by the Buddha. He founded the Vajjiputtaka (Skt. Vātsīputrīya) group, whose offshoot, the Sammitiyas, became one of the four most important sects of early Buddhism (with the Mahāsāṅghikas, the Sarvāstivādins, and the Sthaviras as represented by their major offshoot, the Theravādins). The realist Sarvāstivādins seceded from the Sthaviras in the reign of Aśoka. Meanwhile, the Lokattaravādins emerged as the most docetist and transcendentalist of the Mahāsāṅghika offshoots.

The Mahāsāṅghikas and their later subsects enacted the most significant break from the old tradition and are generally recognized to be the forerunners of the Mahāyāna revolution. The Five Points of Mahādeva presumably represent the first expression of Mahāsāṅghika doctrine, asserting that arahants may have passions, ignorance, and doubt and may receive instructions from others, and that the Path may be attained by a sudden shout. This conflicts with the traditional concept of the arahant as a perfected saint. Since no one claimed that arahants were omniscient, the ascription of ignorance to them has a certain plausibility. But how can there be an arahant who is still not free from passion? Mahādeva may have been groping toward a position in which the true goal of spiritual life would be focused exclusively in terms of Buddhahood rather than arahantship, or he may simply have been attacking the pretensions of pseudo-arahants. While denigrating the arahants, the Mahāsāṅghikas exalted the Buddha and the bodhisattva (Pāli: *bodhisatta*). Their point of view has been compared to that of early Christian docetism.[38] How can a mere human being be regarded as the source of perfect, spiritual truth? After death the Buddha did not follow the common human way. Could he be said to have followed it in prenatal life? According to the *Mahāvastu,* a myth-laden biography of the Buddha which presents itself as the Vinaya of the Mahāsāṅghikas, nothing belonging to the Buddha is similar to what belongs to a common mortal. The birth of bodhisattvas and their children is immaculate and supernatural. Their behavior in public life is merely a play enacted by them to establish rapport with common mortals.

> There is nothing in the Buddhas which can be measured by the standard of the world, but everything appertaining to the great seers is transcendental. . . . The Buddhas conform to the world's conditions, but in such a way that they also conform to the traits of transcendentalism. . . . It is true that they wash their feet, but no dust ever adheres to them; their feet remain clean as lotus-leaves. This washing is mere conformity with the world.[39]

The Mahāsāṅghika concept of the phantasmic Buddha-body is unintelligible without a radical revision of the concepts of mind and matter. Mind may project itself as a material body; it may act spontaneously out of enlightenment; matter may be wholly pure, unobstructive, and unlimited; and the two may be united in one supernatural being. The Mahāsāṅghikas declared that the Buddha's physical body (*rūpakāya*) is limitless in every sense and that the mind is naturally luminous and is soiled only by accidental factors. The Buddha is eternally absorbed in the contemplation of truth. Though he never speaks a word, his saving influence operates on account of his inherent resolve to help mortal beings.[40] The Mahāsāṅghika belief in pure matter and original mind takes them very near Mahāyāna. This impression is strengthened if we recall Paramārtha's statement that the Lokottaravādins regarded natural elements as unreal because they were the product of delusion. Only the supernatural element is real. It consists of the way and the goal. The latter includes the two sorts of emptiness (*sunnatā*). The way is the insight which leads to the goal.

The Theravādins and the Sarvāstivādins defended the doctrine of no-self, *anattā*, against the Vajjiputtakas and Sammitiyas, who argued that it was reasonable to affirm the reality of the person or *puggala* as bearer of the elements and components of the personality. The person is neither identical with any one of the five aggregates, nor is it different from them.[41] The reality of the *puggala* is directly perceived, and it is the *puggala* that transmigrates. Nibbāna, they held, is neither identical with nor different from the elements (dhammas). They also believed that the arahant could fall. The abandonment of passions takes place gradually just as spiritual insight also takes place gradually. They held that matter is the product of kamma and hence good or bad. In the seventh century C.E. they had considerable sway in India. They had an *Abhidhamma* of their own, which they attributed to Sāriputta. Their importance is clearly shown by the fact that the *Abhidharma-kośa* deals with them at length.[42] In early Buddhist literature there are far too many references to *puggala* and *attā* for the personalist theory to be dismissed as simply baseless. To speak of will, moral effort, character, or making one's future, is unintelligible unless a personal self is postulated, and the canon contains statements that point in this direction: "Why do you not seek the self?" "I have made the self my refuge."[43]

The Theravādins, to whom practically all Buddhist monasteries in Southeast Asia belong, are generally regarded as the most ancient of the Hīnayāna sects, the preservers of the Sthavira tradition. The fact that they possess a complete canon in an ancient Indian language lends plausibility to this view. The principles of Theravāda found their first systematic expression in the *Abhidhamma-piṭaka*. *Abhidhamma* is the analysis of the dhammas, or irreducible elements. A dhamma, defined as "that which has its own nature," is held to be a momentary function. It has a fixed nature but hardly any duration. In the spiritual context the peculiarity of this concept is that it seems to demolish any fundamental difference between the subjective and the objective poles of experience. As a result modern interpreters sometimes regard the concept as positivist, sometimes as phenomenalist. Both inter-

5. *Buddha Calling on the Earth to Witness*. India, Bengal, Pāla Period, 9th century. Black chlorite. 37 inches.

pretations are misleading, for *Abhidhamma* does not regard either external reality or mere experience as final. It merely concentrates on their dependent givenness. From the point of view of spiritual practice its aim is to reduce the notion of personality to a mere flux of events determined by causal order. Constantly contemplated, this point of view is held to emancipate one from the delusion of personality. The Theravāda *Abhidhamma* divided dhammas into four principal categories: mind, mental functions, matter, and nibbāna.

The Sarvāstivādins appear to have spread particularly in Kashmir and Gandhara. During the time of Kaniṣka a great Council of the Sarvāstivādins took place, the Fourth Council, sectarian like the Third. Just as the *Kathāvatthu* gives a summary of the Buddhist sects and their views in the third century B.C.E. from the Sthavira point of view, the *Mahāvibhāṣā*, supposedly compiled at the Fourth Council, contains a vast documentation on the Sarvāstivāda and other sects. The principal Sarvāstivāda tenet was that past and future dhammas are substantially real. Nevertheless the duration of compounded (*saṃskṛta*) dhammas is only momentary, for they have the four marks of production, duration, destruction, and cessation or impermanence. Although mutually contradictory, these marks act together. The first brings the element from the future to the present, the second holds it there, the third destroys it, and the fourth consigns it to the past. The Sarvāstivādins felt it necessary to accept the reality of past and future elements because not only are they the objects of mind; they are also implied by the law of kamma. hat exactly constitutes the difference between the three phases of time is, however, a difficult question.

The Sarvāstivādin view had a dangerous similarity to the eternalism of Sāṃkhya Yoga. The Sautrāntikas, who seceded from the Sarvāstivādins, rejected this extreme realism, pointing out the impossibility of the dhammas having an eternal nature but only a temporal being. The Vaibhāṣika Sarvāstivādins (followers of the *Mahāvibhāṣā*) had added nonmental constructs to the four kinds of dhamma recognized by the Theravādins. The Sautrāntikas rejected these; external objects could only be inferred, not directly perceived. They believed that a subtle mind (Skt. *jñāna*) is the root as well as the continuing element in the flow of the skandhas.[44] Instead of relying on the sūtras, they defended their distinctive point of view through logical argumentation. In opposing Sarvāstivāda realism they too adumbrated some basic tendencies of Mahāyāna.

Hīnayāna orthodoxy is characterized by the following beliefs: (1) The Buddha was a mortal human being who attained superhuman knowledge and powers by personal effort. His physical body (*rūpakāya*) was corruptible. The body of his doctrines (*dhammakāya*) remains the living guide for Buddhists. (2) There is no soul: thoughts and acts are real but there is no thinker or agent apart from them. (3) Human experience depends on the interaction of a plurality of momentary reals. (4) There is also a changeless and permanent entity which it is the purpose of human life to know because its knowledge frees one from the incessant travails of life. However, if the human being is nothing but a flux of events, "if suffering arises and passes without a sufferer," who is it that is to be freed? What is the meaning of freedom and peace except perhaps as the end of life and experience? But would not this be the annihilationism (*ucchedavāda*) expressly rejected by the Buddha? These difficulties prompted the Theravādins and the Sarvāstivādins to ever-subtler analysis, which nevertheless failed to satisfy many. While the personalists appealed to canonical references to "man" and "person," an alternative, later fully developed in Mahāyāna, was to regard the mind as the ultimate ground of human bondage and emancipation. Theravāda and Sarvāstivāda developed a pan-objectivist outlook, wherein nibbāna itself became one among many objects, positive or negative. The abhidhammic analysis of experience into its simplest momentary elements was a process that seemed to have no end and whose value for spiritual practice became increasingly less evident. What religious aspiration needed was a powerful God, not dead and inert elements.

As Buddhism spread into the frontier regions of the northwest and the southeast, the search for a divine figure led to an apotheosis of the Buddha in the various Mahāsāṅghika sects. Even Sarvāstivāda, spreading in the northwest, was powerfully influenced by this tendency. In the older Hīnayāna conception stream-enterers, once-returners, arahants, bodhisattvas, and Buddhas differ only in their knowledge and attainments, not in their constitutive essence. They are all human beings in different stages of the spiritual path. Theravāda regarded the Buddha as a human person subject to death. The Mahāsāṅghikas made the living and dying person an unreal image, a mere appearance. The real Buddha is nothing but the eternally self-subsistent principle of spiritual enlightenment, which serves as the source of spiritual inspiration. While making the Buddha superhuman, the Mahāsāṅghikas robbed him of personality. The ideas of *nirmāṇakāya* as well as of *saṃbhogakāya* may be traced to them.[45] The divinity of the Buddha consisted in his being the source of grace, not creation. At the popular level this might be understood in terms of a dualism which attributed evil to kamma and māyā, and grace to the Buddha. For the serious spiritual aspirant, however, it made the Buddha an ever-living principle, inspiring hope, faith, and devotion. The Mahāsāṅghika image of the Buddha was one of eternal and silent contemplation, omnipresent and radiant.[46] The historic Buddha was seen as an appearance projected in the human world as an expedient. If the Buddha is supernatural, a similar question is bound to arise about the bodhisattva.

One view was that Buddha is constituted by bodhi,[47] leaving the bodhisattva as a historical person unaffected. Alternatively, bodhisattvas could be regarded as a distinct class of supernatural beings destined to be Buddha. The radical difference between the Hīnayāna and Mahāyāna conceptions of the bodhisattva had not yet emerged.

Notes

1. I have given the Pāli form of Indian terms and names, except where the Sanskrit form is more familiar in English (as in the cases of bodhisattva, Sarvāstivāda).
2. *The Collection of the Middle Length Sayings,* trans. I. B. Horner, I 295.
3. Ibid., 207 (my translation).
4. C. A. F. Rhys Davids, *What Was the Original Gospel in 'Buddhism'?* (London: Epworth, 1938) 56–57.
5. *Middle Length Sayings,* I 210.
6. Ibid., 103–5.
7. Ibid., 106.
8. Ibid., 297–301.
9. *The Book of the Gradual Sayings,* trans. F. L. Woodward and E. M. Hare, III 267.
10. *Middle Length Sayings,* I 301.
11. Ibid., 302.
12. Ibid.
13. Ibid., 303.
14. Ibid., 211–12 (my translation).
15. *Udāna* I 1 (my translation); *Minor Anthologies of the Pali Canon* II, trans. F. L. Woodward, 2.
16. *Middle Length Sayings,* II 97–101.
17. *The Book of the Discipline,* trans. I. B. Horner, IV 20.
18. See Marco Pallis, *A Buddhist Spectrum* (New York: Seabury, 1981) 52–71.
19. *Book of the Discipline,* IV 15.
20. *The Book of Kindred Sayings,* trans. C. A. F. Rhys Davids and F. L. Woodward, II 2; cf. II 13: "Everything exists: —this is one extreme. Nothing exists: —this is the other extreme. Not approaching either extreme the Tathāgata teaches you a doctrine by the middle [way]: —Conditioned by ignorance activities come to pass . . . ."
21. *Minor Anthologies,* II 98.
22. *Middle Length Sayings,* III 52–57.
23. See *Dialogues of the Buddha,* trans. C. A. F. Rhys Davids and T. W. Rhys Davids, I 56–95.
24. *Middle Length Sayings,* III 3–6; *Dialogues of the Buddha,* I 300–320.
25. *Middle Length Sayings,* II 102–7.
26. Ibid., III 346–50.
27. C. A. F. Rhys Davids, *Journal of the Royal Asiatic Society* (1902) 481.
28. *Dialogues of the Buddha,* III 168–94.
29. For the following account, see Pe Maung Tin, *The Path of Purity, being a Translation of Buddhaghosa's Visuddhimagga* (London: Pali Text Society, 1975) 340–75.
30. *Middle Length Sayings,* III 124 (my translation).
31. Mahasi Sayadaw, *The Progress of Insight* (Kandy, Sri Lanka: Forest Hermitage, 1965).
32. *Dialogues of the Buddha,* II 71–191.

33. Ibid., II 107–8.
34. Ibid., 171.
35. *Book of the Discipline,* V 407–30.
36. C. A. F. Rhys Davids, *Sakya, or Buddhist Origin* (London: Kegan Paul, 1931).
37. For his missionary initiatives and as an embodiment of the Buddhist ideal of monarchy, Aśoka is one of the most significant figures in the history of Buddhism. His personal attitude to Buddhism is perhaps best shown in the famous Bhabru edict: "The Kind-seeing ruler of Magadha, having greeted the Saṅgha, conveys his good wishes. It is, indeed, known to you how much faith and reverence we have toward Buddha, Dhamma and Saṅgha. Sirs, whatever has been spoken by Buddha has been well spoken." In general, however, what his edicts designate as Dhamma lacks all the distinctive features of Buddhism. He denounced sectarianism and declared that there is an essential unity in the spiritual aims of different sects, and that it is only prejudice which keeps them apart. Aśoka's Dhamma is an integral ethical system, at once personal, social, and political; it includes the principles of *rājadhamma* [kingly law] conceived in terms of a paternalistic welfare state, and the Buddhist principle of "Dhamma-conquest" as opposed to conquest by war. Aśoka's belief in the unity of all faiths and his policy of helping all of them created a favorable situation of which Saṅgha was able to take full advantage, reorganizing itself and undertaking extraordinary missionary activity. After the Third Council Moggaliputta sent preachers to different frontier regions to propagate the Dhamma. Aśoka sent missions of his own, perhaps in coordination with those of the Saṅgha. The vast imperial organization of the Mauryas, its network of routes facilitating trade and movement of armies and officials, its security and official benevolence, favored wide propagation of the Dhamma.
38. Masaharu Anesaki, "Buddhist Docetism," in *Encyclopaedia of Religion and Ethics* 4:835–40.
39. *The Mahāvastu,* trans. J. J. Jones, I 125, 132–33.
40. André Bareau, *Les sectes bouddhiques du petit véhicule,* 57ff.; S. N. Dube, *Cross Currents in Early Buddhism,* 120ff.
41. *The Debates Commentary,* trans. B. C. Law, 9–43.
42. *Abhidharmakośa,* 9th *Kośasthāna.* The personalists argued that one may validly speak of the person as reality dependent on the skandhas just as one may speak of fire as dependent on the fuel.
43. For an interesting discussion of this problem, see Steven Collins, *Selfless Persons.*
44. Bareau, *Les sectes bouddhiques du petit véhicule,* 159.
45. S. N. Dube, *Cross Currents in Early Buddhism,* 139–40.
46. Bareau, *Les sectes bouddhiques du petit véhicule,* 58, 59, 60.
47. Ibid., 248.

Bibliography

Sources

The Book of Gradual Sayings. Translated by F. L. Woodward and E. M. Hare. London: Pali Text Society, 1972–82.

The Book of the Kindred Sayings. Translated by C. A. F. Rhys Davids and F. L. Woodward. London: Pali Text Society, 1975–82.

The Collection of the Middle Length Sayings. Translated by I. B. Horner. London: Pali Text Society, 1975–77.

The Dhammapada. Translated by Irving Babbitt. New York: New Directions, 1965.

The Dhammapada. Translated by S. Radhakrishnan. London: Oxford University Press, 1966.
Dialogues of the Buddha. Translated by T. W. Rhys Davids and C. A. F. Rhys Davids. London: Pali Text Society, 1977.
The Jātaka. Edited by E. B. Cowell. London: Pali Text Society, 1981.
The Minor Anthologies of the Pali Canon, II. Translated by F. L. Woodward. London: Oxford University Press, 1948.
The Minor Anthologies of the Pali Canon, III–IV. Translated by H. S. Gehmen, and I. B. Horner. London: Pali Text Society, 1974–75.
The Sutta-Nipāta. Translated by H. Saddhatissa. London: Curzon Press, 1985.
The *Sutta Piṭaka.* Published by the Pali Text Society, London. Dates given are those of the reprints distributed by Routledge & Kegan Paul, London, Henley, and Boston.

The *Vinaya Piṭaka*

The Book of the Discipline. Translated by I. B. Horner. London: Pali Text Society, 1966–82.

Other Accounts of the Buddha's Life

Aśvaghosa's Buddhacarita or Acts of the Buddha. Edited and translated by E. H. Johnston. Delhi: Motilal Banarsidass, 1978.
The Mahāvastu. Translated by J. J. Jones. London: Pali Text Society, 1973–78.
The Saundarananda of Aśvaghosa. Edited and translated by E. H. Johnston. Delhi: Motilal Banarsidass, 1975.

The Early Schools

Asoka: Edicts. Translated by N. A. Nikam and Richard P. McKeon. Chicago: University of Chicago Press, 1958.
The Debates Commentary. Translated by B. C. Law. London: Luzac (Pali Text Society), 1969. A commentary on the *Kathāvatthu.*
Dīpavaṃsa, The Chronicle of the Island of Ceylon. Translated by B. C. Law. Ceylon: The Saman Press, 1959 = *The Ceylon Historical Journal* 7 (1957–58).
History of Buddhism by Bu-ston, I–II. Translated by E. Obermiller. Heidelberg: Harrassowitz, 1931–32. Reprint, Tokyo: Suzuki Research Foundation, 1964.
The Mahāvaṃsa. Translated by Wilhelm Geiger. London: Luzac (Pali Text Society), 1964.
Points of Controversy. Translated by Shwe Zan Aung, and C. A. F. Rhys Davids. London: Pali Text Society, 1979. Distributed by Routledge & Kegan Paul. A translation of the *Kathāvatthu.*
Strong, John S. *The Legend of King Aśoka: A Study and Translation of the Aśokāvadāna.* Princeton: Princeton University Press, 1984.
Tāranātha's History of Buddhism in India. Simla: Indian Institute of Advanced Study, 1970.

Studies

Bareau, André. *Les premiers conciles bouddhiques.* Paris: Presses Universitaires de France, 1955.
——. *Recherches sur la biographie du Bouddha dans les Sūtrapiṭaka et les Vinayapiṭaka anciens.* Paris: École Française d'Extrême-Orient, 1963–71.
——. *Les sectes bouddhiques du petit véhicule.* Saigon: École Française d'Extrême-Orient, 1955.

Basham, Arthur L. *History and Doctrines of the Ājīvikas.* London: Luzac, 1951.
Bond, George D. "The Development and Elaboration of the Arahant Ideal in the Theravāda Buddhist Tradition." *Journal of the American Academy of Religion* 52 (1984) 227–42.
Carter, John Ross. *Dhamma: Western Academic and Sinhalese Buddhist Interpretations.* Tokyo: Hokuseido Press, 1978.
——, ed. *The Threefold Refuge in the Theravāda Buddhist Tradition.* Chambersburg, PA: *Anima,* 1982.
Collins, Steven. *Selfless Persons.* Cambridge: Cambridge University Press, 1982.
Dube, S. N. *Cross Currents in Early Buddhism.* New Delhi: Manohar, 1980.
Dutt, Nalinaksha. *Early Monastic Buddhism.* Calcutta: Oriental Book Agency, 1960.
Dutt, Sukumar. *The Buddha and Five After-Centuries.* London: Luzac, 1957.
Hofinger, Marcel. *Étude sur le Concile de Vaiśālī.* Louvain: Bureaux du Muséon, 1946.
Holt, John C. *Discipline: The Canonical Buddhism of the* Vinayapiṭaka. Delhi: Motilal Banarsidass, 1981.
Jayatilleke, K. N. *Early Buddhist Theory of Knowledge.* London: Allen & Unwin, 1963.
——. *Ethics in Buddhist Perspective.* Kandy: Buddhist Publication Society, 1972.
——. *The Message of the Buddha.* New York: Free Press, 1976.
Johansson, Rune E. A. *The Psychology of Nirvāṇa.* London: Allen & Unwin, 1969.
Kalupahana, David J. *Causality: The Central Philosophy of Buddhism.* Honolulu: University of Hawaii Press, 1975.
Kalupahana, David J., and Indrani Kalupahana. *The Way of Siddhartha: A Life of the Buddha.* Boulder and London: Shambhala, 1982.
Lamotte, Étienne. *Histoire du bouddhisme indien.* Louvain: Publications universitaires, 1976.
——. "La Légende du Bouddha." *Revue de l'histoire des religions* 134 (1948) 37–71.
Nakamura, Hajime. *Gotama Buddha.* Los Angeles and Tokyo: Buddhist Books International, 1977.
Oldenberg, Hermann. *Buddha: His Life, His Doctrine, His Order.* Varanasi: Indological Book House, 1971.
Pande, G. C. *History of the Development of Buddhism.* Lucknow, 1962. In Hindi.
——. *Śramaṇa Tradition.* Ahmedabad, 1978.
——. *Studies in the Origins of Buddhism.* Delhi: Motilal Banarsidass, 1983.
Pérez-Remón, Joaquín. *Self and Non-Self in Early Buddhism.* The Hague: Mouton, 1980.
Prebish, Charles. "A Review of Scholarship on the Buddhist Councils." *Journal of Asian Studies* 33 (1974) 239–54.
Przyluski, Jean. *Le Concile de Rājagṛha.* Paris: Geuthner, 1926–28.
Rahula, Walpola. *What the Buddha Taught.* New York: Grove Press, 1962.
Reynolds, Frank. "The Many Lives of Buddha." In *The Biographical Process,* ed. Frank Reynolds, 37–61. The Hague: Mouton, 1976.
Saddhatissa, H. *Buddhist Ethics.* London: Allen & Unwin, 1970.
Takeuchi Yoshinori. *The Heart of Buddhism.* New York: Crossroad, 1983.
Thomas, Edward J. *The Life of the Buddha as Legend and History.* London: Routledge & Kegan Paul, 1975.
Warder, A. K. *Indian Buddhism.* Delhi: Motilal Banarsidass, 1980.
Welbon, Guy Richard. *The Buddhist Nirvāṇa and Its Western Interpreters.* Chicago: University of Chicago Press, 1968.

2

Indian Buddhist Meditation

Paul J. Griffiths

Meditational practice has always been of central importance to Buddhist soteriology and Buddhist philosophical theory. The intellectuals of the tradition, past and present, frequently say that such practice is a necessary condition both for the attainment of nirvāṇa and for reaching correct philosophical conclusions about the nature of things. One can, it seems, neither attain salvation nor engage in effective philosophizing without practicing meditation. Although meditational practice in Buddhism has always been, in actuality if not in theory, a strictly virtuoso affair (that is, not many people actually do it and those who do are almost all male, celibate, and monastic), the exalted place given it by the tradition means that an enormous amount of energy has been expended by Buddhists in creating systematic theories about it, as well as in developing and teaching specific meditational techniques.

In this short study I will set forth some of these theories and describe some of these practices. In doing so I shall draw only on sources from the Indian subcontinent (including Sri Lanka) belonging to the first fifteen hundred years of Buddhist history (roughly, 500 B.C.E. to 1000 C.E.). Even though the textual sources available to us for the reconstruction of the Indian Buddhist tradition are fragmentary, their quantity is overwhelming and nothing approaching a systematic survey of them will be offered here. A millennium and a half of intensive intellectual and spiritual activity cannot be effectively summarized in a short encyclopedia article. Further, I shall for the most part treat the meditational practices and ideas of Indian Buddhists synchronically rather than diachronically: more attention will be paid to the content of the key concepts and the structure of the systems in which they are embedded than to the historical changes they underwent.

Meditational practice—here provisionally understood as a self-conscious attempt to alter, in a systematic and thoroughgoing way, the practitioner's perceptual, cognitive, and affective experience—is intimately linked in the Indian Buddhist tradition with both ritual and magic. It is probably only a slight exaggeration to say that no Buddhist ever systematically undertook meditational practice without placing it in an appropriate ritual context and without considering the techniques employed in that context to have strictly magical efficacy. Unfortunately, neither of these important elements of the Buddhist understanding of what meditation is can be treated here, since to consider them would require a discussion of Buddhist devotionalism, Buddhist ritual practice, and (above all) Buddhist tantra, matters beyond the scope of this article. Tantra has been defined as ". . . a technique for magically storming the gates of Buddhahood";[1] many of the practices to be discussed here can also be understood in just this way, even though the exposition given them here will not stress that aspect. It should not be forgotten that the techniques described here in a detached, abstract, and scholastic manner were part of living religious practice, practice which from the earliest times included the belief that it is possible to deify oneself, and the belief that the practitioner necessarily will, as a result of the practice of meditation, attain all kinds of magical powers, from clairvoyance to teleportation.

Terminology

Some initial comments need to be offered on terminology. Indian Buddhists developed a rich and complex technical terminology (in Sanskrit) for the description and analysis of meditational practices and their resultant altered states of consciousness. There is also, of course, a comparably rich and technical vocabulary (in English, drawn mostly from Latin and Greek) used by ascetical theologians for the description and analysis of somewhat similar matters within the Christian tradition. But translation from one technical vocabulary to another is no simple matter, as use of the term "meditation" itself shows. "Meditation" has precise and technical connotations in many Christian contexts. For example, by some ascetical theologians it is used to refer to the practitioner's discursive and repeated consideration of and imaginative identification with the events of Christ's passion and resurrection; the term is also frequently used to refer to the inculcation of an intimate and precise awareness of one's own sins. It should scarcely be surprising that no term in the technical lexicon of Indian Buddhist meditation theory reflects just these emphases. There are, it is true, more general senses in which the term "meditation" is used in English, to denote, among other things, ruminating or pondering upon some particular topic, and (since the 1960s) almost any non-Western consciousness-altering method. But here too there is no Sanskrit term used by Buddhists to discuss these matters that has a similar degree of nonspecificity. Much the same applies, *mutatis mutandis,* to other English words often used to discuss Buddhist meditation and to translate technical Sanskrit terminology.

There are, then, the usual technical and conceptual difficulties involved in translating a set of precise technical terms from one language into another. Methods often used to deal with such problems include (1) neologism (the coining of new words in the target language to reflect important semantic aspects of terms in the source language, such as *shimpi-shisō* in Japanese to reflect the English "mysticism"); (2) borrowing (the direct adoption of words from the source language into the target language, as with the naturalization of the Sanskrit term "karma" into English, or the adoption of the Sanskrit "dhyāna" into both Chinese–*ch'an*[*na*]–and Japanese–Zen); and (3) concept matching (the use of a term or terms in the target language whose connotations have, or appear to have, sufficient conceptual similarity with those of the relevant term in the source language to make it appropriate as a translation term). Each method has its disadvantages. Excessive use of neologism and borrowing issues in incomprehensibility, and facile use of concept matching may often lead to radical semantic alteration. In what follows I shall make use of all of these methods and thus try to minimize the disadvantages of each.

I use the term "meditation" very generally to refer to any self-consciously undertaken consciousness-altering technique that does not make use of chemical substances external to the practitioner in order to produce the desired alteration. That is, "meditation" will refer to any technique designed to alter the practitioner's state of consciousness without using drugs. On this definition, engaging in sexual intercourse, listening to a Beethoven quartet, or contemplating the good qualities of the Buddha will all be examples of meditation. Drinking a bottle of claret or ingesting cocaine will not. Buddhist theorists sometimes use the term samādhi in something close to this very general sense, but I shall not translate samādhi by "meditation" and do not, for the most part, intend my use of the latter term to reflect any particular Sanskrit term.

Among the more important technical terms used by Buddhists are the following. First, samādhi. I shall, fairly consistently, represent this by "concentration." This seems appropriate since the standard gloss given to samādhi in Indian Buddhist texts is "one-pointedness of mind" (*cittasyaikāgratā*), and this idea of directing attention to a single object is also central to the English "concentration." Second, bearing a close connection to samādhi, is the term "dhyāna." I shall leave this untranslated. It refers, in its more technical usage, to a precise set of altered states of consciousness (usually four in number). The nature of these altered states will be discussed below; at this point it must suffice to say that they are enstatic, aimed initially at withdrawing the practitioner's senses and thoughts from interaction with the external world and finally at bringing all mental activity to a halt. Etymologically dhyāna is derived from a verbal root (*dhyai-*) meaning something like "to ponder, consider, think closely about," but it is clear that the technical Buddhist use of the term which is of interest for my purposes does not reflect this discursive sense. It will not be misleading to think of the altered states referred to by the term "dhyāna" as instances of altered states produced by concentration (samādhi).

Perhaps the most general term used for meditational practice is *bhāvanā:* I shall translate this by "cultivation." It is a causative nominal form derived from the verbal root *bhū-*, meaning simply "to be." Literally, then, *bhāvanā* means something like "to cause to come to be, to effect, to bring about, to develop, to cultivate." It is used by Buddhist theoreticians in meditational contexts to refer to the cultivation of specific techniques, and is thus usually compounded with other terms, among which are *śamatha-bhāvanā*, "the cultivation of tranquillity." This compound connotes, as also do dhyāna and samādhi, the development of enstatic practices, practices aimed at the reduction of the contents of the practitioner's mental life. Such reduction, as I shall show, was sometimes seen as an end in itself, and in such cases the "cultivation of tranquillity" is presented as issuing in the cessation of any mental activity whatsoever. It was also seen, though (and perhaps more frequently), as a preliminary practice, one that would act as an appropriate propaedeutic for *vipaśyanā-bhāvanā*, "the cultivation of insight." To cultivate insight is to transform one's cognitive and perceptual faculties in accordance with Buddhist philosophical doctrine. This phrase denotes, then, a set of techniques that involve repeated contemplation of key items of Buddhist doctrine, for example, the doctrine that everything is impermanent, in such a way that those items are internalized in a radical way. The practitioner learns not only to give intellectual assent to their truth but also to alter her faculties in such a way that both perception and cognition occur only in the ways prescribed by the doctrine(s) in question. She learns, that is, not merely to assent to the proposition "everything is impermanent" but also to directly perceive the impermanence of everything.

An important instance of the techniques used to cultivate insight in this manner is *smṛti*, "mindfulness." "Mindfulness" is somewhat clumsy as a translation term, but it has by now become established as standard. The Sanskrit term *smṛti* often means something close to "memory"; but it also often connotes the paying of close attention to some phenomenon, and it is this meaning that is stressed by the Buddhist use of the term. To practice mindfulness is, at least at first, simply to pay close and careful attention to the phenomena of one's mental and physical life. It is thus not, according to Buddhist theoreticians, designed as a consciousness-altering technique, since its use does not require the practitioner to attempt the alteration of any of his states, but only to observe them. In this it differs from the enstatic techniques and altered states denoted by dhyāna, concentration, and the cultivation of tranquillity. But mindfulness can be appropriately considered an example of meditation as defined above, since the very effort of closely observing the phenomena of one's mental life inevitably changes those phenomena. It is difficult, for example, to be enthusiastically and single-mindedly full of rage or lust if one is simultaneously engaged in carefully observing the rage or lust in question and noting "here is an instance of intense rage" or the like. And, as I shall show, mindfulness is considered by the Buddhist tradition itself as a paradigmatic instance of the cultivation of insight.

Finally, there is the important general concept of "mārga," "path." Buddhist soteriology has always been conceived as a path from here (saṃsāra) to there (nirvāṇa), a path that leads the practitioner nowhere when saṃsāra and nirvāṇa are regarded as identical, but which nevertheless has dramatic effects on its practitioner's epistemic condition. Meditation, broadly conceived, is an essential (though by no means the only) part of this path. It comprises the last two "limbs" (*aṅga*) of the eight-limbed path into which Buddhist soteriological practice has been traditionally divided since the earliest times ("perfect mindfulness" and "perfect concentration"), and its practice was itself divided and subdivided by Buddhist intellectuals into ever more complex meditational paths. Something will be said below about the variety and internal structure of these meditational paths (mārga).[2]

Dhyāna as Preparation for the Attainment of Cessation

The four dhyānas are best understood as a series of altered states of consciousness characterized by an increasing degree of enstasy. The term "enstasy" literally means "standing within." An enstatic practice, then, is one aimed at the withdrawal of the practitioner's senses and thoughts from contact with the external world and at the reduction of the contents of her consciousness. An image frequently used to describe this process, in both Buddhist and non-Buddhist texts, is that of the tortoise withdrawing its limbs and head into its shell. The tortoise's limbs usually represent the practitioner's senses (including the mind, the organ of thought): their proper place, the image suggests, is within, turned away from the potential disturbances and disruptions of contact with sensory objects external to the practitioner. The following stereotyped description of the four dhyānas appears to describe a series of altered states of consciousness leading toward just such a goal.

> [The practitioner], separated from desire and negative states of mind, attains to and remains in the first *dhyāna;* this originates from separation and is accompanied by applied thought, sustained thought, joy, and happiness. Upon suppressing both applied and sustained thought [the practitioner] attains to and remains in the second *dhyāna;* this originates from concentration, consists in inner tranquillity and one-pointedness of mind, is free from applied and sustained thought, and is accompanied by both joy and happiness. Upon detaching himself from joy [the practitioner] remains in equanimity; mindful and aware, he experiences that physical happiness of which wise men say "the mindful possessor of equanimity remains happy." So he attains to and remains in the third *dhyāna.* Upon abandoning happiness and sadness as well as former elation and depression, [the practitioner] attains to and remains in the fourth *dhyāna;* this is without happiness and sadness and is characterized by that purity of mindfulness which is equanimity. (*Saṃyutta-Nikāya* 5:307)

This stereotyped description delineates a process of separation or isolation (*viveka*), a process by which the practitioner dissociates himself from a succession of mental factors. Each dhyāna is described both in terms of what the practitioner who attains it is isolated or separated from, and what psychological factors he still possesses.

Thus, the first dhyāna involves dissociation from "desire" (*kāma*) and from negative states of mind generally. These negative states of mind are not specified in the extract cited, but they are usually identified by Buddhist thinkers with a standard list of five "hindrances" (*nivaraṇa*), including such things as desire for sensory pleasures, ill will, sloth, torpor, agitation, remorse, and doubt. The negative states of mind from which the practitioner is separated in attaining the first dhyāna are thus affective rather than cognitive or perceptual. They have to do with the practitioner's emotional reactions to and involvements with her environment, and with crippling psychological weaknesses that might prevent the overcoming of these emotional entanglements. Present in the first dhyāna are four mental factors, two of them cognitive and two of them affective. The cognitive factors are "applied thought" (*vitarka*) and "sustained thought" (*vicāra*): the first of these is often likened to a honeybee's first approach to an attractive flower and the second to that bee's alighting on the flower and extracting nectar from it. So "applied thought" is a term used to describe the mind's initial attention paid to some object of cognition, and "sustained thought" refers to the mind's detailed analytical thought about that same object. Both terms have to do with the mind's activity in appropriating, classifying, and thinking about objects with which it comes into contact through the senses. Such activities are closely connected with discursive thought and with language; their inclusion in the list of psychological factors associated with the first dhyāna is intended to show that such activities, which, as seen by Buddhists, are essentially constructive and necessarily error-laden, are still present for a practitioner in the first dhyāna.

The affective terms "joy" (*prīti*) and "happiness" (*sukha*) are usually differentiated one from another by giving "joy" a more intense affective tone than "happiness." Their joint presence in the first dhyāna, as well as the absence of any other affective terms, shows that the only kind of affect available to a practitioner in the first dhyāna is a generalized sense of well-being ("happiness"), together with occasional, more intense joyful reactions ("joy") to sensory impressions as they are appropriated and classified by the mind. In sum, the first dhyāna is an altered state in which, though the basic cognitive/verbal functions are still fully operative, the range and intensity of the practitioner's affective life has been greatly reduced.

As the practitioner ascends through the remaining three dhyānas, she loses first the cognitive and verbal faculties denoted by *vitarka* and *vicāra* (in the second dhyāna); then the more intense affect denoted by *prīti* (in the third dhyāna); and finally all affect apart from that tranquil even-mindedness denoted by the term "equanimity" (*upekṣa*, in the fourth dhyāna). In this fourth and culminating altered state, then, affect has been reduced almost to nothing, and the analytical and classificatory activities of the mind have also been reduced to zero.

These four dhyānas are frequently connected in Buddhist meditation texts with another sequence of five altered states, a sequence consisting of the "four formless states" and a fifth "attainment of cessation" (*nirodha-samāpatti*). The ninefold series that results (four dhyānas plus four formless states plus one attainment of cessation) is even more obviously enstatic than the four dhyānas taken alone, since it explicitly aims at and culminates in the cessation of all mental events whatsoever. The stereotyped description of the four formlessnesses and the attainment of cessation runs thus:

> By completely transcending all concepts of form, by disposing of concepts based upon sense-data, by paying no attention to concepts of manifoldness, thinking "space is unending" [the practitioner] attains the realm of infinite space and remains therein. By entirely transcending the realm of infinite space and thinking "consciousness is unending," [the practitioner] attains the realm of infinite consciousness and remains therein. By entirely transcending the realm of infinite consciousness and thinking "there is nothing," [the practitioner] attains the realm of nothing at all and remains therein. By entirely transcending the realm of nothing at all [the practitioner] attains the realm of neither-conceptualization-nor-non-conceptualization and remains therein. By entirely transcending the realm of neither-conceptualization-nor-non-conceptualization [the practitioner] attains the cessation of sensation and conceptualization and remains therein. (*Dīgha-Nikāya* 2:71)

The practitioner enters the first three formless states—"infinite space," "infinite consciousness" and "nothing at all"—by dissociating himself from the concepts that characterize the immediately preceding state and by consciously paying attention to and inculcating the characteristics of the state he is about to enter. So, in the case of the first formless state, the practitioner rejects or suppresses all concepts having to do with physical form or with the variety and plurality of physical objects, and then consciously thinks "space is infinite." As a result he enters an altered state of consciousness in which the only thing present to his mind is precisely that: the infinity of space, unencumbered by material objects. A similar progression occurs as the practitioner passes through those altered states called "infinite consciousness" and "nothing at all." This last is perhaps misnamed, since it appears from the description given it, cited above, that a practitioner who has reached it can still think "there is nothing." So still higher and more tenuous altered states must be possible, in which not even that thought can occur. And this is what we find in the description of that formless state which consists in "neither-conceptualization-nor-non-conceptualization": the description of the attainment of this condition, cited above, does not contain any reference to thought on the part of the practitioner, since the occurrence of verbalizable thought would require the existence of at least some "conceptualization" (*saṃjñā*), and if there is any of such in the fourth formless state it is sufficiently tenuous that the condition can properly be described as consisting in neither conceptualization nor its absence.

A still more exalted altered state is possible, however, and this is called the "cessation of sensation and conceptualization" or, more simply, the "attainment of cessation." While this condition is not given precise definition in the extract cited above, it is extensively discussed in many Buddhist texts on meditation. It consists in the complete absence of all mental events and is often called a "mindless" (*acittaka*) condition. A practitioner who attains this state is perhaps most like a catatonic or a patient in deep coma: the only things that distinguish such an individual from a dead person are the continuance of the autonomic functions of the nervous system, such things as minimal heartbeat, body heat, and (perhaps) respiration. Response to external stimuli is impossible, as is initiation of action. Attaining cessation in this way is the culmination, perhaps the *reductio ad absurdum*, of enstatic meditational technique.

Many stories are told in Buddhist texts to indicate the nature and effects of this altered state. One of the most famous concerns Mahānāga. Mahānāga, it is said, attained cessation in the meditation hall of a monastery, and while he was still absorbed in the attainment, the meditation hall caught fire. All the other monks, quite naturally, gathered their belongings and fled. Mahānāga did not. Since he had attained cessation he was not capable of responding to external stimuli, not even stimuli as urgent as a blazing fire, and so he sat unmoved as the monastery burned around him. The story usually ends with Mahānāga's safe emergence from the attainment of cessation and his surprise that anything untoward had happened while he was, as it were, otherwise engaged.

There are also many purely logical problems posed for Buddhist intellectuals by the descriptions and recommendations in the texts of their tradition of a condition of this kind. The most pressing of these involves the necessity of offering some rational explanation of the process by which emergence from the attainment of cessation occurs. If a practitioner in the attainment of cessation is really without mental events of any kind, it becomes difficult to explain the causal mechanism by which mental events can begin again for him. But to pursue these questions would require an excursus into the realms of Buddhist causal and metaphysical theory, and for that there is no space here.

Soteriological methods are always linked with soteriological goals: what you do to get saved depends closely on what it is you think you need to get saved from. Enstatic meditational practice is no exception to this general rule. It is connected (conceptually at least) with the idea that the fundamental soteriological problem consists in passionate attachment, in intense affect. It should not be hard to see that the enstatic meditational path outlined in this section provides an effective answer to that problem. The four dhyānas gradually reduce both cognitive and affective activity; the four formless states reduce both still further until the practitioner reaches the attainment of cessation, wherein no hint of either remains. At that point, clearly, the soteriological problem has been answered: no passionate attachment remains, and the causal connection between such attachment and continued rebirth (with its concomitant suffering) has been broken.

On this reading of the tradition, the attainment of cessation, which is the culmination of the enstatic path, should be identical with nirvāṇa, and there are some elements in the textual evidence which suggest that at least part of the early Buddhist tradition was prepared to make this identification. However, there are also other (and much stronger) indications which suggest that most of the tradition was ambivalent, if not downright negative, in its judgments about the soteriological significance of the higher enstatic states, especially the four formless states and the attainment of cessation. A good example of this ambivalence may be found in one of the stories about the Śākyamuni Buddha's pre-enlightenment life. In this story we are told that Śākyamuni studied under two teachers before he attained enlightenment himself. The first teacher, one Ārāḍa Kālāma, was able to teach him to reach the stage of "nothing at all" (the third formless state), and the second teacher, one Udraka Rāmaputra, taught him to attain the stage of "neither-conceptualization-nor-non-conceptualization" (the fourth formless state). As the story goes, the Buddha found both states soteriologically unsatisfactory, and, since his teachers were not able to teach him anything more, he left them and went to seek enlightenment on his own. This negative attitude toward the enstatic states is further reflected in the stories of the Buddha's attainment of enlightenment: he does this without making use of the formless states or the attainment of cessation, which strongly suggests that these altered states were not regarded as necessary for the attainment of salvation.

In spite of this ambivalence, enstatic method and its resulting altered states of consciousness have always been and still remain a significant part of Buddhist meditational practice. It is usually, as I shall show in the next section, subordinated to the practice of what I shall call analytic method and used as a propaedeutic for that; alternatively, it may be recommended only for certain character types, those especially troubled by intense affective reactions to stimuli. But a good deal of attention is paid by the tradition to these altered states of consciousness, and there are certain specific techniques that are thought to be of special significance to their development. A brief consideration of one of these will conclude my discussion of dhyāna as a preparation for the attainment of cessation.

The Sanskrit term *kṛtsna* in its normal everyday usage is an adjective meaning "whole," "entire," "complete" and the like. In its technical usage by Buddhists the term refers to ten "totalities," ten kinds of material device, any one of which may be taken as an object for meditation by a practitioner. The material device most commonly used (or at least most commonly discussed extensively in the texts) is the "earth totality": this is a disk of (usually) clay, its color as neutral as possible and its surface as smooth as possible. The practitioner sets this clay disk on a pedestal and sits down directly in front of it, a short distance away. He then concentrates all his attention upon this physical clay disk, excluding from awareness all other sensory stimuli and all other concepts and emotions. Eventually, after long and hard practice, the practitioner is able to form a mental image of the clay disk, a mental image without any of the small imperfections of shape and color which necessarily are present in any physical object. This mental image then replaces the physical object as the object of meditation, and the practitioner can at this point continue the meditational practice without being in proximity to the physical object with which she began. At this stage the mental image in question can be "totalized," or extended, as the texts put it, in all directions until (from the practitioner's viewpoint) it fills the whole universe.

Even from this brief account it should be clear that "totality" practice of this kind is purely enstatic: it reduces the content of consciousness to a single, all-embracing percept, which, in the case of the "earth totality," is a mental image of pure earth. This technique (and others like it) is instrumental in producing the higher enstatic states, and therefore something of the ambivalence surrounding these states is found also in connection with totality practice. It is rarely presented as a technique independently sufficient for the attainment of nirvāṇa.

Dhyāna as a Preparation for Observational Analysis

"Observational analysis" denotes those practices aimed either at close observation of the practitioner's psychophysical processes (of which the paradigm case is mindfulness, treated in the next section), or at the repeated contemplation and internalization of key items of Buddhist doctrine (as discussed briefly here and in more detail below, pp. 54–60). As I use the term, it will cover many of the same practices and altered states denoted by the Buddhist terms "cultivation of insight."

The preceding section showed that dhyāna is often seen as a preparation for the higher enstatic states and finally for the attainment of cessation. But it is also often set in the context of observationally analytic technique and seen as an appropriate preparation for that kind of practice. For example, one of the most common progressions from dhyāna practice to observational analysis has the following form. First, the stereotyped description of the dhyānas is given (as translated and discussed in the preceding section) and then the following is said:

> When [the practitioner's] mind is concentrated thus [i.e., with the attainment of the fourth *dhyāna*], purified, cleansed, clear, free from defilements, flexible, supple, firm, and motionless, then [the practitioner] applies and turns his mind to knowledge and insight. He knows this: this body of mine is material; it is made of the four great elements, born from father and mother, nourished on boiled rice and sour milk, subject to being rubbed away, pounded up, broken and disintegrated. Also, this consciousness of mine rests on it and is bound up with it. (*Dīgha-Nikāya* 1:76)

The key elements in this unit of tradition are, first, the directing of the practitioner's mind to "knowledge and vision" (jñāna and *darśana*), and second, the (propositionally expressible) knowledge that results, knowledge having to do with the compounded nature of the body and the intimate connection between consciousness and the body, the mental and the physical. The use of the terms "knowledge" and "vision" is significant: they can appropriately be glossed as indicating something like the Western distinction between

6. *The Great Miracle at Śrāvastī*, India, Gandhāra, Peshawar area, early Kushāṇa Period, ca. 100 C.E. Gray schist.

"knowing that" (jñāna, in this context giving assent to propositions, knowledge by description) and "seeing as" (*darśana*, in this context direct experiential appropriation, knowledge by acquaintance). This is characteristic of what almost all forms of observational analysis are meant to produce: meditation on items of Buddhist doctrine is meant to result, as here, not only in knowledge that certain things are the case, but also in the alteration of the practitioner's cognitive and perceptual experience to accord with that knowledge. Naturally, other items of Buddhist doctrine can be treated in this manner (and, as I shall show below, later developments in Buddhist thought about meditational practice came to include all the most significant elements of Buddhist practice under this rubric).

This connection of the dhyānas with observational analysis is only the first stage in one of the standard Buddhist presentations of the path to awakening. It is followed by the development and exercise of various magical powers (including the creation of magical self-duplicates, clairaudience, clairvoyance, telepathy, and the like), development of the ability to remember one's own previous lives, to directly perceive the past and future lives of all beings, and, finally, to realize the destruction of all those "fetters" holding one back from the attainment of nirvāṇa. Thus the practitioner reaches awakening (bodhi) proper and becomes an awakened one (Buddha).

This presentation of the path to awakening has very deep roots in the Buddhist tradition. Some of the accounts of the Buddha's enlightenment follow a pattern very much like this. It is also a vision based on a somewhat different view of what the basic soteriological problem is from that found in the presentation and recommendation of enstatic technique discussed above. Central to the use and recommendation of observational analysis as a meditational technique is the idea that what needs to be remedied is the practitioner's ignorance, not her passions. The fundamental problem, on this view, is that human beings have an ingrained tendency to misperceive and misconceive the nature of the universe in both its human and nonhuman aspects, and that this ingrained tendency can only be corrected by a radical internalization of the truth about these things. Such truth, of course, is identified by the Buddhist tradition with Buddhist doctrine, and it is the main elements of this that need to be internalized by the practitioner. The view that ignorance is the main soteriological problem is not, of course, necessarily incompatible with the view that this honor should be given to passionate attachment. The two can be combined in various ways. It may be that, as some Buddhist theoreticians suggest, passionate attachment is a product of ignorance, and that if the cause is removed the effect will also vanish. On this view, it is our misperceptions and misconceptions that lead us to be inappropriately attached to things. Alternatively, it may be that passionate attachments are, for most of us, the chief barrier to clear and accurate cognition: if they are removed, accurate knowledge will result. Finally, it may be that the balance and causal connections between ignorance and passionate attachment differ in different individuals, and that different degrees and admixtures of enstatic and observationally analytic technique will therefore be appropriate for different individuals. All these views (and various combinations of them) can be found in the Indian Buddhist traditions. Whichever is taken to be normative, there is no doubt that this tension between enstasy and observational analysis and the soteriological theories that go with each) provides a useful way of looking at the Indian Buddhist traditions about meditation.

Mindfulness: A Paradigm Case of Observational Analysis

The practice of "mindfulness" (*smṛti*), close and continuous observational analysis of every process that goes to make up the psychophysical life of a practitioner, is given an extremely high valuation by the tradition. Descriptions and recommendations of it are often introduced in the following way:

> This, monks, is the path which leads to one [goal], which effects the purification of beings, the transcendence of sorrow and lamentation, the destruction of pain and grief, the attainment of the path and the realization of Nirvana—namely, the four mindfulnesses. (*Dīgha-Nikāya* 2:290)

The "four" in question are the four topics to which the practitioner's close attention is to be directed. The first is the body (*kāya*), its physical and its physiological processes; the second is affective sensation (*vedanā*) in all its varieties; the third is the mind (*citta*) in all its possible states; and the fourth is doctrinal formulas (*dharma*), key items of Buddhist doctrine. It will not be possible to treat all of these in detail, but something of the flavor of the practice and its intended results can be obtained by looking in some detail at the "mindfulness of breathing"—one of the subdivisions of the first of the "four mindfulnesses," that which takes as its object the physical. Mindfulness as applied to the breathing process is given more space and attention, both by the classical texts of the tradition and by contemporary apologists for the efficacy of Buddhist meditation in South and Southeast Asia, than any other element of the practice, and in some of its versions (notably the one translated below), it presents itself as a complete and self-sufficient soteriological method.

> *Stage 1*
> On this matter, monks, a monk who has gone to the forest, to the roots of a tree or a deserted place, sits with crossed legs and a straight back and places

his attention in front of him. Mindfully he breathes in and mindfully he breathes out. (i) Breathing in a long breath he knows "I am breathing in a long breath"; breathing out a long breath he knows "I am breathing out a long breath." (ii) Breathing in a short breath he knows "I am breathing in a short breath"; breathing out a short breath he knows "I am breathing out a short breath." (iii) He trains himself: "Experiencing [the breaths] throughout the whole body, I shall breathe in"; he trains himself: "Experiencing [the breaths] throughout the whole body, I shall breathe out." (iv) He trains himself: "Calming the bodily function [of breathing], I shall breathe in"; he trains himself: "Calming the bodily function [of breathing], I shall breathe out."

Stage 2
(v) He trains himself: "Experiencing joy, I shall breathe in"; he trains himself: "Experiencing joy, I shall breathe out." (vi) He trains himself: "Experiencing happiness, I shall breathe in"; he trains himself: "Experiencing happiness, I shall breathe out."

Stage 3
(vii) He trains himself: "Experiencing the functioning of mind, I shall breathe in"; he trains himself: "Experiencing the functioning of mind, I shall breathe out." (viii) He trains himself: "Calming the functioning of mind, I shall breathe in"; he trains himself: "Calming the functioning of mind, I shall breathe out." (ix) He trains himself: "Experiencing the mind I shall breathe in"; he trains himself: "Experiencing the mind I shall breathe out." (x) He trains himself: "Gladdening the mind, I shall breathe in"; he trains himself: "Gladdening the mind, I shall breathe out." (xi) He trains himself: "Concentrating the mind, I shall breathe in"; he trains himself: "Concentrating the mind, I shall breathe out." (xii) He trains himself: "Liberating the mind, I shall breathe in"; he trains himself: "Liberating the mind, I shall breathe out."

Stage 4
(xiii) He trains himself: "Contemplating impermanence, I shall breathe in"; he trains himself: "Contemplating impermanence, I shall breathe out." (xiv) He trains himself: "Contemplating dispassion, I shall breathe in"; he trains himself: "Contemplating dispassion, I shall breathe out." (xv) He trains himself: "Contemplating cessation, I shall breathe in"; he trains himself: "Contemplating cessation, I shall breathe out." (xvi) He trains himself: "Contemplating renunciation, I shall breathe in"; he trains himself: "Contemplating renunciation, I shall breathe out." (*Saṃyutta-Nikāya* 5:311–12)

Stage 1 describes the practice of careful close observation of the breathing process, a process often called "bare attention" by contemporary apologists for the technique. The practice involves simply observing and mentally noting what is happening as one breathes. No attempt is made at first (in substages i and ii) to alter or disrupt the rhythms of one's breath. Observation is the key. It is only with substages iii and iv that one self-consciously alters one's breathing, first by extending one's breaths imaginatively throughout one's whole body, and then by "calming" or reducing the frequency and depth of one's inhalations and exhalations.

Stage 2 introduces exercises to alter the practitioner's emotional states (about which more is said in the next section). Here, the breaths are used as vehicles for the inculcation of happy and joyous mental states. With stage 3 the practitioner begins to observe the workings of his mind (substage vii), and then to alter those workings in various ways (substages viii–xii). Other texts describe in much more detail what is meant here. Simple observation of the mind's workings is similar to observing the breath: one watches and mentally notes what goes on as one's mind responds to external stimuli, initiates thought patterns, and changes its emotional condition. Nothing at first is done to alter any of these things. Simple observation is itself a demanding spiritual discipline and requires, as most of its teachers stress, many years of continuous practice for proficiency. There are extensive and complex Buddhist intellectual traditions called *abhidharma*, whose main rationale is an attempt to develop classification systems for all the kinds of mental events that might occur. An important part of learning to observe one's own mental life as a Buddhist, then, is learning and internalizing these classification systems so that one will have an appropriate label for every kind of mental event that might happen along.

The practice of mindfulness as presented in the text translated above (and as presented by most of its contemporary apologists) thus appears to be based on a clear separation between techniques aimed at observation of one's mental life and techniques aimed at its alteration. In fact, though, as already suggested, it appears difficult to neatly separate the practice of simple observation from those practices designed to alter the workings of the practitioner's mind. Observation necessarily produces alteration. A simple illustration: suppose that a particular practitioner is an especially lustful character, and suppose that as she sits in meditation, observing her mental processes, she observes an instance of lustful imagination and, as her teacher has taught her, makes a mental note of it: "Here is an instance of lustful imagination." The very action of making that mental note will almost inevitably reduce the intensity of the lustful imagination in question, and there seems little doubt that precisely this effect is intended. The practice of "bare attention," then, is a necessary and appropriate propaedeutic for those subsequent practices which are more explicitly designed to alter the practitioner's state of consciousness.

With stage 4 (substages xiii–xvi) the practitioner passes to techniques designed to internalize key items of Buddhist doctrine. Thus she meditates (still using the breaths) on impermanence, dispassion, and the like; he inhales the basic Buddhist idea that everything is impermanent with every breath, and exhales dispassion. The aim of such practices is to make these Buddhist doctrinal ideas coextensive with the cognitive and emotional life of the practitioner.

It should now be clear why I have called mindfulness a "paradigm case of observational analysis": it begins with bare observation, passes naturally from there through a series of techniques designed to reduce the intensity of the practitioner's mental life, and arrives finally at an intensive analysis or filtering of all phenomena through the fine mesh of such Buddhist doctrines as that everything is impermanent or that everything is unsatisfactory. Learned and practiced under the direction of a competent teacher, this set of practices is generally regarded as a simple, efficacious, and self-contained soteriological path.

Techniques Designed to Manipulate the Emotions

Techniques of this kind have already been touched upon in the discussion of mindfulness. But since it is of central importance to Buddhist soteriology that the practitioner's emotional states be under control and not excessively intense (intense affect of any kind is regarded as a barrier to the attainment of that kind of dispassionate clear vision of reality which is a *sine qua non* for the attainment of nirvāṇa), it is not surprising that the tradition preserves many other techniques aimed explicitly at altering the practitioner's affective states. I shall mention only two of these here.

The Four Ways of Living like Brahma

A tetrad of affective attitudes is thought by the Buddhist tradition to be of special importance. They are friendliness (*maitri*); compassion (*karuṇā*); sympathetic joy (*mudita*); and equanimity (*upekṣa*). All of these are more or less relational in that they have to do with the way in which the practitioner relates to and interacts with other living beings. Friendliness is an antidote to hatred, enmity, and anger. Compassion, traditionally the attitude that enabled the Buddha to spend his life preaching the truths he had discovered even though he was aware that few of those who heard him would be able to comprehend what he was saying, is thus usually associated with an attitude that allows (or requires) active attempts to relieve the sufferings of others. Sympathetic joy is associated especially with the attitudes necessary for harmonious living between groups of people: discussions of it in Buddhist texts, as might be expected, often have to do with the ways in which inhabitants of a particular monastic establishment might learn to live together in harmony. Equanimity, finally, is a mental attitude that in some degree goes beyond what would usually be considered emotional response of any kind. Its full development translates the affective experience of the practitioner altogether out of the usual realm of affect to an area where emotional response becomes irrelevant because the barriers between individuals, the differences which make love, hatred, sorrow, and joy appropriate responses, have been finally broken down. This happens because the practitioner sees that such barriers are merely mental constructs: all perception of difference—but paradigmatically the perception of difference between oneself and the other—is removed, and only when this happens is the full development of equanimity possible.

These four attitudes are called "ways of living like Brahma" (*brahmavihāra*) because, when properly practiced, they are supposed to result in rebirth in the heavenly cosmic realm in which the deity Brahma lives. This is not, of course, the same as nirvāṇa: desire for rebirth in the Brahma realm is almost always characterized in Buddhist texts as a preliminary soteriological goal, and it thus follows that the techniques used to attain it are also preliminary. They are not usually presented as a self-sufficient soteriological path (as was, for example, the practice of mindfulness described above), but as either a set of practices especially useful for those with particular character defects (such as a tendency toward excessive hatred or excessive aggression) or a set of practices whose main point is to encourage appropriate attitudes toward others.

The usual description of the four ways of living like Brahma runs as follows:

> [The practitioner] lives pervading one direction with a friendly mind; and so also, in a similar way, he lives pervading the second, third, and fourth directions, pervading them above, below, and in every direction, pervading the entire world with a friendly mind which is far-reaching, extensive, immeasurable, peaceful, and without enmity. [The practitioner] lives pervading one direction with a compassionate mind, and so also, in a similar way, he lives pervading the second, third, and fourth directions, pervading them above, below, and in every direction, pervading the entire world with a compassionate mind which is far-reaching, extensive, immeasurable, peaceful, and without enmity. [The practitioner] lives pervading one direction with a mind of sympathetic joy, and so also, in a similar way, he lives pervading the second, third, and fourth directions, pervading them above, below, and in every direction, pervading the entire world with a mind of sympathetic joy which is far-reaching, extensive, immeasurable, peaceful, and without enmity. [The practitioner] lives pervading one direction with a mind of equanimity, and so also, in a similar way, he lives pervading the second, third, and fourth directions, pervading them above, below, and in every direction, pervading the entire world with a mind of equanimity which is far-reaching, extensive, immeasurable, peaceful, and without enmity. (*Majjhima-Nikāya* 1:297)

The key term here is "pervading": the practitioner is intended to make a conscious effort to inculcate the emotional attitude in question and then to extend it universally, to fill every corner of the cosmos with it, to apply it in her responses to and interactions with every living being. In developing these attitudes, the practitioner is usually instructed to begin by applying them to a close and beloved friend (though preferably not one of the opposite sex, since too much friendliness and so forth directed toward one such is, according to the tradition, likely to incite lust), then to apply them to someone to whom she feels indifferent, and finally toward a person who is hostile or whom she actively dislikes. The practitioner thus progresses from the easy cases—who finds it difficult to feel friendly toward a friend?—to the difficult ones, and is finally able to apply the attitudes inculcated universally, without making any distinctions. The effects of these techniques on ethical practice are, of course, far-reaching, but beyond the scope of this article.

Cultivation of the Horrible

Cultivation of the "horrible" (*aśubha-bhāvanā*) consists in close contemplation of corpses in various stages of decay. There are usually said to be ten kinds of corpse, ranging from the newly dead, bloated with corruption, through the "gnawed" (corpses that have been partially eaten by jackals or other scavengers), to the "bleeding" (corpses that are smeared with blood), and arriving finally at the "skeleton" (a corpse of which there is nothing left but bones). The various categories of corpse are described in loving detail by the texts. A good example is the description of a "livid" corpse by Buddhaghosa, a fifth-century Buddhist intellectual:

> That which has patchy discolouration is called 'livid' . . . what is livid is vile because of repulsiveness . . . this is a term for a corpse that is reddish-coloured in places where the flesh is prominent, whitish coloured in places where pus has collected, but mostly blue-black if draped with blue-black cloth. . . . (*Visuddhimagga* VI.1)

The methods used to meditate on such things are much the same as those described above in the discussion of the "earth totality." Here, as there, the practitioner centers her mind upon the relevant physical object (in this case one of the ten varieties of corpse) until she is able to form a mental image of the object and contemplate that image without necessarily any longer being in the presence of the actual corpse. Thus there is a sense in which this practice, like "totality" practice, is enstatic: it involves the withdrawal of the practitioner's senses from interaction with the external world and a centering of attention upon a mental image. But there is also a significant difference.

Contemplating the "horrible" is designed specifically for those persons who have an excessive attachment to the beauties and attractions of the (living) physical body, especially those who are unduly troubled by sexual impulses. Cultivating the "horrible" is designed to alter this kind of positive affective reaction to the physical body and replace it with what (from a Buddhist viewpoint) is a more realistic reaction. It is also designed to act as a propaedeutic for the realization of the fundamental Buddhist doctrines concerning impermanence and unsatisfactoriness. Using the "horrible" as one's meditation object one may begin to see the attractions of the human body (and, by extension, of all things) as impermanent, transient, subject to decay; one may also begin to see that what appear as attractions are really only appearances that reveal themselves in their true light at death.

This connection between cultivating the "horrible" and the realization of these fundamental Buddhist truths is made explicit in some texts entitled *Yogācārabhūmi*—"the stages of the practice of Yoga." "Yoga" is yet another general term for meditational practice, one used throughout India and one that has been effectively naturalized into English. The compound term "yogācāra," meaning either "the practice of Yoga" or "those who engage in the practice of Yoga," became the name of an important Buddhist philosophical school in India from about the fourth century C.E. on; but it was also used—and it is this sense that interests me here—as a generic title for texts concerned with setting forth the stages of such practice. Texts with this title were produced in India from the earliest years of the Christian era, and in two of the earliest of them are found listed the following five sets of practices: first, cultivation of the "horrible," designed to counteract sensual desire; second, the cultivation of friendliness (*maitri*), designed to counteract anger; third, the cultivation of understanding related to the universal fact of causality, designed to counteract ignorance; fourth, the cultivation of meditation on the breathing process, designed to counteract excessive analytical thought; and fifth, the cultivation of meditation on skeletons, designed to counteract egotism. Here the attempt to make connections between the cultivation of the horrible (which is of limited soteriological efficacy taken alone) and other meditational practices aimed more directly at removing ignorance is explicit and clear. The cultivation of the horrible has been embedded in its proper place as one of a larger set of meditational practices: it has been made part of a meditational path.

This interest in creating systematic meditational paths out of disparate and sometimes almost contradictory traditions about meditational practice (how, for example, does one reconcile the attainment of cessation and the practices leading to it with mindfulness and its associated soteriological goals?) has always been an important part of Buddhist theorizing about meditation.

The Yogācāra traditions just mentioned are one, somewhat undeveloped, example of this tendency. Others, much more explicit, systematic, and complex can be found in texts explicitly devoted to developing and elaborating such meditational paths. Since it is largely by studying such texts and using them as the basis for practice (always under the guidance of an appropriately qualified teacher) that Buddhist scholastics have for almost two millennia gained access to the conceptual and soteriological riches of their meditational traditions, I shall present in the next section one of the most influential systematic models of progress through meditational paths to be found in such texts.

A Systematic Meditational Path

One of the most important scholastic texts produced by the Indian Buddhist tradition is called *A Commentary Upon the Treasury of Metaphysics* (*Abhidharmakośabhāṣya*), a work attributed to the great Buddhist thinker Vasubandhu and dating from probably the fifth century of the Christian era. It is difficult to overestimate the importance of this text: almost since the time of its composition it has been used by Buddhists of many schools in many different cultures as a teaching tool, an authoritative and systematic summary of key Buddhist teachings. A substantial part of it is devoted to an explanation of the relations between the various meditational practices contained in the Buddhist tradition and to a systematic attempt to show how these fit together into an ordered meditational path (*mārga*).

Vasubandhu's exposition begins with the "path of preparation" (*prayoga-mārga*).[3] This is where novices, ordinary people, begin their religious practice; those upon the path of preparation are not yet "noble beings" (*ārya*). This path begins with the acquisition of the four "noble attitudes" (*ārya-vaṃsa*), attitudes that consist largely in contentment with the life of a monk. That the path begins here indicates once again that the meditational practices under consideration were intended by most Buddhist theoreticians only for monks. Following the acquisition of the four noble attitudes, the practitioner makes use of a number of preliminary practices, including several that have already been discussed: first, mindfulness of breathing; then meditation on the horrible; then the application of mindfulness to body, affective sensation, mind, and doctrinal formulas; and finally, the acquisition, as a result of properly practicing these techniques, of the four "aids to penetration" (*nirvedha-bhāgīya*), mental states that make it possible for the practitioner to pass from the purely preliminary path of preparation to the "transcendent path of vision" (*lokottara-darśana-mārga*). In summary, the path of preparation is a path upon which the practitioner becomes a monk (if he is not already) and learns to rest content with the materially unsatisfying aspects of the monastic life. He then begins to practice some preliminary meditative techniques and through them gains some initial insight into the conditioned and unsatisfactory nature of all existents. And at this point he is ready to pass from there to the "noble path" (*ārya-mārga*), the saving path proper.

It is worthy of note that some techniques which I earlier suggested were often seen as independently soteriologically valid—especially the practice of mindfulness—are here characterized as preparatory. This downgrading, as it were, of previously independently important methods, was to some extent made necessary by the systematic nature of the enterprise Vasubandhu and others like him were engaged in: the impulse was to account for all the various meditational techniques witnessed by the tradition, to provide a slot for each of them, and to try to show how each might be connected to all the others. This naturally made it difficult to allow that any one of the techniques by itself was independently sufficient for salvation.

The second major division of Vasubandhu's exposition is labeled the "path of vision." This is essentially a set of analytical practices concerned with the detailed analysis by the practitioner of the various aspects (usually sixteen) into which the four truths (of suffering, the arising of suffering, the cessation of suffering, and the path to the cessation of suffering) of Buddhism are usually subdivided. The detailed and complex conceptual content of each of these sixteen aspects is contemplated and internalized until these categories become coextensive with the perceptions and cognitions of the practitioner. Exactly how this works will be made clearer by examining the detailed subdivisions of the path of vision. It is divided into sixteen elements, including eight "willingnesses" (*kṣānti*) aimed at the attainment of certain kinds of intuitive realization (jñāna), and a corresponding eight kinds of intuitive realization. The two sets of eight comprise together the sixteen elements of the path of vision and correspond in turn to the sixteen aspects of the four truths. With the attainment of each of the sixteen stages a certain number of "proclivities" (*anuśaya*—either passionate tendencies toward wrong action or ingrained habit patterns resulting in false cognitions) are decisively and finally disposed of. This somewhat complex set of altered states of consciousness, together with the proclivities removed by the attainment of each, is charted below on page 56.

What we have here is a list of sixteen altered states, states in which the practitioner either has a "willingness" to gain a certain kind of intuitive knowledge or has actually gained such knowledge. The knowledge in question may itself be of two kinds: either "intuitive knowledge of doctrine" (*dharma-jñāna*) or "consequent intuitive knowledge" (*anvaya-jñāna*). Finally, there are four possible objects for each kind of willingness and each kind

THE PATH OF VISION
(*darśana-mārga*)

REALIZATION OF THE FIRST TRUTH

1 Willingness issuing in intuitive knowledge of doctrine concerning suffering
2 Intuitive knowledge of doctrine concerning suffering
3 Willingness issuing in a consequent intuitive knowledge concerning suffering
4 Consequent intuitive knowledge concerning suffering

[28 proclivities abandoned by the realization of the first truth: 3 kinds of wrong view concerning the existence of an individual person; 3 kinds of extremist wrong view; 3 kinds of wrong view *simpliciter;* 3 kinds of clinging to wrong view; 3 kinds of doubt; 3 kinds of clinging to ethical practice and religious observance; 3 kinds of passion; one kind of aversion; 3 kinds of conceit; 3 kinds of ignorance]

REALIZATION OF THE SECOND TRUTH

5 Willingness issuing in intuitive knowledge of doctrine concerning the arising of suffering
6 Intuitive knowledge of doctrine concerning the arising of suffering
7 Willingness issuing in a consequent intuitive knowledge concerning the arising of suffering
8 Consequent intuitive knowledge concerning the arising of suffering

[19 proclivities abandoned by the realization of the second truth: 3 kinds of wrong view *simpliciter;* 3 kinds of clinging to wrong view; 3 kinds of doubt; 3 kinds of passion; one kind of aversion; 3 kinds of conceit; 3 kinds of ignorance]

REALIZATION OF THE THIRD TRUTH

9 Willingness issuing in intuitive knowledge of doctrine concerning the cessation of suffering
10 Intuitive knowledge of doctrine concerning the cessation of suffering
11 Willingness issuing in a consequent intuitive knowledge concerning the cessation of suffering
12 Consequent intuitive knowledge concerning the cessation of suffering

[19 proclivities abandoned by the realization of the third truth: 3 kinds of wrong view *simpliciter;* 3 kinds of clinging to wrong view; 3 kinds of doubt; 3 kinds of passion; one kind of aversion; 3 kinds of conceit; 3 kinds of ignorance]

REALIZATION OF THE FOURTH TRUTH

13 Willingness issuing in intuitive knowledge of doctrine concerning the path
14 Intuitive knowledge of doctrine concerning the path
15 Willingness issuing in a consequent intuitive knowledge concerning the path
16 Consequent intuitive knowledge concerning the path

[22 proclivities abandoned by the realization of the fourth truth: 3 kinds of wrong view *simpliciter;* 3 kinds of clinging to wrong view; 3 kinds of doubt; 3 kinds of clinging to ethical practice and religious observance; 3 kinds of passion; one kind of aversion; 3 kinds of conceit; 3 kinds of ignorance]

7. *Seated Buddha*, Indian, Gandhāra Region, Kuṣhāṇa Period, 1st half of 3rd century C.E. Grey schist 51 x 31 inches.

of knowledge, and these are the Four Truths themselves. So much for the schema. What of the actual practice? And what is the significance of the distinction between the two kinds of intuitive knowledge and that between a "willingness" for knowledge and knowledge itself?

First, the division between the "willingness" for intuitive knowledge and that knowledge itself: this separation is intended to mark two stages in the abandonment of proclivities. On the first stage, that of "willingness," the practitioner turns her mind toward the relevant knowledge and proleptically reaches it; at the same time she separates herself from the relevant proclivities. But it is only with passage from this "willingness" to firm possession of the intuitive knowledge in question that the practitioner becomes finally and irreversibly separated from the relevant proclivities. The image used by Vasubandhu to describe the process is graphic: the willingness for intuitive knowledge is like finding a thief in one's house and expelling that thief; the intuitive knowledge itself is likened to bolting the door behind the expelled thief so that there is no chance he can reenter. This distinction, then, is intended to do no more than mark the difference between, on the one hand, temporary (and thus possibly reversible) insight together with its concomitant separation from negative proclivities and, on the other, permanent (and thus irreversible) insight and separation.

The distinction between the two kinds of intuitive knowledge—that concerning doctrine and that called "consequent"—is also a scholastic device, intended to mark the difference between the cosmic realm within which certain kinds of suffering are located. Buddhist cosmology regularly recognizes three cosmic realms: the realm of desire, the realm of form, and the realm of formlessness. Each realm has its own characteristics, its own inhabitants, its own potentialities and drawbacks; important for the purposes of this article, each realm also has passions and proclivities that belong uniquely to it. This explains the multiplicity of kinds of passion abandoned by the realization of each truth: the reason why there are so often three kinds of any particular proclivity removed is that one kind belongs to each cosmic realm. In terms of the distinction between intuitive knowledge concerning doctrine and consequent intuitive knowledge, the former has as its object the suffering (or origination, or cessation, or path, depending on which truth is under discussion) which is located in the realm of desire and the latter has as its object the suffering (or origination and so forth) which is located in the other two cosmic realms: those of form and formlessness.

So much for the formal details. To get a more precise sense of exactly what is supposed to happen when a practitioner enters upon the path of vision I shall now offer some more detailed comments on the details involved in realizing the first truth (stages 1–4 in the chart given above). These details can then be generalized and applied to the realization of the other three truths. First, it is important to remember that while following this path the practitioner is engaged in analytical intellectual meditations the objects of which are the philosophical ramifications and entailments of the Four Truths. In the case of the first truth (suffering, *duḥkha*), she will be considering the standard threefold subdivision of the truth of suffering into the "suffering that consists in suffering" (*duḥkha-duḥkhatā*), the "suffering that consists in being compounded" (*saṃskāra-duḥkhatā*), and the "suffering that consists in transformation" (*vipariṇāma-duḥkhatā*). She will analyze this threefold subdivision, intended as a complete classification of all possible types of suffering, consider it from all possible angles, unpack its implications, and finally internalize it, grasp its reality and truth, and make it coextensive with the way in which she perceives, responds to, and cognizes the world. Such a process results finally in "complete comprehension" (*abhisamaya*) of the truths in all their aspects, and at this point the practitioner has disposed of every kind of wrong philosophical views and remains bound only by some residual passions and habit patterns.

These residual habit patterns and proclivities need to be removed, according to Vasubandhu, by a repeated re-presentation by the practitioner to himself of the complete comprehension already obtained on the path of vision. This occurs, Vasubandhu tells us, on the "transcendent path of cultivation" (*lokottara-bhāvanā-mārga*), which the practitioner enters with the attainment of stage 16 of the path of vision. The important point to notice here is that the object of meditative practice does not change when the practitioner makes the transition from the path of vision to that of cultivation; it is still the Four Truths in all their aspects. What does change, though, and strikingly, is the method used. In describing what goes on in the transcendent path of cultivation Vasubandhu introduces the four dhyānas and the four formless states which have already been discussed. This is puzzling, since, as should be clear from the description given those altered states and the techniques used to attain them, they cannot easily accommodate repeated re-presentation of complex propositionally expressible truths, and just this is required by the functions attributed to the transcendent path of cultivation by Vasubandhu. These altered states are, after all, enstatic, aimed at the progressive reduction of the contents of consciousness. As I have shown, in the higher formless states those mental functions which would seem to be a necessary precondition for the kind of analytical thought required (conceptualization and so forth) are, by definition, not present.

There is, I think, a historical explanation for this problem. Vasubandhu's view is that the most important functions of the meditational path are those I have been calling "observationally analytic" rather than those I have been calling "enstatic." He wants to stress those methods which remove cognitive error and transform the practitioner's perceptual and cognitive experience rather than those methods which reduce the contents of the practitioner's consciousness and issue finally in cessation. This explains the importance he gives to the path of vision—which is paradigmatically analytic—and also goes some way toward explaining why he identifies the transcendent path of cultivation with the dhyānas and formless states. These latter must be accommodated into any systematic Buddhist path since they are so prominently present in the tradition, but Vasubandhu, since he places little value on their original soteriological thrust, does this in such a way as to obscure much of what they were originally intended to do. This becomes even clearer when we consider what Vasubandhu does with the attainment of cessation, that mindless condition which I have suggested was the proper goal of the enstatic practices. For him, the attainment of cessation is simply a pleasant resting place, a place for the active practitioner to take a short vacation from the stresses and strains of the path proper. It has no independent soteriological validity as it perhaps had for (some strands of) the early tradition.

Vasubandhu's picture of the meditational path encapsulates what became, after his time, Buddhist orthodoxy on these questions. His classifications and subdivisions and his terminology (most of which, certainly, was not created by him but was given standard form by him) became the standard presupposed for later discussions. The changes that took place in India in this area of thought during the second half of the first millennium of the Christian era did not drastically alter the schema, though they often modified it by altering the conceptual content of the ideas internalized through the practice of meditation. And, where these ideas were sufficiently different to require some new meditational exercises for their proper appropriation, such exercises were developed and incorporated into the tradition. It is to one influential set of such exercises that I shall now turn.

The Perfection of Dhyāna

In the first half of the eighth century of the Christian era the poet and philosopher Śāntideva composed a text in Sanskrit called *Entering Upon the Practice of Awakening* (*Bodhicaryāvatāra*, or perhaps *Bodhisattvacaryāvatāra*). The text is structured, in part, around the traditional Buddhist set of six "perfections" (*pāramitā*), of which the fifth is the "perfection of dhyāna" (treated in the eighth chapter of the *Bodhicaryāvatāra*). A brief glance at the structure and content of this chapter will give a good idea of how (a part of) the Buddhist meditational path was presented at a later period in India: it will be obvious that Śāntideva has somewhat different soteriological concerns than did Vasubandhu, or at least that he stresses things differently.

Śāntideva begins by stating the following twofold necessity: first, for isolating the body (*kāya*) from the world, and then for similarly isolating the mind (*citta*). The former is to be achieved by renouncing physical entanglements, the latter by renouncing discursive thought. Both are difficult, the former largely because of *sneha,* a kind of lubricious involvement with oneself and what pertains to oneself and a concomitant involvement and concern with worldly things, and the latter because of the inherent difficulty in restraining and concentrating the mind. Tranquillity (*śamatha*) is therefore the first thing to be sought in the pursuit of isolating oneself from the attractions of the worldly life.

Śāntideva devotes many verses (vv. 5–39) to describing the dangers of social existence (vv. 9–25) and the delights of solitude, poverty, living in forests, and contemplating corpses (vv. 26–39). In these last verses he suggests many of the same themes that were covered in the material discussed earlier on the contemplation of the "horrible," and he clearly sees such practices as a necessary corrective to our natural tendency to become involved in worldly life. But this is only the first stage. Even when the body has been isolated in this way, when the practitioner has removed herself from physical proximity to worldly distractions, it still remains to isolate the mind. This is done by attempting to first understand and then remove sensual desire (*kāma*) and to consciously restrain and control the mind's discursive thought processes (vv. 40–89). It is here, if anywhere, that Śāntideva provides what little scope he allows for the purely enstatic techniques described above.

But even this is no more than preliminary. When both body and mind have been isolated in this way the practitioner is enjoined to inculcate the "decision for enlightenment" (*bodhicitta*) and the inculcation of active compassion for others. All this, for Śāntideva, is just as much part of the "perfection of dhyāna" as the attempt to isolate body and mind; in fact the former practices have a rationale only insofar as they make it possible for the practitioner to undertake the latter. In explaining how the practitioner is to develop compassionate action Śāntideva stresses the importance of meditationally cultivating the realization that oneself and other living beings are actually identical. The following programmatic verse is important:

To begin with one should effortfully cultivate,
in the appropriate way,
the identity of self and other:
All [beings] are alike in [avoiding] pain and [wanting] pleasure!
I should protect them as I do myself! (v. 90)

The central point here is partly conceptual—that, metaphysically, there is no meaningful distinction to be made between "my" sufferings or pleasures and "your" sufferings and pleasures, since "you" and "I" are not different—and partly meditational. That is, it is not sufficient for the practitioner to realize the conceptual truth of the doctrine that self and other are identical; it is not even enough for him to act as if what counts is the removal of suffering rather than the individual in whom that suffering is apparently located. Instead, she must actually learn to perceive herself as the other and the other as herself, and to do this by mentally exchanging herself with the other:

So whoever wishes to quickly give protection
To both himself and other [beings]
Should practice that supreme secret:
The exchange of self and other. (v. 120)

To take a practical example: on perceiving a person who appears less fortunate than himself—say, a beggar or a cripple—the practitioner would imaginatively identify himself with the unfortunate in question to the extent that he would, in an almost literal sense, become that unfortunate. The cripple's pains or the beggar's hunger would become his and he would do everything in his power to ease them, just as an ordinary person would if the pains or the hunger were truly "his." Thus, in giving to the beggar or nursing the cripple the practitioner does not perceive herself as the giver and the recipient as someone other than herself; for a time at least she sees herself as the recipient and someone other than her (her "real self") as the giver (vv. 155–73). Ultimately, Śāntideva's recommendation of this position leads to some strange paradoxes of language: language (Sanskrit no less than English) is irredeemably person-centered, and a metaphysic predicated on the idea that there are no persons, no "owners of deeds" as the text puts it, leads to genuine linguistic and conceptual difficulties. But from the viewpoint of meditational practice Śāntideva's recommendations are clear enough: the practitioner is to consistently attempt to dissolve the idea of himself as a persisting enduring subject—a "person"—and to do this by repeated and thoroughgoing thought experiments in which he exchanges his (illusory) identity for the (equally illusory) identity of another. For Śāntideva, this practice, when carried out consistently, is the apex of meditational practice, for by engaging in it one can simultaneously realize the truth of Buddhism's most characteristic doctrine (that there are no perduring substantial selves) and provide oneself with what is, from the Buddhist viewpoint, the only possible basis for proper ethical practice.

* * *

If there are common themes to the material surveyed here they seem to be the following. Buddhist meditational technique, as it was theorized about and systematized in India, was of two kinds: first, enstatic, aimed at reducing the contents of consciousness and issuing finally in the complete cessation of all mental events (this was discussed at length in this chapter, and it is in this context that the dhyānas are most appropriately placed); second, observationally analytic, aimed at first understanding and then internalizing key items of Buddhist doctrine. It is this broad category of practice which was of most significance for the systematizers of the tradition such as Vasubandhu; they appear to have felt somewhat uneasy about the first kind of practice. Under the rubric of the observationally analytic should be placed mindfulness, the path of vision, and, though with a rather different flavor, the meditational identification and exchange of self and other. Observationally analytic technique of this kind is transformative in a profound and thoroughgoing sense, since it is always linked with a specific and often highly developed metaphysic: its rationale is simply to embody that metaphysic, to make it necessary for the practitioner to perceive the world and respond to it in accordance with the categories of that metaphysic. And it is the content of the metaphysic more than the specific techniques which makes the meditational practices I have surveyed here peculiarly Buddhist.

Notes

1. Stephan Beyer, *The Cult of Tārā: Magic and Ritual in Tibet* (Berkeley: University of California Press, 1973) 92.
2. See p. 54 below.
3. What follows is based mostly upon material from the sixth chapter of the *Abhidharmakośabhāṣya.*

Bibliography

The bibliography that follows is not, and is not intended to be, complete. Its first section gives details of translations of texts cited in the body of the article or of texts that will provide useful background. Its second section gives some of the more important Western-language works on the topic. Most of the works cited will provide further bibliographical guidance to what is now an enormous field.

Sources

The canonical texts of the Theravāda tradition are almost all easily available in English translations (of varying quality) from the Pāli Text Society. Most of the extracts cited and discussed on pp. 39–53 are from this literature.

The standard postcanonical systematization of theories about meditation in the Theravāda is Buddhaghosa's *Visuddhimagga,* available in excellent English translation by Ñyāṇamoli (Bhikkhu) as *The Path of Purification* (2 vols.; 1st ed. Sri Lanka, 1956, 1964; reprint, Berkeley and London: Shambhala, 1976).

The analogue to the *Visuddhimagga* from the Vaibhāṣika school is Vasubandhu's *Abhidharmakośabhāṣya*. This has been translated into French by Louis de la Vallée Poussin, *L'Abhidharmakośa de Vasubandhu* (6 vols.; Pāris: Paul Geuthner, 1923–31; reprint, Brussels: Institut Belge des Hautes Études Chinoises, 1971).

The early texts called *yogācārabhūmi* have not been extensively studied by Western scholars. The most easily accessible analysis is Paul Demiéville, "La Yogācārabhūmi de Saṅgharakṣa," *Bulletin de l'École Française d'Extrême-Orient* 44 (1954) 339–436.

Later, more strictly philosophical Yogācāra views on meditational practice may be found in Asaṅga's *Abhidharmasamuccaya* (translated into French by Walpola Rahula as *Le Compendium de la Superdoctrine (philosophie) (Abhidharmasamuccaya) d'Asaṅga* [Paris: École Française d'Extrême-Orient, 1971]); in the same author's *Mahāyānasaṃgraha* (translated into French by Étienne Lamotte as *La somme du Grand Véhicule d'Asaṅga* [2 vols.; Louvain: Bibliothèque du Muséon, 1938–39; reprint, Institut Orientaliste de Louvain, 1973]); and in the nirvāṇa chapter of the *Viniścayasaṃgrahaṇī* (translated into German by Lambert Schmithausen as *Der Nirvāṇa-Abschnitt in der Viniścayasaṃgrahaṇī der Yogācārabhūmiḥ* [Österreichische Akademie der Wissenschaften, Philosophisch-Historische Klasse Sitzungsberichte 264; Veroffentlichungen der Komission für Sprachen und Kulturen Süd- und Ostasiens 8; Vienna: Hermann Böhlaus, 1969]).

A standard systematization of Mahāyāna views on the meditative path which may be of Indian origin is the **Mahāprajñāpāramitāśāstra* (translated into French [from Chinese] by Étienne Lamotte as *Le traité de la grande vertu de sagesse* (5 vols.; Publications de l'Institut Orientaliste de Louvain 2, 12, 24–26; Louvain-la-Neuve: Institut Orientaliste de Louvain, 1970–81]. Volumes 2–3 are especially rich in material devoted to the technicalities of the meditative path).

Śāntideva's *Bodhicaryāvatāra* has been translated into English twice recently, first from the original Sanskrit by Marion L. Matics (as *Entering the Path of Enlightenment* [New York: Macmillan, 1970]), and then from the Tibetan version by Stephen Batchelor (as *A Guide to the Bodhisattva's Way of Life* [Dharamsala: Library of Tibetan Works and Archives, 1979]). The eighth chapter is on dhyāna.

Studies

Barnes, Michael. "The Buddhist Way of Deliverance." *Studia Missionalia* 30 (1981) 233–77. Especially useful for its copious comparative material from the *Mahābhārata*.

Bronkhorst, Johannes. *The Two Traditions of Meditation in Ancient India*. Alt- und neuindische Studien 26. Stuttgart: Franz Steiner, 1986. A detailed textual study (including much interesting Jaina material) exploring the tension between the enstatic and observational modes of praxis.

Conze, Edward. *Buddhist Meditation*. London: Allen & Unwin, 1956. (Frequent paperback reprints.) A general survey, somewhat dated and with some anti-Theravādin bias.

Cousins, Lance S. "Buddhist Jhāna: Its Nature and Attainment According to the Pāli Sources." *Religion* 3 (1973) 115–31. Especially useful for its discussion of the term *jhāna* (Sanskrit *dhyāna*).

De Silva, Lily. "Cetovimutti Paññāvimutti and Ubhatobhāgavimutti." *Pāli Buddhist Review* 3:118–45. A detailed technical treatment of a set of Theravādin categories designed to deal with the problem of combining concentrative techniques with analytical techniques.

Eliade, Mircea. *Yoga: Immortality and Freedom*. 2nd rev. ed. New York: Bollingen

Foundation, 1969. An indispensable work and a thoroughly good read. Eliade introduced much of the technical terminology which has since become standard in the discussion of these matters. Not reliable, though, in matters of detail.

Griffiths, Paul J. "Buddhist Jhāna: A Form-Critical Study." *Religion* 13:55–68.

———. "Concentration or Insight: The Problematic of Theravāda Buddhist Meditation-Theory." *Journal of the American Academy of Religion* 49 (1981) 605–24.

———. *On Being Mindless: Buddhist Meditation and the Mind-Body Problem.* La Salle, IL: Open Court, 1986. A detailed analysis of the historical and philosophical problems surrounding the "attainment of cessation" (*nirodha-samāpatti*).

———. "On Being Mindless: The debate on the reemergence of consciousness from the attainment of cessation in the Abhidharmakośabhāṣyam and its commentaries." *Philosophy East and West* 33 (1983) 379–94.

Gunaratana, Henepola. "A Critical Analysis of the Jhānas in Theravāda Buddhist Meditation." Ph.D. dissertation, American University (Washington, DC), 1980. A very thorough linguistic and textual analysis of the development of theories about the jhānas in the Theravāda tradition.

Heiler, Friedrich. *Die Buddhistische Versenkung: Eine religionsgeschichtliche Untersuchung.* Munich: Reinhardt, 1922. One of the pioneering works in the Western study of Buddhist meditation. Heiler based his views mostly on Theravāda materials, but what he says applies much more widely than to Theravāda texts. In some respects his work has still not been surpassed.

Hurvitz, Leon. "Dharmaśrī on the Sixteen Degrees of Comprehension." *Journal of the International Association of Buddhist Studies* 2 (1979) 7–30. A study of the types of realization (*abhisamaya*).

———. "The Eight Liberations." In *Studies in Pāli and Buddhism: A Memorial Volume in Honor of Bhikkhu Jagdish Kashyap,* ed. A. K. Narain and L. Zwilling, 121–69. Delhi: B. R. Publishing, 1979. A collection of materials on the eight "liberations" (*vimokṣa*), a set of categories not discussed in this article but overlapping to some extent with the material analyzed in this chapter.

Katz, Nathan. *Buddhist Images of Human Perfection: The Arahant of the Suttapiṭaka Compared with the Bodhisattva and the Mahāsiddha.* Delhi: Motilal Banarsidass, 1982. Conceptually and methodologically flawed, but containing some interesting material.

King, Winston L. *Theravāda Meditation: The Buddhist Transformation of Yoga.* University Park, PA: Pennsylvania State University Press, 1980.

Kiyota, Minoru, and Elvin W. Jones, eds. *Mahāyāna Buddhist Meditation: Theory and Practice.* Honolulu: University Press of Hawaii, 1978. A collection of essays on various aspects of Buddhist meditation in Mahāyāna texts. The quality of the pieces is uneven, but the pieces by Nagao and Kiyota are first-rate.

Kornfield, Jack. *Living Buddhist Masters.* Santa Cruz: Unity Press, 1977. A fascinating collection of interviews with and studies of contemporary (mostly Theravādin) meditation teachers.

La Vallée Poussin, Louis de. "Musīla et Nāradā: le chemin du Nirvāṇa." *Mélanges chinois et bouddhiques* 5 (1936–37) 189–222. A basic and influential article. Poussin was the first Western scholar to point out and systematically analyze the tensions apparent in Theravādin theories about meditation. Essential reading.

Nyanaponika (Thera). *The Heart of Buddhist Meditation.* London: Rider, 1962. (Frequent paperback reprints.) A treatment of the Theravāda version of mindfulness from within the tradition.

Rahula, Walpola. "A Comparative Study of Dhyānas According to Theravāda, Sarvāstivāda and Mahāyāna." In Walpola Rahula, *Zen and the Taming of the Bull,* 100–109. London: Gordon Fraser, 1978.

Sayadaw, Mahasi (Mahāthera). *The Progress of Insight.* Kandy: Forest Hermitage, 1965. A classic short treatment by a twentieth-century Burmese meditation master of the practice of mindfulness. Originally written in Pāli. The Buddhist Publication Society edition (1973 and reprints) includes the Pāli text as well as an English translation.

Schmithausen, Lambert. "Ich und Erlösung im Buddhismus." *Zeitschrift für Missionswissenschaft und Religionswissenschaft* 53 (1969) 157–70.

——. "On Some Aspects of Descriptions or Theories of 'Liberating Insight' and 'Enlightenment' in Early Buddhism." In *Studien zum Jainismus und Buddhismus,* ed. Klaus Bruhn and Albrecht Wezler, 199–250. Wiesbaden: Franz Steiner, 1981.

——. "On the Problem of the Relation of Spiritual Practice and Philosophical Theory in Buddhism." In *German Scholars on India,* 2:235–50. Bombay: Nachiketa Publications, 1976.

——. "Spirituelle Praxis und Philosophische Theorie im Buddhismus." *Zeitschrift für Missionswissenschaft und Religionswissenschaft* 57 (1973) 161–86.

——. "Versenkungspraxis und Erlösende Erfahrung in der Śrāvakabhūmi." In *Epiphanie des Heils: Zur Heilsgegenwart in Indischer und Christlicher Religion,* ed. Gerhard Oberhammer, 59–85. Vienna: Österreichische Akademie der Wissenschaften, 1982.

——. "Die Vier Konzentrationen der Aufmerksamkeit: Zur geschichtlichen Entwicklung einer spirituellen Praxis des Buddhismus." *Zeitschrift für Missionswissenschaft und Religionswissenschaft* 60 (1976) 241–66.

——. "Zur Struktur der Erlösenden Erfahrung im Indischen Buddhismus." In *Transzendenzerfahrung: Vollzugshorizont des Heils,* ed. Gerhard Oberhammer, 97–119.

This collection of pieces by Schmithausen forms the most significant theoretical contribution by any Western scholar to an understanding of Indian Buddhist meditation. The fact that most of it is written in German has meant that it has not received the attention it warrants from the Anglo-American scholarly community. Some of the pieces deal with Theravāda issues, but most of them are centered on the Yogācāra, in which Schmithausen is a specialist.

Soni, R. L. *The Only Way to Deliverance.* Boulder, CO: Prajñā Press, 1980. Another Theravādin exposition of mindfulness; adds rather little to Nyanaponika's work.

Takeuchi Yoshinori. *Probleme der Versenkung im Ur-Buddhismus.* Leiden: Brill, 1972. A study by the most prominent living member of the Japanese Kyoto School of what the Pāli Canon has to say about meditation. Historically problematic but philosophically interesting.

Vajirañāṇa, (Mahāthera). *Buddhist Meditation.* Colombo, Sri Lanka: M. D. Gunasena, 1962. A systematic rendering of Buddhaghosa's theories about meditation. Uncritical, but useful as a reference work.

There is also an enormous literature in Japanese, much of it excellent, on many of the topics mentioned in this chapter.

3

Abhidharma

Sakurabe Hajime

The Abhidharma Literature

Modern studies in Abhidharma literature are still not sufficiently advanced to permit a full survey of the process by which *abhidharma* (literally, "study in regard to the Dharma") developed within the Indian monastic tradition. Abhidharma has its origin in the *abhidharmakathā* (discourses about Dharma) carried on in the Saṅgha in the earliest days of Buddhism, possibly even in the Buddha's own lifetime. After the Saṅgha split up into some twenty factions, several of the more important ones engaged in abhidharmic studies, and consequently formed themselves into schools with distinctive ontological, psychological, and soteriological theories, eventually building coherent systems of thought with their full complement of precise terminology. We do not know how many of these schools produced a literature; what is extant comes, by and large, from two schools only. In Pāli sources we have the Theravāda *Abhidharma-piṭaka* and the ten or so postcanonical treatises. In the Abhidharma section of the Taishō edition of the Chinese Tripiṭaka are found twenty-eight texts in translation, of which all but one belong to the Sarvāstivāda school. In addition, the Tibetan Tripiṭaka contains a distinct collection of nine treatises of the same school.

Sarvāstivāda

The Sarvāstivāda literature, which exceeds that of Theravāda both in the number of texts and in volume, allows us to distinguish three stages in the development of Abhidharma: (1) an early stage of explaining, organizing, and classifying the terms in the sūtras; (2) a stage in which the distinct doctrinal theories evolved; and (3) a late stage of doctrinal systematization.

1. To the first stage belong the *Saṅgītiparyāya* and the *Dharmaskandha*, each of which is traditionally ascribed to a disciple of the Buddha. The first of these śāstras (treatises) is an exposition of the *Saṅgīti* [*-paryāya*]*-sūtra* in the *Dīrgha Āgama*, a sūtra of abhidharmic cast, each of whose sections deals with technical terms arranged from one to ten; the śāstra gives explanations or definitions of each of these terms, and thus derives directly from the sūtra. The same is true of the *Dharmaskandha*, which deals with twenty-one topics taken from the teachings of the *Sūtra-piṭaka* in the same number of chapters. T. Kimura describes these two texts as "śāstras as expositions of the sūtra." Though some terms and ideas peculiar to Sarvāstivāda are already evident here, most are common to all schools.

2. The śāstras in the second stage are apparently independent of the *Sūtra-piṭaka* and are of a more distinctly Sarvāstivāda hue. They include the *Prajñapti*, which advances cosmological analysis; the *Vijñānakāya*, which analyzes mental functions; the *Dhātukāya*, which investigates mental elements and their concomitants; and the *Prakaraṇa*, a collation of several originally independent works. These texts revel in definitions of technical terms and detailed analyses of the relations between them, and set a headline for the increasingly intricate argumentation of subsequent Abhidharma literature.

The epoch-making *Jñānaprasthāna*—unlike the preceding texts, which had attempted to cover only a particular, limited field—made a general survey of the whole of Sarvāstivāda doctrine. Thus it is sometimes called the "body" śāstra, in contrast to which the six preceding works are the "limb" śāstras. It was long regarded as the principal text of the school. It is not, however, a very methodical composition, and related topics are simply grouped together by section with no attempt to arrange them more systematically. The *Mahāvibhāṣā* (150–200 C.E.), a voluminous commentary on the *Jñānaprasthāna*, represents a still more advanced level of analysis. Generous in its citation of views from various quarters, it is the most thorough compilation of theories of Sarvāstivāda and other schools. It is not a rigid, line-by-line commentary, but allots ample space to topics regarded as important, while others are wholly ignored or dealt with cursorily.

3. A clear progress in organization is marked by the short but systematic presentation of Sarvāstivāda theory in the first seven of the ten chapters of the *Abhidharma-hṛdaya*.[1] Chapters 1 and 2 expound the "logic of dharma," the basic standpoint of the school; chapters 3 and 4 clarify the nature of the present world of delusion; chapters 5, 6, and 7 deal with the realm of enlightenment and the way to it. This scheme is followed by almost all subsequent Sarvāstivāda works, which also imitate this text's procedure of setting forth the theories in concise verse followed by a prose paraphrase.

Vasubandhu was the author of the *Abhidharma-kośa*, in which the development of thought in this line of abhidharmic tracts reaches its peak.[2] This voluminous compendium of precise definitions of Buddhist terms enjoyed wide circulation in India, Tibet, China, and Japan as a basic textbook, and a great many commentaries and doctrinal writings resulted from its study. At times the author criticizes Sarvāstivāda teaching, apparently from a Sautrāntika standpoint, making it doubtful if the text can be taken simply as a Sarvāstivāda work. Yet in both structure and content it is related directly to the *Abhidharma-hṛdaya* and more distantly to the *Saṅgītiparyāya*, and thus certainly belongs to the literature of the Sarvāstivāda school. Indeed, the author himself states clearly that he is following the doctrines of the Vaibhāṣika (i.e., those who study the *Mahāvibhāṣā*). Unlike most other Sarvāstivāda works, this uniquely important text fortunately survives in the Sanskrit original, as well as in Chinese and Tibetan translation.

Theravāda

The Pāli *Abhidhamma-piṭaka* (ca. 100 B.C.E.–100 C.E.) contains seven works whose order of appearance has yet to be clarified. I shall describe them in the order in which they are usually presented.

1. *Dhummasaṅgaṇi.*[3] Chapter 1 discusses the eighty-nine mental elements and the forty mental functions, dividing them into good, bad, and neutral. Chapter 3 discusses existent things in terms of the categories of "threes" and "twos" in 122 entries called the divisions of the *abhidhamma mātikā*, and again in terms of another category of "twos" in forty-two entries, the divisions of the *sutta mātikā* (which coincides in part with the list of terms found in the *Saṅgīti-suttanta* and commented on in the Sarvāstivāda *Saṅgītiparyāya*).

2. *Vibhaṅga.*[4] Like the Sarvāstivāda *Dharmaskandha*, this text explicates discourses from the *Sutta-piṭaka*, proceeding on the basis of *mātikā* found in the *Dhammasaṅgaṇi.*

3. *Dhātukathā.*[5] To clarify the concepts expressed by technical terms, this complex formulaic work examines whether or not they are connotatively or denotatively related.

4. *Puggalapaññatti.*[6] This work, perhaps the earliest of the seven, attempts to provide definitive explanations of terms for the human person taken from the sūtras.

5. *Kathāvatthu.*[7] With the *Paṭṭhāna*, this is the latest of the seven works, and the only one that even in legend is not attributed to the Buddha. It has been identified as the discourses of the elder Tissa, who destroyed heretical views at the Third Council. The entire work is in the form of questions and answers, and without a commentary it is difficult to determine which parties are involved or which school held the heretical views. It is unique in that it expounds Theravāda orthodoxy while crushing the heretical views of another school.

6. *Yamaka.* This work examines pairs of concepts and asks such questions as "Is all of A identical with B, or all of B identical with A?" or "Where A arises does B also arise; or where B arises does A also arise?"

7. *Paṭṭhāna.*[8] This, the largest of the seven works, defines the twenty-four "conditions" (*paccaya*) to which frequent reference is made from the time of the āgamas, and gives the range of associations for each, following the *abhidhamma mātikā.*

Three postcanonical works, the *Peṭakopadesa,*[9] the *Nettippakaraṇa,*[10] and the *Milindapañha* (Questions of King Milinda)[11] contain parts that clearly have abhidharmic characteristics. The first two are handbooks of canonical theory. The third is the record of a conversation between the Greek king Milinda (Menander) and the Buddhist priest Nāgasena, and is unique in the genre of doctrinal works for its focus on practical problems of cultivating the way. It has great historical interest as reflecting the spread of Buddhism and its encounter with Greek culture, and its aesthetic quality has sometimes invited comparison with the *Dialogues* of Plato.

In the Theravāda tradition there is an ancient transmission of commentaries on the Tripiṭaka which were compiled by Buddhaghosa in the fifth century C.E. "The Suttas offered descriptions of discovery; the Abhidhamma, map-making; but emphasis now [in the commentaries] is not on discovery, or even on mapping, so much as on consolidating, filling in and explaining. The material is worked over for consistency."[12] The *Aṭṭhasālinī,* a commentary on the *Dhammasaṅgaṇi,* fleshes out its skeletal analysis, providing a subtle map of psychological states which can serve as a framework for ethical striving and meditative practice.[13] There is also a commentary on the *Vibhaṅga* and one on the remaining five works. These voluminous commentaries follow the original word by word and reveal the progress made in academic study since the appearance of the *Abhidhamma-piṭaka.* The *Visuddhimagga* is closely related to the first two of these commentaries and is believed to be based on the *Vimuttimagga* of Upatissa, who lived two or three centuries earlier. The *Visuddhimagga* is so huge and complex a work that it has been replaced in Theravāda tradition by brief manuals such as Buddhadatta's *Abhidharmāvatāra* and Anuruddha's *Abhidhammatthasaṅgaha.*[14]

Some Abhidharma Doctrines

The Sarvāstivāda Logic of Dharma

In the *Sūtra-piṭaka* the impermanence of all things is a recurrent theme. People are apt to fail to perceive this impermanence and suffer from their attachment to things. To know the truth of impermanence and to rid oneself of attachment is a basic Buddhist aim. What is the reason for the impermanence of all things? All things are *dependent on* (*pratītya*) a number of causes and *arise* (*samutpāda*) as their result. Things are not self-sufficient entities, but come to exist only as the result (*phala*) of an interaction of various causes (*hetu*). When the cause undergoes change, so does the result. The Buddhist view that all things arise out of a cause–result relationship is opposed to such views as that all things derive from one ultimate cause, such as God the creator, or that all things are accidental and without cause, hence the universe is chaos. The reality into which Buddhism seeks to attain insight is not the absolute or the infinite, not the empirical and the contingent, but the logic underlying existence.

Since all things *arise through dependence* (*pratītyasamutpanna*) and are *produced* (*saṃskṛta;* we shall use the word "conditioned") through a number of causes, they are impermanent. When we clearly perceive the impermanent nature of things, our attachments to them vanish, our minds become calm and quiet, and the realm of nirvāṇa, the world of enlightenment, opens up for us. Because the world of enlightenment is not produced through causes, it is called *asaṃskṛta.* A person who does not perceive impermanence as it truly is lives in the world of delusion. This is called *sāsrava,* meaning to be covered with defilements, while the world of enlightenment is *anāsrava.* In terms of the Four Noble Truths, the conditioned world of *sāsrava* is *duḥkha* (suffering) and *samudaya* (the cause by which suffering arises), and the unconditioned world of *anāsrava* is *nirodha* (the extinction of suffering). The former is the world of saṃsāra (transmigration), the latter the world of nirvāṇa. Mārga (the path from suffering to the extinction of suffering) is still conditioned inasmuch as one has not attained nirvāṇa, but it is *anāsrava* since one is already in the process of departing from defilements, the evil passions.

The name Sarvāstivādin, meaning "those who explained that all exists," aptly expressed the "logic of dharma" of this school, on the basis of which they presented detailed proof of the truth of impermanence. The word *dharma* generally has the meaning of order, rule, or law; it may also mean justice, reality, virtue, custom, quality. In Buddhism, it can also mean "event," "existent thing"—a usage probably based on the fact that all existent things follow laws and principles. As a Sarvāstivāda technical term, however, it does not refer to a self-existent "thing" but to the "elements of existence" which coexist in composition. That all existents and phenomena in the experiential world are a flowing composition of countless dharmas, coming together and coming apart in complex cause–result relationships is the basic insight of the "logic of dharma." In the perfected theory, these dharmas are of seventy-five kinds, falling into five categories: *rūpa* (the material elements), *citta* (the mind), *caitasika* (the various mental functions), *citta-viprayukta-saṃskāra* (what is neither material nor mental, and includes elements such as relation, potential, and condition), and *asaṃskṛta.*

That "all exists" (*sarvaṃ asti*) is the central Sarvāstivāda tenet. The past dharma exists, the present dharma exists, and the future dharma also exists. But since conditioned dharmas also "instantaneously disappear," they cannot be of a continuous nature in time. For example, we usually think that if the cup on the shelf remains unchanged from one hour ago, then it has existed continually. However, from the standpoint of the "logic of dharma" it is nothing more than an unbroken series of countless conditioned dharmas instantaneously arising and instantaneously disappearing. That in any one moment a cup exists is merely a coming together in that instant of the round, tall shape of the cup (this is one kind of dharma) and the touch of its hard, smooth surface (this is another kind of dharma) with countless other dharmas to form the phenomenon known as the existence of the cup. In the next instant each of these dharmas disappears completely, and the cup continues to exist only because dharmas of the same kind have taken their place in the same spatial relationship, giving rise to the same phenomenon as that of the cup which existed in the preceding instant. In this process of arising and extinction of noncontinuous dharmas, the cup continues to exist as a stable, undisturbed phenomenon only as long as the succession of dharmas arising remains unchanged or unstopped.

The dharmas do not arise from nothingness, nor do they return to nothingness upon extinction. Arising means that a dharma comes from the future to appear in the present; extinction means that a dharma goes from the present into the past. Dharmas before arising in the present *exist* in the future. Dharmas after leaving the present *exist* in the past. In that one instant when dharmas have arisen from the future realm and are going into the past, they *exist* in the present. Whether past, present, or future, the dharma, keeping its unchanging self-nature (*svabhāva*) continues to exist. How then does a dharma appear from the future to arise in the present? The dharmas in the future realm are countless and without order. From out of that realm, a certain dharma will arise in a certain instant. It is a "cause" that decides which dharma will arise in which instant. Thus, the dharma that a cause brings to arise in that instant is the result of that cause and hence is said to "arise in dependence." If this is the case, what is this "cause" that brings about the arising of a dharma? The answer is: it is another dharma or other dharmas. The cause–result relationship is established between dharma and dharma. Each dharma has its cause in the countless other dharmas and arises as a result of them, and each is the cause of countless dharmas and works to bring about their arising as its results. This complex cause–result relation of countless intertwining dharmas constitutes our present world filled with suffering. On

8. Remains of the Buddhist University, monastery at Nālanda.

9. Remains of the Buddhist University, monastery at Nālanda.

10. Remains of the Buddhist University, monastery at Nālanda.

the one hand, there are the defilements (*kleśa*) that form the basis for wrong acts (*karman*) for which we sink deeper in suffering (*duḥkha*); on the other hand, there is the serene activity of wisdom (*prajñā*) which dispels the defilements one by one and turns us toward the way of enlightenment (bodhi). *Kleśa* and *karman* are the cause of which *duḥkha* is the result; prajñā is the cause of which bodhi is the result.

Sarvāstivāda Soteriology

In the vast reaches of the universe, countless beings are being born and are dying in a steady stream. Each being has repeated this cycle of birth and death from a beginningless past. In Buddhism, beings caught in this cycle are called *sattva.* The Sarvāstivādin Abhidharma divides the modes of existence of *sattva* into three realms (*dhātu*) and five courses (*gati*). Of the three realms two are realms with form: the realm of desire, in which the instinctual desires of living things are dominant, and the realm of form, in which they are less dominant. The realm of desire corresponds to the world under the earth, the surface of the earth, and the lower level of the heavenly world. The realm of form is the middle level of the heavenly world. The third realm, the realm of formlessness, is the top level of the heavenly world. The world under the earth is that of the hell states; the world on the surface of the earth is that of the hungry ghosts, animals, and humans; the heavenly world is that of the gods—these are the five courses of *sattva.* The three lower courses are filled with more suffering than the course of humans, and the gods have a far happier existence than humans do. But even the gods cannot escape change, decay, and death. It is the fate of *sattva* to be born somewhere in the five courses and to remain in the world of saṃsāra as long as the chain of birth and death remains intact.

It is the good or evil actions (*karman*) of the *sattva*'s life that determine the various states of existence. Good *karman* in the past necessarily earns one pleasant circumstances in the present, whereas evil *karman* necessarily earns one unfavorable circumstances filled with suffering. The cause–result relationships are strictly individual. One can neither obtain favorable fruits from another's good *karman* nor transfer to the other the unfavorable results of one's own bad *karman.* This law is the basis of Buddhist morality. But however desirable it is to be reborn in heaven as the result of one's good *karman,* that is not the ultimate goal. Buddhism seeks instead the world of enlightenment, which transcends the world of saṃsāra and arises at the point where one is released from the shackles of *karman.* By good *karman* is meant that which is good by the standard of worldly morals; it does not go beyond being *sāsrava* good. To be rid of defilements and to reach nirvāṇa, it is necessary to have the *anāsrava* good which accompanies *anāsrava prajñā.* This is the supramundane path (the Noble Path) which transcends worldly morals.

Before entering on this path aspirants after nirvāṇa must undertake a stage of preliminary discipline, in which they endeavor to maintain a pure life and to tame the mind and make it as serene and calm as possible. When this is achieved in a sufficient degree, the practitioner awakens the *anāsrava jñāna* and enters the Noble Path, having now become a noble one (*ārya*). Sarvāstivādin Abhidharma distinguishes two stages: the path of insight and the path of cultivation. The path of insight is the first stage leading to insight into the Four Noble Truths, which rids one of eighty-eight kinds of defilement. However, there remain ten more kinds of defilement, such as lust and hate, which are emotional or psychological defilements and cannot be banished by intellectual understanding only. The path of cultivation—that is, the path of mental cultivation through the repeated practice of samādhi upon the Four Noble Truths—enables one gradually to rid oneself of these defilements. This long, step-by-step process of spiritual cultivation is required so that the one who, in the path of insight, "has entered the stream of the Buddha's teaching" (*srotāpanna*) can become a "worthy one" (*arhat*) free of all defilements and can attain enlightenment.

Theravāda Philosophy of Mind

As a systematic exposition of the teachings found in the *Sūtra-piṭaka,* the Theravādin Abhidharma is not qualitatively different from the Sarvāstivādin. However, there are points at which this school developed its own special theories, for instance, the division of mental processes into the fourteen stages of *citta,* which reflect the course of life from birth to death. The first stage is the first moment of *citta* at birth when life is acquired, and the fourteenth is the last moment of *citta* at death when life ends. The second stage, called *bhavāṅga,* is that of subconsciousness, which is the repository of all psychological activity. Although it has no mental process itself, all mental processes arise from it and return to it. The third stage, deriving from subconsciousness, is the process of conscious manifestation of latent potential. From this stage emerges either any one of the five senses (the fourth to eighth stages) or consciousness. At the ninth stage an object is perceived by one of the senses and regarded as pleasant or unpleasant. At the tenth stage the object is evaluated as joy or sorrow. At the eleventh and twelfth stages the intellectual processes are engaged: the eleventh stage is that of initial intellectual perception, while the full elaboration of the intellectual processes, such as recognition, discernment, and will, is not introduced until the twelfth stage. Consciousness, emerging from the third stage, bypasses the ninth to eleventh and directly enters the twelfth stage. Whereas the third stage required two instants to complete, and only one instant was needed for any of the mental processes of the fourth to eleventh stages, the twelfth requires as many as seven instants to complete. When an object perceived at the twelfth stage is sufficiently clear and definite to make an impression, the impression is preserved in the consciousness. The activity of preserving an image belongs to the thirteenth stage. When the *citta* completes the series of mental processes from the third to the thirteenth stages, it subsides once again into the *bhavāṅga.*

Where the Sarvāstivāda logic of dharma attempts to explain logically the transiency of all things, this Theravāda theory is an attempt to observe human psychology carefully. Sarvāstivāda speculation reflects interchange with non-Buddhist thought and other Buddhist schools, whereas Theravāda is based more on diligent practice and samādhi.

* * *

The Abhidharma systems have often been accused of lacking all pertinence to the spiritual life. They seem to typify the attitude of the person struck by an arrow who is more concerned with discovering all about the arrow than with healing the wound. These systems were the product of an intellectual elite within the Saṅgha and do not reflect the concerns of the Saṅgha as a whole, much less those of the mass of devout Buddhists. Nevertheless, the Abhidharmists were not freethinkers. Their labors were devoted to the elucidation of the Buddha's teaching as found in the sūtras and to the service of the Dharma. The advances in subtle analysis, logical coherence, and architectonic perfection which these scholastics achieved as they created the first Buddhist philosophy must have seemed to exhibit the truth of the Dharma in all its splendor.

Nor should it be forgotten that, were it not for these systems, the later history of Buddhist thought might never have produced the broad and elaborate systems which future chapters in this volume will describe. The Mādhyamika critique of the Sarvāstivādin Abhidharma and the reappropriation of Sarvāstivādin analysis in Yogācāra, provided Mahāyāna philosophy with its architecture.[15] The Mādhyamika theories of emptiness (śūnyatā) and absence of self-nature (*niḥsvabhāva*) are clearly intended to refute or go beyond the Sarvāstivādin concept of dharma. The Yogācāra theory of store-consciousness (*ālaya-vijñāna*) is intimately connected with the Theravāda concept of *bhavāṅga.* One may also note that the doctrine of tathāgatagarbha is not unrelated to the Mahāsaṃghika concept of the basic nature of mind, and that the Sautrāntika concepts of "seed" (*bīja*) and "impression in the mind" (*vāsanā*) were adopted in Yogācāra and tathāgatagarbha doctrine. Thus some key concepts of Mahāyāna thought derive from or are intimately connected with abhidharmic Buddhism.

Abhidharma must also be credited with focusing the problem of the human condition and its solution with lucid fidelity to basic Buddhist insights. It clearly demonstrates that the problem and the solution lie within the human mind and are not dependent on an omnipotent God or a universal principle. Furthermore, it inculcates awareness that the establishment of one's true inner self cannot be achieved by self-assertion, but only by the regulation and control of one's self through an absolute spiritual quiescence. It shows a radical lucidity, too, in its account of the moral realm as conditioned and samsaric and in its aspiration to transcend this conditioned realm entirely in order to reach the absolute good—or, better, the quiescence and extinction—of nirvāṇa.

Notes

1. *The Essence of Metaphysics: Abhidharmahṛdaya*, trans. Charles Willemen (Brussels: Institut Belge des Hautes Études Bouddiques, 1975).
2. *L'Abhidharmakośa de Vasubandhu*, trans. Louis de la Vallée Poussin (6 vols.; 2nd ed.; Brussels: Institut Belge des Hautes Études Chinoises, 1971).
3. *A Buddhist Manual of Psychological Ethics*, trans. C. A. F. Rhys Davids (London: Pali Text Society, 1974; distributed by Routledge & Kegan Paul).
4. *The Book of Analysis*, trans. P. A. Thiṭṭila (London: Luzac, 1969).
5. *Discourse on Elements*, trans. U Nārada Mūla Paṭṭhāna Sayadaw (2 vols.; London: Pali Text Society, 1977).
6. *Designation of Human Types*, trans. Bimala Charan Law (London: Pali Text Society, 1979).
7. *Points of Controversy*, trans. Shwe Zan Aung and C. A. F. Rhys Davids (London: Luzac, 1979).
8. *Conditional Relations*, trans. U Nārada Mūla Paṭṭhāna Sayadaw (2 vols.; London: Pali Text Society, 1969, 1981).
9. *The Pitaka-Disclosure*, trans. Ñāṇamoli (London: Pali Text Society, 1979).
10. *The Guide*, trans. Ñāṇamoli (London: Pali Text Society, 1977).
11. *Milinda's Questions*, trans. I. B. Horner (2 vols.; London: Luzac, 1963, 1964).
12. Bhikkhu Ñyāṇamoli [Ñāṇamoli], trans., *The Path of Purification* (Berkeley and London: Shambhala, 1976) 1:xxix.
13. *The Expositor*, trans. Pe Maung Tin (London: Pali Text Society, 1976).
14. For the *Visuddhimagga*, see the section on meditation in Winston King's treatment of Theravāda in Southeast Asia (chapter 4, below).
15. See the essays of Kajiyama Yuichi (chapter 7, section I), Tachikawa Musashi (chapter 8, section I), and John Keenan (chapter 8, section II) below.

Bibliography

Bareau, André. *Les sectes bouddhiques du petit véhicule.* Saigon: École Française d'Extrême-Orient, vol. XXXVIII, 1955.

Conze, Edward. *Buddhist Thought in India.* Part II. London: Allen & Unwin, 1962.

Frauwallner, Erich. "Abhidharma-Studien." *Wiener Zeitschrift für die Kunde Süd- und Ostasiens* 7–17 (1963–73).

Guenther, Herbert V. *Philosophy and Psychology in the Abhidharma.* Berkeley and London: Shambhala, 1976.

Norman, K. R. *Pāli Literature.* A History of Indian Literature 7/2. Wiesbaden: Harrassowitz, 1983. Pp. 96–153.

Renou, Louis, and Jean Filliozat. *L'Inde classique,* II. Hanoi: École Française d'Extrême-Orient, 1953. Chapter xi.

Stcherbatsky, Theodor. *The Central Conception of Buddhism and the Meaning of the Word "Dharma."* Delhi: Indological Book House, 1970.

Van den Broeck, José. *Le saveur de l'immortel.* Louvain-la-Neuve: Institut Orientaliste de l'Université Catholique de Louvain, 1977.

Van Velthem, Marcel. *Le traité de la descente dans la profonde loi de l'Arhat Skandhila.* Louvain-la-Neuve: Institut Orientaliste de l'Université Catholique de Louvain, 1977.

4

Theravāda in Southeast Asia

Winston L. King

The spread of Buddhism into Southeast Asia must be seen as an integral part of the commercial and cultural Indianization of the region. For some centuries before the Christian era and throughout the first millennium C.E., India was the dominant civilization in South and Southeast Asia. This cultural dominance was seldom exerted in any political or military activity outside the subcontinent, perhaps because the attempts to achieve political and social unity within India occupied all available energies. Landless princelings from various Indian states occasionally established themselves as sovereigns in some small "nation" or other. But in no case was there a military conquest. These rulers were welcomed, sometimes invited, as representatives of a superior civilization and as experts in kingcraft. India was not a single political entity even in the Mauryan (ca. 320–185 B.C.E.) and Gupta periods (third to fifth centuries C.E.), the periods of greatest political unity, but its culture was amorphously unified within a multiplicity of variant forms collectively known as "Hinduism," whose variety and flexibility enabled it to penetrate the surrounding regions to the south and east. Indian culture was carried into these areas by traders and settlers, and strongly affected the culture and institutions of most Southeast Asian lands. Many tried to imitate Indian cultural and political institutions and continually imported experts from India to perform various functions.

Thus the spread of Buddhism into Southeast Asia from India should not be interpreted only in terms of its own inherent character. In India itself, that character had already undergone change in its contacts with Brahmanic-Upanishadic Hinduism (which produced Mahāyāna) and its early abstraction from that contact (which produced Theravāda). Both forms of Buddhism played an important role in the formation of Southeast Asian Buddhism, even though in the end Theravāda became dominant. In addition, the copresence of Hindu-influenced political-cultural models and various forms of Hinduism itself throughout the region gave rise to a variety of interactions between the mother and daughter religions, ranging from competition and hostility to cooperation, functional complementarity, and some degree of mutual incorporation. Sometimes these varied interactions occurred simultaneously, and they involved social, political, cultural, and religious factors. Finally, the indigenous religion and culture, the "little" tradition on which the "great" traditions of Hinduism and Buddhism were superimposed, was an important ingredient in the resulting mixture.

Beginnings in Southeast Asia

The date of the first entrance of Buddhism into the various parts of Southeast Asia is uncertain. In many cases, a datable event or inscription indicates the presence of Buddhism but gives no clue to the time of its entry. The devout Theravāda tradition invariably opts for the earliest possible dates. Theravādins, the followers of "the teaching of the elders" (*thera*s or the Buddha's personal disciples), insist on the pristine purity of their faith as directly derived from Gotama Buddha himself—hence their legends of airborne visits of Gotama to various Theravāda countries, as evidenced, for example, by his footprint left on Adam's Peak in Sri Lanka. Burma has a legend of two pious Mon merchants who brought back from India head-hairs of the Buddha, now enshrined in the Shwedagon pagoda in Rangoon. Other relics of the Buddha or of his leading disciples are claimed here and there, notably the Tooth Relic in Kandy, Sri Lanka.

Undoubtedly there were Buddhists among the traders and settlers who fanned out from India, by sea and by land, during the late centuries B.C.E. and the early centuries C.E. But the first semihistorical account of Buddhist missionary effort is the account in the Sri Lankan chronicle *Mahāvaṃsa* of how Aśoka (274–232 B.C.E.) sent Buddhist emissaries to various Southeast Asian countries. One country is named "the Land of Gold," usually taken to be western Java but identified by some Burmese historians as Thaton in southern Burma. Better accredited historically is the *Mahāvaṃsa*'s statement that Aśoka sent his own son Mahinda and daughter Saṅghamitta to Sri Lanka to establish Buddhism there. It is not surprising that there should have been no Buddhist missionary effort before this. For though Buddhism is claimed to have been universalistic in its inception and first interpretations, historical evidence seems to suggest that in the first two centuries or so of its existence, Indian Buddhism was a relatively minor religious sect among many others, still engaged in defining its own nature and institutions in a Hindu Brahmanical context, and largely confined to a monastic expression. But the avowed discipleship of Aśoka and his generous though not exclusive material support projected Buddhism into the front rank of Indian religions and gave it a strong sense of its historical mission and destiny. The *Mahāvaṃsa* presents Aśoka as a very active Buddhist layman and a model Buddhist king or *dhamma rāja*. This tradition, though questioned by some historians, is an important element in Sri Lankan Buddhist self-identity, instilling a strong sense of Sri Lanka's seniority in the Buddhist fold and its continuing obligation to preserve the pristine purity of the faith.

The entry of Buddhism into the rest of Southeast Asia, whether by the settlement of immigrants or by missionary effort, cannot be dated as confidently, nor is it always clear whether it was Mahāyāna or Hīnayāna that first entered a given region. Mahāyāna came into its own as a distinct sect early in the period of Buddhist expansion outside India. No doubt its self-designation as the Greater Vehicle helped strengthen the Theravāda sense of self-identity also, though for some time Mahāyāna and Hīnayāna sects lived together in harmony. The headquarters of missionary activity in India were Nalandā in the north (probably mainly Mahāyāna) and Hīnayāna centers near Madras. Sometimes Buddhist propagation followed the sea-lanes, as in the cases of Java and coastal Cambodia (Mahāyāna) and the Thaton area of southern Burma, an early center of Theravāda. It was by the overland trade to China that Mahāyāna reached Pagan, its first Burmese center, around the fifth century, and from there it penetrated into north Thailand and inland Cambodia. Despite its supposed Aśokan origin, the Buddhism of Java was Mahāyāna. During the seventh and eighth centuries it achieved its greatest strength under the Sailendra dynasty, when the massive Borobudur structure was built. It was imported from there into Cambodia, reaching Vietnam in the ninth century, and it spread east to Sumatra in the tenth.

Hindu–Buddhist Interaction

Buddhism shared many of the religious representations of Hinduism: belief in endless rebirths, karma, the desirability of release (mokṣa) from karma-governed existence, and a multiplicity of superhuman beings or gods. Each of these was given a specific Buddhist form; in particular the gods, their powers, and their worship were reduced in scale. The Hindu–Mahāyāna link, because of long mutual influence in India, was closer and friendlier than the Hindu-Theravāda one. Theravāda saw the gods as the Buddha's lay helpers, desirous of using their superhuman powers for the advancement of the Dhamma, but inferior in spiritual understanding even to a worthy monk. Some centuries after the birth of Buddhism, Hinduism accepted the Buddha as an avatar of Viṣṇu. Mahāyāna Buddhists could live in relative harmony with Hindu god-worshipers. Hinduism itself developed a two-level conception of Ultimate Being: *nirguṇa* Brahman, Brahman without discernible qualities, and *saguṇa* Brahman, Brahman with qualities who took the form of Īśvara, a specific god, for his worshipers. All Buddhists objected to Hindu sacrifice of animals and to caste distinctions, but these elements were deemphasized in export Hinduism. Thus it could happen that when the eighth-century Javanese dynasty became Śaivite rather than Buddhist as heretofore, there was no great dislocation. "The return of a Śaivite rule to central Java brought no antagonism between Buddhists and Hindus; their relationships everywhere were excellent."[1]

Sri Lanka offers a rather unexpected pattern of Buddhist–Hindu interaction. Despite periods of hostility, as when in the eleventh century the Hindu-Tamil Coḷas imposed a persecutive regime on Sri Lankan Buddhists, Buddhists and Hindus worshiped cheek by jowl in a number of "Buddhist" temples; or perhaps more accurately, many Sri Lankans, nominal Buddhists we may suppose, performed both types of worship in the same temple compound. In several cases, the central sanctuary contained Buddha images and ritual paraphernalia in its inner precincts, while on the outside of the walls were shrines of Hindu gods. The functionaries of the two religions lived in separate quarters in the same temple grounds. In their thought and practice Buddhists seem to have made a division of functions, approaching the Buddha for the high-level matters of accumulating good karma and seeking release from saṃsāra, but praying to the gods, both Hindu and local, for this-worldly good fortune, health, and prosperity. One notes a remnant of the caste structure of Indian society in that several of the Theravāda sects refuse admission to the lowest classes into the monkhood. The other Theravāda countries' worship patterns contain little that is so explicitly Hindu, because the Hindu presence there was never as strong.

The Role of the Monarch

Another facet of the relation between Hinduism and Buddhism in Southeast Asia is the difference in their conceptions of kingship. The actual content of the ideal kingly role was much the same in both cases, since Buddhism largely took over the Indian (Hindu) institution of kingship as its own. The virtuous king, we are told, gives gifts (to monks and priests?) and is affable, beneficent, and impartial. He is to have true counselors, avoid oppression, punish the evil, and reward the good. His kingly virtues should be almsgiving, justice, penitence, meekness, peaceableness, mercy, patience, charity, and moral purity. It was this ideal that Aśoka sought to fulfill. Buddhism at first subscribed to the ideology of the *deva rāja* or god-king. As manifestation and embodiment of a deity, often Śiva, for a certain place and time, the god-king had absolute power over his subjects and was technically the owner of the whole kingdom and its inhabitants. All of his just and benevolent acts were acts of condescending grace. Reverential respect for him was therefore a form of worship; priests and rituals surrounded and fortified the throne. The secret lore of the correct, or efficacious, rituals by which a Hindu king was enthroned and by which he performed his royal duties was highly prized, and its priestly technicians were considered indispensable.

Buddhism did not propose an alternative to monarchical rule but constructed a new model of kingship, the *dhamma rāja,* already nascent in the *Jātaka* stories in which Gotama Buddha in his former lives rules as a bodhisattva king. Many monarchs in Southeast Asia gave at least lip service to this ideal after the time of Aśoka. This should have made them more peaceful, less bent on conquest, and more humane than their Hindu god-father-king counterparts. In fact, however, it was often difficult to distinguish a *dhamma rāja* from a *deva rāja.* Theravāda monarchs who espoused the *dhamma rāja* ideal still kept the Hindu-Brahmanical court establishment of soothsayers, fortune tellers, astrologers, and court ritualists. The Hindu religious overtones of these activities do not seem to have worried them. Mahāyāna monarchs were still less concerned. The reverence given to a *dhamma rāja* by his subjects differed little from that given to a *deva rāja,* at least in outward form. Nevertheless, the *dhamma rāja* ideology was a valiant, and occasionally successful attempt to modify and humanize the fierce, raw power of god-kingship. Sometimes the roles of *deva rāja* and *dhamma rāja* tended to fuse. Birth as a king signaled a great accumulation of merit in past lives. This high degree of dhamma virtue combined with the intrinsic power and prestige of the *deva* ruler expressed in the traditional enthronement rituals. A Khmer ruler, Jayavarman VII in the thirteenth century, called himself a living Buddha—Buddha having become a Hindu-style god; the Thai monarch is considered to be a near-Buddha.

Both Mahāyāna and Theravāda monarchs, especially the latter, were defenders of the faith and patrons of the Saṅgha, which was the guarantor of orthodoxy in doctrine and practice. In this relationship the sovereign was the dominant partner, as the primary builder of pagodas and monasteries, the provider of monastic privileges and estates, munificent gifts, and official patronage and protection. Following the alleged example of Aśoka, the king was also called upon to be the arbiter of doctrinal controversies and to settle intra-Saṅgha disputes. Thus Anawrahta in eleventh-century Burma backed the monk Shin Arahan and established Thaton-type (Pāli Canon) Buddhism in Pagan, unfrocking the Mahāyāna-tantric Saṅgha. A century later a Mon monk, trained in Sri Lanka, felt that the Burmese Saṅgha had become lax and began a new and stricter order, called the Latter Order, but the king made no clear decision, thus allowing a new sectarian division. In the late fifteenth century, King Dhammazedi sent a delegation of Burmese to Sri Lanka for reordination—a way of renewing the Saṅgha after a period of social disturbances. Burma returned the favor in the seventeenth century, helping to mend the damage done to Sri Lankan Buddhism by the Portuguese. These Burmese examples of kingly intervention are typical of all Theravāda countries.

The advantages and disadvantages of this power of the sovereign over the Saṅgha were reciprocal. It was seldom that Buddhist monarchs followed the example of Duṭṭhagāmāṇi (161–137 B.C.E.) in Sri Lanka, who took a body of monks with him into battle to guarantee his success—and later had them absolve him from the un-Buddhist act of killing. But the support and approval of the Saṅgha was important to almost all Southeast Asian kings. In Sri Lanka it came to be a received tradition that only a Buddhist could be a king; a legitimating ceremonial was practiced, and sometimes a sovereign would "give" his kingdom to the Saṅgha for a few days. Even where the Saṅgha approval and its legitimation of the throne were not formalized, the tacit support of the Saṅgha was deemed necessary to a secure tenure of the throne.

Theravāda as a Reform Buddhism

In most of Southeast Asia, Mahāyāna Buddhism was first in the field, and when Theravāda came, it had distanced itself from both Hinduism and Mahāyāna, and was seen as replacing the former and reforming the latter. This occurred mainly in the second millennium C.E. When Theravāda confronted Hinduism, as in the Khmer kingdom at Angkor, the *deva rāja* pattern of rule withered on the vine. Christopher Pym points out that as the people were gradually converted to Theravāda the rulers found that "all the characteristics of the god-king—sole ruler, arbiter, commander in chief of the armed forces, the god whom everyone had to worship, divinely enthroned ruler, incarnate form of Śiva, Viṣṇu, Brahma, *or Buddha*—were hateful to the worshipers of Theravāda faith."[2] According to G. Cœdès, "the royal dynasty failed any longer to inspire the people with the religious respect which enabled it to accomplish great enterprises. . . . [The sovereign's] prestige diminished, his temporal power crumbled away, and the god-king was thrown down from the altar."[3] In Burma this meant that Anawrahta destroyed the Ari Mahāyānism of the eleventh century. In Thailand the vigorous discipleship of kings from the fourteenth century on removed the Mahāyāna forms and firmly established Theravāda. In both cases, there was a series of reinfusions of Pāli Canon teaching and practice emanating from Sri Lanka, occasionally reciprocated. Thus there was a mutually helpful reformative process among the predominantly Theravāda nations.

The success of Buddhism in Southeast Asia was largely due to the high esteem that Indian civilization enjoyed during these centuries. Both Hinduism and Buddhism contained a world philosophy, an inclusive ethic and social ideal, a reasoned way of life, and a way of salvation quite superior to anything the indigenous cults had to offer. Buddhism in time displaced Hinduism, largely because of its democratic, casteless ethical beliefs and practices, and the adaptability of its doctrine and practice at certain points. It never denied the existence of gods and spirits; it simply demoted them to a subordinate but still important status as helpers to the Buddha and powerful benefactors in worldly matters. Converts, thus able to keep their old gods and worship-magic patterns to some degree, found Buddhism superior but not strange and forbidding. Images of the Buddha had by this time become popular in Theravāda, which had at first resisted them, so that people had a concrete object of worship, vividly represented. The exemplary life of the Saṅgha also held before them a concrete representation of the path to release from suffering and an attractive invitation to take refuge in the Buddha, the Dhamma, and the Saṅgha and to pledge obedience to the five precepts.

Meditation

The principal Theravāda contribution to spirituality is undoubtedly its preservation of the early Buddhist practices of meditation. The Buddha himself attained to the perfect enlightenment of Buddhahood by meditation; he taught its methodology to his disciples during the forty-five years of his public career, and never wavered in presenting it as the sole means of finally escaping the round of birth and death (saṃsāra). Since Theravāda strives after complete fidelity to the Pāli Canon as the verbatim record of the Buddha's teachings, scriptural statements on the role and method of meditation are taken to be the final authority on the subject. An abundant commentarial literature has arisen on all the important topics discussed therein, including meditation, which is treated most comprehensively and most systematically in *The Path of Purification* (*Visuddhimagga*), composed by the great Indian Buddhist scholar Bhadantācariya Buddhaghosa in Sri Lanka in the fifth century C.E. In Theravāda, this has always been the standard authoritative textbook on meditational theory and practice. It has never been considered canonical, but it is often mentioned in the next breath after the canon when meditation is spoken of. It is a massive compilation of a thousand years of thought, practice, and tradition formation in regard to meditation, including excerpts from scriptures and commentaries, traditional accounts of meditation techniques, anecdotes about meditators, as well as an extensive scholarly excursus into some basic Buddhist doctrines and the Buddhist theory of the cycles of world destruction and renewal. This varied material is organized in accord with the progression from the initial steps on the meditational path to final enlightenment. Though this progression is hard to follow and though the style is sometimes crabbed and pedantic, the work is unrivaled as a mine of information and abhidharmic analysis.

The purpose of the work was to conserve the orthodox Pāli Canon tradition, which seemed to Buddhagosa's patrons in the Anurādhapura monastery to be endangered by the teaching of the new sects. A secondary aim was to reestablish the ancient ascendancy of the host monastery. The requirements of the task were clear: the work had to adhere closely to Pāli Canon authority and embody the central orthodox Theravāda tradition and practice of meditation. The received canonical teaching could not be spiritualized or demythologized. Contemporary materials and commentarial additions were to be used only as illustrative of the eternal truth, not as additions to it. Did Buddhaghosa expect that subsequent meditators would actually follow—book in hand, so to speak—his charted course? Was he himself a meditator of depth or only a scholar who knew the literature and tradition intimately? This is impossible to ascertain. Whether one sees the work as having been a practicable guide and sourcebook for scholar monks and even meditation masters, lighting up the terse scriptural statements and ensuring the orthodoxy and efficacy of practice, or whether one admits the suspicion that it has been honored more in verbal homage than in practical use, it remains the touchstone for any understanding of the goals and means of Theravāda meditation, ancient or modern, complicated or simple in presentation and practice.

The considered and mature Theravāda meditational pattern presented in *The Path of Purification* is structured as a three-stage progression. The elements of each stage are implicit in every other and are fully developed and fully interactive in the summit attainment. The first and foundational stage is *sīla*, or moral conduct and character; the second is samādhi, or mental concentration, an essential technique throughout; the third is *pañña*, or liberating knowledge of the nature of human existence, the *sine qua non* of the achievement of enlightenment.

Sīla, or right ethical attitude and practice, is both preliminary to and foundational in the total meditative structure. Indeed, enlightenment itself is perfected morality. Not only must one begin with and continue in the observance of the five basic precepts, but these rules for outward conduct are increasingly deepened and internalized by meditational progress. The mere avoidance of killing any living creature, for example, finally becomes the perfection of a benevolence that is completely incapable of aversion, hatred, or anger. There are also some methodological avoidances even for the lay meditator, such as worldly entertainment, high luxurious beds, and bodily unguents. For the "professional" meditators, the monks, there are over two hundred regulatory measures with regard to clothing, eating, personal life, and social conduct which are presumed to enhance spiritual growth and meditative progress. That morality should be thus foundational even for a solitary meditator is not surprising, given the Buddhist interpretation of the nature of enlightenment. Buddhism began its separate career in Brahmanical India as a moral rather than a ritual way to salvation; in the view of the Buddha no ritualism, however ancient or precisely carried out, could free the human being from saṃsāra. Only a complete ethical transformation of the individual, reversing most of the usual ideas about and attitudes toward the nature and meaning of human life, could do this. For what ties humanity to perpetual rebirth is greed, hatred, and delusion in their varied forms. Greed and hatred spring from delusion (ignorance) about the nature of embodied existence and its ordinary perception as innately desirable; and the avid pursuit of this-life goods and intense abhorrence of this-life evils are self-love in disguise—disguised even from oneself. Only through detachment from the ordinary appetites, ambitions, false hopes, and aversions can humankind be released from perpetual rebirth.

The *Visuddhimagga* instructs the beginning meditator—presumably under the supervision of a teacher—to concentrate on some devotional or ethical theme suited to the beginner's character. Five types of character are recognized: devotional, intellectual, passionate, dull, irritable; and the forty traditional subjects for meditation are parceled out among them in varying proportions. For the beginner, or even for beginning any meditational period at any level of attainment, such subjects as the Buddha, the Dhamma, peace, loving-kindness, compassion, unselfish joy, and serenity are fitting, though the last four of these are capable of carrying the meditator to higher levels of attainment. The first three lead only to the initial stage of mental concentration called neighborhood or access consciousness—access to the genuinely samadhic states. Neighborhood consciousness is a mildly concentrated state of attention in which distracting elements are largely shut out of consciousness, but in which consciousness is not yet fully one-pointed to the exclusion of all content but the specifically chosen subject.

The second level in the meditational structure is samādhi, or intensely one-pointed concentration on a given subject or object. Generally the subjects suitable to this second stage have a physical basis; breathing, repulsiveness of food, stages of body decay, and the *kasiṇas* are capable of producing the various levels of samādhi. Loving-kindness, compassion, unselfish joy, and serenity, unphysical in nature, are practiced at this stage by directing them in imagination toward objects and persons. By continued concentration of this kind the jhānas are produced. Jhāna (the Pāli form of Sanskrit *dhyāna,* later becoming Chinese *ch'an* and Japanese *zen*) signifies a state of trance in which all sensory input, aside from the subject of meditation, is totally excluded from awareness. At the higher jhanic levels the meditator is also incapable of speech or movement, and in the highest possible, attention is said to be without ordinary consciousness and to reach the trance of cessation. According to the Pāli Canon, Gotama reached Buddhahood (enlightenment) by means of the four classic jhānas, gained by concentrated attention on the (unspecified) meditational subjects he had chosen. They are described as progressively eliminating emotional accompaniments and resulting in an awareness "purified by equanimity and mindfulness."

The *kasiṇas* (colors, circular shapes) are capable of a development beyond the four jhānas into what are called the four formless meditations. The meditator gazes at some circular shape or distinctively colored area with such total and continued concentration that after continued practice he can produce its image before his "sight" with or without the original stimulus. When this is accomplished the second step is to dematerialize it and free it of limits. Thus a circular *kasiṇa* made of clay becomes pure and shining like the full moon to the meditator's vision, all of one brightness, without any inner markings. Then it is progressively shorn of its limits by imagining it as larger and larger until it becomes infinite, so to speak. Thus the meditator arrives at the perception of the infinity of space. Using each attained state as a springboard to the next higher state, he progressively attains infinity of consciousness, nothingness (no-thingness?), and neither perception nor non-perception. In this eighth jhanic-type state of awareness the meditator has erased all awareness of subject–object distinctions and is one with his awareness; the state is described as a luminous vacuity.

It may be questioned whether these four formless states were a part of the original jhanic method; but by the time of Buddhaghosa, Buddhism's Brahmanical jhanic heritage had reasserted itself and they had become integral to it. However, it should be noted that jhanic expertise by itself cannot achieve either the highest possible this-life experience of nibbanic bliss or full enlightenment (arhatship). These require a further factor, present, it must be presumed, in Gotama's four jhanic attainments but not explicitly mentioned in the canon until Gotama's post-enlightenment statement about freedom from saṃsāra. This factor is *pañña,* or the liberating knowledge of the true nature of self and existence, without which enlightenment cannot be gained. The type of meditational awareness that produces *pañña* is *vipassanā,* or insight. This is the meditative application of the central Buddhist insight that all phenomenal life and conscious experience are impermanent (*anicca*), empty of substantiality or essence (*anattā*), and intrinsically permeated by dissatisfaction, even suffering (*dukkha*). This insight must be applied by the meditator existentially to his own person and situation. He must see himself and his conscious life as full of impermanence, emptiness, suffering.

The key point for the vipassanic attack is the ingrained sense of selfhood—one's awareness of being an integral self that remains identical with itself through the passage of time and changing states and conditions. This is necessary in the Buddhist view because this delusive view of integral selfhood is the core of the human samsaric predicament; for the "self" is attached both positively and negatively to its states, experiences, ideas, and desires. Indeed, "self" is but a name for attachment, and this attachment to unreal, impermanent entities is what projects the human being into forever-repeated rebirths. The method of destroying this enslaving attachment is twofold: intellectual and emotional. First, by means of sustained introspective observation and analysis of body and mind states, the individual becomes aware that "self" is but a continuing series of mental-physical states, an ever-flowing stream of consciousness. The second prong of meditative attack is emotional; the lustful person, for example, may need to observe the decaying human body, or a glutton to think of the repulsive process of the digestion of food. Such analysis must of necessity be applied even to jhanic states immediately after emergence from them, lest their attainment be taken for nibbāna.

The final result of the achievement of liberating knowledge through insight meditation is the attainment of the conditions of stream-enterer (*sotāpanna*), once-returner (*sakadāgāmīn*), non-returner (*anāgāmīn*) and released one (arhat). Stream-enterers will never again be born in any less-than-human form and have at most seven more lives before release; once-returners have only one more human birth; non-returners will achieve nibbāna in a future life from some heavenly realm; arhats will enter nibbāna at death. Gotama Buddha was the Supreme Arhat, of course. While an arhat remains alive, he is in the condition of *kilesa-parinibbāna*, or extinction of defilements; when he dies, he achieves *khandha parinibbāna*, the final extinction of all rebirth-causing body-mind factors, and is a completely released individual.

The trance of cessation (*nirodha-samāpatti*), the very highest meditative state (though it does not by itself achieve enlightenment, nor is it necessary to its attainment) can only be experienced by an *anāgāmīn* or arhat who has attained to the state of neither perception nor nonperception. In this state the meditator is without perception or feeling and appears to be dead; such a state can last for up to seven days. It is seen as the enjoyment of the flavor of nibbāna for "as long as we like," to quote a disciple of the Buddha. It is the fullness of that Path-awareness which first came to the stream-enterer in instantaneous flashes, strengthening and lengthening until it reaches its climax in this trance. It is the maximization of the *direct* awareness of nibbāna. Though this is the highest possible this-life experience of nibbanic bliss, it is not essential to enlightenment. Only fully existentialized vipassanic knowledge of the true character of embodied existence is absolutely essential. Therefore, though Buddhaghosa writes condescendingly of the "dry-visioned saints" or the "bare-insight workers," that is, those meditators who have bypassed the jhanic attainments altogether and concentrated on *vipassanā*, he must admit that this approach to enlightenment is successful, for it contains the essential factor of liberating knowledge. Jhanic skill is helpful in deepening and stabilizing even vipassanic meditation, and in many ways it is complementary to it. But it is not essential for the achievement of samsaric release; *vipassanā* as the absolutely indispensable meditational discipline can be pursued in its own legitimate right without jhanic admixture.

Indeed, contemporary Theravāda meditation, wherever found, is increasingly vipassanic only. It may legitimately be asked, without hope of a sure answer, whether the full-scale jhanic-vipassanic path was *ever* followed extensively in the 2,500 years of Buddhist history. Certainly this tradition has been kept alive by at least a few "experts" in each generation, but for the most part the full jhanic-vipassanic attainments have probably remained a lofty ideal, increasingly attributed mainly to the saints of the first ages of Buddhism. Today, with the growing number of lay meditators, as well as foreign followers of the Dhamma, *vipassanā* is coming into its own. The reason is that the full course of jhanic-vipassanic development requires a monk's mode of life, one given over almost exclusively to meditation. The modern monkhood in most Theravāda countries is very aware of its obligations to the laity, as teachers of the Dhamma, counselors, and celebrants of rituals. In most Theravāda societies lifetime monks are becoming fewer; most remain in the monkhood for only a few years. Further, in Sri Lanka and Thailand and to some extent in Burma, there has been increasing agitation for a more socially active monkhood. These developments tell against full-time meditation except at sporadic intervals.

Since the Buddha predicted that his Dhamma would decline in purity and power, and his disciples in their devotion to it, beginning some five hundred years after his death, modern Theravādins have a strong sense of the need to use the easiest and quickest methods for enlightenment. The inclusion of laity in the meditators' ranks, from which they were long excluded by traditional usage (though not by the scriptures), has made ease of attainment even more essential. Since *vipassanā* is the essential meditational element and since it requires only a relatively low level of concentrational skill, it is ideal for the lay meditator. It is often urged that the noisy, turbulent world in which we live requires some mode of release from saṃsāra that is faster and more efficient than the traditional one which was suited to the isolated, retired mode of life. This altered mood and situation have also had an effect on the method itself, allowing for a closer integration of the meditative and active lives. *Vipassanā* can be practiced for short intervals every day and in conjunction with one's daily work. Some teachers suggest that work itself may be made into a meditational discipline by complete concentration in it, by what may be called "mindfulness in work"—a combination of care for what is involved in the work and detachment from any personal benefits that may result from it. Again, vipassanic meditators are encouraged to focus on present experience, cultivating awareness of bodily sensations and the arising and ceasing of emotional states and trains of thought. High value is placed on the *present* realization of the peace given by that detachment which comes with the recognition and acceptance of embodied existence as completely and ineradicably impermanent, unreal, and pain-filled. Some avant-garde interpreters suggest that in the Buddha's core teaching nibbāna was never more, or other, than present-life liberation from evil dispositions and enslaving attachments, a transformation of character, though the Buddha sometimes used rebirth-ending language as a device necessary for his ignorant hearers. But regardless of how distant they may feel themselves to be from its attainment, the vast majority of Theravādins continue to long for nibbāna as the final ending of embodied existence.

Notes

1. D. G. E. Hall, *History of Southeast Asia*, 63.
2. Christopher Pym, *Ancient Civilization of Angkor*, 183.
3. G. Cœdès, in Hall, *History of Southeast Asia*, 114.

Bibliography

Sources

Buddhaghosa, Bhadantācariya. *The Path of Purification (Visuddhimagga).* Translated by Bhikkhu Ñyāṇamoli. 2nd ed. Colombo: A. Semage, 1964.

Manual of a Mystic. Translated by Frank L. Woodward. London: Pāli Text Society, 1982. Distributed by Routledge & Kegan Paul.

Upatissa, Arahant. *The Path of Freedom (Vimuttimagga).* Translated by N. R. M. Ehara Thera. Colombo, Sri Lanka: D. Roland Weerasuria, 1961.

Studies

Buddhadasa, Bhikkhu. *Ānāpānasati: Mindfulness of Breathing.* Translated by Nagasena Bhikkhu. Bangkok: Sublime Life Mission, n.d.

Byles, Marie. *Journey into Burmese Silence.* London: Allen & Unwin, 1956.
Conze, Edward. *Buddhist Meditation.* London: Allen & Unwin, 1956.
Goldstein, Joseph. *Experience of Insight: A Natural Unfolding.* Santa Cruz: Unity Press, 1976.
Hall, D. G. E. *A History of Southeast Asia.* New York: Macmillan, 1961.
In Search of Southeast Asia. Edited by D. J. Steinberg. New York: Praeger, 1971.
King, Winston L. *Theravāda Meditation: The Buddhist Transformation of Yoga.* University Park, PA: Pennsylvania State University Press, 1980.
Kornfield, Jack. *Living Buddhist Masters.* Santa Cruz: Unity Press, 1977.
Le May, Reginald. *The Culture of Southeast Asia.* London: Allen & Unwin, 1954.
Sayadaw, Mahasi. *The Progress of Insight.* Kandy, Sri Lanka: Forest Hermitage, 1965.
Ñyāṇamoli, Thera. *Mindfulness of Breathing (Ānāpānasati).* 2nd ed. Kandy, Sri Lanka: Buddhist Publication Society, 1964.
Nyanaponika, Thera. *The Heart of Buddhist Meditation.* 3rd ed. London: Rider, 1962.
Pym, Christopher. *The Ancient Civilization of Angkor.* New York: New American Library, 1968.
Religion and Legitimation of Power in Thailand, Laos, and Burma. Edited by Bardwell L. Smith. Chambersburg: Anima Books, 1978.
Saddhatissa, H. *The Buddha's Way.* London: Allen & Unwin, 1971.
Smith, Bardwell L., *Religion and Legitimation of Power in Sri Lanka.* Chambersburg: Anima Books, 1978.
——. *The Two Wheels of the Dhamma.* Chambersburg: American Academy of Religion, 1972.
Sobhana Dhammasudi. *Insight Meditation.* 2nd ed. London: Committee for the Advancement of Buddhism, 1968.

5

Theravāda Lands

I. *Sri Lanka*

Maeda Egaku

In 1981, Sri Lanka had a population of 14.9 million, of whom 74 percent were Sinhalese and 18.2 percent were Tamils. The majority of the Sinhalese were Theravāda Buddhists; most of the Tamils were Hindus, and Muslims and Christians made up a further 15 percent of the population. The Constitution of the Democratic Socialist Republic of Sri Lanka states: "The Republic of Sri Lanka shall give to Buddhism the foremost place and accordingly it shall be the duty of the State to protect and foster the Buddha *sāsana* [church], while assuring to all religions the rights granted . . ." (article 9). The three major sects or orders (*nikāyas*) are the Siyam (11,474 monks in 1973), Amarapura (5,034 monks), and Rāmañña (3,514 monks). The Siyam Nikāya is divided into four or six subsects and the Amarapura Nikāya is said to have twenty-six subsects, which do not seem to possess much unity. There is no central unifying organization. Even more than the ordinary temple monks, who devote their energies to social works, the five hundred or so forest-dwelling monks, whose hermitages are centers for training in meditation, enjoy high popular regard. In many temples, shrines are provided for the worship of devas such as Viṣṇu, Kataragama, and Nātha.

Theravāda Buddhism originated in Sri Lanka, and it is Sri Lanka that transmitted the Pāli Tipiṭaka, as well as numerous commentaries, synopses, chronicles, and grammars. The legend in the *Dīpavaṃsa* and other chronicles that the Buddha visited the country three times is widely believed in present-day Sri Lanka. As far as is known, Buddhism was first introduced when Mahinda, said to be the son or younger brother of King Aśoka, established the Saṅgha at the start of the reign of King Devānaṃpiya Tissa (ca. 250–210 B.C.E.). The king built the Mahāvihāra in the capital Anurādhapura, and the Saṅgha centered there was long recognized as the orthodox school of Buddhism in Sri Lanka. The Buddhism of South and Southeast Asia inherited the Mahāvihāra tradition and thus owes its origin to the establishment of this monastery.

The Age of Establishment

Helped by an unbroken state of peace and royal protection, Buddhism gradually increased its influence. The Sinhalese were constantly engaged in conflicts with Tamil invaders from the Indian coast. King Duṭṭhagāmaṇī Abhaya (161–137 B.C.E.) obtained a victory over the invaders and extended his power over the whole island. Thirty years later King Vaṭṭagāmaṇī Abhaya built the Abhayagirivihāra, dedicated to his friend, the senior monk Mahātissa. Because of problems concerning the Vinaya, Mahātissa was criticized by the monks of the Mahāvihāra and expelled from the Saṅgha. He reacted by establishing his own sect, the Abhayagiri, which prospered under royal protection, while the Mahāvihāra went into decline. The Mahāvihāra bhikkhus, fearing the extinction of Buddhism, began the transcription of the Tipiṭaka (which until then had existed only as an oral tradition). The Abhayagirivihāra monks were liberal in outlook, and because they offered permanent residence to followers of Mahāyāna, their discipline became rather loose. The Mahāvihāra, resenting this, appealed to the king and tried to have the Mahāyānists banished. A Mahāyāna monk was able to gain the confidence of King Mahāsena (276–303) and take revenge on the Mahāvihāra. When the monk was slain by a minister who rebelled against the king, Mahāsena had to change his policy, but he could not bring himself to favor the Mahāvihāra. He built the Jetavanavihāra in their compounds, and this became the third of the major Sri Lankan sects.

The Chinese monk Fa-hsien, who visited Sri Lanka in 410–412, mentions the prosperity of the Abhayagirivihāra and says that they had five thousand monks, while there were three thousand in the Mahāvihāra and two thousand in the Cetiyapabbatavihāra. A few years later the Southern Indian monk Buddhaghosa wrote the *Visuddhimagga* and presented it to the Mahāvihāra, and, with all the Buddhist texts in the Mahāvihāra at his disposal, Buddhaghosa composed an extensive set of Pāli commentaries. His work was continued by Buddhadatta and Dhammapāla, and as a result of these commentaries Theravāda doctrine was firmly established.

The Dark Ages

From the end of the fifth century, Theravāda Buddhism in Sri Lanka rapidly declined as a result of the waning power of its royal patrons. Until the eleventh century, no conspicuous Buddhist activity is observed. On the Indian

11. Buddhist monks in Malvatta Vihare, one of the main temples of the Siam Nikāya School; Kandy, Sri Lanka.

continent the religion was also in decline. Mahāyāna influences on Sri Lanka are visible from the third century and continued until, at the end of the sixth century, the Indian monk Jotipāla demolished the Mahāyāna doctrine in an open debate. There were no more converts to Mahāyāna, and the Mahāvihāra recovered its lost prestige. Around 638 the Chinese monk Hsüan-tsang traveled all over India but did not go as far as Sri Lanka because he had heard that not only was the country in political disarray but there were also no outstanding learned monks. He wrote that there were in Sri Lanka at that time more than ten thousand monks and that the Mahāyāna-Sthavira (Abhayagirivihāra?) prevailed over the Hīnayāna-Sthavira (Mahāvihāra?).

According to Chinese accounts, Vajrabodhi (671–741), who introduced Tantric Buddhism to China, visited Sri Lanka twice, staying at the Abhayagirivihāra. His disciple Amoghavajra (705–774) is said to have been born in Sri Lanka. In accord with his master's last will, in 741 he traveled from China to Sri Lanka in order to transmit the sacred scriptures of Tantric Buddhism. It is said that Tantric Buddhism was flourishing then in the country and that Amoghavajra received there the initiation ceremony by sprinkled water, and took more than five hundred scriptures back with him to China.

From the latter half of the eighth century, the maintenance of Anurādhapura became difficult, and the capital was moved to Polonnaruwa. The religious world was also often in disarray. There is very little mention of Tantric and Mahāyāna Buddhism in the chronicles of these centuries. Instead, there was influence from Hinduism, reflecting the faith of the Indian masses. The Mahāvihāra reached the limits of decay, and at one time there was not a single Mahāvihāra monk in Sri Lanka. At the beginning of the eleventh century, the Coḷa invasion reduced Anurādhapura to ruins. The Mahāvihāra, Abhayagirivihāra, and Jetavanavihāra were completely destroyed. The Coḷa were believers in Śiva and persecuted Buddhism without mercy.

The Age of Prosperity

Whereas Buddhism in India, after the destruction of the Saṅgha, was completely replaced by Hinduism, which won the adherence of the masses, in Sri Lanka the king and the populace remained Buddhist despite the disappearance of the Saṅgha. King Vijayabāhu I (1055–1110) recaptured Polonnaruwa from the Coḷa invaders and made the city his capital. Having restored stability, he gave his attention to the reestablishment of the monastic order. He sent an emissary to the Burmese king Anawrahta and reintroduced Buddhism from that country. He encouraged the Tipiṭaka and Buddhist activities in both countries. After his death, there was again unrest in the country and strife among the monks. This was finally overcome by the great king Parakramabāhu I (1153–1186). In 1165 he held a conference of leading monks, which resulted in the reunification of the three sects under the Mahāvihāra. A reform was implemented with special emphasis on the following points: (1) study of the scriptures; (2) times and places at which it was allowed to leave the monastery; (3) prerequisites for accepting new disciples. The king built several monasteries, and his literary activity marks the beginning of the "Augustan Age of Ceylonese literature." The best-known scholar of the period is Sāriputta, whose many works, including the *Vinayasaṅgaha*, a summary of the commandments, won a wide following.

In the Polonnaruwa period there were several changes in Buddhist practice. First, a great loss to the Saṅgha was the sudden disappearance of the order of Buddhist nuns. The reason for this is not altogether clear, but there are no traces of persecution. Second, Buddhism as an ethical system yielded to folk Buddhism, marked by the increasing popularity of spirit chanting. Third, pilgrimages to Mount Śrīpāda grew in popularity and were patronized by royalty. Fourth, the Tooth Relic at Kandy, received from the Kaliṅga Royal House of India in 311, and long a popular object of worship, became the main symbol of royal authority, so that the princes fought for its possession. In the period after the removal of the capital to Kōṭṭe in the fifteenth century, Sri Lankan Buddhism was admired and imitated by visitors from Burma, Thailand, and Cambodia.

The Age of Modern Buddhist Revival

From 1505 Sri Lanka was colonized by Portugal, Holland, and England in turn. At that time the island was divided into the three states of Kōṭṭe, Jaffna, and Kandy, which were unable to take joint action against the invaders. The Portuguese goals were "Christianity and spices," and with their overwhelming military power they succeeded in gradually subduing the island. The majority of the population of Kōṭṭe were Buddhists, while in Jaffna Hinduism predominated. But it was the Muslims in both states who were the strongest rivals of the Portuguese in both religion and trade, and who were the first object of their attacks. Since the Portuguese considered Hinduism and Buddhism to be primitive religions, they did not think of studying them. The Franciscan missionary Vincente arrived in 1505, followed by Dominicans and Jesuits, who preached in the vernacular, lived and ate with the people, helped the poor, and built schools and hospitals, winning many converts. For Buddhism this development was a bolt from the blue. The conversion of Sinhalese kings to Christianity, beginning with King Dharmapāla in 1557, was a heavy blow. As a result of such conversions, Kōṭṭe and Jaffna became predominantly Catholic, and Buddhism and Hinduism completely lost the traditional royal sponsorship. The decline of Buddhism accelerated. Portugal brought the powerful Renaissance culture of Europe to Sri Lanka, every aspect of which seemed superior and worthy of imitation. The variety of ceremonies and rituals in the Buddhism and Hinduism of the time facilitated the adoption of Christian customs. Buddhist temples were destroyed and many monks victimized; temple property and the income that the temples received from the villages were transferred to Christian churches.

It was during the reign of Vimaladharmasūriya I (1592–1604), king of Kandy, that the first emissary of Holland arrived in Sri Lanka. The only wish of the king was to get rid of the Portuguese, so he welcomed the Dutch with open arms. However, when, with their help, the Portuguese were expelled in 1658, the Dutch took their place. Their religious policy, implemented through schools opened by Calvinist missionaries, was to convert to the Dutch Reformed faith not only the Buddhists and Hindus but also the Catholics. When a school was built in a village, the children were obliged to attend, and, along with reading and writing, the catechism and the prayers of the Dutch Reformed Church were the main subjects of study.

The kings of Kandy, an inland area less important to Western traders and not so heavily affected by the successive dominations of Portugal and Holland, had continued to be zealous reformers of the Saṅgha. The reign of Kīrti Śrī Rājasīmha (1747–1781) was a period of Buddhist revival, marked by the activity of the founder of the Siyam Nikāya, Vālivita Saraṇaṃkara. He became a *sāmaṇera* at the age of sixteen and was a popular preacher, widely respected for his personality and erudition. He had to remain a *sāmaṇera* for a long time, since Buddhism was in a situation of extreme decay and not enough bhikkhus were available in Sri Lanka to confer higher ordination. In 1753 the king welcomed a Buddhist delegation from Siam led by Upāli. Saraṇaṃkara, then aged fifty-five, at last became a bhikkhu, along with seven hundred others. He was appointed Saṅgharāja (Ruler of the Order), and under his leadership a great revival of Buddhism took place. Saraṇaṃkara was a prolific author and is regarded as the father of the revival of arts in the country.

In 1762 the British emissary Pybus visited Kandy and asked for a settlement and for trade. The king, who was constantly at loggerheads with the Dutch, welcomed the arrival of the British. In 1780 the British declared war on the Dutch, and in 1796 all Dutch possessions in Sri Lanka fell into the hands of the English East India Company. In the early period of British rule, the government of Sir Thomas Maitland (1795–1806) feared that the king could use Buddhist and Hindu monks to rouse the Sinhalese and Tamils to resistance. Maitland's policy was to divide and rule by fomenting rivalry between the monks. He put the Anglican and Dutch churches under government control and managed to receive the support of the Catholics as well.

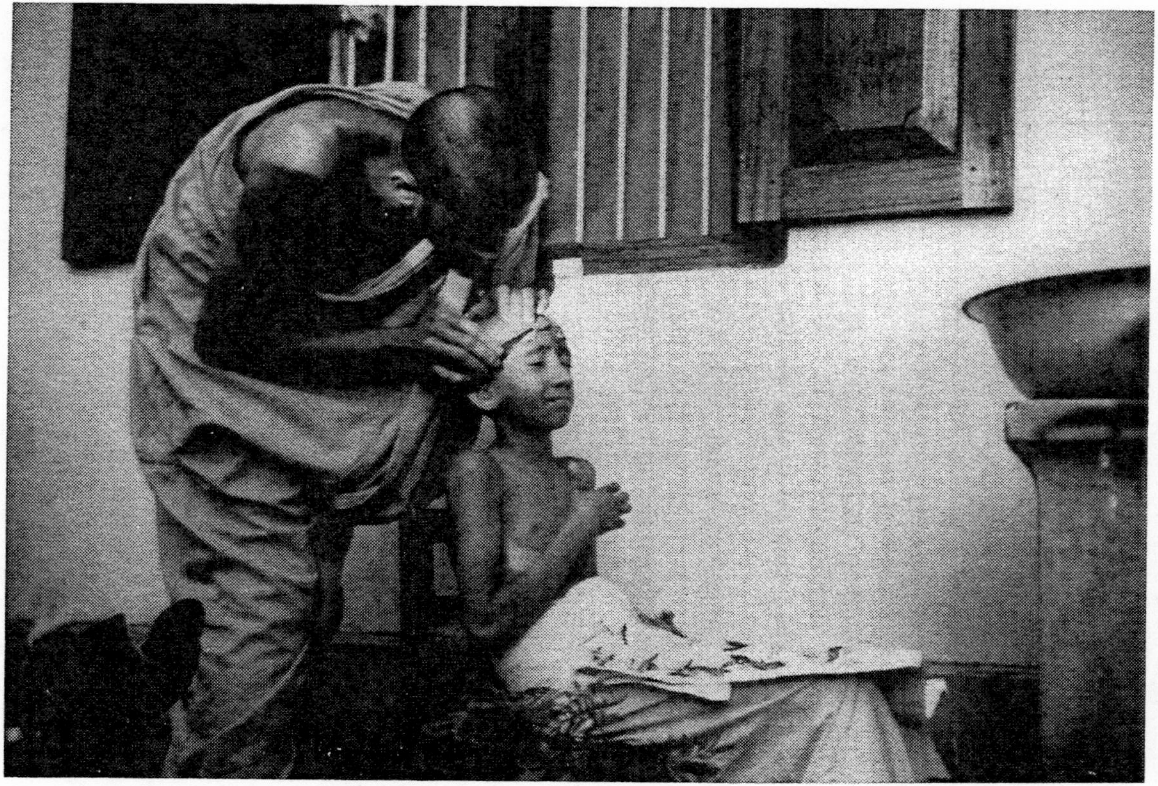

12. A young boy (aged 11) has his head shaven as part of the ceremony to become a Buddhist monk; Kurunegala, Sri Lanka.

The churches related to England and the Dutch Reformed Church received government support; their ministers were paid from public funds. The government did not lend any support to Buddhism; the governor did not fulfill the role that the kings had performed in the Buddhist ceremonies, nor did he show the monks the respect that they had received from the kings; instead, they were obliged to pay homage to him.

As a result of religious revival in England, several Protestant denominations sent missionaries to Sri Lanka. In 1812 the Baptist Mission arrived, followed by the Wesleyan Missionary Society in 1814, and the Church Missionary Society in 1815. Today the non-Catholic churches in Sri Lanka include the Anglicans, Presbyterians, Wesleyan-Methodists, Baptists, and the Salvation Army, all of which have followed the Dutch Reformed policy of using schools to propagate Christianity. This method was not adopted by the Catholic Church. This church had found itself in a disadvantageous position in the Dutch period. Under British rule, its position improved a little, though it did not receive government support. Its strong organization facilitated intensive missionary work, and its solemn ceremonies and rituals had immense popular appeal.

The seeds of revival sown by Saraṇaṃkara bore fruit in centers for Buddhist learning opened by his disciples in the areas dominated by the Dutch. It is regrettable that he introduced the caste system in the Saṅgha, which was originally without any discrimination. The Siyam Nikāya, which he founded, forbade people of all castes other than the farmers' class to enter the Saṅgha. Those who were excluded went to Burma to receive the precepts and founded the Amarapura Nikāya. A reform movement within the Siyam led to the establishment of the Rāmañña Nikāya. Buddhists became aware of the need for organization if their religion was to survive. They established associations using the same methods as the Christian churches. Books and pamphlets explaining Buddhist doctrine were published. Buddhists started comparing their faith with Christianity, and a number of open debates were held between the two religions. In 1873 Mohoṭṭivattē Guṇānanda engaged in a historic debate with Rev. David de Silva and Mr. F. S. Sirimanna before Buddhist and Christian leaders and a large crowd. Contrary to the expectations of the Christians, the debate persuaded the people that Buddhism was superior to Christianity and boosted the recovery of Sinhalese self-confidence.

Helena P. Blavatsky and Colonel H. C. Olcott, the first Westerners to understand Buddhism and to become Buddhists themselves, were deeply impressed by this controversy and, after founding the Theosophical Society, came to Sri Lanka in 1880, establishing there the Buddhist Theosophical Society with the purpose of founding schools in which children could receive a Buddhist education. Olcott published a Buddhist catechism and a Buddhist newspaper. Anagārika Dharmapāla (1864–1933), the father of the Buddhist revival in Sri Lanka, studied Pāli on the advice of Madame Blavatsky and devoted himself to the study and propagation of Buddhism, social service, and political enlightenment. In 1891 he went to India and was shocked to discover that the places sacred to the Buddha were in the hands of nonbelievers and in ruins. His appeal to the Buddhists of the whole world led to the restoration of the sacred places. The Mahā Bodhi Society which he founded for this purpose has chapters throughout the world. In 1898 a group of about twenty young Buddhists, under the leadership of C. S. Dissanayake, a convert from Catholicism, met in the headquarters of the Buddhist Theosophical Society. This was the beginning of the Young Men's Buddhist Association, which contributes very actively to the social education of Buddhists, including Sunday schools. In 1919, the YMBA created the All Ceylon Buddhist Congress, the first national organization of Buddhist laymen, which conducts influential political campaigns for the protection of Buddhist rights. As part of its international service department, the World Fellowship of Buddhists was founded in 1930; it restarted after the war with G. P. Malalasekera as president. After Sri Lanka attained independence in 1948, Buddhism became the central pillar in the formation of the new nation, and its leading ideology. Buddhism now faces the task of finding its place in an independent country without a king. The monks, awakened to their political responsibilities, started a movement to make Buddhism the state religion. It is in that context that the present constitution of Sri Lanka was promulgated. The new political significance of the religion is reflected in the phenomenon of so-called political monks making street speeches. However, there is also an increase in monks who practice meditation at the hermitages, aiming to return to the original way of the Buddha.

Bibliography

Adikaram, E. W. *Early History of Buddhism in Ceylon.* Colombo: M. D. Gunasena, 1953.

Ariyapala, M. B. *Society in Mediaeval Ceylon.* Colombo: K. V. G. De Silva, 1956.

Geiger, Wilhelm. *Culture of Ceylon in Mediaeval Times.* Edited by Heinz Bechert. Wiesbaden: Harrassowitz, 1960.

Malalasekera, George Peiris. *The Pāli Literature of Ceylon.* London: Royal Asiatic Society, 1928.

Malalgoda, Kitsiri. *Buddhism in Sinhalese Society: 1750–1900.* Berkeley: University of California Press, 1976.

Nicholas, C. W., and S. Paranavitana. *History of Ceylon.* Colombo: Ceylon University, 1959–1973.

Rahula, Walpola. *History of Buddhism in Ceylon: The Amurādhapura Period.* Colombo: M. D. Gunasena, 1966.

II. *Burma*

Winston L. King

Although Theravāda Buddhism may have taken root in Thaton and Pegu as early as the second century c.e., and although Pagan was a Mahāyāna stronghold from around the fifth century, the verifiable history of Burmese Buddhism begins only in the reign of Anawrahta (1044–1077), the ruler who made Burma a major political force in Southeast Asia, establishing the first Burmese "empire." This monarch provided sanctuary to a monk named Shin Arahan, who had fled from Thaton to Pagan, because of the growing encroachments of Hinduism (and Mahāyāna?) on Thaton Pāli Canon Buddhism. Shin Arahan persuaded Anawrahta of the superior truth and orthodoxy of Theravāda and inspired him to outlaw the local Ari variety of Buddhism (apparently a Mahāyāna form, which had become affected by tantrism). With Shin Arahan as his counselor, later his primate, the king undertook a thorough reform, executing recalcitrant Ari leaders, conscripting the body of monks into the army, and having an entirely new monkhood ordained. The new monks were to follow the Vinaya code, no longer indulging in intoxicants, associating with women, and carrying on other practices inconsonant with Theravāda standards of morality. Anawrahta respectfully requested a set of the Pāli canonical texts, of which he had no copy, from the king of Thaton, but was rudely refused. In 1056 he mounted a military campaign and captured Thaton, its king, and his scriptures. Seeking to be a true *dhamma rāja* after the model of Aśoka, Anawrahta built many pagodas and temples, initiating the surge of construction whose still-impressive ruins cover several square miles in the Pagan region. He worked to establish Theravāda elsewhere in his spreading domain, which either by direct rule or tributary kinglets included most of modern Burma and some of Thailand.

The main characteristics of Theravāda as Anawrahta established it survive in modern Burma. The Pāli Canon is the standard of belief and practice and a blueprint for reform when needed. It is the responsibility of the Saṅgha to maintain the strength and purity of this scriptural tradition both in doctrine and in Vinaya observance. They provide the laity with a field for creating merit by giving alms to them. They also have a responsibility to teach the Dhamma, though a few are allowed to assume the special vocation of full-time meditators or forest hermits. All monks renounce lay occupations and concerns, shaving their heads, donning the yellow robe, possessing nothing but their robes and begging-bowl, medicine, a needle, and a water-strainer—and these are actually the property of the Saṅgha. Their life is devoted to the quest of nibbana and to aiding others in this quest. Monks may leave the Saṅgha without discredit, for any reason that seems important. The nun's vocation has not flourished, despite provisions for it in the canon; nuns are few and their functions menial.

The lay person's chief obligations are to observe the five precepts and to support the Saṅgha. The goal of lay practice is to produce merit, thus ensuring a fortunate rebirth and laying the remote basis of the attainment of nibbāna. Lay men sometimes adopt the monastic life for a time, thus adding to their store of merit. Lay devotion is centered on the pagoda and the Buddha image. Some pagodas are believed to enshrine relics of the Buddha or one of his disciples, notably the Shwedagon in Rangoon, said to contain some hairs of the Buddha. But any pagoda having a Buddha image in some niche in its spire or seated at its foot is the sacramental presence of the Buddha's power (*paya*) to the lay people who circumambulate it and, kneeling, offer flowers. Even simple pagodas in field or village, without a Buddha image, are considered sacred.[1] There are only a few other lay rituals, including the Triple Refuge, recited three times, led by a monk, and the *shimbyu* initiation ceremony, held in most families, in which a boy of puberty age acts the part of Prince Gotama living in splendor and then renouncing the world to take a monk's robe (which the boy does for a week or so, begging for his food like a monk).

For all his zeal for Theravāda, Anawrahta was unable to root out folk religion, firmly embedded in popular local festivals. The cult of the Thirty-Six Lords, with Mahagiri of Mount Popa at their head, was dominant, and all Burmese saw themselves as subjects of one or other of these lords (popularly called *nats*). Though he demolished all the great public *nat* shrines, Anawrahta was eventually obliged to adopt the *nats* into the household of faith, giving them a subordinate position. Thagyamin, the Pāli Canon Sakra, king of the gods, who dwells on Mount Sumeru, was made the thirty-seventh and supreme Lord, displacing Mahagiri, and in pagodas images of the thirty-seven lords, placed on the same platform as the Buddha, depicted them as worshiping the Buddha.[2] This set the pattern for Burmese Buddhism, in which gods and spirits, now many more than the original thirty-seven, are powers to be honored and placated in the proper context, but always in subordination to the transcendent power and worth of the Buddha. This is a variant of a pattern warranted by the canon, which never denied the Hindu gods, but left them subject to impermanence, and taught that humans with proper karma can become gods and that even at their best the gods' knowledge of ultimate truth is less than that of a virtuous monk. The *nats* are helpful in

13. A procession of Buddhist monks in contemporary Burma on their daily rounds of soliciting alms.

this world—Premier U Nu honored them for their assistance in overcoming insurgency shortly after Burmese independence in 1948—and few Burmese see any impiety in appealing to them in mundane matters as guardians of the otherworldly Buddha, housed in spirit-shrines on pagoda grounds. In many Buddhist usages, remnants and disguised forms of the native cults may be observed. A boy who receives initiation must be kept indoors for seven days before the ceremony to protect him from spirits, and he is sometimes marched to the *nat* shrine during the rites. Loud shouts of "*Shwe*" ("Lord"), signifying his entry into manhood, are a Hindu element. Again, the three-day New Year festival in the spring and the Feast of Lights in the autumn, though given a Buddhist gilding, are doubtless equinox celebrations. Despite the accommodations between them, there is a residual tension between *nat* and Buddha, and autonomous forms of *nat* worship, with shrines, priestesses, mediums, and harvest fertility rites, can be found in rural areas.

Anawrahta also set the pattern of the relationship between throne and Saṅgha. The Saṅgha was to be detached from the business of government. This otherworldly role could not always be strictly maintained. The king's piety was of concern to the monks, since it was expressed in material support for the Saṅgha. The prosperity, or even the survival, of the Saṅgha depended on the king's disposition toward them, for he alone had the resources for the building of pagodas and the granting of lands. Moreover, as Buddhist kings followed the *dhamma rāja* rather than the *deva rāja* power pattern, they sought from the Saṅgha a sacral legitimation of their kingship, which, intangible though it might be, greatly strengthened their rule. Anawrahta's successors included such pious and generous kings as Nadoungmya (1210–1234), the last great pagoda builder before the Pagan Kingdom succumbed to Shan incursions in the later thirteenth century; Dhammazedi, reigning in Pegu (1472–1492), who instituted a reform of the Saṅgha; Bodapawya (1782–1819), reigning from Amarapura near Mandalay, the last empire builder, who regularized the Saṅgha and promoted Buddhist learning;[3] and Mindon (1853–1878), ruler over a Burma diminished by British conquest, who sought to make Mandalay a great center of a renewed Buddhism and had all the scriptures and some of the commentaries engraved on stone. Variation in the strength and extent of central rule throughout these centuries caused frequent disorganization and consequent undiscipline among monks. Under a strong king, who appointed a primate (such as Shin Arahan under Anawrahta), the Saṅgha was kept in order; the king seldom intervened directly, but the primate had the prestige of royal backing. Saṅgha reforms nearly always looked to a model in the past. In 1192 Chapta, a Burmese monk trained in Sri Lanka and convinced that Buddhism there was more "orthodox," persuaded King Narapatisithu (1173–1210) to reform the regnant Thaton

Buddhism by having many monks reordained. These monks formed the Latter Order, in contrast to the Former Order. In 1474 King Dhammazedi sent twenty-two monks to Sri Lanka for reordination and enforced reform and reordination on all monks in his realm. In the eighteenth and nineteenth centuries the Saṅgha was split by the robe dispute: should monks in public cover both shoulders or only one? Under pressure from King Bodapawya the dispute was settled in favor of both shoulders. Most of the present sectarian divisions stem from the indecision of King Mindon. Shwegyn Sayadaw, protégé of the king and trainer of his sons, called for a return to the Vinaya rules: no sandals, no umbrellas, no monks' attendance at worldly festivals. Mindon recognized the Shwegyn sect, but did not disestablish the existing Thudhamma sect; the division continues, the Thudhamma being the larger of the two. Other sects are the Dwaya, which is close to the Shwegyn, the small Hngetwin group which frowns on such popular lay practices as worship of Buddha images, lighting of candles, and food offerings, and the highly conservative Pakokku sect, which prides itself on its monks' learning. In addition to these there are many evanescent subsects, each with its special traits but all claiming to be pure Theravāda.

British rule (1885–1948) was a misfortune for Buddhism. It ended state support for Buddhist institutions; no provision was made for Saṅgha supervision by a primate; and missionary or government schools replaced the traditional monastery schools. The Saṅgha became disorganized and undisciplined, and children were weaned from their Buddhist upbringing. In the restive 1930s the British made a belated effort to authorize national supervision of the Saṅgha, but it was ineffective. Protests against Britishers wearing shoes within pagoda precincts developed into a strong pro-independence movement in the Saṅgha, producing a martyr or two. Independence did not bring immediate improvement, for U Nu, though helping Buddhism in every way he could, was preoccupied with the survival of his government. In his final premiership (1960–1962) he sought to make Buddhism the state religion: a Buddhist calendar was instituted; Buddhist institutions were given state support, as were those of other religions in due proportion; monastic schools for the early years were strengthened; a "Buddhist socialism," neither capitalist nor communist, was attempted at state level. The holy experiment lasted only two years. After the military takeover in 1962, the state was secularized and the monks sent back to their monasteries. Lay practice was not greatly affected. A novel feature of contemporary Burmese Buddhism is the popularity of lay meditation, stimulated by U Nu; this is the primary offering of Burma's new missionary outreach to the West.

Notes

1. Buddha images, introduced in the last centuries B.C.E., are probably a Mahāyāna innovation, with no warrant in the Pāli Canon, yet they have taken an unshakable hold on the popular imagination in Theravāda countries.

2. See Maung Htin Aung, *Folk Elements in Burmese Buddhism,* 73–75.

3. He hoped to be designated a Future Buddha, as Alaungsithu (1112–1167) and Alaungpaya (1752–1760) had been, but was refused the honor. See Maung Htin Aung, *A History of Burma,* 89.

Bibliography

Aung, Maung Htin. *Folk Elements in Burmese Buddhism.* London: Oxford University Press, 1962.

——. *Burmese Monks' Tales.* New York: Columbia University Press, 1966.

——. *A History of Burma.* New York: Columbia University Press, 1967.

Aung-Thwin, Michael. *Pagan: The Origins of Modern Burma.* Honolulu: University of Hawaii Press, 1985.

The Glass Palace Chronicle of the Kings of Burma. 1923. Translated by Pe Maung Tin and G. H. Luce. Rangoon: Burma Research Society, 1960.

King, Winston L. *A Thousand Lives Away: Buddhism in Contemporary Burma.* Cambridge, MA: Harvard University Press, 1964.

——. *In the Hope of Nibbāna: An Essay on Theravāda Buddhist Ethics.* LaSalle: Open Court, 1964.

Mendelson, E. Michael. *Saṅgha and State in Burma.* Ithaca, NY: Cornell University Press, 1975.

Ray, Nihar Ranjan. *An Introduction to the Study of Theravāda Buddhism in Burma.* Calcutta: University of Calcutta, 1946.

Ray, N. *Theravāda Buddhism in Burma.* Calcutta: University of Calcutta, 1956.

Sarkisyanz, E. *Buddhist Backgrounds of the Burmese Revolution.* The Hague: Nijhoff, 1965.

Spiro, Melford E. *Buddhism and Society: A Great Tradition and Its Burmese Vicissitudes.* New York: Harper & Row, 1970.

——. *Burmese Supernaturalism: A Study in the Explanation and Reduction of Suffering.* Englewood Cliffs, NJ: Prentice-Hall, 1967.

III. *Buddhism in Thai Culture*

SUNTHORN NA-RANGSI

BUDDHISM HAS LONG been recognized as the state religion of Thailand, and the vicissitudes of its development are associated with the historical fortunes of the country. Although the kingdom of the Thai people was established in the Indo-Chinese peninsula only in 1238,[1] their relationship with Buddhism began in the first century C.E., when they were living in their ancient kingdom called Ailao in Yunnan, with the conversion of King Khun Luang Mao to Buddhism.[2] Presumably the Buddhism professed in this period was that of some Hīnayāna sect. When the Ailao kingdom was conquered by the Chinese in 255, the Thai people lost their independence. The majority remained in their homeland under the Chinese rule, but a great number migrated southward, and in the course of time many of them moved as far as the Chao Phraya river valley of present-day Thailand. In 651 the Thais in Yunnan rose against China and established the Nanchao kingdom, which remained independent until it was conquered by the army of Kublai Khan in 1253, causing a second massive migration southward. The prevalent form of Buddhism in the Nanchao kingdom was Mahāyāna, which had come from China during the T'ang dynasty. The Chinese annals of the T'ang dynasty record that "the people of Nanchao were of high culture, devoted to Buddhism, and they recited the sūtras with great reverence."[3] The annals of the Yüan dynasty state that the people of Nanchao could travel with relative ease to India; that an altar for the Buddha image could be found in every house, rich or poor; and that the people of Nanchao, old and young alike, always held the rosary in their hands ready for use at the time of daily prayer.[4]

In 1238 the Thai people revolted against the Khmer who ruled over the region which is now Thailand and set up the Sukhothai kingdom. The Thais who had lived in the Indo-Chinese peninsula for generations followed either the Theravāda Buddhism of the Mon or the Mahāyāna Buddhism of the Khmer, the indigenous races of Indo-China. Those who joined them after the fall of Nanchao brought their Mahāyāna tradition with them. The introduction of the form of Buddhism dominant today was the work of King Ramkamhaeng the Great, who ruled from 1297 and greatly expanded the Thai kingdom. Impressed by the calm appearance and learned attitude of Sri Lankan monks who came to propagate Theravāda Buddhism in Nakorn Sridhammaraj (some 800 km. south of Bangkok), he invited some of them to establish Theravāda Buddhism in his capital. As they preferred to live in a quiet place, he ordered the construction of a forest monastery for them. A stone inscription reads: "To the west of this city of Sukhothai there is a monastery of the forest monks. King Ramkamhaeng founded it and offered it to the Venerable Preceptor, learned in all the Three Piṭakas, in erudition excelling all other monks in the whole land."[5] King Ramkamhaeng offered the title of Saṅgharāja (Ruler of the Order) to the leader of the monks. This group ordained a great number of Sukhothai youths, and Theravāda Buddhism of Ceylonese lineage thus became firmly established in the kingdom.

This was the beginning of a long history of religious relations between Thailand and Sri Lanka. In the reign of King Lithai (1347–1374) a Sri Lankan bhikkhu, Sumana Thera, was welcomed by the king and was invited to pass the rainy season (Vassa, the Buddhist lent) in a newly constructed monastery in the mango grove. King Lithai himself entered the monkhood for a temporary period, the first reigning Thai king to do so. This is presumably the origin of the later custom, still observed, whereby young men temporarily ordain as monks for a three-month period of Vassa. King Lithai is celebrated as a Buddhist scholar. Consulting the Pāli Tipiṭaka, commentaries, and about thirty other independent Pāli works, he wrote a treatise called *Tebhūmikathā* (Sermon on the Three Worlds), describing the three planes of existence in Buddhist cosmology and the kamma (action) leading to them. Another expression of the vitality of the Theravāda tradition in this reign is the art of the school of Sukhothai, which may be admired in the exquisite image of the Buddha called Jinarāj in the grand temple of Pitsanuloke (about 400 km. north of Bangkok), and in the Phra Buddha Jinasīha and Phra Srisasadā in the main chapel and the vihāra of Wat Bovoranives in Bangkok. After this reign the kingdom of Sukhothai declined until in 1438 it was annexed to the Ayudhya kingdom, which had been founded by King Uthong in 1350.

Ayudhya inherited Theravāda Buddhism from Sukhothai and religious life in this period continued smoothly. Buddhism continued to play an important role as the national religion and the source of morality. King Boromkot (1733–1758) was able to repay Sri Lanka's kindness to Thailand by sending Upāli to reestablish a pure and correctly ordained Saṅgha there, in response to the request of Kittisirirājasīha, king of Kandy. When Ayudhya was sacked and destroyed by the Burmese in 1767, King Tak Sin the Great, then a general of the Thai army, was able to liberate his motherland within seven months. He established Thonburi, opposite present-day Bangkok, as the capital, and ascended the throne. Although he tried to restore Buddhism to its former state and undo the damage of the war, the brevity of his reign prevented him from achieving very much. Buddhism recovered its former stability and prosperity in the Bangkok period. Although King Rama I, who founded Bangkok as the capital, had to wage many wars against the invading enemy, he found time to advance the prosperity of Buddhism. He sponsored a Buddhist Council, which produced a standard, purified Pāli Tipiṭaka written on corypha palm leaves. Many of the major monasteries of Bangkok were built at his command, and the study and practice of Buddhism were encouraged.

A reform of disciplinary practice undertaken by the later King Mongkut during his twenty-seven years of monastic life led to the emergence of the Dhammayuttika Nikāya, a new Buddhist sect strictly observing the rules of discipline laid down by the Buddha. The Thai Buddhist Church has since then been divided into two sects: the Dhammayuttika, and the traditional

Saṅgha, called the Mahānikāya, which has the majority of monks and novices. As sovereign, King Mongkut, although the founder of one of them, rendered impartial support to both sects. His successor, King Chulalongkorn (1868–1910), continued the tradition of royal support for Buddhism. He founded two Buddhist academies, Mahāmakuta-rājavidyalaya of the Dhammayuttika and Mahāchulalongkorn-rājavidyalaya of the Mahānikāya, which later developed into two Buddhist universities, and he initiated the first printing of the Pāli Tipiṭaka in Thai script.

It can be said that the way of life of Thai people is inseparably connected with Buddhism from birth to death. When a child is born, the parents approach a monk for an auspicious name for him. Children are taught to pray and to pay homage to the Triple Gem (Buddha, Dhamma, Saṅgha) before going to bed, and to pay respect to monks. Many Buddhist families give food to the monks every morning; this is regarded as a way of accumulating merit and fulfills the duty of lay Buddhists to support the monks who preserve the Buddha's teachings for the world. When a young man reaches twenty years of age the parents arrange for his temporary ordination as a monk, and he remains in the monkhood for at least the three months of Vassa.

Public education in Thailand was formerly organized in monasteries, found in almost every village. Monasteries performed the function of school, college, or even university. Parents who wanted their sons to be educated in literary or vocational knowledge had to bring them to monasteries, which served as both lodgings and place of study. Education was free of charge at every level; the daily class timetable was not very systematic, as it had to be accommodated to the times each monk was free. The boys served their teachers in necessary domestic tasks. The modern system of education in Thailand began in the reign of King Chulalongkorn. As most of the primary and secondary schools are situated in monastery campuses, Buddhist monks in Thailand still have some role to play in national education.

The impact of Buddhism on Thai architecture and art has also been immense. The construction of monasteries has been motivated not only by wholehearted devotion but also by the desire to exhibit a monument of artistic achievement to the public and to posterity. Architects and artists lavished their skill on the chief buildings of monasteries such as the pagoda, the shrine hall, and the vihāra. These buildings serve as living textbooks for the architects and artists of younger generations. As sacred places for people of all classes they have played an important role in preserving national architecture and works of art throughout the long history of the nation.

Notes

1. Rong Syamananda, *A History of Thailand* (Bangkok: Thai Watana Panich, 1977) 8.
2. Mahamakut Buddhist University, *Buddhism in the Kingdom of Thailand* (Bangkok: Mahamakuta Rajavidyalaya Press, 1972) 26.
3. Ibid., 21.
4. Ibid., 23.
5. H. H. Prince Dhani Nivat, Kromamun Bidyalabh, *A History of Buddhism in Siam* (Bangkok: The Siam Society, 1965) 5.

IV. *Thai Spirituality and Modernization*

SULAK SIVARAKSA

> King Ramkamhaeng . . . commanded his craftsman to carve a slab of stone and place it in the midst of the sugar palm trees. On the day of the new moon, the eighth day of the waxing moon, the day of the full moon and the eighth day of the waning moon, one of the monks . . . goes up and sits on the stone slab to preach the Dharma to the throng of lay people who observe the precepts. When it is not the day for preaching the Dharma, King Ramkamhaeng, lord of the Kingdom of Sri Sajjanalai and Sukkothai, goes up, sits on the stone slab, and lets the officials, lords and princes discuss affairs of state with him.[1]

THE SPIRIT OF THAI BUDDHISM is already clearly evidenced in this most important inscription of Thai history, dating from 1292. The text reveals a mutual proximity and influence of ruler and subjects. The king was not only a political leader but an ethical teacher. Spiritually, the monkhood was placed even higher than the king: when the monk sat on the stone slab, the sovereign remained on the floor, with his subjects, listening to the sermon, as is still the custom today.

The inscription also shows the festive character of Thai Buddhism:

> At the close of the rainy season, they presented robes to the monks [Kathina ceremonies]. . . . Everyone goes to the Forest Monastery. . . . When they are ready to return to the city, they walk together, forming a line all the way from the Forest Monastery to the parade ground. They repeatedly do homage together, accompanied by music . . . whoever wants to make merry, does so; whoever wants to laugh, does so; whoever wants to sing, does so.

No expression of religious fervor is complete without the element of enjoyment, or *sanuk*, a key word in Thai culture. But the elements of fear and of ignorance are also prominent, especially for those of us who are unenlightened lay people. Animistic beliefs, derived from Khmer culture, are evidenced by the following inscription:

> There are mountain streams and there is Brah Krabun. The divine spirit of that mountain is more powerful than any other spirit in this kingdom. Whatever lord may rule this Kingdom of Sukhothai, if he makes obeisance to him properly, with the right offerings, this kingdom will thrive, but if obeisance is not made properly or the offerings are not right, the spirit of the hill will no longer protect it and the kingdom will be lost.

Another text that illustrates the rich texture of Thai Buddhism is King Lithai's *Sermon on the Three Worlds,* a work that seeks to make the spiritual dimension of Buddhism more accessible to the laity.[2] Lithai inserts into a cosmological framework legends about Buddhist deities, descriptions of heavenly realms and hellish beings, and other elements which, though not always compatible with Theravāda orthodoxy, could serve to communicate the Dhamma to those who possessed only a minimum of Buddhist learning. The cosmological scheme is correlated with the more psychologically oriented analysis of consciousness and material factors that are constitutive of Theravāda doctrinal orthodoxy, and with Theravāda conceptions of human social order and hierarchy. The work inculcates such themes as the negative effects of sinfulness and the positive results of meritorious activities, the impermanence that characterizes all samsaric existence, the ideal of life on the Noble Eightfold Path, and the realization of nirvāṇa. Combining a claim to Theravāda orthodoxy with the strong popular appeal of residual Mahāyāna and Brahminist cosmological representations, this text, perhaps the most important and fascinating work in the Thai language, has had a powerful influence on religious consciousness, literary and artistic development, and social, political, and ethical attitudes throughout the centuries.

The worldview expressed in these texts became problematic for many thoughtful Buddhists when they were exposed to Western science and ideology. Not only the cosmological imagery and symbolism but also the ritual and communal patterns correlated with them became the subject of skepticism and were often attacked as archaic and even antithetical to the pristine teaching of the Buddha. King Mongkut (1804–1868) felt the need to go beyond Lithai's *Three Worlds.* That work had relied on the commentaries and subcommentaries to the Pāli Canon. Mongkut studied these as secondary sources, but gave more attention to the original Tipiṭaka itself. Thus he could discriminate the essential and pure teaching of the Buddha from its mythological and popular overlay, mixed with magical beliefs and Brahministic rites. He practiced meditation on mindfulness and the austerities prescribed in the Pāli Canon and traveled to many parts of the kingdom, mixing with his people in various walks of life, collecting alms from them and giving them spiritual advice, thus gaining experience and insight not available to the nobility and princely families. In 1833 he discovered Ramkamhaeng's inscription together with the stone slab it mentions. He interpreted the inscription as a Magna Carta of the Thai nation and took the example of Ramkamhaeng as his guide, using the stone slab as his throne at his own coronation in 1851.

Mongkut believed that if Thai Buddhists were to survive Western imperialism they must (1) return to the original teaching of the Buddha, beyond *The Three Worlds,* and (2) reinterpret Ramkamhaeng's message in light of Theravāda Buddhism, so that the king would be a *dhamma rāja* rather than a *deva rāja;* the Ayudhyan monarchs had reverted to the latter model, appropriating the Brahministic Khmer concept, especially after the Thai conquests of Angkor around 1367 and in 1432. Mongkut held that the king had the right to rule as long as he was righteous, and that if the people did not want him on the throne, they had the right to remove him.

The Theravāda tradition inherited from Sri Lanka divided the monkhood into two categories: town dwellers, who concentrated on the study of the scriptures, and forest dwellers, who devoted themselves to meditation practice. The former task was later pursued especially by two of Mongkut's sons: Prince Vajirañānavarorasa (1892–1921), who introduced Dhamma studies nationwide for monks of both sects, as well as for lay men and women, and King Chulalongkorn. Another educational venture was the presentation of Buddhism to the younger generation and the defense of it against foreign missionaries by Chao Phya Dipakaravamsa (1812–1870), author of *The Modern Buddhist,* a pioneering critique of *The Three Worlds.* The preface to the English translation describes it as follows:

> *The Modern Buddhist* assumes religion to be the science of man, and not the revelation of God. He does not think that the comprehension of the Deity, or the firm persuasion of the exact nature of heaven, is of so much consequence as that just idea of one's own self which he believes he finds in Buddhism purged of superstitions. . . . He has a firm faith that whatever truths science may reveal, none will be found opposed to the vital points of Buddhism. He freely criticises his sacred books by such small lights of science as he possessed. He states his opinion that Buddha, although he knew everything, was careful not to teach that which the people of his age were not ripe to understand, and therefore refrained from many topics he might have referred to, had he lived in a more advanced age. . . . The missionaries again and again feel hopeful that the day of conversion is at hand, yet are ever doomed to disappointment. I cannot but think that the money and energy expended on their work is in great measure lost, and that the labour of many of them would be better employed in their own country.[3]

14. Forest monks in Thailand. In the midst of an illegally logged forest, Phra Prajak (right) gestures to his disciples as he speaks about conservation and logging issues.

In the Saṅgha, Mongkut set up a strong tradition of deep meditation practice. The Dhammayuttika Order of the Northeast in particular has carried on this tradition, especially through charismatic meditation masters such as Venerable Phra Acariya Mun (1871–1949). His biography by his disciple, Ven. Phra Acariya Mahā Boowa, the doyen of living masters, has been translated into English.[4] Ven. Phra Acariya Cha, another living master, was a close disciple of Ven. Phra Acariya Mun and has spread his life-style, his method of meditation practice, and his strict adherence to Vinaya discipline to the majority of monks in the Mahānikāya Order, and also to Western monks who set up communities in Britain, the United States, Sri Lanka, New Zealand, and Australia. There are a number of other groups that claim to be older than the reform of King Mongkut and tend to accept superstitions and supernatural powers, in the spirit of *The Three Worlds.*

In the north, Kru Ba Srivijaya (1873–1937) refused to acknowledge the spiritual and temporal authorities of Bangkok. He was regarded as a holy man, with deep spiritual insight, who led the multitudes to rebuild many important Buddhist monuments, but he ordained monks in defiance of the requirements laid down by the first Ecclesiastical Act of 1902. There are still a few meditation masters who claim to be direct disciples of his. They are known for their art of healing by traditional herbs, as religious psychiatrists using holy water and other spiritual mediums, and as astrologers. But they have not continued the social activity and political dissent of Kru Ba. In fact, the royal court, the military, the civilians, as well as the business communities regard meditation masters, of all schools and lineages, as their great supporters, spiritually, socially, politically, and economically.[5]

The Santiasoka sect is the only one that has rebelled against the present established Saṅgha. Its founder, Phra Bodhiraksha (b. 1934), was ordained in both the Dhammayuttika and Mahānikāya, but was satisfied with neither. His sect dates from 1975, when he gave ordination in defiance of the Ecclesiastical Law of 1962. He has also attracted lay followers by his puritanism and vegetarianism, and his abstention from all kinds of ceremonies. He claims to be enlightened spiritually, combining scholarship with meditation, and stressing social reform rather than upholding the *status quo.* Yet his Buddhist scholarship and his grasp of Thai social reality do not seem sufficiently deep to guarantee that Santiasoka will become a movement of any significance. The government and the Supreme Council of the Saṅgha have ignored its challenge rather than take it on legally.

The Dhammakaya school, established in 1970, traces its existence to the Ven. Luang Poh Sod (1884–1959), who claimed to have rediscovered a meditation technique lost to the Saṅgha for hundreds of years, presumably since the Thai were converted to Sinhalese Buddhism. This technique, akin to some

Tantric practices, has become popular, especially among Japanese Buddhists of the Shingon sect. Luang Poh Sod's best-known follower, Kittivuddho Bhikkhu (b. 1936), works closely with the military; he once said that to kill a communist to preserve the nation, the religion, and the monarchy is not sinful. Many Buddhists doubt whether peace and nonviolence are still of importance to this monk and his admirers. The school claims to represent the only authentic teaching of the Buddha, not revealed in the scriptures. It has not attacked the established Saṅgha, and it also works well with the capitalist tendency in the Thai society, enjoying close links with the royal palace and the military. Buddhist clubs in most universities have been dominated by lay followers of this school.

In 1932 the traditional monarchical social order was challenged by the Western ideology of liberal democracy. In the same year a young Thai monk, dissatisfied with the division of the Saṅgha into meditators and textual scholars, left Bangkok and returned to his native village in the South, at Chaiya, and founded Suan Mokha, the Garden of Liberation. This monk, the Ven. Buddhadasa Bhikkhu (b. 1906), has the vision and scholarship of Mongkut, but he has gone far beyond the great king. Not being interested in ceremonial detail and going beyond the literary message in the Pāli Canon, he was able to grasp the essential teaching of the Buddha. He was freed from founding a new sect or criticizing the established hierarchies. Indeed, Buddhadasa is the first Thai monk to acquire a critical understanding of the Pāli Tipiṭaka and to give serious consideration to Mahāyāna tradition as not inferior to the Theravāda school. He has also studied Christianity and Islam in the spirit of dialogue without any feeling of superiority or inferiority. He is much admired by Thai Christians and Muslims alike. However, he has been attacked by some Thai and Sri Lankan Buddhists who regard the Pāli text, especially the *Abhidhamma-piṭaka* and Buddhaghosa's commentaries, as sacred, and allow no reinterpretation or criticism. His comments on social reforms and dhammic socialism have also given him a reputation in certain circles as a communist. Yet his influence in the monkhood, of all sects, is tremendous. Both scholars and meditation masters look up to him as a very important guru, although he only claims to be a Good Friend (*kalayānamitta*). He has made a major contribution to the hermeneutics of Thai tradition. In reading texts like *The Three Worlds* one must be able to distinguish between the dhammic language and the worldly language, going beyond those things that would normally be regarded as myths, superstition, miracles, or deities, neither accepting them easily nor rejecting them outright, but using one's wisdom to interpret them for one's spiritual growth, enlightenment, and liberation.

An American scholar writes:

> Buddhadasa's vision of the good and just society coincides with his view of an original state of nature or an original human condition, one of mutual interdependence, harmony and balance. By its very nature this state of nature is selfless–individuals are not attached to self for its own sake. But with the loss of this state of innocence individuals are subject to the bondage of attachment (*upādāna*) and unquenchable thirst (*tanhā*). Consequently, sentient beings need to find ways to return to or restore this condition of mutual interdependence and harmony, love and respect. On the personal level the attainment of wisdom (*bodhi*) through the methods of awareness (*sati*), continuous attention (*sampajaña*) and focussed concentration (*samādhi*) serves to break through the conditions of greed, ignorance and lust (*kilesa*); while on the social level those in positions of power promote economic and political policies which after meeting basic physical needs promote a balanced development in which matters of spirit (*citta*) assume their rightful dominance. Buddhadasa's notion of a truly human community is a universal vision shared by all religions. This socialist society is one governed by love (*mettā*). In the language of Buddhist millenarian expectations, it is the age of the Buddha Maitreya. But Buddhadasa's teachings regarding Buddhist Socialism cannot be consigned to an otherworldly messianism. His vision serves as a critique of Western political theories of capitalism and communism, and provides the basic principles for a political philosophy with the potential to guide not only Thailand in the coming years, but all societies struggling to create a just and equitable social, political and economic order.[6]

The quantity and quality of his written work have excelled all living Theravāda scholars. He has even been compared with Buddhaghosa of Sri Lanka and with Nāgārjuna of India. It is too early to say whether these comparisons are valid, but his works have been studied critically by Thai and foreigners as the crowning expression of contemporary Thai spirituality and a signpost to its future.

Notes

1. See A. B. Griswold and Prasert na Nagara, "Epigraphic and Historical Studies no. 9," *Journal of the Siam Society* 59 (1971) 179–228.
2. See *Three Worlds According to King Ruang: A Buddhist Cosmology*, translation with introduction and notes by Frank E. Reynolds and Mari B. Reynolds (Berkeley, CA: Asian Humanities Press, 1982).
3. See Henry Alabuster, *The Wheel of the law or Buddhism illustrated from Siamese Sources* (London: Trubner, 1871). The author later joined the Thai government and established his family in Bangkok. His grandson, Sitthi Sawetasila, has become Thai Foreign Minister.
4. There are two English versions of this biography: one by Ruth Inge Heinze, published in the Asian Folklore and Social Life Monograph Series, Teipe; another by Siri Buddhasukh (Bangkok: Mahamakut Rajavidyalaya Press, 1976).

5. See Stanley J. Tambiah, *The Buddhist Saints of the Forest and the Cult of Amulets* (Cambridge: Cambridge University Press, 1984)

6. Donald K. Swearer, ed., *Buddhadasa's Dhammic Socialism* (Bangkok: Thai Inter-Religious Commission for Development, 1986).

Bibliography

Gabaude, Louis. *Introduction à l'herméneutique de Buddhadhasa Bhikkhu.* Paris: École Française de l'Extrême Orient, 1979.

Rajadhon, Phys Anuman. *Popular Buddhism in Siam and other Essays.* Bangkok: Sathirakoses-Nagapradipa Foundation (forthcoming).

Rajanubhab, Prince Damrong. *Monuments of the Buddha in Siam.* Translated by S. Sivaraksa and A. B. Griswold. Bangkok: The Siam Society, 1973.

Rajavaramuni, Phra (P. Patutto). *Thai Buddhism in the Buddhist World.* Bangkok: Mahachulalongkorn Rajavidyalaya, 1985.

Sivaraksa, Sulak. *Buddhist Vision for Renewing Society.* Bangkok: Thienwan Press, 1986.

———. *Siamese Resurgence.* Bangkok: ACFOD, 1985.

"Symposium: Religion and Society in Thailand." *Journal of Asian Studies* 36 (1977) 239–326.

6

Monasticism and Civilization

ROBERT A. F. THURMAN

THE BUDDHIST TRADITION begins with the young Gautama Siddhartha's spectacular renunciation of the world and is commonly thought of as essentially "otherworldly."[1] While appreciating the spiritual vision and yogic virtuosity of the Buddhists, scholars—Eastern and Western, ancient and modern, insiders and outsiders—tend to ignore altogether Buddhism's vast contribution to civilization on the planetary and millennial scale.

We cannot evaluate precisely the spiritual contribution of the Buddha if we neglect the import of the story that he was predicted to be either a Cakravartin (world emperor) or a perfect Buddha. In the eyes of his contemporaries, he chose the latter path in order to have a greater impact on this planet. In Indian myth, a Cakravartin is a political messiah who creates world peace for his own generation. The Buddha, or Jina, enlightened conqueror, was a spiritual and social messiah whose whole life was dedicated to saving the entire world from suffering and to bringing permanent peace to all. His conquest was not political or military, but it had immediate social impact. He renounced kingship and the use of force, seeking instead to conquer hearts with his Holy Truth (*saddharma*). Nonetheless, he could not realize his educational aim without an institution, a new community founded on his civilizing ethic. Though it embraced lay men and women of all social classes, this community, the Saṅgha, was monastic at the core, thus reflecting in its structure the supremacy of the interests of its individuals over its own collective interest.[2] Aware that it would be a long time before the planet was civilized enough for the manifest realization of a society whose relationships would be based on selfless wisdom and love, the Buddha designed monasticism as a specially protected society within society, in which the seeds of the Buddha-land of the future could mature and which could set an extraordinary standard of ethical, religious, and intellectual life oriented to transcendent individual and social fulfillment. He established the first "monastery" in history in the town of Rājagṛha, with the encouragement of King Bimbisāra of Magadha and the financial support of a wealthy merchant of that town.[3]

Buddhist monasticism emerged from the Axial Age in India and swept throughout Asia, transforming the landscapes, the cultures, and the politics of all its nations, as well as countless individuals. It is even likely that it influenced West Asia, North Africa, and Europe through lending its institutional style to Manicheanism and Aramaic and Egyptian Christianity.[4] The view that monasticism is a revolutionary institution is supported by descriptions of the role of Christian monasticism during the difficult ages of European history—as a bastion and harbinger of spirituality, culture, and even civilization.[5] Recent works on specific periods in Buddhist history are providing abundant data to substantiate a similar global account of its role in the East.[6] I shall present ten theses which may allow us to reexamine the historical record from this perspective.[7]

I

> Enlightenment transcends all dichotomies, and is just as powerful in the social realm as it is in personal experience. The core insight of selfless emptiness immediately implies the inexorable relatedness of the selfless individual to all others. Thus emptiness is "the womb of compassion." (Nāgārjuna)

All forms of Buddhism agree in defining a Buddha as one who has reached the peak of evolution. His attainment satisfies completely his own personal interests and enables him then to help others with their relative and ultimate concerns. The Vinaya texts of all the Hīnayāna (Individual Vehicle)[8] schools show Śākyamuni as a powerful moving force in Ganges Valley society, demonstrating supreme competence as a teacher and an organizer of teaching institutions. He is a "tamer" or civilizer of human societies, a founder of a new utopian community. In Mahāyāna (Universal Vehicle) schools, his public competence is called "great compassion" (*mahākaruṇā*) and "skill in liberative art." His ultimate social achievement is called "perfection of the Buddha-land." Because he was a bodhisattva, his messianic vow is not to attain Buddhahood until all other beings have attained freedom from suffering. Thus, in theory, a Buddha's enlightenment must be his achievement of a perspective from which all other beings, including his society and his planet, simultaneously achieve freedom and happiness. He cannot leave even a single being behind. The perfect outcome of all evolution must be totally present to the Buddha-mind, and his every word and gesture must manifest that presence to others who have not yet come to see it. His very body must become a Body of Beatitude (*saṃbhoga*) and Emanation (*nirmāṇakāya*), an inexhaustible engine of loving action, and his every social act must contribute strategically to effecting the perfect goodness and beauty of the Buddha-land.

Though the Individual Vehicle lacks an explicit doctrine of perfected altruism, it exhibits an awareness of Buddha's society-transforming role. The Buddha's life as a Buddha is presented as the evolutionary culmination of a series of lives as royal figures who, one after another, save their social worlds by astounding acts of generosity, self-sacrifice, and tolerance. Compassion is a central virtue that a Buddha is said to possess even more than a benevolent world emperor. He turns down the latter role, arguing that such a monarch cannot protect his people from their real enemies: birth, sickness, old age, and death. This has been taken to imply a repudiation of life and its value, simply because we do not deem it possible for *anyone*, even a God, to protect beings from these inevitable sufferings. But the Buddhist claim is that a Buddha is a being who has achieved a superior type of monarchy and can protect other beings from suffering.

The *Mahāparinibbāna* and *Mahasudassana Suttas* state that a perfectly enlightened Buddha eclipses the glory of a world emperor a million-billion-fold.[9] In Indian myth, a world emperor is a person who effortlessly conquers the entire planet. He has the not inconsiderable help of a gigantic magic wheel that goes around humming powerfully in the air over the capitals of other nations, causing them to submit to him at once. He is invariably a good ruler, benevolent and uncorrupted by power. His supreme worldly success is due to his vast store of merit from his own previous generosity, morality, and tolerance. He pacifies all the continents of the earth and enjoys a long and pleasant reign over loving subjects, using his complete authority to help them further their own highest aims. This is the mythic social fulfillment that the Buddha is presented as turning down in his last life in favor of an even greater success. To say that he was turning away from altruistic concerns, resigning himself to the hopelessness of the world, seeking an otherworldly triumph, is too simplistic. It also amounts to an accusation of selfishness against the greatest figure in Asian history. To refute this misinterpretation, we must uncover the historical perspective from which he can be seen to exert an even more beneficial sway over the destinies of beings on the planet than the greatest political rulers ever managed to do.

II

Buddhahood is far more than political Cakravarti-hood; it is the complete Truth-conquest of the whole world, the creation of the pure Buddha-land, which appears as atemporal unfolding to the unenlightened people trapped in ordinary time or history.

If a perfect Buddha is so much greater than even a universal monarch, he must conquer his entire world permanently and bring everlasting peace to all beings, in a conquest by means of Dharma, not by force. A perfect Buddha must be a Dharma-emperor, completely successful in Dharma-*vijaya,* truth-conquest. Śākyamuni can accept Buddhahood then only when his world has become a "Pure Land," and "Buddha-field." In the *Vimalakīrti Sūtra,* when Śāriputra points to the inconsistency between Śākyamuni's definition of Buddhahood and its Buddha-land and the reality of this world, the Buddha chides him and miraculously reveals that the land is, after all, perfect, pure, and beautiful, like a land of jewel bliss. But after a moment, Buddha withdraws his power, and the assembly is back in ordinary perception, ordinary history.[10] This incident shows that the Buddhist tradition is highly aware of the paradox of theodicy (or "Buddhodicy")—a world must be perfect, for a perfect Buddha to arise in it, and so we are saved; yet our perception of historical imperfection is also relatively valid, and we must strive to perfect ourselves and the world, even though we know that when we reach our goal we will understand how it has all along already been perfect!

In the Buddhist psychology of the Path, this paradox cannot easily be solved, nor can it be dismissed. Its liberative impact can be sustained at first by faith. It can be intensified by critical investigation and one-pointed contemplation. It can be incorporated and reconciled ultimately only by intuitive wisdom whereby one becomes enlightened, selfless, a holy one. One discovers that others also have reached that stage, and one joins them as a member of the Community Jewel, created by the interrelationships of people who live in awareness of the immanence of the Buddha-land. Its focal nodes are called "abodes" (vihāra), or monasteries, which are institutions precursory to the universal Buddha-land, functioning for ordinary society in an ethical/legal, religious/medical, and scientific/educational manner.[11] Buddhahood must be world-transformative as well as self-transformative, since the ultimate self-fulfillment is an experience of selflessness which is simultaneously interconnectedness with all living beings.

III

The Buddha's compassion effects the transformation of the planet, which unfolds through history as the process of the taming of violence by nonviolence.

A perfect Buddha himself/herself can see the perfection of the transformed, purified world, because of his or her transcendence of time-objectification.

A Buddha can show its potential to unenlightened persons for an instant, as in touching the ground with his toe in the *Vimalakīrti Sūtra.* And a Buddha's view of timeless perfection makes possible a precise awareness of timely evolution of living beings, of their inexorable progress into their own enlightened awareness.

The Buddha lived in a time when the combination of tribal sacrificialism and incipient imperialistic urbanization was initiating a cycle of violence that has continued up to its present outer limits in the nuclear age. He was the first to teach that "hatred will not cease by hatred; it can only cease by love." He clearly understood that one cannot effectively oppose evil by becoming evil. To stand up to evil with evil is to surrender to evil. The enemy can only be defeated by love, violence only by nonviolence. So he abandoned all sides of the many conflicts of the day. He became a mendicant, abandoning the upper-class identity. He entered a spiritual family, abandoning his racial and national identity. He became propertyless, abandoning competition for wealth and all identity of ownership. He became viewless, abandoning all ideological identity, and all fanatical dogmatisms. He became selfless, abandoning all personal clamor for recognition. He became lifeless, abandoning all violent claim to air, food, water, and other valuable resources. Thus abandoning all ordinary roles, he created a new role, that of the bhikṣu mendicant or monk, who connects himself and therefore others to a transcendent reality that puts the demands of relative reality into a better perspective.

He set an example, gave a teaching, and founded a community (the Three Jewels) based on self-conquest through self-transcendence. These three spread throughout the world, mirrored in the lives of numerous leaders, saints, and sages. Today it is clearer than ever that the value of self-conquest through self-transcendence, of conquering violence through nonviolence, is not at all unrealistic idealism, but is indispensable to life itself. If the planet survives, which the omniscient Buddhas must have already seen it as doing, then the triumph of civilization as truth-conquest will be complete; human beings will at last have tamed their hatred and violence, and the Buddha-land will be openly manifest.

IV

> Truth-conquest, or Buddha-land-building, can only proceed nonviolently, since individuals can only be conquered from within, from their hearts, by their own free understanding. Their insight itself is what liberates the energy of good will that constitutes the perfected land.

Truth-conquest cannot be implemented by force, by doctrine, or by magic, for human minds cannot be converted through passive acquiescence, but only through their own understanding. According to Mātṛceta's famous verse, "Buddhas do not wash away sins with water; they do not heal by laying on of hands; they do not transmit their own understanding into others; they introduce to liberation by teaching true Reality." The Buddha gave this missionary charge:

> You, monks, are freed from all snares, both those of gods and those of men. Walk, monks, on tour for the blessing of the manyfolk, out of compassion for the world, for the welfare, the blessing, the happiness of gods and men. Let not two of you go by the same way. Monks, teach dhamma that is lovely at the beginning, lovely in the middle, and lovely at the ending. Explain with the spirit and the letter the Brahma-conduct completely fulfilled, wholly pure. There are beings with little dust in their eyes who, not hearing dhamma, are decaying; but if they are learners of dhamma they will grow.[12]

The Buddha thus felt that his Dhamma was universally applicable and was zealous to spread it far and wide. Yet it could not be taken up merely as a belief system. One had to change one's way of life and one's inner understanding as well as one's emotional habits. Especially this last had to come from within each individual and could not result from any sort of coercion. Therefore, Buddhists never waged a crusade or a holy war. They operated even transnationally on the social and cultural level and not on the political one.

V

> Perfect Buddhas must carry on their truth-conquest by means of education in the liberal sense, which is neither indoctrination nor training. The insight of psychological "selflessness" is the source of the creative individualism Buddhism has always nurtured, and of its world-transforming dynamism of ethical selflessness.

The Buddha sought to conquer the world by means of *education* in the True Dharma, which has both scriptural and practical forms. The scriptural (*āgama*) Dharma consists of the Tripiṭaka. The practical (*adhigama*) Dharma consists of the ethical (*sīla*), psychological/religious (*citta/samādhi*), and intellectual/scientific (*prajñā*) higher educations (*adhiśikṣa*).[13] Thus "Dharma" involves a whole pattern of culture and civilization. The Dharma cannot spread as an external phenomenon, a set of texts, or symbols, or buildings, but must be incorporated in the actions, emotional patterns, and levels of understanding of individual people. This can come about only through gradual and systematic education.

VI

The educational institution Buddha founded is the Saṅgha, which functions on the moral, spiritual, and intellectual levels as the anchor of the new ethics, religion, and science.

The Buddha was confronted with great difficulties in seeking to teach a new pattern of ethics, a new religion, and new sciences. The laws were under the control of the kings, their armies, and police. The brahmins controlled religious orthodoxy and kept it within a strictly defined circle. They also controlled the sciences of the day, which aimed at a magical, ritual manipulation of the forces of nature and society rather than at rational inquiry into the riddles of causation. Clearly, in such circumstances, the Buddha needed to found a "school," an academy. He could have settled for an *āśrama*, an ascetics' retreat in the wilderness. But the price of such comfortable retirement would have been to abandon the enterprise of transforming the larger society, as such retreats could never accommodate large numbers of aspirants from all walks of life.

So the Buddha gradually evolved the institutional form of the urban, or perhaps suburban, monastery. This was to found a new community (saṅgha) within the existing social world (*loka*), the boundary between them a change of identity so drastic as to involve a psychic death and rebirth. The monk or nun had to abandon race, caste, family, name, property, occupation, clothing, adornment, hair, even genetic involvement through sexuality. The seriousness of this boundary was essential to insulate the monastic core of the new community from the powerful demands of the larger social whole. The monks and nuns soon thereby came under the protection of the religious awe already felt in India for the renunciant ascetic. Yet they remained in constant proximity to the laity, going to town every day for food, and then preaching for the donors. In the new community, the insiders could relate to one another without violence, exploitation, or roughness. As each was seeking transcendent liberation, there was a new consideration for the individual, a new sensitivity toward others as ends in themselves, a new respect for freedom, personal attainment, and wisdom. They could put the Buddha's psychological methods of self-cultivation into practice to free themselves from debilitating negative notions and passions, and enjoy the happiness of the positive emotions. Even women and members of the lower castes could adopt the penetrating philosophical teachings of the Buddha, criticize conventional notions imbibed from the culture, and attain liberative and transformative insight into the nature of the self and of reality. Thus, the new community was an ethical proving ground for a future Buddha-land society, a psychological asylum and meditative retreat, a philosophical school and cultural center, a fountain of goodness (by systematic restraint of evil), a haven of peace (by concentration of mind and cultivation of positive emotion), and a center of learning, understanding, and knowledge (through systematic inquiry into the true nature of reality).

VII

Monasticism is the core of the new community, and is an original invention of the Buddha; it is the institutionalization of transcendental individualism, society's acknowledgment that its highest interest is the self-fulfillment of its individuals.

The new community was not constructed in a single organizing moment. The Buddha was aware that the rules of the new community and its patterns of connection to the old society must evolve naturally. Slowly, more and more people began to share his vision and feel the need for a new pattern of living, while the outsiders became accustomed to having these saintly and eccentric "enlightened" folk in their midst. Indeed, the new was very closely tied to the old—the old society had to feed the new people, provide space for them, and allow their own relatives, employees, and subjects the freedom to join the new community.

The Mūlasarvāstivāda *Vinayavastu* (Foundation of the Discipline)[14] begins rather surprisingly with a long account of the wars conducted between the king of Aṅga and King Mahāpadma of Magadha, a few years before the birth of the Buddha. The Magadhans lose rather badly and have to pay a tribute to the Aṅga king, as the bodhisattva looks on from Tuṣitā Heaven. Then the bodhisattva enters the womb of Māyādevī in his six-tusked white elephant form, and simultaneously four princes are conceived in four of the major Gangetic kingdoms, Bimbisāra as the son of Mahāpadma. Even in this Individual Vehicle Buddhist myth, there is already a clear sense of the messianic destiny at work in the Buddha's life. The myth presents the whole country as taken over through a kind of supernatural infiltration via reincarnation. Bimbisāra soon grows up and learns about the humiliating tribute to the Aṅga king. He leads out his five hundred princely playmates and destroys the Aṅgan army, kills the king, and adds Aṅga to the Magadhan empire. Thus, when he becomes the foremost royal patron of the Buddha and his community, he is already the most powerful king of central India. These myths show that the Saṅgha understood its existence, function, and destiny as inextricably intertwined with the social history of the time.

In the Theravāda Vinaya, the Buddha at one point refuses to dictate the *Prātimokṣa Sūtra* (Rule for Individual Liberation). He says to Śāriputra that he must wait, that the Lord will know the right time. "The Teacher does not make known the course of education for disciples or appoint the Rule of Individual Liberation until some conditions causing contamination appear here in the community."[15] The rule is not then yet needed because at that early stage all the monks are already changed in consciousness, already whole in their own internal wills, and need no rule. Actually, most stories agree that the rule is not formally recited as a whole until King Bimbisāra requests the Buddhist monks to recite the central covenant of their community. Thus, the Rule of the Discipline emerges from the life of the Saṅgha, each of the hundreds of rulings occasioned by particular incidents being the judgment with attendant reasoning given by the Buddha in that particular case. All of the rulings are given from an explicitly multifocal perspective, in terms of their impact on the individual, on the rest of the Saṅgha, and on the world, allowance being made for the future as well as for the present. The Buddha always recites ten reasons when he gives a ruling:

> For this reason, monks, I will make known the course of education for the monks, founded on ten reasons: for the excellence of the saṅgha, for the comfort of the saṅgha, for the restraint of evil-minded men, for the ease of well-behaved monks, for the control of the contaminations in the here and now, for the combatting of the contaminants in future worlds, for the benefit of outsiders, for the increase in the number of insiders, for establishing the dhamma, indeed, for following the rules of discipline.[16]

VIII

> Monasticism is a mediating institution, centrist in every sense, midway between city and wilderness, priest and hermit, noble and commoner, indirectly providing both social cohesion and mobility.

The monk has a social role without precedent, midway between the pre-existing hermit-ascetics (śramaṇa) and brahmin priests. The role of the nun was also an innovation, as there were no female ascetics or priests. Sometimes the Buddha referred to himself and his monks as ascetics (śramaṇa), redefining asceticism in terms of inner mental effort, purity, and understanding, in opposition to spectacular mortifications. He considered the Indian tradition of using asceticism in order to obtain power or pleasure through rebirth among the gods to be merely another form of entrapment in saṃsāra. The Buddha less often referred to his monks as priests (Brāhmaṇa). While many rulings in the *Discipline* serve to distinguish them from priests, not allowing them to tell fortunes, perform rituals of baptism, marriage, funeral rites, and so forth, not allowing them to develop priest–client relations with the laity, the *Dhammapada* redefines the meaning of Brāhmaṇa to fit the enlightened monk or nun who is pure in motive, word, and deed.[17]

The Buddha's discovery of a "middle way" between hedonism and asceticism resulted in a middle social type, a renunciant who represented a middle way between ascetic and priest. Again, the Buddhist monastery can be seen as an institution midway between the traditional rural ascetics' *āśrama* and the city priests' temple compound. These monasteries were usually in groves or gardens on the outskirts of the cities, midway between downtown and wilderness.

The Saṅgha served a number of mediating functions, incidental to its main functions as retreat center, school, and research academy, but probably quite important for its rapid and successful spread throughout Northern India. It was the first institution to grant access to any sort of education to members of the castes who were outside the "twice-born" elite of the Vedic religion, and actually formed the majority of the population. It was the first institution that was transnational, in that Buddhist monks and nuns at one end of the "Sixteen Countries" that constituted central India were theoretically more closely related to monks and nuns at the other end than they were to the non-Buddhists of their own countries. And it was the first institution that was transsexual, in that both males and females were free to join the community, although within it there was careful segregation of the sexes as well as a hierarchical superiority of monks to nuns. In spite of this, the songs of the early sisters of the community graphically express the tremendous relief these women felt as a result of their liberation from their very confining social situation, as well as from the transcendental liberation some of them achieved.[18] Thus, the Saṅgha became an important avenue of social mobility as well as a mechanism of social cohesion. It is perhaps for this reason that the most important of the rising new classes of Indian society of those times, the mercantile classes, some of whom came from the lower rungs of the Vedic hierarchy and some from the outsider castes, found a number of their needs and aspirations satisfied by the Saṅgha and were its most important supporters. In the Buddha's time the kings of the sixteen main states were vying with one another for imperial domination of all of India. One of the reasons they supported the Saṅgha was its great popularity among the merchants. Kingly acceptance of monasticism marked the birth of functioning social individualism in Indian civilization.

IX

The main rival of monasticism, whose origin lies in the same era, is universalistic, imperialist militarism. The greater success of monasticism may be partly due to its natural alliance with mercantilism and the bureaucratic state.

Socrates was put to death for "corrupting the youth of Athens." The Duke of Lu and other petty rulers were not willing to let Confucius spread his ethical and philosophical ideas too widely in their kingdoms. Yet the Buddha's community, with its monastic core, had by comparison a phenomenal success, spreading throughout all the north Indian kingdoms until in the time of Aśoka it had become an "establishment" in India. One expects kings to dislike monasticism, which encourages potential soldiers to seek salvation rather than serve their country, diminishes the ranks of farmers, artisans, and other producers, attracts donations, and can remove substantial landholdings and revenues from the royal tax rolls. For these reasons monasticism could not take root in West Asia and East Asia until more than seven centuries after Buddha's time. In Buddha's and Aśoka's India, there must have been a surplus of recruits, land, and treasure, and monasticism must have provided a safety valve for the liberationist energies of potential idle malcontents. It must have provided a contemporary, effective source of legitimation, its universalistic tendencies contrasting with the tribalistic brahmin traditions and their regional ritual lineages. It was the religious wave among the all-important powerful merchants, who financed royal adventures. Finally, it provided the kings themselves with a cosmic scheme more credible than that of Vedic kingly ritual, within which their persons, deeds, and reigns acquired significance. When we analyze the role of the Saṅgha in the edicts of Aśoka, we can clearly see the ethical and educational contribution it made to the task an emperor faces after concluding his expansive conquests—the maintenance of a peaceful, self-balancing order, based on the cheapest and most effective of all means of social control, a sensible, coherent, hence easily internalized ethic.

There is a connection between militarism and monasticism. Some aspects of the Saṅgha reflect the military practices of ancient India. It was an anti-army, in a sense, an army of ascetic, transcendence-seeking spiritual soldiers, striving to conquer the entire world of living beings by the Holy Truth of selflessness. Śākyamuni's campaign was extremely long-range, of course, and victory could be measured only by the number of souls who turned their own wills inward to achieve self-conquest. But before it went underground at the time of the barbarian invasions at the end of the first millennium, his army conquered culturally most of Asia. What happened to it subsequently is a subtle question, precisely because of his nonviolent strategy of going underground in response to violent opposition.

X

Three phases of Buddhist monasticism can be distinguished: (1) the revolutionary, and radically dualistic, phase of the Individual Vehicle; (2) the evolutionary, or educatively nondualistic, phase of the Universal Vehicle; (3) the fruitional, or pervasively nondualistic, phase of the Diamond Vehicle.

The first phase covers roughly the first five to seven hundred years in India, during which Śākyamuni and his successors worked to establish the original institution. In subsequent interactions with other cultures, this initial phase of establishing an "extraworldly" institutional space on the new land, as it were, was always a slow and difficult process. Well documented in China were the Confucian critiques and the Buddhist defenses of the idea of monasticism, the creation of a sphere theoretically outside the emperor's control. In Tibet and Japan, sponsoring monarchs had an easy time making public shrines for the rituals of the new religion, but it took centuries for the more conservative forces in the cultures to accept the idea of an unproductive, free, potentially subversive monastic space. Today in the West, while there are many lay Buddhist organizations, the necessity of genuine monasticism (with celibacy, poverty, and political immunity at its core) is just beginning to be understood, and it still has not taken firm hold after more than a century.

The first phase terminates automatically when its socioethical, cultural-educational, and scientific-ideological goals have been achieved. "Achievement" here means that the larger society has become more civilized, gentler, "tamed," with a better tolerance for individualism, and it is no longer so essential for the seeker of enlightenment to withdraw into monastic seclusion. Now the monastic centers develop a more aggressive relationship to the larger society, intervening more openly in the affairs, debates, and customs of the lay community. They adopt a more "immanent" approach to social transformation, developing a stronger interest in lay education. With the rise of Mahāyāna and the spread of the bodhisattva ethic, the monasteries began to serve the entire society in an educational sense, becoming the core of the largest universities on the planet during the first millennium. The messianic program of Buddhism could afford to come out in the open, as it were.

Western scholars, predisposed to interpreting Asian history as a record of error, decline, and decay, have seen Mahāyāna as arising from a failure or decadence of the Monastic Vehicle, but it seems clear that it arose in response to the needs of a gentler, more civilized society. As Buddhism spread through Inner and East Asia, this second phase coexisted with the earlier phase in some of the new cultures. The second phase preserved the monastic core of the first phase intact at its center—Messianic Buddhism never considered Monastic Buddhism institutionally obsolete, even though sometimes individual bodhisattvas may have chided individual monks for narrow-mindedness or philosophical crudeness. The great monastic universities of first-millennium C.E. India were the typical institutions of this second phase, institutions that still existed in Tibet and Mongolia into this century. Their heirs still flourish in Sri Lanka, Thailand, the Chinese fringe nations, South Korea, and Japan, in the form of the numerous Buddhist colleges and universities of those nations.

The final, fruitional, nondualistic phase is most difficult to discuss, for it has almost nowhere yet come into existence. In Pala-dynasty India, and to a lesser extent T'ang-dynasty China, the two greatest alluvial civilizations at their zenith were centered on monastic universities. The bodhisattva missionaries of the time transcended individual reliance on any institution and created the style of the Great Adept (*Mahāsiddha*). Their missionary outreach touched previously inaccessible realms—the uneducated and the outcast in Indian society, and the outlying barbarian areas of Southeast, Inner, and East Asia. They used the esoteric lore of the Tantras as well as unconventional, iconoclastic approaches like Ch'an, Great Perfection, and Great Seal.[19] Their movement outward from the centers of civilization into the fringe realms such as Tibet, Indonesia, and Japan was fortunately timed, for the second millennium brought great barbarian invasions into the civilized areas, Turkic Muslims in India, Mongols in China, and eventually Portuguese, Dutch, French, and British into both areas.

Only in Kamakura Japan, Phagmodruba Tibet, and certain Mongolian nations was monasticism allowed to develop further. It reached its high point of fruitional possibility in the Dalai Lama era of Tibet, consolidated in the seventeenth century.[20] The social dualisms of the earlier phases ended with the monastery taking complete responsibility for the world, producing a government, a bureaucracy, a complete culture. This represented a fascinatingly exact mirror-opposite of what was happening in the same centuries to European monasticism. There the Reformation collapsed the social dualism of medieval Europe into the unified secularized industrial culture of Northern Europe. In Switzerland and Tibet, the monastic quest for a truly gentle, ethical civilization realized opposite types of millennial fruition; the former by dissolving the monastery into the world, into corporations, universities, government bureaucracies, hospitals, and the latter by dissolving the world into the monastery, having its monks and nuns assume all those responsibilities in a systematic, rationalized way. Today these social mirror-images have finally come into close confrontation.

In the face of our mutually genocidal threat of nuclear obliteration, we will finally tame our passions and realize a heavenly peace on earth; or we will remain savage and create a hell on earth. Many Buddhist monastics today are refugees, some in heavenly retreats, as His Holiness the Dalai Lama in his Himalayan headquarters, some in the hellish din of camps of holocaust survivors, as in the Cambodian camps on the Thai borders. In the midst of all their apparent institutional self-obliteration, they exude a quiet optimism which wells up from the foundations of their Jewel of a Community, which, as I have tried to elucidate, stands on the Buddha's seeing beyond the holocausts to the Buddha-land destiny of this planet.

Notes

1. Max Weber, *The Religion of India* (New York: Grove Press, 1967) 204–90, and "The Social Psychology of the World Religions," in *From Max Weber: Essays in Sociology* (London: Routledge & Kegan Paul, 1970) 267–301.

2. This definition of monasticism may startle those who think of the Buddhist *anatma* as "lack of individuality" rather than simply "selflessness." I have refuted this conflation of Buddhist spiritual individualism with Brahmin mystical monism in "The Emptiness that is Compassion: An Essay on Buddhist Ethics," *Religious Traditions* 4/2 (October–November 1981).

3. This early "abode" (vihāra) in the Prince Jeta's garden only gradually became structured into an organized monastery. The space for the new community was incredibly costly, as the donor had to cover almost all of its surface with gold coins. This is an excellent symbol of the difficulty a society has in allowing part of its space to be turned over to the quest of ultimate freedom.

4. This has been surmised by various scholars, though no one yet has given serious study to the hypothesis, rendered plausible by the seven-century priority of Buddhist monasticism, the long coexistence in the Bactria-Iran area (reflected in Mani's third-century claim of descent from Buddha, Zoroaster, and Christ), and the strong tradition of Indian cultural influence on the Hellenic world through Alexandria.

5. Jean Decarreaux, *Monks and Civilization* (New York: Doubleday, 1964); Jean Leclercq, *The Love of Learning and the Desire for God* (New York: Fordham University Press, 1982).

6. See the works of Collcutt Gunawardana, Joshi, Mendelson, Miller, Tambiah, and Welch in the bibliography.

7. See R. A. F. Thurman, "The Politics of Enlightenment," *Lindisfarne Letter* 8 (1979).

8. I use the pair "Individual Vehicle"/"Universal Vehicle" for early Monastic Buddhism as a whole and later Messianic Buddhism as a whole in contrast to each other. I feel this gives us a nonderogatory equivalent of the unfortunate term *Hīnayāna.*

9. See T. W. Rhys Davids, *Pali Suttas* (New York: Dover), 1973.

10. See *The Holy Teaching of Vimalakīrti,* trans. R. A. F. Thurman (University Park, PA: Pennsylvania State University Press, 1976) chapter 1.

11. These non-"religious" functions of Buddhist monasteries have been hard for modern scholars to discern, as one of the phenomena of modernity is the reduction of religious institutions to a very narrow range of functions, as social services previously rendered by them have been taken over by various secular agencies.

12. *The Book of the Discipline,* trans. I. B. Horner (London: Pali Text Society, 1966–82) IV 28 (modified).

13. In this respect, it is interesting that the Buddha was celebrated as the discoverer of causation and cessation, rather than as the recipient of some religious revelation. The Skt. *sikṣa* is usually translated "training," to distinguish it from the modern, supposedly

"secular," "education." The Central Government of India, however, still uses *Sikṣa* for its Ministry of Education, and the kind of growth the Buddha sought to foster certainly fits with the inner unfolding we seek for our students in liberal education.

14. I am familiar only with the Tibetan version, *Kanjur,* Vol. *'Dul-ba ka.*

15. *Book of the Discipline,* vol. I.

16. Ibid.

17. *The Dhammapada,* trans. Irving Babbitt (New York: New Directions, 1965) chapter XXVI.

18. *Psalms of the Early Buddhists,* trans. C. A. F. Rhys Davids (London: Luzac [Pali Text Society], 1964).

19. The similarities between the Tantric siddhas of late first millennium India and the Ch'an masters (Bodhidharma, Hui Neng, Ma Tzu, Hang Po), and the Tantric siddhas of late first millennium East Asia (Amoghavajra, Hui Ko, Kūkai) have been noticed by Tucci, Blofeld, and Govinda, but are not widely recognized. They are important for a revised interpretation of that period of Indian history, supposed to be decadent while the contemporaneous period in East Asia is supposed to be a renaissance.

20. The achievement of the Great Fifth Dalai Lama in completing the construction of a fully monasticized society in the 1640s and 1650s has only just begun to be understood. See Franz Michael and Eugene Knez's *Rule by Incarnation* (Boulder, CO: Westview, 1982).

Bibliography

Bunnag, Jane. *Buddhist, Monk, Buddhist Layman.* New York: Cambridge University Press, 1973.

Collcutt, Martin. *Five Mountains: The Rinzai Zen Monastic Institution in Medieval Japan.* Cambridge, MA: Council on East Asian Studies, Harvard University, 1981.

Gunawardana, R. *Robe and Plough: Monasticism and Economic Interest in Early Medieval Sri Lanka.* Tucson: University of Arizona, 1979.

Joshi, Lal Mani. *Studies in the Buddhistic Culture of India.* Delhi: Motilal Banarsidass, 1967.

Mendelson, E. Michael. *Saṅgha and State in Burma.* Ithaca, NY: Cornell University Press, 1975.

Miller, Robert James. *Monasteries and Culture Change in Inner Mongolia.* Wiesbaden: Harrassowitz, 1959.

Tambiah, Stanley J. *World Conqueror and World Renouncer.* New York: Cambridge University Press, 1976.

Welch, Holmes. *The Practice of Chinese Buddhism 1900–1950.* Cambridge, MA: Harvard University Press, 1967.

Part Two

MAHĀYĀNA

7

The Sūtras

I. *Prajñāpāramitā* and the Rise of *Mahāyāna*

Kajiyama Yūichi

After the time of King Aśoka (d. 232 B.C.E.) Buddhist monks and nuns lived in community in large monasteries, economically supported by kings and wealthy merchants. Having neither financial problems nor domestic and social duties, they were able to devote themselves to doctrinal (or abhidharmic) studies, prolonged meditation practice, and the search for emancipation, activities far beyond the capacity of lay followers. Monastic Buddhism became "professional," and monks and nuns tended to discriminate against lay Buddhists because of their inferior attainments. During the last centuries B.C.E. and the early centuries C.E., the Bactrians, Saka-Scythians, Parthians, and Kushans successively invaded Northwestern India and penetrated deep into the Indian subcontinent. People suffered from wars, pillage, murder, and poverty. In this time of upheaval, people who had lost their families, farms, and possessions had to resort to evil deeds to make their living. Stories of the period tell how brahmins abandoned ancient Vedic rituals and submitted to serfs; social ethics degenerated; wives betrayed husbands; boys only eight years old married; five-year-old girls bore children; and people killed one another as if they were chasing deer.[1] The Hīnayāna saints of that period taught karmic retribution and transmigration, emphasizing the merits of meditation and a religious way of life, but this teaching failed to relieve the anxiety people felt or to offer a path of salvation practicable under the conditions of everyday life.

Between the later Mauryan dynasty (which fell ca. 180 B.C.E.) and Kaniṣka's establishment of the second Kushan dynasty (ca. 129 C.E.), India was exposed to foreign civilizations, Greek, Egyptian, Iranian, and, to a certain extent, Chinese, as attested by polished stone pillars and rocks bearing inscriptions, the architecture of the palace at Pātaliputra, the golden coins of the Kushan empire, and the earliest Buddhist images. In religion, these intercultural contacts catalyzed new developments: heavenly saviors such as Viṣṇu and Amitābha, the notion of bodhisattvas, and the philosophy of emptiness (śunyatā), which was developed in conscious opposition to the conceptual realism, distinctionism, and dualism of the Abhidharma schools.

Emptiness and the Perfection of Wisdom Sūtras

The Sarvāstivāda philosophy was a pluralistic realism, analyzing all phenomena into their indivisible, singular elements or principles (seventy-five dharmas in five groups), seen as separate and distinct from one another and as having an intrinsic own-being (*svalakṣaṇa, svabhāva*), which remained unchanged throughout past, present, and future. When combined with operation these unchanging essences became manifest as present phenomena, much as the frames of film on the reels of a projector, passing from upper to lower reel, project momentary ever-changing pictures on the screen, while existing permanently in the film on the reels. Mahāyāna thinkers, in contrast, contended that things had no own-being and that they simply appeared when all the causes and conditions were provided and vanished in absence of any of the latter. As sound from a lute is produced because of the body and strings of the instrument, a plectrum, and the player's effort, any and every thing, without having own-being, appears and disappears depending on the sufficiency or insufficiency of its causes and conditions. That which depends on other things for its production and existence is without own-being or reality, like a dream or an illusion. Since all things are equally empty of own-being, they are not different from one another with respect to emptiness. This philosophy found its first radical expression in the large corpus of writings known as the *Prajñāpāramitā,* or Perfection of Wisdom sūtras.

The earliest of these texts date from around the first century C.E., and new compilations were developed from these by expansion and contraction for about one thousand years, in four phases: (1) the period of formation of the *Sūtra of Perfect Wisdom in 8,000 Lines* (*Aṣṭasāhasrikā-prajñāpāramitā-sūtra*), which is the basic Perfection of Wisdom sūtra (before 100 C.E.), itself having older and newer layers; (2) the period of enlargement (100–300), during which the basic sūtra was enlarged to form the *Sūtras on Perfect Wisdom in 18,000 Lines, 25,000 Lines,* and *100,000 Lines,* prose compositions named after the number of thirty-two-syllable śloka (stanzas) they contain; (3) the period of condensed scriptures in prose and verse (300–500), such as the *Diamond Sūtra* (*Vajracchedikā*) and the *Heart Sūtra* (*Prajñāpāramitā-hṛdaya*); (4) the Tantric period (600–1200), in which scriptures were composed under the influence of Tantrism. The most important of these sūtras were translated into Chinese several times, and Hsüan-tsang compiled a six-hundred-volume collection of almost all the Perfection of Wisdom sūtras.

These scriptures have as their central theme the compassion and self-sacrifice of the bodhisattvas, who, until they had saved everyone in this world, would not enter the nirvāṇa of absolute quiescence. Refusing to enjoy enlightenment for themselves alone, they did not leave ordinary society behind, but walked together with everyone else. The bodhisattva ideology developed apace with actual religious practice. In contrast to the monks of the conservative cloisters, Mahāyāna followers, when they were monks, actively guided the laity who worshiped stūpas. More frequently, the bodhisattva was himself a layman. The image of the religious person changed radically. Until now practitioners had either lived in a monastery or meditated in the wilderness. But the bodhisattvas who figure in the *Sūtra on Perfect Wisdom* are usually rich and powerful men who live in splendid mansions in the cities, models of education, virtue, and eloquence, respected and loved by everybody, handsome and surrounded by female admirers, and, as occasion demands, energetic and heroic. They can be described in essentially secular, social, and active terms. In the bodhisattva, the religious and the profane merge into one.

The story of the head of the family in the *Sūtra on Perfect Wisdom in 8,000 Lines* illustrates this ideal. He leaves on a trip with his family and dependents, and they become lost in a jungle. When his fellow travelers, among whom are women and children, become frightened and disorderly, he tells them, "Don't be frightened. I'll soon lead you out of the jungle." No matter how pressed by difficulties and dangers, he does not forsake his people and try to escape by himself. He devises suitable methods for each occasion and defends them from each new danger. In the end, he leads them all back to his own city. Although he realizes the truth and arrives at the gate of salvation, because he cannot forsake his fellow beings, the bodhisattva renounces his own nirvāṇa in order to walk the path of suffering in this world together with everyone else. This compassion is grounded in the bodhisattva's insight that there is no salvation apart from life in this world. It is not true that either delusion or enlightenment has an intrinsic nature, for the two do not exist as separate entities. They are nondual and defy essential differentiation. The religious order is within the profane. Enlightenment does not exist apart from delusion.

The *Sūtra on Perfect Wisdom* lists six perfections (pāramitā) as the religious practices of the bodhisattva: perfect charity, perfect observation of precepts, perfect perseverance, perfect energy, perfect meditation, and perfect wisdom. Here the word "perfect" has a special meaning. Charity does not mean to give to others when one has more than enough, but to give whatever one has, up to and including one's life. Moreover, as long as one is self-conscious, one's charity cannot be said to have the perfection of a purely selfless act. The religious practice of meditation likewise involves more than controlling one's mind by sitting and meditating on an object. Perfect meditation breaks through the outer form of meditation. True meditation can exist in the midst of social action. Perfection depends on the realization that *no practice has its own intrinsic nature.* When one insists on a virtue called charity, believing it to have some intrinsic quality, charity is not perfect. Only when charity does not have the intrinsic nature of charity—when it is empty (*śūnya*)—does it become perfect. Enlightenment too, if insisted on as enlightenment, turns into illusion. Thus, perfect wisdom means to know that no thing has an intrinsic nature, or that everything is empty. In some circumstances even poison can become a miracle drug; if poison had an intrinsic nature, this transformation could not occur. The distinction between defilement and purity is ultimately a question of egotistic attachment.

In Abhidharma philosophy, each datum is classified according to categories, and in the datum thus categorized, it is held that there is an inherent, unchanging own-being: water has its own quality of moisture, and fire of heat. From this viewpoint, nirvāṇa, which is unconditioned and unchangeable, is a completely different realm from changing and conditioned phenomena. Data are differentiated from mind; mind is differentiated from mental functions, each possessing a different own-being. A good act is essentially different from a bad act. One thing cannot alternately be good and bad; or there cannot sometimes be enlightenment and sometimes illusion. The *Sūtra on Perfect Wisdom* opposed this philosophy of distinction, and its metaphysical and religious dualism. So-called unchanging own-being is merely the result of attachment to the forms of perception and language. It is not that there is an own-being of color-form in red or white objects, or that there is an own-being of impurity in love. "Own-being" is arbitrarily attached by human beings to the flux of ever-changing data. In the original form of emptiness and purity, there is no distinction between data and mind, enlightenment and delusion, or any other dichotomy. In this original form, everything is nondual, undifferentiated.

The Abhidharma philosophy represented rationalism within Buddhism at that time. However, from the very beginning Buddhism had mystics who repudiated rationalistic tendencies. The *Sūtra on Perfect Wisdom* is the work of people who saw meditation as the one and only path for fathoming reality. When one concentrates one's attention on a certain object and meditates on it, the name and form of this object disappear. As the objects of thought, representation, and feeling all disappear, one apprehends the highest reality, which remains to the end and which neither comes into being nor passes away. Nor does it manifest itself in any form, being limitless and boundless both temporally and spatially, and free from all designations, pure, quiescent, and alone.

Three kinds of meditation (samādhi), also called the three entrances to liberation, represent the fundamental religious attitude of Mahāyāna Buddhists toward all things. They are meditation of emptiness (śūnyatā), signlessness (*animitta*), and wishlessness (*apraṇihita,* the state that is free from desire). Emptiness, the negation of own-being (*niḥsvabhāva*), is the highest reality of original purity; signlessness, equivalent to noncognition (*anupalabdhi*), is the epistemological character of this reality; and wishlessness, nonattachment (*asaktatā*), is its psychological character. A person who intuitively apprehends the highest reality no longer supposes that there is any own-being in things, or considers it possible that things can be recognized by certain characteristics or grasped by definitions. Consequently, such a one does not become attached to any being, hold it fast, or have desires concerning it.

In the highest order of reality, things are intrinsically empty and cannot be characterized by any sign. The mystics of the *Sūtra on Perfect Wisdom* did not trust human language and cognition. Concerning the highest reality, whatever one says is merely a verbal symbol. Like words, the ordinary perceptions, judgment, and cognition are also without objective validity. These mystics had not yet developed a subtle epistemology like that found in later Buddhist philosophies. Rather, in meditation, they actually experienced the gradual disappearance of perception and judgment in regard to objects. The intuition that finally remained could not be expressed by any means. The highest reality is sometimes described as the "pure and bright mind." Since even the distinction between mind and data does not arise in the world of intuition which transcends language, it is one and the same to say a thing is originally pure and to say the mind is pure and bright. The *Sūtra* does not carry its account of the highest reality any further. However, the idea that everything besides this purity—the perceptual images and verbal forms, and the value judgments, defilements, and actions that arise from them—is arbitrarily assigned by human subjects had great influence on the later thought of the Mādhyamika, Vijñānavāda, Tathāgatagarbha, Hua-yen, and Ch'an schools.

Against the abhidharmist distinctions between good and evil, sacred and profane, enlightenment and defilement, nirvāṇa and saṃsāra, the philosophy of emptiness upheld a standpoint of nonduality, arguing from the impossibility of drawing hard and fast distinctions between things void of own-being. This standpoint of nonduality is beautifully expressed in the *Vimalakīrti Sūtra.* A goddess scatters divine flowers upon many guests who have gathered in Vimalakīrti's house. Flowers alighting on Mahāyāna bodhisattvas drop off them and fall to the ground, whereas those falling on Hīnayāna monks stick to their bodies. Thinking that as a mendicant who has renounced the worldly life he should not decorate himself with flowers, Śāriputra, the sage representing the Hīnayāna monks, exerts all his effort in vain to remove the flowers which cling to his body. The goddess, laughing at him, says that it is only Śāriputra's discrimination which distinguishes between the worldly and the unworldly. Śāriputra contends that the Buddha taught people to attain emancipation by getting rid of the defilements of greed, hatred, and ignorance. The goddess answers that this teaching is only for those who are attached to themselves, and that the Buddha taught nonduality of defilements and enlightenment to those free of such pride. Vimalakīrti asks the thirty-two bodhisattvas surrounding him to explain the Buddha's teaching about "entering into nonduality." Each presents a different account of what nonduality means: the identity of good and evil, saṃsāra and nirvāṇa, defilements and enlightenment, the worldly and the unworldly, and so forth. Bodhisattva Mañjuśrī shows the inadequacy of these replies and declares that the nonduality taught by the Buddha is the attitude of freeing oneself of words and concepts. Then Mañjuśrī requests Vimalakīrti to give them his own interpretation. Vimalakīrti remains silent and utters not a word.

The Social Context of the Mahāyāna Philosophy

The immediate social context for the emergence of Mahāyāna is the practice of *stūpa worship.* According to the *Mahāparinibbāna-suttanta* (*Digha Nikāya*, No. 16), in answer to Ānanda's question about how to deal with the remains of the Buddha after his demise, the Buddha enjoined that Ānanda and the other ascetics should devote themselves to their religious quest without being worried about the matter, and that cremation, erection of a stūpa containing the Buddha's relics, and memorial services should be entrusted to lay Buddhist followers, including brahmins, kṣatriyas, and wise commoners. In the same sūtra the Buddha teaches in detail how his body is to be placed in the coffin, how it is to be cremated, how to build a stūpa, and how to worship it with flower garlands, incense, colors, umbrellas; to which the Chinese version of the sūtra (T 1.20b) adds music and dancing. Neither the Pāli nor the Chinese version can date back to very early times, but the former was known in the time of Aśoka, who erected many stūpas, designated the four sacred places of the Buddha, and made pilgrimages to them. The Vinaya texts of the Mūlasarvāstivāda and Dharmaguptaka schools describe how on the occasion of a Buddhist service at a stūpa many merchants gathered to open a market and made offerings of gold, silver, clothes, pearls, and other

15. Copy of the *Diamond Sūtra*, dated 868.

jewels, intended solely for maintenance of the stūpa; their use for the orders of monks and nuns was forbidden.

Since their precepts forbade monks and nuns to listen to music and worldly tales, to watch dancing, to enter a marketplace, and to pluck living flowers, they were not able to hold services at stūpas together with laypeople. Chinese Vinaya texts of various schools reveal that stūpas were under the care and management of lay Buddhists, not of monks and nuns, while the older Pāli Vinaya texts make no mention of services at stūpas.[2] It is clear that from a fairly early time lay followers, gathering around Buddha stūpas, began to form a "Buddhism of faith" separate from the "Buddhism of truth" maintained in the monasteries. As it is older than the *Sūtra on Perfect Wisdom in 8,000 Lines*, the *Great Amitābha Sūtra* (T 12. 300–320) is recognized to be a pre-Mahāyāna sūtra. It describes the twenty-four primal vows made by the bodhisattva Dharmākara, prior to becoming Amitābha. He vows that he will accept into Sukhāvatī, his Buddha-land, sons and daughters of good families who worship Buddha stūpas, that he will make them bodhisattvas in that land if they have faith in him (sixth vow), and that he will let ascetics (śramaṇa) practicing the six perfections be born in his land and will make them irreversible bodhisattvas (seventh vow). These separate vows for laity and monastics indicate that around the first century C.E. some of the lay worshipers of Amitābha became monks and nuns, probably to meet the call for leaders as these groups grew, or that some monks and nuns from Hīnayāna schools joined the group of worshipers of Amitābha. Since conservative Hīnayāna monastics refused to recognize present Buddhas such as Amitābha, the ascetics mentioned in the above seventh vow must have lived outside Hīnayāna monasteries.

The Sthaviravāda and its subschools such as the Sarvāstivāda and Vibhajyavāda were among the Hīnayāna schools which held that in the past there had appeared only seven Buddhas, of which the seventh was Gautama the Śākyamuni. The present time belongs to the age of Śākyamuni, which is to continue until the appearance of Maitreya, the future Buddha. Progressive schools such as the Mahāsāṅghika and its subschools tended to believe that there were many Buddhas residing at present in the ten directions, if not in India. Some of these schools, the Caitika (Cetiya), for example, must have been associated with stūpas, as the name itself suggests—"caitya" (cetiya) being equivalent to "stūpa." The laity who used to bow and pray in front of a Buddha stūpa could never have accepted the Hīnayāna monastic teaching that the Buddha in the stūpa had long been dead; they refused to believe that no Buddha existed in the age in which they lived. Even before Mahāyāna Buddhism arose, new Buddhas such as Akṣobhya and Amitābha were revered by the laity and the progressive monastics, as is evidenced by the frequent references in the *Sūtra on Perfect Wisdom in 8,000 Lines* to Akṣobhya, whose Buddha-land is in the East, and to other Buddhas and bodhisattvas. Stūpa-worshipers, both lay and monastic, were called "sons and daughters of good families" and came to be called "bodhisattvas," probably in the first century C.E. when the *Sūtra on Perfect Wisdom in 8,000 Lines* was being compiled. Many Mahāyāna sūtras, when enumerating their audience in the introductory parts, mention a "group of bodhisattvas" (*bodhisattva-gaṇa*) or "order of Bodhisattvas" (*bodhisattva-saṅgha*) separately from the (Hīnayāna) "order of disciples" (*śrāvaka-saṅgha*). This suggests that there were groups of Mahāyāna followers as distinct orders.

The Bodhisattva Cult

One of the most vivid innovations of Mahāyāna spirituality is the development of *the notion of the bodhisattva.* Gautama the Buddha was thought to have been a follower of other Buddhas in many previous lives. The existence of many Buddhas in the past and the future meant that there could be many aspirants to Buddhahood, or bodhisattvas, in any age, and these need not be monks. We cannot ascertain the exact date of the first appearance of Jātaka stories, in which in the extant forms the word *bodhisatta* (Skt. *bodhisattva*), referring to the previous incarnations of Gautama the Buddha, is found repeatedly. Since reliefs depicting scenes from Jātaka stories are found on stūpas at Barhut which, according to an inscription, were built during the Śuṅga dynasty (ca. 180–70 B.C.E.), the stories must have originated at the latest by the middle of the second century B.C.E. The word *bodhisattva*, however, emerged later than the Jātaka stories and was interpolated into them. The idea of the bodhisattva as a sentient being destined for full enlightenment originated from the famous story of Buddha Dīpaṃkara, one of the seven past Buddhas, making a prediction to the youth Megha, a former incarnation of Gautama, who attained the mind of full enlightenment on seeing Buddha Dīpaṃkara. He offered five stalks of flowers to the Buddha and spread his long strands of hair on the muddy ground to let the Buddha walk on them. The Buddha predicted that Megha would be a Buddha called Śākyamuni. After hearing this prophecy, Megha, conscious of his future enlightenment, endeavored to practice the six perfections of a bodhisattva. Thus, he represents exactly what the word *bodhisattva* means—a being destined for, or seeking, full enlightenment. This concept became commonly known by 100 B.C.E.[3]

The compound word *bodhisattva* can be analyzed in many ways, but only three interpretations are well attested in Buddhist literature: (1) In Pāli sūtras the Buddha often says, referring to his past experience: "When I was a bodhisattva, and not yet fully enlightened, it occurred to me that . . . ." The context clearly shows that *bodhi* means enlightenment and *satta* (*sattva*) a sentient being. *Bodhisattva* thus refers to a sentient being seeking full enlightenment. (2) The Pāli word *satta* can be equivalent to Skt. *sakta,* which means "attached to, devoted to." Buddhaghosa, the illustrious commentator on the Pāli Canon, takes the word *bodhisatta* to signify a being devoted to enlightenment. However, the *Sūtra on Perfect Wisdom in 8,000 Lines* and the one in *25,000 Lines* stress that a Mahāyāna bodhisattva should not be attached to anything, not even to enlightenment and Buddhahood, because perfect wisdom is empty of own-being. (3) The *Sūtra on Perfect Wisdom in 8,000 Lines* and the great commentators Haribhadra and Kumārajīva interpret *sattva* as meaning "intention" (*abhiprāya*), "mind" (*citta*), or "heroic mind" (cf. Vedic *satvan*), so that *bodhisattva* denotes a being whose mind or intention is directed toward full enlightenment.

In the *Sūtras on Perfect Wisdom* and other Mahāyāna sūtras the word *bodhisattva* is often combined with the word *mahāsattva* (a great being, or one who has great intention). Commenting on the words *bodhisattva mahāsattva* Haribhadra says:

> Bodhisattvas are these whose *sattva,* or intentions, are directed towards the completion of their own interests, namely, enlightenment as non-attachment to all things. One may contend that even *śrāvakas* (Hīnayāna monks) can be like that. Thus, the word *mahāsattva* is added. Those whose minds are directed towards the completion of great benefit for others are called *mahāsattvas.* An objection may be raised that a *mahāsattva* or a being with great altruistic mind can be found elsewhere, as in the case of a good non-Buddhist. Thus, the word *bodhisattva* is used as well.[4]

In India the bodhisattva concept developed in four stages: (1) Bodhisattva as Gautama before his enlightenment: Gautama from his birth in this historical world up to the time of his enlightenment, by which he became a Buddha, had been a bodhisattva, a religious practitioner aspiring to Buddhahood. He is sometimes called a bodhisattva even when in the Tuṣita Heaven before his birth in this world. (2) The *Jātaka:* Ancient Indian popular fables, in which not only men and women of all classes and professions but also animals, birds, and other creatures play major roles, were introduced into Buddhism. The Buddhist monastics identified the leading characters of the stories with the various incarnations of Gautama the Buddha in his innumerable former lives. Forbidden to listen to or to tell worldly stories, they resorted to this adaptation for the purpose of spreading Buddhist teachings. They called the protagonist of a story a bodhisattva. The stories were later incorporated into the Buddhist canon under the name of *Jātaka* or stories of the Buddha in his former births. (3) Heavenly bodhisattvas: Even before the appearance of Mahāyāna Buddhism heavenly saviors such as Avalokiteśvara, Maitreya, and Amitābha manifested themselves in response to the earnest desires of the suffering masses. These are beings of grace who save sinful people. Some of them, such as Avalokiteśvara and Maitreya, are called bodhisattvas, while others, such as Akṣobhya and Amitābha are addressed as Buddhas. Nevertheless, the former are to become Buddhas in the future, and the latter were bodhisattvas before their attainment of Buddhahood. (4) Bodhisattva as "any and every Mahāyāna Buddhist":[5] Mahāyāna sūtras taught the stūpa-worshipers that they should endeavor to become not arhats, the highest sages of Hīnayāna Buddhism, but Buddhas, by practicing the six perfections. Thus, all Mahāyāna followers, laity and monastics alike, came to be called bodhisattvas (seekers after Buddhahood) in distinction from śrāvakas (disciples, or Hīnayāna monks). In Mahāyāna sūtras many lay bodhisattvas appear as heroes and heroines.

Buddhist ethics and discipline were reformulated in light of the bodhisattva ideal. In Hīnayāna Buddhism monks and nuns observe two to three hundred precepts, but lay followers keep only five precepts. Mahāyāna sūtras advised sons and daughters of good families or bodhisattvas, lay as well as monastic, to abide by the path of the ten good acts, observing the following rules: (1) not to kill, (2) not to steal, (3) not to commit adultery, (4) not to tell lies, (5) not to use harsh words, (6) not to utter words causing enmity between people, (7) not to engage in idle talk, (8) not to be greedy, (9) not to be angry, (10) not to have wrong views. The first four coincide with the first four of the Hīnayāna lay precepts (the fifth was not to drink intoxicants). Shortly before the emergence of Mahāyāna, the "three learnings," consisting of precepts, meditation, and wisdom, which had been the fundamental practices since early Buddhism, were enlarged to make six perfections (pāramitā): charity (*dāna*), observation of precepts (*śīla*), perseverance (*kṣānti*), energy (*vīrya*), meditation (dhyāna) and wisdom (prajñā), of which the last, *prajñā-pāramitā*, is to guide the first five as their intimate principle. Perfection of wisdom, or perfect wisdom, is the wisdom of emptiness, which constitutes the omniscience of a Buddha, and which is the true nature of all things (*dharmatā*). The first five remain merely worldly good practices unless they are founded on perfect wisdom; just as blind persons without a guide cannot reach their destination, as the sūtra adds. Each of them comes to be called "perfect" only upon being accompanied by the sixth, perfect wisdom. While other Mahāyāna sūtras, especially the *Lotus Sūtra,* encourage people to worship stūpas, the *Sūtras on Perfect Wisdom* teach that the omniscience or perfect wisdom of a Buddha is far more important and worthy of respect than the remains of his body contained in a stūpa. *Prajñāpāramitā* is the mother of all Buddhas, for all of them were enlightened by its guidance and protection. This idea led to the development of two significant aspects of Mahāyāna Buddhism: (1) Buddhist followers were advised to *copy a sūtra* rather than to worship a stūpa, and even to this day, the copying of a sūtra, especially of the *Heart Sūtra*, is practiced widely by Japanese lay Buddhists. (2) The concept of the *Body of Truth* (*dharmakāya*) appeared perhaps around 200 B.C.E.[6] The *Sūtras on Perfect Wisdom* stressed that a Buddha should be regarded not as a physical body (*rūpakāya*), but as the Body of Truth.

The spiritual and ethical originality of Mahāyāna Buddhism is shown also in its reinterpretation of the *twelve-membered dependent origination* in terms of emptiness. The abhidharmists explained the twelve-membered dependent origination as the process of a sentient being's transmigration. This "periodic theory of dependent origination" was first expounded in the *Jñānaprasthāna* and finally systematized in the *Mahāvibhāṣā* (ca. second century C.E.). The completion of the theory coincides chronologically with the appearance of Mahāyāna Buddhism. The Sarvāstivādin asserted that each of the twelve members of the dependent origination is endowed with the five aggregates (skandha) or all elements of body and mind, but is named according to the element that prevails most strongly in the given period or stage of an individual's life. The school regarded the first two members, "ignorance" and "volition" (saṃskāra), as belonging to one's past life; the eight members from "consciousness' (*vijñāna*) to "existence" (*bhava*) as belonging to the present life, and the last two members, "birth" (*jāti*) and "old age and death" (*jarāmaraṇa*), as belonging to the future life. Thus, the twelve-membered dependent origination came to mean the transmigration of a being who, owing to his ignorance and evil deeds (volition) during his past life, comes to be born in the womb of a woman as a group of elements represented by consciousness, consolidates his individuality (name-form), develops organs (six organs), comes out of his mother's womb, cognizes (contact) and feels (feeling) external objects, and accumulates passions (desire, attachment) and evil deeds (existence) in the present life to be reborn (birth) in the future, in which he repeats the same process of suffering (old age and death).[7]

Mahāyāna Buddhists conceded that this was the most distinguished traditional interpretation, but tried to transcend it without losing its conventional or moral significance. As Schopenhauer said, a great truth that promises salvation needs a vehicle of myth to descend to the world of practical use. The doctrine of karmic retribution and transmigration is the vehicle of the truth of Buddhism in the moral sphere. The periodic interpretation of the twelve-membered dependent origination is a realist myth created for the purpose of relating morality to religion. What was the Mahāyāna alternative? The sixth chapter of the *Daśabhūmika-sūtra* gives ten different interpretations of the twelve-membered dependent origination, in apparent conformity with the Sarvāstivāda theory of transmigration. But at the end comes the sudden statement: "The bodhisattva perceives by the wisdom of enlightenment that there is no self, no sentient being, no life, no human being, no substance, and that dependent origination is empty of an individual who acts and suffers." The *Śālistamba-sūtra,* which the Mādhyamikas revered, also explains the twelve-membered dependent origination according to the Sarvāstivāda interpretation. But it adds:

> No subject migrates from this world to the other, but merely the effects of deeds appear when their causes and conditions are all provided. Just as the reflection of your face is seen on the clean surface of a mirror not because the face moves onto the surface of the mirror but only because all the causes and conditions are present, just so the effect of a deed appears not because someone, dying in this world, is born in the other. . . . Fire does not burn when any of its causes and conditions is lacking, but it burns when all its causes and conditions arise. In the same way, a seed of consciousness, produced by karma and defilements, comes to be born in the womb of a woman, and produces the sprout of name-form, provided that none of the causes and conditions is missing, although, like space and illusion, all these things do not belong to anyone nor are they possessed by anybody. (T 16.823a14–24)

Transfer of Merits and the Beginning of Pure Land

The Buddhist theory of transmigration in the five courses, which seems to have been established in the late third century B.C.E. around the time of the first schism of the Buddhist order,[8] also underwent a radical transformation in Mahāyāna thought. The five courses, or five forms of sentient life, comprise the inhabitants of hell, hungry ghosts (*preta*), animals, human beings, and celestial beings. Later a widespread form of the theory added devils (*asura*) between the animals and human beings. Every sentient being leads either the relatively happy life to which celestial beings and humans ascend, or the miserable life which is the lot of hungry ghosts, animals, and the inhabitants of hell—a matter determined by one's past deeds. Even if one is born in heaven, one must fall into the human world or hell once one has exhausted the merits of past good deeds. A sentient being transmigrates infinitely, life after life, through the five forms in their respective worlds. This contrasts with Zoroastrian or Christian eschatology, in which the individual is believed to go to a determined place eternally. A good deed, however meritorious it may be, promises the performer only temporary happiness in heaven or in the human world, which is not the place of supreme bliss but merely one of the worlds in which he transmigrates. As transmigration is a principle which relates good or bad deeds to happy or unhappy results, moral virtue is not sufficient to liberate a being from the world of transmigration. Celestial beings, though happier than humans, were also in need of being saved. Ancient Indian polytheism had no creator God who saved souls by grace, so there could be no principle of salvation in the doctrine of transmigration. Before the rise of the cults of Viṣṇu and Amitābha, the only principle that emancipated one from transmigration was mystic intuition. In the Upanishads it was intuition of the identity of an individual self and Brahman, the absolute, cosmic principle; in Buddhism it was realization of the disappearance of defilement and suffering. In both Buddhism and Brahmanism this intuition could be attained through meditation (yoga), a way open only to a small religious elite.

The two principles of karmic retribution and transmigration taught by Hīnayāna Buddhism are (1) good and evil deeds produce corresponding happiness and suffering; and (2) the results return to none other than the performer of the deeds. However, ideas that opposed and transcended the two principles began to appear in the later Pāli literature and in abhidharmic philosophy. Finally, in the *Sūtra on Perfect Wisdom in 8,000 Lines* the concept of *parināmanā,* which means merit transfer as well as merit transformation, emerged. Apace with the development of the doctrine of transfer and transformation of merit, gods of grace such as Viṣṇu and Amitābha manifested themselves in response to the quest of suffering people. Many stories in the *Petavatthu* of the Pāli Canon indicate that divine beings, hungry ghosts, and other inaccessible beings are unable to receive offerings directly from a donor, and that to be of benefit to them one should make offerings directly to a virtuous monk or a Buddhist community, by which act one can transfer merits to them. The abhidharmic *Jñānaprasthāna* and *Abhidharmakośabhāṣya* say that Buddhas or arhats can transform karma that ripens as life into karma that ripens as happiness, or vice versa, thus curtailing or prolonging their life-span. These texts, although not yet using the term *parināmanā,* already express the idea that karma and merit are transferable from one person to another, and that their content can be altered, contrary to the above two principles of karmic retribution. According to the *Sūtra on Perfect Wisdom in 8,000 Lines* the six practices of a bodhisattva, which are themselves deeds of worldly good, are transformed into omniscience, whereby they come to be called six perfections (pāramitā); the sūtra also talks about transformation of merits of good deeds—that is, happiness—into supreme and perfect enlightenment, which is unworldly wisdom.

The theme of gods of grace underlies the beginning of the Pure Land tradition. According to the *Great Amitābha Sūtra,* which represents the oldest form of the *Sukhāvatīvyūha-sūtra,*[9] Dharmākara, the boddhisattva, prior to becoming Buddha Amitābha, says in the fifth of his twenty-four vows:

> If innumerable beings, including heavenly beings, human beings, and even insects which fly and wriggle, despite the fact that they have committed evils in their former lives, after hearing my name when I shall have become a Buddha, should direct their thoughts incessantly to being born in my country, and should reflect upon themselves, repent their misdeeds, perform good acts for the cause of Buddhism, and recite sūtras, then I will cause them to be born in my country without their going back to hell and the states of animals and hungry ghosts; and if they so wish, I will make them Buddhas by virtue of this vow of mine. If this vow of mine is not realized, then may I not become a Buddha. (T 12.301b14–20; author's translation)

Thus Amitābha is able to cause all sentient beings, including the most defiled, to be born in his Buddha-land and to become Buddhas by transferring to sentient beings the merits accumulated during his eons of religious practice.

According to the *Larger Sukhāvatīvyūha-sūtra,* in the immeasurably distant past, after hearing the Buddha Lokeśvararāja's sermon, the boddhisattva Dharmākara made forty-eight primal vows to save all sentient beings. After obtaining Buddhahood, he would possess infinite light and infinite life; his own land would be superior to all other Buddha-lands, an ideal country without defilement, suffering, or delusion, and those who believed in him and who sincerely desired to be born into his country would have all their wishes realized and could there pursue perfect religious lives leading to Buddhahood. After immeasurable years of discipline, filled with difficulties, Dharmākara, who had vowed that he would not become a Buddha until all his vows had been fulfilled, finally obtained Buddhahood. He is called Amitābha. He is now preaching his doctrine and calling to all people, promising that they will be born into his country by simply thinking of him. Designated *Sukhāvatī,* or Land of Bliss, his country lies to the west beyond countless Buddha-lands. Both the *Larger* and the *Smaller Sukhāvatīvyūha* sūtras[10] describe its features in detail, exhausting the hyperbolical power of Indian imagination to express its wonders, both religious and worldly. In Mahāyāna such vows were made by all bodhisattvas. However, Dharmākara, after examining all the vows of Buddhas and bodhisattvas and their countries, made his vows to establish a country that surpassed all the Buddha-lands. In portraying Amitābha and the Land of Bliss as supreme among the innumerable Buddhas and Buddha-lands, the two sūtras succeeded in conferring on them a quite distinctive status in subsequent piety.

A Mahāyāna bodhisattva can be compared to one who leads across an endless desert a large caravan of rough-tempered young men, ignorant old men, women and children, camels and horses, bearing a great number of commodities. Such a task requires strong resolution and thorough preparation, to a degree unimaginable to minor merchants aiming at their own prosperity (Hīnayānists seeking only their own salvation). Before starting, the leader must prepare water and provisions; he must be familiar with the geographical features of the route and be able to foresee all the danger and damage that might occur. He needs wisdom to discern the minds of the people, practical knowledge, ingenuity, expedient measures against emergencies, and compassion in order to lead the group to their destination without losing one of them, enduring all hardships by himself alone. The bodhisattva's vow is like the travel plan of this caravan leader. It is permeated by a valiant spirit and an exhaustive knowledge of people's ignorance and evil passions. It reckons the causes and conditions of delusions and sufferings and projects the people's delight and prosperity upon their arrival at their destination. The people who follow this leader have absolute trust and are filled with happiness before they start on the journey. Amitābha worship in its oldest form in India and in its later developments in China and Japan regarded pure faith in Amitābha, thinking of him, or recitation of his name as the sole condition necessary for one's rebirth in the Land of Bliss. However, in India and Central Asia, where worship of Amitābha spread widely in the early centuries C.E., meditation on Amitābha in which the Buddha is visualized as a *manifestation of the Truth of Emptiness* also came to be an important feature of this type of Buddhism. The *Pratyutpanna-buddha-saṃmukhāvasthita-samādhi-sūtra* (T 13.897) stresses that one is able to see Buddha Amitābha and listen to his preaching while in deep meditation, without going to Sukhāvatī, using divine eyes and other supernatural powers, and that, hence, Amitābha is nothing other than one's mind which is empty of own-being. The Buddha neither comes from any place nor goes anywhere; he appears and disappears according to the sufficiency and insufficiency of causes and conditions, such as a worshiper's earnest desire to see him, deep meditation, and so forth. The *Amitāyur-dhyāna-sūtra* (T 12.340) also describes in detail how to meditate on Amitābha and his Buddha-land in order to gain a clear vision of both. This sūtra, too, identifies Amitābha with the meditator's mind, on the grounds that the Buddha is nothing but mind full of compassion.

Vasubandhu, in his commentary on the *Sukhāvatīvyūha*, after enumerating and praising seventeen kinds of supernatural embellishments or merits of the Land of Bliss, eight of Amitābha, and four of bodhisattvas in the Land of Bliss, says that all twenty-nine can be summed up in One True Word (*eka-dharma-pada*), "purity" (*pariśuddhi*), and that purity means the Unconditioned Dharma-Body (*asaṃskṛta-dharmakāya*) as True Wisdom. This purity is twofold: pure environment and the purity of sentient beings. The former refers to the Land of Sukhāvatī embellished by the seventeen kinds of merit, and the latter to Amitābha endowed with the eight embellishments and the bodhisattvas endowed with the four embellishments. Thus, it is the purity of the Unconditioned Dharma-Body as True Wisdom which manifests itself as Amitābha, the bodhisattvas, and Sukhāvatī. As "purity" is another name for emptiness (śūnyatā), Vasubandhu actually sees Amitābha, the bodhisattvas, and Sukhāvatī as being no different from emptiness, which in turn reveals itself as the three. In the same commentary Vasubandhu stresses that a worshiper of Amitābha should pursue five mental practices, which include concentrating one's mind (*śamatha*) with serious desire to be born in the Land of Bliss, and observing in meditation the physical and mental splendors of the Land of Bliss, Amitābha, and the bodhisattvas residing in the Land (*vipaśyanā*). Therefore, to Vasubandhu, meditation was the central practice of the cult of Amitābha.

Notes

1. *The Mahābhārata,* Books 2–3, trans. J. A. B. Van Buitnen (Chicago: University of Chicago Press, 1975) 593–97; *Cakkavatti-sīhanāda-suttanta, Dīgha Nikāya,* No. 26; *Sukhāvatīvyūha,* Section on Five Sins, in T 12, No. 362, 361, 360; *Fu-fa-tsang-yin-yüan-ch'uan,* T 50.315–17.

2. A. Hirakawa, *Shoki daijō no kenkyū* (Studies on Early Mahāyāna Buddhism) (Tokyo: Shunjūsha, 1968) 617–43.

3. A. L. Basham, "The Evolution of the Concept of the Bodhisattva," in *The Bodhisattva Doctrine in Buddhism,* ed. Leslie S. Kawamura.

4. See Y. Kajiyama, "On the Meanings of the Words 'Bodhisattva' and 'Mahāsattva' in Prajñāpāramitā Literature," in *Indological and Buddhist Studies,* ed. L. A. Hercus et al. (Canberra: Faculty of Asian Studies, The Australian National University, 1982).

5. M. Shizutani, *Shoki daijō Bukkyō no seiritsu katei* (The Process of Formation of Early Mahāyāna Buddhism) (Kyoto: Hyakkaen, 1974) 238ff.

6. The word "Body of Truth" does not appear in the earliest layer of the *Sūtra on Perfect Wisdom in 8,000 Lines* (cf. Chinese version, T 8.425ff.); Nāgārjuna (150–250 C.E.), however, uses the word.

7.

Cause [past life]:	1. *avidyā* (ignorance)
	2. *saṃskāra* (volition = *karman*)
Effect [present life]:	3. *vijñāna* (consciousness)
	4. *nāma-rūpa* (name-form)
	5. *sadāyatana* (six organs)
	6. *sparśa* (contact)
	7. *vedanā* (feeling)
Cause [present life]:	8. *tṛṣṇā* (desire)
	9. *upādāna* (attachment)
	10. *bhava* (existence = *karman*)
Effect [future life]:	11. *jāti* (birth)
	12. *jarā-marana* (old age and death)

8. See *Samyutta Nikāya,* V, 474ff.; *Samyukta Āgama,* T 2.114; *Smaller Samyukta Āgama,* T 2.488. Agreement of the theory in the Pāli and Chinese scriptures suggests its early origin.

9. The *Larger Sukhāvatīvyūha-sūtra,* extant in the Sanskrit original and a Tibetan translation, represents a later development of the sūtra. Among the five Chinese translations,

the so-called *Great Amitābha Sūtra* (T 12.300, No. 362), which is inferred by scholars to be a pre-Mahāyāna sūtra, retains the oldest form of the *Sukhāvatīvyūha*. In China and Japan, however, a Chinese translation (T 12.265, No. 360) of the *Larger Sukhāvatīvyūha* is regarded as the standard sūtra.

10. In Pure Land Buddhism in China and Japan the *Larger Sukhāvatīvyūha* (T 12.265, No. 360), *Smaller Sukhāvatīvyūha* (T 12.346, No. 366), and *Amitāyur-dhyāna-sūtra* (T 12.340, No. 365) form the basic sūtras on Pure Land doctrine, being called "the Three Sūtras."

Bibliography

Sources

Conze, Edward. *The Short Prajñāpāramitā Texts.* Totowa, NJ: Rowman & Littlefield, 1974.

——. *The Perfection of Wisdom in Eight Thousand Lines.* Bolinas, CA: Four Seasons Foundation, 1975.

——. *The Large Sutra on Perfect Wisdom.* Berkeley: University of California Press, 1975.

——. *Buddhist Wisdom Books.* London: Allen & Unwin, 1975.

Cowell, E. B., Max Müller, and J. Takakusu. *Buddhist Mahāyāna Texts.* Delhi: Motilal Banarsidass, 1965.

Lamotte, Étienne. *Le traité de la grande vertu de sagesse.* Louvain: Bureaux du Muséon, 1944–80.

Studies

Conze, Edward. *The Prajñāpāramitā Literature.* 's-Gravenhage: Mouton, 1960. Reprint, Tokyo: Reiyūkai, 1978.

——. *Thirty Years of Buddhist Studies.* Columbia: University of South Carolina Press, 1968.

Dayal, Har. *The Bodhisattva Doctrine in Buddhist Sanskrit Literature.* Delhi: Motilal Banarsidass, 1975.

Dutt, Nalinaksha. *Aspects of Mahāyāna Buddhism and its Relation to Hīnayāna.* London: Luzac, 1930. Reprinted as *Mahāyāna Buddhism.* Calcutta: Firma K. L. Mukhopadhyaya, 1973.

Hirakawa, Akira. "The Rise of Mahāyāna Buddhism and its Relationship to the Worship of Stūpas." *Memoirs of the Tōyō Bunko Research Department* 22 (1963) 57–106.

Kawamura, Leslie S., ed. *The Bodhisattva Doctrine in Buddhism.* Waterloo, Ont.: Wilfrid Laurier University Press, 1981.

Kimura, R. *A Historical Study of the Terms Hīnayāna and Mahāyāna.* Calcutta: Calcutta University, 1927.

Lamotte, Étienne. "Sur la formation du Mahāyāna." In *Asiatica: Festschrift Friedrich Weller,* 377–96. Leipzig: Harrassowitz, 1954.

Prajñāpāramitā and Related Systems: Studies in Honor of Edward Conze. Edited by Lewis Lancaster. Berkeley: University of California Press, 1977.

II. *The Vimalakīrti Sūtra*

NAGAO GAJIN

THE VIMALAKĪRTI-NIRDEŚA-SŪTRA (Sūtra Expounded by Vimalakīrti) is one of the earliest Mahāyāna sūtras that followed the prototype of the *Prajñāpāramitā-sūtra;* it dates from before the second century C.E. The Sanskrit original is lost. There were no fewer than seven Chinese translations, the most popular being that of Kumārajīva. The ninth-century Tibetan translation retains the flavor of the Sanskrit.

The name Vimalakīrti means "one who has a spotless fame." He is a rich citizen of Vaiśāli (present Besarh). Although a layman, his understanding of the Buddha's teaching is profound and he is called a "bodhisattva" by the Buddha; the depiction of the bodhisattva ideal under his name is perhaps one of the intentions of the sūtra. Vimalakīrti is clearly not a historical person, though there may have been a historical prototype.

The sūtra has several unique characteristics. First, as its title indicates, it mainly consists of the eloquent discussions of this layman, while the Buddha Śākyamuni's sermons occupy little space. The title "sūtra" is merited because Vimalakīrti's wise utterances won the approval of the Buddha. Second, the work skillfully employs dramatic technique. Many characters appear on the stage in dialogue with the protagonist. His lucid eloquence, with its puzzling paradoxes, incisive wit, and bitter irony, overwhelms his interlocutors. Third, the idea of śūnyatā (emptiness) is extensively expounded, clarified, and deepened. The entire work is permeated by an air of śūnyatā; this sūtra is more "empty" than the *Prajñāpāramitā-sūtra.*

The sūtra consists of twelve chapters in the Tibetan version.[1] The first chapter, the prologue of the drama, begins with the hymns to the Buddha by Ratnākara and five hundred other youths. In answer to their questions, the Buddha teaches them what the Buddha's land, the Pure Land, is. For the Buddha, all sentient beings, their mental activities, are the Buddha-land that he cultivates, changing the defiled land into the Pure Land. The sūtra declares: "When the mind is pure, the land is pure." This is the orthodox interpretation of the Pure Land. The idea of śūnyatā is implied here, for only when things are empty can defilement be converted into purity.

Vimalakīrti appears for the first time in the second chapter. He is lying in bed, ill, but his illness is not physical. It is the illness of a bodhisattva:

"because sentient beings are all sick, I am also sick." At that time, the Buddha Śākyamuni was staying with his disciples in a suburb of Vaiśāli. He wants to send somebody to inquire after Vimalakīrti's health and requests the ten great disciples and four bodhisattvas to take on this task, but none of them are willing to do so, because all of them have had experiences of being cruelly embarrassed by Vimalakīrti on certain issues. They confess this one by one (chap. 3). These confessions reveal Vimalakīrti's sharp-witted personality, which is nothing other than an embodiment of śūnyatā. Bodhisattva Mañjuśrī sighs with admiration: "Vimalakīrti is a person hard to deal with, subtle in reasoning and eloquent in speech, master of paradox and of rigorous logic. There is nobody who can stand up against his wit and eloquence."

However, in the end it is Mañjuśrī who reluctantly accepts the duty of visiting Vimalakīrti. A multitude of people who want to observe the dialogue between these two great sages follow from behind. Being aware of this, Vimalakīrti empties his small sick room and welcomes them inside. The dialogue which occupies chapters 4 to 9 is full of sharp-witted debates whose frequently paradoxical tenor may be illustrated by Vimalakīrti's welcome to his visitor: "In a way not coming, you have come; in a way not meeting, we have met." Mañjuśrī answers in a similarly enigmatic way. After this exchange, although both are aware that Vimalakīrti is only pretending to be ill, they discuss the significance of inquiring after illness and the real nature of illness. They move on to such themes as wisdom and skillful means, the domain of the bodhisattva (chap. 4), the meaning of Dharma, the supreme doctrine of "inconceivable liberation" (chap. 5), love toward sentient beings, the baselessness of life (a goddess joins them at this point, chap. 6). In chapter 7, after explaining the bodhisattva's way of practice in an entirely paradoxical fashion, Vimalakīrti answers a question about the family of a bodhisattva: "The perfection of wisdom (*prajñāpāramitā*) is his mother, skillfulness in means (*upāyakauśalya*), his father."

The climactic chapter 8 elucidates the doctrine of nonduality. Thirty-one bodhisattvas explain one by one what the nonduality of the world means. Lastly, Mañjuśrī, the thirty-second, explains it perfectly, saying that nonduality lies in excluding all words, not expressing anything, not designating anything. Contrary to these explanations in words and concepts, however, Vimalakīrti in his turn remains perfectly silent. Mañjuśrī applauds this total silence. This utter negation of words is celebrated in Sino-Japanese tradition and there is a saying: "Vimalakīrti's silence rolled like thunder." When the ultimate truth is experienced, it surpasses all verbal expression and is represented only by silence. Yet without some device of communication the ultimate truth can never be manifested. Chapter 9 deals profoundly with the problem of how to expound the Dharma. In this world, the Buddha

Śākyamuni is forced to employ "severe words" such as *hell* or *heaven*, *good* or *bad*, *false* or *true*, *death* or *birth*. The concluding chapters 10 to 12 deal with the Buddha's activities in the whole universe, the doctrine of "the exhaustible and the inexhaustible," and the inexistence of the Tathāgata in the realm of time and space.

At the end of the sūtra, as is usually the case in the Mahāyāna sūtras, the sūtra is entrusted to Maitreya and Ānanda and its name is explained. Three names are given: (1) Exposition by Vimalakīrti, (2) Establishment of Paired and Inverted Phrases,[2] and (3) Chapter of the Inconceivable Liberation. The first is the ordinary name. The third refers to chapter 5. It is puzzling that the second appears only in the Tibetan version. I understand "inverted" here to mean "contradictory" or "paradoxical" and the whole title to mean "paradoxical phrases in pairs are well established by Vimalakīrti," an appropriate description of the characteristics of this sūtra.

The keynote of this sūtra is śūnyatā, which is associated with such notions as inconceivability, inexpressibility, nonduality, and total equality. In Sino-Japanese tradition, Vimalakīrti's sickroom is understood to be a small ten-foot-square room. When Vimalakīrti empties this room, the idea of emptiness is already suggested. In receiving the multitude of guests who followed Mañjuśrī, or, later (chap. 5), in receiving thirty-two thousand huge "lion-chairs" sent from the faraway world of the Tathāgata Merupradīparāja, his small empty room did not become cramped. All these miracles are possible only in the world of śūnyatā. Śūnyatā is radical nothingness in which all worldly beings are denied, but this nothingness is the true foundation for the existence of anything whatever. Only through Vimalakīrti's silence (=śūnyatā) is his sharp-witted talk or any exposition of the Dharma (chap. 9) possible. Śūnyatā is called "the baseless base" (chap. 6) because, though itself empty, it is the basis for everything. Only through the death of "nothingness" is the real being of everything revived and resurrected. Realization of śūnyatā means realization of this nothingness and at the same time realization of everythingness. It is simultaneously negation and affirmation.

Therefore, the expression of śūnyatā necessarily takes a paradoxical form: "A bodhisattva is not a bodhisattva, therefore he is a bodhisattva." Phrases of this kind are frequently encountered in the *Prajñāpāramitā* sūtras. Similar paradoxes of śūnyatā are: "Nirvāna is attained without severing defilements (*kleśa*)" (chap. 3); "one follows the way of poverty and yet possesses boundless treasures" (chap. 7); Vimalakīrti's advice to Mahākāśyapa: "You should beg alms in order not to receive alms" (chap. 3); or his reply to Mañjuśrī's question how a bodhisattva practices the way of the Buddha-dharma: "When a bodhisattva follows the wrong way, he follows the way to attain the Buddhahood" (chap. 7).

In this sūtra, Māra, the Tempter, appears several times. Vimalakīrti declares: "All Māras and all heretics are my family members" (chap. 4). "The Māras who play the devil in the innumerable universes of the ten quarters are all bodhisattvas who are abiding in the inconceivable liberation" (chap. 5). Actually, it seems that Vimalakīrti himself is one of those Māra-bodhisattvas in that he severely attacked and cruelly embarrassed the great disciples and bodhisattvas with his keen eloquence. However, it is also true that in our ordinary world the most evil one often pretends to be the supreme one, or a devil appears (to some believers) as if a god, as the case of Bodhisattva Jagatīmdhara (chap. 3) suggests. Māra, surrounded by twelve thousand heavenly daughters, approaches Jagatīmdhara in the guise of the god Indra and proposes to offer these daughters to the bodhisattva as his servants. Vimalakīrti appears and exposes the true identity of Māra; he takes these daughters as his own servants, and, preaching to them, converts their minds from carnal desire to the pleasure of faith in the Dharma. When the daughters have to return to Māra's palace, Vimalakīrti gives them a famous lesson called "inexhaustible lamp." When from a single lamp new lamps are lighted one after another endlessly, the light, no matter how feeble it may be, will never go out, but increase in brilliance. In a similar way, as the Dharma is transmitted from one to another, the good increases, never diminishes. This story suggests the immortality of virtue. It is especially interesting to note that the light of Dharma could be ignited even in Mara's palace, where the darkness of evil prevails.

The sūtra often deals with the problem of how to teach the Dharma. In chap. 3 we hear how Vimalakīrti criticized the preaching methods of Maudgalyāyana and Pūrna. Chapter 9 describes how in the land named Supreme Fragrance, the Dharma is taught only through using scents, and people are enlightened by fragrance, while in our world, the *Sahā*-world, the Buddha Śākyamuni is obliged to make use of "severe words," because the sentient beings here are so hard-hearted that they can be tamed only in this way. This passage, together with the story of Vimalakīrti's silence, is a suggestive comment on the limitations of language in general and the missionary problem in particular.

The wit and irony of the sūtra are also products of śūnyatā. Śāriputra, wisest of the Buddha's disciples, plays the role of a clown in this drama. Listening to the dialogue between Mañjuśrī and Vimalakīrti, he feels anxious about chairs (chap. 5) or worries about the noon meal of the assembly (chap. 9), while Vimalakīrti jeers: "Did you come to seek the true Dharma or to search for chairs?" He is also teased by a goddess who has long lived in Vimalakīrti's house (chap. 6). Overwhelmed by her wisdom and eloquence, Śāriputra asks her, "Why do you not transform your woman's body?" However, after discussing womanhood, the goddess, through her power of superknowledge, changes Śāriputra into the likeness of a goddess, and her own body into the likeness of Śāriputra, and says, "Why do you not transform your woman's body?" But Śāriputra can do nothing. The banter of the goddess continues: "If you can transform this woman's body, then all women should be able to transform themselves too. Just as you are a woman now, so are all women women." What the goddess attacks here is Śāriputra's attachment to discrimination—between nirvāṇa and saṃsāra, male and female, and so on. In śūnyatā, such discrimination disappears; hence, "in all things there is neither male nor female." And yet the goddess is naturally a woman, just as Śāriputra is naturally a man.

The sūtra has enjoyed immense popularity wherever Mahāyāna has prevailed. Especially in the East, from China to Japan, it has been devoutly studied by many monk-scholars, and many literati were also familiar with it. More than sixteen Chinese commentaries are edited in the Chinese Tripiṭaka, and ten additional ones, mostly fragmentary, have been discovered in Tun-huang. In Japan at least five commentaries have been composed. The dialogue of Mañjuśrī and Vimalakīrti is a common theme of the frescoes and sculptures of Tun-huang, Yün-kang, and Hōryūji, and there are excellent statues of Vimalakīrti in Kōfukuji, Hokkeji, and other temples in Japan. There are many translations into modern languages: Lamotte's is the most academic and is fully annotated, and Thurman's, the most recent, is very readable.

Notes

1. I follow the Tibetan numbering.
2. For the discussion of this title, see the introduction to Lamotte's translation.

Bibliography

L'enseignement de Vimalakīrti. Translated by Étienne Lamotte. Louvain: Publications universitaires, 1962. Eng. trans. *The Teaching of Vimalakīrti,* rendered into English by Sara Boin. London: Pali Text Society, 1976.

The Holy Teaching of Vimalakīrti: A Mahāyāna Scripture. Translated by Robert A. F. Thurman. University Park, PA, and London: Pennsylvania State University Press, 1976.

Lu, K'uan Yü (Charles Luk). *The Vimalakīrti Nirdeśa Sūtra.* Berkeley and London: Shambhala, 1972.

III. *The Avataṃsaka-Sūtra*

Luis O. Gómez

Although in East Asia the *Avataṃsaka-sūtra* (Chinese *Hua-yen ching;* Japanese *Kegon-kyō*) is cherished in different schools of Buddhism for its subtle and profound philosophy, it never achieved the popularity of the *Lotus* or the *Heart Sūtra.* Its teachings and imagery are abstruse, and it is not a single literary piece but an unwieldy compilation of disparate texts held together by a thin narrative thread. Attempts to synthesize this heterogeneous collection were made only for a brief though fruitful period in China from the mid-seventh to the early ninth century. The Chinese school of interpretation known as the Hua-yen Tsung provided the philosophical basis for subsequent projects of doctrinal synthesis in East Asian Buddhism. Unfortunately, there were no equally comprehensive efforts elsewhere in the Buddhist world. An interpretation of the meaning of the text in its Indian context is thus hampered by the absence of an exegetical tradition.

Everything suggests that the sūtra was originally composed in Buddhist Sanskrit. Unfortunately, only two books survive in the original language: the *Daśabhūmika-sūtra* (On the Ten Stages of the Bodhisattva), and the *Gaṇḍavyūha-sūtra* (On Multiple Manifestations). These texts circulated in India and China as independent works. No references to the *Avataṃsaka* as a corpus, or to the title *Buddha-avataṃsaka-sūtra,* are found in Indian scholastic or exegetical literature. We must rely, therefore, on extra-Indian sources for the title of the text, as well as for most of our information on its plan and contents. The title conveys the double meaning of "Discourse Describing the Buddha's Garlands (Ornaments)" and "Discourse Describing Garlands (interconnected series) of Buddhas." Three "complete" versions of the whole collection survive, one in a Tibetan translation and two in Chinese translation: the "*Avataṃsaka* in 60 Scrolls," translated by Buddhabhadra and his staff from 418 to 420 C.E., and the "*Avataṃsaka* in 80 Scrolls," translated by Śikṣānanda's team between 695 and 699.[1]

The work developed gradually, either by accretion, through the incorporation of whole texts into a fluid collection, or by piecemeal expansion and interpolation on the framework of a "primitive" *Buddha-avataṃsaka-sūtra.*

If the *Avataṃsaka* did not grow from one germ text, but includes preexistent texts or sets of texts, it does not make much sense to ask for the original text of the sūtra. However, if one assumes that there is a certain plan to the collection, and that this plan reflects the "intention" of earlier strata in its composition, one may propose a single line of development. It seems highly probable that the final compilation took place in Central Asia, where the work was already known by the middle of the fourth century. At least from that date on, many Buddhists have regarded it as a single work with a specific message. We shall adopt this view as a working hypothesis here.

Paul Demiéville described the *Avataṃsaka* collection as a genre of Buddhist literature "characterized by overflowing visionary images, which multiply everything to infinity, by a type of monadology that teaches the interpenetration of the one whole and the particularized many, of spirit and matter" and by "the notion of a gradual progress towards liberation through successive stages and an obsessive preference for images of light and radiance."[2] D. T. Suzuki prized the work for its historical significance and profound religious meaning. He called it "the climax of Indian creative imagination" and summarized its teaching as the "balancing of unity and multiplicity or, better, the merging of self with others."[3] The grandeur of its vision is achieved through an original combination and poetic elaboration of earlier notions of (1) the visionary powers of meditation, (2) causal interdependence, (3) the equality or sameness of all things in emptiness, and (4) the freedom of those who experience emptiness. Buddhas and bodhisattvas are able to reveal or give sensory form to the reality of emptiness by displaying the universe as one sees it in enlightenment—with all things equally empty, equally dependent on each other. In plan and structure, as well as in doctrine and imagery, the work expresses the complexity of the universe as reflected in the unity of enlightenment. Its imposing structure embodies the plurality of spiritual paths that lead to the awakening of Buddhas, and the infinite opportunity and forms open to enlightened beings for the manifestation of the one, fundamental enlightenment. It is, the most common metaphor states, as if the higher contemplative states (samādhi) of Buddhas and bodhisattvas manifested a universe on the tip of every hair on their bodies, and each of these universes in turn reflected all other worlds. Accordingly, Far Eastern exegesis of the sūtra considers that its main topic is the world seen from the perspective of perfect enlightenment, from the Plane of Dharma (*dharmadhātu*). In this way the tradition recognizes that the *Avataṃsaka* is a visionary text (Demiéville) as well as a summary of the deepest meaning of Buddhist thought (Suzuki).

The collection centers on the figure of the Buddha Vairocana, whose name ("Sun" or "Sunlight") conveys the idea of an awakened being who is a source of light and life for the whole universe. This Buddha, therefore, stands for the underlying presence of enlightenment and its manifestation in all things. In mythic time and space, Vairocana appears as the Buddha of a universe called the Lotus Universe.[4] Connections between this universe and the conventional world in which we move are established by various means: the identity is explicitly recognized; the Lotus Universe is declared to be the field in which former Buddhas practiced the Path; the Lotus Universe appears in the same spot where the Buddha sits; the Lotus Universe contains all world systems; the three times, past, present, and future, are said to be manifested simultaneously in Vairocana's samādhi.

The close link between the experiences of Vairocana, Śākyamuni, and the bodhisattvas is established at the opening of the sūtra, where the mythic and doctrinal stage for the rest of the work is set:

> At one time the Buddha was staying in the country of Magadha, at the site where he practiced the forest discipline, and had attained awakening. He had just attained Perfect Awakening. The place upon which he sat was of solid diamond (vajra), resting upon a circle of splendid jewels, upon a lotus formed by many jewels. Pure Maṇi jewels were his ornament; a sea of all possible colors appeared in all directions without end. Banners embroidered with Maṇi jewels emitted dazzling lights incessantly, producing marvelous sounds. . . . A forest of jewel-trees appeared, with shining branches and leaves. By virtue of the Tathāgata's extraordinary psychic powers, the Tree of Enlightenment emitted marvelous voices, explaining the nature of all things. . . .
>
> From Buddha-fields in the ten directions came bodhisattvas as many as all the dust particles in the world-system. . . .
>
> All of these bodhisattvas in the distant past had collected the roots of good in the company of Vairocana the Tathāgata. With him they had practiced the bodhisattva career. As a result of this, they could now perceive the three worlds in all samādhis. (T 10.1b–5b)

As in this passage, throughout the *Avataṃsaka* Śākyamuni Buddha is the central figure. Yet Vairocana Buddha is constantly in the background, either as the source of the power and virtue of all Buddhas and bodhisattvas or as the former Buddha of mythical time. In the same manner, though he never speaks, Śākyamuni is consistently seen as the source of the arrays of cosmic manifestation appearing throughout the text. His mouthpieces are the bodhisattvas who participate in or form part of the apparitions created by his samādhis. Through the power of his mental concentration, he transforms the world of the ordinary into the world of spiritual visions. The bodhisattvas use similar powers to manifest their state of freedom (inconceivable liberation, *acintya-vimokṣa*) and their capacity for indefatigable, altruistic action (*samantabhadra-caryā*) according to their vows:

> Bodhisattva Samantabhadra entered the ocean of the Tathāgata's virtues by entering an ocean of skillful means—gates to inconceivable liberations. One of these gates to liberation was . . . establishing the ocean of all the vows of the bodhisattva stages. Another was the manifestation of countless bodies, as many as all the atomic particles in the plane of dharma. Another gate was explaining the inconceivable number of different names of all the Buddha-fields. Another gate was the manifestation of the full scope of all the wondrous powers of the bodhisattvas in every particle of dust. One gate was the manifestation in one instant of thought of the arising and ceasing of all events taking place in all cosmic ages in the past, the present, and the future. (T 10.21c6–18)

Thus, bodhisattvas, as beings on the way to enlightenment, and as enlightened beings, manifest the full range of the path in a single instant and in every atom of the universe. For their liberation is a form of knowledge: "To have a mind that sees all beings as equal, not to give rise to any discrimination, and to enter into the realm of truth—this is the task that should be performed" (T 10.64b4–5). This knowledge of "oneness" is at the same time the wisdom of the bodhisattva as an ethical being, which is expressed in the metaphors of psychic powers: "Give rise to a mind of great compassion in order to rescue and protect all living beings. Forever forsake heavenly and human rebirth. . . . Lift up the boundless universe, drink up the water of the oceans, with the extraordinary knowledge and power of psychic attainment" (T 10.64a21–22 and 64b6–7). The bodhisattva's vow summarizes the primary motivations for the bodhisattva path, the point of departure and the goal of the "perfect conduct" (*samantabhadra-caryā*):

> [The bodhisattva] reflects, and pronounces this vow: "I will become the light of the world, possessing the virtues of the Buddha—the ten powers, his omniscience. All sentient beings are burning in the flames of covetousness, hatred, and confusion. I will rescue them all by extinguishing the suffering of the evil destinies." (T 10.259b11–14)

The sūtra not only describes a world beyond the limitations of fact and natural laws; it also challenges our notions of unity, argument, and purpose. It does not even pretend to depict historical events. Its compilers were not interested in a cohesive narrative referring to individual human beings. Even the mythical audience is shifting constantly, as if to undermine our notions of causal order and connection. No attempt seems to have been made to erase obvious traces of earlier stages of composition, in which the books stood alone, as independent works. Nevertheless, there is an underlying order, and setting and audience serve to indicate some of the intentions of the authors and compilers. In the version in eighty scrolls there are thirty-nine "discourses" delivered to eight different audiences, or "assemblies," in seven locations.[5]

Three of these locations are in the human world: the first assembly takes place around the tree of enlightenment in Bodh Gaya, the second and the seventh at the Hall of All-pervading Light, near the Tree of Awakening, and the last begins in the Jetavana, then extends to a pilgrimage throughout South India. The other locations are in heavenly realms: the third assembly is on Mount Sumeru, the fourth in Yama's Palace, the fifth in the Tuṣitā Heaven, the sixth in the highest heaven of the world of desire. The locations gradually rise higher and higher but return to the human world in the end. The seventh location brings us back to the point of departure of the sūtra—Śākyamuni's enlightenment. Then an eighth location places this experience in the practical context of the bodhisattva's career, since the last section is that of the pilgrimage of a layman, Sudhana, who stands for the human reader or hearer.

It is difficult to go beyond this general outline to try to establish closer connections between the various books. Nevertheless, following the Chinese tradition one can propose approximations to a unifying theme for each of the eight assemblies: (1) the Buddha at the moment of enlightenment is one with Vairocana (books 1–5); (2) the Four Noble Truths form the basis for the bodhisattva's practice and liberation (books 6–12); (3) the bodhisattva's progress, from initial aspiration to the highest station in the bodhisattva's path: ten vihāras (books 13–18); (4) ten types of conduct (*caryā*) of bodhisattvas (books 19–22); (5) ten dedications of merit (books 23–25); (6) ten stages of the bodhisattvas (books 26–37); (7) a summary of the themes that form the core of the collection (themes 3 to 5 of this list; book 38); (8) the bodhisattva's career and inconceivable liberation (book 39). Thus the collection can be seen as a complete map of Buddhist practice.

The last book, the *Gaṇḍavyūha-sūtra,* can be regarded as emblematic of the whole collection.[6] In this well-known sūtra, a layman by the name of Sudhana meets Bodhisattva Mañjuśrī and asks him for instruction on the bodhisattva's course of conduct. After offering Sudhana an answer to his questions, Mañjuśrī sends him to seek a spiritual friend, who will further explain the bodhisattva vows and conduct. Sudhana then travels throughout South India and the central province of Magadha, and also visits a few mystic spheres. One by one, each of fifty-two teachers refers Sudhana to another spiritual friend. The fifty-first encounter is a meeting with Bodhisattva Maitreya, whose towerlike abode is a symbol of the universe of the enlightened: the bodhisattva's home is the universe or, rather, a universe in which are reflected all possible universes. After absorbing this vision of enlightenment in the world, Sudhana returns to Mañjuśrī, who sends him to his fifty-third teacher, whose very name, Samantabhadra, betokens the bodhisattva's perfect conduct. He teaches Sudhana about the bodhisattva's capacity to meet and manifest all the Buddhas of the universe.

In doctrinal content the *Gaṇḍavyūha-sūtra* does not differ from the rest of the *Avataṃsaka*, but its rich symbolism highlights elements that are not always transparent in other books of the collection. For instance, the protagonist is not Vairocana, nor any of the fifty-three teachers visited by Sudhana, but the lonely pilgrim himself, a beginner in the Path. He stands for the reader, seeking a conception of the Path that will place the bodhisattva's activities in this world. Though he is a wealthy merchant's son, he is nevertheless a layman, and his teachers—all implicitly acknowledged to be advanced bodhisattvas—include laymen, laywomen, Brahmins, and female nightspirits. This places the *Avataṃsaka*'s visions of spiritual grandeur in their proper context, one of immanence rather than transcendence. The women among Sudhana's teachers do not have to become men; lay persons do not have to become ascetics in order to be enlightened teachers and wonderworking bodhisattvas with full access to the cosmic vision of the *Avataṃsaka.*

The presence of enlightenment *in the world* and the bodhisattva's determination to discover and reveal it are expressed elsewhere in the *Avataṃsaka* by a different metaphor:

> There is not a single sentient being who is not endowed with the knowledge of the Tathāgata. Still, because sentient beings are attached to deluded and erroneous views they are unable to realize this. Only when they abandon their deluded conceptualizations will omniscience—natural knowledge, unhindered knowledge—appear before their eyes. Son of the Buddha, it is as if there were a large sūtra scroll, as large as the three thousand world-systems, and in it were recorded exhaustively, without exception, all things in this world-system. . . . Yet, though it was the same size as the world-system, it was all contained in one particle of dust. And it was contained in every particle of dust as it was contained in this particle of dust, equally in all.
>
> Now, suppose that at that time a certain person, who had clear, penetrating wisdom, . . . were to see that this sūtra scroll was inside every particle of dust, and yet it did not benefit sentient beings in the least. Immediately it would occur to him, "Why don't I . . . break up a dust particle and let out this sūtra, that it may benefit all sentient beings?" . . .
>
> Son of Buddha, it is also like this with the knowledge of the Tathāgata, it is measureless and not hindered by anything, and is able to assist all beings in every way. It is present in the body of every sentient being, yet they are deluded, attached to their deluded conceptualizations, ignorant, unawakened, so that their knowledge serves no purpose. Then, a Tathāgata . . . thoroughly examines all beings in the cosmic realm and says: "Isn't it surprising, surprising indeed. Why is it that these living beings, though they are endowed with the knowledge of a Tathāgata, are nevertheless deluded, confused, bewildered, ignorant and blind? I will lead them by means of the Noble Path, that they may abandon forever their deluded thoughts and attachment. They will be able to see the vast and magnificent knowledge of the Tathāgata in their own bodies. They will be equal to the Buddha." (T 10.72c5–29)

The doctrine of the Buddha's extraordinary psychic powers does not eclipse the sūtra's religious and ethical message: the metaphor of the Buddha as magician in fact reveals the nature of liberation and asserts its power.

Mahāyāna Spirituality in the *Avataṃsaka*

The *Avataṃsaka* grew out of the common ground of Buddhist spirituality. Rooted in traditional ideas regarding the enstatic experiences (samādhi) of Buddhas, it shared in ancient beliefs that the fruits of spiritual cultivation include both freedom from suffering and supernormal psychic power. Much of the *Avataṃsaka* can be interpreted as a development of these early conceptions. As a Mahāyāna text, however, the *Avataṃsaka* displays a multidimensional spirituality, encompassing the inner world of spiritual visions, the path of self-cultivation, the path of saving grace, and the ethical aspects of spiritual power. Thus its spirituality is not exclusively visionary but centers rather on the transformative power of awakening. Buddhas and bodhisattvas, transfigured by self-cultivation, appear in a corporeal frame that is both the embodiment of emptiness and an accurate reflection of the universe. A Buddha,

> Realizing that the nature of things
> Is incorporeal, serene, and nondual,
> Displays a body of form,
> Adorned with the marks of purity,
> Pervading the whole world.[7]

Statements describing the "body" or personality of a Buddha define at the same time the two dimensions of holiness: the Holy itself (the object of veneration) and the sanctified person (the goal of spiritual cultivation). The bodhisattva path includes both devotion to cosmic Buddhas and bodhisattvas in their many supernal manifestations, and ethical and spiritual growth leading to realization of the state of a Buddha. The sphere of mythical marvels is correlated with that of personal growth.

Plans for spiritual progress are described in more than one section of the *Avataṃsaka.* For instance, the Sūtra on the Ten Abodes (book 15) and the *Daśabhūmika* (book 26) describe the stages through which the aspirant bodhisattva must pass to reach full Buddhahood. Maps of the Mahāyāna path always include the initial stage of the vows, which defines the goal of the path: spiritual cultivation for the sake of sentient beings. This is a key to understanding the *Avataṃsaka,* providing the context for its restatement of traditional values by means of the imagery of supernatural powers. The Mahāyāna expansion of the ideal of individual spiritual growth to encompass the liberation of the universe appears clearly in the Sūtra on the Ten

Actions [of the bodhisattva] (book 21). Some of the ten perfections (pāramitā) here discussed correspond to earlier models. *Śīla*, for instance, is described in traditional ascetic terms, though the vow to save all sentient beings is here the primary motive for the morality of abstention; self-cultivation has the motive of helping others attain the goals of the spiritual path (T 10.103b15–21; 103c12–16).

But it is not enough to practice virtue on this universal and heroic scale; virtue itself must be transcended, until the bodhisattva is free from all ideas of virtue: "they do not see themselves nor the object they give, nor the recipient of the gift. They do not see the field of merit, they do not see a deed, or its results, or its fruits, great or small" (T 10.103a27–29). This detachment is part of the realization of emptiness, and it is emptiness that makes possible the magical apparitions of spiritual cultivation and liberating action. "All along they will not be attached to self, they will not give rise to thoughts of me and mine, and in every single hair-tip they will spend all future cosmic ages cultivating the practices of bodhisattvas" (T 10.106b6–8; 10–12). The same experience that liberates from the world liberates the bodhisattva from conceptions of spirituality and transcendence. The goal of dhyāna and prajñā is detachment from body, but it is also detachment from "doctrine (dharma), thoughts, vows, samādhis, calm or insight, . . . teaching and training, . . . entering the Plane of Dharma" (T 10.106a9–11). Although the perfections liberate the bodhisattvas from the confusion and distraction of the world, they also enable them to be free from spirituality in order to practice their vow in the world:

> In this way bodhisattvas understand the depth of all things, the serenity of all worlds. They understand that . . . the qualities of enlightened beings are no different from the qualities of the world, the qualities of the world no different from the qualities of enlightened beings. (T 10.105b13–16)

In this state of mind bodhisattvas carry out the vows—the oneness of prajñā becomes the impartiality of altruistic action:

> Though they may understand that all sentient beings are unreal, they do not abandon the world of sentient beings. They are like ship captains who do not stay on one shore or the other, and do not stay at sea, but ferry sentient beings across from one shore to the other, making their trips back and forth, without rest. (T 10.106c11ff.)

They remain in the world not only because there still are beings to be saved, but also because they see that a safe, transcendent spiritual realm is a trap. Thus they remain "without reaching their spiritual goal, without not reaching it, without grasping, without not grasping. . . . They are not beings of this world, but they are not beings of the Buddha realm. They are neither common persons, nor attainers of the higher fruits of the Path" (T 10.107a3–6).

This paradox signals the importance of freedom from the spiritual realm no less than from the realm of the passions. The term that describes the functional value of this paradox is *upāya,* skillful means, the seventh of the ten perfections. The potential aloofness of detachment from the world for the sake of liberation is tempered by its compassionate complement: detachment from liberation for the sake of the world. This is called the skillful application of the principle of detachment. *Upāya* is actually defined as "the practice of nonattachment" (T 10.105c19ff.). Although in certain contexts *upāya* may be understood as an attempt to extenuate the rules of training of Buddhist spirituality,[8] it actually refers to detachment applied to images of purity and spiritual hierarchy and achievement: "In an instant of thought they see numberless Buddhas, yet their mind is not attached to any of these Buddhas. . . . They see the splendor and light of Buddhas, they hear the preaching of the Dharma by these Buddhas, but they are not attached to any of this" (T 10.105c26–29). This liberation from the holy is affirmation of the profane, a return to the world:

> When they see impure worlds they have no aversion. Why? Because these bodhisattvas, having examined all the qualities of awakened beings, know that the qualities of awakened beings are neither defiled nor pure, neither dark nor bright, neither different nor identical, neither real nor false, neither calm nor disturbed. . . . (T 10.106a6–9)

This special skill allows the bodhisattva to use the ideals of the spiritual life without turning them into ends in themselves: "Although they use words, their minds are not attached to words. . . . Though they master the samādhis, and are able to enter and abide in them, their mind is not attached to samādhis" (T 10.106a12–14). This is not a way around ideals, but a clarification of them, for the two spheres, emptiness and form, the spiritual and the worldly, ultimately coincide. Bodhisattvas "examine the Plane of Dharma and the Plane of Sentient Beings, and they see that both are boundless, empty, without existence, without marks, without substance, without location, without support, without activity" (T 10.103a25–27). On the central Mahāyāna concept of *upāya* are based the ideals of liberation and altruism, symbolized by the pure body of the Buddha (one and all-encompassing, yet many and present everywhere in multiple forms) and by the magical power that allows Buddhas and bodhisattvas to manifest their bodies conforming to the aspirations of living beings.

* * *

The *Avataṃsaka-sūtra* could be regarded as an encyclopedic compendium of Mahāyāna Buddhism; however, it is more than a survey or a representative text. In the style of its books (which must be described as a separate genre of Buddhist literature), and in its idealized visions (the most daring in the visionary world of Buddhism) the *Avataṃsaka* expresses a view of spirituality that must be considered one of the crowning creations of Indian Buddhism. Paradoxically, the recondite imagery of the *Avataṃsaka* draws our attention—as it did for its Chinese readers—away from the abstractions of Buddhist philosophy to the immediacy of enlightenment. It leads the reader from the capricious world of the supernatural, to a world in which the miraculous is only another name for the freedom of emptiness. It transforms the world-denying values of Buddhist monasticism into detachment from literal emptiness. In the image of an unattainable Buddha one is made to realize a Buddha whose deepest concentration reaches out to all beings, embodying the bodhisattva's vows of compassion. The *Avataṃsaka* gave Mahāyāna Buddhism new symbols of practice, which may have contributed to the development of lay Buddhism. The sūtra also made an important contribution to the development of Buddhism as a universal religion: first, in its probable place of compilation, in the Indian northwestern frontier, then as a bridge between the mysticism of India and the philosophy of China.

Notes

1. T 9.395–788, No. 278, and T 10.1, No. 279. All references here are to Śikṣānanda's version. The *Daśabhūmika* and *Gaṇḍavyūha* sūtras correspond, respectively, to book 26 and book 39 of Śikṣānanda's translation (22 and 34 in Buddhabhadra's version).

2. Louis Renou, Jean Filliozat, et al., *L'Inde classique: Manuel des études indiennes* (Hanoi: École Française d'Extrême-Orient; Paris: Imprimerie Nationale, 1953) 2:434.

3. D. T. Suzuki, *Zen Buddhism and Its Influence on Japanese Culture* (Kyoto: Eastern Buddhist Society, 1938) 113, 226. In *Essays: Third Series* he used the term "interpenetration" for this central doctrine.

4. More accurately, "The World-System Existing Within a Lotus." Vairocana, as Śākyamuni's spiritual alter ego, presides over a Buddha-field in which an ocean of perfume water rests on a disk of wind. From that ocean rises the lotus that forms the seat of Vairocana. It is the receptacle for as many world systems as there are particles of dust in the whole universe.

5. Here we assume that the collection has an overall plan. It is possible to make such an assumption for exegetical purposes, but its historical basis is questionable. Each book may easily be read as an independent work, and the connections between books are in no way transparent.

6. Suzuki considered it the most important, and devoted a good part of his *Essays: Third Series* to discussing its contents.

7. *Gaṇḍavyūha*, ed. Suzuki, 240; see also p. 504: "Magic processes and formulas are incorporeal and unmanifest, yet by arousing the mind they can make visible magical

apparitions of many forms. In the same way, the arising of the thought of perfect awakening, though it is incorporeal and unmanifest, can make manifest the whole Plane of Dharma, accompanied by displays of all the ornaments and virtues [of Buddhahood], merely by the power resulting from the arousal of this mind."

8. For instance, in T 10.103b21–22.

Bibliography

Sources

Das Kegon Sutra. Translated by Torakazu Doi. Tokyo: Doitsubun Kegon-kyō Kankōkai, 1978–83. A translation of Buddhabhadra's version.

The Great Means Expansive Buddha Flower Ornament Sutra. Institute for the Translation of Buddhist Texts. City of the Ten Thousand Buddhas, Talmage, CA: Dharma Realm Buddhist University, 1979–84. A translation of Śikṣānanda's version. The volumes have not appeared in sequence, and fewer than half of the chapters have been translated so far.

Honda, Megumi. "Annotated Translation of the *Daśabhūmika-sūtra.*" In *Studies in South, East, and Central Asia: Presented as a Memorial Volume to the Late Prof. Raghu Vira,* edited by Denis Sinor, 115–276. Śatapitaka Series, Indo-Asian Literatures 74. New Delhi: International Academy of Indian Culture, 1968.

Studies

Chang, Garma C. C. *The Buddhist Teaching of Totality: The Philosophy of Hwa Yen Buddhism.* University Park, PA, and London: Pennsylvania State University Press, 1971.

Cleary, Thomas. *The Flower Ornament Scripture: A Translation of the Avataṃsaka Sūtra.* Boulder and London: Shambhala, 1984.

Ehman, Mark Allen. "The *Gaṇḍavyūha-sūtra:* Search for Enlightenment." Ph.D. dissertation, University of Wisconsin, Madison, 1977.

Fontein, Jan. *The Pilgrimage of Sudhana: A Study of Gaṇḍavyūha Illustrations in China, Japan, and Java.* The Hague: Mouton, 1967.

Gómez, Luis O. "Selected Verses from the *Gaṇḍavyūha-sūtra.*" Ph.D. dissertation, Yale University, 1967.

———. "The Bodhisattva as Wonderworker." In *Prajñāpāramitā and Related Systems,* ed. Lewis Lancaster and Luis O. Gómez, 221–61. Berkeley Buddhist Studies Series 1. Berkeley: Institute of Buddhist Studies, 1977. Contains translation of one chapter from the *Gaṇḍavyūha-sūtra.*

Guenther, Herbert V. "Excerpts from the *Gaṇḍavyūha Sūtra.*" In *Tibetan Buddhism in Western Perspective,* 3–35. Emeryville, CA: Dharma Publishing, 1977.

Idumi, Hōkei. "The Hymn on the Life and Vows of Samantabhadra." *Eastern Buddhist* 5/2–3 (1929–31) 226–47.

Paul, Diana Y. *Women in Buddhism: Images of the Feminine in Mahāyāna Tradition.* Berkeley: Asian Humanities Press, 1979.

Robinson, Richard. *Chinese Buddhist Verse,* 49–60. London: John Murray, 1954.

Suzuki, Daisetz Teitaro. *Essays in Zen Buddhism: Third Series.* New York: S. Weiser, 1973.

IV. *The Lotus Sūtra and the Essence of Mahāyāna*

MICHAEL PYE

THE INITIAL CREATIVE PHASE of Mahāyāna Buddhism, usually assigned to the first century B.C.E., was a subtle combination of devotional, meditational, and intellectual adjustments to traditional Buddhism. The pattern of these adjustments seen in the earliest parts of the *Perfection of Wisdom* and the *Lotus* sūtras can be regarded as a searching commentary on existing Buddhism. However, this pattern so quickly developed a dynamic of its own that these sūtras themselves were dramatically expanded and many others were compiled in the same vein. Moreover, the relations between the key ideas and practices were such that themes which at first were only lightly adumbrated came strongly to the fore in subsequent strands of Mahāyāna. Important themes of this kind are the teaching of "consciousness-only," the assertion that all beings possess the Buddha-nature, the three-body (trikāya) doctrine concerning the nature of the Buddha, or rather of the Buddhas in their multiplicity, the practice of calling or recalling the name of a Buddha or a bodhisattva, and the radical opening of a lay path in Buddhism. The unfolding of these ideas was accompanied by a wonderful elaboration of the cosmological and mythological perspective and a continuous enrichment of popular devotion. How did all this come about? What was the driving religious experience behind it? What is the essential spiritual perspective that allows the combination of such a wide range of ideas and practices?

Mahāyāna Restatement and the Notion of Skillful Means

The essence of Mahāyāna lies not in one particular teaching but in a spiritual attitude or direction that enables all the elements of the Buddhist tradition to be seen in a new light. The dramatically transcendent appearance of the Buddha in the *Lotus Sūtra,* for example, which has often been remarked upon, does not in itself make it a Mahāyāna text. The *Mahāvastu* of the Mahāsaṅghika school in its own way sets out a similar view of the Buddha, who is described in one famous passage as supramundane (*lokottara*).[1] According to this teaching the Buddha appears in human form only to match the requirements of the world. In his true being he is above and beyond the world, unlimited in time and space. This conception may be regarded as one of the ingredients that made Mahāyāna possible, and yet it does not in itself provide the essence of Mahāyāna spirituality. It is a cosmological projection of the principle of Buddhahood which gives to the Buddha a status beyond that of a mere human exemplar, a mythological statement of the belief that the enlightenment achieved by the historical Buddha is at one with the very stuff of the universe. This trend can be observed even in the Buddhism of the Pāli texts and, iconographically, in the gigantic images that display the Buddha as "superman" or "great being" (*mahāpuruṣa*).

In the *Lotus Sūtra* we have to do with a transfigured Buddha preaching at Vulture Peak, able with the light between his eyes to illumine vast numbers of other worlds, filling his assembled hearers with numinous awe. But in what way does the teaching of such a Buddha go beyond that of the *Mahāvastu?* Western readers sometimes work their way through the extravaganzas of the text and fail to discern any new content at all. The search for new items of doctrine leads them on to chapter 16, where they grasp at the idea of a Buddha whose length of life is unlimited, a Buddha whose nature transcends the eighty years of Śākyamuni's historical life-span:

> In all the worlds, gods, men, and asuras all say that the present Śākyamunibuddha left the palace of the Śakya clan and at a place not far removed from the city of Gayā, seated on the Platform of the Path, attained *anuttarasamyaksambodhi* [supreme perfect enlightenment]. And yet, O good men, since in fact I achieved Buddhahood it has been incalculable, limitless hundreds of thousands of myriads of millions of nayutas of kalpas.[2]

But the real originality of the *Lotus Sūtra*'s Buddhology lies in the subtle, reflective dialectic between the Buddha of unlimited life-span and the Buddha of earlier tradition. That is to say, we are called upon to interpret the Buddha's apparent life-span of eighty years and subsequent entry into nirvāṇa in a new way as a device (*upāya*) skillfully displayed to give confidence in the attainability of nirvāṇa:

> The Thus Come One [*tathāgatha*], seeing the beings' desire for a lesser dharma, their qualities thin and their defilements grave, preaches to such persons saying, "In my youth I left my household and attained *anuttarasamyaksaṃbodhi.*" However, since in fact I achieved Buddhahood it has been as long a stretch of time as this. It is merely by resort to an expedient device, in order to teach and convert living beings, to enable them to enter upon the Buddha Path, that I speak such words as these.[3]

The attainability of nirvāṇa requires demonstration to living beings locked into the karmic sequences of birth-and-death (saṃsāra). At the same time, to continue to think of the life-span of eighty years and the progression from the one state of saṃsāra to another state called nirvāṇa would be to remain fixed in the very realm of discriminative thinking from which release is sought. The vision of a Buddha whose life-span is unlimited is intended to get over this deadly spiritual danger.

With this in mind the whole tenor of the *Lotus Sūtra* will become clear. Again and again it stresses that the Buddha taught with a great variety of devices to attract and guide living beings. The dispositions and the karmic status of living beings are very diverse, but they all need the same Dharma in adapted form. Thus they are like so many grasses, herbs, and trees which are all in need of the same rainwater from a common source (chap. 5). In the allegory of the burning house, the principle is set out in story form (chap. 3). There we read, with much circumstantial detail, how a wealthy householder entices his children out of a huge rambling house, which, unnoticed by them, is on fire. The house figures the triple world, ravaged by birth, old age, illness, death, and constant anxiety. Since the children are engrossed in their playthings, their father offers them carriages for their sport, outside. These carriages will be drawn variously by goats, deer, and oxen. Once safely outside, the children ask for their carriages and each is given the same superb, bejeweled carriage drawn by a white ox. The carriages drawn by goats are said to represent the elementary hearers of the Buddha's teaching (śrāvakas); those drawn by deer stand for those who in harmony with the Buddha's teaching seek self-authenticating knowledge and quietude (pratyekabuddhas); and those drawn by oxen stand for disciples who follow the path of the Buddha in its fullness until they themselves can bring deliverance to others (bodhisattvas). Of these three "vehicles" the third is the Mahāyāna insofar as it is differentiated from the others. However, the polemical relationship between them is resolved by the appearance of the superior carriage pulled by a white ox, which is what may be called inclusive Mahāyāna. Thus one is not to be spiritually ensnared by the new vehicle understood as the way of the bodhisattva, any more than by the previous understandings of Buddhism. At the heart of the Mahāyāna lies the attempt to relativize its own forms of expression.

The connection with the thought of "emptiness" is everywhere implied in the *Lotus Sūtra* and occasionally clearly stated. Thus, a blind man who has regained his vision is a model for one who is released from the karmic chain of rebirth but must still go on to "attain to all the dharmas." This means that "he sees the world of the triple sphere in its ten directions as empty, a fabrication, a mock creation, a dream, a mirage, an echo. He sees all dharmas as unoriginated, unsuppressed, unbound, unreleased, not dark, not bright."[4] Thus he is freed from the polarity between karmic rebirth and extinction. In this regard the *Lotus Sūtra* is at one with the *Perfection of Wisdom* sūtras and the *Teaching of Vimalakīrti.* "Wisdom" so conceived is one of the golden threads running through all Mahāyāna spirituality, being the highest of the six "perfections" to be cultivated by an aspiring bodhisattva. The meaning of this "wisdom" is, however, very precise. It is not a moralizing wisdom or a general wisdom of life. Rather, it means *insight* into the true nature of the elements or factors of experience (dharmas), the perception that these factors are "empty" of substantial metaphysical import, or in the phrase of the *Heart Sūtra,* that they are empty in their "own-being."[5]

Many of the similes regularly used to convey this meaning—a dream, a mirage, an echo, a fabrication—appear in sūtras that are not always closely related to each other. It is of particular interest that this whole way of thinking, or seeing, is characteristic not only of the *Perfection of Wisdom* sūtras but also of the *Laṅkāvatāra Sūtra.*[6] This work also displays a strong tendency to regard the forms of teaching as provisional constructs, to be used and then abandoned. At the same time the *Laṅkāvatāra Sūtra* has a flavor of its own. It stresses the need for an inward turning (*parāvṛtti*) to overcome the ordinary workings of the mind. Normally we perceive the world as if from a vantage point, the separate vantage point of our own subjective selves. The world without is objectified, sorted, and assessed by our constantly roving mental activity. This leads to attachments and illusions of all kinds. To overcome this a radical reorientation is needed, a turning back toward the starting point of conscious activity. By this means the presumed self disappears and in its place is perceived a wonderful "storehouse-consciousness" (*ālaya-vijñāna*), which embraces the whole of the universe hitherto considered to have existed, so to speak, objectively. There is no self, no world, no discrimination—just an all-inclusive consciousness. This approach saw substantial further development in the form of the Yogācāra school and was influential on both Tantric and Zen Buddhism.

These related strands of early Mahāyāna thinking all have two significant features in common. First, they are all expansive meditations on themes already widely discussed in Buddhism: emptiness, consciousness, analysis of the factors of experience. Second, and at the same time, they all seek to unsettle fixed notions, not indeed for the sake of mere philosophical polemic but in order to achieve a spiritual state free from attachment to particular points. "A bodhisattva should not seize on either a dharma or a no-dharma,"[7] as it says in the *Diamond Sūtra.* Thus, the Mahāyāna has a theory not only of the relativity of the factors of experience but also of the relativity of the forms of Buddhist teaching itself. Moreover, this understanding of the very nature of the Buddhist message was claimed to be true to the original. This explains why, in the *Lotus Śūtra,* there is an extended repetition of the old story of the Buddha's decision to teach rather than to remain silent. The story, in its modified form (chaps. 2 and 7), stresses the provisional character of the teaching and hence permits those advancing in insight to be freed from attachment to this or that point.

Universal Buddhahood

A theme implicit but not strongly developed in the earlier Mahāyāna sūtras was the teaching of the Buddhahood of all beings. It became particularly popular in China near the beginning of the fifth century C.E. with the publication of translations of a Mahāyāna form of the *Mahāparinirvāṇa Sūtra.*[8] This work is a freely ranging meditation on the story of the Buddha's final nirvāṇa. It should not be confused with the pre-Mahāyāna Sanskrit parallel to the well-known sūtra in Pāli on the last stage of the Buddha's life.[9] The Mahāyāna text has much in common with the *Lotus Sūtra,* to which it explicitly refers. For one thing it also takes up the theme of the unlimited duration of the Tathāgata's life, which arises naturally out of reflection on his presumed entry into nirvāṇa. The subjective importance of this lies in not being attached to the idea that the Buddha lived for eighty years. Instead one is invited to revere a Buddha who is, in effect, ever present. Linked with this, and also shared with the *Lotus Sūtra,* is the emphasis on skillful means and the idea that particular forms of teaching are given to suit the needs of the hearers. It is little wonder that the later T'ien-t'ai system classified the *Lotus* and the *Nirvāṇa* sūtras together as the culmination of the Buddha's teaching.

It is in this light that the idea of the Buddhahood—or, more precisely, the Buddha-nature of all living beings—must be understood. Once again we are presented with a paradoxical manner of speaking. Countless living beings are seen to be treading their path toward a goal where, in their true nature, they already abide. Just as in the *Lotus Sūtra* all dharmas are said to possess from the beginning the quality of nirvāṇa, so here all living beings are declared to possess the Buddha-nature. This "Buddha-nature" should not be thought of as some newly perceived metaphysical reality. It is in fact simply a synonym for the nature of a tathāgata, that is, the quality of being "thus arrived," or for "liberation," or for nirvāṇa. The Buddha-nature, like space, is not a conditioned or compound element or aspect of existence. Thus it may be said that it is "with characteristics, without characteristics, and neither with characteristics nor without characteristics."[10] About all this there is nothing unusual. What, after all, is Buddha-nature, if it is not "gone altogether beyond" (*Heart Sūtra*)?[11] The paradox arises in the predication of such Buddha-nature with respect to living beings, who most certainly are compound existences with a great variety of characteristics. The key to understanding the paradox lies in seeing it not statically but dynamically. Thus "Buddha-nature" is a designation that assists in the departure from characteristics. Though living beings have characteristics, it is possible to cease to be attached to these. This is effected by seeing things in another way, in this case by seeing living beings as having "Buddha-nature."

The difference between living beings as normally regarded and living beings regarded in terms of their Buddha-nature is a qualitative one. For this reason the *Nirvāṇa Sūtra* was a source of inspiration for those who, like Tao-Sheng (fl. 397–432) and others after him, were fascinated by the idea of *sudden* enlightenment. If there is no distance to cover, how can the journey be a long and gradual one? However, there is also clear evidence in the sūtra itself that Buddha-nature was regarded as a latent quality that could become clear through steady practice of the religious way. Thus, "just as sentient beings cannot see the roots of grass and underground water because they are hidden in the ground, the same is true of the Buddha-nature, which sentient beings cannot perceive because they do not practice the holy paths."[12]

In more cryptic style the theme is also adumbrated in the *Laṅkāvatāra Sūtra,* where the fundamental basis of all true being is described as the "tathāgata-womb" (*tathāgata-garbha*). This is identical with the seat of consciousness or "store-consciousness" (*ālaya-vijñāna*), which in one aspect gives rise to a differentiated view of the world, separating out a presumed objective area of reality from a searching, willing principle of selfhood, but in another aspect is none other than an integrated reflection of these apparently diverse phenomena. The differentiated view is based on illusion. If one departs from this illusory differentiation and turns back to the unity of the store-consciousness, then the tathāgata or "thus gone" quality of all things will become clear. This quality is not a new, distant achievement. On the contrary, it is the original quality of all things, present from the beginning in the very matrix of consciousness.

The Three Buddha-Bodies

The three-body (trikāya) explanation of the Buddha is a doctrinal construct that has had a particular appeal to the Western imagination. This doctrine is not found in the earliest Mahāyāna sūtras but arose somewhat later in order to correlate different perceptions of the Buddha in actual experience. It should be seen as one attempt among several to formulate what it means when Buddha-nature is perceived to be present everywhere. Even in pre-Mahāyāna Buddhism the number of Buddhas in preceding worlds and in spatially different worlds had increased dramatically, as may be seen clearly in the *Mahāvastu*. Thus there was a general problem about the relation between various manifestations of Buddhahood which increasingly came to be regarded as resolved in terms of the three-body doctrine.

A fine example of an early Mahāyāna Buddha-vision is to be found in chapter 11 of the *Lotus Sūtra*, where the "extinct" Buddha Prabhūtaratna (Many Jewels) appears in the heavens to certify, in a cosmic perspective, the teaching of the present Buddha, Śākyamuni. But how can a Buddha who has long since entered final nirvāṇa reappear? The first sign of his presence is the appearance of a beautiful stūpa suspended miraculously in the sky. This stūpa contains, in condensed form, the "self-being" (*ātmabhāva*) of the Tathāgata Prabhūtaratna. It appears thus, on the occasion of the proclamation of the *Lotus Sūtra*, as a result of a vow that he made eons before, previous to his entry into final nirvāṇa:

> Such are that Buddha's supernatural penetrations, such the force of his vow that in the worlds of all ten directions, wherever anyone preaches the Scripture of the Dharma Blossom, his jeweled stūpa invariably wells up before that person, his whole body in the stūpa giving praise with the words, "Excellent! Excellent!"[13]

Śākyamuni is presented as rising to meet the celestial stūpa, the front of which he then opens. Inside is seen the figure of an ascetic Buddha, described in the text as the "frame of the tathāgata" (*tathāgatavigraha*). Such a "frame" is a projection from the indestructible principle of Buddha-nature, which can thus be made visible in thousands of worlds. To complete the vision, Śākyamuni enters the stūpa and sits down beside Prabhūtaratna, thus indicating that all Buddhas are equivalent to each other. The whole scene dramatizes the reliability of any one Buddha who appears at a particular time and place to lead living beings into enlightenment. The theme of the two Buddhas sitting side by side was iconographically popular in Central Asia and Northwest China.[14]

The appearance and activity of the great savior figures of Mahāyāna Buddhism—Amitābha, Avalokiteśvara, Bhaiṣajyarāja (Medicine King), Samantabhadra, and others, is based on their power to work in a manner that transcends time and even nirvāṇa. The vows of a great bodhisattva to save all living beings work on indefinitely, as long as there are living beings to be assisted. Thus the distinction between a bodhisattva and a Buddha loses all practical meaning for the devotee. Avalokiteśvara is theoretically a bodhisattva who takes on many different forms to assist others in the Buddha-way (*Lotus Sūtra*, chap. 24),[15] whereas the bodhisattva Dharmācara has already become the Buddha Amitābha, who resides in his Buddha-field (*buddhakṣetra*) and welcomes those who rely on his vows. This relationship is taken up in the *Laṅkāvatāra Sūtra*, where we read: "the others . . . are those who have finished practicing the deeds of a Bodhisattva; they are forms of the Transformation Buddha. With skillful means born of their fundamental and original vows they manifest themselves among the multitudes in order to adorn the assemblages of the Buddhas."[16]

With the notion of "transformation Buddha" in the *Laṅkāvatāra Sūtra* we reach one of the main forerunners of the three-body doctrine. This sūtra speaks of the *nirmāṇa-buddha* who gives elementary teaching on meditation and morality. Such a Buddha appears among the ordinary contingencies of everyday life, as did, for example, Śākyamuni Buddha. His teaching is necessarily couched in terms of the differentiations normally made by living beings when dealing with their environment. The task of leading the living beings beyond this view of things falls to the *niṣyanda-buddha*, a glorious projection of ultimate Buddha-nature that inspires the devotee to appreciate the "emptiness" of ordinary phenomena and to transcend the distinction between being and non-being. Third, but ontologically prior, is the *dharmatā-buddha*, Buddha-nature in its own true mode, not decked out with characteristics addressed to the needs of those who require to be saved and guided. These three aspects of Buddha-nature may be interpreted as corresponding to the sequence Hīnayāna, Mahāyāna, and realized Mahāyāna. The older distinction between the *rūpakāya* and the dharmakāya, that is, the body of earthly form and the body of Dharma (replacing the historical Buddha after his decease), is complemented here by a third focus which reflects the typical Mahāyāna spirituality.

The trikāya formulation was particularly favored in the Yogācāra tradition and took systematic, scholastic form in chapter 9 of the *Mahāyāna-Sūtralaṃkara.*[17] Here we find the most frequently quoted, though relatively late, terminology: *svabhāvika-kāya* (body of own being), saṃbhogakāya (body of bliss, or enjoyment), nirmāṇakāya (body of transformation). A similar account is given in *The Awakening of Faith in the Mahāyāna*, which was almost certainly composed in China in the sixth century C.E.[18] The traditional ascription of this work to Aśvaghoṣa led to the common but mistaken assumption that the three-body doctrine was current during the early formative period of Mahāyāna Buddhism. That its influence was widespread, however, may be seen from the fact that the *Suvarṇaprabhāsottama-sūtra* contains a whole chapter on the subject (also not extant in Sanskrit).[19] In this account the dialectical relation between the bodies with characteristics, on one hand, and the dharmakāya without characteristics, on the other hand, is made abundantly clear.

Other sūtras that celebrate a closely related vision of many Buddhas

16. Vulture Peak, site of the preaching of the *Lotus Sūtra*.
The vulture-shaped rock from which the mountain gets its name.

17. An overview of Vulture Peak, site of the preaching of the *Lotus Sūtra*.

emanating from one reality are the *Avataṃsaka* and the *Śūraṃgamasamādhi* sūtras. In the latter we read of many tathāgatas which are unborn, uncompounded, nondifferentiated, fundamentally equal and equal also to all dharmas in their vacuity. But how does a Tathāgata who has thus "penetrated the equality of all dharmas" continue "to manifest his wonderful material body to living beings"? The answer is that this is due to the continuing power of his previously practiced samādhi.[20] In Kumārajīva's Chinese version the tathāgatas are declared, in their equality, to be "truly real," but Lamotte points out that while in the Tibetan version they are described as equally "unreal" it scarcely matters which term is used.[21] To put it succinctly, the reality of a tathāgata lies in his immutable quality of not being ensnared by the characteristics of an illusory and changing existence. In the vast *Avataṃsaka Sūtra* we read of immeasurably numerous Buddhas in all the Buddha-lands of the ten directions (eight quarters, zenith, and nadir). All of these Buddhas manifest themselves in "bodies" equal in number to the specks of dust found in all the worlds. But it is the calling of a bodhisattva, having striven to understand the teachings of all these Buddhas, to realize also that the Buddhas are "unreal." Their true character is plumbed by cultivating prajñā.[22]

Devotional Practices

The Indian imagination experienced no difficulty in supplying vast numbers of Buddhas with names full of light and treasure such as Buddha Flower Glow (*Lotus Sūtra,* chap. 3) or Buddha Many Jewels (chap. 11). Nor did the Chinese translators fail to use the resources of their remarkable writing system to provide expressive, literal renderings. Thus the very names of the innumerable Buddhas could be used as a focus of a devotional form of meditation that managed to jump the language gap from India to China. The practice is known in Sanskrit as *buddhānusmṛti* and in Chinese as *nien-fo.* These terms refer to the recollection of a specific Buddha by name. The name is usually pronounced, but physical utterance is not indispensable. At the beginning of the formula, including the name, stands the word *namaḥ* (Chinese *na-mo;* Japanese *namu*) meaning "hail to." It concludes with "Buddha" or "Bodhisattva." Elementary examples are therefore "Hail Śākyamuni Buddha" and "Hail Avalokiteśvara Bodhisattva." In the latter case it is assumed that calling on the name of the bodhisattva will assist in times of peril.

> If, again, a man who is about to be murdered calls upon the name of the bodhisattva He Who Observes the Sounds of the World [Avalokiteśvara], then the knives and staves borne by the other fellow shall be broken in pieces, and the man shall gain deliverance.[23]

This practical value is assumed to have contributed to the popularity of the *Avalokiteśvara Sūtra* (current both independently and as part of the *Lotus Sūtra*) on the caravan routes of Central Asia.

The most famous of all invocatory practices in Mahāyāna Buddhism is surely that of calling on the name of Amitābha Buddha. Indeed, the Japanese equivalent of *nien-fo* is *nenbutsu*, which refers in ordinary usage to the invocation of this Buddha alone. Amitābha Buddha is the Buddha of Immeasurable Light or the Buddha of Immeasurable Life (Amitāyus), whose vows are set forth in the *Sukhāvatīvyūha Sūtra*.[24] The essential point emphasized by Chinese and Japanese devotees of this tradition is that those who call on his name with the formula *Namo-Amito-Fo* (Chinese) or *Namu Amida Butsu* (Japanese) with a sincerely believing mind will be reborn in the Pure Land in the western quarter, which is not only pleasant in itself but also a place where final nirvāṇa will surely be attained.[25]

How widespread this practice was in early Mahāyāna is best illustrated by the *Buddha-names Sūtra* (T 14.114, No. 440, *Fo ming ching*), which contains hundreds of such formulas addressed to many different Buddhas. The practice was also transferred to sūtra-centered devotion, as seen in the concentration on the title of the *Lotus Sūtra* in the Chinese formula *Namo miao fa lien hua ching*, later widely current in Japan as *Namu myōhō rengekyō*. The point of all these meditational devices is that they provide a clear and easily pronounced symbol for what is taken to be the quintessence of the whole tradition. Although later centuries have seen rivalry between various alternatives, the spirit of the early Mahāyāna sūtras demands that these be seen as essentially equivalent to each other. In a work of the Chinese Pure Land adept Shan Tao (613–681) entitled *Kuan nien fa men*, the recollection of the Buddha Amitābha's name is closely linked with the visualization (*kuan*) of the same Buddha as an exercise in its own right. This is not surprising, as the third of the sūtras fundamental to the Pure Land Buddhist tradition is entitled *Kuan wu liang shou ching*, that is, "Sūtra on the Visualization of the Buddha of Immeasurable Life."[26] Although the Sanskrit name has been reconstituted by some as *Amitāyūrdhyāna Sūtra* no text of this name or with the same contents has yet been discovered in modern times. Nor does dhyāna necessarily imply the specific sense of seeing conveyed by the Chinese character *kuan*. In fact this sūtra is nothing less than a meditational instruction on how to see or visualize the Buddha Amitāyus (identified with Amitābha). It belongs to a class of sūtras that were probably developed toward the end of the fourth century C.E., including among others a sūtra on the visualization of the bodhisattva Samantabhadra (T 9.389, No. 277), which is commonly associated with the *Lotus Sūtra*, and another on the visualization of Bhaiṣajyarāja and Bhaiṣajyasamudgata (T 20.660, No. 1161), who are both associated with healing. These meditations are based on the general ability of most people to banish optical impressions and then to conjure them up again. This is learned, for example, by regarding the setting sun resting like a drum on the western horizon, closing the eyes and recalling the image, which can soon be done at will. In further stages the image to be conjured up is first described by means of verbal description and iconography. When it comes to visualizing a Buddha one is assisted in that one's own mind latently possesses the thirty-two characteristics by which a Buddha is identified. Thus in one respect the visualized Buddha is a projection from the mind of the meditator and in another respect it is none other than a form of the dharma-body that is identical in all instances and therefore is able to reappear when circumstances are conducive.

The revering of the sūtras themselves was widespread in the early Mahāyāna period. It arose as a result of the practice of placing sūtras in stūpas, where formerly Buddha-relics had been preferred. This substitution was no doubt encouraged by the scarcity of relics but demonstrated forcefully the replacement of the Buddha by his Dharma, or indeed the identity of the two (see *Lotus Sūtra,* chap. 10). Sūtra-veneration is a mark of bodhisattvahood:

> If there is a man who shall receive and keep, read and recite, explain, or copy in writing a single gāthā of the Scripture of the Blossom of the Fine Dharma, or who shall look with veneration on a roll of this scripture as if it were the Buddha himself, or who shall make to it sundry offerings of flower perfume, necklaces, powdered incense, perfumed paste, burnt incense, silk canopies and banners, garments, or music, or who shall even join palms in reverent worship of it, . . . be it known that this man or any other like him shall have already made offerings to ten myriads of Buddhas in former time, and in those Buddhas' presence taken a great vow. . . . That person is to be looked up to and exalted by all the worlds, showered with offerings fit for a Thus Come One. . . . That person is an emissary of the Thus Come One, sent by the Thus Come One, doing the Thus Come One's business.[27]

These practices of sūtra-veneration have all continued down to the present and form a most important dimension of Mahāyāna Buddhist spirituality, not least in the context of lay Buddhism. One of the roots of sectarian proliferation within Mahāyāna Buddhism lies in the fact that most of its sūtras contain a passage declaring it to be the supreme, regal sūtra, worthy above all to be honored.

All of the above practices may be regarded as part of a general broadening out of religious Buddhism that linked the simplest believer with the most advanced practitioner. The essential vehicle for this newly coordinated range of experience was the bodhisattva ideal.[28] Early Buddhism had regarded departure from the household life as a prerequisite for serious advance in the quest for nirvāṇa, and left it open for householders to observe elementary morality and support and revere the monks. Mahāyāna, by contrast, invited all to step immediately onto a vast ladder of spiritual progress with many stages and resting places. Thus the humblest religious act, the slightest inclination of the head, the offering of a single flower with distracted thoughts, will set one on an incomparable path leading to the salvation of myriads of other beings and ultimately to nirvāṇa without residue (*Lotus Sūtra*, chap. 2). The first of the six perfections to be cultivated by a bodhisattva may be taken as a further illustration of this point. The Sanskrit term for it is *dāna*, meaning "donation," "giving," or in effect the quality of generosity. This perfection may be initiated by the simple act of putting some rice in the bowl of a monk, but it may extend to the sacrifice of parts of the body or the laying down of one's life for the welfare of others. The most famous example of this is the story of the prince who slit his own throat so that his flesh could be devoured by a tigress who had no food for her cubs (*Sūtra of Golden Light*, chap. 18).[29] The prince is declared to have been none other than the Buddha himself in a previous existence, that is, when he was in an advanced stage of bodhisattvahood.

The exemplification of the bodhisattva's way in the lives of highly placed lay personages is in any case a common theme in the sūtras. Particularly notable here is the *Śrīmālā Sūtra*, which celebrates not only the virtue of a queen but also her grasp of the Mahāyāna teaching.[30] This includes central themes such as the teaching of a sole vehicle (*ekayāna*) transcending the provisional differentiation between Hīnayāna and the bodhisattva way, and the teaching of the Buddha-nature of all beings. This latter, in principle no different from the position expressed in the *Nirvāṇa Sūtra*, is expressed in terms of the Tathāgata-Womb (tathāgatagarbha) in which all beings are equally discoverable. The assumption that every being is latently, that is, already rather than potentially, a tathāgata, together with the projection of a female lay person as one who understands this, implies a subversion of the traditional distinction between monk and lay devotee. The new spirituality is most finely expounded in the *Vimalakīrti Sūtra*, which exhibits the twin principles of the bodhisattva's career, wisdom and compassion. Vimalakīrti's dialogue partner, Mañjuśrī, is regarded as the epitome of the sixth perfection, wisdom, the *prajñāpāramitā*, while compassion is enacted in the story of Vimalakīrti's illness, through which he shares in the illness of all living beings. Though he is a householder, Vimalakīrti is not impeded by the accessories of household life: to demonstrate the voidness of things he can empty his house magically of its contents. The position reached by Vimalakīrti is the identification of the opposites, applied in particular to the way of the monks and the way of the lay person. The fact that the Chinese phrase *tsai chia ch'u chia,* "to lead the household life is to depart from the household life," has found its way into ordinary dictionaries is an indication of the welcome that this idea met in China. What it meant for many may be seen in R. H. Mathews's explanatory translation "to worship the Buddha quietly in the heart is as good as leaving home to become a priest,"[31] though this does not reflect the paradoxical quality of Vimalakīrti's approach.

The Mahāyāna Heritage

Although there is considerable diversity among the Mahāyāna sūtras, this is mainly due to the independent elaboration of particular themes. This in turn has led to the delineation of schools, and in the long run to the growth of what are in effect denominations, and even sects, which in recent times have little knowledge of each other's preferred texts. In spite of a resultant tendency toward exclusivity in some quarters, there are not really any significant contradictions between the Mahāyāna sūtras themselves. They present a most generously conceived range of religious sensibility and practice for monk and lay devotee alike. It is small wonder that eventually the distinction between the two was further blurred by the acceptance of a married priesthood in most Japanese schools of Buddhism.

The key to this coherence in diversity may be discerned above all in four or five leading concepts. First, it may be found in the new universalism, which is ultimately rooted in the equivalence of all dharmas and hence of all living beings, in their voidness, in their essentially nirvanic quality, or in their Buddha-nature. This fundamental quality of things is discerned through the practice of prajñā. Equally, however, the myriad factors of experience are all known to bodhisattvas high and low, in their differentiatedness. Thus it is essential to develop skill in dealing with all of these factors in such a way that Dharma is expressed but living beings, especially those who have entered the bodhisattva way, are not caught fast in them. This is achieved through the practice of *upāyakauśalya.*[32] For the less experienced bodhisattva it is essentially a learning process. For the more experienced bodhisattva it becomes a question of compassionate intervention to assist others (karuṇa). Why should a bodhisattva wish to postpone nirvāṇa without residue and turn back in acts of compassion? The answer to this question, never asked in Buddhist circles, is simply that it would be inconsistent with insight into the Buddha-nature of all things for a bodhisattva to conceive of attaining nirvāṇa as a differentiated, individual process. Here lies the secret combination of immovable vision and salvific enterprise which characterizes the spirituality of the Mahāyāna sūtras.

Such themes underlie the various specific forms which Mahāyāna Buddhism has adopted all over East Asia and yet they are not dependent on any one denominational or sectarian teaching. The essential insights and the flavor of experience which they inspire are available both within and without traditional religious contexts, and increasingly both within and without Asian forms of culture. Where contemporary people are rootless, individualistic, and anarchic, Mahāyāna Buddhism calls them to self-reflection, interdependence, and compassion. Where prejudice and rigid categorization predominate, Mahāyāna Buddhism leads into flexibility and release. These two notes complement each other, for both are grounded in a unifying perception of emptiness. At this level Mahāyāna Buddhism is a genuine restatement of early Buddhism and by no means out of tune with Theravāda tradition. When awareness of emptiness is practiced, the constraints of fixed and discriminating viewpoints give way to liberation. At the same time the attachments arising out of an illusion of self lose their force.

Notes

1. See *The Mahāvastu*, trans. J. J. Jones.
2. *Scripture of the Lotus Blossom*, trans. L. Hurvitz, 237.
3. Ibid., 238–39.
4. Ibid., 114–15.
5. See E. Conze, *Buddhist Wisdom Books.*
6. See *The Laṅkāvatāra Sūtra*, trans. D. T. Suzuki.
7. Conze, *Buddhist Wisdom Books*, 34.
8. See Ming-Wood Liu, "The Doctrine of the Buddha-Nature in the Mahāyāna *Mahāparinirvāṇa Sūtra*," *Journal of the International Association of Buddhist Studies* 5/2 (1982) 63–94.
9. *Dialogues of the Buddha*, trans. T. W. and C. A. F. Rhys Davids, II 71–191.
10. Liu, "Doctrine of the Buddha-Nature," 69 (T 12.526a), adapted.
11. Conze, *Buddhist Wisdom Books*, 101: *pārasaṃgate.*
12. Liu, "Doctrine of the Buddha-Nature," 72.
13. *Scripture of the Lotus Blossom*, trans. Hurvitz, 184.
14. See J. Leroy Davidson, *The Lotus Sūtra in Chinese Art.*
15. Chapter 25 in Kumārajīva's Chinese version, the so-called *Kannongyō* (*Kannon Sūtra*) in Japanese.
16. *Laṅkāvatāra Sūtra*, trans. Suzuki, 104.
17. See Lévi, *Mahāyāna-Sūtralaṃkāra*, esp. chap. 9.
18. See *The Awakening of Faith*, trans. Yoshito S. Hakeda.
19. See J. Nobel, *Suvarnaprabhāsottama-Sūtra.*
20. *La Concentration de la Marche Héroique: Śūraṃgamasamādhisūtra*, trans. É. Lamotte, 130–31.
21. Ibid., 129n.
22. See *Das Kegon Sutra*, trans. Doi Torakazu, here especially 1:246.
23. *Scripture of the Lotus Blossom*, trans. Hurvitz, 312.

24. A satisfactory critical translation of this work is still awaited, but reference may be made to *The Shinshū Seiten: The Holy Scripture of Shinshū,* compiled and published by The Honpa Hongwanji Mission of Hawaii, Honolulu, 1955.

25. The best introductions to the spirituality of this tradition, from the Jōdo Shinshū point of view, are various works in the Ryūkoku Translation Series (Kyoto, 1961ff.), and writings by Alfred Bloom such as *Shinran's Gospel of Pure Grace.*

26. The Japanese transliteration is *Kanmuryōjukyō.* For the text, see *The Shinshū Seiten* (n. 24 above).

27. *Scripture of the Lotus Blossom,* trans. Hurvitz, 174–75.

28. For a translation of a late Sanskrit work on this theme, the *Bodhicaryāvatāra* of Śāntideva, see Marion L. Matics, *Entering the Path of Enlightenment.*

29. See *The Sūtra of Golden Light,* trans. R. E. Emmerick. This appears as chapter 26 in the Chinese version translated by Nobel (n. 19 above).

30. See A. and H. Wayman, *The Lion's Roar of Queen Śrīmālā.*

31. R. H. Mathews, *Chinese-English Dictionary,* 975.

32. See Michael Pye, *Skilful Means;* idem, "Other-Power and Skilful Means in Shin Buddhism," *The Pure Land* n.s. 1 (December 1984) 70–78.

Bibliography

Sources

The Awakening of Faith. Translated by Yoshito S. Hakeda. New York: Columbia University Press, 1967.

La Concentration de la Marche Héroique: Śūraṃgamasamādhisūtra. Translated by Étienne Lamotte. *Mélanges chinois et bouddhiques* 13. Brussels: Institut Belge des Hautes Études Chinoises, 1965.

Conze, E. *Buddhist Wisdom Books.* London: Allen & Unwin, 1975.

Dialogues of the Buddha. Translated by T. W. and C. A. F. Rhys Davids. Sacred Books of the Buddhists. London: Pali Text Society, 1977.

Entering the Path of Enlightenment. Translated by Marion L. Matics. New York: Macmillan, 1970.

Das Kegon Sutra. Translated by Doi Torakazu. 4 vols. Tokyo: Doitsubun Kegon-kyō Kankōkai, 1983.

The Laṅkāvatāra Sūtra. Translated by D. T. Suzuki. London: Routledge & Kegan Paul, 1932.

The Mahāvastu. Translated by J. J. Jones. 3 vols. London: Pali Text Society, 1973.

Scripture of the Lotus Blossom of the Fine Dharma (The Lotus Sūtra): Translated from the Chinese of Kumārajīva. Translated by Leon Hurvitz. New York: Columbia University Press, 1976.

The Sūtra of Golden Light. Translated by R. E. Emmerick. Sacred Books of the Buddhists. London: Pali Text Society, 1970.

Suvarnaprabhāsottama-Sūtra: Das Goldglanz-sūtra: ein Sanskrittext des Mahāyāna-Buddhismus. Translated by J. Nobel. 2 vols. Leiden: E. J. Brill, 1958.

Studies

Bloom, Alfred. *Shinran's Gospel of Pure Grace.* Tucson, AZ: University of Arizona Press, 1965.

Davidson, J. Leroy. *The Lotus Sūtra in Chinese Art.* New Haven: Yale University Press, 1954.
Lévi, Sylvain. *Mahāyāna-Sūtralaṃkāra.* Paris: H. Champion, 1907.
Mathews, R. H. *Chinese-English Dictionary.* Revised American Edition. Cambridge, MA: Harvard University Press, 1943.
Pye, Michael. *Skilful Means: A Concept in Mahayana Buddhism.* London: Duckworth, 1978.
Wayman, A., and H. Wayman. *The Lion's Roar of Queen Śrīmālā: A Buddhist Scripture on the Tathāgatagarbha Theory.* New York: Columbia University Press, 1974.

8

Mahāyāna Philosophies

I. *The Mādhyamika Tradition*

TACHIKAWA MUSASHI

NĀGĀRJUNA (CA. 150–250 C.E.), the founder of the Mādhyamika or Middle School, furnished the philosophical basis of Indian Mahāyāna Buddhism. The school stood for the middle way between such polarities as "the world exists or does not exist," or "the world is permanent or impermanent." Its history in India may be divided into three periods: (1) the period of its formation, (2) the period of systematization, (3) the later period, in which Mādhyamika was synthesized with Yogācāra, and in which the Mādhyamika philosophy served as one of the most important theoretical bases of Buddhist Tantrism. Although Nāgārjuna's philosophy of emptiness (śūnyatā) was obviously influenced by early Prajñāpāramitā literature, it is original in several important respects. Nāgārjuna adheres to the principles of formal logic, and never has recourse to the famous paradoxical slogan of the *Prajñāpāramitā* sūtras: "Form is emptiness" (*rūpam śūnyatā*). Some features of his argumentation appear to clash with the basic principles of logic, prompting some scholars to find in it the seeds of a special kind of "logic" which is to be distinguished from that of the Western tradition. But this view rests on a misunderstanding. If the philosophy of emptiness involves any illogical elements, they are to be found in later developments. Although his most important work, the *Mūlamadhyamaka-kārikā* (Stanzas on the Middle Path; abbreviated as *MMK*), is a religious text, and as such aims at the understanding of emptiness where verbalization ceases, Nāgārjuna consistently undertakes to articulate the notion of emptiness by means of logic. Nāgārjuna seems to have lived in Vaidarbha (present Benar) in South India and it is supposed that he was supported by a Śātavāhana king. The *MMK*, consisting of about 450 verses in twenty-seven chapters, seems fragmentary because each chapter deals with a separate topic. A close examination of the arguments given in the *MMK*, however, will demonstrate that it deals with a single theme using a consistent method.

Negation of Mundane Reality

Human deeds (*karman*) produce their own effects and cause other deeds to arise. This chain of deeds ties human beings to the world of transmigration. Mental defilements (*kleśa*) such as desire, ignorance, and anger, torment both the body and mind of human beings and pull down people floating on the surface of the ocean of transmigration to its bottom. In order to obtain enlightenment one must annihilate one's deeds and mental defilements. Nāgārjuna says: "One obtains final liberation when deeds and mental defilements have been annihilated" (*MMK* xviii, 5a). According to Nāgārjuna, deeds and mental defilements arise from mental constructs (*kalpana*). "Mental constructs arise from *prapañca*" (xviii, 5b), a term that appears ten times in the *MMK* and has the following meanings: (1) words, (2) the act of expressing by means of words, (3) the meaning or image represented by words, and (4) the objects of words.[1] *Prapañca* is thus coterminous with the entire world, and to annihilate it is to negate the entire world. The word *prapañca*, originally meaning "manifoldness" or "expansion," here denotes the dichotomy that is necessarily involved in making a statement or sentence, inasmuch as a Sanskrit sentence may be considered to consist of two elements: a noun phrase and a verb phrase. This is true at least of the statements Nāgārjuna treats in the *MMK*. He sees the dichotomy between the noun phrase and the verb phrase as the concrete linguistic manifestation of *prapañca*.

Prapañca is annihilated in emptiness (śūnyatā; *MMK* xviii, 5c). Emptiness, which is nothing but ultimate truth (*paramārtha*), awaits the religious practice of human beings. Ultimate truth is not independent of these practices. Although *prapañca* inevitably appears in verbal activity, it is an obstacle to enlightenment, and until it is annihilated, one cannot realize ultimate truth. The arguments given in the *MMK* aim at leading people to the state in which *prapañca* has been extinguished and thus serve to map a path of religious practice leading to ultimate truth. This method of negating the mundane to realize the transmundane may be contrasted with that of the Vaiśeṣika school, for whom the existence of pain (*duḥkha*) in the soul (*ātman*) is to be negated, while the existence of atoms cannot be negated; for them, final liberation (*mokṣa*) is the absence of pain in the soul. In Abhidharma thought, it is the mental defilements in each individual that are to be annihilated, while the dharmas constituting the world cannot be negated. In contrast, Nāgārjuna holds that not only mental defilements and deeds but also the material causes of the world are to be annihilated. Emptiness is the state of wisdom in which all the elements of the mundane world, mental defilements, deeds, and material causes have been negated, so that the transmundane, nirvāṇa, can appear. How then is one to be free from *prapañca?* Nāgārjuna's method is to prove *prapañca* to be nonexistent through a special mode of analysis of our verbal activities.

Fundamental to Buddhism is the theory that things come into existence in dependence on other things and do not possess the grounds for existence in themselves—the theory of dependent co-arising (*pratītyasamutpāda*). Nāgārjuna sees dependent co-arising as a type of relation. In order for a relation to be possible, at least two factors are requisite. Nāgārjuna frequently posits a pair of entities that are inseparably connected and expresses these entities and the relation between them in a statement that can be taken as an expression of dependent co-arising.

> Dependent upon the action there arises the actor.
> Dependent upon the actor there arises the action. (*MMK* viii, 12)

This verse focuses on two entities—the actor (*kartṛ*) and the action (*karman*)—and delineates the relation between them. This is the first stage of all arguments in the *MMK*. In *MMK* I Nāgārjuna deals with an entity (*bhāva*) and the action of its arising (*utpāda*); in *MMK* II he takes up "that which is to be traversed" (*gantavya*) and the action of traversing (*gamana*), or the agent of the action of traversing (*gantṛ*) and the action of traversing; in *MMK* III he deals with "that which is to be seen" (*draṣṭavya*) and the action of seeing (*darśana*), or the agent of the action of seeing (*draṣṭṛ*) and the action of seeing. It is unnecessary to enumerate here all the pairs of this kind appearing in the *MMK*. Any pair of entities can serve as two factors comprising the relation of dependent co-arising, insofar as they and the relation between them are expressed or referred to in a statement or sentence.[2]

Those statements expressing dependent co-arising have common features, which give a clue to the structure of Nāgārjuna's arguments. If we take the sentence

> Space is not existence, and space is not non-existence (Candrakīrti, *Prasannapadā* v, 7),

we note the following logical features: (1) "Existence" and "nonexistence" are complementary to each other. The union of existence and nonexistence is the entire universe. (2) The statement "space is existence" consists of the noun "space" and the verb phrase "is existence." One factor is denoted by the noun; the other by the verb phrase. Their relation is expressed by the syntactical connection of the two. (3) The two statements are false.[3] The following verse illustrates the same structure:

> It is impossible that there is an arising of that which exists, of that which does not exist, and of that which exists and does not exist. (*MMK* vii, 20)

The content of the verse may be expressed by the conjunction of the following three statements:

> There is no arising of that which exists.
> There is no arising of that which does not exist.
> There is no arising of that which exists and does not exist.

"Arising" and "that which exists" are related as a property and its possessor. As in the previous case, we can point out the three features in this formula: (1) The union of that which exists and that which does not exist is the entire universe. The concept "that which exists and does not exist" seems to need some explanation. Logically speaking, there cannot be such a thing. That something exists and at the same time does not exist is a mere contradiction, as such commentators as Buddhapālita and Candrakīrti knew.[4] But it is possible to take "that which exists and does not exist" as referring to the union of the set of "that which exists" and the set of "that which does not exist," that is to say, the entire universe. In any event, the third statement is given no important role; the essential argument is carried by the first two. (2) The statement "there is no arising of that which exists" can be broken down into the noun phrase "arising" and the verb phrase "there is no existing." One factor is referred to by the noun phrase; the other by the verb phrase. Their relation is expressed by the syntactical connection of the two phrases. The other two statements have the same structure. (3) All three statements in the formula are false.

We could unearth a similar structure in statements like the following:

> Errors of those who have already erred do not come into existence.
> Neither do errors of those who have not yet erred come into existence.
> And errors of those who are at present in error do not come into existence.
> (*MMK* xxii, 17–18ab)

The two entities Nāgārjuna treats in those verses are error and someone who has already erred (or someone who does not yet err, or someone who is at present in error). Here "those who have already erred" and "those who have not yet erred" are complementary sets. One can consider "those who are at present in error" as the set complementary to the union of these two sets, and this is eventually the empty set. Nāgārjuna distinguishes the erring in terms of the three modes of time: past, future, and present. Time is represented as a continuum, which may be divided into two parts by a given point. One of the two parts divided by the point represents those who have erred, the other part represents the not-yet erring, and the point stands for those at present in error. The statements found in the formula are all false. The same principles of analysis could also be applied to this final example:

> It is impossible that a cause possesses a similar effect.
> It is impossible that a cause possesses a dissimilar effect. (*MMK* IV 6)

Here the words "similar" and "dissimilar" modify the word "effect." (1) The similar effect and the dissimilar effect stand in a complementary relation. The union of the similar effects with the dissimilar ones is the totality of all effects in the universe. (2) The statement "it is impossible that a cause possesses a similar effect" consists of the noun phrase "a similar effect" and the verb "it is impossible that a cause possesses." One factor is referred to by the noun phrase, the other by the verb phrase. Their relation is expressed by the syntactical connection of the two phrases. The other statement has the same structure.

Thus each of these examples reveals a common underlying structure: (1) Two entities are distributed into a complementary relation, either directly or, as in the last example, indirectly, through modifiers. (2) In each verse the relation between the two factors is expressed by the syntactical connection between the two necessary elements of a statement: the noun phrase and the verb phrase. (3) The statements comprising the content of each verse are all false. Thus in the case of the last example, "a cause cannot possess a similar effect; a cause cannot possess a dissimilar effect," the first step of the refutation is the complementary distribution, according to which, if the statement "a cause possesses its effect" is true, then there are two and only two cases: (1) a cause possesses a similar effect, and (2) a cause possesses a dissimilar effect. Next, Nāgārjuna disproves both. It is important to note that the statement "a cause cannot possess a similar effect" does not imply that a cause can possess a dissimilar effect. Nāgārjuna distinguishes between the negation of terms and the negation of propositions, never confusing the two. In that all the statements found in our examples are false or negated, we can see *prapañca* being annihilated. The statement "a cause possesses its effect," for instance, is shown to be based on *prapañca*, no matter how widely and frequently it is stated and is admitted to make perfect sense by common people in everyday life. As long as there remains any functioning of *prapañca*, no one can obtain ultimate truth.

Emptiness and Dependent Origination

Each chapter of the *MMK* shows how to prove the invalidity of statements expressing the relation of dependent co-arising. By this series of negations of *prapañca* Nāgārjuna aims at approaching emptiness, where every *prapañca* has been annihilated. In what kind of situation, however, does one realize emptiness? What kind of feeling does one have, when one succeeds in touching emptiness? What is emptiness after all? On these questions Nāgārjuna keeps silence. Indeed, in his main works he never uses even the term *prajñāpāramitā* (Perfection of Wisdom). The author of the *MMK* surely believes that there is a moment in which all *prapañca* have been annihilated and one is released from their bondage. But one may not say that emptiness exists; emptiness is not a permanent substance. What is important about emptiness is that it presupposes continuous efforts to negate verbal activities. In answer to the objection "If everything is empty (*śūnya*) then the four noble truths are also non-existent," Nāgārjuna says, "You do not know the purpose of emptiness, and the meaning of emptiness." The former is that which urges us to negate *prapañca*, and the latter is the mundane world as grasped in a new way after the application to it of the principle of emptiness. To the purpose and meaning of emptiness correspond the vectors from mundane to transmundane and from transmundane back to mundane. Thus emptiness is not a pole isolated from the mutual dynamic relation between the mundane and the transmundane.

MMK xxiv, 18, points out an important aspect of Nāgārjuna's thought:

> What is dependent co-arising we call emptiness.
> That is representation by words and that is the middle way.

Dependent co-arising is something positive, insofar as things come into existence according to this principle. But as we have seen, Nāgārjuna's aim is to negate the existence of the factors found in the relation of dependent co-arising. The dedication verse of the *MMK* identifies dependent co-arising with ultimate truth (*paramārtha*). "Representation by words" is the world as seen when, having obtained the power of ultimate truth, or emptiness, one comes back to the phenomenal world. Dependent co-arising is here identified with the mundane world thus reenvisioned. Dependent co-arising thus characterizes all three modes of existence: the mundane, which does not undergo the process of the negation of the *prapañca;* the transmundane, or ultimate truth; and the reenvisioned mundane world, which has obtained rebirth through the annihilation of *prapañca. MMK* xxiv, 18, identifies these three different modes of existence, but this does not spell an abolition of the difference between mundane and transmundane. On the contrary, the verse stresses that difference, while it indicates how the transmundane manifests itself in the mundane, or in more religious terms, how the sacred manifests itself in the profane.

We have seen that the world is resurrected as verbal representation. The

MMK contains several verses in each of which a pair of entities and the relation between them are mentioned in an affirmative statement:

> Dependent upon the action there arises the actor. Dependent upon the actor there arises the action. (*MMK* VIII 12).

In this verse (1) a complementary relation is neither found nor presupposed, and (2) the two statements are true. Here Nāgārjuna does not negate the relation between the two factors, but on the contrary tries to establish the relation of mutual dependence between them, which is an important aspect of dependent co-arising. Therefore, no complementary distribution is needed in this verse. In this manner Nāgārjuna shows the way which starts from the mundane world, leads to ultimate truth, and comes back to the mundane, now transformed by the power of ultimate truth.

Nāgārjuna thus distinguishes between the mundane world and ultimate truth in terms of the "direction" of religious practice. It is the general view of Buddhism that one should escape from the world of transmigration and obtain enlightenment by means of the path of religious practice. Nāgārjuna's thought is not an exception to this general tendency. However, the "distance" between the world of transmigration and enlightenment differs according to a thinker or a school. For Abhidharma thinkers the distance between the two religious poles is so great that one is supposed to undergo an enormous number of stages of practice in order to obtain enlightenment. On the contrary, for Nāgārjuna, the two poles are not so wide apart as in the case of the Abhidharma philosophy. The *MMK* xxv, 19, clearly shows in what relation Nāgārjuna holds transmigration and nirvāṇa (final beatitude) as follows:

> Transmigration is not different from nirvāṇa.
> Nirvāṇa is not different from transmigration.

What is important here is that Nāgārjuna does not identify those two opposite poles directly: he employs the negative expression "not different from" to indicate the relation between them. Let us remember that Nāgārjuna never states the famous paradox "matter is emptiness and emptiness is matter." Nāgārjuna thus expresses the identical relation between the two religious poles through the medium of negation.

We now meet a subtle but critical point: Nāgārjuna does not admit any difference between the mundane world and ultimate truth, while he clearly distinguishes the two poles. When he negates every kind of verbal activity (*prapañca*), he strictly differentiates *prapañca* from ultimate truth. On the other hand, the identity of the two religious poles is never indicated directly, but is only implied by Nāgārjuna. The *MMK* xxiv, 18, might seem to identify dependent co-origination with emptiness. Yet here also Nāgārjuna is cautious about the relation between the two. In other words, he is not merely identifying the two poles. As we have seen, he is expressing the vector of religious practice directed from the mundane world to ultimate truth. In the famous phrase "What is dependent co-arising we call emptiness," he is referring to the process of religious practice directed from the profane to the sacred. He never states "What is emptiness is dependent co-arising," which would refer to practice in a reverse direction. Instead Nāgārjuna says, "That [emptiness] is representation by words and that is the middle way." Here also he does not mention the mere identity of the mundane (the profane) with the transmundane (the sacred). In implying that ultimate truth manifests itself in the mundane world he is referring to the process as directed from the sacred to the profane.

One must proceed on the way leading from the profane to the sacred gradually, step by step. For Nāgārjuna concentrates his chief effort on proving the nonexistence of all *prapañca,* and, as we have seen, the path his negations trace is a long and difficult one, though always surprisingly logical. The mundane world is thus gradually led to the transmundane truth, but the latter "returns" to the former in a moment. That is to say, the "time" of the vector directed from the profane to the sacred is successive. The "time" of the vector directed from the sacred to the profane is simultaneous. If someone wishes to realize emptiness, one must know that there is a long way to go. But at the same time one knows that the world of transmigration is not different from nirvāṇa or ultimate truth. The knowledge that this goal is very close encourages the person walking the road leading to the sacred. Even if one is told that the transmigratory world is not different from nirvāṇa, one should not stop cultivating religious practice which, in the case of the *MMK,* takes the form of examining the structure of language and words. If Nāgārjuna had identified transmigration with nirvāṇa directly without any medium, he would not have been able to convey the importance of religious practice. If transmigration is held to be completely identical with nirvāṇa, one would easily be tempted to stop the operation of negating the existence of *prapañca.* Such a tendency is actually observed in some Buddhist schools of later development.

The Development of the Mādhyamika Tradition

Āryadeva (ca. 170–270), said to have been a direct disciple of Nāgārjuna, lived in South India. Legend tells us that he attacked his opponents so vehemently that he was killed by them. Since his Catuḥśataka is extant only in fragments of the Sanskrit original and in a partial Chinese and an obscure Tibetan translation, its contents are not well known, though Candrakīrti's commentary on it has been preserved in Tibetan. His *Śataśāstra*, extant in Chinese translation, has been much studied in China and Japan. Although Āryadeva's thought differs from Nāgārjuna's in some points, in general he follows the master closely. Rāhulabhadra is said to have been a disciple of Āryadeva. We know little about his life. In the tradition of the panegyric genre of Nāgārjuna, he composed two hymns, the *Prajñāpāramitāstotra* and the *Saddharmapuṇḍarīkastava*. Two old commentaries composed in the early period of the Mādhyamika school have survived: the *Akutobhayā* and Piṅgala's commentary. The former, extant only in a Tibetan translation, was ascribed to Nāgārjuna himself in Tibet. The latter, preserved only in Kumārajīva's Chinese translation, was used as one of the most basic texts of the Mādhyamika philosophy in China and Japan. The arguments given in those two commentaries are often similar.

The middle period of the Mādhyamika school was marked by the conflicts between the Prāsaṅgika school founded by Buddhapālita (470–540) and the Svātantrika established by Bhāvaviveka (d. 570). The former school derives its name from the fact that Buddhapālita and his followers employed the *prasaṅga* method (*reductio ad absurdum*), pointing out the inevitable but undesired contradictions and errors in propositions others try to prove, but never presenting any proposition affirming their own standpoint. This method was attacked by Bhāvaviveka, who tried to prove emptiness by means of autonomous (*svatantra*) inference, that is, by syllogisms. While the Prāsaṅgika hold that ultimate truth cannot be reached by words, which are embodiments of conventional truth, the Svātantrika school holds that the two religious poles can be bridged by words.

According to the Tibetan tradition, Buddhapālita lived in South India in the period contemporary with or prior to Dignāga, who established the system of Buddhist logic. Buddhapālita wrote a commentary on the *MMK*, the *Mūlamadhyamakavṛtti*, which has arguments in common with the *Akutobhayā* and Piṅgala's commentary and makes no reference to Dignāga's system of logic. He transformed the dilemmas or tetralemmas of the *MMK* into two or four *prasaṅga*-type syllogisms. His critic Bhāvaviveka wrote the *Prajñāpradīpa*, a commentary on the *MMK;* the *Madhyamakahṛdayakārikā*, a critique of other philosophical schools; and a commentary on this work, the *Tarkajvālā*. Strongly influenced by Dignāga's system of logic, he believed it could appropriately be used to prove the truth of Nāgārjuna's statements expressing the relation of dependent co-arising, which often go against common sense. For instance, in order to prove the statement "a traverser (or goer) does not traverse (or go)," he set forth the following syllogism:

Thesis: In ultimate truth a traverser does not traverse. Reason: because it is connected with an action. Example: as in the case of a stayer.

Bhāvaviveka held that, according to Dignāga's system, the reason that this syllogism was correct was because it fulfilled the necessary conditions of correct reasoning. The syllogism, however, has a defect, or trick, noted by later Mādhyamika thinkers. Its inference is carried out at two different levels: that of common sense and that of ultimate truth. In the latter nothing is existent. It necessarily follows that what can be applied to the level of common sense cannot be applied to the level of ultimate truth. The intention to prove emptiness by means of syllogisms stems from the conviction that words are capable of indicating ultimate truth. Bhāvaviveka thus held that the two religious poles of mundane and ultimate truth are bridgeable by language.

Candrakīrti's commentary on the *MMK*, the *Prasannapadā*, supported Buddhapālita by criticizing Bhāvaviveka, and consolidated the Prāsaṅgika school. Although Candrakīrti knew Dignāga's logic, he did not utilize it to explain emptiness. He kept his distance from systematized logic, having seen the errors into which it led Bhāvaviveka. Instead of setting forth syllogisms, he tried to point out contradictions implicit in the statements of opponents. This work is the fullest exposition of the Mādhyamika, not merely serving to clarify the logic of Nāgārjuna's elliptic utterances but also bringing out clearly the spiritual purpose of the dialectic. The next great, and probably the last, representative of the Prāsaṅgika school was Śāntideva (ca. 800), author of the *Śikṣāsamuccaya* and the *Bodhicaryāvatāra* (Introduction to the Practice of Awakening). The former work teaches the bodhisattva's practice that leads to the attainment of Buddhahood. The latter describes the advantages of the mind of Awakening. Having prescribed preliminaries, such as offering and homage, it urges pupils to perform the six bodhisattva perfections. Candrakīrti, too, finding logic incapable of reaching ultimate truth, had fallen back on practice, and both he and Śāntideva even show some mystical leanings. According to the Tibetan tradition, Śāntideva was an ardent Tantrist, and the Mādhyamika school began to be closely connected with Tantrism toward the end of the middle period of the school.

Śāntarakṣita

In the late period the difference between Prāsaṅgika and Svātantrika became less important. Svātantrika, which flourished more than Prāsaṅgika, was synthesized with Yogācāra thinking in the Yogācāra-Mādhyamika, which was divided into two subschools: the Sākāravijñānavāda and the Nirākāravijñānavāda. It was Śāntarakṣita, a scholar at the Nālandā monastery, who synthesized Mādhyamika and Yogācāra, and he also played the leading role in the introduction of Indian Mahāyāna Buddhism into Tibet. In 771, having entered Tibet for the second time, he defeated Bonpas in religious debate. With the help of Padmasaṁbhava, a Buddhist Tantrist, who was invited from India in 773, Śāntarakṣita built a Buddhist center in Tibet, the Bsam yan monastery (787), and died soon afterward. At the moment of his death he asked that his disciple Kamalaśīla be invited from India if Tibetan Buddhism should come to a crisis. He apparently foresaw that the newly introduced Indian Mahāyāna tradition would soon be forced to confront the Chinese Mahāyāna tradition, which was already showing many signs of rapid growth in Tibet.

The principal works of Śāntarakṣita are the *Tattvasaṃgraha* and the *Madhyamakālaṃkāra.* The former discusses a number of philosophical topics and criticizes the standpoints of other Buddhist schools and also of Hindu schools. Thus, the first chapter examines the Sāṅkhya system; the second, the theory that God is the origin of the world; the third, the theory that attributes creation to both God and primordial matter (*prakṛti*). The middle part of the work deals with sense perception (chap. 17), inference (chap. 18), and other forms and valid means of cognition (chap. 19). However, for a systematic presentation of Śāntarakṣita's philosophy we must turn to the *Madhyamakālaṃkāra.*[5] In the beginning of this work the author proves himself to be a Mādhyamika philosopher by declaring that any entity (dharma) has neither a simple nor a compound nature. The work's ninety-seven verses may be divided into three parts: a proof of the truth of the author's syllogism by means of reasoning (vv. 1–62), a proof by means of scripture (vv. 63–90), and the conclusion (vv. 91–97). Śāntarakṣita followed Bhāvaviveka's example in attempting to present his main theme in the form of a syllogism; like Bhāvaviveka, he considered words capable of denoting ultimate truth, albeit not directly. He was also strongly influenced by Dharmakīrti, who consolidated the system of Buddhist logic established by Dignāga and himself belonged to the Sākāravijñāna school. Bhāvaviveka in his *Madhyamakahṛdaya* had enumerated several doctrines of contemporary schools without grading them. Śāntarakṣita, however, placed Mādhyamika in the highest rank, and saw other Buddhist philosophies as steps toward Mādhyamika. He held that while the Vaibhāṣikas and the Sautrāntikas admitted the real existence of cognition and matter, and the Yogācārins considered only cognition to be real, the Mādhyamikas did not admit even the existence of cognition.

The *Madhyamakālaṃkāra* starts with the following syllogism:

(Thesis) In ultimate truth those entities postulated as real by our [i.e., Buddhist] and other [i.e., non-Buddhist] schools possess no intrinsic nature (*svabhāva*), (Reason) because they possess neither a simple nor a compound nature, (Example) like a reflection (v. 1).[6]

The logical arguments in proof of this syllogism in the first part consist of replies to the objection that the mark (*hetu:* reason) mentioned in the syllogism is unestablished (*asiddha*). The objections come from Vaibhāṣika, Sautrāntika, and Yogācāra philosophers. Śāntarakṣita comments on the syllogism as follows:

If [any] intrinsic nature exists, it has to be either simple or compound. "Simple" and "plural" are exclusive of [i.e., complementary to] each other. Therefore, the third group [or set] is denied to exist. The constituent elements (skandha), primary causes (*pradhāna*), and the like, which are postulated as real by our and other [schools] do not exist in reality, and they possess no intrinsic nature.

Here Śāntarakṣita distributes all the entities appearing in a domain of discussion into a complementary relationship. As in the case of Nāgārjuna, complementary distribution is a basic apparatus of his arguments. Logically, any entity has to be either simple or compound; if it is proved to be neither, then it follows that it does not exist at all in the world. No one can talk about the simple or compound nature of a nonexistent thing. Śāntarakṣita's ultimate theme is that no entity at all exists in the world. He denies the existence of atoms on the ground that an atom can possess no intrinsic nature. Though usually considered a simple entity, an atom cannot be simple, for it must have several dimensions in order to be related with other surrounding atoms (vv. 11–13). Having thus denied the existence of matter (*rūpa*), he goes on to deny the existence of cognition (vv. 16–60), opposing the views of the Sākāravijñānavāda and the Nirākāravijñānavāda. Despite this criticism, the Yogācāra philosophy was as important as the Mādhyamika to Śāntarakṣita, and he can in fact be called a Yogācāra philosopher. Toward the end of the *Madhyamakālaṃkāra* (v. 93) he compares Yogācāra and Mādhyamika to the two reins of a carriage.

According to the Sākāravijñānavāda, the object of cognition is "that which is to be grasped," and the cognition is "that which grasps." The object of cognition is capable of giving the image of itself to the cognition, and the cognition contains the image of its object in itself. Śāntarakṣita denies that cognition, which is indivisible, can possess these different elements and presents the following argument against this theory:

(Thesis) The image [given by the object to the cognition] cannot be compound,

(Reason) because [the image of the object] is not different from the cognition, which is simple,
(Example) like the essence of the cognition.[7]

To say that the image of the object is not different from the cognition of the object does not imply that the image is identical with the cognition. Image and cognition are identical only if one presupposes that there exists an image of the cognition in the world, but Śāntarakṣita does not make this presupposition. Following the Mādhyamika tradition, he holds that there exists no image at all in the world. If there is no image in the world, the proposition "the image is not different from the cognition" and the proposition "the image is identical with the cognition" can be true at the same time. The Sākāravijñānavādins hold that the simplicity of the cognition is not incompatible with the plurality of its objects, because a number of cognitions such as "it is yellow" and "it is red" appear at one moment. Śāntarakṣita refutes this by referring to Dharmakīrti's theory that heterogeneous cognitions caused by different kinds of organs, such as the eye and the ear, may occur at one moment, while homogeneous cognitions caused by one kind of organ cannot occur at one moment. According to Śāntarakṣita, a cognition cannot possess plural images, which may be considered to be parts of the cognition, for if a cognition possesses parts, then the parts are to be divided until one reaches the size of an atom, which cannot be divided into smaller pieces, and the existence of the cognition would have to be denied in the same manner as that of an atom is denied.

In the beginning of the second part of the *Madhyamakālaṃkāra* the author states that all entities are characterized by conventional (as opposed to ultimate) truth (v. 63). He defines conventional truth as follows:

> One should understand that conventional [truth] is in essence (I) that which is agreeable and acceptable only as long as it is not investigated critically, (2) that which is characterized by arising and decay, and (3) whatever has causal efficiency (v. 64).[8]

Then he states that there exists nothing which can be established in ultimate truth (v. 69), and that ultimate truth is beyond every kind of verbal activity (v. 70).

Kamalaśīla

As Śāntarakṣita predicted, the Indian Mahāyāna tradition introduced into Tibet came into conflict with the Chinese tradition toward the end of the eighth century. Kamalaśīla (ca. 740–797), the Indian disciple of Śāntarakṣita, was invited by the Tibetan king to carry on the work of his teacher. He defeated the Chinese Ho-shang Mahāyāna in debate about religious matters, such as the process of obtaining enlightenment, and from then on the Indian Mahāyāna of Śāntarakṣita and Kamalaśīla became the dominant Buddhist school in Tibet. In later times Tibetans called the school led by the Ho-shang Mahāyāna "simultaneists," and the school of Śāntarakṣita and Kamalaśīla, "gradualists." Ho-shang taught that religious practices, such as the observation of precepts, patience, meditation, and studies of philosophical doctrines, are not essential for enlightenment, which can be obtained through the annihilation of mental activities. For him, emptiness was the mere absence of all the kinds of mental activities, such as perceiving, feeling, and thinking. On the contrary, Śāntarakṣita and his followers held that, in order to obtain enlightenment, one had to undergo a number of stages of religious training, including study of Buddhist philosophies, and practice of the six perfections of a bodhisattva and the ten Budhisattva stages.

Kamalaśīla wrote extensive commentaries on the two main works of Śāntarakṣita, as well as two important works, the *Madhyamakāloka* and the *Bhāvanākrama.* The former expounds the theory of emptiness according to the Yogācāra-Mādhyamika system, which maintains the doctrine of non-production in ultimate truth and production on the level of conventional truth. The general frame of his thought in this work is similar to that of the *Madhyamakālaṃkāra.* The second work expounds Kamalaśīla's "gradualist" position by elucidating the processes of religious practice.

Notes

1. See Lambert Schmithausen, *Der Nirvāṇa-Abschnitt in der Viniśkayasaṃgraha der Yogācārabhūmiḥ* (Österreichische Akademie der Wissenschaften, Philosophisch-Historische Klasse Sitzungsberichte 264; Veroffentlichungen der Kommission für Sprachen und Kulturen Süd- und Ostasiens 8; Vienna: Hermann Böhlaus, 1969) 137–42.
2. See M. Tachikawa, "Pratītyasamutpāda in the dedication of the *mūlamadhyamakakārikā,*" in *Brahmavidya Dr. K. Kunjuni Raja Felicitation Volume, The Adyar Library Bulletin* 44–45 (1981) 639–53.
3. See M. Tachikawa, "A Logical Analysis of the *MMK,*" in *Sanskrit and Indian Studies: Essays in Honour of Daniel H. H. Ingalls,* ed. M. Nagatomi et al., Studies of Classical India 2 (Dordrecht and London: Reidel, 1980) 165.
4. Ibid., 181 n. 6.
5. *The Tattvasaṃgraha of Śāntarakṣita with the Commentary of Kamalaśīla,* trans. G. Jha, vii.
6. *Madhyamakālaṃkāra of Śāntarakṣita,* ed. M. Ichigo, cxxxv, 22.
7. Ibid., 82.
8. Ibid., cxlii, 202.

Bibliography

Sources

Madhyamakālaṃkāra of Śāntarakṣita. Edited by M. Ichigo. Kyoto: Buneidō, 1985.

Mūlamadhyamakakārikā de Nāgārjuna avec la Prasannapadā Commentaire de Candrakīrti. Edited by L. de La Vallée Poussin. St. Petersburg, 1903–13. Reprint, Bibliotheca Buddhica 4. Osnabruck: Biblio Verlag, 1970.

The Tattvasaṅgraha of Śāntarakṣīta. Translated by G. Jha. Gaekward's Oriental Series 80, 83. Baroda: Oriental Institute, 1937–1939.

Tucci, G. *Minor Buddhist Texts, II: First Bhāvanākrama of Kamalaśīla, Sanskrit and Tibetan Texts with Introduction and English Summary.* Serie Orientale Roma IX, 2. Rome, 1985.

——. *Minor Buddhist Texts, III: Third Bhāvanākrama.* Serie Orientale Roma XLIII. Rome, 1971.

Studies

Kajiyama, Yuichi. "Chūgan shisō no rekishi to bunken" (History and Literature of Mādhyamika Thought). *Kōza daijō Bukkyō* (Series of Lectures: Mahāyāna Buddhism). Tokyo: Shunjūsha, 1982. In Japanese.

——. *Kū no ronri* (Logic of Emptiness). Tokyo: Kadokawa Shoten, 1969.

Kalupahana, David J. *Nāgārjuna: The Philosophy of the Middle Way.* New York: State University of New York Press, 1986.

Lindtner, C. *Nagarjuniana: Studies in the Writings and Philosophy of Nāgārjuna.* Copenhagen: Akademisk Forlag, 1982.

May, Jacques. *Candrakirti: Prasannapadā Madyamakavrtti.* Paris: A. Maisonneuve, 1959.

Murti, T. R. V. *The Central Philosophy of Buddhism.* London: Allen & Unwin, 1955. Paperback reprint, London: Unwin Paperbacks, 1980.

Robinson, Richard H. *Early Madhyamika in India and China.* Madison: University of Wisconsin Press, 1967.

Ruegg, David Seyfort. *The Literature of the Madhyamaka School of Philosophy in India.* Wiesbaden: Harrassowitz, 1981.

Sprung, Mervyn. *Lucid Exposition of the Middle Way.* Boulder: Prajñā Press, 1979.

——, ed. *The Problem of Two Truths in Buddhism and Vedānta.* Boston: D. Reidel, 1973.

Stcherbatsky, T. *The Conception of Buddhist Nirvana.* Leningrad: Publishing Office of the Academy of Science of the U.S.S.R., 1927. Reprint, Delhi: Motilal Banarsidass, 1977.

Streng, Frederick. *Emptiness: A Study in Religious Meaning.* New York: Abingdon Press, 1967.

II. *Yogācāra*

John P. Keenan

Yogācāra, a school of Buddhist philosophy founded by the brothers Asaṅga and Vasubandhu in the fifth century, focuses on a critical and reflective understanding of mind, both deluded and awakened. It attempts to make explicit the structure of consciousness and to sketch the dynamic progression toward conversion and awakening. Asaṅga and Vasubandhu, as well as the semilegendary Maitreya, who is reported to have been Asaṅga's mentor and to whom various texts are ascribed, were deeply influenced by the *Prajñāpāramitā* scriptures and their central teaching that all things are empty. They were also steeped in Mādhyamika thought: Asaṅga and Sthiramati (sixth century), wrote commentaries on Nāgārjuna's *Stanzas on the Middle.* The notions of emptiness and dependent co-arising and the theme of the two truths are central in Yogācāra thinking and meditation.

But the Yogācāra thinkers did not simply comment on Mādhyamika thought. They attempted to ground insight into emptiness in a critical understanding of the mind, articulated in a sophisticated theoretical discourse. Nāgārjuna had rejected all theory and all views (*dṛṣṭi*) as illusory and had negated them by the dialectic of emptiness. Asaṅga's aim was to revive theory as dependently co-arising understanding through rethinking the meaning of emptiness. Yogācāra is thus a partial reaffirmation of the validity of abhidharmic analyses and expositions. It no longer presupposes the naïve realism of Hīnayāna Abhidharma, but attempts to make explicit the underlying structure and dynamic functioning of consciousness, as witnessed in the title of its foundational scripture, *The Scripture on the Explication of Underlying Meaning* (*Saṃdhinirmocanasūtra*).

The Yogācāra turn toward conscious interiority, which took place more than a millennium before Kant, was triggered by and evolved within a specifically religious problematic. The Mādhyamika practice of logical refutation through insight into emptiness called into question all truth claims, even those most central to Buddhist doctrine, such as the Four Noble Truths, branding them as illusory "views." Nāgārjuna and Āryadeva practiced a constant vigilance against the setting up of any view as true, insisting that the truth of ultimate meaning goes beyond any verbal or logical formulation.

They recommended a thorough deconstruction of all prior theory, all abhidharmic belief in fixed essences (*svabhāva*) of things. Their aim was to open up anew the experience of realizing awakening by the negation and removal of clinging to verbalized truth. This focus on emptiness and negation was constantly in tension with the affirmative value of dependent co-arising. Mādhyamika explicitly rejected nihilism (*nāstivāda*), and claimed to affirm neither being nor nothingness. Yet the idea that everything was empty was a source of despondency and consternation to practitioners, as *The Analysis of the Jeweled Lineage*, a text that brings together Tathāgatagarbha themes, reports.[1] In a world of negation and essencelessness, there appears to be no refuge and no sure path to cessation. No doctrinal discourse can maintain its validity and no scriptures can present words of awakening.

The tension created by these problems led some to the affirmation of an ultimate reality beyond the scope of emptiness. The texts of the Tathāgatagarbha lineage affirm the ultimate, non-empty (*aśūnya*) reality of the dharmabody, of the seed or womb (*garbha*) of awakening present originally in all sentient beings. A specifically Buddhist version of Indian monism was developed, negating the *Prajñāpāramitā* and Mādhyamika notion of emptiness by reducing its applicability to defiled states, not the originally pure seed or Buddha-nature.[2] Although the pre-Asaṅgan Yogācāra texts of Maitreya appear to have been influenced heavily by these Tathāgatagarbha ideas,[3] the classical Yogācāra thinkers, Asaṅga and Vasubandhu, did not follow this monistic option. They based their thought on the *Prajñāpāramitā* teachings and accepted their notion of emptiness.

But the problem remained. How could one enunciate doctrine without falling into illusory views? Did not the Buddha's teachings remain valid? If things are affirmed to all be empty, how can one validate the basic insight into emptiness? Mādhyamikas asserted that they were not asserting anything and so had no need to validate anything. It was sufficient, Āryadeva argued, to disclose the logical errors in others' assertions without offering any "view" of one's own. Yet Mādhyamika did function as a deconstructive method by basing itself on insight into the emptiness and silence of ultimate meaning. That emptiness is then identified with dependent co-arising; ultimate meaning is held in constant tension with and differentiation from worldly convention. These views needed to be more convincingly grounded. In seeking to steer a course between the perception of nihilism and the monistic assertion of an ultimate, non-empty reality, Asaṅga was led to turn his attention to the internal structure and genesis of both illusion and awakening, to ground insight into emptiness in the dependently co-arisen structure of understanding, and to sketch a path toward the realization of "the conversion of support," that is, of consciousness, from illusion to awakening. Yogācāra spirituality is thus a reflective, critical spirituality. While affirming the conventional validity of dependently co-arisen insight and doctrinal formulation, it maintains the centrality of ultimately meaningful emptiness.

The Structure of Consciousness

The Yogācāra analysis of the structure of consciousness centers on two themes: (1) the container consciousness (*ālaya-vijñāna*) in its constant interplay with the active consciousness (*pravṛtti-vijñāna*) of thinking (manas) and perception and (2) the three patterns (*trilakṣaṇa*) or natures (*trisvabhāva*) of its functioning.

The container consciousness marks the initial thrust of the Yogācāra thinkers into the realm of interiority. Nāgārjuna had criticized all verbal attempts at explanation as fabrication (*prapañca*) based on clinging to essences. *The Explication of Underlying Meaning* proffers its teaching on the container consciousness as a critical understanding of the internal genesis of such fabrication. In each and every sentient being the container consciousness is a storehouse of karmic seeds which, having accumulated from the distant past, form the habitual proclivities according to which each being discriminates and verbally fabricates images and names.[4] Underlying the actively conscious process of thinking, the latent seed impressions deposited in the container consciousness subtly and subconsciously program our minds to construct images and ideas believed to correspond to real essences existing apart from the mind. The container consciousness is the foundational substructure of all mental operations, which, since it is not mediated in words or images, remains unknown in those operations. It accounts for the unity of the different activities of the mind,[5] for the actual consciousnesses of thinking and perception arise in virtue of its basic seed-programming.

Thus the differing perceptions and thoughts of a saint and a criminal are traced to these preconscious habitual proclivities planted in their minds through their differing experiences and actions. The self-justifying reasoning of a thief, that he merely responds wisely to an unfair world, results from latent seeds of greed, anger, and delusion, in the same way as the compassionate practices of a bodhisattva result from the implantation of good seeds. But the interplay between the latent container consciousness and the manifested actual consciousnesses of thinking and perceiving is not a one-way process, for the karmic actions of sentient beings plant new seeds in and remove old seeds from the container consciousness. A thief may become a bodhisattva, although it may take him a long period of time to plant and cultivate good seeds. The relationship between the container and active consciousnesses is thus one of interdependence, like that of two reeds resting upon each other. The structure of mind is synergistic, for its functional unity relies on the interdependence of the container consciousness with all its latent seeds and the active consciousnesses with all the conscious acts and thoughts of the life–death cycle.

A further characteristic of the interdependent structure of mind is the mutual reliance between insight (*darśana*) and image (*nimitta*) in the occurrence of knowing. All the active operations of thinking and perceiving appear through insight into image. Without image, whether visual or auditory, no insight occurs. Without insight, the image remains unthought. All conscious knowing takes the form of a subjective knower (*grāhaka*) apprehending an objective known (*grāhya*) because it arises through insight into images. Since interdependence is the basic structure of mind, the basic pattern of consciousness is the other-dependent pattern (*paratantra-lakṣaṇa*). This other-dependent pattern has both a defiled and a pure aspect inasmuch as it is the pivotal structure of mind accounting for both illusion and awakening. Yet in actual experience the other-dependent pattern gravitates toward illusion because of the latent seeds in the container consciousness. Thus emerges the second basic pattern of consciousness, described in *The Analysis of the Middle and Extremes* as "unreal imagining" (*abhūta-parikalpa*), in which pattern meaning is extroverted in a duality of subject standing over against object—as if meaning were a property of things correctly understood. The other-dependent pattern is the act of imagining what is unreal, experienced initially only in the context of the illusory, imagined pattern.

The imagined pattern (*parikalpita-lakṣaṇa*) is the mistaken grasping of images or insights as if they themselves independently pictured or captured real "meaning units" (dharmas). It is the state of living within an imagined world due to a failure to realize the other-dependent relationship between image and insight. When images are themselves taken to represent objective realities, they close off any possibility of insight. Thus one clings to the imagined reality of fame, profit, etc. (or God, Buddha, etc.) with the tenacity of a fundamentalist faith closed to further questioning. When insights are taken to capture reality and truth, they become views asserted in forgetfulness of their image base, a base conditioned by and dependent on a host of differing linguistic and cultural factors. Furthermore, the imagined pattern functions in disregard of the latent seeds which condition and program the habitual proclivities of our imagining and thinking. It mistakes the insight-image structure of other-dependent knowing for the basic structure of reality. Thus the imagined pattern is likened to dreams, mirages, magical tricks—all of which imply the presence of a seemingly self-enclosed image assumed mistakenly to picture reality. Conversely, propositions and theories become "imagined" when they abstract from their dependency on their language image base and pretend to detect true essences in things.

The third basic pattern of consciousness, the perfected pattern (*pariniṣpanna-lakṣaṇa*) is insight into the illusory nature of imagined realities and recovery of the basic other-dependent pattern of mind. It replaces the naïve realism of the imagined pattern with critical awareness of the interdependent structure of mind. The theme of conscious-construction-only (*vijñapti-mātra*) sums up this critical understanding.

The Yogācāra refrain that all things are conscious-construction-only has often been taken to imply an idealist negation of the objective reality of the external world in favor of the inner reality of consciousness. Indeed, it is not difficult to adduce textual passages that do deny "objective" reality and reduce all things to conscious constructs or ideas (*vijñapti*).[6] However, Asaṅga and Vasubandhu negate not only objective reality but also the reality of a subjective knower: the duality of subject and external object is declared to be entirely illusory and inexistent. The theory of conscious-construction-only understands the genesis of imagined thinking in terms not of the given reality of things but of the appearances of image and insight clung to by the seed impressions of the container consciousness as if they constituted a real object standing over against a real subject. It rejects picture images of reality in favor of a critical awareness of the other-dependent relationships that condition all human thinking.

This turning away from the imagined pattern to the perfected pattern upon the pivoting base of the other-dependent pattern is the conversion of support (*āśraya-parāvṛtti*) wherein one gains insight into the emptiness and non-being of what is imagined and into the dependent co-arisen being of what is dependently co-arisen. The sixth-century commentator Sthiramati offers a threefold analysis of conversion as encompassing a conversion of mind (*citta-āśraya-parivṛtti*), a conversion of path (*mārga-āśraya-parivṛtti*), and a conversion of the proclivities (*dauṣṭhulya-āśraya-parivṛtti*). The conversion of mind is the turning away from the imagined pattern to the perfected pattern whereby one attains insight into the empty and dependently co-arisen being of consciousness and all the meanings it generates. Nāgārjuna taught that emptiness is a designation (*prajñapti*) referring to the essenceless being of dependent co-arising. Asaṅga teaches that it is an idea, a conscious construct (*vijñapti*) based on the other-dependent structure of mind. In virtue of this conversion the path constructed in its serial stages is itself emptied and seen as representing no rigid or fixed progression. The worldly path (*laukika-mārga*) that goes from here to there is converted into a transcendent path (*lokottara-mārga*) of no-abiding, of bodhisattva practice. It is the recovery of the originally present, dependently co-arising practice engaged in deeds of compassion. The conversion of the proclivities is the eradication of the defiled seeds in the container consciousness; liberation for unhindered bodhisattva practice requires this total deprogramming of karmic seeds.

The Spiritual Dynamic

The above account of the structure of mind is at the service of the spiritual dynamism of conversion, whose movement is from insight into emptiness to a reaffirmation of being in the context of emptiness. *The Analysis of the Middle and Extremes* teaches that the middle path consists in a movement through illusory being to insight into the non-being of emptiness, and then on to a realization of the being of emptiness.[7] The other-dependent unreal imagining that marks the unawakened mind appears in the dichotomy of subject and object, presenting being as real essences to the mind. Its imagined being as an essential object over against an essentialist subject is declared to be nonexistent. But, while the *Prajñāpāramitā* scriptures and Mādhyamika philosophy stop at insight into emptiness, exercising therein a constant vigilance lest any essentialist view reappear, the Yogācāra author here goes on to reaffirm that within the other-dependent unreal imagining of everyday thinking, emptiness does exist, that is, the other-dependent pattern underlying the illusory genesis of views is not itself inexistent. Being, shorn of essentialism, is apprehended anew in the context of emptiness: "Therefore all things are said to be neither empty, nor not empty, because of being, non-being, and being—and this is the middle path" (*Madhyāntavibhāga* 1.2). The theme of the three patterns allows Asaṅga and Vasubandhu both to negate imagined being through insight into the emptiness of the objective reality of the subject–object dichotomy and to reaffirm dependently co-arising being through conversion to the fully perfected pattern. The Yogācāra thinkers were then able to discourse on the "wondrous being" of emptiness and could resurrect Abhidharma theory in light of emptiness. Thus they not only inherited the two-truth theme of Nāgārjuna but were able to stress the conventional validity of conventional truth more than was possible in Mādhyamika. It is valid in terms of its dependently co-arising language base seen as a construct-of-understanding-only.

Asaṅga in his *Summary of the Great Vehicle* teaches that dharma-body, the ineffable content of conversion, is characterized by the nonduality of existence and nonexistence, since all things are nonexistent—that is, empty—while their character of being empty does exist.[8] The commentator Asvabhāva goes so far as to say that dharma-body has "emptiness as its essence."[9] Here emptiness, the negation of essence, is described as the essence of awakening, suggesting the nonessential being of empty dependent co-arising. Hsüan Tsang in his rather interpretative translation of this passage defines the ontological issue in terms of the three patterns, explaining that the imagined pattern does not exist, but that the pattern "revealed by emptiness does exist."[10] Asaṅga further states that Buddhas "are characterized by the non-existence of existence."[11] Thus, while there are no Buddhas, they do not not exist. Again Asvabhāva explains that there are no Buddhas because the imagined pattern of other-dependent consciousness is not nonexistent, but that they do not simply not exist because the perfected pattern does exist. Thus the non-existence of existence refers to the ultimate stage of awakening attained by emptiness (T 31.443c15).

Yogācāra spirituality thus acquires a critical understanding of being in the context of emptiness through an interiorization of the *Prajñāpāramitā* notion of emptiness as the negation of the deluded, imagined pattern that generates belief in the essential reality of self and things. Where the Tathāgatagarbha texts limit the scope of emptiness quantitatively to affirm a non-empty ultimate reality, Asaṅga limits its scope qualitatively to negate all understanding within the imagined pattern. Freed from the specter of nihilism, he can understand all doctrine and all path practice as "only" doctrine and "only" path practice. Valid doctrine and practice remain always worldly and conventional and, being dependently co-arisen, can never pretend to an absolute validity, for ultimate meaning remains transcendent to any conditioned formulation.

Asaṅga summarizes his understanding of Mahāyāna in three points: (1) dependent co-arising, which he identifies with the structure of the container consciousness functioning in synergy with the active consciousnesses; (2) dependently co-arisen states, which he identifies with the three patterns in which dependently co-arising consciousness functions; and (3) an explanation of what has been declared in the scriptures, which he identifies with conventionally valid interpretations of the meanings and intentions of scriptural teachings.[12]

The Three Bodies of Awakening

The critical focus of Yogācāra thinking is carried over into its understanding of wisdom and the three bodies of awakening (*buddha-trikāya*). The tendency among pre-Asaṅgan Yogācāra thinkers to adopt Tathāgatagarbha themes surfaces again in their interpretations of wisdom and the Buddha bodies. *The Ornament of the Scriptures of the Great Vehicle* presents all three Buddha bodies of essence (*svabhāvika-kāya*), enjoyment (*saṃbhogika-kāya*), and transformation (nirmāṇakāya) as issuing from the ultimate Dharma realm, suggesting a single, all-inclusive and not empty ultimate reality as the essence underlying all states of awakening and all Buddha bodies.[13] In the presence of such an essential reality, wisdom consists in sweeping away the nonessential impurities that block insight. Thus both the imagined patterns and the other-dependent pattern fall away upon the attainment of the pattern of full perfection.

But such an interpretation did not go unchallenged. Sthiramati reports that "some explain Dharma body as the well-purified dharma realm entirely removed from all adventitious defilement," while "others explain Dharma body as excellent wisdom, functioning in an unattached and unobstructed manner in regard to all the knowable."[14] The first opinion is that found in texts like the *Ornament of the Scriptures*, while the second is that of Asaṅga himself, who in the last chapter "On Wisdom" in his *Summary of the Great Vehicle* explains "the excellence of wisdom as the three bodies of Buddha." He seems concerned throughout this chapter lest people abandon practice, claiming that they are "originally" awakened. In the very last paragraph of the chapter he rejects the proposition that no effort is needed in order to attain awakening, "since Dharma body of Buddhas is beginningless, not distinct [from sentient beings], and infinite."

For Asaṅga and Vasubandhu the fundamental dharma-body, as well as the other two bodies which are grounded on and issue from dharma-body, is not a reality beyond the scope of emptiness, as in some of the Tathāgatagarbha texts. Rather, it is the existence of emptiness, realized through conversion as the wisdom content of full perfection, that is, empty of any imagined being, of any notion of an essentialist absolute. Dharma-body is wisdom attained through conversion in contacting the ultimate realm of imageless and ineffable emptiness. The enjoyment-body, which is the consequent issuance of dharma-body wisdom experienced by meditating bodhisattvas, is also brought within the scope of emptiness. During the time of Asaṅga and Vasubandhu, many Mahāyāna devotional cults to various Buddhas and their Pure Lands flourished. Asaṅga understood these Buddhas and Pure Lands in terms of his critical understanding of the mind of wisdom. They are, he asserts, "Nothing but conscious constructs flowing from wisdom" (*jñāna-niṣyanda-vijñapti-mātra*).[15] As such, just as with their ground, dharma-body, all Buddhas of the Mahāyāna devotional cults are themselves empty of imagined being and cannot be clung to in religious imaginings. The transformation-body, both in Yogācāra and in earlier texts, is a magically wrought creation of the ineffable and invisible dharma-body. It is perceptible to common sentient beings. The historical Buddha was seen as the prime example of such a transformation. The entire "being" and life course of Śākyamuni were then explained as skillfully created fictions aimed at leading sentient beings toward awakening. Thus, the three bodies reflect Asaṅga's understanding of the structure of wisdom in realizing ultimately meaningful emptiness and in embodying that realization in conventionally skillful and dependently co-arising manifestations through enjoyment-bodies to meditating bodhisattvas (i.e., practitioners) and transformation-bodies to common sentient beings.

Notes

1. Takasaki Jikidō, *A Study of the Ratnagotravibhāga (Uttaratantra), Being a Treatise on The Tathāgatagarbha Theory of Mahāyāna Buddhism* (Rome, 1966) 305–6.
2. Takasaki so describes Tathāgatagarbha thought in his article, "Hosshin no ichigenron: Nyoraizō shisō no hō kannen," in *Hirakawa Akira hakase kanreki kinen ronshū: Bukkyō ni okeru hō no kenkyū* (Tokyo: Shunjūsha, 1975–76).
3. John P. Keenan, "Original Purity and the Focus of Early Yogācāra," *Journal of the International Association of Buddhist Studies* 5/1 (1982) 7–18.
4. *Saṃdhinirmocanasūtra: L'explication des mystères*, trans. Étienne Lamotte, 184; T. 16, 692b.
5. John P. Keenan, "A Study of the Buddhabhūmyupadeśa," 187–92.
6. See in particular Vasubandhu's *Wei Shih Erh Shih Lun*, trans. C. H. Hamilton.
7. See Nagao Gadjin, "'What Remains' in Śūnyatā," in *Mahāyāna Buddhist Meditation: Theory and Practice*, ed. Minoru Kiyota, 66–82; idem, "From Mādhyamika to Yogācāra," *Journal of the International Association of Buddhist Studies* 2 (1979) 35–42.
8. *La Somme du Grand Véhicule d'Asanga (Mahāyānasaṃgraha)*, trans. Étienne Lamotte, 271. *The Realm of Awakening: Chapter Ten of Asanga's Mahāyānasaṃgraha*, forthcoming translation by Paul L. Swanson, with introduction, 64.
9. *Realm of Awakening*, trans. Swanson, 64.
10. Ibid., 65; T. 31, 436c.28–29.
11. *La Somme*, trans. Lamotte, 308; *Realm of Awakening*, trans. Swanson, 168.
12. *La Somme*, trans. Lamotte, 132–34.
13. *Mahāyāna-Sūtralaṃkāra: Exposé de la doctrine du Grand Véhicule*, trans. Sylvain Lévi (Paris: H. Champion, 1907) 45; Keenan, *Study*, 167–76.
14. *Sthiramati: Madhyāntavibhāgaṭīkā, Exposition Systématique du Yogācāravijñaptivāda*, ed. Yamaguchi Susumu (Tokyo, 1966) 191; English translation in *Realm of Awakening*, trans. Swanson, 11.
15. *Triśatikāyāh Prajñāpāramitāyāḥ*, in Giuseppe Tucci, ed., *Minor Buddhist Texts* I (Rome: Istituto italiano per il medio ed estremo oriente, 1958) 63.

Bibliography

Sources

Asaṅga: Mahāyāna-sūtralaṁkāra: Exposé de la doctrine du Grand Véhicule. Translated by Sylvain Lévi. Paris: H. Champion, 1907–11.

The Laṅkāvatāra Sūtra. Translated by D. T. Suzuki. London: Routledge, 1932.

Lévi, Sylvain. *Un système de philosophie bouddhique: Matériaux pour l'étude du système Vijñaptimātra.* Paris: H. Champion, 1932.

On Knowing Reality: The Tattvārtha Chapter of Asaṅga's Bodhisattvabhūmi. Translated by Janice Dean Willis. New York: Columbia University Press, 1979.

Saṃdhinirmocanasūtra: L'Explication des Mystères. Translated by Étienne Lamotte. Paris: Maisonneuve, 1935.

La Somme du Grand Véhicule d'Asaṅga: Mahāyānasaṃgraha. Translated by Étienne Lamotte. Louvain: Bureaux du Muséon, 1938–39.

Wei Shih Er Shih Lun, or, The Treatise in Twenty Stanzas on Representation-Only. Translated by Clarence H. Hamilton. New Haven: American Oriental Society, 1938.

Studies

Dasgupta, Surendath. *Indian Idealism.* Cambridge: Cambridge University Press, 1962.

Hamilton, Clarence H. "Buddhist Idealism in Wei Shih Er Lun." In *Essays in Philosophy of Seventeen Doctors of Philosophy of the University of Chicago,* 99–115. Chicago: University of Chicago Press, 1929.

Keenan, John P. "Original Purity and the Focus of Early Yogācāra." *Journal of the International Association for Buddhist Studies* 5/1 (1982) 7–18.

——. "A Study of the Buddhabhūmyupadeśa: The Doctrinal Development of the Notion of Wisdom in Yogācāra Thought." Ph.D. dissertation, University of Wisconsin, Madison, 1980.

Matilal, Bimal Krishna. "A Critique of Buddhist Idealism." In *Buddhist Studies in Honour of I. B. Horner,* ed. L. Cousins et al., 139–69. Dordrecht: Reidel, 1974.

May, Jacques. "La philosophie bouddhique idéaliste." *Asiatische Studien/Études asiatiques* 25 (1971) 265–323.

Nagao, Gadjin. *Chūkan to yuishiki.* Tokyo: Iwanami, 1978.

——. "From Mādhyamika to Yogācāra: An Analysis of MMK XXIV.18 and MV I.1–2." *Journal of the International Association of Buddhist Studies* 2/1 (1979) 35–42.

——. "On the Theory of Buddha-Body." *Eastern Buddhist* n.s. 1 (1973) 25–53.

——. "What 'Remains' in Śūnyatā: A Yogācāra Interpretation of Emptiness." In *Mahāyāna Buddhist Meditation,* ed. Minoru Kiyota. 68–82. Honolulu: University of Hawaii Press, 1978.

Suzuki, D. T. *Studies in the Laṅkāvatāra Sūtra.* London: Routledge, 1930.

Tucci, Giuseppe. *On Some Aspects of the Doctrines of Maitreya and Asangha.* Calcutta: University of Calcutta, 1930.

III. *Buddhist Logic: The Search for Certainty*

Ernst Steinkellner

When the classical systems in India's various philosophical traditions had been elaborated, problems of a more critical order began to shape a new culture of philosophical inquiry. The desire to perfect systems of thought yielded to inquiry into the sources and presuppositions providing thought with its basic legitimation. By the middle of the first millennium C.E. an epistemology, or "theory of (the means of) valid cognition (*pramāṇavāda*)," emerged within those Buddhist and non-Buddhist philosophical schools which had reason to be concerned with this question. Buddhist thinkers played a leading role in this inquiry during the second half of the millennium. Dignāga (ca. 480–540) is regarded as the founder of Buddhist epistemology. His last work, *Summary of (the Theory of) Valid Cognition* (*Pramāṇasamuccaya*), accompanied by a commentary, is based on various older traditions, Buddhist and non-Buddhist. But in combining their mostly heterogeneous material he created a new frame of inquiry and understanding that led to the birth of a school of thought that produced in the final phase of Indian Buddhism some of its finest philosophers. In six chapters, the work deals with valid cognition in general, its definition, objects and types, perception, inference, proof, the meaning of words, and futile rejoinders.

Drawing on older insights into the art of debate and its formal aspects, scientific system and grammar, the need for authority in the mediation of values and goals (*pramāṇa*), and the significance of language in understanding reality, Dignāga argued that the Buddha must be understood as a means of valid cognition (*pramāṇabhūta*) and an authority for everybody who strives for a meaningful existence. It was left to Dharmakīrti (ca. 600–660) to develop this idea so that it provided a veritable philosophical foundation of Buddhism. The significance of epistemology and logic within Buddhism as a tradition of religious practice is explained by Dharmakīrti in his *Pramāṇavārttika*, whose second chapter is a commentary on the benedictory verse of Dignāga's *Pramāṇasamuccaya*, a verse that thus became the spiritual motto of the whole school. Meaningful human activity presupposes valid cognition, cognition coherent with the expected results eventually brought about by the factors of reality which have been cognized. A Buddhist's activity is orientated toward the final goal of emancipation revealed by the Buddha. This goal cannot be discovered by perception and inference, the ordinary means of cognition. It is never present immediately, for if it were, it would not be ultimate. It must, therefore, be indicated by an authority whose highly developed experience puts him in possession of knowledge of it. The Buddha can be accepted as such an authority if he is proved to be in possession of such unique insight and to be one who shows through his conduct that he does not seek to deceive.[1]

The *Pramāṇavārttika* is a verse text of four chapters (on inference, valid cognition in general, perception, and proof) and is conceived as a commentary on Dignāga's *Pramāṇasamuccaya.*[2] Much of the school's later work was devoted to the exegesis of *Pramāṇavārttika.* Śākyamati's (ca. 660–720) subcommentary was the most authoritative exegetical source, and Prajñākaragupta's (ca. tenth century) commentary on the last three chapters is a most original work with a strong emphasis on the interpretation of Dharmakīrti's religious thought. Dharmakīrti's second principal work, the *Pramāṇaviniścaya,* is an independent treatise in three chapters (valid cognition and perception, inference, proof), and, as a mature presentation of his epistemology, an unsurpassed masterpiece.[3] Dharmakīrti practically superseded the authority of Dignāga, who was henceforth understood as interpreted by his successor.

After the middle of the eighth century, exegesis of Dharmakīrti, at first mainly philological, was gradually enriched by more systematic philosophical interpretation (Karnakagomin, Dharmottara, Prajñākaragupta) and concise essays were contributed by Arcata, Śubhagupta, and Dharmottara on such themes as the theory of meaning, logical pervasion, valid cognition, and momentariness. The foremost task of these essays was the explanation of central Buddhist tenets—such as that the nature of being was momentariness—by means of proofs elaborated in all their implications in accord with the standards of the refined logic available at that time.[4] Evidently this application of its art fulfilled a major responsibility of the school to the Buddhist community. This literary genre dominated the last period of the school in India, during which, in the eleventh century, Jñānaśrīmitra, its last original philosopher and a brilliant writer, wrote his superb essays on the major theorems and proofs of the school. Lively discussion and polemics with the Brahmanical schools, mainly Nyāya, Vaiśeṣika and Mīmāṁsā, already a major concern of Dignāga, were continued by his successors, culminating in the almost personal polemics directed by the Naiyāyika Udayana against Jñānaśrīmatra and his pupil Ratnakīrti. After the beginning of the eleventh century, the productive life of the Indian tradition seems to have withered away. Only summaries, handbooks, and doxographic surveys are known from this late stage.

Only two early texts were translated into Chinese, and none of Dharmakīrti's famous treatises, nor any of the real theoretical or religious achievements of the school, was ever known in China. The works and scholarly spirit of the school were eagerly received into Tibet already during the first period of the reception of Buddhism (after the late eighth century). A long and productive original tradition developed in Tibet after Buddhism spread into the country a second time in the eleventh century[5] and flourished up to our times within traditional Tibetan culture. The literary transmission of the Indian school was seriously studied and explained over the centuries, and its issues were developed, at first as a secular branch of learning mainly by the Sa-skya-pa, and after the fourteenth century as a part of religious training by the dGe-lugs-pa, who restored to it its original spiritual status.

If there is one idea that expresses the cultural uniqueness and originality of the school and explains its amazing success and influence, even in non-Buddhist circles, it is that of cognitive certainty as attainable in conceptual knowing. The school presented discursive thought as the medium of intellectual life, meaningful not as an end in itself but as progressing toward a goal that transcends it and confers on it its meaning. The school's nominalist theory of meaning dealt with the gap between mobile and immediate nonconceptual reality and the inevitably static and unreal constructions of conceptual thought, and provided a practical bridge between the two. Its logic provided a theory of logical reason, evidence, its criteria and types, and its necessary connection with what it proves. Logic became the school's foremost concern because certainty and control in the realm of concepts required a careful theory of the deductional process.

A short survey of the school's work on the relation between probans and probandum reveals the general motives and aims of the school. Although the pre-Dignāga period is not very well known because of fragmentary transmission, it seems that two logical theorems were developed during this period which had lasting influence on all later traditions. A Sāṁkhya thinker developed the theorem of a necessary, invariable connection between probans and probandum. Freed from the limits of Sāṁkhya ontology, this notion of a formal logical nexus could serve to conceptualize the very fact of the concomitance of probans and probandum (e.g., smoke and fire) as well as the want of universality in concomitance. The second theorem attempts to do formal justice to the phenomenon of the logical connection and to focus it as the central structure of syllogistic proofs and inferences. It requires the probans to fulfill three criteria: to be present in the subject of proof, to be present in similar, positive instances, and to be absent in dissimilar, negative instances. This theorem was developed in circles representing Buddhist and Nyāya dialectical traditions.

Up to the time of Vasubandhu, Dignāga's teacher, these ideas had not been developed into a coherent logical theory, and in arguments of that period gross errors in reasoning are not uncommon. Vasubandhu, for instance, is familiar with both of the above theorems, but he seems to be undecided as to their logical value, and he still considers appropriate an inference of the absence of a probandum from the absence of a probans. Dignāga threw considerable light on the central function of inferences and proofs, which he was the first to consider logically identical. He improved the theorem of the threefold probans by clearly defining the range of the similar and dissimilar instances, and determining thereby the relation between probans and probandum possible in these cases. The result of this examination is his famous "wheel of logical reasons" (*hetucakra*), which maps all the variations in occurrence of the probans in the similar and dissimilar cases, and is able to demonstrate *why* a certain probans is correct and another incorrect, thus making it possible to formulate inferences and proofs fulfilling the conditions of certainty. The probans is correct if it is present in all cases where the probandum is present or partly present and if it is absent in all cases where the probandum is absent. Thus the theorem of the logical connection is newly formulated as a theorem of universal pervasion: the necessity of logical relations is based on the universality of the pervasion which is to be derived from observing the occurrences and nonoccurrences of the probans.

Īśvarasena objected that Dignāga's notion of pervasion did not guarantee certainty. Dignāga had mapped instances of the concomitance in absence of probans and probandum; these supplied the positive concomitance with high probability but not with necessity. Absolute necessity of concomitance can, in fact, be achieved only if *all* cases of concomitance in absence can actually be observed; and short of omniscience such totality of observation is impossible. Īśvarasena tried to cope with this problem within the frame of the theory of pervasion. He suggested a third kind of valid cognition, "nonperception," as a reliable means for cognizing the absence of the probans in the dissimilar cases. The addition of another criterion for the probans failed, however, to dispel the insecurity caused by the impossibility of observing all positive and negative instances. Nevertheless, he was the first to see the problems of Dignāga's logic, and his proposals prepared for their solution by Dharmakīrti. This solution, building on the idea that there is a basis for the logical connection in reality and on the theorem of the corresponding three kinds of logical reasons, effected a convergence of the different earlier theoretical traditions regarding the core of logical functions into a system of coherent logic.

The logical relation, according to Dharmakīrti, is founded on a relation in reality. It is necessary, and inferential cognition is certain, when the fundamental relation has been ascertained. This fundamental relation in reality is a connection through essence (*svabhāva*) which appears in two ways: as causal relation and as real identity. Two kinds of logical reason correspond to the only possible relations in reality: an essential property can be evidence for another essential property, and effect can be evidence for cause. The third kind of evidence, nonperception of a perceptible, used as evidence for its absence, is based on the same relation as the first kind. The central idea of this logic is that inference of one concept from another is possible only if the realities to which these concepts refer are identical in their *svabhāva*. This theorem of the three kinds of evidence does not replace the theorem of Dignāga, but serves as a substantial explanation of it. The struggle for certainty was won by Dharmakīrti when he devised the corollary methods which have to be applied in order to ascertain the respective real relations. These methodical devices are pre-inferential, of mixed inductive-deductive character, and sufficiently elaborate to guarantee the universal validity of the real basis of logical operations. It is only in his late work that we find both these methods prescribed with the desired clarity. The causal relation is ascertained by an inductive process formalized with certain stages of perception and nonperception, and is secured against the dangers of incomplete induction by an extrapolating argument. The relation of real identity is ascertained through a valid cognition which proves that the evidence does not occur where the opposite of the property to be proved occurs.

Notes

1. Tilmann Vetter, *Erkenntnisprobleme bei Dharmakīrti* (Vienna: Österreichische Akademie der Wissenschaften Phil.-hist. Klasse, 1964) 27–28, 31ff.

2. The second chapter is partly translated in T. Vetter, *Der Buddha und seine Lehre in Dharmakīrtis Pramāṇavārttika* (Vienna, 1984).

3. The first chapter is translated by T. Vetter, *Dharmakīrtis Pramāṇaviniścayaḥ, 1. Kapitel: Pratyakṣam* (Vienna: Österreichische Akademie der Wissenschaften Phil.-hist. Klasse, 1966); the second by E. Steinkellner, *Dharmakīrtis Pramāṇaviniścayaḥ, Zweites Kapitel: Svārthānumānam* (Vienna: Österreichische Akademie der Wissenschaften Phil.-hist. Klasse, 1979) II. For a translation of the *Nyāyabindu*, a small digest of this work, see F. T. Stcherbatsky, *Buddhist Logic*, II.

4. Minaki Katsumi, *La réfutation bouddhique de la permanence des choses (Sthirasiddhidūsana) et la preuve de la momentanéité des choses (Ksanabhangasiddhi)* (Paris, 1976).

5. Leonard W. J. Van der Kuijp, *Contributions to the Development of Tibetan Buddhist Epistemology* (Stuttgart: Franz Steiner, 1983).

Bibliography

Sources

Frauwallner, Erich. "Beiträge zur Apohalehre. I: Dharmakīrti. Übersetzung." *Wiener Zeitschrift für die Kunde des Morgenlandes* 39 (1932) 247–85; 40 (1933) 51–94; 42 (1935) 93–102.
Hattori Masaaki. *Dignāga on Perception.* Cambridge, MA: Harvard University Press, 1968.
Kajiyama Yuichi. *An Introduction to Buddhist Philosophy.* Kyoto: Kyoto University, 1966.
Stcherbatsky, F. T. *Buddhist Logic.* Leningrad, 1932, 1930. Reprint, New York: Dover, 1962.
Steinkellner, Ernst. *Dharmakīrti's Hetubinduh. Teil II. Übersetzung und Anmerkungen.* Vienna: Österreichische Akademia der Wissenschaften Phil.-hist. Klasse, 1967.

Studies

Frauwallner, Erich. "Dignāga, sein Werk und seine Entwicklung." *Wiener Zeitschrift für die Kunde Süd- und Ostasiens* 3 (1959) 83–164.
———. "Die Erkenntnislehre des Klassischen Sāṁkhya-Systems." *Wiener Zeitschrift für die Kunde Süd- und Ostasiens* 2 (1958) 84–139.
———. "Landmarks in the History of Indian Logic." *Wiener Zeitschrift für die Kunde Süd- und Ostasiens* 5 (1961) 125–48.
Hayes, Richard P. "Dignāga's Views on Reasoning." *Journal of Indian Philosophy* 8 (1980) 219–77.
Mookerjee, Satkari. *The Buddhist Philosophy of Universal Flux.* Calcutta: University of Calcutta, 1935.
Steinkellner, Ernst. "Bemerkungen zu Īśvarasenas Lehre vom Grund." *Wiener Zeitschrift für die Kunde Südasiens* 10 (1966) 73–85.
———. "Wirklichkeit und Begriff bei Dharmakīrti." *Wiener Zeitschrift für die Kunde Südasiens* 15 (1971) 179–211.
Tachikawa, Musashi. "A Sixth-Century Manual of Indian Logic." *Journal of Indian Philosophy* 19 (1971) 111–45.
Tucci, Giuseppe. *The Nyāyamukha of Dignāga: The Oldest Buddhist Text on Logic After Chinese and Tibetan Materials.* Heidelberg: Materialien zur Kunde des Buddhismus, 1930. This first interpretation is now being superseded by Katsura Shōryū, "Inmyō shōrimonron kenkyū" (Studies on the *Nyāyamukha*). *Hiroshima Daigaku Bungakubu kiyō* 37 (1977) 106ff.; 38 (1978) 110ff.; 39 (1979) 63ff.; 41 (1981) 62ff.; 42 (1982) 82ff.

9

The Diamond Vehicle

Alex Wayman

Tantric Buddhism does not go back to earliest Buddhist times. The Buddha did not give instruction on "seals" (mudrā; gestures, usually manual), ritual formulas (dhāraṇī, also called mantra), or maṇḍala (the mental content of Tantric samādhi).[1] However, early canonical texts such as the *Saṃyutta-Nikāya* record that the Buddha instructed both the gods and human beings, usually differently, using verses with the former and prose with the latter. The possibility of contacting the gods by following the appropriate procedure was taken for granted; one could also be tempted by such figures as the *devaputra* (son-of-the-god) Māra; in medical theory, certain diseases were credited to spirit possession. Later versions of some Mahāyāna scriptures, the *Laṅkāvatāra Sūtra* for instance, have a dhāraṇī chapter, but this need not mark the beginning of the Tantric literature, for it is probably a concession to the growing popularity of already existing secretive tantric cults, accommodating the aspects least in tension with the rest of the Mahāyāna scripture. To date the emergence of Tantrism in Indian Buddhism to late in the first millennium C.E. is to overlook the fact that, as Buddhism declined, its relations with Hinduism were not such as to favor a borrowing of Hindu theories and practices. It can only have been in an earlier period, that of the Gupta dynasty, that Buddhists adopted the ancient Homa rite along with theories of magical speech, and produced the treatises later called the Tantras, and in fact we first note a minor appearance of such treatises around the fourth century.

Western books on Indian religion often associate the Buddhist Tantra with obscene conduct. This depends on a literal interpretation of certain passages in such works as the *Guhyasamāja-tantra.* If one attempted to interpret the whole work in this literal manner one would find it impossible to do so. These works are accounts of rituals, for Buddhist Tantra is primarily a *practice,* although employing the Mahāyāna doctrines. These texts use words in special arbitrary meanings and deliberately introduce obscurity, so that one does not know from the text itself what is being done. Some Western scholars believe that knowledge of the language (these texts were in almost all cases first composed in Sanskrit) suffices for reading and understanding, but the Tantric tradition contradicts this in assigning to the guru the role of explaining the procedure. The guru is revered as if he were the Buddha—his virtues magnified, his faults minimized. It is he who gives "permission" to summon the deity, a permission held to come from the deity itself. It is he who initiates the disciple into the deity and clan (that is, the maṇḍala), having first ritually identified himself with the deity. The disciples should have faith in the Three Jewels and should have aroused the Mind of Enlightenment (*bodhicitta*). During the initiation they must repeat the appropriate formulas, including vows and pledges, after the preceptor, normally three times. They must be reasonably deft in copying ritual movements such as mudrā. After initiation, they are qualified to receive, again from the guru, the lore of the particular deity cycle. Among their vows is one not to divulge the Tantric secrets to the non-initiate.[2]

The Tantra's claim of superiority to Mahāyāna Buddhism is directed to persons within the Buddhist fold who, in India at least, believed in rebirth and karma, and expected that by practicing the six perfections of giving, morality, forbearance, striving, meditation, and insight they would, after a great many lives (three eons), attain enlightenment. Tantra claims it can speed up the process, perhaps allowing the attainment of enlightenment in one life. Non-Tantric Buddhism concentrated on cultivating the mind: the yogin would sit cross-legged (thus curbing the body) in silence (thus curbing speech), and aim at one-pointedness of mind (samādhi). The Tantra says that here the linkage with the divine is taking place only through the samādhi, whereas in the Tantric process, one shares in the three mysteries of the Buddha, his body by the mudrā, his speech by the incantations or mantra, and his mind by the samādhi on the deity or the maṇḍala. The theory of speeding up the process toward enlightenment relies on these three linkages of human nature with the divine.

When evoking a deity, one must first ascend meditatively to the void (śūnyatā), focusing on an appropriate meditation object and taking it into the void. From the void, also called the void Dharmadhātu (realm of nature), or nonapperception of external object, one generates the deity first as a syllable, then as an emblem, such as *vajra* (diamond) or *padma* (lotus), and finally as shaped with corporeal members (anthropomorphic).[3] One can reach this deity state by pronouncing the mantra many times (sometimes one hundred thousand recitations are prescribed), success being indicated when it seems that the mantra pronounces itself (deity as syllable) and then all at once (deity as the garland of letters). The mantra used to indicate that the performer is linked to a deity is SAMAYAS TVAM ("You are the symbol [of deity]" or "You are the link [with deity]"). In the Buddhist Tantras the word mantra can be employed for all kinds of ritual formulas or magical speech. The incantation for invoking a male deity can also be called *mantra* (in which case *vidyā* is the charm to invoke a female deity). The mantra for a fierce deity is HŪṂ PHAṬ; for a mild deity, SVĀHĀ. The celebrated Indian teacher Atīśa, who came to Tibet in 1042, taught mantras for invoking the following "deities": Gautama Buddha, the bodhisattva Avalokiteśvara (the famous OṂ MANI PADME HŪṂ), the goddess Tārā, and the fierce male deity, the blue Acala.[4] The latter two are tutelary deities, followed and served daily by disciples, who are nonseparate from the deity and who seek from them specific fruits of protection.

The Four Tantra Classes

The Tibetan scriptural collection is divided into the translated revealed scriptures (Kanjur) and the translated exegetical treatises (Tanjur). In both of these, the works on Buddhist Tantra are grouped into four, the Kriyā, Caryā, Yoga, and Anuttarayoga Tantras. The revealed Tantras are not ascribed to human authors; they are discourses by deities, either the Buddha, called Bhagavat (the Lord), or substitutes for the Buddha such as Vajradhara (Vajra-holder). The orthodox explanation is that the Kriyā Tantras were revealed on behalf of the candidates who delight in external ritual more than in inner samādhi, that the Caryā Tantras are for those who delight in external ritual and inner samādhi equally, that the Yoga Tantras are for those who delight predominantly in inner samādhi, and that the Anuttarayoga Tantras are for those who delight in inner samādhi completely. This scheme is too neat, and the Tibetan savants themselves debated the inclusion of certain texts in the given categories. But it is clear that disciples were observed to fall into those groups, although they can scarcely have confined themselves to the texts supposedly intended for them.

Not content with this differentiation in terms of candidates, the classifiers of the canon also found differences in the representation of the deities, arguing from certain passages that the Kriyā Tantra deities were laughing, that the male and female deities in Caryā Tantra were gazing at each other, that those of the Yoga were holding hands, and that those of the Anuttarayoga Tantras were united (sexual union). Thus the four Tantra classes represent stages in courtship of the deities. The aim of this again rather arbitrary scheme is to point to the Anuttarayoga Tantra as showing the male and female deities in union. Since it is the Tantra class in which the candidates are said to delight in inner samādhi completely, there is a claim that the depictions of sexual union on Tibetan *tankas* (temple banners) called *Yab-yum* (Father-Mother) refer to a union taking place within the performer.[5] The representations also correspond to the three kinds of nondiscursive ecstasy, that based on sound (the laughter of the Kriyā Tantra), the mystical experience of "hearing the Lord," that based on sight (the mutual gazing of the Caryā Tantra), the mystical experience of "seeing the Lord," and that based on touch (in the latter two Tantras), implying the mystical experience of being touched by the Lord (as though he placed his hand on the head of the ecstatic human).[6]

Tantrism in the Far East did not adopt this classification of the Tantras. The chief Tantra of the Caryā class is the *Vairocanābhisaṃbodhi-tantra*, known in Sino-Japanese Buddhism as the *Mahāvairocana-sūtra* (Japanese *Dainichi-kyō*). The chief Tantra of the Yoga class is the *Tattvasaṃgraha* (Japanese *Kongōchō-kyō* or Diamond Tip Sūtra). Both these scriptures have been much studied in Japanese esotericism in lineages brought from China in the eighth and ninth centuries; their respective maṇḍalas are the source of the "womb" (*garbha*) and the "diamond" (*vajra*) maṇḍalas depicted on temple banners of the Shingon sect. The Tantras of the Anuttarayoga class were not much appreciated in China, presumably because of their sexual symbolism.

We shall now describe a characteristic practice of each of the four Tantras. The Kriyā Tantra practice of the generation of self into deity has six steps.[7] (1) Using the Mādhyamika dialectic one denies the concepts of singleness and multiplicity. Then one realizes the voidness of one's own mind. These two procedures establish the "self reality." In the realization that the deity to be contemplated and this "self reality" are inseparable, one attains the first deity stage, that of the "reality deity." (2) One realizes the void, in which the sounds of the dhāranī, imagined as the very deity to be contemplated, are the mind's only meditative object, the Sound Deity. (3) One imagines one's own mind as a moon disk in the sky, carrying letters the color of liquid gold, imagined to be the deity to be contemplated, the Letter Deity. (4) One imagines that from those letters come rays of light which are aspects of the deity's body. These rays purify sentient beings from their sins and suffering and delight the Buddhas. The rays are withdrawn onto the moon disk, and thus withdrawn into one's heart, where the moon-mind and the letters are transformed into the perfect body of the Form-deity. (5) One touches with mudrā the crown of the head, the space between the eyebrows, the eyes, the shoulders, the neck, the heart, and the navel, while reciting ritual formulas; these spots being thus empowered, are the Mudrā Deity. (6) Then, while the deity is still vivid, one fortifies the ego by such a sentence as "Om. I am entirely identical with the intrinsic nature of the Dharmadhātu by yoga," and that vivid aspect of the deity as one's sole meditative object is the Sign Deity.

The second chapter of the chief of the Caryā Tantras, the *Vairocanābhisaṃbodhi-tantra,* is an imposing presentation of the "arising of compassion" maṇḍala.[8] The hierophant induces the disciple to remember the Tathāgatas and to take the Mind of Enlightenment, and promises that the disciple will be reborn in all the virtue of the Buddha's family. He imagines that the disciple's head is enclosed in a shining circle radiating in the manner of a blazing garland and that on the crown of the disciple's head is the syllable RA of white color, like the rising (full) moon. Imagining the Buddhas all around, he induces the disciple to throw a flower, and he gives the disciple to the Buddha family of the place where the flower falls. He helps the disciple to pass between the two gates of the maṇḍala, and performs a burnt offering (*homa*). After the disciples give presents to the preceptor, he draws a secondary maṇḍala and on the lotus petals draws bodhisattvas. For the initiation he takes a golden probe and, standing in front of the disciple, speaks these words: "Just as the kings of healing with their probe removed the eye-caul of men, so may the Buddhas remove your film of ignorance, my son." Holding up a mirror, he adds: "The dharmas are like reflected images, clear and pure, without turbulence; ungraspable, inexpressible, arisen from cause (*hetu*) and action (karma)." He gives the disciple the dharma-wheel and a fine conch shell, exhorting him:

> From this day on may you set in motion the wheel of the Dharma for the world, filling it with the supreme conch of the Dharma. From this day on you must not abandon the Illustrious Dharma and the Mind of Enlightenment, even for your life. You must not have envy, or do harm to sentient beings. These pledges are given to you by the Buddha. In the same way as you would guard your life, so you must guard them.

In the Yoga Tantra we find a rather arbitrary classification of spheres of purification according to their mudrās.[9] The four passions to be purified—namely, lust, hatred, delusion, and avarice—correspond to Great Mudrā, Symbolic Mudrā, Dharma Mudrā, and Karma Mudrā, to the four paths of action, and to the four elements. Another correlation, called "fruit of the purification," puts in correspondence the four mudrās, the four Buddha-bodies, the four wisdoms (jñāna), and the four kinds of bodhisattva activity. The sequence of mudrās effects the Yoga Tantra equivalent of the Kriyā Tantra procedure of generating oneself into deity by six deity stages, called generating the Symbolic Being, meaning the person who is linked to the deity or symbolizes the deity. Because this system employs fourfold correspondences, the five Buddhas are reduced to four by combining Amoghasiddhi and Ratnasambhava; the other three are Vairocana, Amitābha, and Akṣobhya.

In the Anuttarayoga Tantra, there are two stages, the stage of generation and the stage of completion.[10] The first of these has much in common with the Yoga Tantra and is conceptual, dealing with the generation of families of Buddhas, who may number either five (Father Tantra) or six (Mother Tantra). Generation means involvement with the four goddesses who personify the purity of the elements, the ten furious deities who ward off and destroy the demons of different kinds, the great bodhisattvas, and the maṇḍala of numerous deities. The stage of completion is the resolution or collapse of the distinct deities. Now the five or six Buddhas (the sixth usually called Vajrasattva) collapse into one primordial Buddha. The various kinds of diversity are reduced to a nondual state. When it is said that the Anuttarayogatantra is meant for the candidate delighting in inner samādhi, the reference is to this collapse of externals into the performer's own inwardness. The Father Tantras emphasize means (*upāya*) as the sequence of the practices leading to the stages of the lights or voids and finally to the Clear Light. The Mother Tantras emphasize the system of cakras, or centers in the body, and experiences of bliss or ecstasy, emphasizing a nondiscursive prajñā.

Rituals for the purpose of gaining certain worldly successes (Skt. *siddhi*) were elaborated in the form of three and then four *homa* (burnt offering) rites.[11] The original aims of mundane *siddhis* were to avert evil by appeasing the deities, to increase prosperity, and to overpower enemies. The third aim was in time divided into two—subduing demons and overpowering enemies. To each aim corresponds a different offering. In Brahmanism one had to know the lineage of fire (Agni) to properly perform the burnt offering. When the *homa* was adopted by Buddhism, it was combined with the Buddhist ethic. Thus the *homa* chapter of the *Vairocanābhisaṃbodhi-tantra* states: "A person possessing great love and great compassion belongs to (can perform) the appeasement *homa*. One possessing sympathetic joy can perform the prosperity *homa*. With the wrath-fire one may practice dreadful magic." The set of four *homa*s is an important part of Far Eastern Tantrism, still practiced in the Japanese Shingon and Tendai sects. They are called external and mundane because the ritual is visible, using expensive materials and perhaps requiring a patron; because of the benefits it confers, the ritual is an occasion for gifts to the institution performing it. In contrast, the "inner *homa*" is supramundane, a burnt offering within the body which aims to burn out defilement for the fruit of liberation or enlightenment.

The Development of Tibetan Buddhism

The Diamond Vehicle revealed its riches most abundantly in Tibet, where it is considered the highest form of Buddhism, surpassing and integrating the other two vehicles, Hīnayāna and Mahāyāna. Tibetan chronicles date the first appearance of Buddhism in Tibet to the reign of Tho-tho-ri-ñan-tsen, presumably in the fourth century C.E. According to the legend, when he was sixteen years old a casket containing texts of Buddhist nature fell from the skies. The king dreamed that in the fifth generation someone would be able to interpret these texts.[12] Western scholars usually date the introduction of Buddhism to the reign of Sron-btsan-sgam-po (late sixth or early seventh century); the Tibetan accounts see him as the one who fulfilled his predecessor's dream by having the previously obtained texts and others translated into Tibetan. This was made possible by Thon-mi Sambhota, who introduced writing to the country, creating the handsome Tibetan script after the model of a late Gupta script of India. At that time Tibet had an extended kingdom, with a suzerainty over Nepal, through which it had direct contact with North India, whose Buddhist traditions included an early form of Tantrism. On the other side of Tibet lay China, where traditions based on one or other Mahāyāna scripture were flourishing. During the seventh and eighth centuries Tibet's extended kingdom also brought it into contact with ideas and practices of Central Asia, including some Greek ideas.[13] Though Tibet had only recently acquired a script, these contacts made it a sophisticated society.

The translation of the complicated Buddhist scriptures required royal sponsorship. In accordance with the first royal decree, from the time of Thon-mi Sambhota through the reign of Khri-sron-lde-btsan (755–797), the *Avataṃsaka Sūtra* and the four *Āgama*s were translated (presumably from Chinese), as well as some *Prajñāpāramitā* works. This reign is marked by the activity of the famous Padmasaṁbhava and the Indian pandit Śāntarakṣita. About 775, when the bSam-yas (Samye) monastery was founded, Śāntarakṣita ordained a select group of Tibetans with Tibet's first ordination lineage, belonging to the Mūlasarvāstivāda Vinaya. Bu-ston in his *History of Buddhism* tells us that various teachers and translators "created a literary language that contained many words unintelligible to the Tibetans. Besides, different translations were made from the Chinese, from the languages of Li [Khotan] and Sahor [possibly Bengal], etc. Owing to this there were many different renderings of words and the study of the Doctrine became very difficult."[14] Toward the end of this reign, between 792 and 794, an important debate took place between the Indian pandits and the Chinese party at bSam-yas.[15] The Indian party, headed by Kamalaśīla, was declared the winner, and the opposing teachers, headed by the Chinese Hva-śan, were ousted from Tibet.

A second royal decree on translation was issued by King Khri Ral-pa-can (b. 805; r. 814–838): texts were henceforth to be translated only from the Sanskrit, with the aid of the Sanskrit-Tibetan Buddhist dictionary called *Mahāvyutpatti*, and the standard equivalences had to be respected so that everyone could study the works. Ral-pa-can was killed by his brother Glan-dar-ma, who succeeded ca. 838. During the ensuing persecution of Buddhism, which was the reaction of the aboriginal Bön-po faith to the threat of the growing religion from India, monks fled to the outskirts of Tibet, taking the translated books with them. The year 841 ends the Sna dar or "former diffusion" of Buddhism in Tibet.

Buddhism is said to have been revived in Central Tibet in 978 by six men from the provinces of dBus and gTsan; this is the beginning of the Phyi dar or "later diffusion." King Ye'ses-'od invited to Tibet the East Indian pandit Dharmapāla, who introduced the second Mūlasarvāstivāda ordination lineage—the lineage from the former diffusion having become suspect. He also employed the great translator Rin-chen-bzan-po (958–1055), who lived on to collaborate in translations with Atīśa. He issued the third decree on translation, commanding the elimination of obsolete nonreligious words in the religious texts. All the earlier translated works had to be edited to make them consistent with the new orthography. At this time many new types of works were translated, namely, the Mādhyamika books and numerous Tantric treatises, and soon the Buddhist logical corpus.

The influence of Atīśa, who came from India in 1042, cannot be overestimated.[16] Besides his own brief summary-type works, such as the celebrated *Light on the Path to Enlightenment,* he brought with him a library of books to be translated into Tibetan. The bKa'-gdams-pa school descends from him through his chief disciple 'Brom-ston. Atīśa stressed the most characteristic Tibetan cults: the Avalokiteśvara of the six-syllable formula OṂ MANI PADME HŪṂ and the Tārā of the ten-syllable formula OṂ TĀRE TUTĀRE TURE SVĀHĀ. In 1073 'Khon dKon-mchog-rgyal-po founded the Sa-skya sect, which carried the Tantric lineage of the *Hevajra-tantra.* About 1110 sGam-po-pa became a pupil of Mi-la Ras-pa (1040–1123) and subsequently founded the bKa'-rgyud-pa sect, whose lineage goes back to the Indian Nāro-pā and the Tibetan Mar-pa, and whose precepts are the "Six Doctrines," known in the West principally through W. Y. Evans-Wentz, *Tibetan Yoga and Secret Doctrines.* As Buddhism was dying out in Northern India, a number of pandits came to Tibet and worked with Tibetan translators, notably the "Kashmir pandit" Śākyaśrībhadra, who brought the third and last ordination lineage of the Mūlasarvāstivāda Vinaya in 1204. Through his disciple, the Sa-skya Pandit, known as Sa-pan, he fostered the study of Buddhist logic in the Sa-skya sect. It was Sa-pan who wrote a celebrated work on Buddhist logic, one of the earliest contributions to the enormous Tibetan literature on the technical ramifications of Buddhism.

The Tibetans were soon to have a dazzling political-religious success. In 1249 Sa-pan was appointed Tibetan viceroy by the Mongols, but he spent much of his time in Peking. Thus the Tibetan form of Buddhism began to penetrate the Mongol court. Sa-pan was succeeded by his nephew, 'Phags-pa, who at the age of nineteen participated in Kublai Khan's great religious conference of 1258 and helped gain the victory for the Buddhists in the debate. Kublai made 'Phags-pa his chief religious advisor and had the Mongols adopt the Tibetan form of Buddhism. All this must have made the Tibetans realize the maturity of Buddhist study and practice in their country. They could take pride in their faithful translations of an immense number of Sanskrit works, which had preserved the canon now lost in India; in their success in digesting this literature and producing their own commentaries; in their legendary yogis; and now in the conversion of the Mongols to their form of Buddhism. But this justified pride also intensified the rivalry between the Tibetan sects. The bKa'-rgyud-pa sect had already split into divergent groups with irreconcilable claims of spiritual lineage, chief among which were the Karma-pa (the Black Hats, to distinguish themselves from the Red Hats).[17] In addition to these sects that had started in the "later diffusion" of Buddhism, there was the Rñin-ma-pa, the sect of the ancients, who claimed to be the heirs of Padmasaṁbhava. The latter part of this period of Sa-skya power is spanned by the life of Bu-ston Rin-chen-grub (1290–1364), the author of an enormous set of books and the redactor of the Kanjur and the Tanjur. His school became famous for mastery of the *Kālacakra-tantra.*

As the Mongol Yüan dynasty of China weakened, the Tibetan group called the Phag-mo-gru-pa overthrew the Sa-skya regime. In 1358 one of them, Byan-chub rgyal-mtshan, formally assumed power. This was just one year after the birth of Tson-kha-pa (1357–1419), founder of the school subsequently called the Gelugpa. He was ordained in the Mūlasarvāstivāda lineage introduced by the Kashmir pandit. His great compendium of the Path, the *Lam rim chen mo,* was written to expound the mental training of the three orders of persons, to clarify Buddhist meditational practice on the basis of Asaṅga's school, and to establish Buddhist philosophy according to the Prāsaṅgīka-Mādhyamika version of Nāgārjuna's school, thus bringing the bKa'-gdams-pa lineage descended from Atīśa to its culmination. His great compendium of Tantrism, the *Snags rim chen mo,* aims to expound the ritual of the four Tantra divisions and to purify it on the basis of the authoritative texts of the Kanjur and Tanjur. In 1408 he was invited to visit the Chinese capital, but instead he sent his disciple Byams-chen chor-rje, who preached the *Kālacakra-tantra* in China. Another disciple, Dge-'dun-grub (1391–1475), posthumously became the First Dalai Lama, while Tson-kha-pa's chief Tantric disciple, Mkhas-grub-rje (1385–1483), posthumously became the First Panchen Lama.

The theory of unbroken lineage of consciousness is the basis of the Dalai Lama and Panchen Lama systems. It was not an invention of the Gelugpas,[18] but is foreshadowed by the Indian theory of yogins gaining the power to control their destiny and to be reborn in appropriate circumstances. The

Six Doctrines of Naropa, especially professed by the bKa'-rgyud-pa sect, teach that a yogin can learn to control the transference of his consciousness principle. That does not mean, of course, that the numerous "incarnations" (Skt. *nirmita;* Tib. *sprul pa*) in the Tibetan sects were really an expression of this fabulous, if not fantastic, yoga power. The belief doubtless serves a political purpose. The method of searching for a child supposed to be the immediate rebirth of the deceased Grand Lama may well result in a more capable sectarian successor than the hit-or-miss method of father–son lineage. Since the Gelugpa lamas take the bhikṣu vows of celibacy, there would be good reason for them to accept the "incarnation" theory as a basis of succession.

The Second Dalai Lama, Dge-'dun rgya-mtsho, had his seat at the 'Bras-spuns (Drepung), founded in 1416, as did his successors. Upon his death he was succeeded by a child who would receive the name bSod-nams rgya-mtsho (1543–1588). Thus by that time the immediate rebirth of the Drepung Abbot was taken for granted. It was this Third Dalai Lama who really established the power of the system through his contact with Altan Khan, chief of the Tumed branch of the Mongols. During their meeting in 1578 near Kokonor, they exchanged titles. The Khan gave him the Mongol name usually written "Dalai," meaning "ocean," but this is precisely the meaning of the Tibetan *rgya mtsho,* which was part of the Grand Lama's Tibetan name. The term "ocean" here means "ocean of knowlege." The lama traveled extensively among various Mongol tribes with remarkable missionary success and never returned to Central Tibet. When he died at the age of forty-five, his successor was found, not fortuitously, in a great-grandson of Altan Khan. This had the immediate result of cementing relations with the Mongol ruling group. However, when a large retinue of Mongols, many of them armed, escorted the child all the way to Central Tibet, this naturally disconcerted and embittered the sectarian rivals of the Gelugpas, especially the Karma-pa of the bKa'-rgyud-pa. It was now 230 years since the Sa-skya-pa vassal of the Mongols had been overthrown by the Phag-mo-gru-pa. The prospect of a return of the Mongols on the side of the Gelugpas was distressing. When the Fourth Dalai Lama was about twenty years old, the king of gTsang, taking the side of the Karma-pa, carried out a raid on the Gelugpa Drepung and Sera monasteries and the Dalai Lama was forced to flee. The Gelugpas turned to their allies, the Mongols, for help. They did not immediately intervene, and the Dalai Lama met an untimely death at the age of twenty-five.

The Fifth Dalai Lama, known in Tibetan history as the Great Fifth, was found in a Rñin-ma-pa family of Central Tibet. This was Nag-dban Blo-bzan rgya-mtsho (1617–1682). Prominent Mongols along with armed followers arrived to do homage to the child and to escort him to Lhasa to be installed in the Drepung Monastery. The Mongols, lacking a strong leader, now consisted of somewhat adventurous bands, which many Gelugpas welcomed to gain an advantage over their sectarian enemies. Eventually, the Fifth Dalai Lama allied himself with Gu-shri Khan, who defeated the king of gTsang, thus destroying the military power of the Karma-pa, and helped the Dalai Lama to extend his sway throughout Tibet. The Gelugpas' rise to power might be defended on the grounds that their ordination lineage goes back to Gautama Buddha's order of monks, the Saṅgha. The other groups were mainly the marrying type, so their Tantra was lay. The Gelugpas, distinguished by their yellow headdress, stressed the monastic drill of non-Tantric Buddhist texts as a preliminary for the Tantra. They spent many years mastering these texts, called Mtshan ñid ("characteristic," in reference to the characteristics of Buddhism). For the Abhidharma they studied the *Abhidharmakośa* of Vasubandhu; for the *Prajñāpāramitā*, the *Abhisamayālaṃkāra;* for the Mādhyamika, the *Mādhyamakāvatāra* of Candrakīrti; for the Vinaya, the *Vinaya-sūtra;* for Buddhist logic, the *Pramāṇavārttika* of Dharmakīrti.

The abbots of the Tashilunpo monastery founded by the First Dalai Lama were called Panchen Lamas. "Panchen" is equivalent to the Sanskrit *mahāpandita* (great scholar), while "lama" is equivalent to the Sanskrit *guru.* The Fifth Dalai Lama had as his tutor the Fourth Panchen Lama, Chos-kyi-rGyal-mtshan (1570–1662), and in recognition of his attainments, the Dalai Lama declared that he would be the first member of an incarnation series. Hence, at his death a child was identified as the second (or fifth) Panchen Lama, Blo-bzan ye-śes, and installed at Tashilunpo. Once there were reincarnational series for both Dalai Lamas and Panchen Lamas, anterior Tibetan incarnations were worked out. The Dalai Lamas were said to belong to the Avalokiteśvara series, and their anterior incarnations were traced back to King Sron-bstan sgam-po. The Panchen Lamas belonged to the Amitāyus incarnation series, and their incarnations went back to Subhūti, a frequent interlocutor in the *Prajñāpāramitā* scriptures.[19] The collected works of the Dalai Lamas and some of their celebrated tutors form an extensive literature. The Seventh Dalai Lama, presumably because he had time to spare during his exile, wrote extensively and seems to have fostered the Guru-yoga cult, especially surrounding the figure of Tson-kha-pa as inspired by the three bodhisattvas—Mañjuśrī, Avalokiteśvara, and Vajrapāni—a cult that may have been started by the First Dalai Lama.[20] This parallels the Rñin-ma-pa cult surrounding the legendary figure of Padmasaṁbhava.

The Japanese photographic reprint of the Peking edition of the Tibetan Kanjur and Tanjur, along with the collected works of Tson-kha-pa and of Lcan-skya Hutukhtu Nag-dban Blo-bzan chos-ldan (1642–1714), for which the final catalogue was issued in 1962, has greatly facilitated access for Western scholars to the Buddhist scriptures in their Tibetan form. The best indigenous

Tibetan compositions match the quality of the Indian classics of Buddhism. Tibet did not simply swallow and duplicate Indian Buddhism. The early Chinese influences and the ideas flowing in through Central Asia in the seventh and eighth centuries and later were also fully integrated into the distinctive character of Tibetan Buddhism.

Tibetan Tantric Buddhism

The many Tibetan monks who were enthusiastic followers of the Tantra believed that by practicing its rituals and by concentrating their minds they were participating in the divine realm, the secret Mind, Speech, and Body. It is important not to forget that there is more to Tibetan Buddhism than Tantra. A monk who hears at midnight the sounding of the *damaru*-drum knows that the mysterious rite of Chöd is being practiced. But he may take less interest in this feature of his culture than in studying Buddhist logic and participating in debates; if he does practice Tantra he may go through the motions, his heart not really in it. In Tson-kha-pa's reform, continued in the Gelugpa sect, the non-Tantric Mahāyāna Buddhism is a stipulated background for the practice of Tantra. This is not new, for the *Vairocanābhisaṃbodhi-tantra* devotes its first chapter to Mahāyāna Buddhism before starting its portrayal of maṇḍala in the second chapter. Followers of the Diamond Vehicle believe it is a "quick path," speeding one's progress to enlightenment, while Mahāyāna (the "Pāramitā Vehicle") is the "slow path" of three eons of rebirths. Tson-kha-pa in his *Mdun legs ma* (Auspicious Preparation) puts it this way:

> Now, for guidance to Complete Buddhahood, there are both the profound Diamond Vehicle and Pāramitā Vehicle. It is well known that the Mantra path far surpasses the Pāramitā path, as the sun surpasses the moon. Some respect this as a true word, but do not try to find out what the Diamond Vehicle is, while posing as wise men. If in such manner they are wise men, who then are the more stupid ones? It is most surprising that one should cast aside this highest path so difficult to encounter. Therefore, I entered and exercised myself with many endeavors in that Deep which is the highest vehicle of the Jina and even more rare than a Buddha and which is the treasure of the two esoteric attainments.

The two esoteric attainments are the mundane (appeasing the deities, prosperity, commanding the spirits, drastic magic) and the supramundane (complete Buddhahood).

In the enormous corpus of texts and commentaries on the Buddhist Tantras translated into Tibetan, the kinds of texts translated in the first diffusion contrast sharply with those of the later diffusion. Typical of the former are two texts commented on by Buddhaguhya, who came to Tibet in the eighth century, the *Vajravidārana-nāma-dhāraṇī*, which deals with the Kriyā Tantra generation of self into deity in six stages as described above, and the *Vairocanābhisaṃbodhi-tantra* of the Caryā class. The fifth chapter of the latter text deals with the four foundational practices: (1) The subjective foundation: one goes through an imaginative sequence, as in the Kriyā Tantra practice, culminating in one's imagining oneself to be the deity, in this case the Buddha Vairocana. (2) The objective foundation: one imagines in front of one a Vairocana, like oneself, and identifies with him. (3) Identification with the Mind of Enlightenment: one imagines that one's mind is in the shape of a moon disk within the heart of the Tathāgata in front. (4) Immersion in sound: one imagines on that moon disk the syllables of the formula to be recited, and one recites it one hundred thousand times. After mastering this kind of yoga, at its culmination the Sign Deity stays in the mind with a brightness as though before the eyes on the side of the mind which is directed outward. The signature or residue of that intense contemplation amounts to the brightness on the inward side of the mind, where the body of the deity appears to be an illusion, or a void accumulation; this is the yoga without signs.[21]

One gets the impression that in the early period of translation into Tibetan, the pandits who had come to Tibet and the Tibetan translators were the chief teachers, while the scriptures themselves remained mysterious documents, studded with the jewels of precepts, as though locked up in a vault. The later diffusion was marked by translation activities on an enormous scale. The lineages brought into Tibet by Indian refugees in the eleventh century are bewildering in their complexity and variety. The Tantra was enthusiastically pursued, but the Tibetans also translated every available commentary on Mādhyamika and on the *Abhidharmakośa*, and tome after tome on Buddhist logic. Their diligent study of these works was accompanied by practice of the complicated procedures of Tantra. But though the Rñin-ma-pa claimed a continuous lineage going back to such Tantras as the *Guhyagarbha*, and though the Gelugpa praised the writings of Buddhaguhya in the highest terms, it is doubtful if any of them tried to meet the requirements for the title of ācārya specified in the *Vairocanābhisaṃbodhi-tantra*, as explained by Buddhaguhya,[22] namely, to imagine thirty-two syllables in spots of the body while being initiated in the maṇḍala of Body, then of Speech, and then of Mind. The link with this early tradition had been broken. If such complex efforts were necessary to be an ācārya, there would be few ācārya anywhere!

In the later diffusion, great emphasis is placed on the lineages, the "permission" to invoke the deity, and the guru's kindness in imparting the precepts to the candidates. The texts give detailed accounts of the precious attributes of the master and what makes a disciple an appropriate vessel. Thus, the treatise *Fifty Stanzas in Praise of the Guru* describes the teacher: "Steadfast, self-controlled, intelligent. . . ."[23] The commentaries require him to be versed in the sūtras and śāstras, and free from basic transgressions (such as reviling the Word of the Buddha, criticizing the guru, revealing the Tantric secrets to the uninitiated). The guru's mantra vow must be intact; otherwise his initiation of disciples is declared a sham. The disciple, on his part, is required to take the triple refuge, generate the Mind of Enlightenment, and take the bodhisattva vow.

The *Sarvatathāgata-Tattvasaṃgraha* (Diamond Sūtra) was translated at the beginning of the later diffusion along with a large amount of exegetical commentary. It presents the magic formulas going with the five Manifest Enlightenments (*abhisaṃbodhi*) of Sarvārthasiddha, a name of Gautama, showing how he became fully enlightened as Śākyamuni. Mkhas-grub-rje describes these five as Gautama experienced them, and the manner in which later candidates may have the experience.[24] (1) The Buddhas of the ten directions are said to have conferred on the bodhisattva the diadem initiation and to have directed him to contemplate the meaning of the mantra "I perform mind penetration." Thereby he realized the true nature of his mind (*citta-dharmatā*) and its sixteen kinds of śūnyatā. Emerging from this samādhi he saw this true nature of his mind in the shape of a moon disk in his own heart and thereby attained the "mirror wisdom" which is the nature of the Buddha Akṣobhya. The Manifest Enlightenment in this case is the one resulting from discrimination. The later candidates attend to the vowels of the mantra so that they change into the moon disk in their heart. (2) The Buddhas bade the bodhisattva contemplate the meaning of the mantra "OṂ, I generate the Mind of Enlightenment." Emerging from this samādhi, he saw the true nature of his mind, void, undefiled, in the form of a full moon disk in his own heart. Thereby he attained the "equality wisdom" which is the nature of Ratnasambhava. This Manifest Enlightenment results from generating the Mind of Supreme Enlightenment. The later candidates associate the consonants with the true nature of their minds. (3) All the Buddhas bade the bodhisattva contemplate the mantra "Stand up, O *vajra!*" Thereby, he attained the discriminative wisdom which is the nature of Amitābha. (4) They bade him contemplate the mantra "I consist of diamond." Thereby all the elements (*dhātu*) of the Body-*vajra*, Speech-*vajra*, and Mind-*vajra* of all the Tathāgatas of the ten directions, entered the five-pronged, white *vajra* of his own heart, and he directly observed that this *vajra* (in his heart) was composed of the finest atoms of the *vajras* of all the Tathāgatas. Thereby he attained the "duty-fulfillment wisdom," which is the nature of Amoghasiddhi. (5) They bade him contemplate the mantra "OṂ. Like all the Thus-gone, so am I." Thereby, because of the transformation of the *vajra* and moon in his own heart, he appeared as Mahāvairocana, the saṃbhogakāya adorned with the thirty-two characteristics and the eighty minor marks, and thus was a Manifest Complete Buddha. Thereby he attained the Dharmadhātu Wisdom which is the nature of Vairocana. As to the later candidates for the last three of the Manifest Enlightenments, their procedure is much the same as that of the bodhisattva. At no stage, however, is the possibility held out that they may share his attainments.

Ritual texts describe the thirteen visions of a yogin.[25] A suitable place is prescribed—for example, a temple hall, a monk's cell, or a room sanctified for the purpose in a home. An altar or a table should be equipped with symbols of the deity's Body (an icon, preferably of metal), Speech (a sacred book of Buddhism), and Mind (a stūpa). Special offerings are placed before the altar and the yogin recites ritual formulas over them; his mental concentration on them is essential. The yogin adopts a sitting posture known as the pose of Mahāvairocana: The feet are in the "diamond" interlock; the hands are in a samādhi gesture (the palms open with the fingers of one hand on those of the other, the two thumbs touching in an apex); the spinal column erect; diaphragm relaxed; head bent like a hook; tongue touching the palate; eyes focused on a point two feet in front of the body. The yogin takes his refuge first in his guru, then in the Three Jewels. He takes a vow to become a Buddha on behalf of all sentient beings, and while reciting these words, he has the following visions: (1) His father is standing at his right, his mother at his left, and sentient beings of the different destinies are ranged around him; the yogin imagines that every one of these beings during uncountable rebirths has at some time or other been mother or father to him; and he determines to rescue them. (This is an exercise in the promotion of compassion). (2) He imagines the deity he serves as seated on a high throne consisting of eight lions, transformed from the eight bodhisattvas. The central deity multiplies itself into many Dharma-transmitting gurus. He imagines that these gurus confer the initiation of fivefold wisdom by pouring sanctified water upon the crown of his head; the water is imagined to pass out of his pores taking with it all the sinful material. (3) The yogin visualizes the deity as himself and becomes one with the deity; this is an inward apprehension in contrast to the outward direction of the preceding visions (mundane in the case of the first, supramundane in the second). At the right is the symbol of the Dharma; at the left the symbol of the Saṅgha; behind are the Protectors of the Dharma, all shining brightly. (4) On a lion throne he sees the founder of Buddhism, Śākyamuni with golden body, right hand touching the ground, left one making the samādhi gesture and holding an ambrosia alms bowl. A great light issues from the Buddha's heart, and the yogin knows him as the primordial teacher. Another light issues from the Buddha's head, making visible a throne above him on which is Vajradhara, the primordial Buddha, colored dark blue, enveloped in transparent light, wearing a jeweled diadem, and surrounded by the eighty-four great masters (*mahāsiddha*) of the past ages. (5) He sees another light issuing from the Buddha's heart. It makes visible at the right the future Buddha Maitreya, surrounded by Asaṅga, Vasubandhu, and others of the lineage of the Yogācāra school which he inspired. (6) Another light from the Buddha's heart reveals at his left the bodhisattva Mañjuśrī, surrounded by circles of spiritual helpers and the lineage of gurus in the school of Nāgārjuna. (7) Rays from Śākyamuni's heart illumine the foreground, and here the yogin sees his own immediate teachers, especially those who initiated him into the mysteries. Below them are the deities of the five or six Buddha families, the bodhisattvas, pratyekabuddhas, śrāvakas, *dakinīs* (deities of the mysteries), and *dharmapālas* (protectors of the faith), and, finally, the books of scriptures which they reveal, all emitting beams of light. (8) The yogin renews and fortifies in himself the Mind of Enlightenment, seeing it under twenty-two images: earth, gold, moon, fire, treasure, jewel, ocean, diamond, mountain, cure-all, great friend, wish-granting jewel, sun, Gandharva-voice, king, gem storehouse, great road, vehicle, fountain, pleasant sound, great river, cloud. (9) The yogin utters sentences expressing the four immeasurables (love, compassion, sympathetic joy, impartiality), of the form, "May all the beings . . . ," and imagines that the form of the supreme teacher on a throne enters him through the top of his head and passes down to his heart. (10) He visualizes a *vajra* standing upright in his heart on the moon disk constituting the Mind of Enlightenment. He utters the sacred spell "OṂ! All the dharmas are intrinsically pure; I am intrinsically pure." Thus, he realizes his oneness with the pure Dharmadhātu. (11) The yogin begins his mystic death and resurrection. As the solid parts of the body begin to pass into water, the yogin has the first sign, a mirage. As the fluid parts dry up in the fire, he has the second sign, of smoke. As the ability to eat, drink, and digest fails, while the fire passes into the wind, he has the third sign, of fireflies. As the life winds transfer from their normal corporeal centers, while the wind passes into the *vijñāna* (understanding) principle, he has the fourth sign, of a changeable lamp in the heart. Then the *vijñāna* principle leaves the body and passes to the Clear Light, or the pure, void Dharmadhātu. This is referred to as abandoning the body of works and obtaining a diamond body. Afterward, the body, thus purified in the Clear Light, returns by the reverse process, recreating the elements.

(12) The yogin utters the four mystic syllables, JAH HŪṂ BAṂ HOH, which go with four steps in bringing down the gnostic aspect (*jñānarūpa*) of the Lord, and he realizes, "The god enters me and I enter the god." Thus this form of the Lord which enters through the crown of the head is the yogin himself. (13) He visualizes the germ syllable, in his heart, emitting rays of light that illumine all the realm of form and the realm of desire (among the three realms, the third being the "formless realm"). These rays of light are then retracted into the germ syllable. He then invokes the appropriate deities for bestowing initiation on his disciples.

All the aspects of the yogin's quest for enlightenment hitherto described recur in connection with various deities in other settings. The large pantheon of deities, comprising those inherited from Indian Buddhism and indigenous deities, are a remarkable feature of the tradition. Among Indian deities invoked in Atīśa's lineage are the four deities of the bKa'-gdams-pa: Munendra, that is, Gautama Buddha, the sole teacher, called Buddha of the Diamond Seat (with Maitreya Bodhisattva and Avalokiteśvara as companions); Avalokiteśvara of the six syllables; Khadiravanī Tārā, who dispels outer hindrances and accomplishes mundane *siddhis;* Blue Acala, who dispels inner hindrances and generates wisdom. Among the most popular indigenous deities are Lhamo, the fierce goddess who rides on a mule, and various other deities mounted on horse or reindeer, each having its own legend. The central figure of the Five Bodies group of deities is Pe-har, greatly adored by the Tibetans, said to have been brought by Padmasaṁbhava from Magadha and bound by solemn oath to protect the great monastery of Samye. During the reign of the Fifth Dalai Lama, he moved to the Nechung monastery near Drepung and took possession of a priest there, whom that Dalai Lama appointed as the state oracle.[26]

Current Tibetan Buddhism

A seven-hundred-year period of intense religious searching and definition came to an end with the Fifth Dalai Lama. Then Tibet entered upon a difficult political era.[27] When the Fifth Dalai Lama died in 1682, the regent Sangs-rgyas rgya-mtsho (author of works on medicine, astrology, and the history of the Gelugpa sect) kept his death secret by various subterfuges while he raised secretly the child picked as the Sixth Dalai Lama, Tsan-dbyans rgya-mtsho. When the deception broke down, the Sixth Dalai Lama was enthroned in 1695. Then, in 1697, a descendant of Gu-shri Khan named lHa-bzang became "king" of the Qoshot Mongols and aspired to get political control of Tibet. The Sixth Dalai Lama complicated matters by his reputation as a libertine. Eventually lHa-bzang killed Sangs-rgyas rgya-mtsho and conspired with the Manchu emperor K'ang-shi to depose the Dalai Lama (who died in 1706). lHa-bzang ruled Tibet from 1705 until 1717, when he was killed by the Dzungar Mongols. The young Seventh remained under Manchu protection at the Kumbum monastery in Kokonor and was eventually escorted to Lhasa by an army of Mongol and Chinese troops, when the Tibetans finally gained the upper hand against the Dzungars.[28] K'ang-shi's death in 1722 brought the Chinese interference to a halt and a lay Tibetan named Pho-lha ruled capably for twenty years, during which the Seventh Dalai Lama was occasionally exiled, exercising temporal power only toward the end of his life (he died 1757, aged fifty).

The Manchu emperors tried to play the Panchen Lama against the Dalai Lama. The Panchen Lamas increased in stature after the Seventh and Eighth Dalai Lamas, because the next four all died in youth, and government was for the most part in the hands of their regents. The Thirteenth Dalai Lama (b. 1876) assumed power in 1895. From then until his death in 1933, he governed almost continuously, with his main effort devoted to keeping his country free, especially from the Chinese, while introducing some social reforms. He knew the danger of communism, which had already destroyed monasteries of Outer Mongolia. His taxation of Tashilunpo estates caused the Panchen Lama to leave for Peking, where he remained in semiexile until the Dalai Lama's death. The Panchen Lama was then invited back to Tibet, but his return was prevented by various problems; he died in 1937. The most recent phase in Tibetan history began with the finding of the Fourteenth Dalai Lama, Nag-dban Blo-bzan bsTan-'dsin rgya-mtsho, born in 1935, and the events of utmost tragedy for Tibet inaugurated by the communist Chinese invasion in October 1949. After the remarkable escape of the Dalai Lama and his party in 1959, the Indian government granted him asylum.[29]

The writings of the regent Sangs-rgyas rgya-mtsho are typical of the encyclopedic works and multivolume collections of the period after the Fifth Dalai Lama, in which new compositions tended to be ritualistic rather than philosophical. The founders of the sect and their immediate followers were supposed to have treated the basic issues definitively. Any new efforts to decipher the meaning of the *Guhyasamāja-tantra* seemed superfluous. Instead, monastic summaries of doctrine, ritual handbooks, and subcommentaries on commentaries were composed. Whereas in the earlier period, works on Buddhism aimed to explain its teachings, now the aim was simplification, achieved by the omission of problematic passages and troublesome details. The great writers of the Sa-skya-pa and the Gelugpa had to sift the canonical works in the Kanjur and Tanjur, designating some as works to be read, while the remainder would not normally be read by anyone. As we approach modern times, the amount of indigenous Tibetan works in every sect had reached such proportions that few could read the bulk of the major works of their own sect, not to mention those of rival sects! Some of these later compilations have considerable value, for instance, the fourteen-volume *sādhana* collection called *Sgrub thabs kun btus.* These works are now known to interested Western scholars as reprinted in North India by Tibetan refugees of different sects, including followers of the Bön-po religion.

As an instance of the ritual yoga of this later period, the *guru-yoga* (which can be referred to by the Sanskrit term *upacāra-krama,* "the steps of honoring")[30] may be mentioned. It is divided into the preliminary section, the main section or body, and the conclusion. The preliminary section is in three phases, taking refuge, awakening the Mind of Enlightenment, and aspiration in terms of the four immeasurables. The main body is in seven sections, including the invitation of the conclave of deities and the offerings. In conclusion, one asks for various *siddhis,* and presents a final prayer. The service is addressed to Tson-kha-pa. The refuge formula: "I take refuge in the gurus and the pledged deities. I take refuge in the Buddhas and Bodhisattvas. I take refuge in the Mothers and *Dakinīs*. I take refuge in the protectors of the religion." To awaken the Mind of Enlightenment means to seek enlightenment for oneself and to set others on the course to Enlightenment. For the four immeasurables one prays: "May all beings be in concord! May they become free from suffering! May they enjoy (religious) success! May they abide in equanimity!" In the main part, at the invitation, the performer imagines Maitreya in the Tuṣitā Heaven; he also imagines Tson-kha-pa there, invites him and his sons, Rgyal-tshab-rje and Mkhas-grub-rje, to the space in front, and praises him as king of the Dharma with shining body. The offerings, said to be pleasing to the mind, are such things as flowers, food, incense, lamps, perfume, which the performer must mentally transform into a field of merit. Then he confesses his sins; sympathetically rejoices for those who avoid the untimely conditions, such as being born when there is no Buddha; entreats the venerable ones imagined in the space in front to pour down the rain of Dharma to germinate the seeds of virtue; and, finally, dedicates all his accumulated merit, whatever it be, to the service of the Dharma and sentient beings. Among the gifts for which one prays at the conclusion is the precept and its threefold meaning, outer (exoteric), inner (esoteric), and secret (mystic): "You [Tson-kha-pa] are all three, the compassionate Avalokiteśvara, the sovereign-of-insight Mañjuśrī, and holder-of-diamond Vajrapāni." One also asks for extension of life, for merits, and for knowledge (to abolish defilements and dispel ignorance). Then one invites the guru (in this case, Tson-kha-pa) to abide in one's heart, and to bestow success of Body, Speech, and Mind. Last, there is the general dedication: "May we in every rebirth enjoy the glory of Dharma unseparated from our true guru. After having accomplished the stages and the merits of the way, may we quickly reap the fruit of Vajradhara." This rite of guru-yoga is said to have been composed by Sangs-rgyas rgya-mtsho.

When lamas migrated to European and other countries, the fine reception they frequently met was prepared for by the appearance of such works as W. Y. Evans-Wentz's editions of translations made by the Lāma Kazi Dawa-Samdup (*The Tibetan Book of the Dead*, 1927; *Tibet's Great Yogī Milarepa*, 1928). The biography and poems of the Tibetan mystic Milarepa (1040–1123) have been perennial favorites in Tibet. He succeeded the translator Marpa in the Kagyut sect and brought into Tibet the lineage from Naropa, the Indian master. Milarepa is the paragon cave meditator, who hears the "ear-whispered secrets" from the *dakinīs*, those "sky-walking" spirits. His relation with the guru Marpa exemplifies the kindness of the guru. In his youth Milarepa had practiced black magic, producing by magic destructive hailstorms, and he had to atone for this. When Tibetan lamas fled the oppression that had descended on their country, they were often patronized by Westerners who looked upon them as compatriots of Milarepa. The establishment of "centers" in the West, even monastery-type edifices, by these migrating lamas has been an extraordinary event. The Tibetan people have of course lost much, but Tibetan Buddhism has not shared the same fate. While in Tibet proper so many monasteries were looted and destroyed, Tibetan Buddhism has moved far and wide and has shown its vitality, aided immeasurably by the Dalai Lama's guidance and inspiration to the refugee Tibetans.

Bön literature need not be discussed here since it is subsequent to and heavily dependent on the Buddhist literature. The early and later Bön partisans practiced savage blood sacrifices, which the Buddhists tried to suppress.[31] It has been suggested that the rite of Chöd, where the participants practice self-mutilation (and believe in magical restoration of the limbs) is a survival of the Bön.[32] Probably the various Tibetan customs regarding the spirit world, such as the "thread-crosses" to catch demons, are other such survivals, as are the "charms" which use drawings of animals and suggest sympathetic magic. However, the mere fact that a Tibetan religious practice is not traceable to Buddhism does not prove it to be Bön, since Tibet received other influences through Central Asia. A feature rarely noted is very evident in the *Sgrub thabs kun btus*, in which numerous passages emphasize that the world consists of poison, for instance this formula:

> OṂ. Homage to the Lord. May I, named so-and-so, a defiled person in the passage of time destroying all the obscuration of poison—become possessed of the three virtues. This earth is the father of poison. This earth is the mother of poison. By these true words of truth, may the three poisons pass into the earth.

The same formula is used for the other elements, substituting *water, fire,* and *wind* for the word *earth.* This view that humanity is poisoned and that it is cured by returning the poison to the four elements from which it comes is not derived from Buddhism. Its wide influence is evidence that the old Bön and Buddhism became quite mixed. The Gelugpa sect were to the fore in opposing Bön practice, while the Rñin-ma-pa is the one most resembling the Bön.

When the monastery Tashilunpo was built in 1447 by the First Dalai Lama, a large statue of Maitreya was erected, and on that occasion he composed this hymn, which may fittingly close our survey:

> Now that an excellent statue of Maitreya has been erected, may these embodied beings who engage in the concordant conditions enter the glory of practicing the Great Vehicle Dharma, before the feet of the venerable Lord Maitreya.
>
> At whatever time Maitreya as a powerful sun rises on the peak of the Diamond-seat Mountain, opening up the lotus of my intelligence, may I refresh the fortunate host.
>
> At that time, may the Buddha Maitreya, very pleased, place his right hand on my head and prophesy the supreme, incomparable enlightenment. Then may I speedily attain Buddhahood for the sake of all living beings.
>
> Also, however many be the magnificent practices of all the Buddhas of the three ages and their spiritual sons (the bodhisattvas) in all their illustrious lives, may I, compressing them together, preach them correctly!
>
> Having recourse to the golden hilt of analyzing the scriptural cloth with its colorful lines of good explanation, may I install in the ten directions the victory banner of the Teaching marked with the jewel tip of the Three Instructions.
>
> May all the persons who are scripture-holders spread and expand upon the Teaching which is the source of benefit and joy! May the Buddha's Teaching, the source of felicity to all embodied beings, forever spread!
>
> May the force of continual contemplation of love (*maitrī*), in three ways, bring the blessing of the Buddha Maitreya who overcomes the Māras by the troops of love and protects all beings by the power of love.[33]

Notes

1. See Prabodh Chandra Bagchi, *Studies in the Tantras, I* (Calcutta: University of Calcutta, 1939) 34f.
2. Alex Wayman, *Buddhist Tantras,* 66–67.
3. Benoytosh Bhattacharyya, *The Indian Buddhist Iconography* (Calcutta: Firma KLM, 1958) 22.
4. A. Wayman, "The Significance of Mantras, from the Veda down to Buddhist Tantric Practice," *Indologica Taurinensia* 3–4 (1975–76) 488–489.
5. Wayman, *Buddhist Tantras,* 33.
6. Ibid., 53.

7. *Mkhas grub rje's Fundamentals of the Buddhist Tantras,* trans. F. D . Lessing and A. Wayman (=*Introduction to the Buddhist Tantric Systems* [Delhi: Motilal Banarsidass, 1978] 159–63).
8. Japanese photo edition of Tibetan canon, Peking, V 249.
9. *Mkhas grup rje's Fundamentals of the Buddhist Tantras,* 231–49.
10. Ibid., 251, 269.
11. Tibetan canon, V 212–14.
12. *History of Buddhism by Bu-ston,* II, trans. E. Obermiller, 182–83.
13. See Christopher Beckwith, "The Introduction of Greek Medicine into Tibet in the Seventh and Eighth Centuries," *Journal of the American Oriental Society* 99 (1979) 297–313.
14. *History of Buddhism by Bu-ston,* II, 196.
15. Giuseppe Tucci, ed., *Minor Buddhist Texts,* 2:30. Paul Demiéville incorrectly calls this debate the council of Lhasa.
16. See Alaka Chattopadhyaya, *Atīśa and Tibet* (Calcutta: Indian Studies: Past & Present, 1967; reprint, Delhi: Motilal Banarsidass, 1981).
17. See H. E. Richardson, "The Karma-Pa Sect: A Historical Note," *Journal of the Royal Asiatic Society* (Oct. 1958).
18. As pointed out by David Snellgrove and Hugh Richardson, *A Cultural History of Tibet,* 182.
19. See Toni Schmid, *Saviours of Mankind: Dalai Lamas and Former Incarnations of Avalokiteśvara* (Stockholm: Statens Etnografiska Museum, 1961); idem, *Saviours of Mankind II: Panchen Lamas and Former Incarnations of Amitāyus* (Stockholm: Statens Etnografiska Museum, 1964).
20. Seventh Dalai Lama, Blo-bzan bskal-bzan rgya-mtsho, *Collected Works,* Peking edition, Vol. Kha, f. 5b-4ff.
21. Buddhaguhya's commentary on the *Vairocanābhisambodhi-tantra,* Japanese photo edition of Peking Kanjur-Tanjur, PTT, Vol. 77, 195–3–5,6,7.
22. Ibid., 207–11.
23. *Mkhas grub rje's Fundamentals of the Buddhist Tantras,* 272–73.
24. Ibid., 29–35.
25. See Ferdinand D. Lessing, "The Thirteen Visions of a Yogācarya," *Ethnos* (1950) 108–30.
26. For these deities, see Réne de Nebesky-Wojkowitz, *Oracles and Demons of Tibet* (London: Oxford University Press, 1956).
27. See Luciano Petech, *China and Tibet in the early 18th Century* (Leiden: E. J. Brill, 1950).
28. See Tsepon W. D. Shakabpa, *Tibet: A Political History,* 138–39.
29. The Dalai Lama has movingly described the torment of his people and his flight from Tibet in *My Land and My People* (London: Weidenfeld and Nicolson, 1962).
30. Here I edit materials from the F. D. Lessing notebook, "Guru-yoga," where he refers to A. von Staël-Holstein, "On a Tibetan Text Translated into Sanskrit under Ch'ien Lung and into Chinese under Tao Kuang," reprinted from the Bull. of the Nat. Libr. of Peiping (Peiping, 1932).
31. R. A. Stein, *Tibetan Civilization,* 235.
32. Thubten Jigme Norbu and Colin M. Turnbull, *Tibet* (New York: Simon & Schuster, 1968) 127–30.
33. Oral information from Geshe Rabten, Spring 1970, Dharamsala, H.P. India, on the occasion when he made the Tibetan text available for my translation.

Bibliography

Sources

Evans-Wentz, W. Y. *Tibetan Yoga and Secret Doctrines.* London: Oxford University Press, 1958.
——. *Tibet's Great Yogi, Milarepa.* London: Oxford University Press, 1962.
——, ed. *The Tibetan Book of the Great Liberation.* London: Oxford University Press, 1954.
Guenther, Herbert V. *The Life and Teachings of Naropa.* Oxford: Clarendon Press, 1963.
——. *The Royal Song of Saraha.* Seattle: University of Washington Press, 1969.
——. *sGam-po-pa: The Jewel Ornament of Liberation.* Berkeley, CA: Shambhala, 1971.
——. *Tibetan Buddhism Without Mystification.* Leiden: E. J. Brill, 1966.
The Hevajra Tantra. Translated by David L. Snellgrove. London and New York: Oxford University Press, 1959.
History of Buddhism by Bu-ston. Translated by E. Obermiller. Heidelberg: Harrassowitz, 1931–32. Reprint, Tokyo: Suzuki Research Foundation, 1964.
Hopkins, Jeffrey, et al. *The Buddhism of Tibet.* London: Allen & Unwin, 1984.
Mkhas grub rje's Fundamentals of the Buddhist Tantras. Translated by F. D. Lessing and Alex Wayman. The Hague: Mouton, 1968.
The Tibetan Book of the Dead. Translated by Francesca Freemantle and Chogyam Trungpa. Berkeley, CA: Shambhala, 1975.
Tucci, Giuseppe, ed. *Minor Buddhist Texts.* Rome: Istituto italiano per il medio ed estremo oriente, 1958.
Wayman, Alex. *Calming the Mind and Discerning the Real.* New York: Columbia University Press, 1978.

Studies

Bell, Charles. *The Religion of Tibet.* Oxford: Clarendon, 1968.
Beyer, Stephen. *The Cult of Tārā.* Berkeley: University of California Press, 1973.
Bharati, Agehananda. *The Tantric Tradition.* London: Rider, 1965.
Bhattacharyya, Benoytosh. *An Introduction to Buddhist Esoterism.* Oxford University Press, 1932. Reprint, Varanasi: Chowkambha Sanskrit Series Office, 1964.
Blofeld, John. *The Tantric Mysticism of Tibet.* New York: E. P. Dutton, 1970.
Bromage, Bernard. *Tibetan Yoga.* New York: Samuel Weiser, 1952.
Demiéville, Paul. *Le concile de Lhasa.* Paris: Presses universitaires de France, 1952.
Guenther, Herbert V. *The Tantric View of Life.* Berkeley, CA: Shambhala, 1972.
Hoffman, Helmut. *The Religions of Tibet.* New York: Macmillan, 1961.
Shakabpa, Tsepon W. D. *Tibet: A Political History.* New Haven: Yale University Press, 1967.
Snellgrove, David, and Hugh Richardson. *A Cultural History of Tibet.* London: Weidenfeld & Nicholson, 1968.
Stein, Rolf Alfred. *Tibetan Civilization.* Stanford, CA: Stanford University Press, 1972.
Studies of Esoteric Buddhism and Tantrism. Kōya-san: Kōya-san University, 1965.
Tucci, Giuseppe. *The Religions of Tibet.* London: Routledge & Kegan Paul, 1980.
——. *The Theory and Practice of the Mandala.* London: Rider, 1961.
——. *Tibetan Painted Scrolls.* Rome: Libreria dello stato, 1949.
Wayman, Alex. *The Buddhist Tantras.* New York: Samuel Weiser, 1973.
——. "Female Energy and Symbolism in the Buddhist Tantras." *History of Religions* 2 (1962) 73–111.
Willis, Janice Dean. *The Diamond Light.* New York: Simon & Schuster, 1972.

10

Pure Land Piety

ROGER J. CORLESS

> Thinking we were sure to be wiped out, we huddled together under the trees on the dark, damp floor of the ravine. All of us were prepared to die. We sat there in breathless silence, with our backs hunched, staring wide eyed into the darkness.—Then one of our men must have lost his nerve, for a voice at one side muttered: "*Namu Amida Butsu—.*"[1]

THE INVOCATION *Namu Amida Butsu* ("Hail! Amita Buddha!"), known as nenbutsu (Chinese *nien-fo*), "Recalling (recollecting; invoking) Buddha," is perhaps the single best-known Buddhist phrase in all of East Asia. The form quoted is its pronunciation in Japan: in Mandarin Chinese it is pronounced *Nan-mo O-mi-t'o Fo,* and it has versions in other Chinese dialects, in Korean, and in Vietnamese. Whatever pronunciation is used, it is a cry for help found repeatedly on the lips of the ordinary Buddhist man or woman of East Asia, as in the above story of frightened Japanese soldiers. On the surface, it is nonproblematic and unphilosophical: it is something one resorts to when one has "lost one's nerve," and, as such, it has often seemed to Western scholars to be unworthy of serious study. But, we might ask, if something is so popular, might it not be because it has often been experienced as effective? And, if so, wherefrom is its effectiveness? That is the topic of this article.

The variety of Buddhism with which the invocation is linked is usually known in English as Pure Land Buddhism. "Pure Land" is a direct, if not very helpful, translation of the Chinese *ching-t'u* and refers to a land, region (*chieh*), or country (*kuo*) many millions of Buddha-lands to the west, so far away, indeed, that it is actually beyond all realms, beyond saṃsāra, unsullied by the passions which drive our world of suffering, and is therefore called "pure." Outwardly, the Pure Land resembles a sumptuous (and so, from a Buddhist point of view, defiling) paradise or deity-realm (*deva-loka*), but inwardly, in its essence, it is unarisen and of the nature of emptiness, so that it is *purifying* as well as being itself pure. The Pure Land is presided over by a Buddha called Amita, a Sanskrit name which becomes, when transliterated, *O-mi-t'o* in Mandarin Chinese and *Amida* in Japanese. Amita, it is said, has resolved that all those who, while living as humans, chant his name, will be, after their deaths, reborn in his Land. Thus, if one says "Hail! Amita Buddha," the power of Amita comes immediately to one's aid, both now and in the future. The practice is simple, but the effect is profound.

In order to study this profundity, we will first look at the general characteristics of Pure Land spirituality within the context of other religions and then investigate its roots in the Buddhist sūtras. Next we will spend a good deal of time looking at the life and teaching of one major figure, Dharma Master T'an-luan, who, in the fifth century B.C.E., was in many ways the architect of the tradition, after which the reasons for the effectiveness of such a simple practice as the invocation of a six-syllable phrase should become apparent. Finally, we will briefly discuss, without in any way presuming to give a comprehensive historical account, something of the development of Pure Land spirituality in China and the remainder of the Far East.

Pure Land Spirituality

The heart of Pure Land spirituality is a distinctive approach to the themes, found in some form in many religions and in other Buddhist lineages, of light and trust.

A Mysticism of Light

Light is commonly found as a spiritual symbol, as in this renowned Hindu prayer:

> From the unreal lead me to the real, from darkness lead me to light, from death lead me to immortality. (*Bṛhad-āraṇyaka Upaniṣad* I.3.28)

It is followed by the explanation "'From darkness lead me to light'; darkness, verily, is death, the light is immortality."[2] The same Upaniṣad (V.14.3) refers to the famous *Gāyatrī* mantra of the Rig Veda, which says, "We meditate on the adorable glory of the radiant sun; may he inspire our intelligence."[3]

In Pure Land Buddhism, light is not only important; it is central. The Pure Land is filled with light; it is, as it were, made of light, and one of the aliases of Amita is Amitābha, "He of Immeasurable Light." In meditation, the light of the Pure Land is glimpsed shining afar, beyond the place where the sun goes to its rest. The picture (as many scholars have noted, not always with approval) is superficially quite Christian. Indeed, the following lines, penned by the Christian poet Henry Vaughan (1621/2–1695 C.E.), might have been written by a Pure Land Buddhist, and they elegantly set the tone for our discussion.

> They are all gone into the world of light!
> And I alone sit lingring here;
> Their very memory is fair and bright,
> And my sad thoughts doth clear.
>
> It glows and glitters in my cloudy brest
> Like stars upon some gloomy grove,
> Or those faint beams in which this hill is drest,
> After the Sun's remove.
>
> I see them walking in an Air of glory,
> Whose light doth trample on my days:
> My days, which are at best but dull and hoary,
> Meer glimmering and decays.[4]

The transformative effects of the light of the Pure Land are similar to those of the light of the Christian God which Saint John of the Cross describes as "a flame that is consuming and painless . . . a consummator and restorer."[5] It is a light "like that of the sun on a window [which] makes it look bright, and all the stains and smudges previously apparent are lost sight of. . . ."[6]

Transformation by, or into, light is apparently recorded in another Upaniṣadic text (*Taittirīya Up.* III. 10). Having attained to the Supreme (according to the Upaniṣadic system), the yogin chants:

> HA VU HA VU HA VU!
> I am Food I am Food I am Food;
> I am the Eater I am the Eater I am the Eater;
> I am the Eating I am the Eating I am the Eating;
> I am Firstborn of the Worldforce;
> I am prior to the gods;
> I dwell at the Eye of the Deathless;
> He who gives me is me indeed;
> I am Food, the Foodeater I eat;
> I have won the world and her spaewning;
> I am burning like the sun!
> Who knows this, knows Truth.[7]

This is an experience of nonduality, or unity, which is so intense that its expression is partly ecstatic nonsense (the first line is mere noises, and line eight is literally something like "Whoever gives me, that one verily indeed me, yes") and which ends with the mystifyingly brief proclamation (on the penultimate line) "gold light!" (*suvarṇa jyotiḥ*), reminiscent of Pascal's cry of "Fire!" in his *Mémorial.* Commenting on this, Śaṅkara says that "gold" means the sun, and Rāmānuja explains that the yogin "becomes a beautiful, intensely shining body."[8] Apparently, he turns into a sun.

A dramatic example, nearer our own time, of transformation by and into light, is given in the account of a conversation between the Russian Orthodox mystic Saint Seraphim of Sarov (1759–1833 C.E.) and his lay disciple Nicholas Motovilov. Saint Seraphim begins to speak of the Holy Spirit as a "light-filled breath" which descends upon Christians, of how Moses' face shone when he came down from Mount Sinai (Exodus 34:30–35), and of the transfiguration of Jesus, in which "his face shone like the sun, and his garments became white as light" (Matthew 17:2). When Nicholas asks if such a transformation is really possible for such as himself, Saint Seraphim assures him that they are both already on fire with the Spirit, and asks why Nicholas does not look at him.

> I can't look at you, Father, because the light flashing from your eyes and face is brighter than the sun and I'm dazzled!

To which Saint Seraphim replied:

> Don't be afraid, friend of God, you yourself are shining just like I am: you too are now in the fullness of the grace of the Holy Spirit, otherwise you wouldn't be able to see me as you do. . . . So, my friend, why not look at me? Come on, look, don't be afraid, for the Lord is with us!

Nicholas then gives this description of Saint Seraphim's appearance:

> Then I looked at the Staretz [i.e., the teacher] and was panic-stricken. Picture, in the sun's orb, in the most dazzling brightness of its noon-day shining, the face of a man who is talking to you. You see his lips moving, the expression in his eyes, you hear his voice, you feel his arms round your shoulders, and yet you see neither his arms, nor his body, nor his face, you lose all sense of yourself, you can see only the blinding light which spreads everywhere, lighting up the layer of snow covering the glade, and igniting the flakes that are falling on us both like white powder.[9]

The light mysticism of Pure Land spirituality is at least as powerful as, if not more than, these examples from Hinduism and Christianity, and it has sometimes been asked if it did not enter Buddhism from elsewhere. When this question is answered in the affirmative, Iran, especially its native system of Zoroastrianism, is often indicated as the source of the sun and light symbolism of the sūtras (to be examined later in this article) on which Pure Land spirituality is based. This is how, for example, Ahura Mazda or Ohrmazd ("Lord of Wisdom"), the Supreme Being of Zoroastrianism, is described:

> It is thus revealed in the Good Religion that Ohrmazd was on high in omniscience and goodness. For boundless time He was ever in the light. That light is the space and place of Ohrmazd. Some call it Endless Light.[10]

Since Amitābha is, as we have seen, an alias of Amita Buddha meaning "He of Immeasurable Light," and since (as we shall see later) his light is understood to symbolize his wisdom, so that his name also means "He of Immeasurable Wisdom," it might seem that the figures of Amita and Ohrmazd arose in some dependence on each other, or that they were even the same entity. That was the view of the Zoroastrian heresy called Manichaeism, the system (which was so influential on Saint Augustine of Hippo) developed by the prophet Mani (216–277 C.E.), claiming that Zoroastrianism, Buddhism, and Christianity were merely three aspects of one religion.[11] Hard evidence for the influence of Zoroastrianism on Buddhism is, however, lacking,[12] and in its absence the theory does not seem necessary. All of the main features of Pure Land Buddhism can be derived from Buddhist sūtras and śāstras. The fact that these texts sometimes contain teachings similar to (though, of course, not the same as) those of other religions need not be accepted as evidence of influence. From the Buddhist point of view, the similarities could be taken to show that, where non-Buddhist religions agree with Buddhism, they have correctly understood the nature of reality as it truly is.

A Spirituality of Trust

Trust in a power greater than oneself is such a common motif in those systems which we call religions that it has sometimes been regarded as a *sine qua non* for identifying a system as a religion rather than, say, a philosophy. Since Buddhism often appears to be ambiguous on this point, it has got itself called, in English, a "religion-philosophy."[13] Pure Land Buddhism, however, is not ambiguous. It speaks explicitly and often of reliance on Amita Buddha as "Other Power" (a term best known in the West in its Japanese form of *tariki*). This has led some scholars to claim that Pure Land Buddhism is not, or is not fully, Buddhist, bringing up the question (already referred to) of Zoroastrian, or perhaps Christian, influence, and so charging that Pure Land Buddhism is a corruption of "true" Buddhism.[14]

The claim can, at first, be addressed in the same manner as that of the supposed Iranian influence on Pure Land Buddhism's light mysticism. The theory is not a priori necessary, since the sources for the spirituality of trust, just as those for the symbolism of light, can be found without going outside the bounds of Indian Mahāyāna. And then, there is no hard evidence to support the claim. What evidence there seemed to have been has mostly turned out to be mistaken. The most embarrassing mistake was that of the Jesuit Father Nicolas Trigault, who, on hearing the invocation to Amitābha as *Tolomé*, presumed that he had discovered a corrupt Christian sect founded by that indefatigable early missionary, Saint Bartholomew (pronounced *Bartholomé* in French).[15]

But, more importantly, the issue is whether or not Amita Buddha is in the final analysis like a Supreme Being, or God. The general tone of Pure Land devotion is certainly very similar to devotion in the theistic systems. In them, the worshiper gives up all possessions to the Worshiped and receives only God (who, to the worshiper, is All), as in this classic prayer to the Christian God by Saint Ignatius Loyola:

> Take, Lord, all my independence.
> Govern my memory, my reasoning and my will.
> My possessions are your gift:
>   I restore them to you,
>   I entrust them to your guidance.
> I ask only for your love and your grace,
>   and that will be my treasure.[16]

In a similar vein, the Hindu God Krishna says:

> Fix your intention on me, let your reasoning dwell on me; then, without any doubt, you will dwell in me.[17]

And, through a Sufi mystic, Allah says:

> My servant ceases not to draw nigh unto Me by works of devotion, until I love him, and when I love him I am the eye by which he sees and the ear by which he hears. And when he approaches a span I approach a cubit, and when he comes walking I come running.[18]

The psychological consequences of this relinquishing of one's own power is the peace that comes from knowing that one is being kept secure by a Power that will not fail. The Jesuit Jean-Pierre de Caussade says that this way of, as he calls it, self-abandonment "is the easiest road which leads soonest and most surely to a deep and invariable peace; it is also a sure guarantee of the preservation of that peace in the depth of our soul throughout the most furious tempests."[19]

However, although the *tone* of Pure Land Buddhist devotion may be theistic, so that a Pure Land Buddhist could find much in the above quotations with which to resonate, its *content* is clearly Buddhist. Amita Buddha is both like and unlike a Supreme Being or God in the following respects:[20] (1) He is unique in his own realm (the Pure Land), but he is not unique in the universe as a whole, being only one of many Buddhas, each unique in his own realm (Buddha-land) and each having distinctive properties. (2) He is the creator of his realm, the source of all good in it, and the parentlike protector and helper (or savior) of its inhabitants, but he does not create, sustain, or destroy the universe as a whole, nor is he the ontological support (a "Ground of Being") for the universe as a whole. (3) He is omniscient and all-seeing within and outside of his realm and is especially concerned with knowing human activity, so that he may remove ignorance; but he does not judge or punish. (4) He is outside "this world"; he is visualized as living in a paradise in the sky and is "Other Power"—that is, other than the passionate, defiled mind of the practitioner; but he does not stand above the worshiper as an ontologically "Higher Power." (5) His life is immeasurably long, but his life is not infinite, since there was a time when he was not a Buddha. Points 4 and 5 above need a little elaboration.

Amita is called upon as "Other Power" (Chinese *t'o-li;* Japanese *tariki*), literally, "that power," normally translated into English as "other power" because it is the antonym of *tzŭ-li,* "self power." The experience of the Pure Land practitioner, as of the theistic devotee, is that one's own power is insufficient to take one to liberation and so it is necessary to trust in the power of Another. In some forms of Pure Land piety the worshiper completely surrenders to Amita, but in all forms the practitioner turns over final responsibility for his or her liberation to Amita. This attitude is called *hsin,* a character usually translated into English as "faith," but (since faith is a slippery word, often implying irrationality) it seems better to translate it as "trust." The practitioner, having heard of Amita's promise, *trusts* that Amita will be faithful to his promise.[21]

The power of Amita is felt as *other* than the practitioner's defiled and limited mind (for, if that were not so, it could not liberate the defiled and limited mind), but it is not felt as *ontologically other* or "higher" than that mind, as God feels to a theistic worshiper. The mind of the Pure Land practitioner and the mind of Amita are, finally, discovered to be nondual, as are (according to general Mahāyāna teaching) saṃsāra and nirvāṇa.

Amita is sometimes known as Amitāyus, "He of Immeasurable Life." It is important not to translate "immeasurable" (Chinese *wu-liang*) as "eternal" (as if the Chinese had been *yung*). Buddhas were not always Buddhas: they began as ordinary beings and, after a very long time (many world cycles) evolved into Buddhas. Therefore, for a Buddha, as distinct from God, "there was a time when he was not" (to adapt a phrase that was the center of an early christological debate). In the case of Amita, his "pre-Buddha" career as the bodhisattva Dharmākara is an important part of his story. Having become a Buddha at a definite time in the past (ten kalpas ago, according to both the *Larger* and *Smaller Sukhāvatīvyūha*), Amita now has a life-span that is immeasurable, that is, incapable of being calculated by our defiled and limited minds.

18. *Folding Triptych, an Eight-Bodhisattva Mandala*, 9th century. Sculpture—Central Asian. Sandalwood with traces of red and green color. 12¼ x 14 inches.

In the above, we have sketched the outlines of Pure Land piety in a few broad brush strokes. We will now go into more detail with a discussion of the sūtras on which it is based.

The Pure Land Sūtras

The Three Main Sūtras

Of the many Mahāyāna sūtras that have at least some mention of the (or *a*) Pure Land, three are given special prominence in Pure Land Buddhism, as they are wholly concerned with Amita's Pure Land. Two sūtras, which exist in Sanskrit and have the same title of *Sukhāvatīvyūha*, are commonly referred to as "larger" and "smaller" because of their great difference in length. The third sūtra exists only in Chinese, and is known by its short title of *Kuan ching*. It is also referred to by the reconstructed Sanskrit title *Amitāyurdhyāna Sūtra*, but this is only a guess. These sūtras will be summarized in order.[22]

The Larger Sukhāvatīvyūha

This sūtra is extant in Sanskrit and may have been composed in the northwest of the Indian subcontinent around 100 C.E. It exists also in Tibetan, and twelve translations are said to have been made into Chinese, of which only five remain, and only that by Saṃghavarman (252 C.E.) is commonly read.

The sūtra is spoken by Śākyamuni Buddha on Mount Gṛdhrakūṭa, in the presence of a large assembly. Ānanda is the first to speak, and he tells the Buddha that he can see his face shining like gold. Śākyamuni asks him if he really sees this himself or is merely reporting something that the gods (devas) have told him. Ānanda replies that he sees it himself, and Śākyamuni congratulates him. This exchange may describe a phenomenon similar to that recounted above between Saint Seraphim and Nicholas Motovilov, and may indicate that both the Buddha and Ānanda had been transformed into deva-like light in preparation for the teaching which follows.

The main intent of the sūtra is to tell how the Pure Land, and Amita Buddha, came to be. Śākyamuni explains that a very long time ago there was a Buddha in the world called Lokeśvararāja, who had a disciple called Dharmākara. Dharmākara wished to make the Bodhisattva Resolve under Lokeśvararāja, and he wished to do it in a special way. He knew that all Buddhas obtain, as a result of their bodhisattva practice, a realm known as a Buddha-land (*buddhakṣetra*).[23] He desired that his realm should be the finest (or purest) of them all. So, he asked Lokeśvararāja to describe in detail the finest Buddha-lands then existing. The account took 10^7 years to complete, after which Dharmākara went into retreat for five kalpas in order to perfect a visualization which combined the best of the best of what he had heard.

On emerging from his retreat, Dharmākara at last made the Bodhisattva Resolve, holding clearly in his consciousness the pure Buddha-land that he had visualized. His Resolve was in forty-eight parts[24] (often referred to as the Forty-eight Vows), each of the general form "If, when I become a Buddha, my Buddha-land should not have the quality 'X' then may I not become a Buddha." According to the law of karma, this meant that, if Dharmākara did become a Buddha then he certainly will have a land with the quality "X." And, says Śākyamuni, that is exactly what has happened. Dharmākara Bodhisattva is now (and has been for a very long time) the Buddha Amitābha in a Buddha-land called Sukhāvatī. Sukhāvatī means "possessing *sukhā*," and *sukhā* is the antonym of *duḥkha;* that is, it is the opposite of all that marks saṃsāra as saṃsāra. Therefore, Sukhāvatī is the best, finest, and purest of all Buddha-lands. Simply, it is "the" Pure Land.

With respect to Pure Land practice, the most important quality "X" in the forty-eight-part Bodhisattva Resolve of Dharmākara is that of devotion to Amita Buddha, especially by visualizing the Pure Land and, even more especially, by chanting his Name. This is the origin of the popularity of the invocation *Nan-mo O-mi-t'o Fo,* "Hail! Amita Buddha." Because of the power of Dharmākara's resolve, reciting this Name ensures one of rebirth in Sukhāvatī.

The Smaller Sukhāvatīvyūha

The date and provenance of this sūtra are probably similar to those of the *Larger Sukhāvatīvyūha,* except that it might be a little earlier. It also exists in Tibetan, and three translations were made into Chinese, of which one has been lost. The translation by Kumārajīva (402 C.E.) is the one commonly read.[25]

The sūtra is considerably shorter than the preceding one, being mainly a description of Sukhāvatī. It begins rather abruptly, with Śākyamuni (in the garden, this time, of Prince Jeta at Śrāvastī) announcing, unasked, that Sukhāvatī exists and that Amitābha is at that very moment preaching Dharma in it. This highly unusual procedure (generally, the Buddha, or any Buddhist teacher, waits for a topic to be requested before speaking on it) is explained by saying that the teaching on Sukhāvatī is so wonderful that even the great disciples did not have enough wisdom to ask about it.[26]

Between this and the larger sūtra it has been claimed that there is a doctrinal difference. Whereas the larger sūtra promises rebirth in Sukhāvatī on the basis of fairly standard merit-bearing practices (powerfully assisted, nevertheless, by the visualization and invocation of Amitābha), the smaller sūtra regards invocation of the Name as sufficient. However, the difference may be due only to the compressed nature of the smaller sūtra. The larger sūtra teaches that one may be reborn in Sukhāvatī through great merit, through small merit, or through invocation, as a result of which one will maintain greater or lesser consciousness during the process of rebirth, the last group going there in a dream. The smaller sūtra, then, may be regarded as mentioning only this last group, and the three kinds of rebirth may be seen as being developed in the last of the three sūtras, to which we now turn.

The Kuan ching

This sūtra exists only in Chinese. Two translations are said to have been made, but only one survives. This is the version of Kalayaśas (424 C.E.). The current presumption is that the sūtra was composed in Central Asia and embellished in China. Its title, *Kuan Wu-liang-shou Fo ching* means "The Sūtra on the Visualization of the Buddha of Immeasurable Life." The common Sanskrit restoration, *Amitāyurdhyāna Sūtra,* is almost certainly wrong, and its use is going out of fashion in favor of *Kuan ching,* an abbreviation of the Chinese title. *Kuan* is sometimes translated "contemplation," but, since it explicitly refers to *seeing,* it is better to translate it as "visualization."

Visualization, indeed, is the heart of the sūtra. Śākyamuni Buddha interrupts a teaching session on Mount Gṛdhrakūṭa to fly through the air and appear before a certain Queen Vaidehī, who has been unjustly thrown into prison, and transmit to her thirteen visualizations on the land of Sukhāvatī and its inhabitants. The story of an evil son who usurps the throne and imprisons his righteous father, and of the virtuous wife who tries to help her husband and is herself imprisoned for her pains, is told with great dramatic flourish, and employed by commentators as a symbol for the condition of all sentient beings, trapped in the prison of saṃsāra.

After transmitting the thirteen visualizations, Śākyamuni Buddha speaks of nine grades of rebirth into Sukhāvatī, divided into three main classes of those who are skilled in meditation, those who cannot meditate well but are strong in their ethical practice, and those who can do no more than invoke Amitābha's Name. These last, in the lowest grade of the lowest class, may have committed gross evil but, on their deathbeds, they turn their minds to Amitābha and invoke him ten times, and are thus assured of rebirth in Sukhāvatī.

The Unity of the Three Main Sūtras

Whatever differences scholars may find between the three sūtras, they are regarded as complementary by Pure Land practitioners. The picture (literally, for it appears often in Pure Land Buddhist art[27]) that then emerges is somewhat as follows:

> Far beyond the setting sun, beyond all the troubles of saṃsāra, there is an intensely beautiful, sparklingly pure realm called Sukhāvatī, the Land of Unalloyed Happiness. It is ruled over by an all-wise and all-compassionate Buddha whose life and wisdom are immeasurable, and who is therefore called both Amitāyus and Amitābha or, for short, just Amita ("Immeasurable"). He sits on an immense throne, higher than many cosmic mountains, and although he himself is dressed in the simple robes of a monk, his throne is richly hung with draperies and set with rare jewels. On either side of him are his chief bodhisattvas, the greatly compassionate Avalokiteśvara and the greatly powerful Mahāsthāmaprāpta, and in front of him is a lake of lotus buds continually opening to reveal those newly born into Sukhāvatī. All around him are jeweled palaces, jeweled trees, and lakes full of jewel-like and perfumed water, and the air is filled with divine music and heavenly incense. All the inhabitants, once they fully emerge from their lotus buds, are great bodhisattvas only one lifetime away from perfect liberation, and they have beautiful, ethereal bodies, as if "walking in an Air of glory." The land is flat and even, without boundaries or obstacles, and as limitless as space. If one wishes to be reborn in that marvelous place, one does not have to leave home and become a monk or nun, or meditate far into the night, one merely has to focus one's mind as much as one can, while attending to one's daily tasks, on Amitābha and Sukhāvatī, and say *Nan-mo O-mi-t'o Fo!* at least ten times. Then, because of the wonderfully powerful fruiting of his Bodhisattva Resolve, Amita Buddha will ensure that one is reborn in his realm, and one can proceed without delay to one's own enlightenment and then quickly return to saṃsāra to help other beings, until saṃsāra is emptied.

Other Sūtras

A number of other sūtras make brief mention of Sukhāvatī or describe other Pure Lands. The sūtras can be read as making a distinction between Pure Lands that exist somewhere else and Pure Lands that are this present reality seen, or transformed, in the proper way, but this distinction tends to be collapsed in Pure Land practice.[28]

A good example of the latter is found in *Vimalakīrti-nirdeśa* 1.[29] From the principle that "[a] buddha-field is pure . . . to the extent that the mind of the bodhisattva is pure" it follows that this realm of humans, seen with pure mind, is a Pure Land, and one of the speakers says "I see the splendid expanse of the buddha-field of the Lord Śākyamuni as equal to the splendor of, for example, the abodes of the highest deities"; that is, he sees the human realm as the Pure Land of Śākyamuni. Śāriputra, however, objects that he sees this earth "as if it were entirely filled with ordure."

Śākyamuni replies that the impurities which Śāriputra sees arise dependent on his impure mind, and, striking the ground with his toe, the Buddha causes the earth to be "transformed into a huge mass of precious jewels . . . until it resemble[s] the universe of the Tathāgata Ratnavyūha." The Buddha asks Śāriputra if he sees the transformation. When Śāriputra answers that he does, Śākyamuni Buddha tells him that the human realm is always like this and that "living beings born in the same buddha-field see the splendor of the virtues of the buddha-fields of the Buddhas according to their own degrees of purity."[30]

A sūtra that somewhat bridges the gap between distant and immanent Pure Lands is the *Pan-chou san-mei ching* (The Sūtra on the Meditation Which Brings Buddhas to Appear and Dwell in One's Presence.)[31] This was first translated into Chinese by Lokakṣema in 179 C.E. and can in a sense be regarded as the scriptural foundation for Chinese Pure Land piety. It recommends concentrating the mind on Sukhāvatī day and night for a week, after which Sukhāvatī will appear before one's eyes.

The sūtra explicitly states that the Pure Land will appear here and now, and that one will not have to die and be reborn there. This method, it states, is effective for any Buddha or Buddha-land one wishes to see. Putting it quite straightforwardly, it says "if you wish to see present Buddhas of the ten directions, you should single-mindedly direct your thought to where they dwell and should not entertain other thoughts. Then you will be able to see them." This "is as if a man gets up at night and observes numerous stars."[32] The reason why the meditation works is simple. We normally "consider the worldly things as existent and never realize emptiness"; that is, as the *Vimalakīrti-nirdeśa* puts it, our world is impure because our minds are impure. But, when we concentrate on reality as it truly is (emptiness, or a Pure Land) then, provided that our practice is strong enough, we will begin to see reality truly.

The trick, however, is in this proviso. The meditation that results in seeing the Buddhas and their Pure Lands here and now is strenuous and is open (with a few rather grudging exceptions) only to monastics, since it requires strict adherence to the Vinaya as well as long periods of intense meditation. But there is hope for laypeople.

> The Buddha [Śākyamuni said], "Bodhisattvas in this land can *see* Amita Buddha by single-mindedly visualizing him. Now, let it be asked what method of practice they should perform in order to be *born* in that Land. Amita Buddha

replies, 'Those who desire to be born should invoke my name unceasingly; then they will attain birth [there].'"[33]

Thus, it appears that the *Pan-chou san-mei ching* teaches invocation of the Name of Amita as a substitute practice for those who are unable to become monks or nuns. And while invocation will not result in a vision during this life, it will bring rebirth in the Pure Land after death, and that, in the end, is just as effective for final liberation. Many practitioners apparently decided that, by and large, this was good enough, and the importance of being a monastic, or having one as a teacher (which this sūtra emphasizes) is, in later Pure Land practice, downgraded.

Two other sūtras that have brief but important passages relevant to Pure Land piety are the *Lotus Sūtra* (discussed earlier in this volume), which has a chapter on Avalokiteśvara, and the *Laṅkāvatāra Sūtra,* which foretells the coming of Nāgārjuna and predicts that he will be reborn in Sukhāvatī.

Lotus Sūtra 24 (in the Sanskrit) or 25 (in the Chinese) praises the wonderful assistance given to sentient beings in all kinds of distress by the bodhisattva Avalokiteśvara, who, in the Pure Land sūtras, is one of the two principal assistants of Amitābha. In the *Lotus Sūtra* he appears as an independent entity, but devotees of Amita have not accorded this difference much weight.

In *Laṅkāvatāra Sūtra,* Sagākatham 163–166, the Buddha is asked who will teach the Mahāyāna after the Buddha has passed. He replies:

> In Vedalī, in the southern part, a Bhikshu most illustrious and distinguished [will be born]; his name is Nāgāhvaya, he is the destroyer of the one-sided views based on being and non-being. He will declare my Vehicle, the unsurpassed Mahāyāna, to the world; attaining the stage of Joy he will go to the Land of Bliss.[34]

This rather gnomic utterance is understood to refer to Nāgārjuna, the destroyer of dualistic views through his system of Mādhyamika, and to predict that, after attaining the first bodhisattva *bhūmi,* he would die from the human realm and be reborn in Sukhāvatī. From a historical-critical point of view, this passage is not given much credence, but it is honored in Pure Land tradition, since a text ascribed to Nāgārjuna, the *Daśabhūmikavibhāṣā-śāstra* (Treatise Explaining the Ten *Bhūmis*) is quoted as a kind of theme text at the beginning of the *Commentary on the Pure Land Discourse* by T'an-luan, to whose important system we now turn.

The Pure Land Vision

T'an-luan

Dharma Master Shih T'an-luan was born near holy Wu-t'ai mountain sometime between 476 and 489 C.E. He appears to have been of peasant stock, and, although he rose to imperial favor, he never lost his common touch. This combination of great learning and mass appeal is frequently found in Pure Land Buddhist teachers.

Having entered a Buddhist monastery at about age fourteen, he threw himself with such youthful zeal into the study of the sūtras that his health broke and he went on a pilgrimage in search of a cure. Becoming healed after seeing a vision of the Gate of Heaven opening in a break in the clouds, he continued his travels, searching for immortality. It is reported that he met a famous Taoist master from whom he received a book or books on immortality. Then about forty years old, he began to move back to the north. On his way he met the Indian Buddhist Master Bodhiruci, who gave him another book or books[35] on "The Greatest Immortal" (*Ta Hsien,* apparently a name for Amitāyus), which impressed him sufficiently that, so the story goes, he burned his Taoist books and devoted himself to Buddhist Pure Land practice. He then returned homeward and, earning the admiration of the emperor for his knowledge of medicine, was given a monastery located about fifty miles southwest of modern Taiyuan in Shanxi, where he died between 524 and 554 C.E., facing the west and surrounded by disciples chanting the name of Amita.[36]

The importance of T'an-luan stems from a text he wrote while staying at his monastery in Shanxi. Entitled *Wu-liang-shou ching yu-p'o-t'i-shê yüan shêng chi chu* (Notes on the Hymn [gāthā] on the Resolution to be Born [in Sukhāvatī] and the Explanation [*upadeśa*] on the Sūtras concerning Immeasurable Life [*Amitāyus*]) and usually referred to as the *Lun chu,* it unifies the teaching of the three Pure Land sūtras and provides a sophisticated explanation, on the basis of learned references to other sūtras and many śāstras, of how the simple practice of visualizing and invoking Amita can be so effective for liberation.[37] The *Lun chu* lays the doctrinal basis for the later developments in Pure Land piety.[38]

In form, the *Lun chu* is cumbersome. Its focus is the hymn (gāthā) on rebirth in Sukhāvatī, attributed to Vasubandhu and appearing in a somewhat obscure Chinese translation under the name of Bodhiruci. The hymn is followed by "Bodhiruci's" translation of "Vasubandhu's" auto-commentary (the "explanation" or *upadeśa*) on the hymn.[39] T'an-luan provides a subcommentary (*chu,* "notes" means a *commentaire au pied de la lettre*), adds an introduction, a

19. *Altarpiece with Amitābha and Attendants*, China, Sui Dynasty, dated 593 C.E. Bronze. 76.5 cm. high.

conclusion, and a question-and-answer section at the halfway mark, and opens with the quotation from the *Daśabhūmikavibhāṣā-śāstra* mentioned above. Since the auto-commentary repeats (in the manner of auto-commentaries) the text of the hymn, and T'an-luan's subcommentary repeats (in the manner of subcommentaries) the repetitions, the text is not designed as a quick read. Its form is, we might say kindly, conducive to sustained reflection. A complete analysis of the text[40] is irrelevant (the reader will be glad to know) to the intent of this article, which will focus on two features controlling later Pure Land piety: other power and purification.

Features of T'an-luan's Vision

Other Power

The fundamental and most necessary exercise of other power by Amita Buddha concerns the setting up of the Pure Land itself, without which all else would be futile. While he was the bodhisattva Dharmākara he realized the first noble truth, that there is no escape from suffering (*duḥkha*) within saṃsāra, that saṃsāra itself is characterized by suffering through and throughout.

> Everything we see is like this: we get things we did not work for, and we live off what we did not save. (T 40.840a10–11)

In consequence, Dharmākara resolved that Sukhāvatī should be exactly the opposite of saṃsāra in every respect; that is, instead of pervasive *duḥkha* there would be pervasive *sukhā*.

> May it be, in my Land, that whoever requests something will receive as much of it as they wish. (T 40.831b9–10)

T'an-luan then describes all the delights of Sukhāvatī, at length and with great relish, explaining how each one is a particular *sukhā* offsetting a particular *duḥkha*. And all this comes about, he says again and again, because of Amita Buddha's inconceivably (*pu-k'o ssŭ-i*) great power.

Where did Amita get such power? From his former practice as the bodhisattva Dharmākara. But, many bodhisattvas have practiced earnestly and have not obtained as much power as Amita Buddha. Why is this? Because, T'an-luan tells us, of the power of Amita Buddha.

> The present lordly, divine power (*tsŭ-tsai shên-li*) of Amitābha Tathāgata depends upon the initial (*pên*) forty-eight Resolutions of Dharmākara Bodhisattva. The completeness of [Amitābha's] power depends upon [Dharmākara's] Resolutions, and the perfection of [Dharmākara's] Resolutions depends upon

> [Amitābha's] power. The Resolutions were not vain, and the power is not empty. The power and the Resolutions fit together, ultimately they are not different. (T 40.840a13–15)

A Western reader is liable to find this argument unconvincing, accusing it of being circular. What needs to be examined, however, is not the nature of the argument but the nature of causation. Western theories of causation tend to be linear, in respect of both space and time, relying on something like billiards as a model for the universe, while Chinese theories are more indebted to chess (which, be it noted, the Chinese invented) and are comfortable with circularity and interdependence.[41]

If the world is like a game of billiards, then a prior event A can cause a subsequent event B across linear, unidirectional time, but a subsequent event B cannot have any effect upon a prior event A. On this model, it makes sense to say that God creates the world, and nonsense to say that the world creates God.

If, however, the world is like a game of chess, then the movement of piece A is controlled by pieces B, C, etc., and itself controls the subsequent movement of pieces B, C, etc. Indeed, it is difficult to know which piece to call A and which B, and so forth. On this model, it makes sense to say both that God (heaven) creates the world (earth) and that the world creates God. Or (what amounts to the same thing) that yin and yang influence each other. When this native Chinese cosmology of patterns and the mutuality of yin and yang is allied with the Buddhist cosmology of the interdependent arising (*pratītya-samutpāda*) of all phenomena in the Net of Indra,[42] T'an-luan's statement that Amita's power and Dharmākara's Resolutions arise together presents itself as perfectly logical, and the Western objection of circularity appears as a perverse delusion of ignorant mind.

Following upon the teaching of the power of Amita is the distinction between the easy and difficult paths to liberation. This is stated in the quotation from the *Daśabhūmikavibhāṣā-śāstra* which opens the *Lun chu* and forms, in a sense, its theme. The Way of Difficult Practice (*nan-hsing tao*), which later Pure Land Buddhists came to call the Holy Path or Path of the Sages (arhats), is the traditional triple practice of meditation, conduct, and study, involving ascetical discipline and encouraging celibacy. It is, for example, the path strongly recommended in the *Pan-chou san-mei ching*. The Way of Easy Practice (*i-hsing tao*) is the way of trusting oneself to the power of Amita. This is the path somewhat grudgingly allowed by the *Pan-chou san-mei ching* as effective for rebirth in Sukhāvatī. T'an-luan quotes Nāgārjuna to the effect that the first way is like walking painfully over land and the second is like sailing easily over water. The difference, then, is between proceeding under one's power and being carried along by a power other than one's own. He takes it for granted that, if one is offered a lift, one would surely accept it.

Purification

The Pure Land having been set up, the other power of Amita can be actualized through the purifying effects of his Land and his Name.

The key to understanding the purifying nature of Sukhāvatī is found not in any specific resolution of Dharmākara but in his entire attitude at the time that he made the forty-eight Resolutions.

> At the beginning [of his bodhisattva practice], the Bodhisattva Dharmākara, in the presence of the Buddha Lokeśvararāja, awoke to the Calm Knowledge of Non-Arising, and established at that time what is known as "Holy Seed Essence." In that essence he made forty-eight Great Resolutions, by the practice of which he gave rise to this Land called Sukhāvatī. This [Land] has been gained with that [essence] as cause, and as we can say that the cause is in the effect, we can speak thus of its essence. (T 40.826c1–4)

"Holy Seed Essence" (*shêng-chung-hsing*) is the "birth into the clan" (*gotrabhū*) of the Holy Ones (*ārya-pudgala*), those who will not again draw back from final enlightenment. The perfection called the Calm Knowledge of Non-Arising (*anutpattika-dharma-kṣānti*) is attained at the eighth bodhisattva *bhūmi*.[43] With it, one realizes that all phenomena are essentially unarisen (*anutpāda*) or empty of inherent existence. Dharmākara, T'an-luan says, having reached that level and realized essential non-arising, caused Sukhāvatī to appear. This means that the effect (Sukhāvatī) must have the essence of non-arising, which was its cause, and that Sukhāvatī is, in fact, outside of saṃsāra (or dualistic mind) altogether.

The model of causation here is similar to the one he uses when explaining the interrelationship of Dharmākara's Resolutions and Amitābha's power, with a slight difference. The interrelationship of the essence of the Resolved Mind of Dharmākara to the essence of Amitābha's Sukhāvatī is that of seed and fruit. An apple is sweet because it came from an apple tree grown from an apple seed, not from a lemon tree grown from a lemon seed. Similarly, Sukhāvatī is "the realm of non-arising" (*wu-shêng chieh*, T 40.839b6), having been grown from a mind of non-arising, "the product of non-production" (*wu-shêng-chih-shêng*, T 40.838c20–21). It then follows that those who are reborn in Sukhāvatī take on its essence; that is, they are "not-born" there. Three of the similes T'an-luan gives to explain this are: river and sea; fire and ice; a wishing-jewel.

As the rivers, when they flow into the sea, do not flavor it but are flavored by it, so the one born into Sukhāvatī does not defile it but rather is purified by it.[44] Then again, as fire and ice, when mixed, annihilate each other, so the one who desires to be born in Sukhāvatī will find, on being born there, that the "fire" of dualistic ideas, like the desire to be born in Sukhāvatī, will be dispersed by the "ice" of Sukhāvatī, which itself, T'an-luan seems to suggest, will disappear: that is, its inherent existence as a "paradise" will be seen to be false.

The simile of the wishing-jewel (*cintāmaṇi*) is most important, because it leads up to the explanation of the transforming power of Amita's Name. According to the *Sūtra on the Perfection of Wisdom in Eight Thousand Lines*,[45] a wishing-jewel thrown into muddy water will clarify it, and if the jewel is wrapped in a colored cloth, the water will take on the color of the cloth. This, says T'an-luan, is how the jeweled decorations of Sukhāvatī cleanse the mind of the meditator:

> That pure Buddha-land has the peerless jewel of Amitābha Tathāgata wrapped in the "cloth" of the perfection of the merits of the innumerable decorations, and it is cast into the "water" of the mind of the one who is to be Born. How could this not convert the false view of "birth" into the wisdom of "no-birth"? (T 40.839a29–b3)

Now, the real jewel of Sukhāvatī is the Name of Amitābha himself (T 40.839a27), which is a "real name": it not only *means* "Immeasurable Light"; it is the expression of the *essence* of immeasurable light, and that light itself is the outer manifestation of an even more interior essence of immeasurable wisdom (T 40.835b13–18).

> When that brilliance suffuses objects, it penetrates from the outside to the inside; when that brilliance suffuses the mind, it puts an end to ignorance. (T 40.837a19–20)

There are, says T'an-luan, two sorts of names: those which are merely conventional labels ("names which are other than things," *ming i fa*) and those which effect what they signify ("names which are the same as things," *ming chi fa*). Taoist spells, Buddhist mantras and dhāraṇīs and, most importantly, the names of Buddhas and bodhisattvas are names that effect what they signify (T 40.835c5–8).

Thus, saying *Nan-mo O-mi-t'o Fo* is not just a petition or, worse, a useless noise, it is the actualization of immeasurable light, and, therefore, of immeasurable wisdom, in the mind of the practitioner. It is, in fact (for T'an-luan, though not always for other Pure Land teachers), a mantra.[46]

The Development of the Pure Land Vision

It is not, as we have stated, our purpose to give a history of the Pure Land tradition in China and the rest of the Far East. However, in order not to leave the discussion of T'an-luan entirely in a vacuum, two developments of spiritual importance will be addressed: the Parable of the White Path and the question of whether or not Pure Land practice should be exclusive.

The Parable of the White Path

A work attributed to T'an-luan, *Sukhāvatī Briefly Explained* (*Lüeh-lun an-lo ching-t'u i*),[47] contains a short parable in which a man crossing a narrow path between two rivers is given as an illustration of Pure Land spirituality. This is quoted by Tao-ch'o (562–645 C.E.) in *Passages on Sukhāvatī* (*An-lo chi*)[48] and elaborated by Shan-tao (613–681 C.E.) in his commentary on the *Kuan ching* (*Kuan ching shu*),[49] who seems to have had a dream based on the parable and the symbolism of the *I Ching*.

In the developed form given by Shan-tao, a man on a long journey to the west suddenly finds, in the middle of a wasteland, that his only way forward is over a narrow white path between a river of fire to the south and a river of water to the north.[50] Pursued by murderous bandits, he rushes toward the path, but draws back when he sees the surging water and roaring flames. Realizing that whichever way he turns he may die, he decides to try to cross. Just then, he hears a voice from behind (the east) and in front (the west) encouraging him and, despite the cries of the bandits that the way is too perilous, he walks on the path and reaches the other shore in safety. Shan-tao then explains the parable as follows:

> The east bank is an analogy of this world. . . . The west bank is a symbol of the precious land of highest bliss. The ruffians . . . are an analogy of the six sense organs, the six consciousnesses, the six defilements, the five skhandhas, and the four elements. The lonely wasteland is the following of bad companions and not meeting with those who are truly good and wise. The two rivers of fire and water are an analogy of attachment, which is like water, and aversion, which is like fire. The white path . . . is analogous to the aspiration for rebirth in the Pure Land which arises in the midst of the passions of attachment and aversion. . . . . The man proceeding on the path towards the west is comparable to one who directs all actions and practices towards the West[ern Pure Land]. The hearing of voices from the east bank encouraging and exhorting him to pursue the path straight to the west, is like Śākyamuni Buddha, who has already disappeared from human sight but whose teaching may still be investigated and is therefore like "voices." . . . Someone calling from the west bank is an analogy of the Resolution of Amitābha.[51]

And reaching the west bank, of course, is being reborn in Sukhāvatī.

This parable became very popular in the Pure Land tradition, for its entire spirituality is neatly encapsulated in it.

Single and Dual Practice

Some Pure Land devotees argued that, since Amitābha was the most powerful Buddha, Sukhāvatī was the best Pure Land, and the Pure Land practice was so easy, no other practices were necessary. Opponents, who were mostly of the Ch'an lineage, maintained that, by making such a sharp distinction between this life and the next, Pure Land piety was dualistic and should not be practiced at all. The debate was long and complex,[52] but its main conclusions are clear: China, Korea, and Vietnam decided in favor of combining devotion to Amita with Ch'an meditation (known in Korea as Sŏn and in Vietnam as Thiền), while Japan divided Pure Land and Zen into separate lineages. In all cases, a tendency developed to collapse the distinction between distant and immanent Pure Lands (see above, "Other Sutras") and say, possibly in reaction to Ch'an criticism, "The Pure Land is nothing but our pure heart."

T'an-luan's recommendations for Pure Land practice are conservative and traditional. They are distinctive only in that they focus on Amitābha and Sukhāvatī, and are prefaced by T'an-luan's claim that the world cycle is in decline, with the result that liberation by one's own power is now the "difficult path." Following the structure in the hymn attributed to Vasubandhu, he divides the practice into five "recollection gates" (*nien-mên*): (1) prostrating to Amitābha; (2) chanting his Name; (3) making the resolution (*praṇidhāna*) to be born in Sukhāvatī; (4) concentrating the mind on a detailed visualization of Sukhāvatī; (5) spreading the benefits of Sukhāvatī by (a) while one still lives here in saṃsāra, distributing the merit obtained from one's practice; (b) after one has been reborn in Sukhāvatī, returning to saṃsāra as a bodhisattva.

It should be noted that T'an-luan regards the other power of Amita and the self power of the practitioner as mutually supportive. Chanting Amita's Name while one's mind is wandering, he says, is ineffective: one must chant with a trusting mind that is genuine, focused, and persistent (T 40.835b24–c2). Quite soon after T'an-luan, Tao-ch'o narrowed the focus of Pure Land practice in two ways. First, he taught that the decline of the world cycle, with its consequence of the disintegration of Buddhism (*mo-fa shih*, "the time of the end of the Dharma"), rendered the way of self-power not only difficult but actually impossible. This viewpoint, which has continued to be a prominent (and controversial) feature of Pure Land piety, lent support to the position that devotion to Amitābha should be practiced exclusively. Second, he focused on the second of T'an-luan's "recollection gates" as the most important. He is credited with the introduction of the rosary into Pure Land practice, with the aid of which both laypeople and monastics people notched up record numbers of *nien fo*.[53]

In Japan, this emphasis on invocation and exclusivism was taken to term by Hōnen and Shinran. Hōnen (1133–1212 C.E.) regarded the nenbutsu as not merely the supreme practice but the only practice. He concentrates on a passage from Shan-tao which recommends "saying Amita's Name single-heartedly, whether walking, standing still, sitting, or lying down, regardless of the occasion"[54] and makes it absolute:

> The method of salvation that I have propounded is neither a sort of meditation, such as has been practiced by many scholars in China and Japan, nor is it a repetition of the Buddha's name by those who have studied and understood the deep meaning of it. It is nothing but the mere repetition of the "*Namu Amida Butsu,*" without a doubt of His mercy, whereby one may be born into the Land of Perfect Bliss. The mere repetition with firm faith includes all practical details. . . . Thus [one] should fervently practice the repetition of the name of Amida, and that alone.[55]

Hōnen's disciple Shinran (1173–1262) went even further. He practiced constant nenbutsu for many years as a monk on Mount Hiei, but, feeling no nearer to enlightenment than when he began, he abandoned not only practices other than the nenbutsu but even the nenbutsu itself as a *practice.* When the impure mind tries to purify itself, he taught, we are doomed to failure.

> Though we rush to act, rush to perform practices as though driving fire away from our heads, all our deeds must be termed good acts poisoned and irresolute, acts empty, transitory, and false. . . . Aspire though one may to attain birth in the Land of Immeasurable Light through such empty, transitory, and poisoned good acts, it is altogether impossible.[56]

Thenceforward, Shinran taught Absolute Other Power (*tariki*), in which the self power of the practitioner is overwhelmed and negated by the other power of Amida. He transformed, we might say, a spirituality of *trust* into a spirituality of *surrender,* in which, although one continued to perform acts of proper conduct, meditation, and study, one did so out of thankfulness and gratitude for *having been* liberated by the power of Amita, rather than as a "practice" with which one might *earn* liberation.[57] He then wrote a brilliant and learned defense of his position (generally known by its short title of *Kyōgyōshinshō,*[58] quoting extensively and deftly (some would say deviously[59]) from the sūtras and śāstras, with pride of place given to T'an-luan.

Shinran's understanding led to the foundation of a new lineage, the Jōdo Shinshū "True Pure Land Lineage," often referred to merely as Shin Buddhism, which became the dominant Japanese lineage.[60] Its dominance has spilled over into Buddhology, and the reader should be warned that many studies, whether by Japanese or non-Japanese scholars, which record a "development" in Pure Land practice from T'an-luan through Tao-ch'o and Shan-tao to

20. Illustration of the Parable of the White Path between raging waters and fire

Shinran's "consummation" of Other Power, are written from the perspective of Shin orthodoxy. This perspective is worth studying in its own right, as the self-understanding of an important lineage, but it should not be regarded as a viewpoint accepted by other lineages.

In China, Pure Land chanting is balanced by Ch'an meditation, usually on the basis of the explanation of Yen-shou (904–975 C.E.) that the two reinforced each other, like "a horned tiger" (i.e., a dragon-tiger, an animal combining yin and yang). The combination is literally built into the monastic architecture, which will often contain both a Meditation Hall for Ch'an practice and a Buddha Recitation Hall for Pure Land practice.[61] The recitation is often done while walking in a "serpentine" pattern, and according to a five-tone chant developed by Fa-chao (seventh-eighth century C.E.).

The Korean Master Chinul (1158–1210 C.E.) explains the balance between Pure Land and Sŏn as follows:

> I have briefly assessed the cause for the development of faith and understanding regarding the Sŏn transmission, as well as the gain and loss accompanying birth and death and passing from the mundane world into the pure land . . . because I want those of you who enter this community and wish to cultivate the mind to be aware of the roots and branches of practice, to cease from wrangling, and to distinguish between the provisional and the real. Then you will not waste your efforts. . . .[62]

In Vietnam, Pure Land and Thiền practices are regarded as different methods appropriate for different people, as in this quotation from Thảo-Đường (d. eleventh century C.E.), who introduced the union of Ch'an and Ching-t'u from Sung dynasty China.

> Though you may practice Buddhism in many ways, in summary there are three main methods: meditation, visualization, and Buddha's-name-recitation. The method of meditation has no definite way to follow and is therefore a difficult practice. If you do not have an enlightened master or a capable mind, you may stop midway in your progress or remain mistaken for your entire life. Visualization is a very subtle method; without a good teacher or prajñā wisdom, complete enlightenment is hard to attain. Buddha's-name-recitation (Vietnamese: *Niệm-Phật*) is a quick and easy method. In all the ages past both intelligent and dull, both men and women have been able to practice *Niệm-Phật.* Nobody makes a mistake with this method. . . . Putting worries aside, you may therefore proceed with a decisive heart.[63]

This is an excellent summary of Pure Land piety. Simple and direct, but securely based on the sūtras and śāstras, it is a practice suitable for anyone, monastic or lay, young or old, male or female, intelligent or dull. That is its enduring appeal.

Notes

1. Michio Takeyama, *Harp of Burma*, trans. Howard Hibbett (Rutland, VT, and Tokyo: Charles E. Tuttle, 1966) 15.

2. *The Principal Upaniṣads*, edited with introduction, text, translation, and notes by S. Radhakrishnan (London: Allen & Unwin, 1953) 162–63.

3. Ibid., 299.

4. *The Metaphysical Poets*, selected and edited by Helen Gardner (Penguin Books, 1957) 273–74. The spelling follows the conventions of the time.

5. *The Collected Works of St. John of the Cross*, trans. Kieran Kavanaugh, O.C.D., and Otilio Rodriguez, O.C.D. (Washington, DC: Institute of Carmelite Studies Publications, 1979) 562.

6. Ibid., 515.

7. My translation of the Sanskrit as given in *The Principal Upaniṣads*, 562.

8. *The Principal Upaniṣads*, 562; my translation.

9. Valentine Zander, *St. Seraphim of Sarov*, trans. Sister Gabriel Anne, S.S.C., from *Seraphim von Sarow* (Crestwood, NY: St. Vladimir's Seminary Press, 1975) 88–91.

10. From the Greater Bundaḥishn, chap. 1. *Textual Sources for the Study of Zoroastrianism*, ed. and trans. Mary Boyce (Manchester, England: Manchester University Press, 1984) 45 (selection 2.3.1).

11. Mary Boyce, *Zoroastrians: Their Religious Beliefs and Practices* (corrected ed.; London and New York: Routledge & Kegan Paul, 1987) 111–12.

12. Mary Boyce mentions the evidence, but only in passing (*Zoroastrians;* see "Buddhism" in index).

13. See, for example, the cover of *Buddhism* by Christmas Humphreys (Baltimore: Penguin Books, 3rd ed. 1962 and subsequently). This mysterious phrase has survived since at least the second edition (1955), and was possibly on the cover of the original edition, to which I do not have access.

14. This charge is still alive enough to be inquired into (and answered, albeit somewhat equivocally, in the negative) in a recent book by Paul Williams, *Mahāyāna Buddhism*, 275–76.

15. Henri de Lubac, S.J., *Aspects du Bouddhisme*, 2:331.

16. My translation from the Latin.

17. *Bhagavadgītā* 12:8; my translation.

18. Abū Naṣr as-Sarrāj, *Kitāb al-luma' fi't-taṣawwuf* 59, quoted in Annemarie Schimmel, *Mystical Dimensions of Islam* (Chapel Hill, NC: University of North Carolina Press, 1975) 133.

19. Book 1, Letter 1, in *The Spiritual Letters of Father P. J. de Caussade, S.J. on the Practice of Self-Abandonment to Divine Providence*, trans. Algar Thorold (London: Burns & Oates, 1934) 1.

20. The following list is modified from my article "Monotheistic Elements in Early Pure Land Buddhism," *Religion: Journal of Religion and Religions* 6:2 (Autumn 1976) 176–89, which see for the argument supporting the conclusions here presented.

21. It should be carefully noted that, although much of Pure Land devotion may remind one of Hindu bhakti, this term does not appear to underlie the Chinese word *hsin*, which seems more likely to be based on the Sanskrit word *śraddhā*. While the devotional energy of bhakti often has sexual overtones, *śraddhā* is more concerned with loving trust in a superior, such as a teacher or parent. This problem is complex and has not, to my knowledge, been addressed. It certainly deserves further study.

22. For a translation of all three, the first two from the Sanskrit and the third from the Chinese, see *Buddhist Mahāyāna Texts,* Sacred Books of the East 49/2.

23. See Fujita Kōtatsu, "Pure and Impure Lands," in *The Encyclopedia of Religion,* ed. Mircea Eliade (New York: Macmillan, 1987) vol. 12.

24. There are only forty-six parts in the Sanskrit text, which has, especially at this point, significant variations from the Chinese. This fact should be borne in mind when the English translation (see n. 22 above) is read.

25. In addition to the translation referred to in n. 22 above, see Takahatake Takamichi, *The Sūtra of the Buddha Amitābha AMIDA-KYŌ* (English and French versions in one volume), and Tripiṭaka Master Hua, *A General Explanation of The Buddha Speaks of Amitābha Sūtra.*

26. Tripiṭaka Master Hua, *A General Explanation of The Buddha Speaks of Amitābha Sūtra,* 108, 111.

27. See Okazaki Jōji, *Pure Land Buddhist Painting.* Although this work is limited to Japanese examples, many of these are modeled after, or are even direct copies of, Chinese pieces.

28. See below, "Single and Dual Practice."

29. This sūtra is discussed earlier in this volume; chapter 7, section II, by Nagao Gadjin.

30. *The Holy Teaching of Vimalakīrti,* trans. Robert A. F. Thurman, 18–19.

31. *Pratyutpanna-buddha-sammukhāvasthita-samādhi-sūtra.* For a translation, see Inagaki Hisao, "Pan-Chou-San-Mei-Ching" in *Indian Philosophy and Buddhism: Essays in Honour of Professor Kōtatsu Fujita on His Sixtieth Birthday,* 49–88.

32. Ibid., 60, 64, 65.

33. Ibid., 60–61 (slightly adapted; italics added).

34. *The Laṅkāvatāra Sūtra,* trans. Daisetz Teitaro Suzuki (London: Routledge & Kegan Paul, 1932) 239–40.

35. The identity, and even the number, of Buddhist and/or Taoist books is a matter of conjecture. The text of the biography is quite ambiguous.

36. This account is summarized from the official Buddhist biography (T 50.470a13–c15). See also Ching-fen Hsiao, "The Life and Teachings of T'an-luan" (Ph.D. dissertation, Princeton Theological Seminary, 1967), available from University Microfilms International, Ann Arbor, Michigan.

37. T 40.826–844. In this article, all translations from this text are my own.

38. This basis is, however, largely implicit. For unknown reasons, explicit reference to the *Lun chu* is rare until Shinran's extensive and enthusiastic quotation of it in twelfth-century Japan (see below). I have suggested that T'an-luan's instant fame as a (Taoist) physician might have obscured his less newsworthy, but more original, contributions to Buddhism. See Roger J. Corless, "T'an-luan: Taoist Sage and Buddhist Bodhisattva," in *Buddhist and Taoist Practice in Medieval Chinese Society,* ed. David W. Chappell, 36–45. For a more detailed discussion of T'an-luan's importance see Roger J. Corless, "T'an-luan: The First Systematiser of Pure Land Buddhism," in *The Pure Land Tradition: History and Development,* ed. James Foard and Michael Solomon (Berkeley Buddhist Studies Series 3; in press).

39. The authenticity of the hymn and its explanation, neither of which exists in Sanskrit, and the attribution of the translation to Bodhiruci are all matters of scholarly debate.

40. For which see Roger J. Corless, "T'an-luan's Commentary on the Pure Land Discourse: An Annotated Translation and Soteriological Analysis of the *Wang-shêng-lun chu* (T 1819)" (Ph.D. dissertation, University of Wisconsin, Madison, 1973), available from University Microfilms, Ann Arbor, Michigan.

41. The chess analogy was suggested by Paul K. K. Tong in "A Cross-Cultural Study of *I-Ching*," *Journal of Chinese Philosophy* 3:1 (December 1975) 73–84.

42. See the discussion on the *Avataṃsaka Sūtra* above, chapter 7, section III, by Luis O. Gómez.

43. Har Dayal, *The Bodhisattva Doctrine in Buddhist Sanskrit Literature*, 290.

44. T 40.828c5–6. The image is reminiscent of Saint Augustine of Hippo, who records that God said to him "I am the Real Food (*cibus grandium*). Grow, and eat me. I will not be changed into you, as is the case with ordinary food (*sicut cibum carnis tuae*), you will be changed into me" (*Confessions* 7.10; my translation).

45. *Aṣṭasāhasrikāprajñāpāramitā-sūtra*, Vaidya edition, p. 49, lines 25–30. I am indebted to Professor Kajiyama Yuichi for this reference.

46. There are many parallels between T'an-luan's Pure Land spirituality and Tantra. See Roger J. Corless, "Pure Land and Pure Perspective: A Tantric Hermeneutic of Sukhāvatī," *The Pure Land* n.s. 6 (1989).

47. T 47.1–4. English translation by Leo Pruden, "A Short Essay on the Pure Land by Dharma Master T'an-luan," *Eastern Buddhist* n.s. 8:1 (May 1975) 74–95. Most Japanese Buddhologists do not accept the text as authentically T'an-luan's.

48. T 47.4–22 (esp. lines a27–b14). English translation in *Sources of Chinese Tradition*, compiled by W. Theodore de Bary et al. (New York: Columbia University Press, 1960) 1:345.

49. T 37.272c15–273b8. English translation in *The Buddhist Tradition in India, China and Japan*, ed. W. Theodore de Bary, 204–7.

50. It does not seem accidental that, in the Later Heaven or King Wên arrangement of the eight trigrams in the *I Ching*, fire (*li*) is to the south and water (*k'an*) is to the north.

51. *Buddhist Tradition*, ed. de Bary, 206–7 (adapted).

52. Since, according to Mahāyāna (especially Yogācāra), outer (distant) and inner (immanent) are interdependent, the controversy does not, finally, seem to have much force.

53. The rosary is not unique to Pure Land Buddhism, or even to Buddhism as a whole, but it has special characteristics in the tradition. See Roger J. Corless, "The Garland of Love: A History of Religions Hermeneutic of Nembutsu Theory and Practice," in *Studies in Pāli and Buddhism: A Memorial Volume in Honor of Bhikkhu Jagdish Kashyap*, ed. A. K. Narain and L. Zwilling (Delhi: B.R. Publishing, 1979) 53–74. See pp. 55–56 for a discussion of the ambiguous evidence on whether T'an-luan advocated the use of a rosary or not.

54. Adapted from Shan-tao's commentary on the *Kuan ching* as quoted in *Notes on Once-calling and Many-calling: A Translation of Shinran's Ichinen-tanen mon'i*, ed. Ueda Yoshifumi (Kyoto: Hongwanji International Center, 1980) 5.

55. From Hōnen's "One-Page Testament" (*Buddhist Tradition*, ed. de Bary, 331).

56. From the *Kyōgyōshinshō* as quoted in *Notes on Once-calling*, ed. Ueda, 11.

57. Shinran's "practice" is sometimes called that of "faith alone," his insight being explicitly compared to that of Martin Luther in the Christian tradition. However, rather than contrasting "works" and "faith" I suggest it is more helpful, and more consonant with a Buddhist understanding, to compare "work" (in the singular) and "play." See Roger J. Corless, "The Playfulness of TARIKI," *The Pure Land* n.s. 3 (December 1987) 34–52.

58. *The True Teaching, Practice and Realization of the Pure Land Way: A Translation of Shinran's Kyōgyōshinshō*, ed. Ueda Yoshifumi. See also the selections in Ueda Yoshifumi and Dennis Hirota, *Shinran: An Introduction to His Thought*.

59. Rather than accuse Shinran of deception, I argue that he was a visionary whose experience allowed him to see something in the texts never seen before, and so to bring about a paradigm shift in Buddhism. See Roger Corless, "Shinran's Proofs of True Buddhism" in *Buddhist Hermeneutics*, ed. Donald S. Lopez, Jr. (Honolulu: University of Hawaii Press, 1988) 273–89.

60. This is presumably the Buddhism of the frightened soldiers mentioned in the story quoted at the beginning of this article.

61. Holmes Welch, *The Practice of Chinese Buddhism 1900–1950*, chaps. 2, 3.

62. Robert E. Buswell, Jr., *The Korean Approach to Zen: The Collected Works of Chinul*, 124.

63. Thich Thien-An, *Buddhism and Zen in Vietnam*, edited, annotated, and developed by Carol Smith, 89. I have changed "contemplation" to "visualization."

Bibliography

Sources

Buswell, Robert E., Jr. *The Korean Approach to Zen: The Collected Works of Chinul*. Honolulu: University of Hawaii Press, 1983.

The Holy Teaching of Vimalakīrti. Translated by Robert A. F. Thurman. University Park, PA, and London: Pennsylvania State University Press, 1976.

Tanaka, Kenneth K. *The Dawn of Chinese Pure Land Buddhist Doctrine: Ching-ying Hui-Yüan's Commentary on the* Visualization Sutra. Albany: State University of New York Press, 1990.

Thich Thien-An, *Buddhism and Zen in Vietnam*. Edited, annotated, and developed by Carol Smith. Rutland, VT, and Tokyo: Charles E. Tuttle, 1975.

Ueda Yoshifumi, ed. *The True Teaching, Practice and Realization of the Pure Land Way: A Translation of Shinran's Kyōgyōshinshō*. 4 vols. Kyoto: Hongwanji International Center, 1983–87.

Studies

Chappell, David W., ed. *Buddhist and Taoist Practice in Medieval Chinese Society*. Honolulu: University of Hawaii Press, 1987.

Corless, Roger J. *The Vision of Buddhism*. New York: Paragon House, 1989.

Dayal, Har. *The Bodhisattva Doctrine in Buddhist Sanskrit Literature*. London: Routledge & Kegan Paul, 1932. Reprint, Delhi: Motilal Banarsidass, 1970.

de Bary, W. Theodore, ed. *The Buddhist Tradition in India, China and Japan*. New York: Modern Library, 1969.

de Lubac, Henri, S.J. *Aspects du Bouddhisme*, t. 2, Amida. Paris: Editions du Seuil, 1955.

Fujita Kōtatsu, "Pure and Impure Lands." In *The Encyclopedia of Religion*, ed. Mircea Eliade, vol. 12. New York: Macmillan, 1987.

Hua, Tripiṭaka Master. *A General Explanation of The Buddha Speaks of Amitābha Sūtra*. San Francisco: Buddhist Text Translation Society, 1974.

Inagaki Hisao. "Pan-Chou-San-Mei-Ching." In *Indian Philosophy and Buddhism: Essays in Honour of Professor Kōtatsu Fujita on His Sixtieth Birthday*. Kyoto: Heirakuji Shoten, 1989.

Okazaki Jōji. *Pure Land Buddhist Painting*. Translated and adapted by Elizabeth ten Grotenhuis. Tokyo: Kodansha International, 1977.

Takahatake Takamichi. *The Sūtra of the Buddha Amitābha AMIDA-KYŌ*. Montréal: Centre Monchanin, 1979.

Ueda Yoshifumi, and Dennis Hirota. *Shinran: An Introduction to His Thought.* Kyoto: Hongwanji International Center, 1989.

Welch, Holmes. *The Practice of Chinese Buddhism 1900–1950.* Cambridge, MA: Harvard University Press, 1967.

Williams, Paul. *Mahāyāna Buddhism: The Doctrinal Foundations.* London and New York: Routledge, 1989.

Part Three
CHINA

11

The Three Jewels in China

WHALEN LAI

The Seeds of the Tradition

THOUGH CHINESE CULTURE prized the way of moderation, it nevertheless knew an extravagant flight of the spirit during its medieval Buddhist period, which lasted from the third century to the twelfth. That period of enthusiasm embarrasses Chinese scholars, weaned away from it by the Sung dynasty Neo-Confucian revival, and they tend to see it as a plague of Indianism, fortunately checked when Buddhism was Sinicized as Ch'an. Yet such a seduction of the spirit cannot be explained simply as the ascendancy of one culture over another (any more than its waning can be explained by the overthrow of this ascendancy). China was not Indianized; it was converted to the truth of the Dharma. Nor should we see Chinese Buddhism as just a tailoring of the Dharma to local taste; rather, it represents the dynamic unfolding of the Dharma, which could embody itself as well in Chinese as in Indian culture, and to which neither could claim the monopoly. If Chinese pilgrims sought it in India, Indians also came to Ch'ang-an to pay it homage. Therefore I shall relate the history of Sinitic Mahāyāna as an unfolding of the spiritual vision lodged in the Three Jewels: the Buddha, the Dharma, and the Saṅgha.

Rumors of a Foreign Immortal

The Chinese Buddhist calendar places the Buddha's birth in 1132 B.C.E., when heaven sent down auspicious signs, as recorded in ancient Chinese chronicles. Three centuries later King Aśoka spread Buddha relics all over the world, and those which came to China marked the sites where pagodas were to be built. These legends are recounted by Tsung Ping (375–443) in his *Ming-fo-lun* (Elucidating the Faith; T 52.9b–16a); in reality Śākyamuni lived around

566–486 B.C.E., and Buddhism did not spread into Central Asia until the first century B.C.E. It is impossible that there were missionaries from India in the reign of the First Emperor of Ch'in (r. 246–210, contemporaneous with Aśoka, r. 273–232), and even stories of Chinese envoys coming across the tradition in Central Asia in the second century B.C.E. are not to be trusted. Wei Shou, author of a chapter on Buddhism in the *Wei-shu* (Wei Record), compiled sometime after 520 (T 52.101a),[1] relates a popular legend of the epiphany of Buddhism, already found in the *Hou-Han shu* (History of the Later Han) of Fan Yeh (398–445). In a dream, Han emperor Ming (r. 58–75) saw a golden man, resembling a Taoist immortal, flying into the palace. Upon learning from his advisors that this was an Indian sage, the emperor sent envoys to the West and they brought back (as we learn from other sources) the first scripture, the *Sūtra in Forty-Two Chapters* (T 17.722a–724a), on a white horse, as well as an image of the Buddha. These were then enshrined in the White Horse Temple in Loyang. According to some accounts, they also brought back two attendant foreign monks. This simultaneous arrival of the Three Jewels is a late and contrived story. For one thing, the sūtra in question, which relates the life and teachings of the Buddha, draws on the Chinese *Āgamas* not yet in circulation. The real significance of this legend is that it shows Buddhism coming in the guise of Taoism; gold symbolizes both Taoist immortality and Buddhist enlightenment. Levitation is a shared symbol of freedom from the material world, and the flight of the golden man into the palace no doubt reflects the Buddhist cultivation of imperial patronage, which was to continue in the following centuries.

The worship of the Buddha as a god at court is, however, a fact recorded in the same *Hou-Han shu.* A half-brother of Emperor Ming, Prince Ying (d. 71 C.E.), and other *upāsakā* (laymen) were already honoring the Buddha (*fou-t'u*) in Ch'u (Kiangsi and Shan-tung in the East), side by side with Lao-tzu and the Yellow Emperor—a custom retained by Emperor Hsüan (r. 147–167). Buddhists do not like to recall this episode because Prince Ying probably offered wine to the Buddha. This beverage of gods and immortals was prohibited in Buddhism. A century later (ca. 193 C.E.), in the same area, Chia Yung, an official of transportation, still laid out food and wine along the road for the five thousand people who came to view a Buddha-image he installed in a hall. This perception of the Buddha as a foreign immortal was natural. The difference between these two traditions would not be clarified until China had learned more from the sūtras about this alien faith. The first translations were not made until An Shih-kao (ca. 150 C.E.), and even then the dhyāna tradition was presented in a Taoist guise.

The Early Interplay of Buddhism and Taoism

The Han Taoists had a tradition of "inner learning" that aimed at "cultivating life, refining the spirit." Of the sūtras translated into Chinese by An Shih-kao, the most popular was the *An-pan shou-i ching* (*Ānāpāna-sūtra;* T 15.163a–173a), which effected a blend of this meditative tradition with Hīnayāna mindfulness of breathing (*ānāpāna anusmṛti*). As An presented it, this dhyāna seemed to Taoists to be only a variant of their practice of nurturing the ether (*yang ch'i*), the vital impulse of human beings, living things, and the universe itself. In Buddhism, breath does not carry that cosmic meaning. Ether is only one of the four great elements, not the substance of all reality. The mindfulness of breathing was meant to inculcate the awareness of the three marks of suffering, impermanence, and no-self. By focusing attention on and counting the inhaled and exhaled breath, one acquires single-mindedness of intent. As the senses are gradually pacified (*chih, samatha*), one meditates on certain insight formulas (*küan, vipaśyanā*) intended to reverse the process of ignorance and to permit correct perception of the impermanence of self and world. In Taoism, the same exercise had a different aim: by lessening desires, to "calm the mind and make pliant the breath (spirit)"; by cultivating non-action, to return to the Origin and achieve immortality. In the notation added to the *An-pan shou-i ching* in An's translation, the Chinese Buddhists interpreted the word *ānāpāna* as *ch'ing-ch'ing wu-wei,* purity, quietude, and the absence of action (T 15.164a). In one of the earliest Chinese commentaries on any sūtra—a Wu commentary (T 33.9b–24c) on An's translation of the *Yin-chih-ju ching* (Sūtra on the Five Aggregates, the Six Faculties, and the Twelve Elements; T 15.173b–180c)—it is acknowledged that "in *ānāpāna* meditation, one can see in the one breath, the working of the five skandhas of form, sensation, perception, will, and consciousness" (T 33.17a). But elsewhere in the same commentary, the author speaks of the One Ether and the return to the Origin (T 33.10ab). Buddhist pluralism and Taoist monism mixed.

Thus Taoism helped to introduce Buddhism, but in the process it left a legacy of preconceptions that would affect even the great masters of the T'ang. For example, the Taoists had applied the yin-yang scheme in analyzing and evaluating the mind and its functions. The mind (*hsin*), being the passive element, always turns out to be good; however, active mentation—called *i* (intention, incipient idea), *nien* (present or momentary thought), or *shih* (subsequent object-knowledge, consciousness)—is always judged undesirable, for it is extroverted and deluding. This simple scheme underlies the Han Buddhist teaching that in order to preserve the purity of mind, one must guard well the intentions characteristic of active mentation. The term "guarding the intention" (*shou-i*) thus appeared in the Chinese title of the *An-pan shou-i ching* itself (Sūtra on Breathing Exercises and on Guarding the Intentions; the original was Sūtra on Mindfulness of Breathing).

A fusion of Buddhist ideas of mind and Taoist notions of spirit also led to a hybrid theory of the three bases of consciousness. In the *A-han ch'eng-hsing ching* (Sūtra of the Noble Career of the Arhant; T 2.833b–884b), we find death and transmigration explained in terms of the triad of *shih, hsin, i:* "Within the human body, there are three matters. When the body dies, the consciousness goes, the mind goes, the intention goes. These three always chase after one another [causing suffering and rebirth] (T 2.883b). The meaning of this text is that the soul is other than the body and that when the body dies there is a disintegration of consciousness: first the five senses (*shih*) disintegrate; then even the sixth, the mind (*hsin*), goes; but the intention, meaning the subtle karmic impulse (*i*, the saṃskāra or *cetanā*), continues to the next life; after assuming an embryo, it too disintegrates. Once there is form, there are new sense organs, and then consciousness, mind, intention (the whole mental process) will begin again.

Controversy and Apologetic

An Shih-kao had made the Buddhist Dharma known to Han China without dispelling the popular perception of the Buddha as an immortal. Since the Chinese were then forbidden by law to "leave home," the Saṅgha did not yet pose a threat to the state and the family. Lack of knowledge of the fellowship is shown in the confused usage of the terms for full monk, novice, and layman in Han writings. By the end of Han, however, the peculiar obligations of the Buddhist "man of the way" were better known. The monk's dress, diet, celibacy, and—something foreign to native "men of the Way"—his ignoble begging began to invite comments. In an emerging conflict between the two traditions, the author of the Taoist *T'ai-p'ing ching* (Classic of the Great Peace) found much to criticize in this barbarian faith.

The Confucians also raised their voice, prompting Mou-tzu, a lay Buddhist, to answer them in the work *Mou-tzu* (T 52.1a–7a). To the Sinocentric Confucian critic who believed that anything worthwhile had to be in the classics and who asked why nothing concerning the Buddha was found therein, Mou-tzu had two simple answers. First, there were more things in heaven and earth than were dreamt of in Confucius's philosophy. One cannot really just "review the old" and expect to "learn anew" (T 52.2bc). Second, Mou-tzu trusted the Dharma because it was true. Here is a declaration of faith, *hsin*, a word traditionally denoting the virtue of trust among friends, but which at this time took on a new and central meaning in human life.[2] In reply to the charge that monks were unfilial in abandoning the family, practicing celibacy to the harm of the ancestral line, and immolating by tonsure the body that belonged to their parents, Mou-tzu cited cases of ancient sages who had resorted to similar unfilial expedients and argued that, for example, to save a drowning father, a son may improperly turn him upside down (T 52.2c). These are weak arguments, for it is unclear how one's leaving home is comparable to saving a drowning father, nor can a monk's calling be classed as an expedient.

The most basic tenet that Mou-tzu shared with all Han Buddhists concerns the immortality of the soul. As Wei Shou put it later:

> The core of the (Buddhist) scriptures is as follows: The varieties of living beings all come into existence because of their own deeds. There are past, present, and future, and the conscious soul which lives through all three eras never perishes. Whenever one does good or evil, one is sure to have one's retribution. (T 52.101b)

For the Buddhists, the karmic theodicy was self-evident, as it could not be to non-Buddhists. Theodicies involve questions of meaning, which, as Max Weber reminds us, can never be derived directly from fact. An ethical fiction, karma is as difficult to prove as its moral impact is evident. It infuses the actual with the normative, bringing every conceivable human action into a template of perfect, universal justice. Mou-tzu did not try to prove karma, fortunately, for those who did try were inevitably drawn into a confusing debate about the soul (*shen*). The Buddhists did endorse a surviving consciousness, but in accordance with the doctrine of anātman (no-soul), they referred consistently to it as "not subject to destruction" (*pu-mieh*), never as "permanent" (*ch'eng-chu*). The *vijñāna* which survived death would disintegrate once the embryo was conceived. This is a canonical doctrine, not a Taoist corruption.

Karma was controversial because of the new conception of justice it implied. Confucians trusted in the goodness of the universe; while they could tolerate some degree of injustice in life, they expected it to be redressed in the future by society itself. Buddhists, on the contrary, saw the good earth as painful saṃsāra, insisted on an iron law of karma and on individual culpability, and, seeing justice as an obvious impossibility in this world, placed their hope in future lives. Religious Taoists combined elements from both attitudes. They believed that the sins of the parents were visited on the children, a familial karma called "carrying over the (ancestral) burden." If we judge only by the words or even the practices of these three groups, it is sometimes not easy to see where they differ. Wei Shou's description of the Buddhist method of "refining the spirit" seems indistinguishable from the Taoist program:

> Thus one accumulates superior works, smelting out one's baseness, passing through innumerable forms, and refining the spirit, until one effects no-birth and attains the Ultimate of Buddhahood. The mental stages traversed in this process are many and varied. In every case one lays hold of the shallow and makes one's way to the profound, makes use of the imperceptible and achieves the preeminent. The essential lies in accumulating humility, purging out desires, practising quietude, and achieving pervasive illumination. (T 52.101b)

However, the differences were real enough. The Confucians sought only social immortality, the Taoists sought immortality through psychic communion with the Tao of nature, while Buddhists sought total pneumatic liberation from this fallen world.[3]

The curious or the critical often asked Buddhists why the Buddha was not visible. The sense of the question is: "If the Buddha is omnipotent, why can he not make himself visible to enlighten me?" (T 50.70a–72a). It shows the puzzlement occasioned by a new conception of divine omnipotence, one unknown to the classical Chinese religions.[4] There was no simple answer, yet the same question could not have arisen about Lao-tzu. One apologist drew a curious parallel: the Buddha did what Confucius did; he "only transmitted and did not author"—meaning here, however, that he did not force his presence upon people. In the end, as the presence of Christ is for Christians, the acceptance of the presence of the Buddha had to remain a matter of faith.

Buddhism thus introduced a more lofty notion of the divine and a spiritual cosmos that defied the rational limits of classical China. China was no longer the Middle Kingdom. Its Mount Kun-lun was displaced by Mount Sumeru; its squarish Nine Continents by circles of land and water masses; its heaven above and Yellow Springs below by layers of deva heavens above and chambers of hells below. Of course, the three Buddhist realms of desire, form, and formlessness were worlds of a spiritual order; at least the upper ones required the perfection of the four dhyānas (trances) before they could be seen. Mahāyāna had an even more expansive universe, proportioned to the extravagance of its spirituality, and this too was gradually absorbed in China. The decentering of China prompted pilgrimages to places beyond China's borders and produced many travelogues, including accounts of journeys to the Tuṣita Heaven above and the Avīci hells below, to galaxies without and within. In this period travelers saw and avid readers imagined things that dwarfed all classical imagination.

The Han Taoist interest in Buddhist meditation was selective; Mou-tzu, the apologist for the nascent tradition, showed limited understanding. As long as the Han Confucian order lasted, a new God and a new cosmos could not hope to prevail over the worldview on which this order was based. Even after the collapse of Han Confucian orthodoxy in 220 C.E., Buddhism had still to prove itself against the Neo-Taoist experiment of the Wei-Chin period (220–420). The Neo-Taoists sensed the limitations of the Han Confucian teaching of names (*ming-chiao*). Ho Yen (d. 249) and Wang Pi (226–249) argued that Confucians knew the Tao even better than Lao-tzu and that the true quest in life was for the higher freedom of spontaneity (*tzu-jan*, naturalness). So it was that the monk Chih Tun (314–366) came across a group of gentlemen at the White Horse temple who were discussing the *Hsiao-yao* (Roving Freedom) chapter of the *Chuang-tzu* and were of the opinion that freedom was simply following one's given nature, *hsing*. Chih Tun asked, "If so, would not the evil kings [the last kings of Hsia and Shang] who followed their nature in killing also be counted as men of the Way?" They could not answer him. Chih Tun then composed his commentary on the *Chuang-tzu*, after which he vanished into the mountains, never to be seen again. The story exposes the poverty of the Neo-Taoist philosophy and shows why the Buddhist monk was to hold such attraction for the new era.

A New Man for a New Era

The gentlemen were probably following Kuo Hsiang's reading of *Chuang-tzu*. In Chuang-tzu's parable of a roc and a cicada, the flight of the roc represents the freedom of one who abides in the Tao and the hop of the cicada stands for the limited world of the common person. But Kuo Hsiang (d. 312), while recognizing the roc's greater freedom, also defended the cicada's claim to a lesser one. In conformity with its nature, which is to hop short distances and not attempt anything more, the cicada too participates in the all-comprehensive way of nature itself. Freedom becomes here a "recognition of necessity" (Spinoza). Because he collapses these ultimate opposites, Kuo Hsiang has been called the supreme mystic, an ancient existentialist, a pure fatalist, as well as an apologist for the status quo who succeeded in rising from his *han-men* (poor families) background into the elite Neo-Taoist circle of *hou-men* (magnate families). But Kuo Hsiang avoided the pitfall into which the gentlemen at the White Horse temple fell. The problem lies in their use of the word *hsing* (nature), often interchangeable with the word *ch'ing* (emotion) in Han usage. Feelings were included within nature. If so, since evil impulses are emotions and therefore a part of nature, must not following them be considered freedom? The Neo-Taoists were ill-equipped to disclaim this consequence, not only because of the linguistic ambiguity but also because Neo-Taoism had somehow lost its original moral force. By the time of Juan Chi, who considered the "great man" to be above common morality, it had made a cult of unbridled romanticism. Neo-Taoists were notorious for their indulgence of impulse, in which they saw the essence of their new-found freedom.[5] To get drunk, or to go naked as one nudist did, was freedom. Crying one's heart out at funerals and for days afterward was judged excellent, though such "mourning unto death" was contrary to the moderation of "mourning unto life" that the rites prescribed. To visit friends at the most ungodly hours on impulse and to turn back at the door because the mood was gone were seen as proof of spontaneity. These Epicureans of the undisciplined were unable or unwilling to distinguish sheer abandon and cultivated freedom and were thus unable to answer the Stoic question of Chih Tun: Is one free when one is ruled by impulse? The Neo-Confucians of a later age could have answered that easily, having then distinguished the goodness of *hsing* from the selfish impulses of *ch'ing*, following the example of the Buddhist monk who perfected the yogic art of rational self-control.

This sense of transcendental freedom is what we suspect was aired in Chih Tun's commentary on the *Chuang-tzu.* He used the word *li* (Principle) in a new transcendental sense and spoke of the freedom of one who "though concoursing with things in the world of things, is somehow never himself turned into a thing among things." The Neo-Taoists were men of the world (*ming-shih,* men of renown) still possessed by the things they possessed, whereas the monk renounced world and possessions. The Neo-Taoists might cut charming figures in the tales told of them, but these salonists were elitists as the monks were not. Disillusioned with politics, they made a show of defying convention, but held onto their wealth and social renown. The monks, in contrast, were known as the "poor men of the Way" (*pin-tao*), and their fellowship accepted men from all classes, including social nobodies like Seng-chao, who rose by talent alone. Unlike the effete Neo-Taoist gentlemen who painted their eyebrows, the monks made an art of simplicity. The Neo-Taoists might discourse on *tzu-jan* (naturalness), but these armchair romantics seldom left the urbane drinking parties held on their private estates to smell the grass or taste the rain. It was the monks who dwelt amidst hills and waters, and their success in making these marginal lands habitable was envied: "Of the famous mountains under Heaven, the monks owned most of them." The fortunes of the Neo-Taoists declined throughout the later third century, and their comfortable life-style ended with the barbarian sack of the Chinese capitals in 311 and 316. Too refined to escape on horseback, the gentlemen were slaughtered on the streets. One of them, waving a duster about him in a theatrical gesture, made an elegant plea: since he had never meddled in the dusty affairs of politics, his life should be spared. This did not avail to stop the barbarians from beheading him. Confucian critics could see his fate as illustrating the fatal weakness of Neo-Taoism. In the lawlessness that followed, the ascetic was a law unto himself, a pillar of strength as the world crumbled around him, for he alone had virtues not yet developed in the indigenous traditions: compassion, a spirit of selfless service, and the meekness of the peacemaker. These virtues made him a source of blessings for everyone who came into contact with him.

With the loss of the North to the barbarians, the Chin court moved South. The Saṅgha had been until then relatively small, but the prestige conferred on it by the Neo-Taoist interest and the conversion of such eminent figures as Chih Tun increased its popularity and gave it for the first time a predominantly Chinese membership. The issue of whether monks owed loyalty to the throne became a burning one in 340, when the Saṅgha faced a charge of misplaced loyalty. This was quickly silenced by powerful supporters of the faith in court, but it surfaced again in 403, when the usurper Huan Hsüan insisted that the monks pay the throne homage. Supported by pious magnate families traditionally opposed to centralized rule, the Saṅgha found a defender of its calling in the revered Hui-yüan (344–416). His defense showed the same spiritual autonomy as Chih Tun's. Referring to the monk as a *fang-ai chih-shih,* a man who lives beyond the square (*fang,* shape) of the earth, Hui-yüan placed him beyond the laws of common society (like the *sannyāsin* of India). The monk acquired this status by virtue of the *shen* (spiritedness) he had perfected. Until recently, the soul has been thought of as having some shadowy form, like a ghost. But a more metaphysical appreciation of *shen* had been proposed in a thesis titled *Shen wu hsing lun* (On the Soul Having No Form). Building on this, Hui-yüan saw the monk as one who had returned to a state of spiritedness, that is, to a state in which yin and yang were still undifferentiated. He cited the *I ching* (Book of Changes) in support of this account of spirit as dynamic yet passive, as both yin and yang, a bivalence material things do not have. Since this spirit precedes existents, it is not bound by mortal limits. The holy man as the axis of the state, upholding its welfare, should be freed from the duty of bowing to worldly rulers. This argument is partly derived from the traditional Han view of the cosmic status of the sage, but coming two centuries after Mou-tzu, Hui-yüan spoke with the authority and conviction of a man of the calling. More than his words, his hermit life-style contrasted sharply with the life of the Neo-Taoist torn between courtly duties and escape to nature. Hui-yüan's conversion was occasioned by a lecture on emptiness given by Tao-an (312–385). He had his head shorn and uncompromisingly declared Confucianism, Taoism, and the nine Learnings mere dregs in comparison with the treasure he had found. He retired to Mount Lu and became an exemplary instance of a "man living beyond the world," steeped in the vision of Pure Land piety, his converse with the world limited by his resolution never to step across the Tiger Creek that separated his nirvanic retreat from the "dusty world." He lived and died as a monk should, observant of the precepts to the very end, refusing to take any medicine laced with alcohol. In him, the Buddhist calling had found an unshakable foothold, the starting point for the growth of the Saṅgha from about the year 400.

Century of the Holy Man: North China 311–439

The division of the kingdom into North and South after the sack of Loyang and Ch'ang-an in 311 and 316 affected Buddhism too, so that from this point on it is necessary to trace separately the course of its development in the two areas. In the South, Neo-Taoist interest in Buddhist ideas persisted even as Buddhist monks such as Hui-yüan disengaged themselves from worldly involvement. In the North, which had no leisure for speculation, Buddhist monks became hierocrats actively involved in politics. The revolt of the barbarian nomads had been followed by that of sixteen tribal kingdoms, creating conditions of war for an entire century, a century during which the "holy man" acquired a social prominence comparable to that which similar figures had in the late antiquity of the Roman West. Incredible feats were ascribed to these charismatic figures. These legends deserve study for the light they throw on the age which produced them. Holy men of this type are found only in this century and only in the North. They form a peculiar triad with the despot and the people in the institutional structure of this culture. Later they were to be replaced by the Saṅgha, to produce the three classes of soldier, clergy, and peasant, as in feudal Europe. The holy man was a living institutional embodiment of the sacred. He differed from holy men in other periods and other traditions in one respect: his power seldom extended beyond his lifetime. Indeed, the century that conferred such glory on the holy man could also reward him with death and dishonor, as we shall see.

The paradigmatic figure in the genre was Fo-t'u-teng (T 50.383b–387a). Teng arrived in China around 310, just at the commencement of the barbarian revolt, and witnessed the massacres at the capital. To help the sufferers, he decided there and then to "civilize the barbarian (Shih Lo, founder of the later Chao dynasty, which lasted from 328 to 352) by feats of magic." In pursuit of this aim, he first attached himself to a general serving Shih Lo, soon proving himself such a flawless war prophet that Shih Lo eventually asked for him. At their first meeting, Teng awed and converted the bloody warrior by magically drawing a dazzling blue-green lotus from a bowl of water (T 50.383c). Later, as the Great Reverend serving the state, Teng was able to "halve the massacre" the Shihs could have committed. This outline of a fantastic life indicates three salient characteristics of holy men: their compassion, their role as war prophets, and their miraculous powers used for good ends. Most studies focus on the episode of "Teng bewitching the barbarian with magic," and they treat Shih Lo as if he were taken in by a mere sleight of hand. But if the "lotus from the basin" was a miracle, it was no ordinary one, but carried a symbolic meaning: the blue-green (*ch'ing*) lotus is the pure (*ch'ing*) lotus, and the basin clearly represents the monk's begging bowl. The buddhophanic message clearly is that the Dharma that transcends the world, as a lotus rises above the mud, has, since the death of the Buddha, been entrusted to the monk to whom even rulers should bow. Shih Lo was not dazzled by magic; he submitted to the higher law in a classic confrontation of power and authority.

There is no question here as yet of the religious legitimation of rule. The barbarians were still engaged in conquest, rather than rule. Hence the chief function of the holy men was to be prophets of war; the infallibility of Teng, Tao-an, Seng-lang, Kumārajīva, and Dharmakṣema in this role was celebrated. This is in ironic contrast to the teaching of nonviolence (*ahiṃsā*) these monks were obliged to uphold. The precepts forbid monks even to be near a battle, and there is no reason to believe these pillars of the Buddhist community broke that rule. How could they then justify their role as "military advisors"? The answer may be sought in the Mahāyāna sūtras that evoked the power of the Four Heavenly Kings to protect the faithful. These sūtras probably reflect a political climate in Northwest India not unlike that faced by the nomadic tribes in China. As in ancient Israel, national destiny was now associated with faith, and the inevitable result was that Buddha, like Yahweh, was associated with war. One may doubt, however, if Teng really advertised his prophetic powers to Shih Lo. A monk could be a confessor, and this is probably what the general, a lay Buddhist who later took the precepts from Teng, looked for and found in him. (He may be seen as seeking out Teng just as much as Teng sought him out.) It was as a chaplain, then, that Teng begged the Buddha's protection of his flock in battle. However, since all victories were attributed to this protection, while defeats, as always in the higher religions, were ascribed to human faults, Teng was retrospectively credited with flawless predictions.

The holy man was not holy because he had power to work miracles; he demonstrated those powers because he was a holy man, as can be seen from the careers of Teng's disciples, Tao-an and Seng-lang. A literatus who never pretended to possess special powers, Tao-an (T 50.351c–354a) was drafted nonetheless as a military advisor to Fu Chien, the ruler of Former Ch'in (351–394), who almost took the South in 383 but met a crippling defeat there at Fei-sui. Seng-lang lived in retirement at T'ai-shan and had refused all offers of office (T 52.354b). Nonetheless, petitions came to him from all men of destiny, who thanked him for lending them "divine help" and "prophetic predictions," his repeated disclaimers notwithstanding (T 52.322abc). His holiness alone sufficed to make him a king-maker.

The power of the holy man was symbolic; he had access to the symbols of rule and could legitimize reigns and grant rulers the authority they sought. Using the symbol of the Two Wheels of religious law and earthly power, Teng prophesied the fortunes of war using a "twin wheel" bell. The only time he prophesied by harking to the chime of a "single wheel" bell was when Shih Hu assassinated the heir apparent to pave his own way to the throne; only one bell rang then because the other had been silenced by that bloody deed (T 52.384b). Shih Hu taunted Teng on several occasions. For instance, he would ask him what was the first rule in Buddhism–knowing too well (he was brought up in a monastery) that it was "Not to kill"–in order to see how Teng could justify his ruler's bloody life. Such confrontations, however, often brought out the best in the saint (T 52.385ab). As in ancient Israel, the true prophet proved his worth when prophecy failed. In one battle Teng's prayers to the Buddha had gone unanswered. Hu, surrounded by enemies on three sides, angrily declared the Buddha to be inefficacious, and was ready to put Teng to death for misleading him. Teng used no magic, but simply appealed to common sense. "Why blaspheme the Buddha for such daily fare as a slight set-back in war?" Then he baited Shih Hu by relating that in a former life sixty arahants had promised Shih Hu, then a merchant who supported the Saṅgha, that for his piety he would gain the throne of China. To chastise Shih Hu for his rash anger Teng inserted a threat by recalling how the merchant had to suffer first an interim rebirth as a rooster (in India, associated with cockfights and violent lives). Shih Hu realized at this point that he had gone too far, and he apologized to Teng (T 52.385a). Thus was the ethical fiction of karmic theodicy applied to politics. Not by power, which can only breed anarchy, but by righteousness in a former life, was the throne acquired.

Although Buddhist symbols of rule might have a restraining effect on some men of power, in general they were more impressed by other men of power. The saint, in time of war, was seldom all meekness; he too had demonstrable power, as the yogin Hui-shih showed in a confrontation with the barbarian Ho-lin Po-po. Po-po and his band had just swept into the capital. Angered that the citizens had let an enemy escape hidden among monks, the army was slaughtering monk and lay alike. Hui-shih refused to flee before the sword. What happened next became one of the most retold legends of the time. A soldier plunged his sword into Hui-shih's body but it came out leaving him unscathed. This was reported to Po-po, who came and struck Hui-shih with his jeweled blade; it too left hardly a mark on Hui-shih's body. Terrified, Po-po asked for forgiveness, and the massacre came to an end (T 52.392bc). Here, the saint who had conquered "life and death" could quite literally not suffer death. Again, fact and fiction come together in this legend. The form of Hui-shih's indifference and immunity to harm probably derives from an *avadāna* telling of the Buddha practicing the *kṣānti-pāramitā* (perfection of forbearance) in a former life. The Buddha emits no cry of pain and shows no anger against his killer; or miraculously his severed head grows back on his shoulder. Hui-shih could imitate this because this Master of White Feet was a living Buddha who walked barefoot in Śākyamuni's footsteps. Lily-white soles unpollutable by this dusty world were one of the supernatural marks of all Enlightened Ones. In the confrontation with Po-po, Hui-shih acted as a temporary peacemaker between two hostile races. His miracle was the miracle of reconciliation of invincible barbarian force and immovable Chinese will. Po-po had to coerce the Chinese populace to compliance; he could not afford to appear weak, but neither could he slaughter all his Chinese subjects. Hui-shih stepped into this impasse and interceded for the Chinese. The barbarian ruler Po-po promised clemency in exchange for Hui-shih's promise of divine protection and compliance from the people. The Chinese promised an end of hostility in exchange for the holy man's divine intercession and protection of his flock.

The legend of Hui-shih's immunity, which stems from the grateful Chinese, shares its structure with the set of legends of monks chasing off bandits who had been hounding innocent villagers or travelers or of mountain ascetics scaring away man-eating tigers. The Buddhist triumph of right (right view, etc.) over might (the sword) was supported by the feats, the yogic might, of the ascetic. In a sense all monks participated in such power. An Shih-kao the translator was no great yogin. Yet one day, confronted by a young robber who threatened to take his life, he simply told him that if he did so it would be because it was his karma to die and the youth's to be the instrument of his death. No blade was plunged into An's body, but the robber fled, awed by his detachment (T 50.323b). The sword could not intimidate a monk who had for so long renounced life itself. Ascetic self-control allowed the renunciate to be a law unto himself when the rest of the world was in chaos. The monk was, in Wei emperor T'ai-tsu's words, the "exemplar of the Way," a living witness of nirvanic freedom from suffering, whom even the most lawless of men could not help admiring (Edict of 386; T 52.101c).

The spiritual power of the holy man had very concrete political functions in this period. These were judged so essential to the state that it even happened that wars were waged to secure the release of such men of peace. We have already seen how Shih Lo demanded Teng from his general. When Teng passed away, Tao-an became the prize. Fu Chien sacked Hsiang-yang in 379 to gain access to Tao-an, whom he was never to let go (T 50.352c). When Kumārajīva's fame reached China, Fu Chien dispatched an army under his general Lu Kuang to "secure his release" from Kucha, his birthplace. Lu Kuang eventually decided to keep Kumārajīva for himself. Later, Yao Hsing of Later Ch'in (384–417; r. 393–410) again released him from alleged abuse at Lu's hands in Liang-chou, but no sooner was he brought to Ch'ang-an in 401 than the same abuse—forced concubinage—was practiced on him (T 50.331b–332c). Of all the holy men in the North, only Seng-lang managed to stay out of harm's way by refusing to leave his mountain valley. The holy man was prized because he provided the symbols of rule and solace to the troops, and because he interceded for all before the Buddha after death. (In folk belief, when a person's sin or karma is being weighed after death, one's preceptor presents one's case before the Buddha.) Moreover, the holy man usually brought with him his entourage of disciples, attracted still others, and claimed the loyalty of those who received the precepts from him and whose dharma-name sometimes betokened that lasting tie. This following gave the holy man a political stature that could give his patron a leading place among his compatriots and make him the envy of his enemies. In what was often a confederation of Buddhist tribes under the Dharma, Buddhism was the paratribal ideology, the standard for diplomatic exchange, often taking the form of pledges of brotherhood. Monks served so often as carriers of messages or political overtures between nations that the *Brahma Net Sūtra* (T 24.997a–1010a), following traditional precepts, sought to have them banned from such business. The holy man was an effective mediator not only between the barbarian tribes but also between them and the Chinese. A three-way covenant was sealed in the person of the holy man, pledges being formally made to him by each party to be conveyed to the others. He filled the gap left by the destruction of the traditional Confucian bureaucratic channels of mediation between the ruler and the ruled as a result of the barbarization of North China.

As monks, the holy men in the North were as politically neutral as Hui-yüan. By recognizing no distinction between barbarian and Chinese, they were able to serve both for the common good, teaching compassion (karuṇā) to the powerful and forbearance (*kṣānti*) to the powerless. The potentates and the poor could identify with the holy man because he embodied the virtues characteristic of both. Thus it became common for the holy man to receive hierocratic office (Great Reverend, National Treasure, Nation's Preceptor) from the barbarians he "converted," while massive households from the Chinese he "saved" adopted the faith. He was the one link between the people and the Buddha at the spiritual level, and at the same time the indispensable link between the members of the body politic, without whom it could not be held together. But the weakness of this institution was that since the authority of the holy man lay in the personal guarantee he offered to both parties, that influence seldom extended beyond his death. Furthermore, war prophecy lasted only as long as wars lasted, and the mediating office of the holy man was potent only as long as racial tension was severe. When, after a hundred years or so, intermarriage between Chinese and barbarians, at first unacceptable to both, became a common practice, and when traditional Han channels of communication between ruler and ruled were restored, the office of holy man lost one of its major functions.

Wei Emperor T'ai-wu (r. 424–451), drawn like his predecessors to the Taoist cult of Huang-Lao (the amalgam of the Yellow Emperor and Lao-tzu), was persuaded by his Confucian minister Ts'ui Hao to accept a revelation received from Lao-tzu by the southern Taoist master K'ou Ch'ien-chih to the effect that the True Ruler of the Great Peace proclaimed in the Taoist *T'ai-p'ing ching* was coming from the North, in the person of Emperor T'ai-wu himself. Ts'ui Hao's motive in dispelling the emperor's initial skepticism is far from clear. Though he had ties to religious Taoism, it seems that he was first and foremost an arch-Confucian, who sought to protect and extend the Chinese influence in court and who pursued a rather antiquarian program of restoring Chou ideals and eliminating the barbarian influence of Buddhism. With Ts'ui as his military advisor and K'ou as his new war prophet, T'ai-wu plotted to take Liang-chou in order to complete the unification of the North. The war prophet of his enemy, the charismatic Dharmakṣema (d. 433), lost his life in the ensuing strife. Another famous holy man, Hsüan-kao, suffered an untimely death in a conflict between pro-Buddhist and pro-Confucian forces after the conquest of Liang-chou and the evacuation of its population to the Wei capital. The age of the holy man was passing. The confrontation of ruthless killer and selfless saint became obsolete with the transformation of conquerors into rulers, and the role of these singular hierocrats devolved on the leader of the Saṅgha.

Founding of the Saṅgha Jewel

"Follow the Dharma, not the person" is a basic dictum of Buddhism. People took refuge in the holy man and expressed their gratitude to him in legends, yet the holy man never sought his own glory but that of the Three Jewels. Fo-t'u-teng taught the Dharma to Tao-an and others, built Buddha stūpas, and founded Saṅgha fellowships at every opportunity. His magic he saw only as an expedient means, which could never be a substitute for wisdom (prajñā) or charity (*dāna*). The eclipse of the holy man was not due simply to the changes in political culture described above. It was also a result of his voluntary self-effacement in favor of the Saṅgha. Up to this point there had been monks and novices in the North, but no real Saṅgha. Teng is rightly considered to be the father of the Northern Saṅgha though he had little material with which to build and few disciples who knew what the true fellowship entailed. Preceptory consciousness began with his student Tao-an, who late in life realized that the precepts were "the foundation of the faith." But he had no access to the Vinaya (monastic code) and had to make do with some innovations of his own (T 50.353b). Only in the generation of his student Hui-yüan do we see an approach to a full understanding of what the precepts entailed. As for the Southern Saṅgha, Chih Tun was credited with setting up the first "precept platform," but that is pure legend. He was a gentleman in retirement, independently wealthy, who once clipped the wings of cranes to make them stay around his hermitage. Again, Ho Ch'ung's "monastic manor" was a gentleman's private estate conveniently converted into a monastery, which no doubt merited the accusation of worldliness brought against such places.

Although there was no overnight change, the 400s can be reckoned as the real beginning of the Saṅgha. For the first time, the full vocation—and a Mahāyāna one at that—could be implemented, chiefly as a result of Kumārajīva's clarification of the notions of prajñā (wisdom) and karuṇā (compassion) and his introduction of some forms of Mahāyāna meditation (other meditative masters of renown arrived soon after). Furthermore, the complete Tripiṭaka, including especially the Vinaya, was now made available, so that at last monks could be fully trained in *śīla,* samādhi and prajñā. Kumārajīva had with him the Sarvāstivāda Vinaya, but Fa-hsien brought back in 414 the code of the Mahāsāṅghika, which was preferred. Although these 250 or so rules were never fully implemented in China,[6] the existence of the tradition made it a point of reference. Relapses notwithstanding, even the South embraced the Vinaya, under the influence of Buddhabhadra, who taught the Chinese monks to wear Indian gowns, baring one shoulder, to sit on hard ground, and to eat only one meal daily before noon (T 52.77b–79b). Even Tao-sheng, who flouted the last rule (saying that the sun, being the zenith of heaven, could never pass that midpoint) (T 50.366c) was aware of the prohibition, and when he was expelled from the community (for daring to contradict the letter of the scripture with his Buddha-nature doctrine), he was expelled on Vinaya grounds. However, different Buddhist communities had different styles, and even if they had the same set of rules, there were different degrees of their implementation.

To understand how the Saṅgha unfolded in this period, one must consider the character of each major community, how it interacted with others, and what group was dominant at any given time. Unlike the much more unified Buddhist culture of Sui and T'ang, that of the early fifth century had several major centers: Ch'ang-an and Yeh, Lu-shan and Chien-k'ang, Liang-chou and Tun-huang. K'uai-ch'i in the deep South, Shan-tung to the East, and Szechwan were of less consequence politically.

The Center and the South

These two regions were in proximity and, as monks then traveled freely across frontiers, maintained close communication despite the political divisions. In the first decade of the fifth century the community at Ch'ang-an under Kumārajīva was the grandest, and under Hui-kuan as many as three thousand monks gathered there (T 50.332c). Many of these worked on the translation project, which bore the stamp of their Kucha master's powerful personality. Kumārajīva was a Hīnāyanist abhidharmist before he was converted to Mahāyāna emptiness, and the predominantly philosophical nature of his interests is reflected in his decision to translate such texts as the *Vimalakīrti* and *Lotus* sūtras and the *Prajñāpāramitā* corpus including the *Ta-chih-tu-lun*, a voluminous commentary on the *Mahāprajñāpāramitā-sūtra.* He also translated some works dealing with meditation, but the influence of these was not as extensive or as penetrating, and his legacy to the monks of the Southern dynasty who later inherited the Ch'ang-an tradition, was a one-sidedly gnostic one.

A dark cloud hangs over Kumārajīva's status as a monk. This virile figure acquired the title of National Preceptor, but he was not and could not be the actual leader of the Saṅgha. He lived in a separate "grass hut" (a euphemism) with his concubines, a circumstance which the tradition piously views as forced upon him by his patron Yao Hsing, with a view to securing his charismatic offspring; the story is suspiciously unparalleled in the dealings of rulers with holy men. Kumārajīva was obliged to confess, in a confrontation with the disciplinarian Buddhabhadra, that he was a "lotus in the mud" (T 50.332c). The relative weakness in precepts in the Ch'ang-an community is thus understandable. Yet Kumārajīva's dilemma bears out the Mahāyāna paradox that "form (*rūpa:* color, sex) is emptiness (*śūnyatā*) and emptiness is form." This solid reminder of sin might even explain the other, more personal aspect of his faith: he translated the Pure Land *Amitāyus Sūtra,* and taught Hui-yüan to meditate on Amitābha.

Kumārajīva brought his entourage from Liang-chou, and his fame attracted others (including the yogin Hui-shih) to Ch'ang-an. Because of Yao Hsing's support "nine out of ten households" adopted Buddhism, and the Ch'ang-an community grew so large and was so well endowed that the three basic offices of abbot, rector, and keeper of the records were established for the first time, as the *Seng-shih-lüeh* (A Brief History of the Saṅgha) relates (T 54.242c). The abbot had charge of the community; the rector dealt with holdings and properties; and the two monks who kept the records ensured the just distribution of goods. Thus the Saṅgha became a self-administrating community, with offices probably based on election rather than appointment. Despite this auspicious beginning, the community did not survive the defeat of Yao Hsing and the destruction of Ch'ang-an. The monks were dispersed, mainly to the North and South.

In the South, the most brilliant community was that of Hui-yüan at Lu-shan near the capital. In the last decade of the fourth century, it had been an abhidharma stronghold under Saṅghadeva (T 50.328c–329a), but through its contact with Ch'ang-an it was reoriented toward Mahāyāna. Lu-shan is famous as the site of the first "Lotus" or Pure Land gathering. The group, however, was devoted to meditative visualization of the Pure Land rather than to reliance on Amitābha's vows. It was an elite group that, as Chia-tsai later charged, "benefited no one" (i.e., did not reach out to the common people; T 47.83b). It had no peasant and no female members. Enjoying sanctuary from search by soldiers, Lu-shan remained a home of gentlemen in retirement. Though it had effectively withstood the pressure to bow to the ruler, the community nevertheless disintegrated soon after its holy man, Hui-yüan, passed away in 416. The center of Southern Buddhism then shifted to the capital, Chien-k'ang. In 420, the Chin fell and there was a succession of four dynasties in the South, all founded by warriors who, with one exception, patronized the faith. Buddhism was tinged by the power and wealth of the capital, in which the monks lived in relative comfort as popular public figures known for expertise in philosophical exegesis. There was a paucity of preceptual or meditating monks. Endowed temples had serfs and elder monks had pages. On one occasion, the monks demanded still better treatment, although their diet already included meat and wine. Emperor Wu of Liang reminded them at length but in vain that their favorite *Nirvāṇa Sūtra* forbade eating meat (T 52.294b–303c).

To its credit, the Southern Saṅgha continued to stand fast against imperial demands that monks should bow to the throne—less, however, from Hui-yüan's motive of detachment than as an assertion of the power the monks had by then acquired. Their political involvement was such that some monks (and nuns) were solicited by those who wanted a hearing at court. This situation is only tangentially similar to the role of the holy man in the North because these monks and nuns were not working for the welfare of the people but were the richly rewarded servants of special interests. This influence of monks at court was due to several factors. First, to the military upstarts who became rulers they offered Buddhist (karmic) legitimacy of rule. Second, there was often a subtle symbiosis of militarism and mysticism, inasmuch as soldiers in battle who had to suspend normal standards of right and wrong took solace from monks who aspired to a state that was also somehow beyond good and evil. The mystic who saw all action, good no less than bad, as karma could in turn accept the military man as he was. The monk was obliged to hate killing, but equally obliged not to hate the killer (or anyone else); the soldier knew impermanence at first hand and tended to accept his lot fatalistically as due to karma, which could not be changed in this life but which might be in a future one, perhaps by the supreme act of wisdom or boon of grace that in one stroke can annihilate all karma. (This psychodynamics also lies behind the later alliance of Ch'an with the military art of *kung-fu*, of Zen with Bushido, and of the samurai life with Pure Land devotion.) Thus in lieu of a stable core of "middle-class morality," the two extremes of action and contemplation complement each other to hold at bay the social anomie of which they are symptomatic. Similarly, the fascination of the chaste nun went together with the infamous debauchery of the Southern Court, and sudden conversions from one to the other extreme were not unknown. In this period of extremes, China had Aśokas like Liang emperor Wu in the South and Caligulas like Ch'i emperor Wu in the North.

These new religious trends soon spread from the capital to the more stable countryside. The older "monastic manor" continued, and the number of temples and monks in the Southern dynasties remained fairly constant, except for a sudden increase in the number of monks under Emperor Wu, whose patronage encouraged a "black and white" (impure) Saṅgha. In contrast, there were dramatic fluctuations in the numbers for the turbulent North, where the experiments of brotherhood under the Dharma had the state up in arms. The stability of Buddhism in the South suggests that it had never posed as great a challenge to the traditional order and that while it preached the opposite, it succeeded only in pacifying guilty consciences and reinforcing the status quo.

The North and the Northwest

The Northern Saṅgha was founded by Fo-t'u-teng, who is supposed to have converted ten thousand households around Yeh. Teng operated on the assumption of the coterminality of the Wheel of Dharma and the Wheel of Rule. Tao-an never bowed to rulers, but he did not shun the challenge of politics either, openly confessing that "without reliance on the rulers, matters of the Dharma could not be established." Despite some allegations of corruption—for example, the charge that people were avoiding worldly obligations such as tax by joining the Saṅgha—this Northern community seems to have been fairly pure and circumspect. These attitudes were in evidence when the victorious Emperor T'ai-tsu of the Wei dynasty and his troops, passing through areas where these two had taught, were greeted by monks lining the road. When he had pacified the territory, T'ai-tsu decreed that the faith deserved support and that the monks were worthy of support, as exemplars of the divine traces were worthy of trust. He appointed Fa-kuo, a central Asian, head of the Saṅgha, thus giving a foreign leader to the Chinese śramaṇa. Fa-kuo, no charismatic, was chosen for "his learning and purity of conduct" (T 52.102a). In a classic confrontation scene, there was no miracle: Fa-kuo simply bowed before T'ai-tsu, recognizing him as Tathāgata king. This has repeatedly been cited as proof that Northern Buddhism was a state religion, but this is a simplification of the relationship between the two institutions, state and Saṅgha, which were in the process of consolidating themselves. It is true, and no accident, that Fa-kuo was not a holy man like Teng. He was not the axis of a covenant between ruler and people; he represented the monks alone, not the people. Nor could the monks be seen as representing the people; in fact, monks were housed in "official residences" which T'ai-tsu had repaired. They were sent by the next emperor, T'ai-tsung, probably as official emissaries, to pacify the countryside (T 52.102a).[7] Fa-kuo was chosen for his knowledge of the precepts, and the precepts made clear that monks should not bow to rulers. Nevertheless, Fa-kuo argued that he bowed only before the Buddha, but that the king, as supporting the Dharma, was in virtue almost similar to the Buddha. The ambiguity was intended; his submission had a hidden sense. Fa-kuo preserved his celestial authority, to which, in matters of the spirit, the terrestrial emperor deferred. In fact, in the same episode, the emperor bowed to him in turn, though less publicly: he visited Fa-kuo in his hermitage, the gate of which was so low that he had to stoop to enter. (To preserve his royal dignity, the gate eventually was widened to accommodate the royal carriage [T 52.102a]). In this story state and Saṅgha reach mutual accommodation as two permanent institutions. If Fa-kuo stooped, he also conquered. Despite the limitation placed by the state on the quota of monks for a given population, the Saṅgha outgrew it under Wei patronage.

There was another Buddhist community then not yet under Wei rule, in the obscure Northwestern frontier region of Liang-chou, and it posed a greater threat to the established order than the Southern Saṅgha did. Liang-chou was the first of the four military colonies that linked China, through Tun-huang (the most remote of the four), to Central Asia. A stronghold of Buddhism since the early third century, Liang-chou saw a lot of traffic between Ch'ang-an

21. *Casing Slab from a Buddhist Monument,* ca. 525 C.E.
Sculpture—Chinese. Northern Wei Dynasty (386–534 C.E.)
Buff sandstone. 27 3/4 x 25 inches.

and the West. Dharmarakṣa, the Tun-huang bodhisattva (late third century; T 50.326c–327a) traveled freely between the two. Tao-an's sūtra catalogue noted an entire separate set of scriptures that had been translated in this center. Political unrest in the Central Plains after 311, however, had cut off that traffic. Now a relatively peaceful backwater, Liang-chou had a century to evolve its own brand of Buddhism. In the early fourth century, Meng-hsun ruled the area, attended by the resident hierocrat Dharmakṣema (T 50.335c–337b), a war prophet and miracle-worker second only to Fo-t'u-teng. Less renowned than Kumārajīva, Dharmakṣema translated a far wider and more representative set of works. The Vaipulya scriptures he rendered appealed to the whole Buddhist community: there were Jātaka (birth) stories of the Buddha for the young and old, the *Golden Light Sūtra* for rulers, the *avadāna* (myths of origins) explaining the expanding Mahāyāna pantheon, magical dhāraṇī for all occasions, the *Upāsaka-śīla-sūtra* (Sūtra of Lay Precepts), and the *Bodhisattva-śīla-sūtra* (Sūtra of Bodhisattva Precepts) for the creation of lay and monastic communities based on Mahāyāna precepts, and texts more in the philosophic line of Kumārajīva, such as the *Karuṇā-puṇḍarīka* (Lotus of Compassion), which celebrates the *ekayāna* (one vehicle), and the *Mahāparinirvāṇa-sūtra,* which teaches universal Buddhahood. No other community had at its disposal so formidable a range of scriptures. Dharmakṣema reinforced this comprehensiveness by creating the first Mahāyāna preceptory community in China, including generals as well as common people under a code as liberal in its rules as it was demanding in its principle (T 50.326c–327a). It appears that Liang-chou monks kept up wayfaring; they traveled about much more than Southern monks and never resided in propertied temples. They mingled well with the laity, who housed them on their rounds; in guiding the people, they felt few inhibitions in compiling teachings or sūtras or in diluting the Dharma as expediencies. They were diligent propagators of the precepts; the confessional and the liturgical tradition originated among them. They were the popularizers of Buddhism. They were also known as those who kept the ascetic tradition alive. They maintained the old forest-dwelling ideal, but substituted grottoes for the forests.

This most dynamic of Buddhist communities was isolated in the Northwest and had little impact on the rest of China until the Wei conquest of this area in 439, which marks a watershed in the Saṅgha history of the North. In the reign of Emperor T'ai-wu (424–451), the Three Teachings headed for a confrontation, and an expedient alliance of Confucianism and Taoism eventually brought about the first persecution of the Buddhists. The emperor initially supported the Dharma, befriended monks, and attended the festival of Buddha's birthday. Liang-chou was the last stronghold he needed to bring under his rule. He took the first step to secure compliance, in asking

Meng-hsun to hand over his resident saint Dharmakṣema. Meng-hsun found an excuse to let Dharmakṣema go free. T'ai-wu, furious that his will had been defied, ordered Meng-hsun to send soldiers after Dharmakṣema and have him killed. Meng-hsun, lamenting the impermanence of worldly power, sighed: "Dharmakṣema was my precept master (to whom one owed eternal debt) and it would be fitting that I should die with him" (T 50.326c). T'ai-wu reinforced his army with able-bodied monks whom he had defrocked, and in 439 he marched against Liang-chou. During the siege of the walled city occurred the first recorded case of monks taking part in battle: three thousand of them helped to defend the city. That Dharmakṣema's disciples might have flouted the rule of *ahiṃsā* to avenge his death and to prevent a similar fate for themselves is understandable. However, they may actually have been following a precept in so bearing arms. The sūtra that justified this was none other than the Dharmakṣema-translated *Nirvāṇa Sūtra.* This scripture was read quite differently in North and South. The Southern Nirvāṇa school focused almost exclusively on its teaching on the universality of Buddha-nature, whereas the Northern reading stressed the eschatological prediction of imminent threats to the Saṅgha and the demise of the Dharma "within sixty years." Nor did it forget the earlier teachings in the sūtra that denied Buddha-nature to the *icchantika* (cursed one), legitimized the bearing of arms in defense of the Dharma, and taught that the killing of an *icchantika* could be no sin. Thus the episode of the armed monks was no aberration; it was in fact a dramatic demonstration of the activism of Liang-chou Buddhism.

However, the defense of Dharma by arms failed. After the city fell, the population was enslaved and transported back to P'ing-ch'eng, the Wei capital. But soon the Liang-chou community claimed new adherents in its new surroundings. The crown prince and the Wei nobility acquired the Liang-chou practice of housing the monks in their residence, much to the chagrin of the arch-Confucian prime minister Ts'ui Hao. In 444, it was decreed that such hoarding of monks be prohibited. Then in 445 a discovery of arms in a temple in Ch'ang-an allowed Ts'ui Hao to conjure up other charges and push for a persecution of Buddhism (T 50.102b). The crown prince and his privately kept monk Hsüan-kao tried to intercede. Hsüan-kao staged the Golden Light Confessional to heal the split between king and prince, father and son, invoking the power (dream appearances) of the (pro-Buddhist) ancestors. Ts'ui thwarted this promising initiative with a charge of witchcraft, and had Hsüan-kao strangled (T49.354ab). After Buddhism was officially banned in 446, Liang-chou monks who refused to defrock hid themselves among a supportive laity, patiently awaiting their chance. In 452, T'ai-wu died and the ban was lifted. A successful revival ensued and Buddhism regained more ground than it had lost, by means of a daring program of expanding Saṅgha membership that literally redrew the religious map of China.

The Creation of a Liberal Mahāsaṅgha

The creation of the "great fellowship" (*mahāsaṅgha*) produced a legendary figure of three million "monks" (*seng*), before its magnitude courted the next persecution in 574 C.E. The title *mahāsaṅgha* is appropriate, for as the liberal Mahāsaṅghika preceded Mahāyāna in India, this liberal community in the North preceded the rise of Sinitic Mahāyāna. Three million is an impossible number, for even at the peak of Buddhism in T'ang, the count reached only seven hundred thousand. Clearly not all three million were monks in the narrow sense. Ninety percent were peasants who counted themselves as "monks" (*seng-chia*) because they officially belonged to and were organically a part of a preceptory *mahāsaṅgha* created by the Buddhist revival.

The success of this institution corrects the Weberian misperception of Buddhism as an otherworldly mystical religion designed for a handful of "spiritual virtuosos" or "exemplary prophets" emulating in their selflessness the impersonality of nirvāṇa. Buddhism gives clear injunctions on how to conduct oneself in the real world in compliance with the will of the Enlightened: the precepts and noble paths of Hīnayāna, the perfections of the bodhisattva required in Mahāyāna. For householder and monk alike, the first rule is *dāna,* giving or charity in view of human brotherhood. The wisdom formula that accompanies it—let there be neither donor, gift, nor recipient—might suggest Weber's "acosmic love," yet in practice it is no different from the detachment accompanying Christian charity, whereby the right hand does not know what the left is doing. The Buddhist theory of human brotherhood is based on the interdependence of all beings, or on the fact that we must have, through an infinity of rebirths, been connected as sons and daughters, brothers and sisters, spouses and relatives to all sentient beings. Hence the obligation of repaying to all the kindness once received from all. One does not, however, repay ills; karma takes care of "an eye for an eye." This message of charity broke with the Confucian insistence on the priority of kin. The clan organizations set up by Confucians for the care of the widowed and orphaned and the free hostels of religious Taoists were surpassed by the Buddhist institution of the cooperative merit-field which enabled an injunction of universal charity to be put into effect. The ideology of merit might later seem to some a lesser path, but it effectively reminded people that it is better to give than to receive, to transfer merit to others than to claim it for oneself, to give anonymously or to strangers than to give publicly or to those one knows.

Around 470, in response to the distress of another enslaved population, from Shan-Tung in the East, who were finding it difficult to adjust to being slaves on an imperial estate, the Liang-chou monk T'an-yao, head of the Saṅgha, devised a charitable solution that was to have widespread consequences. The administrator having passed away, T'an-yao petitioned that the estate be put under clerical administration. Pious Emperor Kao-tzu approved the request, knowing the great merit acquired by a ruler who releases people to the Saṅgha in this way. This was the beginning of the merit-field of compassion known as the Saṅgha household. In this system a peasant family could accrue merit by donating an amount of grain to the Saṅgha; Saṅgha householders were counted as part of the family of monks (*seng-chia*); they could claim a share of the Saṅgha grain as relief in times of need and could also share in monastic privileges such as exemptions from tax and corvée labor. In return for the donation, the peasant would no doubt receive the lay precepts then being popularized by an apocryphal sūtra composed for the purpose, the *T'i wei Po-li ching* (*Trapusa Bhallika Sūtra*), which aligns the five precepts with the Confucian five virtues, the five elements and other sets of fives in Han cosmological correlations. Within the *seng-chia,* its adopted members called themselves brothers and sisters. They even imitated the fortnightly confessions of the monks. This charitable estate grew rapidly, as peasants donated their fields to the Saṅgha, acquiring both spiritual benefits and material protection. What began as an administrative office ended in creating a propertied Saṅgha, eventually fabled to own one-third of the land. This was not the original style of Liang-chou, and its secularizing effect became apparent when the community faced its first charges of corruption, coming from the monks themselves.

Development of the Dharma

While the barbarian North developed the institution of the Saṅgha, the cultured Chinese South laid the foundation for the digestion of the Dharma. Two overriding concerns occupied Buddhist thinkers there up to the end of the Liang dynasty (552): the meaning of *emptiness* and the promise of *Buddha-nature.* The emptiness philosophy came from the *Prajñāpāramitā* sūtras, whose recurrent theme is: "Form is emptiness, emptiness is form; saṃsāra is nirvāṇa, nirvāṇa is saṃsara." The Chinese took this to imply transcendence of the world of appearances through a *via negativa,* followed, as befitted the Mahāyāna bodhisattva, by a return from the nirvanic to the samsaric realm, through insight into their nonduality. The doctrine of Buddha-nature comes from the *Nirvāṇa Sūtra* and inspired in the Chinese the hope of locating this divine spark in humanity and the causes and conditions for the eventual fruition of this "seed of the highest enlightenment." These two topics informed the objective ontology and the subjective psychology of these Southern gnostics. In introducing them here, our focus is less on the original Indian notions than on the unique aspects of the Sinitic exegetical understanding.

Buddhist Emptiness and Taoist Void

The Neo-Taoist encounter with Buddhism in the fourth century generated the practice of *ko-i,* or concept-matching exegesis of Buddhism. Although Chinese Buddhists in Han had already paired native and foreign ideas, interpreting the Hīnayāna basics of skandha, *āyatana, dhātu* with native concepts of ether (*ch'i*) and soul (*shen*), *ko-i* denotes the matching of the śūnyatā of the emptiness sūtras introduced since the time of Chih Ch'an to the Void or Nothingness (*wu*) discovered by the Neo-Taoist Wang Pi.

Wang Pi, reacting against the Confucian fixation on this world of being, sought behind the façade of facts a transcendental principle (*li*), an ultimate meaning (*i*) beyond all forms (*hsiang*) and words (*yen*). This is non-being or nothingness and is the origin, ground, and substance of all things. We do not know if Wang Pi was influenced by the emptiness sūtras, of which he makes no mention. But we do know that later Neo-Taoists, being less Sinocentric, were receptive to the wisdom of India and open to the irrational. (One of them collected reported encounters with spirits in the *Shou shen chi* [In Search of the Daemonic].) During Eastern Chin when these gentlemen retreated more and more from politics and political criticism (*ch'ing-i*) and indulged in pure conversation (*ch'ing-t'an*), emptiness was a favorite topic of speculation. Six theses on emptiness—to call them "schools" would be too generous—appeared. Often regarded as separate opinions, they actually constitute a series of attempts to appropriate the Mahāyāna understanding of emptiness. Their dialectical unfolding went through typical phases of thesis, antithesis, and synthesis.

1. The first, basic thesis identified emptiness (emptiness of self-nature, *svabhāva-śūnyatā*) with Original Non-being (*Pen-wu,* a term already used for rendering *tathatā* and *śūnyatā*). This view was put forward by Fa-shen (286–374). Lao-tzu's statement that "being comes from non-being" (chap. 40) had inspired Wang Pi to declare non-being the ground of all being. Following this, Fa-shen took or mistook the dictum "form is emptiness" to mean that all things are born of a "gaping hole" or non-being, the "empty space" that preceded the rise of the four great elements:

> Chu Fa-shen says that for all dharmas to be originally nonexistent, hollow, and formless is the truth of supreme meaning; the arising of the myriad

phenomena is called the mundane truth. Therefore the Buddha answered the brahmin, "The Four Elements arise from emptiness." (T 65.93b.5–7)[8]

This position confuses emptiness with the Void and Buddhist causation with Taoist cosmogony. Emptiness is not some nebulous potentia out of which all things sprang. But since most Chinese then considered spiritual practice to be the reduction of activity (*wei;* karma) until nonaction (*wu-wei;* nirvāṇa) was reached, few noticed the fallacy. Tao-an developed this position as follows:

> When the Tathagāta appeared in the world he propagated his teaching by means of Original Nonbeing. Therefore the vast collection of sūtras all clarify the Original Nonbeing of the five aggregates. . . . Nonbeing existed originally before this world of transformations, and emptiness came at the beginning of all forms. People became mired in the later state of Being. If the mind is entrusted to Original Nonbeing, then one's various thoughts will come to an end. (T 65.92c.16–20)

2. It took an observant monk, Chih Min-tu, who came South sometime between 325 and 342, to expose the nihilistic bias of *Pen-wu.* Versed in the *Prajñāpāramitā* corpus, he noted that the sūtras never said there was no form (*rūpa,* matter). Form, however empty, continues to exist as form. Since the objects of the senses clearly exist, he argued that they appear not to exist only as the mind of the subject consciousness is emptied:

> The mind is negated with regard to myriad phenomena, but the myriad phenomena are not nonexistent. The meaning of this interpretation is that when the sūtras teach that all dharmas are empty, it means that one should seek to physically and mentally consider them vain and not be attached to them. . . . It does not mean that external phenomena are empty, or that the phenomenal objects are empty. (T 42.29a.2528)[9]

This *Hsin-wu* or Mind as Empty antithesis dealt such a blow to the simplistic *Pen-wu* thesis that it set off a series of counterattacks from the Southerners, who, when they could not win their case, resorted to slandering Min-tu. Most scholars consider this *Hsin-wu* thesis to be inspired by Chuang-tzu's idea of "no-mind." But whereas Chuang-tzu meant by "no-mind" the absence of deliberate thought, Min-tu apparently took the term to mean the absence of the psyche. He could invoke the sūtras, where not just form but also consciousness had been declared empty. It was for this that he was so maligned by his fellow Buddhists. He grasped the meaning of anātman (no-soul) when they still held the belief that there must be a soul that transmigrates. Even Tao-an, who amended Fa-shen's thesis in response to Min-tu's critique ("emptiness is not a gaping hole; things as-such are suchness [*tathatā,* natural, *tzu-jan*]"), could not abandon the theory of a transmigrating consciousness.

3. Two defenders of the theory of the indestructibility of the soul now

arose. They accepted Min-tu's view but sought to subsume it under mundane truth (in the context of the double truth theory) so as to safeguard the existence of the soul as the highest truth. Sometime after 362, the monk Yü Fa-k'ai (306?–365), while agreeing with Min-tu that mundane reality was indeed a function of consciousness and that an empty mind would indeed see no form, claimed that beyond this lower subject–object consciousness there lay the transcendental Mind:

> This triple world is a dwelling for a long night. Mental consciousness is the subject of a great dream. If one awakens to the fundamental emptiness of this triple world, deluded consciousness will be exhausted. (T 65.94c.22)

> The assembly of existents which is perceived now are all perceptions in a dream. If one awakens from the great dream after dawn brightens this long night, then delusions are overturned, the deluded consciousness is extinguished, and the triple world is seen to be empty. At that time there is no place from which anything arises, yet no place which has no arising. (T 42.94b.4–7)

Freed from the dream in which there is a dichotomy of subject and object, this Mind becomes *shen* (soul, spirited) and united with emptiness.

unreal dream	perceived by	deluded consciousness
true emptiness	one with	the enlightened soul

This is the theory of *Han-shih* (Mind incorporates consciousness as its mundane function) or *Shih-han* (the world of objects, mundane reality, is subsumed under the function of deluded consciousness).

4. Tao-i also accepted the dependence of reality on consciousness. Sometime after 365 he proposed that the mind is like a magician that can create objects of illusion. However, he insisted that beyond this illusion of life and death that constitutes the mundane truth, there lies the "real self" (soul) that cannot be untrue:

> All dharmas are the same as magical illusions. Because they are the same as magical illusions they are called the mundane truth. The mind and spirit are real and not empty; this is the highest truth. If the spirit is empty, then to whom are the teachings given, and who cultivates the Path from ignorance to sagehood? Therefore it is clear that the spirit is not empty. (T 65.95a.4–7)

illusions of the mind	the mundane truth
true spirit of the sage	the highest truth

This *Huan-hua* (Reality is Illusion) thesis advanced beyond the *Pen-wu* thesis. The latter saw being as evolving out of non-being. Here being (reality) is non-being (illusion).

5. Another thesis claiming to show how form can be real and empty at the same time came from Yü Fa-lan (d. 355). This *Yuan-hui* or Confluence of Conditions thesis argued that phenomena when reduced to their component parts can be shown to be unreal. Although it avoided a *reductio ad nihilum*, it hardly moved beyond Nāgasena's argument for the provisionality of the chariot in the *Milindapañhā*. It realized the whole was unreal, but it still accepted the reality of the parts. This was the most Hīnayānist of the attempts to digest Mahāyāna emptiness. Surviving records do not indicate if the issue of the *shen* was involved here.

6. Although both Tao-i and Yü Fa-k'ai already tried to combine the *Pen-wu* thesis and the *Hsin-wu* antithesis, the boldest synthesis came with Chih Tun, who performed a dialectical triple turn. First, he reduced reality to emptiness, probably by the *Yuan-hui* method. Then he reaffirmed the reality, agreeing with Min-tu that forms remained form no less.

Form is empty   Form is form
nonbeing   being
being and nonbeing are of the mind
higher than mind is soul

Finally he traced both of these opposing positions to the discrimination innate to the mind. By emptying this mind, being and non-being can be overcome and one awakes to the eternal soul. This *Chi-se* (Abiding with Form) theory was connected with an interpretation of the Roving Freedom chapter in the *Chuang-tzu*, according to which the sage abides physically in the world of form (hence *chi-se*), while in spirit he roves freely in the mysteries, being thus "a thing in relation to things without becoming ever a thing among things"; that is, the sage is "in but not of the world."

Whatever the flaws of these six theses, they emulated the bodhisattvic calling to transcend saṃsāra and yet be faithful to the earth; to intuit emptiness in the midst of form. Still, these fourth-century figures had not the benefit of knowing Kumārajīva's translation of the Mādhyamika śāstras of Nāgārjuna and Āryadeva. They were all biased in some way and failed to comprehend the Middle Path, though they fared better than those who showed an obsession with ātman in disputing Min-tu's thesis. Kumārajīva corrected both mistakes and approved Seng-chao's critique of them in the latter's *Pu-chen k'ung lun* (Emptiness of the Unreal). The first expositor of Mādhyamika in China, Seng-chao drew the curtain on the early theses. He did so by demolishing the three representative theses. First he faulted the *Pen-wu* for its ontological nihilism. "It made the mistake of prizing nonbeing at the expense of being," thus missing the Middle. He went on to undermine the *Hsin-wu* thesis, faulting it for its psychological reductionism. "It failed to prove the emptiness of form in and of itself," resorting instead to what was really a Hīnayāna theory of the *dhātu,* to the effect that an object is real only when sight and consciousness are intact. Finally he took to task the *Chi-se* thesis, a poor schizophrenic solution, one that had the body abiding with other bodies while the disembodied spirit roved in emptiness. He accused Chih Tun of a causalist destruction of reality, and of emptying form only in relation to other forms. "Form as form is empty; it needs not be emptied relative to other existent forms."

Seng-chao detected the common flaw in all six theses, which may be stated as follows: they all assumed the existence of two separate categories of realities, being or form on the one hand, and non-being or emptiness on the other. It was only after that that they sought the coincidence of the opposites. Thus the *Pen-wu* school began with form and ended with emptiness. In avoiding that nihilistic reduction, Min-tu fell into the other trap, the independence of form. The dualism was even more obvious in the division of the two levels of truth in Tao-i and Yü Fa-k'ai. Even Chih Tun failed to get out of that quandary. After successfully emptying form, he reasserted its being again "different from emptiness." Even as he eulogized the freedom of the sage, that led him to dissect him into body and soul, one half with things and the other half above things. Seng-chao showed that the dictum "form is emptiness" does not collapse two entities into one. There is only one reality to begin (and to end) with. The innate unreality of form is what is meant by emptiness; the self-sufficiency of concepts is exposed as self-negating. That is the substance of his essay on the "Emptiness of the Unreal," which its title reflects.

The Satyasiddhi Detour

One might have expected Seng-chao's rigorous application of Mādhyamika dialectics to put an end to the errors of his compatriots. That, however, was not to be. In fact, he himself was not counted as the first in the lineage of the later San-lun (Mādhyamika, Three Treatises) school. For the next century and a half, there was a regression to a diluted version of the emptiness philosophy known as Satyasiddhi or Ch'eng-shih, named after a thesis by Harivarman (no longer extant in Sanskrit) translated by Kumārajīva late in his career. Prized originally for its criticism of Hīnayāna Abhidharma, the *Ch'eng-shih-lun* (T 32.239–373), still trapped by some of the same assumptions, led the Southerners astray.

Yet no detours of the mind are ever taken without reasons. Why was it that these Southerners ranked Harivarman on a par with Nāgārjuna? What integrity did they find in their own system to which the later dismissals of it may blind us? The intellectual climate of the fifth century was more complicated than is commonly supposed. First, there was no continuity between the prajñā interest of the fourth century and the Nāgārjuna-guided scholarship of the fifth. In between came the recent legacy of Abhidharma to which even Tao-an, the leading *Pen-wu* prajñā-theorist, inclined in his last years. Whereas Kumārajīva's arrival was delayed, Saṅghadeva's was not. The latter introduced Abhidharma to China and taught it at Lu-shan in the last decade of the fourth century. That legacy Kumārajīva attacked with passion in his *Ta-chih-tu-lun*, but lesser minds under him, including even Seng-chao, could not dislodge it. Both North and South felt that abhidharmic impact, the latter not awakening to the mistake until the arrival of new San-lun masters from the North in the sixth century.

Second, further complications were created by the arrival of the *Nirvāṇa Sūtra*, a text unknown to Kumārajīva, and for which he had not prepared his students. (Tradition, of course, regarded his *Lotus Sūtra* as anticipating its doctrine and even granted him insight into Buddha-nature.) The new doctrine of a Buddha-nature (*gotra*) was one that Nāgārjuna's *Mādhyamika-kārikā* explicitly disallowed. Harivarman of course knew no better, but it happened that his Satyasiddhi did posit One Truth (higher than the Two Truths) as the real truth, *satya*, which by sheer coincidence was what the *Nirvāṇa Sūtra* also called its one, real Truth, namely, the Buddha-nature *qua mahātman*. But what Harivarman had as his One Real Truth is simply the third of the old Four Noble Truths: *nirodha* (nirvāṇa) was judged real because it liberates; the other three (suffering, its cause, and the path) were deemed provisional because they all come under saṃsāra. This was a costly confusion, for it would drag the epistemic double-truth theory back into the ontological dualism of the Four Noble Truths.

Third, Seng-chao was not entirely free of Taoist assumptions and could therefore not prevent his being misread later. In his *Wu pu-ch'ien-i* (Things Do Not Move), he might even have taught the Ch'eng-shih masters not so much critical dialectics as linguistic license. In seeking to demonstrate the fallacy in the common assumption of the reality of motion, Seng-chao lapsed back momentarily into the Sarvāstivāda division of past, present, future as three discrete time brackets, so defined that things of one time could not logically move into another. His ultimate goal, however, was not to show that things do not move, but that what people take to be motion, the knowledgeable one does not, and, moreover, that things can be both moving and not moving at the same time. This could be read as a three-tiered vision of truth, in which motion is the commoner's view, immovability the sage's view, and the identification of the two the highest truth.

This interest in finding the necessary unity of the two truths in a third (and final) truth was not present in the *Mādhyamika-kārikā*. It seems, in any case, to have inspired the next round of speculation on form and emptiness, on the mistaken assumption that by the Middle Path is meant some unity of being and non-being in a higher truth. The simplest version of this would be as follows:

Highest Truth	True but empty
————————	Paradoxes meet in the Middle
Mundane Truth	Real but False

Clearly, some sophistry is involved in the equation. The new Two Truths speculation snowballed in complexity. In practice it meant explaining how a thing can be real at one level and yet unreal at another, and how the two merge in the One Real. An early reviewer of attempts made to date was the lay thinker Chou Yung. He typologized the major options as three in his *San-tsung-lun* (On Three Schools):

To empty the provisionally real	Nihilism
To not empty provisional reality	Realism
To see the provisionally real as empty	Middle

A good explanation by way of analogy of what the three meant was offered in the early fifth century by Seng-ch'üan, one of the founding figures of the new San-lun school being established in Mount She.

Nihilism:	Rodent-gnawed-empty chestnut no meat within but a shell without
Realism:	A melon bobbing in and out of water now you see it, now you don't
Middle:	(no metaphor: total union of opposites) the provisional as the empty

The first two positions cheat in their account of how things can be real yet false. The first empties the substance but retains the appearance of reality, thus dividing the two truths spatially, inner versus outer. The second overcomes this, but only by substituting a temporal distinction, whereby the same reality is *in toto* there or not there depending on circumstance. Only the last position sees how form is directly empty and emptiness is immediately form. As usual, the last option is never fully explained.

It is not always clear either where Chou Yung's own choice falls. Sometimes he is judged to be holding the third position (which is natural); sometimes he is put in the second (in retrospective evaluation); sometimes he is placed at some Archimedean point overseeing all three (a position he deserves; see below). The new San-lun masters at She-shan eventually dismantled the Satyasiddhi school by exposing some of their basic mistakes. I shall mention only one. If the earlier six theses of emptiness misread emptiness, then the Ch'eng-shih masters basically misread the Middle Path, by taking it positively, like the Confucian Mean or the Taoist Harmony, as necessarily uniting the two truths, like yin and yang, in some higher Ultimate. Orthodox San-lun knew better: emptiness is not some entity and the Middle Path does not affirm; the empty is the middle, the neither/nor that functions as a means to being free from all ontic assumptions. It knew that all words were play, all theses mere fingers pointing to the moon.

The Ch'eng-shih masters might not have realized true emptiness, but they did taste freedom from the bondage of reason to the extent that they were able to transcend the Taoist categories of being and non-being, and they were in their way liberated from the mundane. We may illustrate this Buddhist sophistication from an exchange between Chou Yung and Chang Jung: the Taoist Chang Jung was arguing that Lao-tzu also knew the identity of being and non-being. Chou Yung pointed out that Lao-tzu only knew "being comes out of non-being" but not "being is non-being." Chang Jung, like other Taoists of the time, had learned to read the "double mystery" in chapter 1 of the *Lao-tzu* in the style of Mādhyamika's *śūnyatā-śūnyatā* (double negation: emptying emptiness).

> These two [being and non-being] appear at the same time
> But are somehow given different names.
> That is the mystery.
> Mystery of mysteries [*chung-hsüan*, double mystery]
> It is the key to all mysteries.

He cited this to show that Lao-tzu knew the same identity of form and emptiness as the Buddha. A believer in the unity of the Three Teachings, Chang Jung died with the emptiness sūtras on one side, the *Tao-te ching* and the *Analects* on the other. But on this occasion Chou Jung hinted that his own position transcended all three schools. His position was no position, but consisted purely in the exposure of the limits of other positions. In this he anticipated the Prāsaṅgīka ideal of San-lun and could indeed be seen as its forerunner, rather than merely as the proponent of the best of the three Ch'eng-shih options.

The Nirvāṇa School

Shortly after Kumārajīva, Nirvāṇa scholarship—studies of the *Nirvāṇa Sūtra*—overshadowed even the interest in the emptiness philosophy per se. Since purist San-lun rejected a positive Buddha-nature, Nirvāṇa scholars aligned themselves eventually with Ch'eng-shih. In the Southern dynasties, Buddhist thinkers devoted much time to speculation on this *mahātman* and its whereabouts in human person. The founder of the Nirvāṇa tradition was Tao-sheng, who discovered the doctrine of "universal Buddha-nature" even before the full text arrived at Chien-k'ang in 430; he was temporarily expelled from the Buddhist community as a result. (Initially the *Nirvāṇa Sūtra* excluded the *icchantikas* from enlightenment; only in a later section was this judgment reversed.) In the end the doctrine became so central to Sinitic Mahāyāna that the Fa-hsiang, or Yogācāra, school, which revived the category of the unredeemable *icchantika*, has been summarily classed as Hīnayānist ever since! Tao-sheng's career reveals the intellectual excitement and confusion of the time and falls into four phases. First, he was initiated by an emptiness theoretician, putting down his roots in Neo-Taoism. Then he studied Abhidharma at Lu-shan under Saṅghadeva, who declared Mahāyāna to be the work of the devil. It was at this time, following apparently Hui-yüan's reading of the Saṅghadeva-translated *Abhidharma-hṛdaya*, that he came up with his first and simplest theory of sudden enlightenment. This text had declared that after all defilements had been replaced by purity, then the final removal of these pure karma that still tie us to saṃsāra is to be "in one moment" and "without gradations." Tao-sheng paraphrased this to form the twin theories of "(ultimate) good produces no (more karmic) retribution" and "enlightenment has (then) to be all of a sudden." Since others at the time also accepted the necessary discontinuity between saṃsāra and nirvāṇa, they saw no cause to contest this expression of old truths in startlingly new epigrams.

However, in his third phase this changed. The news of the arrival of Kumārajīva brought Tao-sheng to Ch'ang-an to study with the Kucha master. Kumārajīva had already acknowledged that the *Lotus Sūtra* had an "esoteric teaching of the Tathāgata"—its *ekayāna* had redeemed the arahant as a Buddha. Tao-sheng now disputed the difference between the Three Vehicles (*triyāna:* those of the śrāvaka, pratyekabuddha, and bodhisattva). Going beyond Kumārajīva, who still accepted three grades of achievement within the ten-stages (*daśa-bhūmi*) scheme for the enlightened trio, Tao-sheng argued uncompromisingly that if the Principle (of *ekayāna*) is One, then enlightenment into the One has to happen at one stroke. This controversial claim divided him from the Three Vehicle theorists. Yao Hsing and his brother Yao Sung joined in the controversy, and Seng-chao, representing the *Prajñāpāramitā* tradition which accepted the *triyāna* distinction, was recruited to defend gradualism. That he did, in the essay "Nirvāṇa is Nameless." Thus far, the debate did not involve the *Nirvāna Sūtra*, but even before the controversy ended, Tao-sheng discovered the doctrine of universal Buddha-nature unaided by scripture. It was only when the full text arrived that he was vindicated and only still later, in a preface to the Southern text of the *Nirvāṇa Sūtra,* that he added "recognizing one's innate Buddha-nature" to his prior instant-enlightenment argument. Later the Ch'an tradition taught a similar but actually more radical formula, and it claimed Tao-sheng as its own.

In fusing the traditions of emptiness, *ekayāna,* and Buddha-nature, instant-enlightenment Tao-sheng was in many ways ahead of his time. He had no real successor except perhaps Fa-yao. Most Nirvāṇa scholars were gradualists. They embraced Satyasiddhi and accommodated *triyāna.* In their analysis of Buddha-nature, they tended to be ontic in approach (where is it?) and causalists in practice (what four causal modes are there?). These mistakes were later corrected by the San-lun masters after they had adjusted Mādhyamika to accept the doctrine of a not-empty Buddha-nature (*aśūnya-tathāgatagarbha*), and by the revival of *ekayāna* by the T'ien-t'ai (Lotus) school that absorbed the Nirvāṇa scholarship under itself.

Emperor Wu of Liang and the Synthesis of Schools

Nirvāṇa and Satyasiddhi scholarship flourished together in the Liang dynasty under Emperor Wu, who came to the throne, like his predecessors, through bloodshed, but who was a great patron of the faith. This most cultured of dynasty founders was brought up on the classics and nurtured by religious Taoism before his change of heart, after which he renounced Taoism and ruled as a bodhisattva disciple of the Buddha, modeling himself and his reign after the teachings of the *Aśoka Sūtra.* He built stūpas, released criminals, suspended capital punishment, and even pledged himself as a serf to a temple so that the court had to ransom him back more than once. He was pious enough to retire from active rule, eventually losing his kingdom to more worldly men.

It was during his reign that Fan Chen disputed once more the Buddhist belief in the immortal soul. The best of such critics, whose Socratic dialectics recalls the *Milindapañhā,* Fan Chen compared the *shen* to the keenness of the blade of a knife, the body being the knife. Indeed, the *shen* is the life of the body, but no matter how keen its intelligence, who has ever heard of it surviving the body? One might as well speak of the function of a blade surviving the destruction of the substance that is the knife. So powerful was the thesis that Emperor Wu convened the court to answer it. In the end, Emperor Wu himself defended the Dharma in a treatise wherein he identified the "indestructible" soul with the "permanent" Buddha-nature; this seems to be the first time the two qualifiers were confused. The emperor was following the Satyasiddhi and Nirvāṇa scholarship of the time. Since the *Nirvāṇa Sūtra* had limited Buddha-nature to sentient beings ("Tiles and stones have no Buddha-nature"; they do not suffer and have no use for liberation from suffering), most Nirvāṇa scholars accordingly located it in the heart-mind. Thus the monk Pao-liang, a protégé of the emperor, identified the transcendental tathāgatagarbha (embryonic Buddha) mind as the Buddha-nature. Since the tathāgatagarbha in man is paradoxically taintless yet tainted, fully enlightened though temporarily trapped in the body, Pao-liang also considered it to be the locus for the Unity of the Two Truths. Here in the mind, saṃsāra and nirvāṇa would meet. Thinking along similar lines, Emperor Wu identified the transmigrating consciousness with the Buddha-nature, a risky move since this Mahāyāna *mahātman* should be more than a Hīnayāna skandha. However, he divided the *hsin-shen* (mind-spirit) into two parts—the mind, which is transcendental, and the spirit or consciousness, which transmigrates—and, more significantly, he turned Fan Chen's materialist paradigm of substance–function on its head. Rather than see the mind as function of the body, he saw the transcendental mind as substance and the transmigrating consciousness as function. Conceding that this deluded consciousness disintegrates with the fleeting phenomena, he claimed that beyond it lies the unchanging Buddha-nature which is destined for enlightenment:

Mind as Buddha-nature	Invariable substance	One with Principle
Mundane Consciousness	Mutable function	Dies with phenomena

This is a variation of the Han-shih thesis we met earlier.

This debate on the immortality of the soul was the last and the most meaningful of the series. By T'ang, most Chinese accepted karmic theodicy and the judgment of the soul; most informed Buddhists also recognized that the real issue is never one of body versus soul, but rather of form (*rūpa*) and consciousness (*citta*). The emperor, by making the enlightened mind the substance behind the deluded consciousness, may have initiated a development of great historical significance, in that the same mode of thinking is found in the *Awakening of Faith in Mahāyāna* (probably a sixth-century Chinese composition), which was to influence all schools of Buddhism in the Far East.

The Ascendancy of the Buddha Jewel

Images of the Buddha

The rule "Follow the Dharma, not the person" that Śākyamuni taught could not be applied to the Buddha himself, who, as the one who discovered the

Dharma and founded the Saṅgha, was revered by all. In Hīnayāna he was considered extinct and the world was seen as now without a Buddha; yet the presence of his refuge was never questioned. This felt presence was what inspired the *Lotus Sūtra* to declare his extinction a charade and to proclaim the Buddha everlasting and able to manifest himself at any time, even to the common person lacking spiritual vision. This claim was made vivid by artistic representation. Buddhism was originally aniconic; enlightened realization of *anātman* and nirvāṇa defied anthropomorphic representation. The Buddha was represented only by such symbols as the stūpa, his footprint, a sun-wheel. Images of the Buddha first appeared in Mathura and in Gandhāra, the latter a place exposed to Greek influence. These made him a living, approachable personality, giving birth to a new type of image contemplation. To the extent that Mahāyāna glorified the Buddha in its teaching and meditated on him in practice, Buddhist art aided its rise and remained an indispensable part of its cause. It helped to elevate the Buddha above the Dharma and the Saṅgha, making him the head and the others the limbs, as the *Nirvāṇa Sūtra* puts it.

Although Buddhism spread into Central Asia in the first century B.C.E., the images followed only in the second half of the first century C.E., reaching China later. Prince Ying of Han (d. 71) had at best only a picture; Chia Yung (ca. 120) possessed a statue—a surprisingly large one considering the date. In the Chin period, Buddha-images remained rare. The few artists knowledgeable enough to produce them were mostly Central Asians. The names of some Chinese painters of the Buddha have been preserved, but that their names are known indicates how rare they were. In the early fifth century, Hui-yüan owned a small jeweled image, a rarity. For an image on a larger scale, the Lu-shan circle apparently had to be satisfied with a shadow of the Buddha that appeared on a cliff. In any case, the Southern monks probably felt little need of statues, enthralled as they were by the formless dharmakāya. They tended to make the form of the Buddha, the *rūpakāya,* a mere expediency. Tao-sheng, a lover of emptiness rather than form, went so far as to say that the Buddha, meaning Enlightenment itself, really had no *rūpakāya,* or none that mattered. He also saw Pure Lands as sheer fictions, creations of the mind.

In the North, in contrast, Dharmakṣema's emphasis on the liturgical tradition had prepared the Buddhists there to appreciate the Buddha-form as transcendence incarnate, as what the trikāya (Three Bodies) theory would later recognize as the numinous and power-endowed Bliss Body or saṃbhogakāya. The Jātakas he translated also reminded men of the human Buddha; these became a major motif in later cave art. Liang-chou also had better access to central Asian artistry and probably inherited its iconic Pure Land meditative tradition more fully. The flow of Buddha-images was impeded after 311, and it was not until the area was conquered and the route between China and India reopened in 439 that there was suddenly a flood of "sūtras and images eastward," as Wei Shou recalled. The Liang-chou monks who ended up in P'ing-cheng brought with them their artists, so that in 444 when the edict was posted banning "private household monks," it also indicted "privately kept artisans." In 446, three thousand artisans were brought from Ch'ang-an to P'ing-cheng. The nomads had apparently been content to live in tents, but now these wood and plaster artisans were to build new palaces for them. During the Buddhist revival in 452, these artists must have cooperated with their Central Asian counterparts in glorifying the Buddha, for when, around 460, the Yung-kang project started, the monumental size and consistency of style there indicate that we are dealing with work teams (mostly Chinese then) under the supervision of master craftsmen (mostly Central Asian). By about 480, a change of style under Chinese influence was already visible. Later, when the Wei capital was moved to Loyang (494), the new Lung-men cave projects showed even more Sinicization of the figures and their features. It is clear that the craft of image-making was no longer the monopoly of an esoteric few.

That many private parties had images before 444 can be seen in the Chinese-compiled *Brahma Net Sūtra,* which prohibited the impious sale of statues (a reference to the persecution that prompted such sale). This was much more the case in Loyang, where, by the second decade of the sixth century, cheap replicas of Buddha-images were mass-produced for easy sale, to the annoyance of the author of the *Hsiang-fa chueh-i ching* (Sūtra to Resolve Doubts in the Age of the Semblance Dharma), who lamented the traffic in these "reprehensible products lacking the complete set of marks . . . and deplorable half-bodied busts." Monks who had once had control of the production of sacred images were understandably incensed by such trade in paper gods. What they and the conservative purist who wrote this sūtra overlooked was that such cheap replicas made popular private devotion to the Buddha possible for the first time. Art had, if not created, at least enhanced a lay-dominated and Buddha-centered piety. This development undercut the monastic order and its older, more sober, elder-centered piety.

Architecture and the Rise of Temple Communities

Architecture, too, aided the rise of this new Buddha-centered piety. Worship required the proper setting in Buddha-temples, *saṅghārāma.* Temple-centered piety flowered in Loyang in the North and Chien-k'ang in the South in the early sixth century. The difference between monasteries and temples is that temples celebrate the Buddha Jewel, while monasteries organize the Saṅgha refuge. Historically, Buddha temples originated with the stūpa, which housed the Buddha ashes representing the Buddha after his death. Monasteries began with the vihāra housing the Saṅgha, cloister cells that went back to simple sheds used during the monsoon retreat. Originally these two institutions were separate; the Buddha was supposed to have entrusted the stūpa to the laity and the Dharma to the monks. (In fact, the Buddha is recorded to have asked that his ashes be scattered without commemoration.) The laity were allowed to worship relics to gain a better rebirth, while the monks were told to be a lamp unto themselves, to seek out nirvāṇa by following the Dharma, not the person. Nāgasena the Elder still openly disapproved of stūpa cults. Acceptable for the laity, such idolatry could never lead to nirvāṇa. The Mahāsāṅghika school judged such worship more meritorious, but even the *Prajñāpāramitā* sūtras, which stressed the dharmakāya, disapproved of stūpa worship. It is the Buddhayāna wing of Mahāyāna, the *ekayāna* of the *Lotus Sūtra,* that promoted this cult. Thus, the two lines of development originally ran parallel. But when stūpa grew into pagoda and vihāra became monastery, we find each promoting the other in one site. That the Buddha and the Saṅgha should be found in one complex, as in all Buddhist countries today, was a later development, violating the principle of the separation of the jewels which prohibits the commingling of their separate properties. By the time Buddhism entered China in the Han dynasty, that principle had been relaxed or judiciously circumvented. There, from the beginning, stūpa and cloister merged.

Buddhist architectural plans could not be well known then, and monks were few in number. Modeled on an ancestral hall with the Buddha as the ancestor, the hall in which Chia Yung installed his Buddha-image was large enough to hold three thousand visitors, and may therefore be called a temple, though such early structures are not to be identified with the mature temple complex. The earliest surviving example of a classic temple structure, modeled on Sui at the earliest, can be seen in Nara Japan. The classic temple is one with a large, public atrium in the foreground where the pagoda and the Buddha-hall are located, and a monastic cloister at the back.

	monk-cloister	nirvanic withdrawal
Buddha Hall Pagoda	public atrium	nirvāṇa=saṃsāra
	temple market	samsaric involvement

Each part has its own history and symbolic meaning. The monk-cloister preserves the old vihāra structure; the domain of nirvanic monks, the area is out of bounds to laymen (or tourists). The atrium extends to the courtyard the cells shared. Here monks gathered for their fortnightly confession, which laymen who observed the eight abstinences on that day were allowed to attend. Into this atrium the stūpa was introduced. Images came later and had then to be housed separately, in what is now the Buddha hall. (By T'ang, as images displaced relics, the Buddha hall displaced the pagoda.) Unlike the cloister, the atrium is for Buddha-devotion, and here the layman is made welcome, and usually served by monk-clerics. Caught between the nirvanic withdrawal of the cloisters and the samsaric entrapment of the temple market outside the main gate, the atrium symbolizes the nirvanic Buddha living among samsaric men. This is where "saṃsāra is nirvāṇa; nirvāṇa is saṃsāra."

The temple, already in India, created its own form of piety, differing from that of the monastery. The expansive atrium allowed greater lay participation; the image encouraged devotion; the size of the Buddha (sixteen feet high) would dwarf any monk, however holy. The laity could directly approach the Buddha, bypassing the mediation of the monk, and might even claim access to the Dharma, previously monopolized by the Saṅgha and prohibited by the Vinaya from "being taught to the unqualified." This development greatly affected the Saṅgha, and created division in its ranks: should it reject or incorporate, ignore or assist, this extracanonical, extramonastic development of lay-led Buddha-centered devotionalism?

The Three Jewels and the Patterns of Conversion

In the pattern of Chinese conversions to Buddhism, the successive centrality of Dharma, Saṅgha, and Buddha in the lives of the converts may be detected. This has been brought out indirectly by an analysis Miyakawa Hisayuki made of the biographies of the eminent monks. It appears that the early converts to Buddhism during the Wei-Chin were touched primarily by ideas or the Dharma. They tended to be men of good family background who were enticed by the emptiness philosophy at a relatively mature age. Hui-yüan, who left the world upon hearing Tao-an lecture and who then judged Confucianism and Taoism inferior to the Buddha-dharma, was a classic convert of this type. Chih Tun apparently did not keep the vow of poverty: he had enough money held in private trust (which is permissible) to contemplate buying up a hillside for his final retirement at scenic K'uai-chi (which is a bit extravagant). This reflects the better-than-average background of many of these early converts. This is not to say that Buddhism was an intellectual toy of the rich and famous. Many of the unrecorded converts must have come from poorer backgrounds.

22. *Buddhist Stele*,
ca. 535–45 C.E.
Sculpture—Chinese.
Western Wei Dynasty
(535–557 C.E.).
Dark grey limestone.
98 x 31¾ x 13 inches.

Still, the elitist bias of the reports underlines the fact that before the fifth century the finer rules of the Vinaya were not yet known and the Saṅgha had not yet become sufficiently endowed to recruit at will. The ideal that "the four castes (in India) should flow like four streams into the one body" in the brotherhood of monks could not, because of material limitations, yet be realized.

A change occurred in the fifth century. The number of monks jumped; the average age when they joined the order dropped; and there were more cases of monks whose family backgrounds were not notable enough to be included in their biographies. Seng-chao was a poor copier; Fa-hsien entered the monastery at the age of three. The Saṅgha was becoming increasingly self-sufficient and could recruit from a larger social base and from every age-group. Now the catalyst of conversion was not love for abstract ideas but rather personal tragedies that brought an awareness of life's transience and human suffering. Thus, Seng-tu, a presentable youth of Eastern Chin, betrothed to a Miss Yang, awoke to the fact of impermanence through the sudden deaths of his widowed mother and of Miss Yang's parents, and thereupon renounced the world, leaving his betrothed to take care of the funerals. She then pleaded for his return in a series of poems, voicing Confucian and Taoist sentiments:

> The great Way is endless,
> Heaven and earth will endure . . .
> Though man born into this world
> Passes through it like a fleeting shadow,
> Still fame and glory may flourish
> If one but daily prepare for them,
> As music pleases the ears
> And fine gowns the body adorn.
> So why should you, your head shorn,
> Deny being through your nihilistic escape? (T 50.351a)

Seng-tu wrote a Buddhist response:

> Neither fate nor chance comes to an end.
> Even rocks will crumble one day.
> So upstream (from the polluted world) I fare,
> Leaving all mundane glories behind.
> With head aloof, I chant a simple tune,
> My body warmed well by a cotton gown.
> Pleasurable this world might be,
> But what then of the next?
> Good and evil are my karma due,
> I would lose myself for others' sake. (T 50.351b)

Miss Yang eventually joined him by becoming a nun herself. Though the Dharma played a part in the conversion, it is not abstruse emptiness, but suffering, impermanence, karma, and rebirth that led Seng-tu to leave the world. These urgent sentiments reflect the social dislocation of the time, which impelled people to take refuge in the Saṅgha. This is clearer in Miss Yang's case. Her plea went out only when she realized that she, an orphan by her parents' death and a widow by his desertion, had "no support to lean on." The nunnery as refuge provided her both life and livelihood. This service the Saṅgha provided throughout the six dynasties.

We can detect a new pattern of conversion as early as the sixth century in Loyang and Chien-k'ang (though it is more salient in the T'ang): conversion becomes centered on the Buddha in a temple context, the average age of converts drops further by T'ang, and what triggers the conversion is often the emotional appeal of Buddhist art. The occasion of conversion is now neither intellectual nor painful anxiety, but, as it were, a sense of the sublime. Thus it is related that a three-year-old was brought to the temple by his mother and became so attached to the beauty of a Buddha-image that he refused to leave. The mother then entrusted him to the temple's care and he became a full monk on attaining the proper age. The intellectual deliberation of a Hui-yüan or the renunciation of a Seng-tu can scarcely be expected in the case of so young a convert. The child's longing to stay at the temple was conditioned by a culture converted to Buddhism, and by family life receptive to the calling. If the pious mother had not actually already pledged the child to the temple as part of a Buddhist vow, she was quite willing to accede to his wish. Many such cases come from the T'ang period, when future monks were often recruited from within the temple population itself. The old tension between filial piety and leaving the world had faded away. Parents wanted a son to be a priest and recognized the "greater filiality" of the renunciate. This hardly meant renouncing name and fame. Prestige, power, and wealth due the priesthood made it a standard way to achieve upward mobility through talent. The attractiveness of the calling led to an increase, from the sixth century on, in the number of eminent monks with good family background. The rapid development of art and architecture at the Buddha temple in late fifth-century China marked a watershed in Buddhist spirituality, one that pointed ahead to the increasing secularizing trend in T'ang.

The Saṅgha Household in Peril

That the Buddha should receive more veneration than the Saṅgha was not surprising. It was in the tradition almost from the start. Even now in Theravāda countries, the stūpa always attracts most donations, despite the saying, so often repeated by monks, that the Saṅgha is the unsurpassed field of merit! It is widely believed that donation to the Buddha, purest of all souls, generates more merit than donating to the Saṅgha, just as it is more meritorious to give to the pure Saṅgha than to ordinary folk. The Saṅgha, therefore, found it hard to object to the veneration of the Buddha, until there was cause for alarm, as happened at one time in India and then again in China. In the sixth century, in the North, the urban Buddha temples were draining the resources of the rural Saṅgha monasteries. In some cases, the Saṅgha grain was being used to build temples, contrary to T'an-yao's original design of creating a field of merit under the Saṅgha specifically in order to help the poor and needy. By law the goods of the Saṅgha are held in common trust for all members, to help them in need, and during T'an-yao's lifetime the Saṅgha grain was never used except by or for Saṅgha members. He was careful not to put peasants or grain under the Buddha-household which he also founded. The Buddha-household was made up of freed slaves and pardoned criminals, who tended to the Buddha, sweeping and washing the stūpa area (still the standard act of piety for stūpa devotees). By canon law based on the doctrine of the separation of the Three Jewels, property of any one jewel could not be freely appropriated by another. Had the peasant and his grain been placed under the Buddha Jewel, the whole welfare program would have been thwarted. The grain would have had to rot at the stūpa site (T 50.351b).

In the peace and prosperity of the Loyang period (494–520), urban economy and needs arose. There was a corresponding decline of the rural manor. Urban temples prospered, as both public and private resources, gold and silver, were lavished on the Buddha. The extravagance indicates that part of the Saṅgha grain must have been spent on this purpose. Critics of this trend defended the "merit-field of Saṅgha compassion" and lamented the plundering of the grain by secular and clerical officials, for in building another pagoda in the "merit-field of Buddha reverence," these heartless men neglected the needy. This was the burden of the *Hsiang-fa chueh-i ching*, otherwise known as the scripture calling for "aid to the orphaned and widowed." Ironically, the success of the Saṅgha household program had favored these abuses, for it was the newly acquired wealth of the Saṅgha, wealth such as Liang-chou had not previously enjoyed, that corrupted the program. Some of the clerical officials in charge of the grain became very wealthy; others were political appointees; sometimes the office was given to the highest bidder. T'an-yao, in popularizing the Buddha-image (though not the urban temple; he loved the suburban caves still), unwittingly made possible the ascendancy of Buddha over Saṅgha, and in consequence, of temple over monastery, and of city over countryside.

But criticism of the sea of humanity happily bowing before pagodas and Buddha halls need not detract from the positive aspect of this urban piety.

Mahāyāna itself was a product of "secular cities" such as Vaiśālī. Loyang's powerful lay patrons (householder bodhisattvas) therefore appreciated the Mahāyāna learning of the South. They identified with the figure of Vimalakīrti, long a Southern favorite, who now left his mark also on the North.

Urban Temples and the Genesis of Mahāyāna Lay Piety

The ascendancy of the urban temple may have occurred at the expense of the rural monastery, but it was to the advantage of the laity. Devotion to the Buddha liberated the laity from monastic tutelage. The city might be heartless but it was also the breeding ground for the truly generous householder-bodhisattva whose charity and wisdom put him on a par with the monk-bodhisattva. The atrium of a temple might not be as pure as the withdrawn cloisters; there was always some buying and selling afoot, usually of religious goods by the religious themselves. Yet this was where saṃsāra concretely met nirvāṇa: the nonabiding Buddha found his abode in the eternal in-between of cloister and marketplace. An oblique, and rather gossipy, testimony to this temple piety is given by a literary classic of this period, Yang Hsüan-chih's *Lo-yang ch'ieh-lan chi* (Record of the Loyang Temples; T 51.999a–1022b), which depicts the new Buddha-centered and lay-dominated piety of the city with unique vividness. Most temples it mentions were of the elite, but scholars make too much of this when they conclude that Loyang piety was elitist. More significant is the fact that only two temples were built by native monks; the majority were built by lay patrons, the more gorgeous ones naturally by the aristocracy; but all were open to even the poorest beggar. This contrasts with the days of Fo-t'u-teng and Tao-an, when stūpas and cloisters were built primarily under their guidance and few of these "monasteries" were in the public domain as tourist attractions.

Loyang *saṅghārāma* were, however, basically temples, not monasteries. Not all had cloisters for monks. Many private chapels only hired them to perform services on special occasions. Still others were simply residences turned into merit cloisters for the departed owner. Many more (not recorded) were simply shrines set up with no clerics in attendance. Even when monks were involved as sponsor or staff, they were typically not renunciate or contemplative, but rather Dharma masters, lecturers or preachers, leading Buddha devotion and acting as communal fund-raisers. Many temples were communal projects with donations from different wards or guilds to furnish a stone lamp, a pavilion, a shrine. To call these *ssu* "monasteries" or to call the piety there atypical or elitist is to misread the phenomenon of urban piety. As the sponsorship was mainly lay, the devotion was primarily to the Buddha. The temple legends accordingly told of the powers, not of holy men, but rather of the Buddha relics, etc. Relics appeared mysteriously at every temple site to mark its superhuman origin (T 51.1000a). Pagodas lost in mundane fires would take transmundane flight to show that the Buddha Body could never die (T 51.1002b). Images that walked and talked, shook their head or sweated (T 51.1007c), held a peculiar attraction, seeming not mere plaster and stone but the living, edifying incarnation of the Buddha himself. Since pious Loyang was also secular Loyang, the sacred and the profane fused. Temple *avadāna* told of both the holy and the downright earthy. Far too many of them are concerned with materialistic themes and with rumors of fortunes, both political and economic, made and lost overnight in the city (T 51.1010c). In one tale the Buddha was drafted as a policeman protecting temple property (namely, the golden statue of the Buddha himself) from thieves enticed no doubt by the extravagance of its display. This lack of discernment was part of the nature of urban lay piety, which was more zealous than rational. Unguided, it could and often did lapse into excess. Instead of the monk's cool discernment of saṃsāra and nirvāṇa, the citizens of Loyang were caught up in rumors of heavens and hells. A famous "living ghost" drove up the price of cypress coffins with a story of how people might be drafted into being soldiers in hell (T 52.1013a). Another report about the requirements for gaining admission into paradise had the city buying up new insurance by sponsoring sūtra-chanters and contemplatives (T 52.1005bc). Such popular emotional piety could, if tapped and led, bring great innovations. Reformations have often resulted from an optimum combination of popular zeal and learned reflection. The religion of the heart could also inspire the heartless city to generous action and even large-hearted theologies. Loyang was the foster parent to the universalist vision of the glorious T'ang, challenging the more parochial village piety of a darker era.

Meanwhile, immoderate times bred immoderate reactions. The city fell into the grip of a crisis, both political and religious, in 520. When, in that year, the magnificent Yung-ning pagoda went up in flames, the citizens wept and monks threw themselves into the flames (T 52.1002b). There was "not a day of peace" after this. The capital was sacked, its elite were massacred, and it was finally abandoned in 535 as the Wei empire disintegrated in civil war. When Yang visited the city before he wrote the memoirs, it lay in ruins. It is sad that whereas once the holy man predicted the rise of empires, the legends of Loyang temples after 520 could only prophesy the demise of reigns. Nor could relics, pagodas, and images save the temple itself from its doom. The concentration of wealth and power at the capital had brought disaster. The inequitable relations between rich and poor, city and countryside, had fomented discontent, creating an unprecedented schism within the Saṅgha. The tension between the new urban Buddha-devotion geared to cultivating private merit and the older commitment to Saṅgha welfare of the preceptory communities in the countryside led to a confrontation between the high priests serving the state in Loyang and the lower clerics working among the people in the farms. Not too long before, wayfaring monks spreading the gospel were considered normative, temple residency being seen as attachment to a site. Now in late Wei, this changed. Peasant uprisings were led by these itinerant lower clerics, regarded by the elite as impostors and agitators. A band of bandits who counted one killing as one rank in the *bodhisattva-bhūmi* is reported in 520, and the first Maitreyan revolt occurred soon after in Sui.

When Loyang eventually fell, Wei was split in two, and the illusion that Loyang was "a Buddha-kingdom on earth" (Bodhidharma in Yang's *Record*) crumbled. From this sudden disillusion rose the new Buddhism of Sinitic Mahāyāna.

The Passing of an Era

Dark rumors, such as always attended the end of a dynasty, were in circulation ever since the Yung-ning Temple, a monument of the Eternal Peace hoped for in the regency of Empress Dowager Hu, went up in smoke in 520. One rumor, said to have alarmed the once-pious Chou emperor Wu and turned him against the faith in 574, concerned the "black-capped" taking the kingdom away from him. Though this may not have referred only to black-capped monks, it indicates the renewed conflict between the Three Teachings and the shadow side of the alliance of politics and piety in the North since its founding.

Buddhist politics—state Buddhism is a misleading term—took different forms, some mild and nominal, others bold and absolute, depending less on theory than on implementation. When Wei emperor T'ai-tsu laid claim to being Buddha and king, he still bowed to Fa-kuo in matters of the spirit. Likewise, Emperor Shih-tsu (T'ai-wu) at first still celebrated Buddha's birthday, showering the parade of his statue with flowers from atop the gate. This smooth balance of the Wheels of the Dharma (secular rule and Buddha law) had been the ideal of Fo-t'u-teng. Teng's risky but effective magical dealings with warrior kings gave way to Fa-kuo's less charismatic and confrontational methods. As the Saṅgha became bureaucratized, the monks on the royal payroll were increasingly unable to withstand state pressure—unless they had the support of magnate families, as Southern monks had. The balance of the Two Wheels was increasingly tipped in favor of the ruler.

In contrast to Teng's buddhocratic ideal, whose dualistic framework is close to Hīnayāna, some post-Aśokan sūtras grant the ruler more power and present the Buddha as entrusting the Dharma directly to the ruler, charging him with the Aśokan duty of "purifying the Saṅgha" if conditions called for it. After the death of Emperor Shih-tsu and the end of the persecution of 446–452, the new ruler became the first to assume this role, acting as precept master and readmitting the defrocked monks into the Saṅgha. Though the South had no Tathāgata kings, there are indications of a similar trend. Thus, Liang emperor Wu, a "bodhisattva-disciple emperor," proposed himself as head of the Saṅgha, in order to form a closer alliance of the two wheels of power and authority. Though this proposal was repulsed by the monks, they were not necessarily any less worldly. Unlike Hui-yüan, these court monks wielded power and meddled in politics, often in an arrogant way; they too were seeking new ways to bridge might and right.

The North undertook a bold new religiopolitical venture based on the fact that the Buddha had the same set of supernatural marks as the Cakravartins (Cosmic Kings), and that Buddhist kings had always looked eagerly for these marks to verify their destiny as world conquerors. In furtherance of a monistic conception of Tathāgata kingship, five past Buddhas at Yün-kang were aligned with five past emperors, and commissioned images of the Buddha were found to exhibit a body mark of the current ruler. This radical monism generated new tensions. If the five (past) Buddhas went with the five past emperors, then could not the current ruler be identified with Śākyamuni, the sixth, and might not his future successor be regarded as Maitreya, the Future Buddha? Such notions underlay the Maitreyan peasant revolt later in Sui. The peasants did not politicize religion; they merely learned from their masters. Again, the monistic Dharma overseeing both secular and sacred could be so absolutist as to rule out accommodation with other ideologies, preparing further quarrels and persecutions.

This monistic religiopolitics had come from Liang-chou and ultimately from Dharmakṣema. Since Liang-chou Buddhists would take up arms and risk lives to defend the Dharma, this program cannot have been a passive accommodation to imperial rule. A Tun-huang fragment from this Liang-chou tradition shows that monks there never bowed to a ruler without demanding the same in return. It boldly cites the *Aśoka Sūtra* to the effect that even kings should never lie about the homage they paid in private to a śramaṇa: when a novice was asked not to reveal his king's homage to him, he responded by magically jumping into a bottle and asking the king to deny that spiritual feat. This text may have been part of the imperially approved clerical code issued in 493 in which the Saṅgha was granted full autonomy. Thus, it cannot be claimed that it was servility toward the state that brought about the next persecution of the Buddhists in 574. It was the very power and independence of the *mahāsaṅgha* created by Liang-chou monks after the first persecution, and the grassroots support of the Saṅgha household, that pitted them against the Tathāgata-king, who sought to regain control of the religion.

The Final Conflict between the Three Teachings

However, the threat to the Saṅgha came not from Tathāgata-kings, whose title obliged them to defend the Dharma, but from Taoist and Confucian ideologues. The Confucian bureaucracy had grown in size and power, as the barbarian rulers themselves had increasingly adopted Chinese ways, as symptomized by the transference of the capital from the steppes to Loyang. Chou emperor Wu (r. 561–577), in a historic innovation, summoned and chaired a debate between the Three Teachings in order to judge their relative merits. The Three Teachings were well represented (Taoism had by this time a sizable canon of its own), and the ruler acted neither as adversary nor as advocate of any tradition, but as final judge. The Buddhists and the Taoists traded the usual charges without realizing that the way the debate was set up was not in either's favor. The Confucians were inevitably victorious, for it was their tradition that granted the ruler the right to adjudicate between religions. The Chou emperor who modeled his rule after the classical Chou dynasty eventually supported Confucianism and proscribed both Buddhism and Taoism in 574. It is ironic, though understandable, that a Sinicized barbarian ruler in the North was converted to Confucian humanism to become more Chinese than the Chinese themselves in insisting on a classical purism when the Confucian rulers of the South had already generally granted Buddhism the same niche of liberty traditionally allowed to Taoism. The South now became the refuge of Buddhist monks fleeing the persecution in the North.

By 576, the victorious Chou army brought the persecution of Buddhism to Ch'i. A confrontation took place between the emperor and the monk Ching-yin Hui-yüan (523–592). Hui-yüan stood up to the emperor, acknowledged the presence of abuse in the Saṅgha (which should be corrected) but defended the sacred Saṅgha Jewel (which should not be destroyed). Seeing the emperor unmoved, Hui-yüan invoked his authority and threatened him with the bottomless Avīci hell if he should persist (T 50.490c). But no miracle occurred to shore up Hui-yüan's authority. The emperor turned purple with anger but, composing himself, replied that for the good of the people, he would go ahead with his plan and brave the devil himself. This was not a barbarian speaking. It was Confucius himself in his humanistic indifference to "matters beyond this life." The scholarly Hui-yüan was silenced. Even yogins would be impotent before such worldly wisdom. As a demonstration of his cool reason, the emperor let Hui-yüan and others flee southward.

It is commonly said that this led to the blending of the Northern practice (Ch'an meditation and Pure Land devotion) and Southern theory (Buddha-nature and emptiness) which produced the synthesis of Sinitic Mahāyāna. That is the view from a distance, but as the situation was then perceived by the Buddhists, the traumatic persecution signaled an irreversible step in the degeneration of the Buddhist Dharma. While, in Hinduism, the Dharma goes through cycles of birth and decline, in Buddhism, since the Dharma as teaching has a beginning in time, its decline is linear and can occur in a specific historic period. Speculation on how long the True Law would last went back to early Buddhism, as did the belief in a restoration under Maitreya the Future Buddha. These notions were already present in China in the fourth century, when eschatological texts were produced by both Buddhists and Taoists. In the early fifth century, Kumārajīva and his circle accepted a timetable of decline. The sense of urgency was, however, greater among Dharmakṣema's followers, largely because they were receptive to that dimension of the *Nirvāṇa Sūtra.* But though Chinese Buddhists know that the age of the True Dharma had gone, there was no popular anxiety about any immanent extinction of the Dharma until the second half of the sixth century in the North, at which time a complete scheme of the Three Ages of the Dharma (True Dharma, Semblance Dharma, Demise of the Dharma) was widely accepted. Even then, the last of these ages would have remained in a remote future, were it not for a 520 debate between the Buddhists and the Taoists that helped to move the date of the last age much closer.

Taoists claimed that Lao-tzu must have lived before the Buddha, that he had gone to India to instruct the Buddha, and that Buddhism was only a corrupt version of Taoism. In the debate of 520 at Loyang the Buddhists insisted on the temporal priority of the Buddha and countered the Taoist theory with the claim that Lao-tzu (and even Confucius) was only a manifestation of the Buddha (or certain bodhisattvas). Since for some time now the Confucians had also been blaming the patronage of Buddhism for shortening the lengths of the dynasties, it was doubly in the Buddhists' interest to push the date of the Buddha back, preferably to China's golden age, Chou. The monk T'an-mo-tsui placed the Buddha's birth long before Lao-tzu in early Chou: the Buddha was born in 1132 B.C.E., lived till eighty, and entered nirvāṇa in 1052 B.C.E.; this became the official dating in the Buddhist calendars of China, Korea, and Japan. Unfortunately, this change from the earlier, more modest date of 607 B.C.E. for the Buddha's *parinirvāṇa,* brought the decline of the Dharma nearer in time. One of the eschatological timetables had counted the True Dharma as lasting a thousand years and the Semblance Dharma another five hundred. This scheme gained widespread currency after 566. Suddenly, it appeared that the Degenerate Dharma age had dawned in

552, fifteen hundred years after *parinirvāṇa* according to the new dating. The recent disasters confirmed this, and the North succumbed to widespread hysteria; when the persecution came it seemed an inevitable doom.

Sinitic Mahāyāna can be interpreted existentially as the creative response to this crisis. To some, the fall of Loyang meant that the Buddha-kingdom ultimately was not to be built on earth. To others, the death of Emperor Wu of Liang showed that religion and politics should not mix. The initial responses of the two capitals to the crisis were, however, not that clear-headed. In the South, two bizarre mystagogues bewitched the capital: Chih-k'ung, whose soothsaying had people brooding anxiously on every remark he dropped; Master Fu (497–569), who claimed to be the teacher of all seven Buddhas and who drove a number of his followers to immolate themselves in his stead, presumably as a way to ward off the impending doom. Both were claimed by the Ch'an school later. The immediate reaction in the North was only slightly saner. Loyang's citizens had been looking for shortcuts to salvation. Now during the persecution, extreme ascetics forsook their bodies "in defense of the Dharma" and in emulation of Bodhisattva Medicine King of the *Lotus Sūtra,* who turned himself into a human candle to light up the universe. This was the ultimate *dāna,* the giving of oneself to save the Truth itself. Though scarcely compatible with the Buddha's Middle Path, this method could be defended in extreme circumstances, and it was not an impossible one, given the power of yogic *tapas,* a potent *citta-karma,* to avert lesser karmic fates. But neither the frenzy of the laity stirred up by mystagogues nor the extremism of the ascetics provided the lasting answer to the crisis. The new Buddhism that rose as a phoenix from the ashes of persecution had a different origin.

Prophetic Voices: Between City and Forest

Sinitic Mahāyāna is of Northern provenance, but was not born in Loyang. To speak of it as deriving from the synthesis of Northern practice and Southern theory caused by the migration of Northern monks to the South during the 574–576 persecution better describes its dynamic growth than its initial germination. Before this infusion of Southern theory into Northern practice, the vogue of "Southern learning" had already been introduced by Emperor Kao-tsu (r. 471–499), in the era of Loyang. If we read the expository writings produced by Northern masters in Loyang or in Yeh, it is hard to see how the North could be said to be poor in theory or why it needed a further infusion from the South. The migration of the Northern monks only enhanced a synthesis already begun; the further fusion aided the spread of Sinitic Mahāyāna in the South, but was not its cause. Nor may one say that

Sinitic Mahāyāna schools were born of Loyang learning. They were all critical of outward temple piety, of good works seeking earthly rewards, and of learning not rooted in practice. Yet they were anything but unlearned. They were characterized by urbane intelligence rather than rural parochialism, though reacting to the limitation of both city and countryside, village and forest, *saṅghārāma* and *āraṇyaka*. As so often in Buddhist history, the creative impulse came from both and neither, from that in-between twixt withdrawal and involvement.

This tension goes back to the Buddha, to primitive Buddhism, to the Theravāda polarity of village-dwelling and forest-dwelling monks, to the Mahāyāna contrast between urbane Vimalakīrti and wayfaring Subhūti. What was new in this sixth-century monastic reformation that became Sinitic Mahāyāna was the recent urban revival which had been followed so suddenly by collapse. The Sinitic Mahāyāna schools were born close enough to Loyang to catch the excitement of new ideas, but not so close as to be drawn into its secularity or the hysteria following its fall. The new Yogācāra of the Daśabhūmika or Ti-lun school at Loyang produced several scholars, but did not develop to become one of the Sinitic Mahāyāna schools; it was too bookish and cerebral. Yet this school touched the lives of T'ien-t'ai masters and inspired the Hua-yen school later. Again, T'an-luan of the Pure Land faith did not belong to Loyang circles, yet he possessed Vasubandhu's commentary on the *Pure Land Sūtra* and his temple was close enough to the capital to capture imperial attention in time. Still more typical was Bodhidharma, who visited the two capitals but chose to retire to Mount Sung outside Loyang, where he acquired a small but distinguished following.

The Three Periods Sect

Before examining these new schools, we must look at a school—or, rather, sect—which was quite unlike them and was disowned by them as they were by it. It appeared in Sui but should be considered here, for it was the only sect still solidly rooted in the tradition of Liang-chou piety. A common trait of the Sinitic Mahāyāna schools is their critical attitude to the donative piety of the six dynasties. As Bodhidharma said, "[Such merit-making is] of no merit whatsoever." Instead of the path of good works, they espoused faith, speculative wisdom, and mysticism. Against a faith in history and the historical Buddha, they showed a marked disillusionment with history as they looked either to a transcendental Śākyamuni, to cosmic Vairocana, to the Pure Land, or to some timeless Buddhahood within. The Three Periods sect, though endorsing these "higher paths," never abandoned the older, more down-to-earth hope in this world and reliance on simple, materialistic "good works."

The founder of the Three Periods sect was Hsin-hsing, a meditating monk like Bodhidharma. He took full cognizance of the arrival of the Degenerate Dharma, as Pure Land masters would. He was precept-conscious; even when he renounced the *bhikṣu-vinaya,* it was only so that he might return to the more demanding life of servitude befitting a novice. But instead of selecting one Buddha and one exclusive path to liberation, Hsin-hsing decided to worship all Buddhas and adopt universal practice. His followers honored all beings, dogs and cats included, as fellow Buddhas, in a world of infinite Buddhahood informed by the Hua-yen worldview. Monks of other schools were encouraged to join separate Three Periods halls set up within their monasteries. The most famous institution of this school was its merit-field of compassion: instead of the Saṅgha grain store tied to land and manor-membership, it had its store in cosmopolitan centers based on voluntary donations from all and even adjusted it to fit a grander Mahāyāna vision. It encouraged perpetual donation to the Inexhaustible Treasure located in major cities, from which the needy and the poor could borrow, in a celebration of the inexhaustible realm of the Lotus Womb.

The tension between Buddha and Saṅgha, temple and monastery, city and countryside that we have depicted as a natural development did not seem inevitable to Hsin-hsing, who hoped to avoid such conflicts by the spirit of universalism, a spirit not merely expressed in words but carried into effect institutionally. To prevent the excess of donations to the Buddha, Hsin-hsing urged "universal" donation, that is, gifts with no specified recipient or intended use, in order that the sect leaders could distribute the funds equally to the Three Jewels: one third for rebuilding stūpas, one third for spreading the Dharma, and one third for helping the needy. If need be, resources could be redirected to meet the greatest perceived need. Whereas the Sinitic Mahāyāna schools turned inward and produced more personal faiths, this *dānavāda* sect committed to "outer works" never forgot the priority of this-worldly community. There was nothing wrong with this-worldly benefits if equally shared; there would be much wrong with spiritual liberation if it was a mere escape from the real. From the Inexhaustible Treasure, open loans went out, generating interest to sustain its inexhaustibility. By its own generous rules, it could not dun those who were unable to repay their loans, and the only threat it could make against defaulters was that of inevitable karmic justice. The Three Periods sect was a "universal" sect. But its claim to inclusiveness in the end alienated the Sinitic Mahāyāna schools. They did not come to its aid when it was banned by the government, which had grown fearful of its popularity, its wealth, and the power that came with it. So disappeared one of the most daring experiments in the history of Chinese Buddhism.

The Restoration of the Three Jewels in Sui

The suppression of Buddhism in 574–577 was a blessing in disguise, inasmuch as from the soul-searching that it made necessary was born the Sinitic Mahāyāna tradition, flowering in the T'ien-t'ai, Hua-yen, Pure Land, and Ch'an schools. External persecution might be a sign of the age of the Degenerate Dharma, but the cause of the Dharma's decline had always been traced primarily to the sin of the Saṅgha, its keeper. Even cool-headed Ching-yin Hui-yüan, who trusted that the *paramārtha-dharma* could never degenerate, conceded to Emperor Wu that the Saṅgha had to purify itself. The same self-criticism was applied to the prevalent misconception of the other two jewels. The Buddha had to be more than temples and images; the Dharma had to be more than doing good deeds in expectation of rewards on earth. This soul-searching led to a fundamental reform of monastic life, an internalization of the Buddha, now freed from outer trappings, and, above all, a diligent probing of the Dharma in the course of which each school interpreted its message for that historical hour. Even as that inward search was going on, the Three Jewels were being restored by the new dynasty of Sui, founded in 581, and ruling over a reunited China after the conquest of the southern Ch'en dynasty in 589.

Although the first two Sui emperors, Yang-chien Wen-ti and Yang-ti, were inspired in peacetime by the Confucian Mandate and even Taoist immortality, it is clear from their patronage of Chih-i that their hearts were with Buddhism. The restoration affected all Three Jewels. First, Wen-ti (r. 581–604) emulated Aśoka in magically "dividing the relics of the Buddha and enshrining them in stūpas all over the world," installing identical stūpas in state temples all at the same time. This was a far bolder project than anything in Wei or under Liang emperor Wu. It served to sanctify rule in a way comparable to the grand rite to heaven at T'ai-shan, which the Sui rulers also tried. Regular liturgical rites to honor the Dharma and the emperor were instituted, during which the *Golden Light* and *Jen Wang* (Virtuous King) sūtras were chanted to commemorate the Buddha and the imperial house. Meanwhile, eminent monks were invited to teach and to take up residence in the capital, a practice that made Ch'ang-an the hub of Buddhist learning. The fusion of Northern and Southern Buddhism under Sui auspices surpassed the exchanges of the Liang period. The concentration of talent at Ch'ang-an, the interaction between contending currents of thought, and imperial patronage in various forms provided the conditions which allowed the great Sinitic Mahāyāna schools to emerge.

Throughout the Sui-T'ang period, regional schools, those not invited into the capital, were overshadowed by those in Ch'ang-an. Imperial sponsorship meant that the succession of schools was in large measure due to changes in the political climate. This pattern changed after the An Lu-shan revolt destroyed Ch'ang-an in 755. Then monks at the regional centers rose to eminence, especially in the South, which was then beginning to prove itself the more prosperous economic center. The weakening of the central authority and the rise of the regional military heads who supported the regional schools particularly benefited Southern Ch'an (Zen), whose golden age falls in this political interim.

Part of the ideology of the Sui restoration was the theory that the fortunes of Buddhism coincided with those of the state. To enhance that relationship, a pseudo-Mahāyāna argument invited monks to renounce renunciation, that is, to take up secular office in secular gown, serving saṃsāra as if it were nirvāṇa, as true bodhisattvas should. A similar proposal had been made to Chou emperor Wu by an advisor and one-time monk, Wei Yüan-sung, who argued that since saṃsāra is nirvāṇa and the Chou ruler was both Tathāgata and ruler, the Saṅgha should be dismantled as a separate institution and its elders made to serve as moral officials. Fortunately, the persecution showed too well the danger of that equation, and no monk of consequence accepted the offer then or later in T'ang.

T'ien-t'ai

Nothing reveals the piety of the Sui rulers more clearly than Yang-ti's (r. 605–616) enthusiastic support for Master Chih-i (538–597) of the T'ien-t'ai school, whom he invited to lecture at the palace, and who was eventually to become the sage in residence, serving as bodhisattvic precept master and personal confessor. Though he conducted rites for the state, Chih-i never had to tailor his T'ien-t'ai philosophy to serve its interest. The root of T'ien-t'ai was entirely spiritual. It was based on the *ekayāna* (One Vehicle) ideal of the *Lotus Sūtra* and the philosophy of Nāgārjuna. The encounter of the school's second patriarch, Nan-yüeh Hui-ssu (515–577), with his disciple Chih-i established a paradigm for all other Sinitic Mahāyāna schools. At Mount Ta-su, when the two met, they were said to recall hearing together in a prior life the Buddha's exposition of the True Law of the Lotus on Vulture Peak. This T'ien-t'ai *avadāna* telling of karmic preconditions is based on the myth form in chapter one of the *Lotus Sūtra* itself, in which the authority of that scripture is justified. There the Mahāyāna bodhisattva Mañjuśrī tells the forgetful (Hīnayāna) Maitreya that this new True Law is no devilish innovation, but the most ancient of Dharmas taught by an ancient Buddha (predating even Dipaṃkara), and that they both have heard it in a prior life, though Maitreya has forgotten about it. Thus the T'ien-t'ai school claimed unchallengeable authority based on direct transmission from the Buddha. By having Chih-i learn directly from the Buddha himself the *hsüan-i* ("hidden meaning") of the *Lotus*, the school repealed all exoteric authorities, such as Fa-yun (467–529) and even Kumārajīva, the translator of the scripture. The validity of the claim resides in the fact that T'ien-t'ai philosophy was a historical breakthrough of unprecedented proportions, both in its grasp of *ekayāna* and in its transformation of the Two Truths theory of Nāgārjuna (from whom direct transmission was also claimed) into an inspired arabesque of criss-crossing Triple Truth.

The T'ien-t'ai school in Sui was not as popular as the Three Periods sect. Chih-i's talks, recorded by Kuan-ting, could not have reached a large audience. Yet, scholastic and monastic as T'ien-t'ai was, it succeeded in refashioning the three jewels and the three baskets. For *sūtra-dharma,* it chose the *Lotus* as the inclusive One Vehicle; it revered the eternal Śākyamuni as its central Buddha; from the bodhisattvic *śīla-vinaya,* it created its own ordination lineage, the first indigenous Chinese *tsung.* It introduced as the summit of samādhi the vision of "3,000 worlds telescoped into one instant of thought." It is the most comprehensive of the Sinitic Mahāyāna schools and can be seen as the foster parent of the others, which developed an awareness of their lineage in a similar way.

Strength and Weakness of the New Buddhism

The Sinitic Mahāyāna schools of Sui and T'ang were distinguished by intellectual attainments which contemporary Confucianism and Taoism could not begin to rival and to which all later Buddhist developments in China, Korea, and Japan referred back. Yet this supreme form of the Buddha-dharma had to be contented with being just one teaching among three. No longer did Buddhism provide the major symbols of rule. In the debates between the Three Teachings before Chou emperor Wu, the emperor was a nonparticipant who presumed to be the arbiter. State policy on religion in T'ang had a similar air of deliberation. Though the policing of faith was not perfected until the Ming dynasty, the new statecraft sought out rational safeguards against religious abuse. Although the Saṅgha still retained many of its privileges, the relative independence that it enjoyed in the Southern dynasties was subtly but definitely curtailed. The Northern Saṅgha in Wei used virtually to run itself. The clerical bureaucracy was separate from the civil bureaucracy and judged all its cases except murder. It had legal rights to the Saṅgha grain, and the land grant system then favored rural manorialism. Such grants to monks and peasants still existed in T'ang, and some temples prospered, but under the new taxation system the Saṅgha grain that went to the Saṅgha bureau disappeared. Later the Sung taxation virtually destroyed the old land-and-household economic basis of the Saṅgha. At the same time, monks were being tried in civil courts and local monasteries were being made answerable to local authorities. Wayfaring was already curtailed in 493, when monks needed written permissions from the abbot to leave a district; when Ennin traveled in China, that permit had to come from secular officials.

In any religious institution, recruitment has to be a sacred right. By late Wei, clerical offices were up for sale. After Sui initiated state registration, the limit placed on the number of ordination certificates led to the worst abuse of religion by the state. As the sale of the certificate became a source of income for the state, monkhood suffered under such commercialization and the Saṅgha lost virtual control of its own membership. Numerically the Saṅgha shrank, in part because its new leaders conscientiously reverted to a purer monastic life, cutting back the *mahāsaṅgha* T'an-yao created. Despite the Mahāyāna slogans about the equal status of monk and lay bodhisattvas, T'ang Buddhism reintroduced a practical divide between the two.

The ideal of a Buddhist fraternity also suffered in T'ang. The wars and conflicts of the age of disunity had often pulled different groups together in self-defense against common enemies. Manorialism had encouraged non-familial host–client relationships, while monastic Saṅgha households and villages adopted into a monastic family were experiments in universal brotherhood, which the looser political organization of the period allowed. With lasting peace and order in T'ang, the more Chinese structures of the family and the imperial state replaced the *communitas* of these nonclan fraternities. T'ang monks referred to themselves as subjects and publicly acknowledged the higher duty of bowing before parents, producing the cloyingly sentimental *Filial Sūtras* that celebrated *jen-ching* (human feelings) rather than nirvanic detachment. The disruption of the old host–client fellowship between the monk family and the peasant householders bore the greatest ill. As money economy undercut manorial self-sufficiency, the Saṅgha householders found themselves becoming hereditary serfs or tenant farmers serving a temple landlord no kinder than his secular counterpart.

The Flowering of the Dharma in the T'ang

The Dharma was the pride of T'ang Buddhism. From the founding of the dynasty (618) to the An Lu-shan revolt (755), a succession of great minds and the schools they championed laid a philosophical foundation for the future of Mahāyāna Buddhism. These schools–T'ien-t'ai, Hua-yen, Pure Land, and Ch'an–can also be seen as bringing to maturity different forms of piety, stretching back to Indian origins. It is hard enough to see any unity to

Mahāyāna in India, much less to discern a teleological structure in Sinitic Mahāyāna. Yet the emergence of these four schools was not a fortuitous event, but accorded with the four optimal poles in Mahāyāna Buddhology. Buddhas could be either *laukika* or *lokottara* (mundane or transmundane), oriented to either prajñā or karuṇa (wisdom or compassion). These two sets of variables provide four optimal combinations of Buddha qualities: (a) historical didactic, (b) supramundane wisdom, (c) transcendental salvific, and (d) living exemplary, represented best by (a) Śākyamuni, (b) Vairocana, (c) Amitābha, and (d) the Patriarch—the central figures, respectively, of (a) T'ien-t'ai, (b) Hua-yen, (c) Pure Land, and (d) Ch'an.

	wisdom		compassion
transmundane	VAIROCANA		AMITĀBHA
	Hua-yen	(b) (c)	Pure Land
historical	ŚĀKYAMUNI	(a) (d)	PATRIARCH
	T'ien-t'ai		Ch'an
	theory schools		practice schools

Early Buddhism knew only (a) the "historic didactic" Buddha. The idealization of the Buddha began within the Mahāsāṃghika school, which marked the shift from the historical to the transhistorical, from (a) to (b). It was with Mahāyāna that (c) emerged; compassion was given equal status with wisdom in a host of new salvific Buddhas and bodhisattvas. A total rehumanization of the Buddha (d) was accomplished only in China. In a study of the identifiable and datable Buddha-images at the Yün-kang caves, Tsukamoto Zenryū reveals a shift in the object of devotion during the period from the six dynasties to the T'ang. The popular figures at the beginning of this period were Śākyamuni and Maitreya, "historic didactic Buddhas"; the popular figures in T'ang were Amitābha and Avalokiteśvara, "transmundane compassionate types." Meanwhile, the cult of the "transmundane wisdom" Vairocana was also growing. Vairocana images, first appearing in the late sixth century, were few, as these could be properly executed only by depicting his cosmic size; but usually only kings in their imperial ambition took to Vairocana and could afford such monumental-sized sculptures. This ultimate dharmakāya wisdom Buddha is usually too distant in his transcendental height and too cold in his dimensionless wisdom for most mortals, except when tantricized into a popular magical icon. The latest stage in this shift in Buddha-ideals is manifested in portraits of the Buddha in his rehumanized form, especially Ch'an portraits of the Buddha as patriarch and the patriarch as Buddha, which could be seen as responsible for the eclipse of the plastic grotto and monumental art. Their human proportions and immanental emphasis required a more personal medium such as ink scrolls and a more private setting such as a niche in a temple or a room.

The movement from (a) to (d) may be correlated with the circuit of the bodies of the Buddha:

(b) Vairocana Dharmakāya Buddha	(c) Amitābha Saṃbhogakāya Buddha
(a) Śākyamuni Nirmāṇakāya Buddha	(d) Ch'an Patriarch Trikāya of the Mind

The *Lotus Sūtra* did not know of trikāya and even the term *dharmakāya* appears only in the Devadetta chapter. In this work, Śākyamuni was in fact nirmāṇakāya, dharmakāya and saṃbhogakāya rolled into one. In the dramatic episode of a transmundane stūpa suddenly rising out of the earth, Chih-i recognized that the earthly manifestation was Śākyamuni; the eternal Dharma was the Lotus Saddharma; and the transmundane manifestation was Buddha Prabhūtaratna (Abundant Treasure) in the stūpa. There was no need for the separate hypostases of a dharmakāya Buddha Vairocana and a saṃbhogakāya Buddha Amitābha. In T'ien-t'ai buddhology Śākyamuni subsumed both functions, even in his humanity. The T'ien-t'ai school was therefore the comprehensive school (a) that contained the seeds of (b), (c), and (d). It included in its teachings the paths of Hua-yen, Pure Land, and Ch'an—wisdom, devotion, and mysticism: Hua-yen through Chih-i's later writings, Pure Land through his Pure Land piety, Ch'an through his treatise on meditation. The clearest link was to Ch'an: Tao-hsin, later claimed as the fourth patriarch in Ch'an, was tutored by a disciple of Chih-i before he broke off to found his own Eastern Mountain teaching. The affinity with Pure Land is seen in the case of Tao-ch'o, who shared the T'ien-t'ai interest in the *Nirvāṇa Sūtra*, but turned to T'an-luan for the security of the Pure Land path as the only way to liberation in the last age. T'ien-t'ai distinguished between authentic and expedient Pure Lands. The former are the realms of saṃbhogakāya Buddhas and are accessible only to bodhisattvas who gain insight into them through purification of mind. The latter, which admit noncontemplative common people, belong to nirmāṇakāya Buddhas who employ them only as a means. Amitābha's Pure Land belonged to the latter category. The Pure Land school eventually reversed the T'ien-t'ai judgment on Amitābha's land. T'ien-t'ai *ekayāna*, known for its synthesis of theory and practice, always had niches within its system for these two practice paths.

The Theoretical Schools in Early T'ang

T'ien-t'ai, so favored in Sui, enjoyed no particular patronage from the first two T'ang rulers. In fact, the house of T'ang saw themselves as heirs of Laotzu, officially placing Taoism above Buddhism. That posed no real threat yet, for imperial Taoism was a palace concern that did not serve the interest of the people; its priesthood and its network of temples did not extend to the countryside, and there were far fewer Taoists than there were Buddhist monks. Neither Taoism nor Confucianism could compete with Buddhism for the heart and soul of the people. Monks had acquired a near monopoly of the soteriological portion of all Chinese funeral rites, at a time when the Han theory of two (yin-yang) souls merging back with nature (one going to heaven and one to earth, hanging around the grave) no longer sufficed, and a third soul going to hell or to the Pure Land had been added.

The relationship between Buddhism and the state changed somewhat when the pilgrim Hsüan-tsang (600–664) was received with great honor at the capital on his return from India. Emperor T'ai-tsung lent his support to Hsüantsang's drive for translations and retranslations of scriptures, a means of spreading the teaching of the Wei-shih (Vijñaptimātratā or Consciousness-Only) school, a brand of Yogācāra Idealism he learned at Nālandā University. The emperor was at first interested only in the pilgrim's knowledge of the frontiers. The awe he later expressed at the intricacies of the Dharma remained at best the curiosity of the cultured. The Wei-shih school was very technical. It did not provide legitimacy to rule. Nor did the Wei-shih philosophy last long. In repealing the doctrine of universal Buddha-nature, it invited the defense of that Tathāgatagarbha tradition by the Hua-yen patriarch, Fa-tsang. Legend has it that Fa-tsang founded his own school as a result of a disagreement with Hsüan-tsang about the *Awakening of Faith*, a text attributed to Aśvaghoṣa but most probably a mid-sixth-century Chinese digest of Yogācāra basics. Its peculiar theory of Mind did not fit well with Yogācāra but was expressive of the Tathāgatagarbha tradition. It may have been the same text that separated the Ch'an patriarch Tao-hsin from his T'ien-t'ai master. Now it drove a wedge between Hua-yen and Wei-shih as Fa-tsang defended "the old school against the new." The old school comprised the earlier Yogācāra representatives of the Ti-lun (Daśabhūmika) school rooted in sixth-century Loyang and the She-lun (Saṃgraha) school based on Paramārtha's translations of works by Asaṅga and Vasubandhu. The two schools had found their home in Ch'ang-an during the Sui. In the early seventh century, interest in their analysis of mind and consciousness was growing, but discrepancies between them had become apparent. Using the line "the three realms are of the mind only" in the *Daśabhūmika* (now in the *Avataṃsaka Sūtra*), Fa-tsang demolished the inferior Consciousness-Only position. Drawing on the Suchness Mind, expressed in the *Awakening of Faith*, he claimed for Hua-yen an immediate knowledge of the dharma essence (*fa-hsing*, *dharmatā*, suchness) and charged Wei-shih with knowing only the superficial appearances or dharma characteristics (*fa-hsiang*, *dharma-lakṣaṇā*). Fa-tsang fused Mādhyamika dialectic, Yogācāra causationism, and Tathāgatagarbha (Buddha-nature) realism. T'ien-t'ai, which derived its philosophy primarily from Mādhyamika and shared an old suspicion of the newer Yogācāra, lost its leading intellectual position to the new Hua-yen school.

When Empress Wu usurped the throne and founded the Chou dynasty, Buddhism reached a peak of prosperity. Because of a patriarchal bias in both Confucianism and even Taoism, empresses and dowagers, like pious mothers and grandmothers in ordinary households, had traditionally been great patrons of the more egalitarian Buddhist faith. Empresses who could not build their own monuments could and did build temples. Following in the footsteps of Lady Feng at P'ing-ch'eng and Lady Hu of Loyang, Empress Wu went beyond them by assuming rule. Buddhism provided her a legitimacy hard to come by in the native traditions. Maitreyan rule had been claimed by Wei rulers, but the peasant Maitreyan uprising in Sui had dampened royal enthusiasm, and Amitābha, politically more harmless, superseded Maitreya in popularity. Hsüan-tsang had recently revived an academic interest in his cult, and now Empress Wu ruled as a feminine incarnation of this Future Buddha in a reign foretold by the *Ta-yün* (Great Cloud) *Sūtra* of suspicious origin. Hua-yen was also half-unwillingly drawn into the celebration of this divine rule. Fa-tsang became the empress's protégé.

Hua-yen celebrates totalism, the mystery of the "one is all, all is one." It perceives the world as a dynamic infinite *dharmadhātu*, in which the matrix of elements, from one second to the next, is generating itself from itself, in a seamless universe in total interdependence. The Sun Vairocana, a rare dharmakāya Buddha, who is depicted with a flaming halo in which each tongue of flame houses a miniature replica of the same Vairocana, and so on *ad infinitum*, is the mythopoeic embodiment of this worldview. A network of provincial temples was planned, emanating from the capital, each housing a miniature replica of the gigantic Vairocana Buddha. A sacred canopy—the

Net of Indra in which every gem reflected the whole—covered the empress's kingdom, a living demonstration of the perfect world, in which part and whole, noumena (*li*, principle) and phenomena (*shih*, fact) interpenetrate and where all elements (*dharma*, *dhātu*) are magically transubstantiated into the Matrix of the Real (*dharmadhātu*) itself. Buddhist scholasticism reached its apex in Fa-tsang, and for a while, it seemed eternity itself had been captured.

The failure of that perfection to last is perhaps in the nature of things, but it also bespeaks the weakness of Empress Wu's reign and of Fa-tsang's idealism. The T'ien-t'ai philosophy too had been called an optimistic reflection of a China united, but unlike Hua-yen, T'ien-t'ai never forgot the suffering of the 574 persecution. Hua-yen was born of peace and it sincerely believed that sin and ignorance were ultimately illusions. Whereas T'ien-t'ai meditation begins with the deluded mind, Hua-yen speculations know only the pure mind. So realist was T'ien-t'ai that it even posited an evil nature for the Buddha Śākyamuni; so idealist was Hua-yen that it knew only Vairocana as timeless perfection. (T'ien t'ai did not say the Buddha is evil, but that, though he had attained "purity through cultivation," nevertheless he willingly retained his "essential [original] evil." This retained humanity is what allowed the Buddha to move freely in saṃsāra to fulfill his bodhisattvic career. In the end, evil and its opposite and their mutual negation are absolved and transcended in T'ien-t'ai Mādhyamika, but, even so, never denied or eliminated.) Hua-yen's triumph was one of speculative reason. When it failed, anti-intellectualism based on faith (Pure Land) and on mysticism (Ch'an) set in.

The Practice Schools in Late T'ang

The fall of Empress Wu was soon followed by the revolt of An Lu-shan in 755 and, after the recovery of "middle prosperity," the great persecution of the Buddhists in 845. Of the Sinitic Mahāyāna schools that survived, Ch'an and Pure Land ruled supreme. The philosophical ideas of these two schools are of less central significance than the personalities around which they grew. *Nien-fo* (Japanese *nembutsu*) spread because Tao-ch'o popularized the rosary and a "bean count" method. Deliverance to Pure Land by *nien-fo* preceded the theory of Shan-tao, who granted such lofty recompense to ordinary mortals. Though Shan-tao was a brilliant thinker, he was remembered as an ardent preacher who held up scrolls depicting the Pure Land on one side and hells on the other. The cult had noble patrons, but Pure Land was never reign-related. It had a larger social base than the much-publicized, but probably little studied, Hua-yen school. The case of Ch'an is more complicated. This practice school engaged in debates, courted imperial favor, and became highly organized. A meditation school based on an esoteric wisdom could

23. *Bodhisattva*, China, Eastern Wei Period, ca. 530 C.E. From the Pai-ma-ssu (White Horse Monastery) near Lo-Yang (Honan Province). Grey Limestone. 196.5 cm. high.

not, however, be popular. The popularization of Ch'an began with Tao-hsin. Since then, the genius of the tradition was that it would insist on a strict personal code of conduct and practice while reaching out to all those who could not follow such a code through public forums known as Dharma or precept platforms, at which initiatory creeds comprising prajñā formula and meditative methods were imparted to all. The eminence of the practice schools changed the tone of Buddhist piety. The theory schools had mastered a universal Dharma, best exemplified by their classification of tenets known as *p'an-chiao.* The practice schools focused instead on the figure of the Buddha, whether located within it (Ch'an) or beyond (Pure Land). In contrast to Hua-yen's submergence of the individual in the flawless *dharmadhātu,* Pure Land reminded people of present imperfections and Ch'an awakened them to the reality of the here and now. Together they freed the individual from the whole. This spirituality coincided with the rise of regionalism and of popular culture in the second half of T'ang.

The return of rule to the house of Li, the original founders of the dynasty, under Emperor Hsüan-tsung brought renewed support for Taoism and accelerated the Sinicization of Buddhism. The last creative phase of Indian Buddhism, Tantrayāna or Esotericism, contributed to this new mix of native and foreign magic. As An Lu-shan destroyed the Buddhist centers in the North, Southern traditions influenced by Taoism emerged in the ninth century, notably, the Hung-chou school of Ch'an branching off from Ma-tsu Tao-i. Chinese-compiled works such as the *Yüan-chüeh-ching* (Sūtra of Perfect Enlightenment), popular in later Ch'an, adjusted Sanskrit terminology to native taste, thus strengthening the Chinese imprint on Buddhism. The *Pao-tsang-lun* (Sūtra of the Treasure Store) attributed to Seng-chao unashamedly paraphrased the *Lao-tzu* in Mādhyamika terms and tailored Yogācāra to fit Chinese cosmogony. This process of domestication is reflected in art in the increasing popularity of Kṣitigarbha (Ti-tsang, Earth Womb), who ferries people out of hell and as Avalokiteśvara (Kuan-yin) then further transports them to paradise. A homely figure, Ti-tsang was no doubt in part the ancient T'u-ti (Lord of Earth) resurrected. Likewise, we begin to see the feminization of Kuan-yin, the fusion of Pure Land with the land of immortals of the Queen Mother of the West, and the transposition of the sacred mountains of India onto those of China; the bodhisattvas would now be permanently based in China.

The health of the Buddhist tradition has always to be measured against the fortunes of the other two teachings. Of the three, it was Confucianism that had best learned the lesson of 755. The disruption of order by the civil war led to a call among the literati to return to matters of practicality, and in the period that followed the seed of Neo-Confucianism was sown. (Han

Yu's defense of the classical way and critique of Buddhism dates from this period.) Neither Buddhists nor Taoists showed a similar awareness of the need for reform from within. Their mutual hostility led to a Taoist accusation that the Buddhists had contaminated a promised elixir of immortality being prepared for a hopeful emperor. A ban on Buddhism followed; the destruction of the Three Jewels was again decreed in 845. This persecution was the result of larger forces, such as a renewed tension between state and Saṅgha, and the hostility between the T'ang and its Central Asian neighbors. The Buddhist establishment was destroyed, as the state decimated Saṅgha membership and confiscated much of its property. Unlike the last persecution, there was no escape from this one to a southern haven, no restoration like that of Sui, no popular support for a revival, and, saddest of all, no rebirth of the tradition. Perhaps the Sui Restoration had been too successful. Perhaps the prosperity of Buddhism in T'ang had erased the memory of the 574 apocalypse. A false sense of security, such as Hua-yen supplied, left people ill-prepared for the holocaust of 845, which contradicted their eschatological timetables and revealed cracks in reality which their totalistic philosophy could not handle. This does not mean that Buddhism has declined ever since. Rather, new forms of piety and organization emerged in time, notably the Ch'an and Pure Land movements, reflecting a renewed bodhisattvic aspiration to reclaim the world as the arena for transformative action.

Notes

1. *Wei Shou: Treatise on Buddhism and Taoism,* trans. Leon Hurvitz.
2. See *Ming-fo-lun,* T 52.11c–12a.
3. This divergence persisted even in the late sixth century, when the Mahāyānist Chi-tsang made the surprising charge that Taoism was more otherworldly than Buddhism. The sharpness of the contrast vanishes only in the Ch'an of the ninth century.
4. Religious Taoism had envisaged its sage as being one with the Tao, and even saw Lao-tzu (T'ai-shan Lao-chun) as the manifestation of the ever dispersing and coagulating primal ether that could take on various earthly appearances; see the Hsiang-erh commentary on the *Lao-tzu* and the *Lao-tzu pien-hua ching* (Scripture on the Transformations of Lao-tzu). This was not the view accepted among philosophers, and it also differed from the more extravagant Mahāyāna idealization of the Buddha.
5. This cult of sheer abandon was recorded in the *Shih-shuo hsin-yu,* translated by Richard B. Mather as *A New Account of Tales of the World.*
6. Chinese monks were essentially novices (śramaṇa), and only foreigners became full bhikṣu. The leader of the Saṅgha was called either "Leader of the Śramanas" or "Leader of the Men of the Way."
7. In this connection one may quote the sensible remarks of a Buddhist apologist of the Northern Chou period: "The teaching of Śākyamuni encourages one to abide in purity and quietude, to look to mildness and harmony. Thus, it can put an end to resentment. Because it teaches karmic cause and effect, fortune and misfortune are regarded

as deserved, and upon that basis the wealthy and the poor can rest and live together in peace."

8. Reported by the Japanese Anchō (763–814).
9. Reported by Chi-tsang.

Bibliography

Sources

Liebenthal, Walter. *Chao-lun: The Treatises of Seng Chao.* Hong Kong: Hong Kong University Press, 1968.

Link, Arthur E. "Biography of Shih Tao-an." *T'oung Pao* 46 (1958) 1–48.

Robinson, Richard H. *Early Mādhyamika in India and China.* Madison: University of Wisconsin Press, 1967.

Shih-shuo hsin-yü: A New Account of Tales of the World. Translated by Richard B. Mather. Minneapolis: University of Minnesota Press, 1976.

"Three Prajñāpāramitā Treatises of Tao-an." Translated by Leon Hurvitz and Arthur E. Link. In *Mélanges sinologiques offerts à Monsieur Paul Demiéville,* 403–70. Paris: Presses universitaires de France, 1974.

Wei Shou: Treatise on Buddhism and Taoism. Translated by Leon Hurvitz. Kyoto: Kyoto University, 1956.

Studies

Ch'en, Kenneth Kuan-sheng. "Anti-Buddhist Propaganda during the Nan-ch'ao." *Harvard Journal of Asiatic Studies* 15 (1952) 166–92.

——. *Buddhism in China: A Historical Survey.* Princeton, NJ: Princeton University Press, 1964.

——. *The Chinese Transformation of Buddhism.* Princeton, NJ: Princeton University Press, 1973.

——. "The Economic Background of the Hui-ch'ang Suppression of Buddhism." *Harvard Journal of Asiatic Studies* 19 (1956) 67–105.

——. "Neo-Taoism and the Prajñā School during the Wei and Chin Dynasties." *Chinese Culture* 1 (1957) 33–46.

——. "On Some Factors Responsible for the Anti-Buddhist Persecution under the Pei-Ch'ao." *Harvard Journal of Asiatic Studies* 17 (1954) 261–73.

——. "The Role of Buddhist Monasteries in T'ang China." *History of Religions* 15 (1975–76) 209–30.

Demiéville, Paul. "Le bouddhisme chinois." In *Encyclopédie de la Pléiade 29: Histoire des religions* I, 1249–1319. Paris: Gallimard, 1970.

Hurvitz, Leon. "Chih Tun's Notions of *Prajñā.*" *Journal of the American Oriental Society* 88 (1968) 243–61.

——. "The First Systematization of Buddhist Thought in China." *Journal of Chinese Philosophy* 2 (1975) 361–88.

——. "'Render unto Caesar' in Early Chinese Buddhism." *Sino-Indian Studies* 5 (1957) 96–114.

Lai, Whalen. "The Awakening of Faith in Mahāyāna: A Study of the Unfolding of Sinitic Motifs." Ph.D. dissertation, Harvard University, 1975.

——. "Before the Prajñā Schools: The Earliest Chinese Commentary on the *Aṣṭasāhasrikā.*" *Journal of the International Association of Buddhist Studies* 6:1 (1983) 91–108.
——. "Chou Yung vs. Chang Jung (on *Śūnyatā*): The *Pen-mo Yu-wu* Controversy in Fifth-Century China." *Journal of the International Association of Buddhist Studies* 1:2 (1979) 23–44.
——. "Chinese Buddhist Causation Theories: An Analysis of the Sinitic Mahāyāna Understanding of *Pratitya-samutpāda.*" *Philosophy East and West* 27 (1977) 241–64.
——. "The Early Prajñā Schools, Especially 'Hsin-Wu,' Reconsidered." *Philosophy East and West* 33 (1983) 61–77.
——. "Further Developments of the Two Truths Theory in China." *Philosophy East and West* 30 (1980) 139–61.
——. "*Hu-Jan Nien-Ch'i* (Suddenly a Thought Rose): Chinese Understanding of Mind and Consciousness." *Journal of the International Association of Buddhist Studies* 3:2 (1980) 42–59.
——. "The Meaning of 'Mind-Only' (*Wei-hsin*): An Analysis of a Sinitic Mahāyāna Phenomenon." *Philosophy East and West* 27 (1977) 65–83.
——. "Nonduality of the Two Truths in Sinitic Mādhyamika: Origin of the 'Third Truth.'" *Journal of the International Association of Buddhist Studies* 2:2 (1979) 45–65.
——. "Sinitic Speculations on Buddha-Nature: The Nirvāna School." *Philosophy East and West* 32 (1982) 135–49.
——. "Sinitic Understanding of the Two Truths Theory in the Liang Dynasty." *Philosophy East and West* 28 (1978) 339–51.
Liebenthal, Walter. "A Biography of Chu Tao-sheng." *Monumenta Nipponica* 11 (1955–56) 284–316.
——. "Chinese Buddhism during the 4th and 5th Centuries." *Monumenta Nipponica* 11 (1955–56) 44–83.
——. "The World Conception of Chu Tao-sheng." *Monumenta Nipponica* 12 (1956–57) 65–103, 241–68.
Link, Arthur E. "The Taoist Antecedents of Tao-an's Prajñā Ontology." *History of Religions* 9 (1969–70) 181–215.
Liu, Ming-Wood. "The Doctrine of the Buddha-Nature in the Mahāyāna *Mahāparinirvāna-sūtra.*" *Journal of the International Association of Buddhist Studies* 5:2 (1982) 63–94.
Maspero, Henri. "Communautés et moines bouddhistes chinois au 2e et 3e siècles." *Bulletin de l'École Francaise d'Extrême-Orient* 10 (1910) 222–32.
——. "Les origines de la communauté bouddhiste de Lo-yang." *Journal Asiatique* 225 (1934) 87–107.
——. "Le songe et l'ambassade de l'Empereur Ming: Étude critique des sources." *Bulletin de l'École Francaise d'Extrême-Orient* 10 (1910) 95–130.
Mather, Richard B. "Chinese Letters and Scholarship in the Third and Fourth Centuries." *Journal of the American Oriental Society* 84 (1964) 348–91.
——. "The Controversy over Conformity and Naturalness during the Six Dynasties." *History of Religions* 9 (1969–70) 160–80.
——. "Vimalakīrti and Gentry Buddhism." *History of Religions* 8 (1968–69) 60–73.
Priestley, C. D. C. "Emptiness in the *Satyasiddhi.*" *Journal of Indian Philosophy* 1 (1970) 30–39.
Tsukamoto Zenryū. *A History of Early Chinese Buddhism.* Translated by Leon Hurvitz. Tokyo: Kodansha, 1985.
Wright, Arthur F. *Buddhism in Chinese History.* New York: Atheneum, 1965.

———. "The Formation of Sui Ideology (581–604)." In *Chinese Thought and Institutions*, 71–104. Edited by John King Fairbank. Chicago: University of Chicago Press, 1957.
———. "Fo-t'u-teng: A Biography." *Harvard Journal of Asiatic Studies* 11 (1948) 321–70.
———. "Fu I and the Rejection of Buddhism." *Journal of the History of Ideas* 12 (1951) 31–47.
Wright, Dale S. "On the Concept of Mind in the *Treatise on the Awakening of Faith.*" *Journal of Buddhist Philosophy* 2 (1984) 37–47.
Zürcher, Erik. *The Buddhist Conquest of China.* Leiden: E. J. Brill, 1959, 1972.

12

Philosophical Schools

San-lun, T'ien-T'ai, and Hua-yen

TAITETSU UNNO

THE SPIRITUALITY developed in the schools of San-lun, T'ien-t'ai, and Hua-yen in the sixth and seventh centuries inherited the highest achievements of Indian Mahāyāna, which had undergone a gradual transformation since the first century C.E. as it encountered the Chinese tradition, characterized by an organic worldview, this-worldly orientation, and harmony both cosmic and social. The common characteristic of these schools was their focus on the phenomenal particular in the here and now. This concrete particular, however, is not the objectified thing grasped in the conventional, dichotomous mode of subject–object thinking; rather, it is that which is realized by non-dichotomous prajñā-insight: dharma-as-it-is[1] or, as some of the later Chinese Buddhists preferred, *shih* (thing, event, entity). Here I follow the classic definition of dharma in Buddhism, as enunciated in the *Ratnagotravibhāga:* dharma as teaching, *deśanā-dharma,* and dharma as realization itself, *adhigama-dharma,* which includes both that which realizes (prajñā) and that which is realized (dharma-as-it-is).[2]

This unity of realized object and realizing subject, dharma-as-it-is, not as a mystical oneness but as an overcoming of all forms of conceptuality, is synonymous with true wisdom and true compassion, the source of spirituality, and the cornerstone of the Chinese Buddhist doctrinal systems. We shall consider three major proponents, each with his distinctive legacy, practical agenda, and historical limitations: Chi-tsang (549–623) of the San-lun school, Chih-i (538–597) of the T'ien-t'ai school, and Fa-tsang (643–712) of the Hua-yen school.

San-lun

The San-lun lineage begins with Kumārajīva, who arrived in China from Central Asia in 401 C.E. His translations of Buddhist texts, especially the *Prajñāpāramitā* literature, were a major stimulus to the study of Mahāyāna Buddhism in this early period, and his distinguished disciples wrought a major shift in the course of Chinese Buddhism. Among them was Seng-chao (374–414), renowned as "first in the understanding of emptiness (śūnyatā)," who expressed one of his basic insights in the following words:[3]

> "Miraculous, indeed, O World-Honored One! Without moving from the reality-limit (*bhūta-koṭi*), you secure positions for all dharmas." It is not that the secured positions exist apart from true reality; the secured positions are themselves true reality. If so, is the way far away? Identical with things (*shih*) is true reality. Is the sage far away? When this is actualized, there is the holy. (T 45.153a3–6)

The "secured positions" refer to the manifestations of concrete particulars, each of which secures its place in the phenomenal world in the eyes of prajñā-insight. As such, each, being a product of dependent co-arising, is simultaneously real and unreal, being and non-being. There is no so-called truth, no reality, or no absolute apart from these phenomenal particulars. "Identical with things is true reality" became the touchstone of the authentic Buddhist life.

This affirmation of the phenomenal was an essential part of Confucianism, whose basic orientation was not toward transcendence but toward a realization of "the secular as sacred."[4] While it stressed *jen* and *li*, manifesting humanity in ritual action, rather than dharma-as-it-is in the Buddhist sense, its primary concern nonetheless was with this world. This is even truer in Taoism (Seng-chao's own background), especially in Chuang-tzu, for whom the Tao was to be found even within the lowliest expressions of life.[5] While Taoist philosophy was rooted in the metaphysical, as found in the emphasis on the One, the Tao was believed to permeate the phenomenal world. But this focus on phenomenal particulars was already inherent in Indian Buddhism, in which truth was not a proposition but reality-as-it-is: thatness (*tattva*), suchness (*tathatā*), and thingness (*dharmatā*), "terms of the simplest prescription of the object."[6] Crucial here is the content of cognitive awareness; thatness, suchness, or thingness, all synonymous with dharma-as-it-is, must not be confused with objective things, grasped by the dichotomous mind. Each term denotes that which is real but empty (*śūnya*), realized by the nondichotomous knowing of prajñā, and forms the content of *tathatā, bhūta-koṭi, animitta, paramārtha*, and *dharmadhātu*.[7] As Seng-chao wrote:

> Within is the solitary mirror's brightness; without, the reality of the myriad dharmas. Although the myriad dharmas are real, they cannot be seen if the light of prajñā is lacking. The correspondence of within and without makes possible this illumination. This is the reason that the Holy One cannot make (the myriad dharmas) the same; each is a dynamic function. Although the inside intuits, it has no knowing; although the outside is real, it has no marks. (T 45.154c6–9)[8]

This classic formulation of prajñā-insight, metaphorically expressed by "the solitary mirror's brightness," which reveals all things, including the self, as they are, contains a contradiction, as found in the concluding sentence, "although the inside intuits, it has no knowing." That is, prajñā sees clearly, yet it does not see. A similar contradiction exists in the "reality of myriad dharmas," constituting the phenomenal world, because "although the outside is real, it has no marks." No marks is synonymous with emptiness, referring to the lack of permanent, identifiable characteristics (*lakṣaṇa*) of the individual dharma, which, however, as the product of dependent co-arising, is real. In short, dharma is, yet it is not. These contradictions within both the subject (brightness of prajñā) and the object (myriad dharmas) in nondichotomous realization are not amenable to a merely rational or logical solution. They are to be resolved only through rigorous religious practice, involving a radical transformation at the core of one's being, such that everything that was grasped as real on the dichotomous plane is now seen as delusory, and true reality is realized as the double exposure of the real and unreal, being and non-being.

An attempt to make this subtle point in contemporary philosophical language is made by Nishitani Keiji. In his seminal work *Religion and Nothingness* he speaks of an "in-itself" (*jitai*), beyond the subject–object dichotomy and manifesting emptiness, which he sharply differentiates from the concepts of both substance (*jittai*) and subject (*shutai*).[9] Aristotelean substance and Kantian subject are based on the field of dichotomous consciousness which cannot escape the "paradox of representation" wherein a thing is lifted out of the elemental mode of being and transformed into an object re-presented to the subject.[10] A thing thus re-presented is grasped conceptually and abstractly from a self-centered perspective from within its own center. When this subject–object mode of knowing is broken through, one experiences conversion into the field of emptiness wherein occurs "be-ification"—all existents emerge in their individual uniqueness, each radiating its own particular light.

Such a perception of reality-as-it-is underlies the twofold truth of Nāgārjuna as interpreted by Piṅgala. According to this commentarial tradition, translated by Kumārajīva, the structure of truth conceived in Nāgārjuna's

Treatise on the Middle, chapter 24, was *twofold* (and not a relationship between *two* truths). Verses 8, 9, and 10 of this chapter read:

> Relying on the twofold truth
> All Buddhas teach the dharma;
> Namely, the mundane truth
> And the truth of the highest object (*paramārtha*).
>
> Those who do not know the distinction
> Between the twofold truth
> Do not know the profound *tattva*
> Taught in the Buddha's teaching.
>
> Without relying on verbal expressions
> The highest object cannot be taught;
> Without reaching the highest object (through practice)
> Nirvāna cannot be attained. (*Chung-lun*, T 30.32c16–33a7)[11]

According to Piṅgala, mundane truth suggests two things: first, that "reality" is seen in inverted form (*viparīta*), regarded as true by the unenlightened but clearly false from the standpoint of highest truth; and second, that the highest truth is expressed in words and concepts of mundane truth in the teaching (*deśanā*) by the enlightened who see reality-as-it-is, denoted in the above verses as dharma, *paramārtha*, and *tattva*, which are synonymous. The identity of these three terms, frequently missed in Western-language translations of twofold truth,[12] is crucial to its precise understanding.

We may schematize this interpretation of the twofold truth in the following way:

A Mundane truth
B Highest truth ⎤
⎬ Twofold truth
A′ Mundane truth ⎦

On level A (mundane truth) the only reality is that which is misperceived and erroneously grasped by the unenlightened as "real"; it is simply an arbitrary conception, a delusion, without any basis in actual life. On level B (highest truth) reality is nothing but emptiness, an emptiness that is none other than the real. But level B is inseparable from level A′ (mundane truth), which is affirmed by the enlightened. The phenomenal particulars, grasped in the dichotomous mode of knowing and constituting mundane truth on level A, undergo negation on level B, to be ultimately affirmed as empty but real—dharma-as-it-is, *tattva*, *paramārtha*—by prajñā-insight. The words and concepts of level A, regarded as "conceptual play" (*prapañca*) by the enlightened, now come alive in the form of a teaching (*deśanā*) which uses words and concepts to reveal that which is true and real. Thus, mundane truth, level A′, becomes a necessary and essential expression of the highest truth, level B, and the two together form the basic structure of twofold truth. When the teaching of the twofold truth is fully realized, culminating in the awakening to reality which is multiple and variegated, the dynamic and creative life called "walking the middle" (*madhyamā-pratipad*) unfolds.

After centuries of misunderstanding and distortion, the philosophy of emptiness found its clear and authentic expression in the San-lun school of Chi-tsang, who inherited the twofold truth as discussed above.[13] Chi-tsang, whose aim was to "destroy erroneous views and manifest the true," devoted his efforts to crushing the "inverted" views of being and non-being, obstinately held by various thinkers in India and China, both Buddhist and non-Buddhist. This destruction of "inverted" views simultaneously meant the revelation of the true nature of reality (*tattvasya lakṣaṇa*) and the affirmation of the Middle Way as the principle of enlightenment to be manifested in everyday life. The basic thrust of the Middle Way, beginning with the Noble Eightfold Path and culminating in the twofold truth, was that it is both a process to the supreme goal of enlightenment and the highest expression of that goal in the everyday world.

In order to accomplish his mission, Chi-tsang developed the dialectic of the four levels of twofold truth. On the first level is found mundane truth which affirms being, as upheld by the Abhidharmists, whereas the highest truth affirms non-being. On the second level is the mundane truth which holds to both being and non-being, upheld by the Ch'eng-shih scholars (exponents of the *Satyasiddhi* doctrine), whereas the highest truth is neither duality nor nonduality. On the third level mundane truth speaks of duality and nonduality, as taught by some Mahāyānists, whereas the highest truth is neither duality nor nonduality. On the fourth level mundane truth contains all the preceding levels, which are actually nothing but teaching relying on words, whereas the highest truth is attained when there is nothing to be realized (*Ta-ch'eng hsüan-lun*, T 45.15c5–10). This absolute and thoroughgoing negation of all forms of conceptuality, however, is not the goal of San-lun, for its ultimate aim is the realization of *tattva*, *paramārtha*, or *dharmatā*. This accords with the final aim of Nāgārjuna's negative dialectic in his *Treatise on the Middle*, where the wise is said to perceive true reality (*tattva-darśana*, chap. 26, v. 10).

According to Chi-tsang, this true reality is none other than dharma-as-it-is, seen in the nondichotomous mode of realization. Still retaining vestiges of the technical vocabulary of Indian Buddhism, he writes, "The form (*rūpa*) of provisional name is neither being nor non-being. It is impossible to grasp it by means of the tetralemma. This form is none other than true reality. . . . Thus, provisional name is clearly true reality" (T 42.126c). Provisional name is the designation of that which is delusory but real, the product of co-arising, creating the world of distinctions. Since reality is multiple, distinction in the end is more important than nondistinction. Chi-tsang makes this point when he writes:

> Now, regarding distinction and nondistinction, there is nondistinction where distinction clearly exists. Thus, provisional name without being destroyed is itself true reality. Although nondistinction exists, distinction is clearly evident. Therefore, the saying, "Without moving from the reality-limit (*bhūta-koti*), you secure positions for all dharmas." Such a penetrating insight is possible only by enlightened beings. (T 33.488c)

Chi-tsang undertakes a relentless negative dialectic in pursuing his agenda, destruction-as-manifestation, as evident in his probings into the meaning of the "middle." For example, he clarifies the usage of this key term through four interpretive schemes (*San-lun hsüan-i,* T 45.14a20–14b15). First is the semantic meaning of middle. Words indicate relations to communicate thought but lose their significance from the standpoint of ultimate reality. Here the term "middle" is a pointer to the true nature of reality, which transcends words and concepts. Second is the ultimate meaning of middle. That is, it suggests the ultimate which is "non-middle," negating any form of conceptualization or reification. In fact, the true nature of reality is said to be neither middle nor non-middle. This is not to say that the middle as the negation of extremes is taken lightly but that middle as an assertion or a position is rejected as untenable. Third is the interdependent meaning of middle. The middle and the extremes are mutually dependent, illuminating each other. To put it differently, the extremes are taught in order to awaken people to the middle, and the middle teaches the awareness of the extremes. Finally, there is the indeterminate meaning of the middle: any phenomenal particular in the world of daily life, manifesting the true nature of reality, can be the middle. This underscores Chi-tsang's earlier assertion: "The provisional name itself without being destroyed is none other than the true reality."

This focus on the phenomenal particular as manifesting the true nature of reality is further confirmed by the various usages of the "middle" found in Chi-tsang's *The Profound Meaning of the Three Treatises* (ibid., T 45.14b17–14c15). When middle is used with a singular referent, it denotes the path of enlightenment itself, as found in the Hua-yen statement: "All beings who seek the non-obstructed freedom of emancipation transcend saṃsāra by means of this one path." This single path leads to the realization of *dharmatā, tattva,* or *paramārtha.* When two kinds of middle are mentioned, they include the middle of the mundane truth and the middle of highest truth, the two working together to manifest the true middle. The true middle denotes each reality in the phenomenal world which manifests dharma-as-it-is, as seen by the enlightened ones. When the three kinds of middle are enumerated, they include the previous two plus the third, the middle of neither mundane truth nor highest truth. This is referred to as the middle which is non-middle, the negation of all arbitrary conceptions and the affirmation of reality-as-it-is.

Chi-tsang comes up with yet another scheme to direct the practitioner to the realization of destruction-as-manifestation. He speaks of the *comparative* middle which negates the extremes of eternalism and annihilationism, being and non-being. This is called the medicine that cures all extreme views. Next is the *exhaustive* middle. The sickness of extreme positions is cured or exhausted by the medicine of the middle principle, but there is no special position called the middle that can be asserted. If people should become attached to either the extremes or the middle, this is regarded as a very serious affliction. Third is the *absolute* middle, which arises from the negation of dichotomous consciousness which is one-sided, incomplete, and imperfect. From this radical negation of all *prapañca* thinking arises the *creative* middle. That is, when the absolute middle is realized, spontaneously there appears the pristine reality of individual phenomenon, manifesting its suchness and radiating its own unique light. The creative middle reaffirms both being and non-being, wiping out the confusion of the delusory mind (*vikalpa*) lost in the perplexities of negations. Thus, non-being is taught to those who cling to "truth," and being is given to those who become attached to "non-being." The creative middle is the path of daily life, the arena of the bodhisattva's salvific activity, which is boundless and endless.

While the twofold truth of Nāgārjuna in the tradition of Kumārajīva, Piṅgala, and Seng-chao was meant to reveal the true nature of reality, Chi-tsang has been criticized for being overly involved with the negative use of the twofold truth as an instrument to simply destroy erroneous views without revealing reality-as-it-is.[14] While this is a standard criticism, eventually leading to the popularity of such schools as the T'ien-t'ai, his agenda historically was to clarify the central experience of the Buddhist path, *adhigama-dharma,* which emerges automatically in thoroughgoing negation. Ultimately, "In the highest truth there are two aspects. First is the true nature of reality; therefore, it is called truth. Second is the penetrating insight of the wise in which there is true understanding" (*Chung-kuan lun-shu,* T 42.150c22–24). This non-dichotomous oneness of the realizing subject and the realized object is the basis of true wisdom and true compassion and the source of San-lun spirituality, but the San-lun path was still in the process of Sinification and awaited articulation more attuned to the native tradition.

T'ien-t'ai

San-lun inherited the apophatic tradition of the *Prajñāpāramitā* and *Vimalakīrti* sūtras, whereas T'ien t'ai developed the kataphatic tradition of the *Lotus* and *Mahāparinirvāṇa* sūtras. This is one reason for the immense appeal of the latter and the gradual decline of the former in the subsequent centuries. Yet, although later T'ien-t'ai comes under the heavy influence of Tathāgatagarbha and Hua-yen thought, fundamentally Chih-i's formulation is another manifestation of Mādhyamika philosophy. Chih-i (538–597) traced his lineage through Hui-su to Hui-wen, a legendary Buddhist figure who was acclaimed for his miraculous feats and supernatural powers.[15] Thus, unlike the earlier Chinese Buddhist schools, including San-lun, which regarded scholar-translators such as Kumārajīva as their founders, Chih-i identified himself with teachers renowned and acclaimed for religious practice.[16] His ultimate concern was the realization of the true nature of reality (*tattvasya lakṣaṇa*) through religious practice and its formulation in a comprehensive doctrinal system which was distinctively Chinese.

For this purpose Chih-i received inspiration from Nāgārjuna's *Treatise on the Middle* (24:18):[17]

> That which is dependently co-arising is, we teach, emptiness. This is a provisional name, and this, indeed, is the Middle Way.

He interpreted this verse in the light of an apocryphal Chinese Buddhist text, *P'u-sa Ying-lo-pen-yeh ching* (T 33.714b5–10), which enunciates a three-step progression in awakening: (1) through penetrating insight into provisional form, one realizes emptiness; (2) through penetrating insight into emptiness, one realizes provisional form; and (3) through seeing their unity, one realizes the Middle Way. Since the phenomenal particulars exist as the result of the countless causes and conditions, there are no fixed permanent realities. When the causes and conditions disperse, a given reality will also undergo change. This is emptiness. However, it is because all realities are empty of permanent characteristics or substance that the phenomenal particulars exist. These have provisional forms or designations; they are real but not enduring. Thus, emptiness and provisional form are interdependent or, more precisely, aspects of each other. When the two are thus seen simultaneously, this is the Middle. Although the three are inseparable, we can say that each of the three—emptiness, provisional form, and Middle—contains the other two. This is known as the "perfect harmony of the threefold truth."

These are not three truths but a single truth understood in a threefold way. In the *Mo-ho chih-kuan* Chih-i states:

> One emptiness is all emptiness; there are no provisional forms and no middles that are not emptiness. All is insight into emptiness. One form is all forms; there are no emptinesses and no middles that are not form. All is insight into provisional form. One middle is all middles; there are no emptinesses and no forms that are not the middle. All is insight into the middle. (T 46.55b15–18)

The threefold truth may be expressed tentatively in terms of the subject as "the threefold insight in one mind" and in terms of the object as "the threefold truth in one realm." The perfect union of subject and object is the awakening or enlightenment described as "the three thousand worlds in one thought-instant," the realization of all phenomenal particulars (dharma) contained in a single thought-instant based on the principle of one-is-all and all-is-one of dependent co-arising. Simply put, it is the realization of dharma-as-it-is in the nondichotomous mode of knowing. The dichotomy of subject and object, the disruption of "the threefold insight in one mind" and "the threefold truth in one realm," is caused by the blind passions (*kleśa*) abounding in the unenlightened. This is the reason that *kleśa* becomes the primary concern of Chih-i's elaborate analysis of phenomena and the object of meditative practice.

The threefold truth of emptiness, provisional form, and Middle pervades all aspects of life. When the threefold truth is still latent and hidden in sentient beings, it is called the threefold Buddha-nature. When it appears as the teaching in the world of delusion, it is called the threefold path. Manifested as awakening or insight, they become the threefold wisdom. That which obstructs the realization of the threefold truth is the threefold passions. When the threefold truth becomes manifest as the Buddha, we have the threefold Buddha-body. In this way the whole structure of T'ien-t'ai is based on the threefold truth. Space does not allow us to expand on all of them, but let us review the content of threefold wisdom.

Chih-i inherits the basic structure of awakening found in Seng-chao when he states:

> The constant realm (known) is without characteristics (*laksana*) and the constant subject (knower) is without an object. By means of the prajñā without an object the realm without characteristics becomes its focus. The realm without characteristics harmonizes with the prajñā without an object. Prajñā and realm exist in the darkness of oneness, yet they are called realm and prajñā. Therefore, it is called non-activity. (T 46.9c2–5)

Here is the same relationship found between the knowing subject (which is without an object) and the known object (which is without any knowable characteristics) that we saw in Seng Chao, but with one significant difference. In Seng-chao's thought the possibility of the oneness of subject and object falling into *unio mystica* exists, whereas in Chih-i the distinction of subject and object is underscored when he clarifies the "darkness of oneness" as constituted by the realm (object) and prajñā (subject). Based on this fact, he speaks of the threefold wisdom which contains simultaneously (1) the wisdom that distinguishes phenomenal particulars, (2) the wisdom that sees their equality or sameness, and (3) the wisdom that sees simultaneously universal equality and multiple distinctions. The first affirms phenomenal forms, the second emptiness, and the third the Middle.

If we pursue the relationship between the threefold truth (object) and threefold insight (subject) within the T'ien-t'ai system of thought, the former is called the "essential nature" of reality and the latter the "cultivated nature" of reality. That is, the threefold truth is fundamental to all phenomena in the world, whereas the threefold insight must be cultivated, developed, and fully mastered. But these are not two separate realities, for the actualization of cultivated nature (threefold insight) is nothing other than the essential nature (threefold truth) fully realizing itself. Their relationship is likened to that of a lamp (essential nature) and the light it emits (cultivated nature), the latter being necessary for the former's illumination. Whereas from the standpoint of the essential nature of reality, there is nothing to be abandoned and nothing to be realized, the standpoint of the cultivated nature is one in which we are aware of the distinction between delusion and enlightenment (and ultimately their nonduality). T'ien-t'ai takes as the object of contemplation the delusory thoughts which naturally occupy the foreground of human awareness. This meditation on delusion leads to insight into the nonduality of delusion and enlightenment. The two are fundamentally identical, being nothing but emptiness, and enlightenment is simply freedom from the deep-rooted ignorance that prevents one from penetrating this basic fact.

The objects of T'ien-t'ai contemplation are summarized in the ten realms (*Mo-ho chih-kuan*, T 46.49a28–49c4, 99a16–118b2):

1. The phenomenal realm, the realm of the five aggregates, twelve fields, and eighteen worlds, which constitute life as we experience it.
2. The realm of blind passions, which is unnoticed and remains latent within the psyche but becomes apparent as one deepens contemplation.
3. The realm of illness brought about through unduly rigorous physical discipline.
4. The realm of karmic law, whereby countless previous lives cause our present condition.

5. The realm of demons, which appear in profound contemplation and which agitate the practitioner.
6. The realm of meditation, which can be a major obstacle to insight, if one becomes stubbornly attached to it.
7. The realm of dogmatic views about meditation, especially the view that one is free from all views.
8. The realm of arrogance and pride.
9. The realm of two vehicles, rooted in negative emptiness.
10. The bodhisattva realm, pointing to the attachment to bodhisattva activities, which must be overcome through contemplation and insight.

Each of these realms, including those of delusion, is none other than the realm of truth, *dharmadhātu* (*Mo-ho chih-kuan*, T 46.49c20–21). This focus on the realms or states of delusion is considered to be a unique feature of T'ien-t'ai Buddhism. A later T'ien-t'ai text states:

> The single character, "possess" (*chü*), manifests the essence of this school. The fact that the essential nature of reality possesses good is well known among other teachers but that it possesses the condition of evil is not taught by anyone else. Therefore, the merit of this school is the claim to nature-possession (*hsing-chü*), and that merit is the nature of evil (*hsing-o*) (*T'ien-t'ai-chuan fo-hsin-yin-chi*, T 46.934a12–14).

The majority of Buddhist schools assert that the fundamental nature of man is pure and good but covered over by defilements; hence meditative practice is directed to seeing the immaculate nature of reality. In T'ien-t'ai, however, the stress is on the evil nature of man, because delusion is the common experience of everyone, and the contemplation on evil, rather than good, is accessible to all. This universality of evil means that even the Buddha possesses the nature of evil. Conversely, even the *icchantika*, said to be devoid of Buddha-nature, possesses the nature of good. This is explained by the metaphor of the bamboo containing the nature or potential of fire. While the bamboo has the potential of burning, unless there is fire, it will never burn. But the condition of fire makes combustion a reality; if there is fire, the bamboo will burn. Likewise, evil contains the nature of good. When the conditions are ripe, good appears and overcomes evil. Likewise, the nature of evil is found in good, since evil is essential for the maximum operation of good.

> In the insight of Mahāyāna when one sees the evil mind, it is not the evil mind. Moreover, the evil is at the same time the good. And it is neither good nor evil. When one sees the good mind, it is not the good mind. Moreover, the good is at the same time evil. And it is neither evil nor good. The insight into one mind leads to threefold mind. (*Fa-hua hsüan-i*, T 33.778c26–29)

In terms of the threefold truth, the insight into the good and evil minds leads to emptiness; the insight into the simultaneity of good and evil to provisional form; and the insight into neither good nor evil to the middle.

Evil goes against good, but when one realizes that it, too, is emptiness, then one is liberated from its bondage and realizes freedom. This is the awareness that evil is the product of various causes and conditions and has no enduring, permanent reality. The wisdom to see this dissolves not only karmic evil, but it also becomes the very content of the "great permanence and great bliss" that is dharmakāya. When Chih-i speaks of dissolving evil, he means that the "cultivated" evil manifested in the world of dependent co-arising is destroyed, but that "essential" evil never disappears. Essential evil is a crucial aspect of the true nature of reality, which means that it is necessarily an aspect of Buddhahood. The Buddha does not possess cultivated evil and, hence, is free of evil, but he retains the essential evil so that he can completely identify himself with and effectively work for the salvation of evil beings floundering in the ocean of saṃsāra. Thus, the saying that the Buddha "uses evil all day long, but he is never defiled by evil. Because he is not defiled by evil, he does not create evil."

This penetration of evil into good and good into evil is formulated as the T'ien-t'ai theory of "the mutual containment of the ten realms" (T 46.52c10–11; T 33.693c6–7). Based on the basic Buddhist view that samsāra consists of wandering through the six realms of hellish existence, hungry ghosts, beasts, fighting demons, humans, and heavenly beings, it adds the four enlightened realms—the hearers, solitary Buddhas, bodhisattvas, and Buddhas. Mutual containment means that each realm contains the other nine realms; for example, the realm of hellish existence contains the realm of Buddhas, and the realm of Buddhas contains the realm of hellish existence. More precisely, this means that the nature of Buddhahood is found in beings of hell, and the nature of hellish existence is contained in Buddhahood. These "realms" are the various states that beings are subject to, depending on their karmic past and insight into the true nature of reality. Thus, beings in the first six realms see reality as being; the hearers and solitary Buddhas see reality as emptiness; the bodhisattvas see reality in provisional form; and the Buddhas see reality as the Middle.

In addition to building a comprehensive and systematic doctrine incorporating the major ideas of Chinese Buddhism that had evolved up to his time, Chih-i established the basic forms of religious practice which had a decisive impact on subsequent developments in East Asian Buddhism. Historically, T'ien-t'ai came to have a major influence on Hua-yen practice, it became the basis for the evolution of Ch'an, and in Japan it was to spawn the practice-oriented Kamakura schools. The basic thrust of religious practice was formulated by Chih-i as follows:

> Although religious practice implies forward movement, there is no progression without prajñā. The guidance of practice by prajñā-insight would not be authentic unless it is based on true reality. The eyes of true wisdom together with the feet of true practice lead a person to the realm of coolness and serenity. Thus, understanding is the basis of practice, and practice completes prajñā. (*Fa-hua hsüan-i* T 33.715b17–18)

The practice advocated by T'ien-t'ai can be subsumed under the four types of samādhi, which are focused on the ten realms of contemplation noted above.

The constant-sitting samādhi, which involves ninety days of continuous meditation before the image of Amitābha Buddha, during which time the mind focuses on the true nature of reality, the discriminated phenomenal world as the realm of peace, and the nonduality of saṃsāra and nirvāṇa, self and Buddha, blind passion and enlightenment. One realizes that in the experience of emptiness that which sees and that which is seen are inseparable and that suchness can never be grasped by the conventional, dichotomous mind. This samādhi was newly formulated by Chih-i, based on different practices found in various scriptures.

The constant-walking samādhi, which prescribes the circumambulation of the Amitābha image placed at the center of the training hall. The period of training is set at ninety days, during which time one constantly recites the name of Amitābha, or holds the image of Amitābha in consciousness, until one realizes the nonduality of self and Buddha.

The combination of sitting and walking samādhi, preceded by the purification of sins, which is entirely different from the first two. This may be practiced for seven days, following the prescription of the *Vaipulya Sūtra,* or for twenty-one, following the *Lotus Sūtra,* accompanied by elaborate rituals of worship, bathing, incense purification, repentance, chanting of dhāraṇī and sūtras, circumambulation, and meditative practice. The repetition of these rituals in a sanctified hall is meant to cultivate the insight into emptiness, provisional form, and Middle.

The samādhi which involves neither walking nor sitting. That is, wherever thought is awakened that thought becomes the object of contemplation, whether one is walking, sitting, standing, or lying down. Everyday life is the arena of this practice in which one observes sequentially: the mind prior to thought, the arising of thought, the activity of thought, and the ending of thought. The object of contemplation can be either good or bad thoughts. Good thoughts are observed as containing evil, and bad thoughts as containing good. It is important to practice the samādhi on evil, so that one is not enslaved to evil; in fact, evil is never eradicated but retained as an object of samādhi, for evil is not an obstruction to enlightenment and enlightenment does not hinder evil. This samādhi reveals that any static and permanent division between good and evil is the product of a self-centered human perspective. In meditation, one penetrates through evil to see the true nature of reality. Since the original nature of evil, unveiled, is true reality, when evil appears, the true nature of reality also appears. This is especially important for those of low moral character who have no interest in cultivating good; the only way to teach them samādhi is to have them concentrate on evil and see its true nature.

Religiously speaking, these four types of samādhi have a dual purpose: repentance based on actual "fact," expressed through the rituals of purification and worship of Buddha, and repentance based on fundamental "principle," through insight into the true nature of reality. The latter destroys the root ignorance of karmic evil, and the former does away with evil actions and their consequences.

In sum, Chih-i affirms the true nature of reality, manifested in phenomenal existence. To live with this vision in the midst of a suffering world, sharing wisdom and compassion, was his bodhisattva ideal, an ideal grounded in the real:

> In relating to *dharmadhātu* and contemplating *dharmadhātu,* there is not a single form or single fragrance that is not the Middle Way. This is also true for the realms of selfhood, Buddhahood, and sentient life. The five aggregates and six sense-fields are all suchness; there is no suffering to be abandoned. Ignorance and defilements are none other than enlightenment; there is no cause of suffering to be sundered. Extreme and erroneous views are all the Middle and right; there is no path to be cultivated. Samsara is nirvana; there is no extinction of blind passions to be realized. Because there is no suffering and its cause, there is no such thing as the mundane world. Because there is no path and extinction, there is no such thing as the supramundane world. All is one true nature of reality; besides the true nature of reality, there are no separate dharmas. (*Mo-ho chih-kuan,* T 46.1c23–29)

This grand affirmation was sustained by a life dedicated to relentless and rigorous religious practice whose ultimate goal was the sanctification of this samsaric world as the Pure Land and the affirmation of each individual reality as of supreme worth. True wisdom and true compassion were thus to be realized in the here and now.

Hua-yen

While both San-lun and T'ien-t'ai firmly established their teaching and practice upon the Mādhyamika transmission in China, Hua-yen inherited a different lineage, although it too was based on the philosophy of emptiness. The fundamental difference between the two great rival schools, T'ien-t'ai and Hua-yen, derived from their respective scriptural sources, the *Lotus Sūtra* and the *Avatamsaka-sūtra.* While the former is a great epic of bodhisattva activity in samsāra, filled with every imaginable kind of liberative techniques to save all beings, the latter is the revelation of the accomplished state of Buddhahood that constitutes the universe of enlightenment. While all the other Mahāyāna sūtras are sermons of the Buddha, delivered after emerging from deep samādhi, the *Avataṃsaka* is a series of expositions by various bodhisattvas describing the profound state of samādhi.

The two schools also differed doctrinally because of the prominent place of Tathāgatagarbha thought in the formation of Hua-yen Buddhism, especially in the third patriarch and systematizer, Fa-tsang (643–712).[19] Whereas in India this tradition had never become an independent movement comparable in influence to Mādhyamika and Yogācāra, in China it had an unparalleled impact and some of its major texts, such as the *Awakening of Faith in the Mahāyāna,* took on the status of scripture. Fa-tsang uses two kinds of classification of doctrines (*p'an-chiao*) to highlight the significance of this tradition. One is the Four Tenets classification—Hīnayāna, Mādhyamika, Yogācāra, and Tathāgatagarbha (T 44.243b.23–28); and the other is the Five Teachings—Hīnayāna, elementary Mahāyāna (both Mādhyamika and Yogācāra), advanced Mahāyāna (Tathāgatagarbha), abrupt teaching, and the perfect teaching of Hua-yen.[20] In both Tathāgatagarbha thought is placed at the apex of traditional Buddhism, and in the latter it is also considered to be the basis of Hua-yen doctrine.

One of the primary reasons for this emphasis was to counter the powerful influence of the great scholar-translator, Hsüan-tsang (600–664) and his newly introduced Yogācāra-Vijñaptimātrata ideas by integrating them into the Hua-yen system by resorting to Tathāgatagarbha thought. This resulted in the Hua-yen focus on the world of phenomenal particulars, although on its own terms. That is, Hua-yen sees all things from the standpoint of the accomplished state of Buddhahood; this world, *lokadhātu,* and the world of enlightenment, *dharmadhātu,* are not two separate worlds within the cosmic samādhi of Vairocana Buddha. The only difference between the two worlds is the ignorant attachments of beings to the self misperceived as enduring, to words and concepts mistaken as absolute, and to external forms misconceived as substantial. While T'ien-t'ai does not hesitate to focus on delusory thoughts, Hua-yen chooses to see the world as it is transparently illuminated by Vairocana Buddha. Both schools agree, however, that delusion and enlightenment penetrate each other through and through. "The real embraces the ramifications of delusion, and delusion penetrates to the fountainhead of the real. Essential nature and phenomenal aspects are mutually harmonized without hindrance and without impediment" (*Fen-ch'i-chang,* T 45.499a.19–20).

The Hua-yen analysis of dharma (a term replaced with the Chinese term *shih* by the first patriarch, Tu-shun) forms the basis of the universe of interpenetration and interrelationship of all phenomenal realities. In a small tract, a commentary on the *Heart Sūtra,* Fa-tsang analyzes on three levels the meaning of its opening lines, "form is none other than emptiness, and emptiness is none other than form" (T 33.553a25–553b.24).[21]

1. Where form exists, its negation, emptiness, cannot exist. But where there is emptiness, form cannot exist. "If both existed at the same time, both would be nullified." Thus, on this level, form and emptiness, being and non-being, are contradictory opposites, each asserting its own reality as standing against the other.

2. However, if emptiness is true emptiness (śūnyatā), it does not hinder the existence of form; and if form is really form (*rūpa*), it does not hinder the manifestation of emptiness. If emptiness obstructs form, it leads to the error of nihilism, and if form obstructs emptiness, it falls into the error of eternalism. Both are unacceptable and must be negated. Here we see a relationship between form and emptiness that defies conventional logic. It is clearly not a relationship of mutual dependency or relativity, but what kind of relationship is it? The next section of the commentary provides the answer.

3. The entirety of emptiness is, in fact, nothing but form itself, and the entirety of form is nothing other than emptiness itself. The relationship is such that when one is affirmed, the other is negated, and vice versa. This mutual negation and affirmation are further analyzed in the following way. Emptiness is identical with form, because (1) emptiness is eliminated and form established, where form is revealed and emptiness is hidden; (2) form is submerged and emptiness manifested, where form is exhausted while emptiness is manifested; (3) both emptiness and form are submerged, because dharma-as-it-is cannot be one-sided. Such terms as "eliminated," "hidden," "submerged," and "exhausted" connote negation, implying the affirmation of the other; and such terms as "established," "revealed," "manifested," and "secured" indicate affirmation, implying the negation of the other. Here, affirmation and negation are centered on a single dharma. Thus, each dharma manifests both being and non-being, non-being and being. This is a basic contradiction contained in dependent co-arising itself: phenomenal form is the product of "co-arising," which affirms being; and emptiness is its negation, suggested in the term "dependent." The dharma as product of dependent co-arising, then, is being yet non-being, non-being yet being. "True emptiness is none other than wondrous being."

This understanding of dharma in Hua-yen as the product of dependent co-arising is developed dynamically in terms of the interrelationship of multitudes of dharmas. This contrasts with the *Heart Sūtra,* where the negation and affirmation occur in a single dharma rather than among innumerable dharmas. In the central concept of "the nonobstructed interrelationship of phenomenal particulars with other phenomenal particulars" (*shih-shih wu-ai*) the crucial term is "nonobstructed," which affirms the mutual negation and affirmation taking place among countless phenomenal entities (*shih*). What this means may be shown by analyzing two basic concepts in the thought of Fa-tsang: mutual identification (*hsiang-chi*) and mutual penetration (*hsiang-ju*).

Mutual identification focuses on the spatial dimension of dependent co-arising by clarifying the relationship between being and non-being, which operates as follows:

> First, when self is being, the other is by necessity emptiness; therefore, the other is identified with self, for the self is dynamic because the other lacks own-being. Second, when self is emptiness, the other is by necessity being, therefore, the self is identified with the other, for the other is dynamic because the self lacks own-being. Since they cannot both be being at the same time, nor non-being at the same time, there is nothing that is not mutually identified. If this were not the case, dependent co-arising could not be formed and the fallacy of own-being would persist. (*Fen-ch'i-chang*, T 45.503b.10–16)

Here it is clear that mutual identification is not a simple union, merging, or identification of phenomenal particulars in which the respective identities are lost. It is basically a relationship of contradictory opposites, such that the affirmation of one means the negation of the other. Although expressed in terms of self and other here, it applies to multitudinous selves and others.

In contrast to mutual identification, mutual penetration explicates the temporal dimension of dependent co-arising. It is based on the functional aspect of each phenomenal particular in relation to all other particulars, such that it may or may not possess the power to affect the other in the relationship, depending on the focus of power. Here is Fa-tsang's description of mutual penetration:

> When the self has complete power to affect another, it is said to embrace the other. Since the other is completely devoid of power, it is able to enter the self. But when the other is with power and self is devoid of power (the opposite holds true). Since this does not depend on the substance itself, it is not mutual identification. Functional powers interpenetrate; therefore, there is mutual penetration. Since the two, self and other, cannot both be with power, nor both without power, there is nothing that is not mutual penetration. Since without power (entering) with power and with power (entering) without power are nondual, all dharmas are always mutually penetrating. (*Fen-ch'i-chang*, T 45.503b.17–22)

Mutual penetration is again the relationship of contradictory opposites, each unique and separate, such that when the self possesses the active power to affect another, the other is negated; and when the dynamic power of the other is affirmed, the self is negated. In actuality, they are seen as occurring simultaneously, so that no single dharma continues to dominate.

Both mutual identification and mutual penetration are aspects of a singular dharma occurring in interaction with others, and they do not operate separately or independently. But when mutual identification is taking place, mutual penetration is hidden, and when the latter occurs, the former is hidden. They are both dynamic aspects of phenomenal particulars, interconnecting with all other particulars in the universe of dependent co-arising. Utilizing these two concepts, Fa-tsang develops a detailed analysis of the Hua-yen universe of dependent co-arising, the foundation of which consists of the following: (1) each dharma or *shih* is unique and different; (2) but each pervades all others and contributes to their uniqueness; (3) both of these facts coexist harmoniously; (4) mutual identification occurs among separate bodies; (5) likewise mutual penetration occurs among separate bodies; (6) both substance and function are all-pervasive; (7) mutual identification occurs within a single body; (8) likewise mutual penetration occurs within a single body; (9) both are all-pervasive without any obstruction; and (10) there is complete harmony between separate and single bodies. What is referred to as "separate bodies" points to dependent co-arising *among* countless entities, while "single body" points to dependent co-arising *within* a given entity, both being aspects of the same reality seen from a different perspective (*Hua-yen-ching t'an-hsüan-chi,* T 35.124a.17–125a.11).

The multiplicity of interrelationships among countless dharmas simultaneously negating and affirming each other is succinctly expressed in the fourfold worldview of Hua-yen, as formulated by Ch'eng-kuan but already implicit in the thought of its founder, Tu-shun. The fourfold worldview comprises (1) the world of phenomenal particulars, naïvely affirmed, (2) the world of ultimate principle, (3) the world of the nonobstructed interrelationship between the ultimate principle and phenomenal particulars, and (4) the world of the nonobstructed interrelationships among phenomenal particulars. In this system, the crucial term is again "nonobstructed," which we touched upon earlier. Nonobstructed means first of all that clearly there are distinctions among the multiplicity of phenomenal particulars, *shih-shih,* each unique and separate from each other. This affirmation of multiple dharmas, however, is not a kind of naïve realism, for they are interrelated in such a way that simultaneous negation and affirmation are occurring. Second, the nonobstruction takes place when A is negated and non-A is affirmed, but simultaneously A is affirmed and non-A negated. That is, the "nonobstructed" interrelationship between A and non-A is identical to that between form and emptiness, the difference being that in the latter case it occurs within a single dharma, whereas in the former case it occurs among two or more dharmas.

Thus, the nonobstructed interrelationship among phenomenal particulars does not suggest in any way a merging of individual dharmas where distinctions are obliterated, nor does it establish a oneness where the parts exist only to serve the whole. Rather, it is descriptive of the universe of enlightenment wherein each and every phenomenal reality is the center of a circle without a circumference. This is the Hua-yen formulation of dependent co-arising, but here the affirmation of each individual reality is due to "co-arising," and its negation is suggested by its "dependent" nature. "Nonobstructed" extends this mutual affirmation and negation to countless dharmas in the universe, such that when one is affirmed all others are negated, and when all others are negated, one is affirmed. And this occurs simultaneously and dynamically without beginning and without end. "Each individual reality, besides being itself, reflects in it something of the universal, and at the same time it is itself because of other individuals."[22] Inherent in this relationship are mutual negation and affirmation, and it should not be understood in the simplistic sense of relativity in which no negation occurs. That is, it is totally misleading to think that Hua-yen interdependence means that A is simply dependent on B, B on C, C on D, *ad infinitum,* albeit multilaterally.

Fa-tsang attempts to disclose this interdependency through the teaching of six aspects, each of which contains the other aspects (*Fen-ch'i-chang,* T 45.503b.10–16). The *total* aspect, for example, can be found in the "house" that exists before us. The *distinctive* aspect refers to each component that makes up the house–rafters, beams, pillars, walls, roof, etc.–distinguished from the "house." The *identical* aspect is the common purpose to which the distinctive components work together to realize the house. The *separate* aspect reminds us once again that each component is unique and different, especially when contrasted with one another. The *integrating* aspect denotes the convergence of causes and conditions in dependent co-arising which makes the house possible. The *disintegrating* aspect makes possible the divergence or dispersal of causes and conditions that enables each component to retain its individuality. It is clear that truth in Hua-yen is not a mystical oneness but a plurality of phenomenal particulars in dynamic interaction.

This dynamic interrelationship is also expressed in another key metaphor: the coexistence of master and servant. "Master" affirms a concrete particular in a world of multiplicities, whereby all others are negated and subsumed as "servants." But simultaneously the roles are reversible: the "master" now submits himself to others and becomes a "servant," and the former "servant" now rules supreme as "master" over all others. Since nothing is fixed in the fluid universe of impermanence, each being, thing, or object can become master or servant. Only in this absolute affirmation and absolute negation can we speak of each being the center of a circle without a circumference. Symbolically this is expressed in the legend of the infant Buddha, who took seven steps at birth, signifying the transcendence of the six realms of samsāra, and proclaimed to the world: "Heavens above, heavens below, I alone am the World-Honored One!"

The interrelationship between master and servant is given a contemporary formulation by Nishitani when he writes:

> That a thing *is*—its absolute autonomy—comes about only in unison with a subordination *of* all things. It comes about only on the field of śūnyatā, where the being of all other things, while remaining to the very end the being that it is, is emptied out. Moreover, this means that the autonomy of this one thing is only constituted through a subordination *to* all other things. Its autonomy comes about only on a standpoint from which it makes all other things to be what they are, and in so doing is emptied of its own being.[23]

The truly autonomous being realizes itself simultaneously as independent and interdependent, absolutely absolute and absolutely relative. Only in such a thoroughgoing realization, based on dependent co-arising, can the fullest possibilities of true equality and true freedom be realized.

The Hua-yen world of interpenetration and interconnectedness is not simply a spiritual vision but is rooted in the nature of reality-as-it-is, the product of dependent co-arising, which is being yet non-being, non-being yet being. This contradiction cannot be understood or resolved through rationality alone; it can be realized only through religious practice. Hence, the emphasis on experiential understanding: "It is the realm not comprehensible by words, not attainable by reason; it is called the realm of ultimate experience."[24] This realm, it should be underscored once again, is not that of a mystical experience which submerges both subject and object but that in which subject and object are one, yet two, and two, yet one.

The attainment of prajñā-insight is necessary in order to fully comprehend the Hua-yen universe of interdependency; and this universe (object) is manifested simultaneously with the realization of prajñā (subject). Buddhism is not merely a matter of subjective epistemological or psychological transformation, teaching only a new way to see the world which remains unchanged. Since the radical transformation or turnabout (*parāvṛtti*) in enlightenment experience involves both the subject and object, both the self and the world undergo transformation. Fa-tsang attempts to explicate this problem in the following dialogue:

> Question: If (reality-as-it-is) is dependent on prajñā, it was not originally existent. How can you say that it has always been like this? Answer: If prajñā

> is eliminated, there can be no talk of dependent co-arising. Only by reliance on prajñā can we speak of it as originally existent. Why? If prajñā is not realized, there is nothing to be said. If it is realized, there is neither beginning nor end. Thus, prajñā and dharma are both originally existent.
> Question: Does it depend upon prajñā, or on the nature of dharma? Answer: It depends on prajñā and on the nature of dharma. They co-exist together. (*Fen-ch'i-chang,* T 45.504b.1–6)

The conclusion affirms that neither prajñā nor dharma has priority; they are simultaneously realized. The realization includes both senses of that term, *recognition* and *actualization* of this new world, and is reached in ten stages of knowing, summarized by Fa-tsang (*T'an-hsüan-chi,* T 35.347a.2–b.27). The ten stages show a transition from an epistemological to what might be called an ontological realization. The first three interpret consciousness as subject standing against an object, as projecting the external world, and as the irreducible basis for all mental activities. The next four relate consciousness to *ālaya-vijñāna,* to Tathāgatagarbha, to the absolute principle behind phenomenal particulars, and to the interaction between this principle and phenomena. The final three stages sweep away all traces of individual consciousness and any reference to absolute principle, revealing this world-as-it-is (*dharmadhātu*) in the eyes of the enlightened, as a dynamic realm interwoven by mutual identification and mutual penetration. The world is its own magic.

The Hua-yen universe of interconnectedness and interrelationships, symbolized by the mythical net of Indra, is inexhaustible in its depth. So also are the manifestations of true wisdom and true compassion, which bring all existence, animate and inanimate, to true and real life. Having returned to its own home ground, each being radiates its own unique light to illuminate the universe and serve all others. Here is the living universe of enlightenment wherein the self becomes truly the self by reaching out to all others as itself. In the words of Nishitani:

> In the circumincessional relationship a field can be opened on which contradictory standpoints—where the other is seen as *telos,* and where the self is seen as *telos;* where the self serves others and makes itself a nothingness, and where the self remains forever the self itself—are both radicalized precisely by virtue of their totally being one.[25]

The grand epic of true compassion, the *Avataṃsaka-sūtra,* receives its most systematic formulation at the hands of Fa-tsang. It is a vision reflecting the Ocean-seal samādhi, wherein all reality is affirmed just as it is. But this vision needs to be actualized through the struggles of people, past, present, and future, so that universal liberation and freedom can be fully realized. Such a cosmic endeavor, known as the Flower of Garland samādhi, the adornment of the universe by the salvific activities of countless Buddhas and bodhisattvas, anticipated the rise of Ch'an and Pure Land Buddhism.

Notes

1. For the study of dharma from the standpoint of various Buddhist schools, see Hirakawa Festschrift Committee, ed., *Bukkyō ni okeru hō no kenkyū* [A study of dharma in Buddhism] (Tokyo: Shunjūsha, 1975). I am especially indebted to the articles on San-lun by Hirai Shun'ei and Yasumoto Tōru in this volume. For a good summary of Western interpretations, see John Ross Carter, *Dhamma: Western Academic and Sinhalese Buddhist Interpretations* (Tokyo: Hokuseido Press, 1978).

2. See Takasaki Jikido, *A Study of the Ratnagotravibhāga* (Roma: Instituto italiano per il medio ed estremo oriente, 1966) 182.

3. See Tsukamoto Zenryū, *Jōron kenkyū* (Studies in *Chao-lun*) (Kyoto: Hōzōkan, 1955) 22; and Richard Robinson, *Early Mādhyamika in India and China* (Madison: University of Wisconsin Press, 1967) 123–55. Also informative is Ueda Yoshifumi, "Thinking in Buddhist Philosophy," *Philosophical Studies of Japan* 5 (1964) 69–94.

4. Herbert Fingarette, *Confucius: The Secular as Sacred* (New York: Harper & Row, 1972). While not in total agreement with Fingarette, I support his major arguments.

5. See, e.g., *The Complete Works of Chuang Tzu* (New York: Columbia University Press, 1968) 240–42.

6. Nakamura Hajime, *Ways of Thinking of Eastern Peoples* (Honolulu: University Press of Hawaii, 1968) 240–42. See also *Kegon shisō* (Hua-yen Thought), ed. Kawada Kumatarō and Nakamura Hajime (Kyoto: Hōzōkan, 1960) 97–127, for an analysis of dharma, *tattvasya, lakṣaṇa,* etc. found in Kumārajīva's translations.

7. See *Madhyāntavibhāgatīkā,* trans. Edward Conze, in *Buddhist Texts through the Ages* (New York: Philosophical Library, 1954) 170–72, "The Synonyms of Emptiness."

8. See Robinson, *Early Mādhyamika,* 220.

9. Nishitani Keiji, *Religion and Nothingness,* trans. Jan Van Bragt (Berkeley: University of California Press, 1982) 119–40, and relevant articles in *The Religious Philosophy of Nishitani Keiji: Encounter with Emptiness,* ed. Taitetsu Unno (Berkeley: Asian Humanities Press, 1990).

10. Ibid., 108–9.

11. For a full treatment of the twofold truth we must consider the interpretations of Bhāvaviveka (sixth century) and Candrakīrti (seventh century), but for San-lun Piṅgala's views should suffice. For a brief survey of the three, see John S. Ishihara, "Rethinking the Doctrine of *Satya-dvaya,*" *Journal of the Chikushi Jogakuen College* 1 (1989) 63–86. For Candrakīrti, see *Lucid Expositions of the Middle Way,* trans. Mervyn Sprung (Boulder: Prajna Press, 1979) 230–32.

12. See, e.g., *The Problem of Two Truths in Buddhism and Vedanta,* ed. Mervyn Sprung (Boston: D. Reidel, 1973) 27, 87.

13. For general discussion, see Aaron Koseki, "Chi-tsang's Ta-ch'eng hsüan-lun: The Two Truths and the Buddha-Nature" (Ph.D. dissertation, University of Wisconsin, 1977).

14. See, e.g., Nagao Gadjin, *The Foundational Standpoint of Mādhyamika Philosophy* (Albany: State University of New York Press, 1989) 29–30.

15. For the biography of Chih-i and standard T'ien-t'ai doctrine, see Leon Hurvitz, *Chih-i (538–597): An Introduction to the Life and Ideas of a Chinese Buddhist Monk, Mélanges chinois et bouddhique* 12 (Brussels: Institut Belge des Hautes Études Chinoises, 1960–62).

16. First clarified by Yūki Reimon in "Zuitō-jidai no chūgoku-teki shinbukkyō kōki no rekishi-teki jijō" (Historical considerations in the rise of the new Sinified Buddhism of Sui-T'ang Dynasties), *Nihon bukkyō gakkai nenpō* 19 (1954) 79–96, and expanded in a series of articles in various journals on Shan-tao, T'an-ch'ien, and studies on Hua-yen, T'ien-t'ai, and Fa-hsiang texts. See also Stanley Weinstein, "Imperial Patronage in the Formation of the T'ang," in *Perspectives on the T'ang*, ed. Arthur F. Wright and Denis Twichet (New Haven: Yale University Press, 1973) 265–74.

17. For a careful discussion of the evolution of the Threefold Truth, see Paul Swanson, *Foundations of T'ien-t'ai Philosophy: The Flowering of the Two Truths Theory in Chinese Buddhism* (Berkeley: Asian Humanities Press, 1989).

18. For a fuller discussion, see Ueda Yoshifumi, "Thinking in Buddhist Philosophy," *Philosophical Studies of Japan* 5 (1964) 82.

19. Fa-tsang inherits many of the original ideas first expounded by the second patriarch, Chih-yen. See Robert Gimello, "Chih-yen and the Foundations of Hua-yen Buddhism" (Ph.D. dissertation, Columbia University, 1976). Peter Gregory gives a good account of the centrality of Tathāgatagarbha thought in Hua-yen, "Chinese Buddhist Hermeneutics: The Case of Hua-yen," *Journal of the American Academy of Religion* 51 (1983) 231–49.

20. Fa-tsang's interpretation of the Five Teachings is found in his *Hua-yen i-ch'eng chiao-i fen-ch'i chang*, commonly known as the *Hua-yen wu-chiao-chang*, contained in T 45. For an English translation, see Francis Cook, "Fa-tsang's Treatise on the Five Doctrines: An Annotated Translation" (Ph.D. dissertation, University of Wisconsin, 1970). I am currently preparing my own translation for publication.

21. For an English translation, see Francis Cook, "Fa-tsang's Brief Commentary on the *Prajña-pāramitā-hrdaya-sūtra*," *Mahāyāna Buddhist Meditation*, ed. Minoru Kiyota (Honolulu: University of Hawaii Press, 1978) 183–206.

22. D. T. Suzuki, *Essays in Zen Buddhism, Third Series* (New York: Samuel Weiser, 1971) 87.

23. Nishitani Keiji, *Religion and Nothingness*, 148.

24. Tu-shun, quoted in *Chu-hua-yen fa-chieh-kuan-men*, T 45.686c.25–28.

25. Nishitani Keiji, *Religion and Nothingness*, 284.

II. *Yogācāra in China*

JOHN P. KEENAN

WHEN THE FIRST Yogācāra texts were translated into Chinese shortly after the beginning of the fifth century, Neo-Taoist thought, such as that of Wang Pi (226–249) and Kuo Hsiang (d. 312), had become the dominant philosophic trend among literate Chinese. Thus, when the Buddhist monk-scholars employed their method of "matching concepts" (*ko-i*), the Chinese concepts involved were

Neo-Taoist versions of Chuang-tzu and Lao-tzu. This process of matching concepts was not, however, a simple aligning of Buddhist doctrinal notions with Neo-Taoist parallels. Indian Buddhism was not a monolithic set of defined ideas agreed upon by all. It represented a long and at times tortuous process of doctrinal development moving in different directions and based on different texts. These texts were introduced into China in a haphazard fashion, presenting to the Chinese a bewildering array of scriptural and commentarial sources. They needed to be rearranged in China, producing the *p'an chiao* systems of doctrinal classification and leading to the establishment of specific Chinese schools of Buddhist thinking.

Furthermore, ideas could not simply be matched, because the concerns and meaning contexts of Chinese philosophic questioning were not those of Indian thinking. Philosophic discussion, as with all things, co-arises dependently. Interests vary and meaningful speech is conditioned by consensual contexts of meaning. This can be seen in one of the very earliest pieces of Buddhist apologetic in China, Mou-tzu's *Treatise on Alleviating Doubts.*[1] Mou-tzu proceeds not by Indian analyses and reasoning but by showing that Buddhist doctrines and practices are in harmony with the classics and their teachings, relying on an accumulation of many examples from Chinese history to bring home each Buddhist point. While such argumentation was, it can be assumed, cogent to Chinese scholars and literati, it would have been meaningless to Indian thinkers.

Moreover, the general tenor of Neo-Taoist thinking was strongly ontological. "The Mysterious Learning" (*hsüan-hsüeh*), based on earlier Taoist cosmological descriptions, presented its insights by constructing interlocking insights into the ineffable *tao* as the ground of all that is. A close Indian analogue for this ontological orientation could be found in Abhidharma, not in its enunciated positions but in its ontological thrust toward evolving all-inclusive worldviews, a fact that accounts for the comparatively early translation of such texts as Vasubandhu's *Treasury of Abhidharma.* But more attractive to the Chinese were the Tathāgatagarbha teachings whose mystic affirmation of the non-empty reality of the ultimate seed or womb (*garbha*) recalls the Neo-Taoist insistence on the ineffability of the *tao.*

The core Mahāyāna texts, however, were based on *Prajñāpāramitā* insight into the falsification of *all* worldviews and on the rejection of *any* non-empty essence anywhere. Nāgārjuna's Mādhyamika use of a rigorously reasoned dialectic of negation in favor of unfabricated and immediate insight into the emptiness of all dependently co-arising beings moved in a context that denies meaning to all views. The Yogācāra turn toward conscious interiority and examination of the structure and functioning of consciousness moved in a context of critical awareness wherein meaning had to be grounded within conscious operations as empty and dependently co-arisen. These meaning contexts did not find ready parallels in Chinese thinking. Obvious misrepresentations of Buddhist doctrine were with time and further study easily corrected. But subtle changes in the way central doctrinal themes were understood and doctrinal meanings constructed were more difficult to recognize and probably impossible to correct in the absence of the Indian context.

A prime example of the resultant transmutation was the equation of the Indian notion of emptiness, śūnyatā, with the Neo-Taoist theme of non-being or nothingness, *wu*. For Wang Pi non-being was understood as the one, integrating basis and source for all the multiple and phenomenal beings. Thus the earliest Chinese understandings of emptiness, represented in "The Six Houses," often patterned their interpretation of emptiness on this Neo-Taoist notion of *wu*, despite that fact that in Indian thought emptiness was the negation of both being and non-being.[2]

The Ti-lun and She-lun Schools

The Yogācāra thinking of Asaṅga, Vasubandhu, and later commentators underwent a similar contextual transmutation. In the absence of the critical focus of Indian Yogācāra, their thought had to be matched with the more ontological questions of Chinese thinkers; hence the first Indian texts to be translated tended to be those which amalgamated Yogācāra themes with the Tathāgatagarbha teaching of the one pure reality behind all phenomenal appearances. One of the earliest Yogācāra texts introduced into China was *The Laṅkāvatāra Sūtra* (The Scripture on Entry into Laṅka), translated by Guṇabhadra in 443, a rather disunified scripture which in different sections both identify the container consciousness with the *tathāgata-garbha* and treat it without any such reference.[3]

The early-sixth-century dispute in the Ti-lun school, which was based on Vasubandhu's *Exposition of the Ten Stages* (*Shih-ti ching-lun*), between Bodhiruci and Ratnamati reflects a similar tension. While translating the *Exposition of the Ten Stages*, from which the school derives its name (. . . *-ti* . . . *-lun*), these two men argued over the proper understanding of the container consciousness, whether it was ultimately real and pure or completely defiled and to be eliminated upon realization of the ultimately pure mind. The fact that neither party questioned the reality of that ultimately pure mind seems to reflect not only the Tathāgatagarbha teaching of *Laṅkāvatāra Sūtra*, but also the Neo-Taoist affirmation of the reality of the primal *tao*.

This Ti-lun school was soon eclipsed by the prodigious efforts of Paramārtha (499–569), an Indian scholar-monk who arrived in Nankai (Canton) in 546. Two of his translations, Asaṅga's *Summary of the Great Vehicle* (*She Ta-ch'eng lun*) and Vasubandhu's *Commentary* on the same formed the basis for the establishment of the She-lun school of Yogācāra. Paramārtha accepted the reality of the pure mind of the *tathāgata-garbha* behind all phenomenal defilements. This inspired his rather frequent insertions and additions into the texts of Asaṅga and Vasubandhu. Indeed, he concludes his translation of Vasubandhu's *Commentary* by quoting the concluding verses from *The Analysis of the Jeweled Lineage,* the main treatise of the Tathāgatagarbha lineage, as if to suggest that Yogācāra leads to the affirmation of the non-empty reality of the *garbha.*[4] In his more exegetical works, *The Evolution of Consciousness* (*Chuan-shih lun*), *The Three Non-Natures* (*San Wu-hsing lun*), and *The Appearance of Consciousness* (*Hsien-shih lun*),[5] he identifies a ninth pure consciousness (*amala-vijñāna*) of suchness as a separate, non-empty reality apart from and realized only upon the eradication of the container and active consciousnesses. This not only repeats the Ti-lun position of Ratnamati but also recalls the pre-Asaṅgan Indian sources, especially the Maitreyan *Ornament of the Scriptures of the Great Vehicle.*[6] Paramārtha appears to belong to the lineage of the Maitreya texts that synthesize a critical understanding of defiled consciousness with the noncritical affirmation of the originally pure mind. Just as Maitreya's *Ornament of the Scriptures of the Great Vehicle* treated the other-dependent pattern only as "the basis of the error" of the imagined pattern,[7] so Paramārtha treats the other-dependent pattern as the subjective side of dualistic consciousness dependent on the linguistic projections of imagined essences in naming intended objects. Thus, for Paramārtha not only is the imagined pattern eliminated upon the realization of awakening, but the other-dependent pattern itself, since it is but one pole in illusory dualism, is also completely eradicated. This differs radically from Asaṅga's presentation of other-dependent consciousness as embodying both an impure, imagined aspect and a purified, perfected aspect realized upon the conversion of support.[8] Paramārtha further presents a formulation of the structure of consciousness quite different from any of his Indian predecessors. He describes three levels: (1) the container (*ālaya*) consciousness as the storehouse of seed impressions, (2) the appropriating (*ādāna*) consciousness (which in Asaṅga is synonymous with the container) as a distinct level of conscious clinging to and making one's own the illusions projected in virtue of the seed impressions, and (3) the six-sense consciousnesses as perceptual illusions due to that appropriation.[9] The realization of Pure Consciousness is then the sweeping away of the entire eight consciousnesses. In place of the conversion of support, Paramārtha uses the term "pure consciousness" to emphasize the discontinuity of this awakening with all prior consciousness.[10] One attains the *amala* consciousness of suchness as a distinct ninth level, a level which alone is real and true. This pure consciousness "is permanent and undefiled,"[11] terms used frequently to describe the *tathāgata-garbha.*

Asaṅga explains the conversion of support as a pivoting and purification of the other-dependent pattern of consciousness, but Paramārtha holds that such consciousness is completely eliminated, to be replaced by awareness of a separate pure consciousness now unencumbered by defilement. One first, he says, "dispenses with sense objects in order to empty the mind," and then when "both the sense object and consciousness are dissolved, this is identical with the true nature (*tattva* or *tathatā*). The true nature is identical with Pure Consciousness (*amala-vijñāna*)."[12] The same thrust is seen in his translations of Vasubandhu's *Treatise on the Buddha Nature,* a text that may have been authored by Paramārtha himself,[13] and in his translation of *The Awakening of Mahāyāna Faith,* a synthesis of Yogācāra themes under the dominant rubric of the one pure mind of the *garbha,* which enjoyed immense popularity in China.[14] The basic intent of Paramārtha was then to restrict the critical Yogācāra understanding of Asaṅga to defiled consciousness and to stress the ontological reality of the pure mind, the *garbha,* or the true nature as not empty. In so doing, he not only reclaimed the pre-Asaṅgan thought of some of the Maitreyan corpus, but also managed to present Yogācāra Buddhism in terms easily accessible to Chinese ontological thinking.

The Fa Hsiang School

The presence of a number of Yogācāra texts with their varying interpretations caused Hsüan Tsang (596–664) to become confused. Journeying to India to resolve his doubts, he arrived at Nālandā in 634, where he immersed himself in studying the Dharmapāla lineage of Yogācāra thought. Through Hsüan Tsang and his disciple Ch'i (646–682), Dharmapāla's (530–561) thought became the basis for all later East Asian Yogācāra under the name of the Fa Hsiang School, a name derived from the basic *Explication of Underlying Meaning* in its treatment of the patterns (*hsiang*) of the mental states (*fa*), that is, the three patterns of consciousness. Yet Dharmapāla's role in India seems to have been more circumscribed, for his texts are extant only in four Chinese translations, the principal of which is *The Complete Meaning of Conscious Construction Only* (*Ch'eng Wei-shih lun*), which became the textbook for all of East Asian Yogācāra.[15] Influenced by the Yogācāra dialectician and epistemologist Dignāga (480–540), Dharmapāla championed the conventional validity of other-dependent understanding, arguing against any attempt to subsume or eliminate other-dependency into a monistic Tathāgatagarbha notion.

In his theory of the four aspects (*bhāga*) of understanding, the first two aspects are those presented by earlier Yogācāra thinkers: insight (*darśana*) and image (*nimitta*) as the subjective and objective appearances of understanding. The third aspect, the self-realization (*svasaṃvitti*) of insight into image—that is, the conscious awareness implicit in gaining insight into image—comes from Dignāga. He himself added a fourth aspect, the realization of that self-realization (*svasaṃvitti-saṃvitti*), that is, a critical awareness of the entire process. But for Dharmapāla, insight and image are themselves not illusory but other-dependent. In contrast to Paramārtha, for whom the subject–object dichotomy implies a totally false duality to be eliminated upon the attainment of pure consciousness, in Dharmapāla and Hsüan Tsang they become imagined only when one clings to either as denoting an essential subject or essential objects. Thus Dharmapāla follows Asaṅga in distinguishing defiled and purified aspects within the other-dependent pattern of consciousness. He is then able to emphasize a valid role for conventional truth, expressed in conventional words and ideas and to hold that the structure of consciousness perdures into awakening and wisdom.[16]

He accounted for the possibility of defiled consciousness becoming awakened and purified by maintaining that the container consciousness contained not only impure seeds of illusion, but also pure seeds which, through cultivation in the path, mature until awakening. Here he departs from Asaṅga, who held that the container consciousness, itself completely incapable of bringing about awakening or purification, nevertheless could hear and attend to the doctrine, become gradually transformed by its permeations, and attain conversion because such permeations come from hearing doctrine as an outflow from the most pure Dharma realm.[17]

* * *

Hsüan Tsang's translation efforts, enjoying imperial patronage, soon outpaced and overshadowed the earlier She-lun school, and through the systematization of Ch'i and later scholars, such as the Korean monk Wonch'uk, made Fa Hsiang the orthodox version of Yogācāra throughtout East Asia.

While Hsüan Tsang's translations and interpretations are on the whole more faithful to Asaṅga and Vasubandhu, he seems to have been less attuned to Chinese philosophic concerns. Fa Hsiang, while beyond challenge in its doctrinal sophistication, tended to become a rigid and scholastic orthodoxy, for the Indian critical context behind the Yogācāra endeavor had been lost in China. Fa Hsiang was transmitted in China and Japan apparently without any felt need for new ideas or reinterpretation, signaling a system in decline. By contrast, Paramārtha's Yogācāra-Tathāgatagarbha notions, with their all-inclusive dynamism of the reality of the Pure Mind behind all phenomenal defilements, although disappearing as an independent school in China, spread in other schools, such as Hua-yen. Its notion of Pure Consciousness was more attuned to Chinese mystic thinking and practice.

Notes

1. Paul Pelliot, "Meou-Tseu ou les doutes leves," *T'oung Pao* 19 (1920) 255–433.
2. Nagao Gadjin, "Kū," in *Chūkan to yuishiki* (Tokyo: Wanami Shoten, 1978) 300.
3. For their identification, see *The Laṅkāvatāra Sūtra*, trans. D. T. Suzuki (London: Routledge, 1932) 190; also Takasaki Jikidō, *Nyoraizō shisō no keisei* (Tokyo: Shunjūsha, 1974) 327–28. Katsumata Shunkyō in his *Bukkyō ni okeru shinishikisetsu no kenkyū* (Tokyo: Sankibō Busshorin, 1974) 625, points out passages on the container consciousness where no such identification is made.
4. T 31.270a–b. English translation in *The Realm of Awakening: Chapter Ten of Asaṅga's Mahāyānasaṃgraha*, 259–61 (forthcoming).
5. Studied by Diana Y. Paul in her *Philosophy of Mind in Sixth-Century China* (Stanford, CA: Stanford University Press, 1984). Paul also provides a translation of the *Chuan-shih lun*. This book, the most complete study of Paramārtha in a Western language, sets the standard for future efforts.
6. John P. Keenan, "Original Purity and the Focus of Early Yogācāra," *Journal of the International Association of Buddhist Studies* 5:1 (1982) 7–18.
7. *Mahāyāna-sūtrālaṃkāra, Exposé de la Doctrine du Grand Véhicule*, trans. Sylvain Lévi (Paris: Champion, 1907) I 58. Note also that the *Saṃdhinirmocanasūtra* also speaks of "destroying" the container consciousness, but without any accompanying notion of a Pure Mind or *garbha*. See *Saṃdhinirmocanasūtra: L'Explication des Mystères*, trans. Étienne Lamotte (Paris: Maisonneuve, 1935) 197.
8. *La somme du Grand Véhicule d'Asaṅga: Mahāyānasaṃgraha*, trans. Étienne Lamotte (Louvain: Institut Orientaliste de Louvain, 1973) 125–26, 268.
9. Paul, *Philosophy of Mind*, 97–99.
10. As seen by comparing Paramārtha's *Chüeh-ting-ts'ang lun* with Hsüan Tsang's *Yuga lun*, both translations of the *Yogācārabhūmi*. See Katsumata, *Bukkyō ni okeru shinishikisetsu no kenkyū*, 699ff.
11. *Chüeh-ting-ts'ang lun* T 30.1020b. Translated in Paul, *Philosophy of Mind*, 143.
12. T 31 62c.13–14. Translated in Paul, *Philosophy of Mind*, 99. Also see the *Chüeh-ting-ts'ang lun*, T 30.1020b.
13. Takasaki Jikidō, "Shintai-yaku Shōdaijōron seshin shaku ni okeru nyoraizō-setsu: Hōshōron to no kanren," in *Yūki Kyōju ju-su kinen: Bukkyō shisōshi ronshū* (Tokyo: Daizō Shuppan, 1964) 241–42.
14. *The Awakening of Faith*, trans. with an introduction by Hakeda Yoshito.
15. French translation by Louis de la Vallée Poussin, *Vijñaptimātratāsiddhi: La Siddhi de Hiuan-Tsang*; English translation by Wei Tat, *Ch'eng Wei-shih Lun: Doctrine of Mere Consciousness*.
16. John P. Keenan, "A Study of the Buddhabhūmyupadeśa: The Doctrinal Development of the Notion of Wisdom in Yogācāra Thought" (Ph.D. dissertation, University of Wisconsin, Madison, 1980) 310–18.
17. Ibid., 318–19.

Bibliography

Sources

The Awakening of Faith. Translated by Hakeda Yoshito. New York: Columbia University Press, 1967.

Chan, Wing-tsit. *A Source Book in Chinese Philosophy.* Princeton, NJ: Princeton University Press, 1963.

Hsān Tsang (Hsüan-tsang). *Ch'eng Wei-shih Lun: The Doctrine of Mere-Consciousness.* Translated by Wei Tat. Hong Kong: Ch'eng Wei-shih Lun Publication Committee, 1973.

La Vallée Poussin, Louis de. *Vijñaptimātratāsiddhi: La siddhi de Hiuan-Tsang.* Paris: Geuthner, 1928–29.

Pelliot, Paul, trans. "Meou-Tseu ou les doutes levés." *T'oung Pao* 19 (1920) 255–433.

Studies

Liebenthal, Walter. "New Light on the Mahāyānasroddatpada-śastra." *T'oung Pao* 46 (1958) 155–216.

Liu, Ming-Wood. "The Mind-Only Teaching of Ching-ying Hui-yüan: An Early Interpretation of Yogācāra Thought in China." *Philosophy East and West* 35 (1985) 351–76.

——. "The Yogācāra and Mādhyamika Interpretations of the Buddha-Nature Concept in Chinese Buddhism." *Philosophy East and West* 35 (1985) 171–93.

Paul, Diana Y. *Philosophy of Mind in Sixth-Century China.* Stanford, CA: Stanford University Press, 1984.

Ruegg, David Seyfort. *La théorie du Tathāgatagarbha et du Gotra.* Paris: École Française d'Extrême-Orient, 1969.

13

The Spirituality of Emptiness in Early Chinese Buddhism

PAUL L. SWANSON

THE CONCEPTUAL INTERPRETATION and practical application of Buddhist emptiness underwent many stages during the introduction and assimilation of Buddhism in China, including the attempt to "match" (*ko-i*) Buddhist concepts with Neo-Taoist ideas, most significantly Taoist "nothingness" or "void" (*wu*) with Buddhist emptiness (Skt. *śūnyatā;* Chinese *kung*). This process reached an early climax philosophically in the San-lun interpretations of Chi-tsang (549–623) and in the realms of both philosophy and practice in the Sinitic synthesis of T'ien-t'ai Chih-i (538–597).[1] The understanding (and misunderstanding) of emptiness in early Chinese Buddhist history is best illustrated by the Chinese attempts to interpret the Mādhyamika theory of the two truths—the mundane, provisional, worldly, or conventional truth (*saṃvṛtisatya*) and the real or ultimate truth (*paramārthasatya*). An unfortunate legacy of the *ko-i* practice of matching Buddhist concepts with Taoist terms was the tendency to discuss emptiness and the two truths in terms of *yu* (Being, existence) and *wu* (non-Being, nothingness). The provisional truth was often discussed in terms of *yu* or worldly existence, and the ultimate truth in terms of *wu* or nothingness, that is, emptiness. The ambiguity of these terms is such that *yu* could be interpreted negatively (from the Buddhist standpoint) as substantial Being or positively as conventional, dependently co-arising existence. *Wu* could be interpreted positively as a denial of substantial Being or negatively as nihilistic nothingness. The same could be said for the English pairs of words "Being and non-Being" or "existence and nothingness."[2] This ambiguity, as well as the strong ontological and dualistic implications of these terms, contributed to the confusion concerning these concepts. In this essay I will discuss the early Chinese Buddhist interpretations of emptiness and the two truths with special emphasis on the "spirituality of emptiness" as the Middle Way developed by Chih-i.

Interpretations of Emptiness and the Two Truths

Kumārajīva's definitive translations of major Mahāyāna texts and Mādhyamikan treatises in the early fifth century provided the foundation for advancing beyond the "matching concepts" identification of emptiness with the Taoistic void. Kumārajīva himself, in his letters to Hui-yüan answering questions on the Buddhist view of the nature of reality, denied the validity of speaking in these terms: "In this context it is not possible to speak even in terms of 'neither *yu* nor *wu*,' let alone in terms of *yu* and *wu*" (T 45, no. 1856, 135c27).[3] Nevertheless, the practice continued. Seng-chao, one of Kumārajīva's most outstanding disciples and famous for his understanding of emptiness, wrote influential essays on themes such as prajñā-wisdom, emptiness, and nirvāṇa. In his essay on "the emptiness of the unreal" (T 45.152a–153a),[4] Seng-chao discusses the meaning of emptiness utilizing the framework of the two truths. First he refers briefly to previous interpretations of emptiness, which he classifies into three schools or trends. The first trend was to explain emptiness as "mental negation" (*hsing-wu*): emptiness refers to the state of the mind when it does not conceptualize about or reflect on things and does not mean that things do not exist. Seng-chao criticizes this position by pointing out that, though it is correct concerning the importance of a calm mind, it is incorrect in that it fails to perceive the emptiness, or lack of substantial Being, of phenomenal things. The second trend was to explain emptiness as "identical with form" (*chi-se*). Form, or phenomenal matter, is empty because it is not form "in itself." Seng-chao points out that this is correct insofar as form is not independently existent but depends on other things for its existence. He then criticizes this position for not going one step further to point out that "form is not (substantial) form," and that "emptiness" in itself has no independent existence either. The third trend was to explain emptiness as "original non-Being" (*pen-wu*). All things derive their existence from an original state of nothingness. This view was compatible with traditional Taoist ideas of the primordial nothingness out of which the world emerged, but Seng-chao points out that when the Buddhist scriptures speak of things not existing, the meaning is that they do not have ultimate existence and lack substantial Being. The Buddhist texts are not nihilistically denying all existence nor affirming the idea of a primordial nothingness.

Seng-chao presents his interpretation of emptiness through a discussion of the two truths. After affirming that language is inadequate to describe reality and ultimate truth, he makes a noble attempt to do just that. The content of the "supreme real truth" (*paramārthasatya*) is illustrated with paraphrases from the *Treatise on the Great Perfection of Wisdom* (*Ta chih tu lun;* T 25.57–756), "All dharmas are neither with nor without marks" (T 25.105a7), and Nāgārjuna's *Middle Verses* (*Mūlamadhyamakakārika;* T 30.1–39), "All dharmas neither exist (as substantial Being) nor inexist (as nothingness)" (T 30.7c16). However, the statement "neither existence nor nonexistence" does not mean that one totally denies the reality of all phenomena and suppresses all senses in order to realize the real truth. The conventional (*saṃvṛtisatya*) and the real (*paramārthasatya*) are one. This is explained in stanzas which are considered by some to contain the essence of Seng-chao's teaching:[5] "That though inexistent they exist is what 'not inexistent' means" (T 45.152b5–6).[6]

It is my contention that this position is needlessly obscured by the fact that the Chinese terms *yu* and *wu* are used with two different meanings, depending on whether they are affirmed or denied. Thus *yu* in the sense of substantial Being and *wu* in the sense of a nihilistic nothingness are denied, but *yu* in the sense of conventional, dependently co-arising existence, and *wu* in the sense of a lack of substantial Being are affirmed. Therefore "nonexistence" is affirmed in the sense that though phenomena have conventional existence, they have no substantive Being. "Not inexistent" is affirmed in the sense that though phenomena have no substantive Being, they are not complete nothingness. Seng-chao does not explicitly identify *saṃvṛtisatya* with *yu* and *paramārthasatya* with *wu*, but sometimes comes close to doing so. After quoting the famous statement from the *Large Sūtra on Perfect Wisdom* (*Pancavimśatisāhasrikā prajñāpāramitā Sūtra;* T 8.217–425) that there is no difference between supreme truth and conventional truth (T 8.378c), Seng-chao explains that the supreme truth means non-Being (not-*yu*) and the conventional truth means not a nonexistent (not-*wu*), and that "non-Being" and "not nonexistent" have ultimately the same meaning (T 45.152b17). The argument is taken one step further by pointing out that a Buddhist cannot accept the position that things are nonexistent nothingness, because this is the extreme and heretical view of annihilationism. Neither can he accept the position that things have substantial Being, because this is the extreme and heretical view of eternalism (T 45.152b23–29). Since things are not complete nothingness, annihilationism is wrong. Since things do not have substantial Being, eternalism is wrong. Thus the content of the real truth can be spoken of, at least negatively, as "neither Being nor nothingness." Finally, Seng-chao approvingly quotes the *Vimalakīrti-nirdeśa Sūtra* (T 14.537–557) that "dharmas are neither Being nor nothingness; all dharmas arise through causes and conditions" (T 14.537c15). Phenomena have no substantial Being because they are merely a complex of causes and conditions, but are not nothingness because as a complex of causes and conditions they have conventional existence.

Seng-chao can be credited with pointing out the ultimate unity of the two truths and clarifying the difference between traditional Chinese interpretations of *wu* as primordial nothingness and the interpretation of emptiness in the Buddhist prajñā-wisdom tradition. On the other hand, he continued in the practice of discussing the issue in terms of *yu* and *wu.* He clearly did not mean to identify the conventional truth with *yu* and the supreme truth with *wu,* since he explicitly defined the supreme truth as beyond the confines of this duality, but his discussions are still dominated by this ambiguous terminology.

Positive Interpretations of Emptiness

Counterparts to the "negative" interpretation of emptiness in terms of nothingness were the "positive" interpretations of emptiness reflected in the popular *Mahāparinirvāṇa Sūtra*[7] and the *Ch'eng-shih lun* (*Satyasiddhi Śāstra*).[8] It is no accident that many of the so-called *Ch'eng-shih lun* scholars, such as Seng-min (467–527) and Chih-tsang (458–522), were also authorities on the *Mahāparinirvāṇa Sūtra.* This sūtra presented emptiness in terms of universal Buddha-nature, the notion that all beings have the potential to attain Buddhahood. All beings can attain Buddhahood precisely because emptiness, the lack of any self-existent and substantial Being, is the nature of reality. As it is stated in the famous chapter on Noble Activity, "true reality is the Tathāgata, and the Tathāgata is true reality; true reality is emptiness and emptiness is true reality; true reality is the Buddha-nature and the Buddha-nature is true reality" (T 12.685b25–27). However, the reference is not to a self-existent and substantial reality. Buddha-nature, like emptiness, "neither arises nor passes away, neither comes nor goes, is neither past, present, nor future, is neither produced by causes nor produced without a cause" and so forth (T 12.687b8–10). Emptiness means that Buddhahood is the "natural" abiding nature, or "spontaneous" reality, of all beings, and that one need only awaken to this fact and thus realize one's inherent enlightenment.

Another popular way to interpret emptiness positively was through the analysis of conventional or provisional existence (*chia*) as presented in the *Ch'eng-shih lun.* Conventional existence, or "conventional designation" (*prajñāptirupādāya*), is the positive side to emptiness in that it expresses the lack of substantial Being in the positive sense of being the confluence of causes and conditions such as aggregates, forms, colors, and so forth. The chapter in the *Ch'eng-shih lun* on "the characteristics of conventional designation" (T 32.327c–328c) gives over twenty different variations on the meaning of this term. For example, conventional designation, or existence, is so called because of the arising of phenomena from different dharmas. A bottle depends for its existence on the various factors of color, and so forth, and has no reality in itself (T 32.328a6–8). A chariot is a designation for a certain combination of wheels and axles and so forth, but the name "chariot" and the concept of the chariot do not exist in, nor independently of, this accumulation of things. The wheels, axles, and so forth are the causes and conditions of the chariot, but there is no substantial Being which is referred to by the name "chariot" (T 32.328a 10–14). Moreover, different people perceive the same thing in different ways. When people see a horse some say they see the horse's tail, some the horse's body, some the skin, and some the hair, as in the parable of the blind men and the elephant. Or, upon hearing music, some say they hear the sound of a harp, some the sound of a violin, and so forth. In other words, there is no ultimate consistency to people's experiences. Therefore we cannot say that we see real forms or hear real sounds, but can only give them conventional designations (T 32.328a16–24). Conventional existence depends on relative factors. Things are here or there, long or short, large or small, teacher or disciple, father or son, rich or poor, and so forth (T 32.328c11–14). These various explanations of conventional designation, or existence, were eventually summarized by the *Ch'eng-shih lun* scholars into three categories. Conventional existence was defined as that which is (1) causally arisen, (2) continuous, and (3) relative.

Let us take as representative of this trend a prominent scholar of the *Ch'eng-shih lun* and *Mahāparinirvāṇa Sūtra,* Chih-tsang (458–522), one of the "three great Dharma-masters of the Liang period."[9] Here again the inquiry into the meaning of emptiness proceeds through a discussion of the two truths. Chih-tsang taught that the Middle Way is the essence of the two truths. The two truths are not separate realities with one as the "basis" or "essence" of the other, nor are they simply the same. In Chih-tsang's words, "The two truths are two yet nondual; the two truths are identical with the Middle Way. Since they are nondual yet two, the Middle Way is identical with the two truths. Therefore the Middle Way is the essence of the two truths" (T 45.108a4–6). The two truths as "two" emphasize the conventional distinction between the two truths and the reality of conventional existence, yet fundamentally they are part of one reality which is nondual, the Middle Way. This theory is expanded into the theory of the three aspects of the Middle Way.

1. The first aspect is the Middle Way of the worldly, or mundane, truth (*saṃvṛtisatya*). This category consists of three variations: (a) The worldly truth is not nothingness (*wu*), for it contains the potential causes for realizing the fruit of Buddhahood and the principle of reality. It is not substantial Being (*yu*), for there is no substantial fruit which is attained. This is the Middle Way of causation, the first of the aforementioned three kinds of conventional existence, which means that dharmas are neither Being nor nothingness.

It is the middle in the sense of denying the duality, or two extremes, of *yu* and *wu.* (b) The worldly truth is not eternal, for dharmas are constantly perishing; on the other hand, it is neither nihilistic nor indicative of complete annihilation, for there is continuity. This is the Middle Way of conventional existence as continuity, which means that dharmas are neither eternal nor completely annihilated. It is the middle in the sense of denying the duality, or two extremes, of eternalism and annihilationism. (c) The worldly truth is the Middle Way of relativity. As pointed out above, things are long or short, large or small, and so forth, only in relation to other things. This is the middle in the sense of denying the duality, or two extremes, of unity and differentiation.

This threefold classification of conventional existence is an analysis of the phenomenal in its ontological (causally arising), temporal (continuity), and logical (relativity) aspects. In this view, although the mundane world of phenomena is "real," it is a conventional, dependent, temporary, and relative reality.

2. The second aspect of the Middle Way is that of the real truth (*paramārthasatya*). This refers to the real truth as neither existence nor nonexistence, a common description of emptiness.

3. The third aspect of the Middle Way is that of the harmony of the two truths. This refers to the Middle Way as that which clarifies the harmony of the two truths as neither merely the real truth nor the mundane truth. This is different from the Middle Way of the real truth in that it is neither merely the real truth nor the mundane truth, but a harmony of the two (T 45.108a10–20).

In this theory Chih-tsang has neatly incorporated the three aspects of conventional existence from the *Ch'eng-shih lun* with the doctrine of the middle and the two truths to provide an explanation of the unity of the two truths in one reality which is not adequately described by the contrasting duality of existence and nonexistence or non-Being and nothingness. Nevertheless, it is significant that the explanation of the Middle Way of the mundane truth is both more detailed and clearer than the other aspects, and reflects the attempt by *Ch'eng-shih lun* scholars to interpret reality from the perspective of, or with emphasis on, this mundane conventional existence.

Chi-tsang's Critique of Emptiness

It was Chi-tsang (549–623) of the San-lun school who attacked this emphasis on the positive interpretation of conventional reality and refocused on emptiness itself as the central concept of Mahāyāna Buddhism. His writings are among the earliest which record and discuss previous interpretations and trends in Chinese Buddhism. Chi-tsang's commentary on Nāgārjuna's *Middle Verses* (*Chung-kuan lun-shu;* T 42.1–169) contains a brief outline of various interpretations of emptiness and the two truths among the Chinese Buddhist community and provides us with some information concerning the interpretation of these concepts in and before his day.[10] These early trends are presented in three overlapping groups: the Three Schools, the Seven Trends or Six Schools, and the *Treatise on Three Theses* (*San-tsung lun*) by an eminent layman named Chou-yung. The Three Schools, the first four of the Seven Trends, and the first three of the Six Schools correspond to the three trends discussed by Seng-chao in his essay on emptiness and need not be repeated here. The remaining three are as follows:

1. Only Consciousness. This position is attributed to a Yü Fa-k'ai, who is said to have taught that "this triple world is a dwelling for a long night. Mental consciousness is the subject of a great dream. If one awakens to the fundamental emptiness of this triple world, deluded consciousness will be exhausted" (T 65.94c), and "the assembly of existents which is perceived now are all perceptions in a dream. If one awakens from the great dream after dawn brightens this long night, then delusions are overturned, the deluded consciousness is extinguished, and the triple world is seen to be empty. At that time there is no place from which anything arises, yet no place which has no arising" (T 42.29b4–7). Chi-tsang criticizes this simple idealism, or complete denial of objective existence and reality, by claiming that "if this were true, then when one experiences the great awakening he will not perceive any of the myriad phenomena, and the worldly truth is lost. What, then, is perceived by the Tathāgata's five kinds of eyes?" (T 42.29b7–8).[11] In other words, what is truly perceived by the Buddha in his perfect perception is not an illusion, but real.

2. Magical Illusion. This position is attributed to a certain Dharma Master Yi, to whom is attributed the following interpretation.

> All dharmas are the same as magical illusions. Because they are the same as magical illusions they are called the "worldly truth." The mind and spirit are real and not empty; this is the (truth of) supreme meaning. If the spirit is empty, then to whom are the teachings given, and who cultivates the Path to advance from an ignorant state and attain Sagehood? Therefore it should be known that the spirit is not empty. (T 65.95a4–7)

This position is the opposite of "Mental Negation"; it completely denies any external reality and affirms the continuous and ultimate reality of the mind, or spirit, which sounds suspiciously like an eternal soul. Chi-tsang criticizes this position as follows:

> A sūtra[12] says that the actions of magical illusions have no good or evil retributive value. If all dharmas are the same as magical illusions, then what difference is there between a real person and an illusory person? (Then a person's actions would have no karmic effect and there would be no cause for being reborn in hell or the Buddha's Pure Land.) Also, the sūtras borrow (the notion of) nothingness to destroy (the notion of substantive) reality. When (the notion of substantive) reality is gone, then it puts away (the notion of) nothingness. (This position of "magical illusion") does not recognize this meaning of the sūtras. (T 42.29b12–13)

Thus Chi-tsang rejects both extremes: the one-sided affirmation of mental activity alone, which involves the denial of external reality (the standpoints of "magical illusion" and "only consciousness"), and the one-sided denial of mental illusion, which involves the simple affirmation of external objective existence (the standpoint of "mental negation").

3. Confluence of Conditions. This final position is attributed to Yü Tao-sui, who taught that "existence due to the confluence of conditions is called the worldly truth. The identity with non-Being due to the scattering of conditions (there is no substantial Being since conditions do not continue but scatter and come to an end); this is called the truth of supreme meaning" (T 42.29b 13–14). Also, "existence due to the confluence of conditions is called the worldly (truth). Non-Being due to analysis (of dharmas) is the real (truth). It is like earth and wood being assembled to make a house. The house had no prior substance. It had a name but no reality. Therefore the Buddha said to Rādha, 'When the marks of visible form are extinguished, there is nothing to perceive'" (T 65.95b1–4). In other words, phenomena consist of the coming together of various causes and conditions and have no substantive eternal Being. This position is not problematic as far as it goes, except that it is an overly simplistic and dualistic understanding of the two truths which identifies *yu* (as the confluence of conditions) with the worldly truth, and *wu* (as the lack of substantial Being due to the mere confluence and scattering of causes and conditions) with the supreme truth.

More significant than the above outlined trends are the "three theses" proposed in a work by a layman named Chou Yung. The *Nan Ch'i shu* says that "at the time in the capital there were masters who established various meanings of the two truths. Three schools existed, each espousing a different idea. Chou Yung authored the *San-tsung lun* locating the thread that runs through the three schools."[13] These three theses are (1) conventional designations are not empty; (2) the emptying of conventional designations; and (3) conventional designation is emptiness.

Conventional Designations Are Not Empty

Chi-tsang describes this position as teaching that

> When the sūtras speak of "the emptiness of visible form" this refers to its emptiness and lack of a true substantive nature; therefore it is called empty. It does not mean that conventional visible reality is empty (nothingness?). Since the substantive nature is an empty nothingness, therefore it is called empty. This is the real truth. The non-emptiness of conventional reality is called the worldly truth. (T 42.29b17–19)

Anchō elaborates:

> A sūtra says that the reality of conditioned co-arising is eternal in nature and form whether there is or is not a Buddha. How can one say that it is nothingness (*wu*)? Another sūtra says that all dharmas are empty. This lack of a subject (*svabhāva*) in all dharmas, an inner emptiness or lack of a substantive subject, is called the worldly truth. This lack of a substantive subject in all dharmas itself is the real truth. (T 65.95c10–14)

This is a bit confusing, but the position is clarified by the use of a metaphor, that of a "meatless chestnut." In the *Meaning of the Two Truths* Chi-tsang explains this metaphor as follows:

The two truths theory of the "rodent-gnawed chestnut" school says: the sūtra has elucidated that all forms are empty. This school takes that to mean that there is the absence of a permanent nature to the form but there is not the absence of the form as such. This view is comparable to a chestnut gnawed (empty) by rodents. The meat inside is all gone, but the shell remains intact. The external is as it was. Therefore it is called an "empty chestnut."[14]

In other words, dharmas or phenomena have no eternal substantive Being, but the outer shell of conventional existence does exist. Chi-tsang criticizes this interpretation by pointing out that both the self-existing subject (*svabhāva*), or self-nature, and lack of this subject (*asvabhāva*) are empty. In other words, it is not enough to affirm the lack of a substantial Being *in* all dharmas; the "shell" of conventional reality is also empty. A correct understanding of "conventionally designated things" would recognize their emptiness.

The Emptying of Conventional Designations

This position teaches that "the worldly truth is that all dharmas arise through the confluence of conditions, and therefore have an essence. To analyze the conditions and discover that one cannot find any center is called the real truth" (T 42.29b24–25). This thesis is represented by the metaphor of the "bobbing melon." Chi-tsang adds that "the sunken melon is the real; the floating melon is the mundane" (T 42.29b26). In other words, the real truth is represented by the melon of reality that has sunk beneath the surface and disappeared, for it has no ultimate existence. The mundane truth is represented by the melon of reality that bobs above the surface and can be perceived as existing. The problem with this position is that it tries to have its melon cake and eat it too. It attempts to recognize as valid both the floating and the sinking melon, both existence and nonexistence, both mundane and real truth, without dealing with the nature of the melon (reality) itself and the relationship between the two states of the floating or sinking melon. Chi-tsang criticizes this position by pointing out that "to say that first there are conventional dharmas but that later these are emptied is to return to the position of the 'confluence of conditions.' Therefore it has the fault of 'nothingness due to the analysis and scattering (of dharmas)'" (T 42.29b26–86). In other words, reality as emptiness is not merely a matter of analyzing each component phenomenon and pointing out the lack of substantial Being in each dharma, a practice often attributed to the *Ch'eng-shih lun* scholars.

Conventional Designation Is Emptiness

This position makes an identification of the two aspects of conventional designation and emptiness, and thus the complete meaning of this phrase would read that "emptiness is conventional designation and conventional designation is emptiness." Chi-tsang summarizes this position as teaching that "conventional designation in itself is identical with emptiness" (T 42.29b28–29). Chi-tsang claims that this was the position of Chou Yung, but adds that Chou Yung bases it on Seng-chao's essay on emptiness. Seng-chao is quoted as saying:

> Although *yu*, yet *wu*. Although *wu*, yet *yu*. "Although *yu*, yet *wu*" is a denial of Being. "Although *wu*, yet *yu*" is a denial of nothingness. In this way, it is not that there is no thing, but that things are not truly (substantial) things. If things are not truly (substantial) things, in what way are they yet "things"? (T 42.29c1–3)

Seng-chao is also quoted as saying that "things are not real (substantial) things, therefore they are conventional things. Since they are conventional things, therefore they are empty" (T 42.29c4–5). This concludes Chi-tsang's presentation of the third position. No metaphor is given.

This third thesis thus acts as a kind of synthesis of the first two theses. The first thesis affirms the existence of conventional phenomena by denying its emptiness. The second thesis denies the first by affirming the emptiness of conventional phenomena. The third thesis resolves the tension between the first two by affirming the identity of conventional phenomena and emptiness. This pattern anticipates T'ien-t'ai Chih-i's threefold truth formulation of conventional existence, emptiness, and the Middle, but before we examine Chih-i's contribution, let us finish with Chi-tsang.

The Four Levels of the Two Truths

Chi-tsang's writings on emptiness are vast and complicated, but the concept is well illustrated by his theory of the four levels of the two truths. In his *Commentary on the Middle Verses* the question is first raised as to why this formulation of four levels of two truths is constructed (T 42.28b10–11). The answer is that various people have various capabilities. Those who are clever and have a good understanding of the Buddhist way can awaken to the correct path upon hearing of the first level, and do not need the other levels. Those of middling ability do not attain awakening upon hearing of the first level of the two truths, but enter the path upon hearing of the second level, and so forth. In other words, the two truths are a *teaching* designed to lead one to the correct way, and are not a complete description of the principle of reality, which is beyond verbalization and conceptualization. Thus the four levels of the two truths are progressively sophisticated teachings concerning reality, not the principle of reality itself.

At the first level, Being (*yu*) corresponds to the worldly truth (*saṃvṛtisatya*), and emptiness corresponds to the real truth, or the truth of supreme meaning (*paramārthasatya*) (see chart). In the *Commentary on the Middle Verses* this is illustrated with a quote from the *Large Sūtra on Perfect Wisdom:* "Bodhisattvas dwell in the two truths and preach the Dharma for the sake of sentient beings. They explain emptiness for the sake of those who are attached to Being (*yu*), and explain existence (*yu*) for the sake of those who are attached to emptiness" (T 42.28b15–16).[15] Thus at the first level emptiness is presented as the teaching designed to lead and teach those who are mired in a naïve realism, who accept the substantial existence of phenomena. On the other hand, *yu* as conventional existence is offered as a counterteaching to those who would become mistakenly attached to emptiness. In the *Meaning of the Two Truths,* the contrast is between Being (*yu*) and non-Being (*wu*), and in succeeding passages "emptiness" and "non-Being" are used interchangeably.

At the second level, the duality of both Being and emptiness from the first level becomes the worldly truth, and the denial of this duality, "neither Being nor emptiness," is the supreme truth. Again the *Large Sūtra on Perfect Wisdom* is quoted: "The worldly truth is explained as 'both Being and non-Being.' The truth of supreme meaning is 'neither Being nor non-Being.'"[16] At this

Chi-tsang's Four Levels of the Two Truths

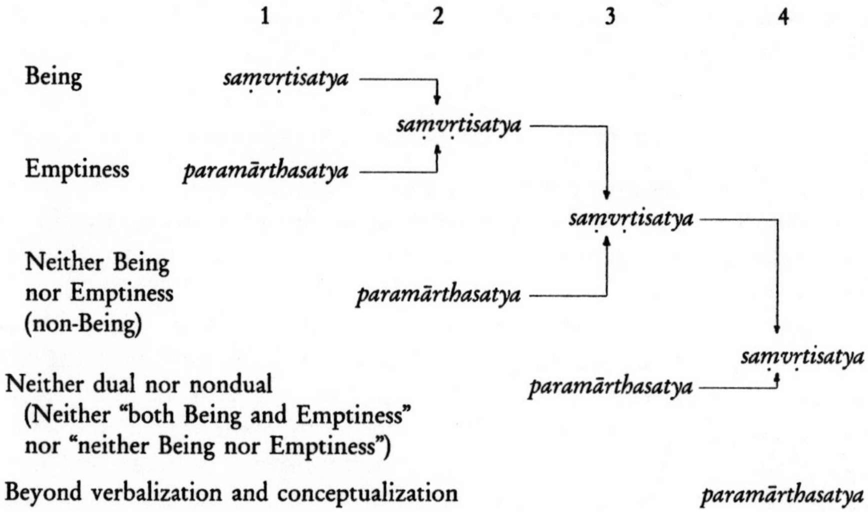

level the affirmation of the duality between existence and emptiness is a conventional, worldly truth, and the denial of this duality is the real, supreme truth.

At the third level the duality of all of the above, both the affirmation and denial of the duality of Being and emptiness, corresponds to the worldly truth, and the transcendence of all dualities corresponds to the supreme truth. Here the *Avataṃsaka Sūtra* is quoted: "Do not be attached to any dharmas of non-duality, for there is neither unity nor duality."[17] At this level the transcendence of all dualities, even the idea of duality itself, is taught.

At the fourth and final level, again all of the preceding levels of verbal expression, the duality of Being and emptiness, of duality and nonduality, and all the teachings of the first three levels, are verbal teachings and thus relegated to the realm of the worldly truth. That which is beyond verbalization and conceptualization is the supreme truth. A long paraphrase of the *Avataṃsaka Sūtra* is given to support this final level:

> When one truly and completely discriminates all dharmas, one sees that (dharmas have) no self-nature but only conventionally given designations. All wish to discriminate the meaning of the worldly truth. Thus bodhisattvas arouse aspiration (for enlightenment). All dharmas without exception are beyond verbal description; the mind and its activity is quiescent and like space. All wish to discriminate the meaning of the real truth. Thus bodhisattvas arouse aspiration (for enlightenment). (T 42.29b19–22; T 9.447a9–12)

Theoretically this progressive affirmation and denial of each previous duality would continue infinitely, but Chi-tsang cuts it off at the fourth level. He has made his point, that the supreme truth is not a description of the principle of reality but refers to that which is beyond verbalization and conceptualization. Any verbal or conceptual description necessarily belongs to the realm of conventional worldly truth. In this sense Chi-tsang escaped the trap of discussing the two truths and emptiness merely in terms of Being or nothingness or some combination thereof.

Emptiness and the Threefold Truth

Chih-i, the founder of the T'ien-t'ai tradition, also succeeded in going beyond the Being/non-Being, existence/nonexistence trap in explaining emptiness by systematizing a "unified theory" which integrated the concepts of conditioned co-arising, emptiness, conventional designation or existence, the two truths, Buddha-nature, and so forth, with the concept of the Middle. This was explained with the concept of the threefold truth. The key inspiration for this concept was a verse from Nāgārjuna's *Middle Verses* XXIV, 18: "All things which arise through conditioned co-arising, I explain as emptiness. Again, it is a conventional designation. Again, it is the meaning of the Middle Way" (T 30.33b11).[18] Chih-i interpreted this verse in terms of the two truths into a threefold truth. These three aspects were, first, emptiness or the absence of substantial Being, often identified with supreme truth; second, conventional existence, or the temporary existence of the world as dependently co-arising phenomena, often identified with the worldly truth; and, third, the Middle, a simultaneous affirmation of both emptiness and conventional existence as mutual aspects of a single integrated reality.

For Chih-i these three aspects were not independent of each other but integral parts of a single reality. The objects of our experience have a temporary reality. We do experience something. Nevertheless, the world which we experience is empty of an eternal, unchanging substance, or Being. Lest one lapse into a mistaken nihilism, one must realize the Middle Way. One must realize the emptiness of phenomenal reality simultaneously with the temporal reality of these empty objects. This Middle Way, however, must not be grasped as an eternal, transcendental Reality; it is, rather, manifested in and through and is identical with temporal, phenomenal reality, which is again in turn empty of an unchanging substance. The circle is complete in itself, what Chih-i calls "a perfectly integrated threefold truth." This is summarized in the *Profound Meaning of the Lotus (Teachings)* as follows: "The "perfect threefold truth" means that the Buddha Dharma is completely included not merely by the Middle Way but also by the real and the mundane (truths). This threefold truth is perfectly integrated; one-in-three and three-in-one (T 33.705a5–7).

A correct understanding of the threefold truth, then, reveals that reality is "one truth," a perfectly integrated unity. In the final analysis even this is reduced to "no truth," for the concept of a single reality, though it stretches the limits of language, is still a conceptualization that is inadequate to describe reality itself. Finally Chih-i is left quoting one of his favorite passages from the *Lotus Sūtra:* "Cease, Cease! No need to speak. My Dharma is subtle and hard to imagine."[19] Reality, emptiness, cannot be grasped conceptually; truth is beyond words.

Yet Chih-i used words and concepts and was quick to point out the necessity to do so. One can make a valid attempt to describe verbally what is ultimately indescribable, as long as one is aware of this limitation. In Chih-i's case this meant describing emptiness in terms of, and in relation to, related concepts such as conventional truth, dependently co-arising existence, and the Middle Way. He thus avoided the false dualism of Being and non-Being and provided a philosophical analysis of emptiness on which one could base one's practice and lead a life of Buddhist spirituality.

The Practice of Emptiness

The nonphilosophically-minded reader may well wonder what the preceding technical discussions have to do with spirituality. It is difficult to know, because of a lack of any extant records, exactly what these concepts meant in the daily lives of most of these Chinese Buddhists and how they were applied to their spiritual growth. Chih-i, however, provided voluminous writings giving detailed instructions on Buddhist practice and the implications of emptiness for the spiritual life. For him, practice and doctrine were like the two wings of a bird, or the two wheels of a cart; they support each other and are meaningless if taken alone.

Chih-i had already studied the Buddha Dharma under many masters when he joined Hui-ssu (515–577) on Mount Ta-su in 560 C.E. His biography states that he chanted and contemplated the *Lotus Sūtra,* and when he reached the twenty-third chapter, which tells of the bodhisattva who burns his own body as a sacrifice to the Buddha, Chih-i attained a "great awakening" of insight into emptiness. His "body and mind were emptied and he entered, quiescent, into contemplation . . ." (T 50.191c28–29).[20] It is said that his teacher Hui-ssu praised him, but pointed out that this realization was but an early stage in understanding the teaching of the *Lotus Sūtra,* equivalent to realizing the emptiness of all dharmas.[21] This was truly a significant insight, but not yet a realization of the integrated nature of emptiness and conventional existence.

From Ta-su, Chih-i went to the capital Chin-ling, where he mingled with the top Buddhist scholars of the day and gave the lectures which are now known as *Instructions on the Gradual Practice of the Perfection of Meditation* (*Shih ch'an po-lo-mi ts'u-ti fa-men;* T 46.475–548). This text gives detailed instructions on how to meditate and gradually advance along the path of contemplation. Chih-i left the capital for Mount T'ien-t'ai in 575 to continue his meditative practices. Details of this stay on Mount T'ien-t'ai are unknown, but he returned again to Chin-lin ten years later to give the lectures now known as his *Commentary on the Lotus Sūtra* (*Fa-hua wen-chü;* T 34.1–150), *The Profound Meaning of the Lotus (Teachings)* (*Fa-hua hsüan-i;* T 33.681–814), and the *Great Cessation and Contemplation* (*Mo-ho chih-kuan;* T 46.1–140). These works contain a synthesis of Buddhist philosophy and practice centered on the threefold truth and threefold contemplation.

Concretely speaking, Chih-i summarized Buddhist practice under the categories of four kinds of samādhi and ten objects of contemplation.[22] Let us take a closer look at one of these, the "samādhi of neither walking nor sitting," as an example of these practices and an illustration of the content of Buddhist spirituality.

The fourth of Chih-i's four samādhis, the "samādhi of neither walking nor sitting," is not merely a miscellaneous category, a grab bag of practices that did not fit into the first three samādhis, but rather is the most applicable of all the samādhis. As Chih-i says, "it includes walking and sitting as well as all other modes of behavior" (T 46.14b27–28).[23] In the *Large Sūtra on Perfect Wisdom* this samādhi is called the "samādhi of an awakened mind (or consciousness)," though it does not elaborate on how it is to be practiced,[24] and Chih-i's master Hui-ssu called it the "samādhi of following one's own mind (or intentions)." The crux of this samādhi is to concentrate on each thought as it arises in the mind. Therefore any and all thoughts, constantly, in any and all situations, are the immediate objects of one's contemplation. The term "awakened mind" is further explained as having an enlightened understanding of and through mental activities. As Chih-i explains, "When the practitioner's thoughts arise, one should reflect upon and contemplate them, not being distracted by their origin or consummation" (T 46.14c2–3). Chih-i goes on to describe one setting for practicing this samādhi, based on the *Sūtra on Petitioning Avalokiteśvara* (**Ṣaḍakṣaravidyā-mantra;* T 20.34–38), with instructions on how to adorn the meditation chamber, to pay reverence to various Buddhas and other Buddhist saints, to kneel, burn incense, scatter flowers, concentrate one's thoughts; "after finishing the offering, assume the lotus position and with body erect and mind regulated, fix the thoughts and count the breaths, with each thought corresponding to ten breaths. When ten thoughts have been completed, rise and burn incense for the sake of sentient beings. Petition the three treasures (of Buddha, Dharma, and Saṅgha) three times; also call on Avalokiteśvara, and join the ten fingers and palms. Then recite the four-line verses . . ." and so forth (T 46.14b–15a).

This samādhi, however, is not limited to monks following the literal and detailed practice of this specific ceremony. It is a practice available for anyone at any time and place to cultivate a spirituality of emptiness in everyday life. The essence of this practice is found in the nature of the mind and specific thoughts. Chih-i illustrates the emptiness of phenomena, and the mind, by discussing four phases of a thought: (1) pre-thought, (2) imminent thought, (3) the thought proper, and (4) completed thought. He argues, following Nāgārjuna's style, that one cannot logically prove how a thought arises from a state of having no thought, but actually thoughts do arise. The thought, however, is not a substantial, eternal thing, but passes away to the phase of a completed thought. The thought arises neither out of nothingness nor out of substantial Being. The mind is not nothingness, for it allows thoughts to arise, but it has no substantial Being, for it lacks eternal, unchanging existence. In Chih-i's words:

> Even when pre-thought has not arisen, it is nevertheless not ultimately nothingness (*wu*). It is like a person who has not yet performed an action and then performs it. It cannot be said that there is no person because the action has not yet been performed. If it is said that no person is present, then who performs the action afterwards? It is precisely because there is a state of pre-performance of the action that there can then be a performance of the action. It is the same with the mind: it is because there is a state of pre-thought that there can then be a state of imminent thought. . . . Although pre-thought is not yet in existence, it does not follow that there are then no thoughts at all. As for completed thoughts, they can be contemplated even though the phase of the thought proper has passed away. It is like one cannot say that a person is inexistent when he has finished doing something. . . . The perishing of mind, or the completed thought, is analogous to this: one cannot say that the perishing is eternal, for this is annihilationism which denies both cause and effect. Therefore, although the state of "completed thought" means that (a thought has) perished, it is still possible to contemplate it. (T 46.15b26–c6)

Thus both the mind and its thoughts are empty. They are not "merely empty," however. The four phases of thought are to be understood in the threefold terms of emptiness, conventional existence, and the Middle. "Although the four phases of thought are empty, one may perceive within emptiness the inclusion of various things in the four phases until one perceives everywhere the Buddha Dharma as numerous as the sands of the Ganges River. . . . This is called the four phases of thought of conventional designation." And "since dharmas arise through causes and conditions, they do not exist substantially. Since they do not exist (substantially), therefore they are empty. Since they are not empty (nothingness), they do exist (conventionally). . . . This threefold truth embraces the Buddha's knowledge and insight, and such is the full understanding of the four phases of thought" (T 46.16a23–28). With this understanding, one should cultivate the ability to spontaneously contemplate each thought, good or evil, as it arises in the mind, and to thus realize the true nature of our existence.

Thoughts themselves are discussed concretely by Chih-i in terms of thought about "good" and "evil" matters. "Good" matters are summarized as the six perfect virtues (*pāramitā*) of charity, morality, patience, diligence, meditation, and wisdom. (1) In all of one's activities one "contemplates sentient beings with the eye of great compassion." This is the perfection of charity. (2) In all of one's activities "there are no beings whom one injures or causes harm, nor does one apprehend (and judge) their sinful or meritorious features." This is the perfection of morality. (3) In all of one's activities "(agitating) thoughts do not arise in one's mind, thus one is unperturbed and without attachment." One's senses are all quiescent, unmoved. This is the perfection of patience. (4) In all of one's activities one is not aware of specific physical actions, like the raising or lowering of one's feet. All activity and understanding are spontaneous; there is no sequence of first having a concept and then realizing it. One realizes that dharmas do not sequentially arise, abide, and then perish. This is the perfection of diligence. (5) In all of one's activities one does not think in dualistic terms of "mind and body" or "saṃsāra and nirvāṇa." There is no dharma (phenomenon) which one dwells on or becomes attached to. One does not savor the bliss of nirvāṇa nor cavort in saṃsāra. This is the perfection of meditation. (6) In all of one's activities one realizes that the senses, sense organs, and so forth are empty and quiescent, and one is neither in bondage nor liberated. This is the perfection of wisdom (T 46.16b26–c6).

It is the contemplation of "evil" rather than "good," however, which is the major focus of Chih-i's analysis. The reason is that "evil" thoughts are the usual fare of our mundane lives, and they are most accessible to one's contemplation. If a desire arises in the mind, do not ignore it but take it by the horns, as it were. Or, in Chih-i's words, "contemplate it minutely in its four phases: pre-desire, imminent desire, the desire proper, and the desire completed" (T 46.17c29–b3). Contemplation of the desire in this fashion will show that that desire is empty of substance and is thus conquered. Chih-i compares this to going fishing: the desire is like a fish, and one's thought the fishing line. "If the fish is strong and the line is weak, it cannot be forcibly pulled in. But if one lets the baited hook enter the fish's mouth and allows it to swim around, diving and surfacing freely, then before long it can be hauled in" (T 46.17c24–26). In conclusion, "when one contemplates in this way, there is no perceiver of the sense object, and no subject opposed to the objective world, yet both are illumined clearly. (The threefold reality of thoughts, desires, and other phenomena) are like illusory transformations (conventionally existent) and empty, and with regard to the nature of reality (the middle) are not mutually obstructive" (T 46.18a24–26). In fact they are integrated and mutually inclusive.

Threefold Cessation and Contemplation

As one can see from these concrete illustrations of Buddhist practice and ideal spirituality, there is basically a threefold pattern underlying the specific instructions. Chih-i refers to this pattern as "threefold contemplation." The threefold truth refers to the reality of the objective (and subjective) realms in terms of emptiness, conventional existence, and the Middle. Threefold contemplation refers to a general pattern of practice which allows one to attain insight into the true nature of reality and the bliss of enlightenment. As Chih-i writes in his commentary on the *Vimalakīrti-nirdeśa Sūtra*, "Reality as the two truths and the threefold truth is the objective realm which is illumined through threefold contemplation" (T 38.525a17–18).

Threefold contemplation actually refers to both threefold cessation (*śamatha*) and threefold insight/contemplation (*vipaśyanā*). Some Western scholars have commented on the tension, and even contradiction, between these two aspects of meditation in Indian Buddhism,[25] but in T'ien-t'ai Buddhism the two are always seen as harmonious and complementary. When the waters are still (*śamatha*), one can see to the bottom of the pond (*vipaśyanā*). Chih-i's mature development of this concept is succinctly presented in *Great Cessation and Insight*, where he discusses the meaning of "cessation and insight" (*chih-kuan*) (T 46.24a–25b).

Chih-i first discusses three kinds of "skillful cessation" in the pattern of the threefold truth: (1) cessation as realizing that the true essence of reality is empty of substantial Being; (2) cessation as realizing expedient conventional existence which arises through conditions; and (3) cessation as putting an end to both extremes of discriminatory conceptual categories.

1. "Cessation as realizing emptiness" describes the stage of spiritual discernment wherein one advances beyond "naïve realism," the acceptance of objective reality as having substantial Being, to the realization of the emptiness of all things. As Chih-i says:

> All dharmas arise through conditions. (Things which arise through) conditioned co-arising are empty and without self-Being. . . . Since one knows the conditioned co-arising, conventional confluence, illusory transformation, and empty nature (of reality), this is called its essence. Conceptualized delusions

> come to an end upon realizing emptiness; therefore emptiness is (the nature of) true (reality). (T 46.24a3–5)

2. "Cessation as realizing expedient conditions" refers to the realization of conventional existence as the coming into being of all things through conditioned and dependent co-arising, which Chih-i calls the "non-emptiness of emptiness." The emptiness of all things does not mean that they are nothingness. Their conventional existence as interdependent entities is real. As Chih-i says:

> Those of the two vehicles (accept only emptiness as) the essence of true (reality), so they do not consider as necessary the "cessation of expediency" (realizing conventional existence). Bodhisattvas understand conventional existence and should put it into practice. They know that emptiness is not empty (not nothingness), therefore this is called an "expedient means." One discriminates and chooses medicine in accordance with the disease, therefore it is called "in accordance with conditions." The mind is at rest with regard to the mundane truth, therefore it is called "cessation." (T 46.24a9–11)

3. "Cessation as an end to both discriminatory extremes" refers to the contemplation and realization of the synonymous nature of both "extremes" of mistakenly understood emptiness and conventional existence. A discriminatory and one-sided attachment to either concept is mistaken; reality is simultaneously empty of substantial Being and is conventionally existent. As Chih-i says:

> (To think that) samsāra flows and moves and that nirvāna is a (constant and inactive) maintenance of an awakened state is a one-sided view of practice and activity, and does not correspond to the Middle Way. Now, if one knows that the mundane is not mundane, then the extreme view of the mundane is put to rest, and if one realizes the non-mundane (nature of conventional existence), then the extreme view of emptiness is put to rest. This is called "cessation as an end to both extremes." (T 46.24a13–15)

Threefold contemplation also follows the same threefold pattern. The three aspects are:

> 1) To enter (insight) into emptiness from (the viewpoint of) conventional existence. This is called the contemplation of the two truths. 2) To enter (insight) into conventional existence from (the viewpoint of) emptiness. This is called the contemplation of equality. 3) These two contemplations are the path of expedient means for attaining entry to the Middle Way, wherein both of the two truths are illuminated. The thoughts of the mind are extinguished and put to rest, and one spontaneously enters the sea of universal wisdom. This is called the contemplation of the Middle Way and the truth of supreme meaning. (T 46.24b5–8)

1. "Entering (insight into) emptiness from conventional existence." At this first level of contemplation, conventional existence refers to the ordinary, mistaken perception of phenomena as existing substantially, and "entering emptiness" means to negate the existence of independent substantial Being in these phenomena. Thus, as Chih-i says, "When one encounters emptiness, one perceives not only emptiness but also knows (the true nature of) conventional existence" (T 46.24b10–11).

2. "Entering (insight into) conventional existence from emptiness." At this second level of contemplation, conventional existence refers to a correct understanding and positive acceptance of objective phenomena as interdependently and conditionally co-arisen. Emptiness here refers to a mistaken attachment to the concept of emptiness, or a misunderstanding of emptiness as merely a nihilistic nothingness. As Chih-i says:

> If one understands ("enters") emptiness, (one understands that) there is no emptiness. Thus one must reenter conventional existence. One should know that this contemplation is done for the sake of saving sentient beings, and know that true reality is not (substantial) true reality but an expedient means which appears conventionally. Therefore it is said, "from emptiness." One differentiates the medicine according to the disease without making conceptual discriminations. Therefore it is called "entering conventional existence." (T 46.24c8–11)

This is compared to blind men who regain their sight. They can then perceive both space (i.e., emptiness) and forms and colors, and can differentiate between various grasses and trees, roots and stalks, branches and leaves, medicine and poison. At the first level one perceives the two truths but is one-sidedly concerned with emptiness and cannot utilize or perceive the reality of conventional existence. If one's eyes are opened concerning the validity of objective conventional reality, one perceives not only emptiness but also the visible forms of conventional existence. One can then understand the minute, conditionally co-arisen phenomena of everyday life and use this knowledge to benefit others.

3. "The contemplation of the Middle Way" refers to the highest level of contemplation, wherein one simultaneously and correctly perceives the validity of both emptiness and conventional existence. As Chih-i says:

> First, to contemplate (and attain insight into) the emptiness of conventional existence is to empty saṃsāra (of substantial Being). Next, to contemplate (and attain insight into) the emptiness of emptiness is to empty nirvāna. Thus both extremes are negated. This is called the contemplation of two (aspects of) emptiness as expedient means to attain encounter with the Middle Way. . . . The first contemplation utilizes emptiness, and the latter contemplation utilizes conventional existence. This is an expedient means recognizing the reality of

both, but when one enters the Middle Way, both of the two truths are illumined (simultaneously and as identical). (T 46.24c21–26)

The above three contemplations have been presented as a graded progression from the first contemplation to the last. Chih-i calls this "progressive contemplation," the detailed and graded practice of contemplation explained in works such as *Instructions on the Gradual Practice of the Perfection of Meditation.* The most superior contemplation, however, and that discussed in *Great Cessation and Insight,* is what Chih-i calls "perfect and immediate cessation and insight." In this case the three aspects of emptiness, conventional existence, and the Middle are contemplated simultaneously and spontaneously, and immediately perceived as being integrated, nondual, and synonymous. As Chih-i says:

> When the truths are contemplated as an object of cessation, (it is realized that) these are three truths yet one truth. When cessation is sustained by means of (insight into) the truth, (it is realized that) these are three cessations yet one cessation. . . . Therefore it says in the *Middle Verses,* "Dharmas which arise through conditioned co-arising are identical to emptiness, identical to conventional existence, and identical to the Middle." (T 46.25b9–18)

The concept and term *chih-kuan* (*śamatha-vipaśyanā,* cessation and contemplation/insight) itself can be interpreted with this threefold pattern to harmonize their apparent tension or contradiction. Cessation involves an "emptying" of the mind of all deluded thoughts, ignorance, passionate disturbances, and other obstacles to clear understanding. Contemplation involves insight into the true features of reality, an understanding of the multifarious aspects of existence. Together they form a harmonious tension in which reality is correctly understood and Buddhahood fulfilled. Cessation and contemplation/insight are attained simultaneously and in a single instant, as one can see clearly to the bottom of a pond when the water is still and clear.

For in Chih-i's final analysis, threefold cessation and threefold contemplation occur, or are present in, one single instant or one single thought. All aspects of reality are contained (at least potentially) in each and every phenomenon, and a single flash of insight in a single moment is sufficient to, even the key to, realizing enlightenment. One should cultivate a state of quiescence which spontaneously includes the perfection of Buddhist virtues, and neither be agitated by nor attached to any conventional, empty phenomenon. This is the goal and ideal state of Buddhist spirituality.

Notes

1. Some of these topics have already been referred to in the articles by Lai and Unno. To avoid repetition I have abbreviated overlapping areas or attempted either to approach the same issues from a different perspective or to add new information. The reader is advised to read this article in tandem with the contributions of Lai (chapter 11) and Unno (chapter 12, section I).

2. Nāgārjuna warns against this common tendency in his *Middle Verses* (*Mūlamadhyamakakārika*): "Those who think in terms of self-existence, other-existence, existence, and non-existence do not grasp the truth of Buddha's teaching." Mervyn Sprung, *Lucid Exposition of the Middle Way: The Essential Chapters from the Prasannapadā of Candrakīrti,* 158. I use the term "Being" with a capital "B" to refer to the idea of reality having substantial existence, precisely what is denied by "emptiness," in contrast to the Buddhists' acceptable idea of existence as arising causally and interdependently.

3. See also Richard H. Robinson, *Early Mādhyamika in India and China,* 184.

4. Or, to put it in terms of the other side of the paradox, "emptiness (does not mean that things are) not real." See Walter Liebenthal, *Chao Lun, The Treatises of Seng-chao,* 54–63, esp. 61 n. 222. See also Tsukamoto Zenryū, ed., *Jōron kenkyū* (Kyoto: Hōzōkan, 1955); Robinson, *Early Mādhyamika,* 140–46; Chan Wing-tsit, *A Source Book in Chinese Philosophy,* 350–56; and Fung Yu-lang, *History of Chinese Philosophy,* 2:264–65.

5. Liebenthal, *Chao Lun,* 57 n. 197.

6. Robinson, *Early Mādhyamika,* 224.

7. *Mahāparinirvāṇa Sūtra.* This refers to the Mahāyāna version of the Buddha's last sermons and his final entry into nirvāṇa. See T 12, no. 374, 365–604, and no. 375, 605–852.

8. The *Ch'eng-shih lun* (T 32, no. 1646, 239–373) is extant only in Chinese translation, and the reconstructed title "*Satyasiddhi Śāstra*" (Accomplishing the Real) is speculative. There is a study and English translation made from a Sanskrit reconstruction of the text by N. Aiyaswami Sastri, *Satyasiddhiśastra of Harivarman* (Baroda: University of Baroda, 1978).

9. For Chih-tsang's biography, see *More Biographies of Eminent Monks* (*Hsü kao-seng chuan;* T 50.461c–463c). Chih-tsang's writings are not extant, and we must rely on the outline of his position given by Chi-tsang in *Treatise on Mahāyāna* (*Ta-ch'eng hsüan lun;* T 45.15–77) and *On the Meaning of the Two Truths* (*Erh-ti i;* T 45.77–115).

10. Chi-tsang's brief comments are expanded in a subcommentary by the Japanese scholar Anchō (763–814) called *Notes on the Commentary on the Middle Verses* (*Chūron shoki;* T 65.1–247).

11. The five kinds of eyes, or eyesight, attributed to the Buddha are (1) physical eyes, or that which is perceived by the physical eyes; (2) divine eyes, or the perception of divine beings, who can perceive the future destiny of sentient beings; (3) the wisdom eye, or the perception of those of the two vehicles, Śrāvakas and Pratyekabuddhas, who perceive the emptiness of all phenomena; (4) the Dharma eye, or the perception of the bodhisattvas, who perceive the entire Dharma for the sake of saving sentient beings; and (5) the Buddha eye, or the perception of the Buddha, which includes all of the above.

12. Kumārajīva's translation of the *Large Sūtra on Perfect Wisdom* contains the following: "'Subhuti, what do you mean? The various illusory things produced magically by a master of illusions, whether they be elephants or horses or cows or sheep or men or women, what about these things? Do these illusions have karmic causes and conditions which function as karmic causes and conditions for falling into hell or being born in the place where there is neither conceptualizations nor no conceptualizations, or not?' 'They do

not, Bhagavan. These magical illusions are empty and have no true reality. How can they be said to have karmic causes and conditions which function as karmic conditions for falling into hell or being born in the place where there is neither conceptualizations nor no conceptualizations?'" (T 8.413b16–22).

13. See Whalen Lai, "Further Developments of the Two Truths Theory in China: the *Ch'eng-shih-lun* Tradition and Chou Yung's *San-tsung-lun*," in *Philosophy East and West* 30 (1980) 139–61; and the section on "The Satyasiddhi Detour" in Lai's article "The Three Jewels in China" (chapter 11 above).

14. See Lai, "Further Developments," 146.

15. Kumārajīva's translation of the *Large Sūtra on Perfect Wisdom* reads, "Śāriputra, the Bodhisattva Mahāsattva dwells within the two truths and for the sake of sentient beings explains the dharmas of the worldly truth and the truth of supreme meaning. Śāriputra, although the two truths are unattainable by sentient beings, the Bodhisattva Mahāsattva practices the perfection of wisdom and utilizes the power of skillful means in order to preach the dharma to sentient beings" (T 8.405a15–18).

16. Kumārajīva's translation of the *Large Sūtra on Perfect Wisdom* has only "The Bodhisattva Mahāsattva speaks of sentient beings as both existing and not existing based on the worldly truth, not on the supreme (truth)" (T 8.378b9–10). It does not mention "neither Being nor non-Being."

17. The *Avataṃsaka Sūtra* says, "From within the wisdom of non-duality / The Lion-man (the Buddha) appears, / Not attached to the dharma of non-duality / For he knows it is neither one nor two (or, 'there is neither unity nor duality')" (T 9.610a21–22).

18. I base my translation on Kumārajīva's Chinese translation, since that was the basis for Chih-i's interpretation. For the original Sanskrit, see volume 4 of the Bibliotheca Buddhica edited by Louis de La Valleé Poussin, *Mūlamadhyamakakārikas (Mādhyamikasūtras) de Nāgārjuna avec la Prasannapadā Commentaire de Candrakīrti* (Osnabrück: Biblio Verlag, 1970) 491; and J. W. de Jong, ed., *Nāgārjuna Mulamadhyamakakārikāh* (Madras: The Adyar Library and Research Centre, 1977) 35. For other English translations of this verse, see Sprung, *Lucid Exposition*, 238; Frederick J. Streng, *Emptiness: A Study in Religious Meaning*, 213; Robinson, *Early Mādhyamika*, 40; Nagao Gadjin, "From Mādhyamika to Yogācāra: An Analysis of MMK XXIV. and MV I.1–2," *Journal of the International Association of Buddhist Studies* 2:1 (1979) 31.

19. See *Scripture of the Lotus Blossom of the Fine Dharma*, trans. Leon Hurvitz, 28.

20. See Leon Hurvitz, *Chih-i (538–597): An Introduction to the Life and Ideas of a Chinese Buddhist Monk*, 109.

21. See Ōchō Enichi, *Hokke shisō no kenkyū* (Studies in Lotus Thought) (Kyoto: Heirakuji Shoten, 1981) 287–88.

22. For a summary of the four samādhis and the ten objects of contemplation, see chapter 12, section I, by T. Unno.

23. For an English translation of the *Great Cessation and Insight*, see Neal Donner, "The Great Calming and Contemplation of Chih-i. Chapter One: The Synopsis."

24. There is an earlier work by Chih-i devoted entirely to this samādhi called the *Commentary on the Samādhi of an Awakened Mind in the Large Sūtra on Perfect Wisdom* (T 46.621–627), which is for the most part repeated in the *Great Cessation and Insight*.

25. See Edward Conze, *Buddhist Meditation*, 17; and Paul J. Griffiths, *On Being Mindless: Buddhist Meditation and the Mind-Body Problem*, 13–14.

Bibliography

Sources

Chan Wing-tsit. *A Source Book in Chinese Philosophy.* Princeton: Princeton University Press, 1969.

Koseki, Aaron. "Chi-tsang's Ta-ch'eng Hsüan-lun: The Two Truths and the Buddha-Nature." Ph.D. dissertation, University of Wisconsin, Madison, 1977.

The Large Sūtra on Perfect Wisdom. Translated by Edward Conze. Delhi: Motilal Banarsidass, 1979.

Liebenthal, Walter. *Chao Lun, The Treatises of Seng-chao.* 2nd rev. ed. Hong Kong: Hong Kong University Press, 1968.

Sprung, Mervyn. *Lucid Exposition of the Middle Way: The Essential Chapters from the Prasannapadā of Candrakīrti.* Boulder: Prajñā Press, 1979.

Scripture of the Lotus Blossom of the Fine Dharma. Translated by Leon Hurvitz. New York: Columbia University Press, 1976.

Studies

Chappel, David W., ed. *T'ien-t'ai Buddhism: An Outline of the Fourfold Teachings.* Tokyo: Daiichi Shobō, 1983. Distributed by University of Hawaii Press.

Ch'en, Kenneth. *Buddhism in China: A Historical Perspective.* Princeton, NJ: Princeton University Press, 1964.

Conze, Edward. *Buddhist Meditation.* New York: Harper & Row, 1969.

Donner, Neal. "The Great Calming and Contemplation of Chih-i. Chapter One: The Synopsis." Ph.D. dissertation, University of British Columbia, 1976.

Fung Yu-lang. *History of Chinese Philosophy.* Translated by Derk Bodde. 2 vols. Princeton, NJ: Princeton University Press, 1973.

Gregory, Peter N., ed. *Traditions of Meditation in Chinese Buddhism.* Studies in East Asian Buddhism 4. Honolulu: University of Hawaii Press, 1986.

Griffiths, Paul J. *On Being Mindless: Buddhist Meditation and the Mind-Body Problem.* La Salle: Open Court Publishing Company, 1986.

Hurvitz, Leon. *Chih-i (538–597): An Introduction to the Life and Ideas of a Chinese Buddhist Monk. Mélanges chinois et bouddhiques* 12. 1960–62.

Kiyota Minoru, ed. *Mahāyāna Buddhist Meditation: Theory and Practice.* Honolulu: University Press of Hawaii, 1978.

Magnin, Paul. *La vie et l'oeuvre de Huisi (515–577): Les origines de la secte bouddhique chinoise du Tiantai.* Paris: École Française d'Extrème-Orient, 1979.

Murti, T. R. V. *The Central Philosophy of Buddhism.* London: Allen & Unwin, 1955.

Ramanan, K. Venkata. *Nāgārjuna's Philosophy as Presented in the Mahā-Prajñāpāramitā-Śāstra.* New York: Samuel Weiser, 1966.

Robinson, Richard H. *Early Mādhyamika in India and China.* Madison: University of Wisconsin Press, 1967.

Streng, Frederick J. *Emptiness: A Study in Religious Meaning.* New York: Abingdon Press, 1967.

Swanson, Paul L. *Foundations of T'ien-t'ai Philosophy: The Flowering of the Two Truths Theory in Chinese Buddhism.* Berkeley: Asian Humanities Press, 1989.

Tsukamoto Zenryū. *A History of Early Chinese Buddhism.* Translated by Leon Hurvitz. Tokyo, New York, San Francisco: Kodansha International, 1985.

Zürcher, Erich. *The Buddhist Conquest of China.* 2 vols. Leiden: E. J. Brill, 1959.

14

Tantric Buddhism in China

Paul B. Watt

Tantric or esoteric buddhism has had a less prominent place in Chinese Buddhist history than the sects commonly regarded as constituting the mainstream.[1] Owing its distinctive character more to its rituals and meditative practices than to its philosophy, it did not win an intellectual following like that of T'ien-t'ai and Hua-yen; nor did it enjoy the sustained acceptance accorded the other "schools of practice," Ch'an and Pure Land. Nevertheless, Tantric Buddhism had greater influence in China than has often been granted. Buddhist texts containing references to Tantric practices, as well as monks acquainted with certain Tantric techniques, appeared early in Chinese Buddhist history and contributed much to the popularity of Buddhism in China. During the T'ang Dynasty (618–906), both foreign and Chinese masters spread this form of Buddhism, and in the eighth and ninth centuries under imperial patronage it became one of the leading sects of Chinese Buddhism. Thereafter, although as a distinct movement it waned, elements of Tantric Buddhist ritual and belief survived until the present century, diffused throughout Chinese Buddhism. It should further be noted that, while the Chinese appear to have added little to the Indian Tantric Buddhism they received, the Tantric sect of the T'ang dynasty played a pivotal role in the founding of the Japanese esoteric traditions of Shingon and Tendai, which developed along distinctive lines and still flourish today.

Since Tantric Buddhism existed only briefly as an identifiable movement in China, materials for its study are relatively limited, if not in quantity, at least in kind. Apart from biographies of monks, the chief sources of information are the extant translations of Tantric texts from Sanskrit into Chinese. Since these translations can be dated, it is possible to trace the spread of Tantric Buddhism into China. Japanese scholars have established a distinction between "miscellaneous" Tantric texts, on the one hand, and "pure" or "systematic" texts, on the other. In general, texts in the miscellaneous category were compiled in India before the seventh century C.E. and incorporate elements of Tantric practice that already had a long history in Hinduism: dhāraṇīs, mantras (incantations), mudrās (hand gestures) and the worship of deities. Though presented as pronouncements of the historical Buddha, these texts have little to do with traditional Buddhist teachings; rather, they are concerned primarily with the magical attainment of blessings and the avoidance of misfortune. The pure or systematic texts, in contrast, were formed in the seventh and following centuries and represent a stage at which Tantric practices adopted from Hinduism were thoroughly rationalized in Mahāyāna Buddhist doctrinal terms. The principal texts of this type introduced into China are the *Mahāvairocana Sūtra* and the several texts grouped under the title of the *Vajraśekhara Sūtra,* of which the *Tattvasaṃgraha Sūtra* is the most important.

In these later texts, the Buddha Mahāvairocana, a personification of the true nature of all that exists, is the protagonist. His name may be translated "Great Luminous One." Various Buddhas and bodhisattvas are introduced as Mahāvairocana's manifestations and guidelines are provided for their depiction in sacred diagrams known as maṇḍalas. In Tantric practice, these Buddhas and bodhisattvas serve, along with certain other objects, as the focus of a complex type of meditation that aims above all at the sudden attainment of Buddhahood. The meditation has a three-part structure, involving the use of dhāraṇīs and mudrās in conjunction with specific objects of concentration. Through this technique, known as the practice of the Three Mysteries (*san-mi*), the individual is enabled to realize his true, Buddha nature by symbolically identifying with Mahāvairocana (or any of his manifestations) in body, speech, and mind.[2]

The first miscellaneous Tantric texts reached China around the third century C.E. In 230, the Indian monk known as Chu Lü-yen translated the *Mo-teng-ch'ieh ching* (T 21.399–410), a text that contains several dhāraṇīs, gives instructions for divination according to the stars, and teaches a rite involving the use of fire that may reflect the influence of the Hindu *homa* or fire ritual. In the fourth century, the introduction of miscellaneous Tantric literature and practices was continued mainly by Central Asian missionaries such as the monk Dharmarakṣa, better known for his translations of the *Lotus Sūtra* and the *Perfection of Wisdom in 25,000 Lines;* Fo-t'u-teng in North China and Śrīmitra in the South, famous for their magical powers and for their knowledge of dhāraṇīs, and T'an-wu-lan, a translator of works containing dhāraṇīs for curing illness and rites for making and stopping rain.[3] The influx of such texts increased in the fifth through seventh centuries. The magical emphasis remained, but there is evidence of a growing prominence of Buddhist doctrine in these texts and of an increasing systematization of ritual. Thus, the *Ta-chi ching* (T 13.1–408), translated by Dharmarakṣema (d. 433), ranks dhāraṇī with morality, meditation, and wisdom as a practice in which a bodhisattva excels. In the second half of the fifth century, T'an-yao, who oversaw the Buddhist artwork done at the Yün-kang caves, translated large parts of the *Ta-chi-i shen-chou ching* (T 21.568–80), which not only describes the preparation of an area in which Buddhist images are to be arranged and presented with offerings (as in certain maṇḍalas), but also points out that each "deity" has its own particular function.

By the seventh century, texts were being introduced that reflect the mature techniques and goals of Tantric Buddhism. Chih-t'ung's translation of the *Ch'ien-yen ch'ien-pi-ching* (T 20.83–90), is one of the first to state that the ultimate aim of Tantric practice is the rapid attainment of Buddhahood. The *T'o-lo-ni chi ching* (T 18.785–898), translated by Atigupta, discusses the Mahāyāna doctrine of emptiness and indicates in detail how numerous Buddhas and bodhisattvas are to be depicted and employed in Tantric ritual and meditation. By the end of this century, the stage had been set for the introduction of so-called pure Tantric Buddhism. The Indian Tantric master Śubhākarasiṁha (Shan-wu-wei, 637–735) and his Chinese disciple I-hsing (683–727) transmitted the *Mahāvairocana Sūtra.* Vajrabodhi (Chin-kang-chih, 671–741), and his disciple, Amoghavajra (Pu-k'ung, 705–774) introduced texts of the Vajraśekhara line. These men were responsible for bringing Tantric Buddhism to its height of popularity in China.

Śubhākarasiṁha and I-hsing

According to one biography, Śubhākarasiṁha was a native of Northeast India and was the son of royalty.[4] He was apparently a precocious child; we are told that he took control of his father's army when he was ten and ascended the throne at thirteen. However, a struggle for power broke out between Śubhākarasiṁha and his brothers. Although he emerged victorious, he decided to turn over the government to the eldest of his brothers and enter the Buddhist clergy. As a monk, he traveled widely, studying and displaying various magical powers, but he finally settled at the great Buddhist university of Nālandā, where he was instructed by Dharmagupta in the practice of the Three Mysteries. He took to the road again, visiting pilgrimage sites and teaching nonbelievers "to look for the Buddha within themselves." Dharmagupta then ordered him to go to China. On his way, he lectured on the *Mahāvairocana Sūtra* to the Turkish and Tibetan people he encountered.

When he arrived in the thriving capital of Ch'ang-an in 716, he was already eighty years old. Emperor Hsüan-tsung (r. 712–756) received the venerable monk at the palace and bestowed on him the title "Teacher of the Country" (*kuo-shih*). Śubhākarasiṁha is said to have "caused the emperor to enter the way of the Tathāgata," but it appears that Hsüan-tsung was more impressed by the feats of magic that the monk performed than by his instructions regarding the attainment of Buddhahood. Even before the Tantric master had arrived, Hsüan-tsung had developed a strong interest in Taoist magic, and he maintained that interest until his death. In Chang-an, Śubhākarasiṁha produced his first translation, the *Hsü-kung-tsang ch'iu-wen-ch'ih fa*, a text containing a dhāraṇī that promised to increase the practitioner's powers of memory (T 20.601–3). In 724, he accompanied the emperor to Loyang, where he continued his work. In 725, he made his most important contribution to the spread of Tantric Buddhism, completing the translation of the *Mahāvairocana Sūtra* (T 18.1–55).[5] The Sanskrit text had been sent from India thirty years earlier by the Chinese monk Wu-hsing, who had died on the way home. The first fascicle sets forth the philosophy on which the sūtra is based; it stresses that knowing one's mind as it really is constitutes enlightenment, and it offers an analysis of the various levels of spiritual awakening. The next six fascicles present the maṇḍala (known as the Womb or Matrix maṇḍala) and the Tantric practices that lead the individual to the realization of the innate, enlightened mind. The maṇḍala based on this text depicts Mahāvairocana seated on an eight-petal lotus, surrounded by four major Buddhas and their attendant bodhisattvas, and then, beyond the perimeter of the lotus, by numerous other bodhisattvas and lesser deities.

Śubhākarasiṁha's disciple, I-hsing, is one of the most remarkable figures in Chinese Buddhist history. As a young man, he studied the Chinese classics, and he was later known for his knowledge of Taoism. He lost his parents when he was twenty-one and began his career in Buddhism as a monk of the Ch'an sect, at one point training under the famous Northern Ch'an master, P'u-chi. By the time his interests had turned to Tantric Buddhism, he not only had studied monastic discipline and the teachings of the T'ien-t'ai sect, but he had distinguished himself in mathematics and astronomy to such a degree that in 721 Emperor Hsüan-tsung called upon him to reform the calendar. I-hsing began his study of Tantric Buddhism with Vajrabodhi, who arrived in Ch'ang-an in 719. Vajrabodhi initiated him into practices associated with the Vajraśekhara textual line. By 724, I-hsing joined Śubhākarasiṁha in Loyang. He helped with the translation of the *Mahāvairocana Sūtra*, and then went on to compile the work that secured his place in Tantric Buddhist history: a twenty-fascicle commentary on the sūtra, reportedly based on lectures given by Śubhākasiṁha (T 39.579–690).[6] No comparable commentary exists for any of the Vajraśekhara texts, a fact that does much to explain the great popularity of the *Mahāvairocana Sūtra* in the later Tantric tradition, not only in China, but also in Japan. Shortly after finishing the project, this multifaceted genius passed away, preceding his master in death by eight years.

Vajrabodhi and Amoghavajra

Little can be said with confidence about Vajrabodhi's birthplace or family background. As a boy he entered the Buddhist clergy and studied at Nālandā. In the following years, he read widely in Buddhist literature, acquiring a thorough knowledge of both Hīnayāna and Mahāyāna doctrine and monastic discipline. At the age of thirty-one he received initiation into the Vajraśekhara line of Tantric Buddhism in South India. In the course of his travels in India, Vajrabodhi heard of the growing popularity of Buddhism in China and set his mind on going there to missionize. With the aid of a South Indian king, he set out from Sri Lanka by sea, finally reaching Ch'ang-an in 719 and Loyang in 720. No sooner had he arrived than he began to erect *abhiṣeka,* or initiation, platforms, replete with maṇḍalas, and to spread Tantric Buddhism. Vajrabodhi quickly came to the attention of Emperor Hsüan-tsung, and, like Śubhākarasiṁha, he was called upon to demonstrate his superhuman powers. He is said to have caused rain to fall on one occasion and, on another, to have saved the life of the emperor's twenty-fifth daughter, who was diagnosed as having a terminal illness. During the twenty-one years he was active in China, he introduced over twenty sūtras and ritual manuals, almost all in the Vajraśekhara textual line. The most important of these was his translation of the opening section of the *Tattvasaṃgraha Sūtra* (T 18.223–53). In contrast to the *Mahāvairocana Sūtra,* this work has no philosophical prologue. From the outset, it is concerned with describing the maṇḍala and the meditational practices understood to lead to enlightenment. The maṇḍala, known as the Diamond, is made up of various subsections or "assemblies"; in its central assembly are five Buddhas—Mahāvairocana, Akṣobhya, Ratnasaṁbhava, Amitābha, and Amoghasiddhi—symbolizing the five types of wisdom characteristic of an enlightened mind.

Of Vajrabodhi's several disciples, the most distinguished was Amoghavajra, who appears to have done more to advance the cause of Tantric Buddhism than any of the masters so far discussed. Amoghavajra was born in 705, most probably in Central Asia. His father was a brahmin from North India; his mother came from Samarkand. After his father's death, he was raised in his mother's homeland until he was ten years old, when he was taken to China by his maternal uncle. It was in Ch'ang-an, in 719, that he met Vajrabodhi and entered the Buddhist clergy. His first training was in Sanskrit and monastic discipline, and only after several years had passed was he initiated into the practices of the Vajraśekhara line of Tantric Buddhism. Amoghavajra served his master until the latter's death, but then in 743 he set off for India and Sri Lanka to collect Tantric material. While in Sri Lanka, he received further instruction in Tantric Buddhism from a certain Samantabhadra. In 746 he returned to Ch'ang-an, bringing with him over five hundred sūtras and commentaries. By the time of his death, in 774, he had translated over one hundred of these texts and established a reputation as one of the greatest translators in Chinese Buddhist history. Among his most influential products was his translation of the opening section of the *Tattvasaṃgraha Sūtra* (T 18.207–23),[7] a more complete version than Vajrabodhi's; in later years it was this version that served as the principal source for the depiction of the Diamond Maṇḍala. Amoghavajra also worked to spread Tantric Buddhism through the establishment of initiation platforms in temples both within and outside the capital, and all three of the emperors who ruled during his lifetime turned to him for the rainmaking and healing miracles they had come to expect from the Tantric monks. When General An Lu-shan rose in rebellion in 755, Amoghavajra was also called upon to perform rituals for the protection of the state. At the time of the monk's death, T'ai-tsung canceled all court activities for three days.

Of Amoghavajra's many outstanding disciples, it was one of the youngest, Hui-kuo (746–805), who had the greatest influence on later Tantric history in East Asia. Two aspects of his career are particularly important. First, Hui-kuo appears to have consciously sought to unify the two lineages of Tantric Buddhism. He had received initiation into the Vajraśekhara line from Amoghavajra, and from Hsuan-ch'ao, a disciple of Śubhākarasiṁha, he received the transmission of the *Mahāvairocana Sūtra* and a related text, the *Susiddhikara Sūtra* (T 18.603–33). While earlier Tantric masters may have had knowledge of both lineages, they tended to specialize in one. Hui-kuo seems to have been the first to hold that they were of equal value. In the immediately following generations, it was common for monks to receive initiation into both. Second, Hui-kuo contributed to the spread of Tantric Buddhism outside China. Among his disciples was the Japanese monk Kūkai (774–835), founder of the Shingon sect of Esoteric Buddhism. The founder of the Japanese Tendai sect, Saichō (767–822), also studied Tantric Buddhism during his stay in China. However, almost nothing is known about his teacher, Shun-hsiao, and the precise character of the transmission he received is unclear.[8] It was not until the monks Ennin (794–864) and Enchin (814–891) visited China and studied with later figures in Hui-kuo's line that Esoteric Buddhism was fully integrated into Japanese Tendai teachings.

The Tantric school did not share in the recovery of Buddhism in the Sung period (960–1279), although some new translations were made, among them a complete version of the *Tattvasaṃgraha* by Shih-hu (late tenth century) (T 18.341–445). During the Yüan dynasty (1280–1368), Tibetan Tantric Buddhism was introduced, but neither the translations nor the contact with Tibet had a reinvigorating effect. Nevertheless, Tantric Buddhism retained a place in the tradition, as can be seen from the careers of two major Buddhist figures of the Ming dynasty (1368–1644), Chu-hung (1535–1615) and Han-shan (1546–1623).[9] Reflecting the general character of Buddhism in this period, they taught a syncretism of Pure Land, Ch'an, and the doctrinal schools; they emphasized the importance of monastic discipline and they paid particular attention to the needs of lay Buddhists. Furthermore, both Chu-hung and Han-shan were practitioners of Tantric Buddhism. They performed the Tantric ritual for rain as well as a rite known as "the feeding of the burning mouths (or hungry ghosts)," a popular ritual for taming malevolent spirits. As the character of these rites suggests, in this period as before, it was the mundane benefits of Tantric ritual that appear to have held the greatest appeal.

Notes

1. The term "Tantric" is derived from the Sanskrit *tantra,* which refers to the ritual and meditation manuals characteristically associated with this movement in India after the eighth century. In Chinese, the appellations *Mi,* "Esoteric," or *Chen-yen,* "True Word," are used to refer to the sect. The former reflects the secret nature of the transmission of its teachings; the latter is a translation of *dhāraṇī* or *mantra.*

2. In terms of the four classes of Tantric literature recognized in India and Tibet, the miscellaneous texts belong to the Kriyā class, the *Mahāvairocana Sūtra* to the Caryā class, and the *Tattvasaṃgraha Sūtra* to the Yoga class. Works in the Anuttarayoga category, which are distinguished by their use of sexual symbolism, had almost no influence in East Asia. See Matsunaga Yūkei, "Indian Esoteric Buddhism as Studied in Japan," in *Studies of Esoteric Buddhism and Tantrism* (Kōyasan: Kōyasan University Press, 1965) 229–42.

3. See, e.g., the *Chou-ch'in ching* (T 21.491).

4. See Chou Yi-liang, "Tantrism in China," *Harvard Journal of Asiatic Studies* 8 (1944–45) 241–332, for a translation and study of the Sung biographies of Vajrabodhi and Amoghavajra as well as Śubhākarasiṁha. On these and other major figures in Chinese Tantric history, see Matsunaga Yūkei, *Mikkyō no sōjōsha: sono kōdō to shisō.*

5. In Japan this text is known as the *Dainichikyō.*

6. For a partial translation of this commentary, see Wilhelm Kuno Muller, "Shingon Mysticism: Śubhākarasiṁha and I-hsing's Commentary to the Mahāvairocana Sūtra, Chapter One, An Annotated Translation" (Ph.D. dissertation, University of California; Ann Arbor: University Microfilms, 1976).

7. The corresponding Sanskrit text has been translated by Dale Allen Todaro, "An Annotated Translation of the Tattvasaṃgraha (Part I), with an Explanation of the Role of the Tattvasaṃgraha Lineage in the Teachings of Kūkai" (Ph.D. dissertation, Columbia University, 1985). Both Amoghavajra's and Vajrabodhi's translations of this work are referred to in Japan as the *Vajraśekhara Sūtra* or *Kongōchōkyō.*

8. See Paul Sheldon Groner, *Saichō: The Establishment of the Japanese Tendai School* (Berkeley, CA: Berkeley Buddhist Studies Series 7, 1984) 52–61.

9. For studies of these individuals see Chün-fang Yü, *The Renewal of Buddhism in China: Chu-hung and the Late Ming Synthesis* (New York: Columbia University Press, 1981); and Sung-peng Hsu, *A Buddhist Leader in Ming China: The Life and Thought of Han-shan Te-ch'ing, 1546–1623* (University Park, PA: Pennsylvania University Press, 1979).

Bibliography

Chou Yi-liang, "Tantrism in China." *Harvard Journal of Asiatic Studies* 8 (1944–1945) 241–332.

Katsumata Shunkyō. "Keika Wajōden no kenkyū." In *Kōbō Daishi no shisō to sono genryū.* Tokyo: Sankibō, 1981.

Matsunaga Yūkei. *Mikkyō kyōten kaisetsu.* Tokyo: Daitō Shuppansha, 1981.

——. *Mikkyō no sōjōsha: sono kōdō to shisō.* Tokyo: Hyōronsha, 1973.

——. "Tantric Buddhism and Shingon Buddhism." *Eastern Buddhist* 2:2 (November 1969) 1–14.

Miyasaka Yūshō, Umehara Takeshi, Kanaoka Shūyū, eds. *Mikkyō no rekishi.* Tokyo: Shunjūsha, 1977.

Osabe Kazuo. *Ichigyō Zenji no kenkyū.* Kobe: Kōbe Shōka Daigaku Keizai Kenkyūjo, 1963.

Ōyama Kōjun. *Mikkyōshi gaisetsu no kyōri.* Kōyasan: Ōyama Kyōju Hōin Shōshin Kinen Shuppankai, 1961.

Taganoo Shōun. *Himitsu Bukkyōshi.* 1933. Reprint, Tokyo: Ryūbunkan, 1981.

Glossary of Technical Terms

[Sanskrit (S), Pali (P), Chinese (C), Japanese (J)]

abhidharma S. Lit., study in regard to the Dharma; scholastic treatises that outline and classify Buddhist teachings.
ācārya S. Spiritual master.
ālaya-vijñāna S. Store-consciousness, or container consciousness, in which all of life's experiences are potentially contained in advance and actually stored after their occurrence, thus providing a basis for continuity and psychic heredity.
amala-vijñāna S. Pure consciousness, identical with the true nature of reality.
ānāpāna S. Breathing meditation; breathing as an aid in meditation.
anātman S. [*anattā* P.] No-self, non-ego, the absence of ātman.
anitya S. [*anicca* P.] Impermanence; the state of flux, changeability, and transiency that characterizes all things.
arhat S. Noble One; worthy one; one who is free from all defilements.
ārya S. Noble beings; holy people.
asaṃskṛta S. Unproduced, or unconditioned, elements.
āśraya-parivṛtti S. The "conversion of the support"; the overturning of the ground of our wayward existence.
ātman S. Ego, a permanent self.

bhāva S. Existence, entity.
bhāvanā S. Cultivation; to cultivate specific techniques in meditation.
bhikṣu S. Mendicant, monk.
bhūmi S. Stage on the path to Buddhahood.
bodhi S. P. Awakening; enlightenment; the conquest of ignorance through the awakening to perfect wisdom.
bodhicitta S. The aspiration for enlightenment; the decision to strive for enlightenment; lit., the "mind" of enlightenment.
bodhisattva S. [*bodhisatta* P.] One who undertakes the path to enlightenment; one who strives to attain the wisdom of the Buddha; a future Buddha; a compassionate being.

brahmavihāra S. P. Ways of living like Brahma; the four divine (brahmic) states: love, compassion, sympathetic enjoyment, and equanimity.
buddha-kṣetra S. Buddha-land.

caitasika S. The various mental functions, as described in the Abhidharma treatises.
chih C. [*śamatha* S., *shi* J.] Cessation; calming; quietude; tranquillity.
citta S. Mind; mental elements.

darśana S. Vision, insight, "seeing as," the action of seeing.
darśana-mārga S. The path of vision; stages in the process of cultivating Buddhist meditation.
deśanā S. Teaching.
dhamma-rāja P. Buddhist king.
dhāraṇī S. Ritual formulas.
dharma S. [*dhamma* P.] Teaching; element, the ultimate constituent of existence; the law that governs all things; the essence or nature of a thing, and hence by association the things themselves; the ultimate truth as taught by the Buddha.
dharmadhātu S. The realm of truth; true reality; this world-as-it-is; the dharma realm, which can be taken either as a general name for "things" or as the underlying spiritual reality regarded as the absolute ground of all that is.
dharmakāya S. The body of Dharma; the body of truth; the totality of the teachings of the Buddha; the eternal essence of the Buddha; the cosmic body.
dharmatā S. The nature of all things.
dhyāna S. [*jhāna* P; *ch'an* C.; *zen* J.] Contemplation, meditation, understood as a process of spiritual advancement involving stages; altered states of consciousness produced by concentration (samādhi).
dṛṣṭi S. False views.
duḥkha S. [*dukkha* P.] Suffering, pain, disquiet, strife, ill, disvalue; the nature of human existence.
dukkha-dukkhatā P. The pain of disagreeable sensations, known to everyone.

garbha S. Womb, matrix, seed.
gāthā S. Hymn, verse.
gotra S. Nature.

homa S. Ritual fire ceremony; burnt offering.

hsin C. Mind.

iccantika S. Cursed one; one who has no nature, or potential, to attain enlightenment.

jhāna P. Insight, concentration, meditation.
jñāna S. Knowledge, wisdom.

karma S. [*kamma* P.] Human deeds and the residue they leave behind them as effects.
karuṇā S. P. Compassion.
kleśa S. Defilement; passionate delusion; blind passions.
ko-i C. Matching terms; a form of exegesis that consisted of "matching" Buddhist technical terms with indigenous Chinese terms.
kṣānti S. Patience, forbearance.
kuan C. [*vipaśyanā* S., *kan* J.] Contemplation; insight.

lakṣaṇa S. "Mark"; identifiable characteristic.
li C. Principle, noumena.

mahākaruṇa S. Great compassion; the compassion of a Buddha.
maitri S. [*mettā* P.] Love, friendliness.
maṇḍala S. The mental content of tantric samādhi; pictures illustrating Buddhist cosmology and used as aids in meditation.
mantra S. Ritualistic formula.
mārga S. Path; way.
moha S. P. Delusion.
mokṣa S. Liberation; release from karma-governed existence.
muditā P. Sympathetic joy.
mudrā S. Ritualistic manual gestures.

nidāna S. P. Causes; the twelve links or bonds or primary causes that make up the chain of dependent origination.
nien-fo C. [*nenbutsu* J.] "Re-calling (recollecting; invoking) Buddha; contemplating the Buddha; later, chanting the name of the Buddha.
nirmāṇakāya S. The body of transformation; the historical incarnation of the Buddha.
nirodha-samāpatti S. The attainment of cessation; complete cessation of mental activity.
nirvāṇa S. [*nibbāna* P.] The final state of release following enlightenment; the extinguishing of the flame (of delusions or passionate desires); the final goal of the Buddhist path.

p'an-chiao C. Classification of doctrines.

paramārtha-satya S. Ultimate truth; supreme meaning.

pāramitā S. Perfection; virtue, of which there are traditionally six or ten. The six are charity (*dāna*), observation of the precepts (*śīla*), patience (*kṣānti*), diligence (*vīrya*), meditation (*dhyāna*), and wisdom (*prajñā*).

pariṇāma-dukkhata P. The pain caused by the passing away of pleasure and happiness.

pātimokkha P. The code of precepts for monks and nuns governing their life-style.

prajñā S. [*paññā* P.] Knowledge or wisdom of the truth attained in enlightenment; the perfect comprehension of the totality of all existence; consummate wisdom; liberating knowledge of the nature of human existence.

prajñapti S. Verbal designation; convention; provisional designation.

prapañca S. Verbal constructs or fabrications; verbal activity; the false dichotomy that is necessarily involved in making a verbal statement; conceptual play.

pratītya-samutpāda S. [*paṭiccasamuppāda* P.] Dependent co-arising; co-origination; dependent origination.

pudgala S. [*puggala* P.] An ineffable self that underlies the five skandhas, the existence of which is denied by Buddhists.

rūpa S. Form; the material elements.

rūpakāya S. The physical body; the body of form.

saddharma S. Holy Truth; the teachings of the Buddha.

samādhi S. P. To settle, fix, compose oneself in meditation or concentration.

śamatha S. [*samatha* P., *chih* C.] Serenity, calm; concentration; stopping of extraneous thoughts and desires. Often compounded with *vipaśyanā*.

saṃbodhi S. Ultimate awakening, enlightenment.

saṃbhogakāya S. The body of enjoyment; the body of recompense.

saṃkhāra-dukkhatā P. The pain caused by the inherent restlessness and transitoriness of all phenomena; the subtlest form of pain, fully appreciated only by the spiritually discerning.

saṃsāra S. P. This world of transmigration; the turning of the wheel of birth and death.

saṃskṛta S. Produced, or conditioned, things.

saṃvṛti-satya S. Mundane, provisional, worldly, or conventional truth.

saṅgha S. The community of Buddhist believers; together with Buddha and Dharma, one of the *triratna* (three treasures) in which a Buddhist takes refuge.
sassatavāda P. The extreme view of eternalism.
śāstra S. Treatise; the second of the Three Baskets (Tripiṭaka), or canon, of Buddhism.
shen C. [*shin* J.] Spirit; soul.
shih C. [*ji* J.] Facts, phenomena, thing, event, entity.
śīla S. (*śīla* P.) Moral rules; moral conduct and character; the rules for a moral life to be upheld by Buddhists and their corresponding commitment to avoid evil deeds.
skandha S. The aggregates or constitutive elements of all existence, including our own existence, considered five in number: *rūpa* (form), *vedanā* (feelings), *saṃjñā* (perceptions), *saṃskāra* (volitional impulses), and *vijñāna* (consciousness).
smṛti S. Mindfulness; paying close attention to a specific phenomenon.
śraddhā S. [*saddhā* P.] Faith, heartfelt inner commitment to the spiritual life, loving trust.
śrāvaka S. A "listener"; disciple; one who hears the teachings of the Buddha; a Mahāyāna term for followers of the Hīnayāna.
śrimaṇa S. Ascetic; mendicant; Buddhist monk.
stūpa S. A tumulus or burial mound for the bones or remains of the dead; also used to contain other sacred relics.
śūnyatā S. [*suññatā* P., *kung* C., *kū* J.] Emptiness; the lack of any substantial being; the fundamental Buddhist conception of ultimate reality.
sūtra S. [*sutta* P.] Scripture, text; the first of the Three Baskets (Tripiṭaka), or canon, of Buddhism.
svabhāva S. Self-nature; the self-existence of anything, that is denied by the Buddhist concept of emptiness (*niḥsvabhāva, śūnyatā*).

taṇhā S. P. Thirst; the attachment to illusion likened to a throat parched and burning with thirst; the flames of lust or desire.
tao C. The Way; the ground of all that is.
tathāgatagarbha S. The womb, embryo, matrix, of Buddhahood; the innate potential to attain Buddhahood.
tathatā S. Suchness; the way things are.
tattva S. Thatness; the way things are; true reality.
trilakṣaṇ / trisvabhāva S. The three patterns or natures of reality as explained in the Yogācāra school: the other-dependent (*paratantra-**), the imagined (*parikalpita-**), and the perfected or pure (*pariniṣpanna-**).
tripiṭaka S. The "Three Baskets"; the three divisions of the Buddhist canon: *sūtra, śāstra,* and *vinaya.*

tzu-jan C. Naturalness; spontaneity; nature.

ucchedavāda P. The extreme view of annihilationism.
upadeśa S. Explanation, commentary.
upāya; upāyakauśalya S. Skillful means.
upekṣa S. [*upekkhā* P.] Equanimity; even-mindedness.

vajra S. Diamond.
vicāra S. The cognitive factor in meditation of "sustained thought."
vijñāna S. [*viññāna* P.] Consciousness.
vinaya S. Precepts, rules for conduct; the third of the Three Baskets (Tripiṭaka), or canon, of Buddhism.
vipaśyanā S. [*vipassanā* P., *kuan* C.] Insight; contemplation. Often compounded with *śamatha.*
vitarka S. The cognitive factor in meditation of "applied thought."

wu C. [*mu* J.] Nothingness, void.
wu-wei C. [*mu-i* J.] No-action; non-action; actionless.

yogācāra S. The practice of Yoga; those who engage in the practice of Yoga; one of the major schools of Mahāyāna Buddhism.
yu C. [*u* J.] Existence, being.

Contributors

ROGER CORLESS is on the faculty of Duke University in Durham, North Carolina. He is a specialist in Pure Land Buddhism and a leader in the developing field of Buddhist-Christian Studies. His numerous publications include *The Vision of Buddhism.*

LUIS O. GÓMEZ is Professor in the Department of Asian Languages and Cultures at the University of Michigan.

PAUL J. GRIFFITHS is Associate Professor of the Philosophy of Religions at the University of Chicago, holding a joint appointment in The Divinity School and the Department of South Asian Languages & Civilizations. He specializes in Indian Buddhist philosophy and is the author of *On Being Mindless: Buddhist Meditation and the Mind-Body Problem* and *An Apology for Apologetics: A Study in the Logic of Inter-religious Dialogue.*

KAJIYAMA YŪICHI is Professor Emeritus of Kyoto University and is currently Professor at Bukkyo University. He is the author of *Studies in Buddhist Philosophy.* He specializes in Pure Land Buddhism, Mādhyamaka philosophy, and Buddhist Logico-epistemology, and has written numerous books in Japanese.

JOHN KEENAN is Associate Professor of Religion at Middlebury College in Vermont. His studies have focused on Indian Mahāyāna and its translation into China. He is the translator of several major Yogācāra texts: *Saṃdhinirmocanasūtra, Mahāyānasaṃgraha, Buddhabhūmyupadeśa,* and *Karmasiddhiprakaraṇa.* His publications include *The Realm of Awakening* and *The Meaning of Christ: A Mahāyāna Theology.*

WINSTON L. KING is Professor Emeritus of Vanderbilt University, having also taught at Grinnell and Oberlin Colleges and Colorado State University in history of religions, specializing in Buddhism. His books include *In the Hope of Nibbana, A Thousand Lives Away, Death was His Kōan,* and *Zen and the Way of the Sword.*

WHALEN W. LAI is Professor and Director of the Religious Studies Program, University of California-Davis, California. He specializes in Chinese philosophy and East Asian Buddhism and has published numerous works in various academic journals and collections.

MAEDA EGAKU is Professor and Head of the Buddhist Studies Department, Graduate School of Letters, at Aichi Gakuin University in Nagoya, Japan, and a member of the Science Council of Japan. He is the author of *History of the Formation of Original Buddhist Texts,* and has edited *Contemporary Buddhism in Sri Lanka.*

NAGAO GAJIN (GADJIN M. NAGAO) is Professor Emeritus of Kyoto University and a member of the Japan Academy. His numerous publications include *The Mahāyānasaṃgraha: An Annotated Japanese Translation, The Foundational Standpoint of Mādhyamika Philosophy, Mādhyamika and Yogācāra: A Study of Mahāyāna Philosophies,* and *An Index to the Mahāyānasaṃgraha.*

SUNTHORN NA-RANGSI is a Thai scholar and Associate Professor of Philosophy at Chulalongkorn University in Bangkok, Thailand. He is a specialist in Buddhist and Indian Philosophy, and Fellow of the Royal Institute. He is the author of several books, including *The Buddhist Concepts of Karma and Rebirth,* and in Thai, *Indian Philosophy: History and Thought, The Philosophy of Theravada Buddhism,* and *Special Topics in Buddhist Philosophy.*

GOVIND CHANDRA PANDE is currently Chairman of the Allahabad Museum. He was formerly Professor and Vice-Chancellor in the Universities of Rajasthan (Jaipur) and Allahabad. He is the author of *Studies in the Origins of Buddhism, History of the Development of Buddhism* (in Hindi), and *Lal Mani Joshi Memorial Lectures on Mahāyāna.*

MICHAEL PYE is Professor in the Department of Religious Studies, Lancaster University. His publications include *Skilful Means: A Concept in Mahayana Buddhism* and *The Buddha.*

SAKURABE HAJIME is a former Professor of Buddhist Studies at Ōtani University in Kyoto, Japan. He is the author of *Kusharon no kenkyū* (A study on the *Abhidharmakośa*), *Bukkyōgo no kenkyū* (A study of Buddhist terms), and *Hanjusanmai-kyō ki* (Notes on the *Pratyutpanna-buddha-sammkhāvasthita-samādhi-sūtra*).

ERNST STEINKELLNER is Professor of Buddhist and Tibetan Studies at the University of Vienna. He is a specialist in the Buddhist tradition of epistemology and logic, both Indian and Tibetan. His works include critical editions and interpretations of major works of Dharmakīrti and a translation of Śāntideva's *Bodhicaryāvatāra.*

SULAK SIVARAKSA is a lawyer, social analyst, nonviolent campaigner, lecturer, and educationalist. He is the president of the Santi Pracha Dhamma Institute of nonformal education and research for alternative development. He is a founder of the International Network of Engaged Buddhists and a member of the international board of the Buddhist Peace Fellowship. He has published a number of books in English including *Siamese Resurgence* and *Seeds of Peace: A Buddhist Vision for Renewing Society.*

PAUL L. SWANSON is a permanent fellow of the Nanzan Institute for Religion and Culture and Associate Professor at Nanzan University. His publications include *Foundations of T'ien-t'ai Philosophy: The Flowering of the Two Truths Theory in Chinese Buddhism.*

TACHIKAWA MUSASHI is Professor at the National Museum of Ethnology in Osaka, Japan. His publications include *The Structure of the World in Udayana's Realism.*

TAKEUCHI YOSHINORI is Professor Emeritus of Kyoto University. One of the leading figures of the Kyoto School of philosophy, he is the author of numerous works on Buddhism and his own Shin Buddhist faith, including *The Heart of Buddhism: In Search of the Timeless Spirit of Primitive Buddhism.*

ROBERT A. F. THURMAN is the Jey Tsong Khapa Professor of Indo-Tibetan Buddhist Studies at Columbia University, founder and president of the American Institute for Buddhist Studies, and Director of Columbia University's Center for Buddhist Studies. He studied at Harvard University and at Namgyal Monastery, Dharmasala, India. He has translated a number of Buddhist texts and has written on all aspects of Buddhism.

TAITETSU UNNO is Jill Ker Conway Professor of Religion and East Asian Studies at Smith College. A specialist in Buddhist philosophical thought, he is the author of *Tannisho: A Shin Buddhist Classic* and editor of *The Religious Philosophy of Nishitani Keiji.*

PAUL B. WATT is Associate Professor and Director of Asian Studies at DePauw University and has taught at Columbia University and Grinnell College. A specialist in Japanese intellectual and religious history, he is the author of numerous essays on Buddhism and on the interaction between religion and Japanese culture.

ALEX WAYMAN is Professor Emeritus of Sanskrit at Columbia University. He has published more than 150 books and articles including *Analysis of the Śrāvakabhūmi Manuscript, The Buddhist Tantras, Calming the Mind and Discerning the Real, Buddhist Insight, Chanting the Names of Mañjuśrī, Ethics of Tibet,* and *The Enlightenment of Vairocana.*

Photographic Credits

The editors and publisher wish to thank the varied museums for providing photographs and granting permission to reproduce the illustrations in this volume. In particular, the editors and the art editor acknowledge the many courtesies and assistance of Kosei Publishing Company not only in providing numerous photographs from their own collection but also in obtaining permissions for other photographs.

1. By permission of Kosei Publishing Company.
2. The Nelson-Atkins Museum of Art, Kansas City, Missouri. (Nelson Fund) 55–105.
3. By permission of Kosei Publishing Company.
4. Photograph by Tsukamoto Keisho. By permission of Kosei Publishing Company.
5. The Cleveland Museum of Art, Dudley P. Allen Fund, 35.146.
6. The Cleveland Museum of Art, Andrew R. and Martha Holden Jennings Fund, 75.102.
7. The Cleveland Museum of Art, Leonard C. Hanna, Jr., Fund, 61.418.
8. By permission of Kosei Publishing Company.
9. By permission of Kosei Publishing Company.
10. By permission of Kosei Publishing Company.
11. Photograph by Sugimoto Yoshio.
12. Photograph by Sugimoto Yoshio.
13. From *Ōgon no pagoda: Biruma bukkyō no tabi* (1989), pp. 39–40. Photograph by permission of Higuchi Hideo.
14. Photograph by Susan Offner.
15. By permission of The British Library. Or 8210/P2.
16. By permission of Kosei Publishing Company.
17. By permission of Kosei Publishing Company.
18. The Nelson-Atkins Museum of Art, Kansas City, Missouri. (Nelson Fund) 44–10.
19. Gift of Mrs. W. Scott Fitz (22.407) and Gift of Edward Holmes Jackson in memory of his mother, Mrs. W. Scott Fitz (47.1407–1422). Courtesy, Museum of Fine Arts, Boston. Acc. #22.407 and 47.1407–1422.
20. Courtesy of the Kawasaki City Museum.
21. The Nelson-Atkins Museum of Art, Kansas City, Missouri. (Nelson Fund) 51–27.
22. The Nelson-Atkins Museum of Art, Kansas City, Missouri. (Nelson Fund) 37–27.
23. Gift of Denman W. Ross in memory of Okakura Kakuzo. Courtesy, Museum of Fine Arts, Boston. Acc. #13.2804.

Index of Names

Index of Subjects

Abhayagiri sect, 94
Abhidharma
  criticism of, 76
  description of, 26
  doctrine, 70–72, 74–76
  influence of, 76–77
  literature, 67–70
  origin of, 67
  philosophy, 140–41
  rationale of, 49
  Sarvāstivāda sect and, 28, 67–69
  teaching and, 26, 28
  Theravāda sect and, 28, 67, 69–70
  Tibetan Buddhism and, 67
Abhidharma-hṛdata, 68, 69
Abhidharma-kośa, 68–69
Abhidharmakośabhāṣya (*A Commentary Upon the Treasury of Metaphysics*), 54–56, 58–60
Abhidharma-piṭaka, 67, 69–70
Absolute Power, 264
Acittaka (mindlessness) condition, 41
Affective sensation (*vedanā*), 47, 48, 49
Ailao kingdom, 109
Ājīvakas, 14
All Ceylon Buddhist Congress, 101
Amarapura Nikāya, 100
Anglican Church, 98, 100
Annihilationism (*ucchedavāda*), 11, 12, 29
Anuttarayoga Tantra, 221, 223–24
Applied thought (*vitarka*), 39, 40
Architecture, 111, 312–13
Art, 111
Ārya-mārga (noble path), 55, 75
Asceticism, 128
Aśubha-bhāvanā (cultivation of the horrible), 52–54
Attainment of cessation, 38–44
Aṭṭhakavagga, 22
Aṭṭhasālinī, 70
Avataṃsaka-sūtra
  bodhisattva and, 161–63, 167–16
  description of, 161–66
  development of, 160–61
  extant texts of, 160
  influence of, 169
  interpretation of, 160
  Mahāyāna sect and, 166–68
  purpose of, 160
Awakening, path to, 46–47
Ayudhya kingdom, 110

Bhāvanā (cultivation), 37
Bodhicaryāvatāra (*Entering Upon the Practice of Awakening*), 60–62
Bodhicitta (decision for enlightenment), 61
Bodhisattva
  Avataṁsaka-sūtra and, 161–63, 167–68
  cult, 145–49
  Lotus sūtra and, 174
  Mahāsāṇghika sect and, 25, 29–30
  Mahāyāna and, 151–52
Bodhisattvacaryāvatāra (*Entering Upon the Practice of Awakening*), 60–62
Body (*kāya*), 47–49, 61
Bön literature, 238–39
Brahmanic-Upanishadic Hinduism, 79
Brahmavihāras ("ways of living like Brahma"), 17–18, 50–54
Buddha
  asceticism and, 128